Global Economic Challenges and Opportunities for the Workplace

Cristina Carrasco-Garrido
Rey Juan Carlos University, Spain

Antonio Martínez Raya
Universidad Politécnica de Madrid, Spain

Carmen De-Pablos-Heredero
Rey Juan Carlos University, Spain

IGI Global
Scientific Publishing
Publishing Tomorrow's Research Today

Vice President of Editorial	Melissa Wagner
Managing Editor of Acquisitions	Mikaela Felty
Managing Editor of Book Development	Jocelynn Hessler
Production Manager	Mike Brehm
Cover Design	Phillip Shickler

Published in the United States of America by
IGI Global Scientific Publishing
701 East Chocolate Avenue
Hershey, PA, 17033, USA
Tel: 717-533-8845
Fax: 717-533-8661
Website: https://www.igi-global.com E-mail: cust@igi-global.com

Library of Congress Cataloging-in-Publication Data

Names: Carrasco-Garrido, Cristina, 1993- editor.
Title: Global economic challenges and opportunities for the workplace / edited by Cristina Carrasco-Garrido, Antonio Martínez Raya, Carmen De-Pablos-Heredero.
Description: Hershey, PA : IGI Global Scientific Publishing, [2025] | Includes bibliographical references and index. | Summary: "This book aims to provide robust theoretical frameworks and business practices on how companies adapt to global economic challenges and seek creative solutions to ways of working"-- Provided by publisher.
Identifiers: LCCN 2024050869 (print) | LCCN 2024050870 (ebook) | ISBN 9798369362891 (hardcover) | ISBN 9798369362907 (paperback) | ISBN 9798369362914 (ebook)
Subjects: LCSH: Sustainable development. | Entrepreneurship. | Organizational change.
Classification: LCC HC79.E5 G59255 2025 (print) | LCC HC79.E5 (ebook) | DDC 338.9/27--dc23/eng/20250115
LC record available at https://lccn.loc.gov/2024050869
LC ebook record available at https://lccn.loc.gov/2024050870

British Cataloguing in Publication Data
A Cataloguing in Publication record for this book is available from the British Library.

Table of Contents

Detailed Table of Contents

an integrative framework that highlights the key role of green HRM in reinforcing CE practices and policies, with a specific focus on B Corps. By examining the intersection of these areas, the chapter seeks to illuminate the synergies between B Corp certification, green HRM practices, and circular economy models. Employing systematic literature review methods and qualitative data analysis with Atlas.ti software, it offers insights into theoretical foundations, practical implications, and avenues for future research. Findings underscore circular economy's transformative potential and advocate for integrating green HRM practices into organizational strategies, fostering sustainability.

With the increasing global concern over food waste and its environmental impacts, there is a growing need to understand and promote sustainable practices throughout the food production and distribution process. This study explores the pro-environmental behaviours of the supply chain actors and their employees that can help minimise food waste within the agricultural supply chain. This study used a thematic literature review method to draw empirical evidence on, to explore the components, factors and impacts of pro-environmental behaviour towards reducing food waste across the agricultural supply chain. The study found that consumer education campaigns, the adoption of innovative technologies for waste management and development of food rescue organisations can help develop pro-environmental behaviours among the supply chain actors to reduce food waste. These findings are useful for policymakers, industry professionals, and researchers to develop effective strategies for minimizing food in the agricultural supply chain.

This chapter presents the applications of blockchain technology within workplace settings and guides future research and organizational adoption. This is achieved through a bibliometric analysis of literature sourced from Scopus and Web of Science between the years 2017-2024. The findings indicate a significant increase in publications on blockchain applications in workplaces since 2019, indicating the technology's rising relevance and potential in workplace contexts. The thematic

There is an extensive body of literature on the factors that condition waste separation behaviors in households; however, the same is not true when analyzing research on the behavior in the workplace. In this study we have carried out a bibliometric analysis of the scientific publications about individual waste separation behavior in their workplaces. The aim is to identify the main issues affecting such behavior, as well as the current state of research on the subject. Given the serious negative impact that waste has on the environment, knowing the reasons that lead individuals to make the effort to separate waste will be a key factor in designing any environmental policy.

This paper aims to verify whether there is a relationship between creative thinking and the entrepreneurial skills of young entrepreneurs to determine the factors that should be included in effective programs to train them as entrepreneurs. For this, a creative thinking test was designed that includes mathematical reasoning, inference and logical-deductive thinking, with software specially designed for this purpose. For entrepreneurial competencies, a validated questionnaire was used, which also served to detect the factors in the training of young entrepreneurs, design and implement a course based on these factors, so that it is confirmed if they are decisive or not. Undergraduate students from a private university in the city of Mérida, Yucatán, in southeastern Mexico, participated in this course, both for the diagnostic study (phase 1) and for the course (phase 2), but it is expected to replicate the study in other groups and companies in the future.

People visiting different destinations around the world demand that tourist attractions be showcased before being visited. This drives us to study which types of adventure

Preface

The global labor market is undergoing profound transformations, shaped by rapid technological advancements, evolving business practices, and the increasing necessity for sustainability. As businesses strive to adapt to these shifts, they encounter a range of challenges and opportunities that demand innovative approaches, greater resilience, and forward-thinking strategies. The workplace itself is changing, not only in terms of the technology that enables it but also in how it aligns with the broader goals of corporate responsibility and social justice.

This book, *Global Economic Challenges and Opportunities for the Workplace*, provides a comprehensive examination of these transformations. As editors, we have sought to bring together diverse perspectives that offer both theoretical frameworks and practical insights into how organizations can navigate the complexities of a rapidly evolving global economy. We explore how companies can capitalize on technological opportunities while remaining committed to sustainable practices and the well-being of their employees. Additionally, we focus on how businesses are addressing global social movements, emphasizing fairness, equity, and social responsibility.

The various chapters in this book cover key areas of current concern: the intersection of economic resilience and technology, the implementation of sustainable business practices, and the emergence of new workplace trends that prioritize flexibility, creativity, and employee satisfaction. From the impact of artificial intelligence and big data to the increasing importance of cybersecurity, we address how businesses can integrate cutting-edge technological opportunities into their operations while promoting ethical practices and environmental sustainability. Moreover, we delve into how organizations are rethinking their workspaces, with the rise of hot desking, open spaces, and teleworking, especially in a post-pandemic world.

As editors, we aim to offer a valuable resource for both practitioners and academics, bridging the gap between theoretical exploration and real-world business practices. Whether you are an entrepreneur, a manager, or a researcher, this book will help you better understand the economic challenges that shape the modern workplace and provide you with tools to foster innovation, sustainability, and resilience in your organization. In particular, the integration of sustainable development goals (SDGs), the growing influence of global social movements, and the importance of ethical entrepreneurship are key themes that we hope will inspire readers to think critically about the future of work and the role of business in a rapidly changing world.

The insights and practices shared in this volume reflect our collective commitment to fostering healthier, more resilient organizations that can thrive in an interconnected, technology-driven world. We hope this book serves as a catalyst for meaningful change, encouraging organizations to embrace the opportunities of the future while addressing the challenges of today.

These chapters collectively provide a rich and diverse examination of the challenges and opportunities that modern businesses face in the context of sustainability, technology, and employee well-being. They offer both theoretical insights and practical solutions for addressing the evolving demands of the global workplace.

Chapter 1: Nurses' Intentions to Implement Sustainable Practices in Public Hospitals: An Empirical Investigation

In this chapter, the authors examine how nurses' intentions to adopt sustainable practices in public hospitals can influence environmental protection efforts. Utilizing the Theory of Planned Behavior (TPB), the study highlights key factors such as attitudes, perceived control, and environmental awareness that shape nurses' behaviors in reducing energy consumption and medical waste. Drawing on data from hospitals in Algeria, this research contributes valuable insights for healthcare policymakers, aiming to promote sustainability in the healthcare sector through the actions of nurses, a group pivotal to the implementation of eco-friendly practices.

Chapter 2: Advancing Circular Economy through B Corp Certification and Green HRM Practices

This chapter explores the intersection of circular economy (CE) principles and green human resource management (HRM) practices, specifically within benefit corporations (B Corps). Through a systematic review of literature and qualitative analysis, the authors propose a framework to understand how B Corp certification and green HRM practices can reinforce CE efforts. The chapter stresses the transformative potential of CE, advocating for businesses to integrate sustainable human resource management practices to align corporate strategies with environmental and social goals.

Chapter 3: Pro-Environmental Behaviour to Minimize Food Waste in Agricultural Supply Chain

Addressing the issue of food waste in the agricultural supply chain, this chapter focuses on the role of pro-environmental behaviors among supply chain actors. By analyzing literature on sustainable practices in food production and distribution, the authors identify strategies such as consumer education, innovative waste management technologies, and food rescue initiatives to reduce waste. The findings offer practical recommendations for policymakers and industry professionals aiming to promote sustainability and reduce food waste in agricultural supply chains.

Chapter 4: Blockchain Technology and the Future of Smart and Safe Workplaces

This chapter investigates the emerging role of blockchain technology in creating smarter and safer workplaces. Through a bibliometric analysis, the authors explore how blockchain can enhance workplace efficiency in areas such as knowledge management, HR practices, and secure data sharing. The study outlines key areas for future research, including prototype testing, regulatory challenges, and the social and environmental impacts of blockchain, providing a comprehensive overview of the technology's potential applications in modern workplace environments.

Chapter 5: Global Challenges and Opportunities of New Technologies for Workplace Conflict Resolution through ADR

Focusing on the application of new technologies, particularly AI, in alternative dispute resolution (ADR) in the workplace, this chapter examines the global challenges and benefits of integrating emerging technologies into conflict management processes. It provides a detailed analysis of how these technologies can improve the efficiency and accessibility of ADR, offering insights into the potential for AI to revolutionize workplace dispute resolution methods.

Chapter 6: Emerging Psychosocial Risks in the Digital Age: Education in Its Dual Role as an Affected Sector and Control Tool

The digital transformation has introduced numerous psychosocial risks in the workplace, impacting employee well-being. This chapter identifies and structures these risks, focusing on the psychological effects of digital work environments. Additionally, it provides educational strategies to help managers mitigate these risks, emphasizing the need for training programs aimed at reducing or controlling these emerging threats in digital workplaces.

Chapter 7: Perspectives and Trends Relating to a Bibliometric Analysis of Hot-Desking Using VOSviewer

Examining the growing trend of hot-desking, this chapter utilizes bibliometric tools to analyze global research on flexible workspace strategies. The chapter highlights key issues such as employee satisfaction, communication, and office design, providing a comprehensive review of the literature on hot-desking from 2010 to 2024. It offers valuable insights for businesses looking to adopt flexible workspaces while addressing the challenges and maximizing the benefits of this practice.

Chapter 8: Teleworking and the Deployment of Dynamic Capabilities

This chapter delves into how the COVID-19 pandemic accelerated the adoption of teleworking, and how organizations can leverage dynamic capabilities—particularly absorption and adaptation capabilities—to enhance their telework processes. Through a survey of Spanish workers, the authors examine the impact of teleworking on employee quality of life, productivity, and organizational performance. The findings offer a solid theoretical framework for businesses seeking to optimize telework strategies and achieve better outcomes in the post-pandemic era.

Chapter 9: Main Topics in Workplace Recycling Behavior Studies: A Bibliometric Analysis

Addressing the growing importance of waste management, this chapter provides a bibliometric analysis of research on recycling behaviors in the workplace. By examining the factors that influence employees to separate waste, the authors aim to uncover key drivers of recycling behaviors and provide insights for designing effective environmental policies in organizations. This chapter underscores the significant environmental impact of workplace waste and highlights the importance of fostering sustainable behaviors in employees.

Chapter 10: Factors for the Effective Training of Young Entrepreneurs: An Experience in Southeastern Mexico

This chapter investigates the relationship between creative thinking and entrepreneurial skills among young entrepreneurs in southeastern Mexico. The authors explore how effective training programs can cultivate these skills, with a focus on the factors that contribute to successful entrepreneurial education. The findings suggest that incorporating creative thinking into entrepreneurship training can help young entrepreneurs develop the competencies needed to succeed in the competitive business world.

Chapter 11: Tourism Marketing: Perspective of Visual Behavior in Adventure Sports

Through eye-tracking analysis, this chapter examines how visual behavior influences tourists' interest in adventure sports destinations. By exploring the differences in how men and women engage with visual content related to adventure tourism, the authors identify key trends and preferences that can optimize tourism marketing strategies. This chapter contributes to the understanding of how visual stimuli can be leveraged to attract visitors to adventure sports destinations, providing valuable insights for marketers in the tourism industry.

Chapter 12: Digital Corporate Identity in the Healthcare Sector: Cross-national Analysis of the HR Marketing of Hospitals

This chapter explores how hospitals in Germany, Austria, and Switzerland shape their digital corporate identity to attract talent in a competitive labor market. By analyzing the online presence of the top 60 hospitals in these countries, the authors highlight areas for improvement in digital HR marketing strategies. The study underscores the importance of a strong digital corporate identity in the healthcare sector, offering implications for hospitals looking to enhance their recruitment efforts in the digital age.

In conclusion, *Global Economic Challenges and Opportunities for the Workplace* provides a comprehensive exploration of the dynamic forces shaping the modern workforce. The chapters in this volume highlight the critical intersection of technological innovation, sustainability, and employee well-being, offering both theoretical perspectives and actionable strategies for addressing the complex challenges faced by businesses today. As organizations navigate the ever-evolving landscape of the global economy, the insights gathered in this book serve as a valuable resource for academics, practitioners, and policymakers alike.

The diverse contributions reflect the wide-ranging impact of emerging technologies, such as artificial intelligence and blockchain, on workplace practices, while also addressing the pressing need for businesses to adopt sustainable and socially responsible strategies. From enhancing workplace efficiency through green human resource management to rethinking the design of workspaces in the age of teleworking, the chapters underscore the importance of adaptability and resilience in the face of change.

Furthermore, the book explores critical social and environmental issues, such as reducing food waste, minimizing workplace recycling, and addressing psychosocial risks in digital environments. These topics are not only crucial for improving organizational performance but also for fostering a more ethical, inclusive, and sustainable business landscape.

As editors, we are proud to present this collection of research and practical insights, which we hope will inspire readers to critically engage with the evolving economic landscape and take proactive steps to shape the future of work. Whether through advancing corporate social responsibility, implementing sustainable practices, or leveraging new technologies to improve workplace dynamics, the contributions in this volume offer a roadmap for creating workplaces that are not only economically resilient but also socially responsible and environmentally sustainable. This book stands as a testament to the importance of forward-thinking strategies in preparing for the challenges and opportunities of tomorrow's global economy.

Chapter 1
Nurses' Intentions to Implement Sustainable Practices in Public Hospitals: An Empirical Investigation

Kamel Mouloudj
https://orcid.org/0000-0001-7617-8313
University of Medea, Algeria

Ahmed Chemseddine Bouarar
https://orcid.org/0000-0001-8300-9833
University of Medea, Algeria

Flaka Hoti
https://orcid.org/0000-0002-4780-5776
University of Gjakova "Fehmi Agani", Kosovo

Dachel Martínez Asanza
https://orcid.org/0000-0002-1830-7137
National School of Public Health, Cuba & University of Medical Sciences of Havana, Cuba

Doruntina Kabashi
https://orcid.org/0009-0008-2696-8390
University of Gjakova "Fehmi Agani", Kosovo

ABSTRACT

Predicting environmentally friendly behaviors in the workplace is crucial for

DOI: 10.4018/979-8-3693-6289-1.ch001

achieving sustainability, as human actions significantly impact the environment. In the healthcare sector, nurses' behaviors can play a pivotal role in environmental protection, such as reducing energy consumption and minimizing the waste of medical supplies and medications. However, research on sustainability behavior among nurses in the workplace remains limited. This study aims to extend the Theory of Planned Behavior (TPB) by incorporating environmental awareness to examine nurses' intentions to adopt sustainable practices in public hospitals in Algeria. Primary data were collected from a convenience sample of 132 participants working in public hospitals through a self-administered paper survey. The results indicate that attitudes, subjective norms, perceived behavioral control, and environmental awareness positively influence nurses' intentions to implement sustainable practices in the workplace. The findings are expected to assist various stakeholders in developing sustainable health policies.

INTRODUCTION

Climate change poses a significant danger to human health, impacting not only the natural environment but also various facets of both natural and human-made systems, such as social and economic conditions, and the operations of healthcare systems (WHO, 2023). In the same context, the healthcare sector contributes to high-density carbon emissions because hospitals and medical facilities consume a lot of energy to offer treatment, which raises concerns for both human health and the environment (Lee et al., 2023). Tiitta et al. (2024) emphasize that understanding the link between climate change and health is crucial for healthcare professionals, making it an important component of nursing education. Accordingly, this sector has a responsibility to take the initiative to reduce emissions and reduce resource waste. In fact, population growth, unhealthy lifestyles, chronic diseases, aging population, and increased access to healthcare will increase the demand for healthcare provision. This, in conjunction with the expected impacts of climate change, emphasizes the need for a sustainable and immediate transformation in the healthcare field (Gaudreau et al., 2024). WHO (2017) describes an environmentally sustainable healthcare system as one that enhances, preserves, or reinstates health while reducing adverse effects on the environment. Such a system seizes opportunities to enhance and rehabilitate the environment for the betterment of the health and well-being of present and future generations.

On the other hand, irresponsible behavior of both organizations and individuals has contributed to environmental degradation due to dramatically increased energy consumption and resource waste (Bouarar et al., 2023). For example, many employees, especially in developing countries, do not care about behaviors to reduce water and energy consumption in their workplaces. Okumus et al. (2019, p. 193) stated that "wing to the growing public concerns about environmental sustainability, the importance of sustainable workplaces has increased." Likewise, Haider et al. (2019) pointed out that the significance of sustainable workplaces has risen due to increasing public concerns regarding environmental sustainability. In the healthcare sector, a few studies have investigated nurses' views on "their professional role in addressing climate change" and identified both enabling factors and obstacles that influence their ability to integrate "climate change into their practice" (Gaudreau et al., 2024). According to Tiitta et al. (2024), nurses are key contributors to addressing climate change and promoting environmental sustainability. Kocoglu-Tanyer et al. (2024) emphasize that nurses play a crucial role in addressing and mitigating environmental challenges. Therefore, creating sustainable workplaces involves implementing practices and principles that minimize environmental impact, promote social well-being, and support economic viability.

During the last decade, there has been a growing and urgent need for environmentally friendly healthcare practices, especially in hospitals. These facilities, being major consumers of resources such as water, electricity, gas, and food for medical services, as well as producers of medical and hazardous waste, have intensified the call for environmentally friendly transformations (Berniak-Woźny & Rataj, 2023). By giving equal importance to sustainability and health objectives, healthcare institutions can minimize waste and pollution, enhance air quality for both patients and staff, diminish carbon emissions, efficiently utilize resources, support biodiversity and ecosystems, eradicate harmful substances, and address the challenges posed by climate change (Al-Surf, 2023). Okumus et al. (2019, p. 193) mentioned that "despite knowing that employees can play a vital role in achieving workplace sustainability, less attention has been paid to understand how employee attitude toward the use of environmentally sustainable work practices can be developed." Similarly, Haider et al. (2019) stated that there is insufficient focus on understanding how to cultivate employee attitudes towards using environmentally sustainable work practices, despite recognizing the pivotal role employees' play in achieving workplace sustainability. In addition, Wesselink et al. (2017) noted that researchers have not sufficiently investigated the factors that influence employees' sustainability behaviors. Consequently, it seems that further research is needed to determine what motivates nurses to adopt sustainable work practices.

Nurses hold a pivotal position within healthcare environments, and their dedication to implementing sustainable practices can exert a substantial influence on hospitals' overall environmental impact. According to Anåker and Marie (2014), sustainability in nursing encompasses six attributes: ecology, environment, future outlook, global perspective, holistic approach, and maintenance. Tiitta et al. (2024) noted that nursing students acknowledge the increasing responsibility they have in tackling climate change. Nursing of the future has the potential to connect local actions with global impact, providing a proactive contribution to improving sustainable healthcare (Goodman, 2011). However, the initial step in implementing sustainable practices in healthcare is to identify and evaluate barriers. A study conducted by Griggs et al. (2017) highlighted the lack of engagement of nurses in environmental sustainability. There are a disparity between nurses' personal values and professional duties, making it difficult for them to influence environmental care in the workplace. Social norms and professional paradigms hinder the adoption of new ways of thinking and working. Consequently, the topic of environmental sustainability does not receive adequate attention in the field of nursing. Furthermore, Aboueid et al. (2023) identified additional factors that are recognized as barriers to implementing sustainable practices in healthcare settings. These barriers encompass various aspects, including personal factors (such as understanding, skills, and mindset), organizational factors (such as finances, planning, and readiness), geographic/structural factors (such as infrastructure and community awareness), political factors (such as laws and incentives), and additional factors (such as patient awareness and comprehension).

The theory of planned behavior (TPB) is one of the theoretical frameworks that have been adopted to investigate environmentally friendly behaviors among customers (e.g., Bouarar et al., 2023; Mouloudj et al., 2023b), farmers (e.g., Erokhin et al., 2024; Mouloudj et al., 2023a), and employees (e.g., Lee et al., 2023). Moreover, several investigations have applied the TPB to examine intentions to implement sustainable practices (e.g., Saleh et al., 2020; Wesselink et al., 2017). Therefore, in this study, we will extend the TPB to include environmental awareness in order to predict nurses' intentions. Environmental awareness involves knowledge about environmental challenges such as pollution, climate change, resource depletion, and biodiversity loss, as well as an appreciation of the importance of conservation and sustainable practices to mitigate these issues.

Even yet, in order to lessen anti-environmental behaviors, it is crucial to support the implementation of sustainable practices in the health sector. To the best of the authors' knowledge, nevertheless, not much study has empirically addressed the determinants of adopting these practices in the setting of Algeria, a country that is making great efforts to attain sustainability. In light of the aforementioned, the purpose of this investigation is to respond to the following two queries: (1) how much does nurses' intention to use sustainable practices at work depend on their awareness of the environment? And (2) how much do the TPB structures influence nurses' intention to adopt sustainable work practices? The remainder of this chapter is structured as follows: Section 2 provides a review of the existing literature and formulates hypotheses. Section 3 outlines the methodology and procedures employed.

The findings are presented in Section 4. Following this, Section 5 discusses the managerial implications and study limitations. Lastly, Section 6 concludes the chapter.

THEORETICAL FRAMEWORK AND HYPOTHESES

Nurses' Workplace Sustainable Practices

Environmentally friendly employee behavior refers to actions taken by employees that reduce their negative impact on the environment. These behaviors can be encouraged and implemented at both individual and organizational levels. According to Haider et al. (2019), achieving workplace sustainability involves implementing "knowledge-based persuasive interventions" to enhance employees' knowledge, attitudes, and intentions regarding the adoption of environmentally sustainable work practices. Tiitta et al. (2024) suggest that nurses can serve as advocates for environmental stewardship by engaging in practices such as waste management, recycling, and encouraging the use of reusable nursing supplies. Therefore, by fostering an environment where environmentally friendly behaviors are the norm, companies can significantly reduce their ecological footprint and contribute to a more sustainable future. Table 1 shows several possible practices for achieving sustainability in the workplace.

Table 1. Initiatives to achieve sustainability in the workplace

Initiatives	Sustainable practices in the workplace
Energy Efficiency	(1) Use energy-efficient lighting, such as LEDs; (2) Implement smart thermostats and HVAC systems to optimize energy use; and (3) Encourage the use of natural light to reduce dependence on artificial lighting.
Waste Reduction	(1) Implement recycling programs for paper, plastics, and electronic waste; (2) Reduce paper use by promoting digital documents and communication; and (3) Use biodegradable or reusable products in cafeterias and break rooms.
Water Conservation	(1) Install low-flow faucets, toilets, and water-efficient appliances; (2) Promote water-saving practices among employees; and (3) Use drought-resistant landscaping.
Sustainable Sourcing	(1) Purchase office supplies and equipment from sustainable sources; (2) Choose furniture and fixtures made from recycled or sustainably sourced materials; and (3) Work with vendors who have strong environmental practices.
Efficient Operations	(1) Optimize processes to reduce waste and improve efficiency; and (2) Implement cost-saving measures that do not compromise environmental and social sustainability.

continued on following page

Table 1. Continued

Initiatives	Sustainable practices in the workplace
Employee Development	(1) Invest in employee training and development programs; (2) Encourage continuous learning and skill development related to sustainability.
Digital Transformation & Green Technology	(1) Move towards paperless operations with digital workflows; (2) Use virtual meeting tools to reduce the need for business travel; (3) Use software and technologies that reduce environmental impact, such as cloud computing; and (4) Implement IoT (Internet of Things) devices to monitor and optimize resource usage.

Source: Authors' own work

By integrating these practices, workplaces can become more sustainable, contributing to the overall well-being of the environment, society, and economy. These practices aim to conserve resources, reduce pollution, promote social equity, and ensure economic viability for present and future generations.

In the field of nursing service, nurses' sustainable workplace practices encompass various actions and initiatives aimed at reducing environmental impact, conserving resources, and promoting eco-friendly operations within healthcare settings. Nurses have the ability to lead initiatives for waste reduction by encouraging recycling practices, implementing sustainable procurement strategies, and advocating for responsible disposal of medical materials (Klein et al., 2020). They also have responsibility for implementing water-saving practices, such as installing efficient water fixtures and appliances, and increasing staff awareness of the importance of water conservation.

In their narrative review, Gaudreau et al. (2024) highlight a disparity between the wide range of roles that nurses could potentially assume in tackling climate change and the extent to which relevant organizations are equipped to establish the necessary conditions to support them in these roles. In this context, nurses play a crucial role in educating patients about the connections between environmental factors and health outcomes. Tiitta et al. (2024) argue that integrating climate change and environmental sustainability into nursing education is essential for preparing nurses to address the health challenges posed by climate change. By providing information on lifestyle choices, sustainable practices, and the impact of pollutants on the environment, nurses empower patients to make choices that positively affect their health and the environment (Fletcher, 2023). They have the opportunity to be actively involved in climate change mitigation efforts. This involves advocating for policies that decrease greenhouse gas emissions, encouraging sustainable transportation alternatives, and participating in community-driven initiatives aimed at improving resilience to climate-related health hazards (Duarte & Pinto-Gouveia, 2017).

In addition, nurses can influence the use of energy-efficient medical devices within hospitals. The utilization of these devices aids in reducing carbon emissions and cost savings. Additionally, they can assist in the use of environmentally friendly products in hospital supplies; promote the use of recyclable materials in clinical settings, thereby reducing the environmental impact of waste (Fletcher, 2023). As we can see, nurses are pivotal in promoting sustainability in healthcare. They lead waste reduction, implement water-saving practices, and educate patients on environmental health. They advocate for climate change mitigation and influence energy-efficient device use, emphasizing the importance of eco-friendly practices. Overall, sustainable practices are crucial for mitigating climate change, preserving biodiversity, and fostering a more equitable and prosperous society.

Planned Behavior Theory (TPB)

TPB is a psychological framework that seeks to explain and predict human behavior, particularly in relation to sustainable and health-related actions. According to the TPB, the stronger an individual's intention to perform a behavior, the more likely they are to actually engage in that behavior. Ajzen (1991, p.181) defined behavioral intentions as "indicators of how hard people are willing to try to perform the behavior indications of how hard people are willing to try, of how much of an effort they are planning to exert, in order to perform the behavior." Similarly, Mouloudj and Bouarar (2023, p. 208) defined it as "the extent of the individual's willingness to complete the behavior". Chan et al. (2014, p. 26) suggested that "ecological behaviour, often led by environmental knowledge, environmental awareness and environmental concern, is a significant factor in predicting hotel employees' intentions to implement green practices." In their study, Okumus et al. (2019) identified that employees' intention to adopt green practices was a significant predictor of ecological behavior. However, Wesselink et al. (2017) pointed out that intention was not significantly related to pro-environmental behaviour in the workplace.

According to previous literature findings, the intention to implement sustainable practices is influenced by many factors, such as personal norm (Chen et al., 2011), environmental knowledge and environmental concern (Chan et al., 2014), and institutional support (Wesselink et al., 2017). In recent years, researchers have extended the TPB with several constructs. Therefore, incorporating environmental awareness into the TPB is expected to improve its predictive power. In this context, scholars have found that environmental awareness and concerns affects intentions to purchase eco-friendly products such as eco-friendly vehicle (Mouloudj et al., 2023a) and energy-efficient home appliances (Bouarar et al., 2023).

Developing Research Hypotheses

Attitude Towards Sustainable Practices

Attitudes are frequently considered as a reflection of an individual's key ideas about the consequence of an action. Attitude, defined as "the degree to which a person has a favorable or unfavorable evaluation or appraisal of the behavior in question" (Ajzen, 1991, p.188). Chen et al. (2011) found that attitudes toward adopting sustainable practices may be influenced by both personal value and past experience. Therefore, if nurses believe that implementing sustainable practices in hospitals is "desirable and favorable, they are more likely to do so" (Erokhin et al., 2024). In this context, many empirical studies have confirmed that positive attitudes play an important role in forming intentions to undertake sustainable practices (Chen et al., 2011; Lee et al., 2023; Okumus et al., 2019; Saleh et al., 2020), save energy (Mouloudj et al., 2023b), water waste reduction (Erokhin et al., 2024), and create green start-ups (Njoku et al., 2024). However, Wesselink et al. (2017) found that Attitude did not significantly influence intention to act pro-environmentally in the workplace. On this basis, the following hypothesis can be proposed:

H1: Attitudes have a significant effect on nurses' intentions to implement sustainable practices in the workplace.

Subjective Norms

According to Ajzen (1991, p.188), subjective norm refers to "the perceived social pressure to perform or not to perform the behavior." So, the term "subjective norm" describes the social pressure that a person experiences regarding whether or not to engage in a particular behavior. In other words, when predicting a person's behavior, it refers to the salient individuals or groups that have an impact on that person's decision regarding whether or not to engage in a particular activity (Lee et al., 2023). Kocoglu-Tanyer et al. (2024) highlight the positive impact of discussing environmental issues within the family on raising awareness. Njoku et al. (2024) reported that the extent of social pressure's impact on intentions to adopt environmentally friendly behaviors varies based on factors such as educational level and individuals' assessment of the quality of information shared by their reference groups. Many previous studies have confirmed the role of subjective norms in influencing the intention to perform sustainable practices (Chen et al., 2011; Lee et al., 2023; Wesselink et al., 2017), adopt green building practices (Saleh et al., 2020), save energy (Mouloudj et al., 2023b), and create green start-ups (Njoku et al., 2024). Based on the above, the following hypothesis can be developed:

H2: Subjective norms have a significant effect on nurses' intentions to implement sustainable practices in the workplace.

Perceived Behavioral Control (PBC)

PBC is defined as "the person's perception of the ease or difficulty of performing the behavior of interest" (Ajzen, 1991, p.183). Therefore, nurses' willingness to adopt sustainable practices in the workplace "depends on how difficult or easy these practices are to implement" (Erokhin et al., 2024). Identified barriers include nurses' limited knowledge of climate change and its connection to nursing practice, resistance to incorporating it into nursing curricula, time constraints in daily practice, and the absence of initiatives that promote environmentally sustainable nursing practices (Gaudreau et al., 2024). Previous research has revealed that PBC is a significant determinant of intentions to implement sustainable behavior, such as promote green healthcare (Lee et al., 2023), save energy (Mouloudj et al., 2023b), water waste reduction (Erokhin et al., 2024), create green start-ups (Njoku et al., 2024), and minimize medication waste (Mouloudj et al., 2023c). Nevertheless, Wesselink et al. (2017) found that PBC did not play a significant role in intention to act pro-environmentally in the workplace. Similarly, other empirical investigations also revealed that intentions to adopt sustainable practices were not influenced by PBC (Chen et al., 2011; Saleh et al., 2020). As a result, the following hypothesis can be proposed:

H3: PBC has a significant effect on nurses' intentions to implement sustainable practices in the workplace.

Environmental Awareness

Environmental awareness refers to the understanding of environmental issues, concerns, and the impact of human activities on the natural world (Saleh et al., 2020). It encompasses the comprehension and mindfulness individuals or groups possess about the environment, comprising its present condition, obstacles, and the consequences of human actions on ecosystems. Chan et al. (2014, p.25) stated that "training and education can normally upgrade employees' skills and environmental knowledge." Farrukh et al. (2022) indicated that employees' consciousness of the serious implications of environmental problems can contribute to making them willing to implement pro-environmental practices, which may result in reducing resource waste and saving costs. Kocoglu-Tanyer et al. (2024) discovered that family environmental awareness influence nursing students' perceptions of environmental issues. Okumus et al. (2019) found that knowledge about "environmentally sustainable work practices" significantly influences employees' intentions to implement these practices. Tiitta et al. (2024) highlight that a holistic approach to climate change within nursing education would not only meet current educational demands but also foster lasting improvements in healthcare settings, supporting environmental sustainability. Farrukh et al. (2022) found that employees' environmental knowledge moderated the "green human resource management"-pro-environmental behaviors relationship. In addition, many empirical studies have found that environmental awareness and knowledge is an important antecedent of intentions to perform green and sustainable practices (Chan et al., 2014), save energy (Mouloudj et al., 2023b), and minimize medication waste (Mouloudj et al., 2023c). Hence, the following hypothesis can be suggested:

H4: Environmental awareness has a significant effect on nurses' intentions to implement sustainable practices in the workplace.

RESEARCH METHODOLOGY

Questionnaire Design

The items within each measurement construct were sourced from existing literature, with slight adjustments made to align with the purposes of this research. Accordingly, attitude towards sustainable practices were measured by using a three statements (items) scale adopted from Okumus et al. (2019). The instrument to measure subjective norm was derived from Erokhin et al. (2024). Furthermore, PBC was operationalized based on the work by Njoku et al. (2024). Environmental awareness was based on the works done by Mohiuddin et al. (2018) and Mouloudj et al. (2023c), and constructed in terms of awareness about implement sustainable practices. In addition, the instrument to measure intentions to implement sustainable practices was adopted from Okumus et al. (2019). The questionnaire was initially composed in English and subsequently translated into Arabic by a language expert. It utilized a 5-point Likert scale, ranging from 1 for "strongly disagree" to 5 for "strongly agree". Subsequently, the authors conducted a pilot study involving 12 nurses to ascertain the clarity and comprehensibility of the questionnaire items. Consequently, some minor adjustments were made to the questionnaire items. Table 1 showcases the survey questionnaire.

Table 2. Measurement of Constructs and Cronbach's Alpha

Constructs Measurement Item (Cronbach's Alpha)	Reference
Attitude towards sustainable practices (0.875) ATT1. I think implementing sustainable practices in public hospitals is quite favorable ATT2. I think implementing sustainable practices in public hospitals is a good idea. ATT3. I believe implementing sustainable practices in public hospitals is quite wise.	Okumus et al. (2019)
Subjective norm (0.834) SN1. Most people who are important to me think I should implement sustainable practices. SN2. My sup-visor expects me to implement sustainable practices. SN3. My colleagues expect me to implement sustainable practices.	Erokhin et al. (2024)
Perceived behavioural control (PBC) (0.807) PBC1. I have resources, time, and opportunities to implement sustainable practices. PBC2. Implement sustainable practices in the public hospital are easy. PBC3. I know how to implement sustainable practices at hospital.	Njoku et al. (2024)
Environmental awareness (0.814) EK1. I am familiar with the specific sustainable practices implemented in public hospitals. EK2. I understand the environmental challenges faced by public hospitals in relation to sustainability. EK3. I believe that sustainable practices are crucial for improving overall public health and reducing environmental impact.	Mohiuddin et al. (2018) and Mouloudj et al. (2023c)
Intentions to implement sustainable practices (0.787) IN1 I intend to turn off computers and lights when they are not being used. IN2 I intend to encourage my co-workers to implement sustainable practices IN3 I will make an effort to implement sustainable practices in the hospital.	Okumus et al. (2019)

Source: Authors' own work

Data Collection

The research targeted participants (nurses) aged ≥18 years, working in Algerian public hospitals. Due to budget and time constraints, a convenience sample of 160 participants was chosen. The authors administered the questionnaire from mid-March to late May 2024. On average, it took 10 minutes to complete the questionnaire. Participants were briefed on the study's scientific objectives, given the freedom to voice their opinions, and informed that completing the questionnaire was optional. All ethical standards, including voluntary participation, anonymity, and confidentiality, were adhered to. Ultimately, 134 questionnaires were collected, resulting in a response rate of 83.75%. Upon review, 2 incomplete questionnaires were deemed invalid, leaving 132 questionnaires for statistical analysis.

Of the total 132 participants, 63 (47.73%) are males and 69 (52.27%) are females. Twenty-seven participants (20.45%) are within the age bracket of 18–30, while 47 (35.61%) fall within the 31–40 age range, collectively constituting over half of the participants. Most of the participants were married (53.79%). Regarding professional experience, 21.21% of participants possess less than five years of experience, 32.58% have between 10-15 years of experience, and 15.91% have accumulated over 15 years of experience in the nursing field. Table 2 presents the more detailed demographic statistics.

Table 3. Respondents' profile (N = 132)

Demographic data	Classification	Frequency	Percentage
Gender	Male	63	47.73
	Female	69	52.27
Age	18-30 years	27	20.45
	31-40 years	47	35.61
	41-50 years	33	25.00
	Over 50 years	25	18.94
Marital Status	Single	53	40.15
	Married	71	53.79
	Other (e.g., Divorced, Widowed)	08	06.06
Years of Experience	Less than 5 years	28	21.21
	5-10 years	43	32.58
	11-15 years	40	30.30
	More than 15 years	21	15.91

Source: Authors' own work

EMPIRICAL FINDINGS AND DISCUSSION

To analyze the data, we employed SPSS version 26 software (IBM Corporation, Armonk, NY, USA). The results depicted in Table 1 indicate that all factors surpassed the recommended threshold of 0.70 for Cronbach's alpha coefficient (Mouloudj et al., 2023c), with alpha coefficients ranging from 0.787 to 0.875. Additionally, normal distribution was assessed (see Table 3). According to Mouloudj and Bouarar (2023), testing for normality is a crucial assumption for conducting multiple regression analysis. The skewness and kurtosis values ranged from -1.700 to 0.717 and 0.017 to 3.726, respectively, as outlined by Njoku et al. (2024), which specifies that data conforms to a normal distribution if skewness values fall within the range of ±2 and kurtosis values within ±7. Consequently, these findings affirm the fulfillment of the reliability condition and the adherence of the data to a normal distribution.

Table 4. Mean, standard deviations, kurtosis, and skewness

Construct	Means	Std. Dev.	Skewness	Kurtosis
ATT	3.853	0.740	-1.072	0.836
SN	2.459	0.545	0.717	0.017
PBC	4.280	0.612	-1.700	3.726
EA	3.010	0.647	-0.177	0.665
INT	4.065	0.568	-0.679	0.540

Source: Authors' own work

To assess the predictive capacity of the extended TPB model relative to the original version, the authors performed a "hierarchical multiple regression analysis". Two models were examined: Model 1 comprised solely the constructs of the original TPB, while Model 2 incorporated the environmental awareness construct. Ensuring the absence of multicollinearity in the data is essential when conducting "hierarchical multiple regression analysis" (Erokhin et al., 2024). Therefore, "variance inflation factor" (VIF) and tolerance tests were employed to assess this concern (Njoku et al., 2024). The results of these tests for the 2 models are presented in Table 4. Tolerance values ranged from 0.64 to 0.96, surpassing the threshold of 0.2. Additionally, VIF indices ranged from 1.03 to 1.55, remaining below the threshold of 5. These findings indicate the absence of multicollinearity in the models (Erokhin et al., 2024).

Table 5. Hierarchical multiple linear regression

Models		B	t	Sig.	Tolerance	VIF	F	Adjusted R^2
Model 1	(Constant)	0.704	1.816	0.072	-	-	41.948	0.484
	ATT	0.371	6.168	0.000	0.643	1.556		
	SN	0.158	2.152	0.033	0.792	1.263		
	PBC	0.361	5.362	0.000	0.750	1.333		

continued on following page

Table 5. Continued

Models		B	t	Sig.	Tolerance	VIF	F	Adjusted R^2
Model 2	(Constant)	0.443	1.128	0.262	-	-	34.440	0.505
	ATT	0.367	6.230	0.000	0.642	1.557		
	SN	0.144	2.001	0.047	0.787	1.270		
	PBC	0.335	5.019	0.000	0.732	1.365		
	EA	0.140	2.550	0.012	0.966	1.036		

Source: Authors' own work

As depicted in Table 4, the outcomes of Model 1 reveal that attitude exerted a positive and significant influence on nurses' intentions to adopt sustainable practices in the workplace ($\beta = 0.371$, $p < 0.001$), thereby confirming H1. Moreover, the findings indicated that subjective norms positively influenced intentions to implement sustainable practices ($\beta = 0.144$, $p < 0.05$), leading to the acceptance of H2. Additionally, the analysis demonstrated a significant impact of PBC on nurses' intentions to implement sustainable practices ($\beta = 0.361$, $p < 0.001$), thus supporting H3. Furthermore, the original TPB constructs accounted for 48.40% of the variance in nurses' intentions to implement sustainable practices.

In Model 2, H4 proposes the direct effect of environmental awareness on nurses' intentions to implement sustainable practices. This hypothesis is also supported (see Table 4). The results indicate that nurses' environmental awareness is a significant determinant of their implement sustainable practices intentions in the workplace ($\beta = 0.140$; $p < 0.05$). Moreover, the empirical findings demonstrate that integrating environmental awareness with the TPB constructs explained 50.50% of the variance in nurses' intentions. Entering the environmental awareness construct explained an additional 2.10% of the variance in intentions to implement sustainable practices (R^2 change = 0.021).

DISCUSSION

This investigation, carried out with a convenience sample comprising 132 nurses from Algerian public hospitals, sought to identify the determinants of nurses' intentions to adopt sustainable practices in the workplace. The results confirmed that attitude play a significant role in shaping nurses' behavioral intentions, serving as influential determinant of intentions to implement sustainable practices in the workplace. This result aligns with results from numerous studies that have identified a significant correlation between attitude and intentions (or behaviors) regarding the adoption of environmentally friendly practices (Chen et al., 2011; Lee et al., 2023; Okumus et al., 2019). In practical terms, the way people feel about a particular behavior, whether positive or negative, strongly influences their likelihood of engaging in it. Positive attitudes towards a behavior typically correlate with higher intentions to enact it (Saleh et al., 2020), while negative attitudes often deter individuals from taking action. Additionally, nurses' attitudes can be influenced by a range of factors including personal beliefs, social norms, and past experiences. Salah et al. (2020) discovered that engineers' attitudes towards adopting green building practices were shaped by their knowledge of sustainable practices and the cost of sustainable materials. Hence, understanding and assessing nurses' attitudes is crucial in predicting and influencing behavioral intentions, as interventions aimed at shifting attitudes towards a behavior can consequently impact nurses' willingness to engage in it. Thus, recognizing the pivotal role of attitudes in shaping behavioral intentions is fundamental in designing effective strategies for promoting desirable behaviors.

The results showed that subjective norms significantly affect nurses' intentions. These norms may include co-workers, senior physicians, senior clinicians, and hospital leaders. Nurses' subjective norms encompass the perceived social pressures or expectations regarding specific behaviors related to their profession. These norms are influenced by the beliefs and opinions of colleagues, supervisors, patients, and broader societal influences. In this context, Xu et al. (2022, p. 2) mentioned that "environmental leaders not only affect followers' common values, commitments and aspirations to deal with environmental problems, but also increase their passion for environmental protection." In the context of nursing, subjective norms can affect various aspects of practice, including adherence to protocols, patient care decisions, and participation in organizational initiatives. This result aligns with results of prior research that have found a favorable association between subjective norms and intentions to engage in environmentally friendly behaviors (Chen et al., 2011; Lee et al., 2023; Saleh et al., 2020; Wesselink et al., 2017). Practically, positive subjective norms can motivate nurses to align their actions with perceived social expectations, fostering a sense of collective responsibility and professionalism. Conversely, negative subjective norms may create barriers to desired behaviors or innovations. Understanding nurses' subjective norms is crucial for healthcare leaders and policymakers seeking to promote positive change and shape supportive environments that encourage sustainable and evidence-based nursing practices.

In addition, the results showed that PBC is a significant antecedent of intentions to implement sustainable practices in the workplace. Nurses' PBC refers to their subjective assessment of the ease or difficulty in executing specific behaviors related to their profession. It encompasses factors such as confidence in skills, access to resources, and perceived barriers or facilitators to action. In this context, nurses' existing and potential roles in tackling climate change remain unclear. As a result, some nurses have advocated for clearer guidance on their responsibilities in addressing climate change and for resources that can help them incorporate this new role into their daily practice (Gaudreau et al., 2024). This result aligns with prior studies that have validated the significant predictive relationship between PBC and individuals' intentions to engage in sustainable practices (e.g., Lee et al., 2023). Therefore, nurses with high PBC are more likely to feel empowered to navigate challenges and adapt to changing circumstances effectively. Conversely, those with lower perceived control may experience feelings of frustration or uncertainty, potentially impacting their ability to perform tasks optimally. Thus, it is crucial to identify and address the factors affecting nurses' PBC to facilitate the transition towards adopting green healthcare practices and to bolster the integration of sustainable initiatives in the workplace.

Finally, our empirical results confirmed that environmental awareness plays a significant role in shaping nurses' intentions to implement sustainable practices in the workplace. This means that increasing environmental awareness is inevitable if hospitals wish to promote sustainable behavior among employees. In fact, environmental awareness often prompts individuals and communities to take actions that contribute positively to environmental protection and sustainability (Chan et al., 2014). Farrukh et al. (2022, p.7) reported that "employees with environmental awareness demonstrate higher environmental care and protection than those with less understanding." Environmental awareness involves recognizing the importance of protecting and preserving natural resources, reducing pollution, and promoting sustainable practices to maintain a healthy planet for present and future generations. Tiitta et al. (2024) stress that incorporating climate change and sustainability into nursing education is crucial for equipping nurses to effectively address the global health challenges arising from climate change. Kocoglu-Tanyer et al. (2024) suggest that incorporating environmental health and social responsibility courses into nursing curricula can greatly influence how students engage with environmental issues. Therefore, environmental awareness often leads to action, such as participating in conservation efforts, supporting eco-friendly initiatives, and advocating for environmental policies and regulations. According to Xu et al. (2022), hospital administrators can improve staff members' green innovation behaviors and raise awareness of green organizations by developing environmental leadership initiatives.

MANAGERIAL IMPLICATIONS

In practice, nurses' workplace sustainable practices include many responsible behaviors such as water conservation, reduction energy consumption, and reduction waste of medical supplies and medications. Based on the empirical results obtained, we may offer some enlightening suggestions to stakeholders, particularly public and private hospitals, to help them improve their ability to create strategies that effectively promote sustainable workplace practices. First, positive intentions toward adopting sustainable workplace practices are significantly shaped by nurses' attitudes. Therefore, in addition to regularly hosting courses and seminars specifically for nurses, it is important to educate nurses about the advantages of sustainable practices and provide a simplified guide to these practices in order to foster favorable attitudes. Second, the results suggest that fostering subjective norms could motivate nurses to embrace sustainable practices in their workplace. Therefore, public hospitals should promote education regarding sustainable practices, organize lectures, and establish mentoring programs for nurses, utilizing reference models to inspire them to integrate environmentally friendly practices. Third, given the significant role of PBC in shaping nurses' intentions, it is crucial to eliminate any obstacles hindering the implementation of sustainable practices in the workplace. This particularly involves ensuring the provision of essential resources and tools needed to adopt such practices. Finally, the results underscore the importance of enhancing awareness regarding the array of sustainable practices viable for implementation in the workplace. It is imperative that nurses are well-informed about the most effective environmentally friendly practices and their associated benefits.

LIMITATIONS AND FUTURE RESEARCH

Notwithstanding its promising results, the present investigation has certain constraints. First, there were just 132 participants in total. Results from a bigger sample size might be more accurate. Second, the sustainability practices of nurses were the only ones assessed in this study. Studies involving physicians, administrative personnel, and medical college students may be carried out in the future. Thirdly, the current study used an extended version of the TPB, and it is expected that by applying other theories, researchers can expand current knowledge of nurses' intentions to implement sustainable practices. For instance, future studies could use the "value-belief-norm" (VBN), social identity theory (SIT), "protection motivation theory" (PMT), or "norm activation model" (NAM) to better understand Nurses' intentions. Finally, in order to investigate the adoption of sustainable practices in other settings, including universities, associations, industrial companies, hotels, and restaurants, future research could adopt the current study's model.

CONCLUSION

The TPB has been widely applied in various fields such as health promotion, waste reduction, sustainable consumer behavior, and organizational behavior to understand and promote behaviors ranging from recycling and energy conservation to healthy eating and implementing sustainability practices in the workplace. It provides a structured approach to understanding the complex interplay of cognitive, social, and environmental factors that shape sustainable human behavior. In the context of sustainability, a green workplace aims to minimize its carbon footprint and contribute positively to environmental preservation and conservation efforts. It encompasses adopting strategies and policies geared towards mitigating the adverse effects an organization imposes on the environment, all the while advocating for conservation and sustainability. This can include initiatives such as reducing energy consumption, implementing recycling programs, using eco-friendly materials, encouraging alternative transportation methods like biking or public transit, and promoting a culture of environmental responsibility among employees. On this basis, sustainable care is essential for the long-term viability of healthcare systems. By focusing on sustainability, healthcare providers can improve patient outcomes, protect the environment, and create a more equitable and resilient healthcare system. Employees adopting practices and behaviors related to environmental protection have become essential to achieving sustainability. Therefore, this investigation sought to understand the drivers of nurses' intentions to adopt work-friendly practices in the workplace. Overall, the study discovered that a number of factors affect nurses' intents, which in turn affect their desire to implement sustainable workplace practices. These factors consist of attitudes, subjective norms, PBC, and environmental awareness. Accordingly, public hospitals should utilize these findings to promote sustainable behavior among employees including nurses.

ACKNOWLEDGMENT

This research received no specific grant from any funding agency in the public, commercial, or not-for profit sectors.

REFERENCES

Aboueid, S., Beyene, M., & Nur, T. (2023). Barriers and enablers to implementing environmentally sustainable practices in healthcare: A scoping review and proposed roadmap. *Healthcare Management Forum*, 36(6), 405–413. DOI: 10.1177/08404704231183601 PMID: 37357691

Ajzen, I. (1991). The theory of planned behavior. *Organizational Behavior and Human Decision Processes*, 50(2), 179–211. DOI: 10.1016/0749-5978(91)90020-T

Al-Surf, M. (2023, August 15). Sustainable Healthcare: Green Practices in the Medical Industry. https://www.linkedin.com/pulse/sustainable-healthcare-green-practices-medical-industry-al-surf/

Anåker, A., & Elf, M. (2014). Sustainability in nursing: A concept analysis. *Scandinavian Journal of Caring Sciences*, 28(2), 381–389. DOI: 10.1111/scs.12121 PMID: 24602178

Berniak-Woźny, J., & Rataj, M. (2023). Towards Green and Sustainable Healthcare: A Literature Review and Research Agenda for Green Leadership in the Healthcare Sector. *International Journal of Environmental Research and Public Health*, 20(2), 908. DOI: 10.3390/ijerph20020908 PMID: 36673663

Bouarar, A. C., Mouloudj, K., Makhlouf, A., & Mouloudj, S. (2023). Exploring Intention to Purchase Energy-Efficient Home Appliances: An Extension of the Theory of Planned Behavior. In Goel, R., & Baral, S. (Eds.), *Handbook of Research on Sustainable Consumption and Production for Greener Economies* (pp. 58–73). IGI Global., DOI: 10.4018/978-1-6684-8969-7.ch004

Chan, E. S., Hon, A. H., Chan, W., & Okumus, F. (2014). What drives employees' intentions to implement green practices in hotels? The role of knowledge, awareness, concern and ecological behaviour. *International Journal of Hospitality Management*, 40, 20–28. DOI: 10.1016/j.ijhm.2014.03.001

Chen, C., Gregoire, M. B., Arendt, S., & Shelley, M. C. (2011). College and university dining services administrators' intention to adopt sustainable practices: Results from US institutions. *International Journal of Sustainability in Higher Education*, 12(2), 145–162. DOI: 10.1108/14676371111118200

Duarte, J., & Pinto-Gouveia, J. (2017). Mindfulness, self-compassion and psychological inflexibility mediate the effects of a mindfulness-based intervention in a sample of oncology nurses. *Journal of Contextual Behavioral Science*, 6(2), 125–133. DOI: 10.1016/j.jcbs.2017.03.002

Erokhin, V., Mouloudj, K., Bouarar, A. C., Mouloudj, S., & Gao, T. (2024). Investigating farmers' intentions to reduce water waste through water-smart farming technologies. *Sustainability (Basel)*, 16(11), 4638. DOI: 10.3390/su16114638

Farrukh, M., Ansari, N., Raza, A., Wu, Y., & Wang, H. (2022). Fostering employee's pro-environmental behavior through green transformational leadership, green human resource management and environmental knowledge. *Technological Forecasting and Social Change*, 179, 121643. DOI: 10.1016/j.techfore.2022.121643

Fletcher, L. (2023). The intersection of nursing and environmental health - A call to action for sustainable practices. *Journal of Advanced Practices in Nursing*, 8(6), 349.

Gaudreau, C., Guillaumie, L., Jobin, É., & Diallo, T. A. (2024). Nurses and climate change: A narrative review of nursing associations' recommendations for integrating Climate Change Mitigation Strategies. *Canadian Journal of Nursing Research*, 56(3), 193–203. DOI: 10.1177/08445621241229932 PMID: 38373438

Goodman, B. (2011). The need for a 'sustainability curriculum' in nurse education. *Nurse Education Today*, 31(8), 733–737. DOI: 10.1016/j.nedt.2010.12.010 PMID: 21232830

Griggs, C., Fernandez, A., & Callanan, M. (2017). Nursing and the barriers to sustainable health care: A literature review. *British Journal of Nursing (Mark Allen Publishing)*, 26(22), 1230–1237. DOI: 10.12968/bjon.2017.26.22.1230 PMID: 29240479

Haider, S., Fatima, F., Bakhsh, K., & Ahmed, M. (2019). Effect of intervention on employees' intentions to use environmentally sustainable work practices: A field experiment. *Journal of Environmental Management*, 248, 109334. DOI: 10.1016/j.jenvman.2019.109334 PMID: 31466182

Klein, A., Taieb, O., Xavier, S., Baubet, T., & Reyre, A. (2020). The benefits of mindfulness-based interventions on burnout among health professionals: A systematic review. *Explore (New York, N.Y.)*, 16(1), 35–43. DOI: 10.1016/j.explore.2019.09.002 PMID: 31727578

Kocoglu-Tanyer, D., Dengiz, K. S., & Sacikara, Z. (2024). Nursing students' conceptualization of environmental problems: A descriptive cross-sectional study. *Nurse Education Today*, 140, 106296. DOI: 10.1016/j.nedt.2024.106296 PMID: 38972168

Lee, P.-C., Huang, C.-Y., Huang, M.-H., & Hsu, M.-J. (2023). The behavioral intention of hospitals to promote sustainable development of green healthcare from the perspective of organizational stakeholders during the COVID-19 epidemic: A case study of hospitals in Taiwan. *Sustainability (Basel)*, 15(5), 4521. DOI: 10.3390/su15054521

Mohiuddin, M., Al Mamun, A., Syed, F. A., Mehedi Masud, M., & Su, Z. (2018). Environmental knowledge, awareness, and business school students' intentions to purchase green vehicles in emerging countries. *Sustainability (Basel)*, 10(5), 1534. DOI: 10.3390/su10051534

Mouloudj, K., & Bouarar, A. C. (2023). Investigating predictors of medical students' intentions to engagement in volunteering during the health crisis. *African Journal of Economic and Management Studies*, 14(2), 205–222. DOI: 10.1108/AJEMS-08-2022-0315

Mouloudj, K., Bouarar, A. C., Bovsh, L. A., Zikii, N., & Kebab, M. (2023a). Investigating the Antecedents of Eco-Friendly Vehicle Purchase Intentions: An Extension of the Theory of Planned Behavior. In Masengu, R., Bigirimana, S., Chiwaridzo, O., Bensson, R., & Blossom, C. (Eds.), *Sustainable Marketing, Branding, and Reputation Management: Strategies for a Greener Future* (pp. 1–16). IGI Global., DOI: 10.4018/979-8-3693-0019-0.ch001

Mouloudj, K., Bouarar, A. C., & Mouloudj, S. (2023b). Extension of the theory of planned behaviour (TPB) to predict farmers' intention to save energy. In *AIP Conference Proceedings* (Vol. 2683, No. 1). AIP Publishing. https://doi.org/DOI: 10.1063/5.0125022

Mouloudj, K., Njoku, A., Asanza, D. M., Bouarar, A. C., Evans, M. A., Mouloudj, S., & Bouarar, A. (2023c). Modeling predictors of medication waste reduction intention in Algeria: Extending the theory of planned behavior. *International Journal of Environmental Research and Public Health*, 20(16), 6584. DOI: 10.3390/ijerph20166584 PMID: 37623170

Njoku, A., Mouloudj, K., Bouarar, A. C., Evans, M. A., Asanza, D. M., Mouloudj, S., & Bouarar, A. (2024). Intentions to Create Green Start-Ups for Collection of Unwanted Drugs: An Empirical Study. *Sustainability (Basel)*, 16(7), 2797. DOI: 10.3390/su16072797

Okumus, F., Köseoglu, M. A., Chan, E., Hon, A., & Avci, U. (2019). How do hotel employees' environmental attitudes and intentions to implement green practices relate to their ecological behavior? *Journal of Hospitality and Tourism Management*, 39, 193–200. DOI: 10.1016/j.jhtm.2019.04.008

Saleh, R. M., Anuar, M. M., Al-Swidi, A. K., & Omar, K. (2020). The effect of awareness, knowledge and cost on intention to adopt green building practices. *International Journal of Environment and Sustainable Development*, 19(1), 33–58. DOI: 10.1504/IJESD.2020.105468

Tiitta, I., Cubelo, F., McDermott-Levy, R., Jaakkola, J. J., & Kuosmanen, L. (2024). Climate change integration in nursing education: A scoping review. *Nurse Education Today*, 139, 106210. DOI: 10.1016/j.nedt.2024.106210 PMID: 38643656

Wesselink, R., Blok, V., & Ringersma, J. (2017). Pro-environmental behaviour in the workplace and the role of managers and organisation. *Journal of Cleaner Production*, 168, 1679–1687. DOI: 10.1016/j.jclepro.2017.08.214

WHO. (2017, February 7). Environmentally sustainable health systems: a strategic document. https://www.who.int/publications/i/item/WHO-EURO-2017-2241-41996-57723

WHO. (2023, October 12). Climate change. https://www.who.int/news-room/fact-sheets/detail/climate-change-and-health

Xu, B., Gao, X., Cai, W., & Jiang, L. (2022). How environmental leadership boosts employees' green innovation behavior? A moderated mediation model. *Frontiers in Psychology*, 12, 689671. DOI: 10.3389/fpsyg.2021.689671 PMID: 35153882

KEY TERMS AND DEFINITIONS

Environmental Awareness: Refers to the understanding and consciousness individuals or groups have regarding the environment, including its current state, challenges, and the impact of human activities on ecosystems.

Environmental management: Refers to the process of overseeing and controlling human activities to ensure they are conducted in a manner that minimizes negative impacts on the environment. It involves assessing, planning, implementing, and monitoring strategies and practices to address environmental issues and promote sustainability.

Green Workplace: Refers to an environmentally sustainable and eco-friendly work environment. It involves implementing practices and policies aimed at reducing the negative impact an organization has on the environment while promoting conservation and sustainability.

Sustainable Healthcare: Refers to healthcare practices and systems that aim to be environmentally, economically, and socially sustainable. The concept of sustainable care focuses on delivering high-quality healthcare services while minimizing negative impacts on the environment, reducing costs, and ensuring equitable access to care for all individuals.

Chapter 2
Advancing Circular Economy Through B Corp Certification and Green HRM Practices

Lydia Murillo-Ramos
https://orcid.org/0000-0003-3436-9861
Universidad Rey Juan Carlos, Spain

Cristina Pérez-Pérez
Universidad Rey Juan Carlos, Spain

ABSTRACT

In today's business environment, sustainability prompts a reassessment of corporate strategies to encompass social and environmental objectives alongside economic goals. However, the convergence of circular economy (CE) with human resource management (HRM), particularly within the context of benefit corporations (B Corps), remains largely unexplored. This chapter aims to address this gap by constructing an integrative framework that highlights the key role of green HRM in reinforcing CE practices and policies, with a specific focus on B Corps. By examining the intersection of these areas, the chapter seeks to illuminate the synergies between B Corp certification, green HRM practices, and circular economy models. Employing systematic literature review methods and qualitative data analysis with Atlas.ti software, it offers insights into theoretical foundations, practical implications, and avenues for future research. Findings underscore circular economy's transformative potential and advocate for integrating green HRM practices into organizational strategies, fostering sustainability.

DOI: 10.4018/979-8-3693-6289-1.ch002

1. INTRODUCTION

In the contemporary business landscape, sustainability has emerged as a crucial concern, necessitating a reevaluation of corporate strategies to encompass social and environmental objectives alongside economic goals. Central to this paradigm shift is the adoption of circular economy premises, which offer a promising avenue for sustainable development. However, the intersection of circular economy with human resource management, particularly within the context of B Corps remains relatively unexplored. This chapter seeks to fill this void by constructing an integrative framework that highlights the pivotal role of green HRM in reinforcing circular economy practices and policies, with a specific focus on the context of B Corps.

As environmental concerns escalate, organizations are prioritizing the implementation of sustainable practices, with circular economy emerging as a key strategy to address environmental challenges. By advocating for resource efficiency, waste reduction, and product lifecycle extension, circular economy frameworks promote a regenerative approach to resource management. Concurrently, the emergence of green HRM practices underscores the importance of embedding environmental considerations into HRM processes, ranging from recruitment to performance management. Through initiatives such as green training and involvement, organizations aim to cultivate a workforce that is aligned with sustainability principles, thus harmonizing organizational goals with broader societal objectives.

This chapter endeavors to provide robust theoretical premises and actionable insights into organizational adaptation and innovative work practices. Drawing upon interdisciplinary perspectives from organizational theory, strategic management, and sustainability studies, the chapter elucidates the intricate interplay between circular economy principles, B Corp certification, and green HRM. Leveraging the qualitative data analysis software Atlas.ti, the chapter employs a systematic literature review approach, utilizing the Web of Science database to access a vast repository of scientific articles. Atlas.ti enables researchers to systematically code, categorize, and analyze textual data from various sources, facilitating the identification of patterns, themes, and relationships within literature. By organizing and managing large datasets, Atlas.ti streamlines the review process, enhancing efficiency and rigor.

This methodological choice offers several advantages, including comprehensive coverage of peer-reviewed literature, rigorous quality control, and the ability to identify key trends and emerging research areas. Specifically, the systematic literature review with the PRISMA model, allows for a thorough analysis of existing research on circular economy, B Corps, and green HRM, providing a robust foundation for the chapter's theoretical and conceptual development.

The general aim of this research is to investigate the potential contribution of the B Corp Certification System to increasing environmental and social awareness within business organizations. It also delves into the impact of green HRM policies on employees' commitment, within the context of circular economy principles. Furthermore, it demonstrates that companies implementing certification programs for recycling services and waste management significantly contribute to advancing the goals of the circular economy. Therefore, some specific objectives of this chapter include:

- RQ1: Evaluation of the theoretical underpinnings of green HRM within the context of circular economy, considering its implications across economic, social, and environmental dimensions.
- RQ2: Development of an exploratory conceptual framework elucidating the synergies between B Corp certification, green HRM practices, and organizational transitions towards circularity.
- RQ3: Identification of research gaps and articulation of future research agendas, aimed at advancing theoretical understanding and practical application in this evolving domain.

Furthermore, the chapter underscores the growing significance of B Corp certification as a voluntary system promoting ethical, environmental, and social responsibility in business operations. By integrating the B Corp mission within HRM practices, organizations can attract and retain top talent, fostering a culture of sustainability and accountability that enhances organizational resilience and competitiveness. Ultimately, this purpose-driven approach not only boosts organizational performance but also contributes to a more equitable and sustainable business ecosystem.

Academically, it advances theoretical understanding by identifying the potential of B Corp certifications and green HRM practices as key factors in meeting circular economy principles and driving structural change in business. By systematically analyzing the intricate interplay between these elements, the chapter provides valuable insights that enrich academic discourse and lay the groundwork for further research in these domains. Moreover, its systematic approach offers practitioners actionable guidance for implementing sustainable practices, enhancing corporate social responsibility, and cultivating a culture of sustainability within organizations. The chapter emphasizes the benefits of integrating B Corp certification and green HRM practices, equipping organizations with the tools to attract top talent, enhance competitiveness, and achieve long-term success in today's dynamic business environment. Specifically, it underscores the critical importance of aligning organizational operations with sustainability principles, providing practical insights for fostering a culture of sustainability and driving green-oriented transformations in HRM strategies.

In conclusion, this chapter serves as a valuable resource for both academics and practitioners alike, offering theoretical insights and practical recommendations for navigating contemporary sustainability challenges. Its integrative framework and actionable insights pave the way for organizations to embrace sustainability as a core value. Moreover, it highlights the intrinsic link between learning and change, underlying the imperative of fostering a culture of organizational learning alongside the implementation of green HRM practices. This dual approach not only facilitates firms' transition to a circular economy but also promotes knowledge acquisition and adaptation to novel sustainable paradigms, ensuring resilience and success in an ever-evolving business environment.

2. THEORETICAL FRAMEWORK

The shift from a linear to a circular ecosystem is driven by growing awareness of the negative externalities linked to organizational impacts on the socioeconomic context and the limitless consumption of resources, which heighten social concerns about environmental sustainability (Boffa et al., 2023). This shift has been further catalyzed by the disruptions caused by COVID-19 on the entrepreneurial ecosystem (Boffa et al., 2023).

In response to these concerns, sustainability and the implementation of environmental practices have become priorities for many companies and governments (Testa et al., 2020). This focus has led to comprehensive analyses of processes and the development of alternative methods to enhance environmental sustainability. The result has been a significant increase in attention to strategic management, sustainability, and supply chain management fields (Daddi et al., 2021; Ferasso et al., 2020).

One of these new paths is the so-called circular economy, which has gradually attracted increasing attention due to its consideration as a relevant driver towards a more sustainable society, encompassing social and economic implications (de Jesus & Mendonça, 2018). The circular economy model is generally understood as an opportunity to transform the traditional linear economy model, unsustainable from both, the environmental and social point of view (Moreau et al., 2017) into a system that acknowledges the finiteness of natural resources (Ghisellini et al., 2016), and therefore aims to keep them in constant circulation to maintain their value (Esposito et al., 2018). Moreover, it seems like an effective method to reconcile economic growth and environmental sustainability given that the main reason behind its use is to create an environmentally friendly economic model (Ghisellini et al., 2016).

The circular economy model understands the production model as a closed-looped system designed to reduce pollution and avoid the overuse of resources while maintaining economic growth (Winans et al., 2017). Initially based on the 3R principles (reduce, reuse, and recycle) framework, the circular economy has further evolved into the 6R principles (reuse, recycle, redesign, remanufacture, reduce, and recover) (Jawahir & Bradley, 2016). Therefore, the circular economy can be defined as a model through which the products are restored and revitalized, and the value and functionality of components and materials are maximized during their lifespan (Elf et al., 2022). This approach aims to produce benefits for companies, society, and the environment by reducing environmental pollution and creating new, distributed, diversified, and inclusive growth opportunities (Elf et al., 2022).

Due to this, the circular economy is expected to revolutionize how people and organizations utilize and consume resources, reshaping the way companies and supply chains deliver goods and services (Klein et al., 2022). Considering this, the generalization of the circular economy requires a compromise of collaboration among all actors, at all social and inter-organizational levels (Kristensen et al., 2021). Moreover, this has led to some authors to emphasize the importance of adopting sustainable practices all along the business processes to encourage the transition towards the circular economy (Obeidat et al., 2023). This includes the HRM processes, which has been said to help advance organizational sustainability through training, the articulation of green teams, or workforce empowerment, among others (Sroufe, 2017). Hence, in accordance with Jabbour and Santos (2008), the importance of tackling the "human side" of companies is undeniable for ensuring the right functioning of the company, and especially the sustainability practices that are to be implemented.

That is why, in this chapter, we will analyze the relationship between circular economy and HRM through a review of the literature on green economy initiatives and environmental management enablers (Teng et al., 2023). These initiatives represent a shift away from traditional growth models towards strategies that prioritize circular economies, low-carbon technologies, and equitable resource access. Although green economy initiatives hold promise, the literature acknowledges the complexities and trade-offs involved in their implementation (Kronenberg et al., 2021). Balancing economic competitiveness and environmental protection requires nuanced policy frameworks that foster innovation while mitigating potential negative impacts (Bai & Li, 2023).

3. METHODOLOGY

A systematic literature review (SLR) was conducted to map and analyze the relevant studies. This method involves several well-established steps, allowing other researchers to validate and replicate the process (Denyer & Tranfield, 2009). We followed the five-step procedure proposed by Denyer and Tranfield (2009): (1) formulating the research question, (2) identifying relevant studies, (3) selecting and evaluating the studies, (4) analyzing and synthesizing the data, and (5) reporting and utilizing the findings. Figure 1 illustrates the research design using a PRISMA (Preferred Reporting Items for Systematic Reviews and Meta-Analyses) flow diagram (Page et al., 2021).

The primary aim of this study is to investigate the overlap between circular economy principles, green HRM, and the corporate social responsibility model of B Corps. This exploration seeks to uncover the shared aspects and synergistic effects among these fields. Following the approach of Maqueira et al., (2022), we utilized the Web of Science (WoS) Core Collections database, which offers a comprehensive sample of high-impact journal articles.

By analyzing previous studies (e.g. Kirst et al., 2021; Yong et al., 2019) and conducting brainstorming sessions, we identified the most frequently used keywords in this research area. The resulting search string employed simple operators, including truncated characters (e.g., *), exact phrases, and Boolean operators (e.g., AND, OR), targeting the "topic" (TS) field in WoS, ensuring the keywords appeared in titles, abstracts, article keywords, or keywords plus. This process identified 93 documents published between 2017 and May 2024 (see Figure 1).

Next, we applied criteria to determine which studies to exclude or include. First of all, only articles and reviews were selected, thus decreasing the results sample to 82. Next, to ensure the quality of the papers, we followed Langhof and Güldenberg (2020) example, using the ABS Journal Quality Guide from the British Association of Business Schools. We excluded studies published in journals not listed in the ABS Journal Ranking 2021, reducing the number of papers to 33. We then scrutinized the titles, abstracts, and keywords, eliminating ten articles due to their peripheral focus on green urban development efficiency or non-financial information disclosure, rather than our primary research topics. After this screening, 23 articles remained, which were then thoroughly reviewed to confirm their relevance. Figure 1 shows the exclusion steps and the final selection of papers.

Lastly, in the analysis and synthesis phase, the selected articles were thoroughly examined and coded. We created a spreadsheet database to capture each study's key research topics, findings, and supplementary information. Multiple researchers participated in this process to reduce bias and enhance the reliability and accuracy of the results (Denyer & Tranfield, 2009). Additionally, forward and backward searches (snowballing) from the references of identified papers were performed to find any missing primary sources (Thomé et al., 2016). This led to the addition of 19 articles, ensuring a comprehensive review. This part of the process was supported by the ATLAS.ti Desktop software, which provided robust features for conducting the literature review. By uploading the documents into ATLAS.ti Desktop, we maximized the software's capabilities to explore the literature, run word frequency checks, and generate textual reports for codes and quotations, ensuring alignment with the research topic (Mohamad, 2024).

Figure 1. Systematic literature review process

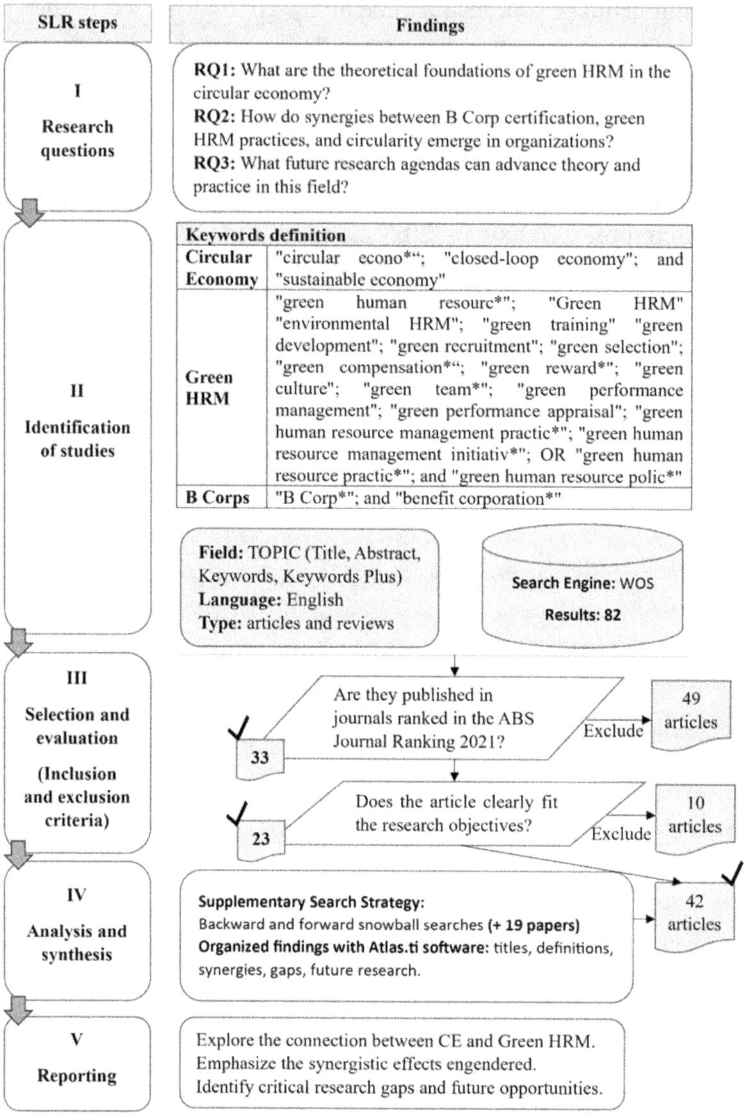

Adapted from Maqueira et al. (2022)

4. RESULTS

4.1 The Theoretical Underpinnings of Green HRM Within the Context of Circular Economy

The circular economy refers to an economic system intentionally designed to replace the concept of "end-of-life" with an emphasis on renewable energy sources and the efficient use of materials throughout the entire production, distribution, and consumption cycle (Kirchherr et al., 2017; Marrucci et al., 2023). This system has become a new business model that is being applied by private companies and public organizations to assist them in achieving their sustainable goals (Wan et al., 2023) in the wake of the increased interest in the green aspects of businesses and transactions (Gusmerotti et al., 2020). However, among all the topics that have been analyzed in the literature, the human side of the circular economy is underrepresented (Jabbour & Santos, 2008), not addressing yet how the HRM initiatives may impact the implantation of circular economy initiatives (Esposito et al., 2018).

This emerging field, termed green HRM, encompasses efforts to align HRM practices with sustainability objectives, including initiatives such as employee empowerment and fostering a sustainable organizational culture (Renwick et al., 2013). Given its comprehensive approach, which considers the interplay between production activities, environmental impact, and the potential influence of HRM, the field of green HRM has garnered increased attention from both scholars and practitioners (Ahmad, 2015; Chaudhary, 2020; Marrucci et al., 2023).

As per different authors, green HRM represents an innovative approach that improves environmental sustainability, reduces waste production, improves economic welfare, and engages employees in green behavior in the workplace (Renwick et al., 2013; Tang et al., 2018). It plays a pivotal role in enhancing the overall sustainability of organizations (Chaudhary, 2020; Farrukh et al., 2022), striving to achieve long-term social, financial, and ecological objectives (Mariappanadar & Kramar, 2014). This entails aligning HRM strategic decisions with environmental goals (Gholami et al., 2016), and implementing eco-focused practices such as recruitment, selection, training, and assessment processes, as well as cultivating an environmentally conscious organizational culture across all HRM facets (Jabbour & Santos, 2008; Renwick et al., 2013). Ultimately, the aim of green HRM is to establish a suite of human resource management practices that significantly contribute to company success without compromising sustainability principles.

That is why, regarding the areas included in the green HRM research, we find a wide range of topics, like corporate reactions to climate change, the development of environmentally friendly products, or the synergies between green HRM and organization practices (Govindarajulu & Daily, 2004; Hoffman, 2005). This broad research agenda underscores the multifaceted nature of green HRM's role in improving an organization's environmental performance. As such, continuous advancement in the field of green HRM is essential to pave the way for a new sustainability paradigm where the integration and execution of green initiatives are central to the circular economy model (Obeidat et al., 2023).

Considering the aforementioned factors, it is evident that green HRM primarily aims to enhance an organization's environmental performance by fostering employee awareness, knowledge, skills, and engagement (Marrucci et al., 2023). Additionally, green HRM practices serve as fundamental pillars within firms. These encompass initiatives such as promoting employee engagement, providing robust management support, cultivating a culture of environmental responsibility, and implementing Environmental Management Systems (EMS) like ISO 14001. Recognized as significant drivers of green process innovation, these elements offer a structured approach to address environmental challenges and advance sustainable practices within organizations (Teng et al., 2023).

4.2 Elucidating the Synergies Between B Corp Certification, Green HRM Practices, and Organizational Transitions Towards Circularity

In today's business landscape, companies face mounting pressures, both internally and externally, to adopt environmentally sustainable practices. These pressures emanate from diverse sources, including regulatory requirements, shifting consumer preferences, and societal expectations (Dai et al., 2023). Consequently, organizations are increasingly compelled to integrate green approaches into their operations to meet these evolving environmental demands.

However, amidst these efforts, one critical aspect often overlooked is the role of employee development. As emphasized by Teng et al. (2023) the success of green initiatives critically depends on the capacity building of employees. Hence, organizations must invest in robust training and development policies to equip their workforce with the requisite skills and knowledge to effectively implement green practices.

With the growing interest in research on green HRM, significant attention has been directed towards its correlation with circular economy systems (Jabbour et al., 2019). Scholars argue that aligning these initiatives can culminate in a cohesive green organizational strategy that promotes circular economy principles (Obeidat et al., 2023). This convergence of green HRM and circular economy concepts holds particular significance as it enables companies not only to contribute to sustainability and society but also to gain competitive advantages and enhance market positions (Obeidat et al., 2023).

Furthermore, similar to green HRM, reverse logistics is considered an environmental practice (Kazancoglu et al., 2021). Reverse logistics activities are gaining prominence due to economic and environmental concerns in the circular economy, involving the reverse flow of materials, information, human resources, and finance among stakeholders (Kazancoglu et al., 2021). The bundle of activities and initiatives brought by green HRM practices not only fosters environmentally friendly companies but also positively impacts circular economy, employee satisfaction, and organizational performance (Subramanian & Suresh, 2022). These practices contribute to reducing the need for raw materials, and increasing resource recycling, reuse, and remanufacturing, thereby minimizing waste, and enhancing firm performance (Despeisse et al., 2017).

In the realm of HRM, circular economy promotes changes in teamwork practices, learning culture, employee empowerment, performance assessments, and rewards, thereby improving firm sustainability and fostering the adoption of green supply chain practices, which directly impacts firm results (Jabbour & Santos, 2008; Marrucci et al., 2023). These initiatives also promote innovation, resource utilization, and efficient management (Batista et al., 2019; Pieroni et al., 2019). In this context, green HRM practices have emerged as a winning strategy for manufacturing firms to gain and sustain a competitive advantage (Waqas et al., 2021). They facilitate the development of green differentiated products through green innovation and human resource practices, addressing environmental challenges effectively. However, these authors further stated that to encourage the green innovation and the adoption of green HRM practices, the top-level management should focus on implementing big data analytics and promoting the information-sharing climate within the manufacturing firms (Waqas et al., 2021).

Additionally, innovation in sustainable business models is crucial for successful circular economy implementation, making companies more responsible in reducing environmental and social burdens while maintaining economic benefits (Ghisellini et al., 2024). This necessitates the adoption of business models aimed at fostering environmental sustainability, efficient resource utilization, and the incorporation of ethical and social values (Boffa et al., 2023)

Herein lies the significant role of B Corps as an emerging managerial model. In the literature, both Benefit Corporations and Certified B Corps are referred to as B Corps. Benefit Corporations, are described as "purpose-oriented" rather than "market-oriented" organizations, as their actions aim to generate not only economic benefits but also social and environmental ones (Mion & Loza Adaui, 2020). In contrast, Certified B Corps hold a sustainability certification valid for three years, which guarantees high standards of transparency and verified social and environmental performance (Gazzola et al., 2023).

Due to these attributes, B Corps, which are certified to produce positive impacts for stakeholders, the environment, and society, are recognized as effective mechanisms for advancing circular business models (B Lab, 2018). These organizations implement cleaner production practices and promote sustainable consumption, aligning with circular economy principles (Franco, 2017). Certified B Corps are uniquely positioned to reconcile sustainability and profit objectives, adhering to the Triple Bottom Line approach to sustainability (Liute & De Giacomo, 2022)

Defined as "hybrid organizations," B Corps must adhere to higher standards of purpose, accountability, and transparency than traditional companies (Mion and Loza Adaui, 2020). The certification process includes a rigorous B Impact Assessment (BIA) that evaluates social and environmental performance, leading to enhanced financial performance and increased stakeholder trust (Krause, 2018). By obtaining sustainability certification, companies can improve their financial performance, as consumers are more willing to pay a premium for socially responsible products, and stakeholders can trust that the company is not engaging in greenwashing (Ferioli et al., 2022).

In essence, the synergies between B Corp certification, green HRM practices, and organizational transitions towards circularity offer a pathway towards sustainable growth, profitability, and societal well-being (see figure 2). By integrating these elements, businesses can navigate the complexities of today's environmental imperatives while fortifying their competitive edge in the market. Through purpose-driven actions, enhanced employee development, and alignment with circular economy principles, organizations can not only contribute to environmental sustainability but also foster innovation, efficiency, and stakeholder trust.

Figure 2. Circular Economy Adoption: Visualizing Synergies with Green HRM and B Corps

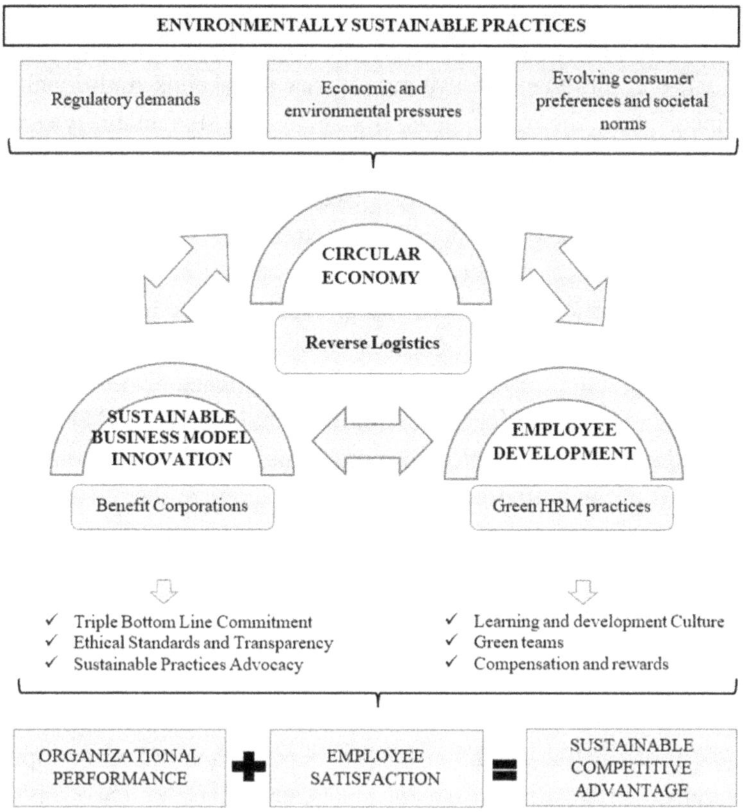

Source: Own elaboration

4.3 Identification of Research Gaps and Articulation of Future Research Agenda

Despite the growing body of research on both green HRM and circular economy in recent years, the intersection of these topics remains underexplored. Many important aspects have not yet been addressed (Pham et al., 2019). While it is well recognized that employees and HRM are crucial for achieving a more sustainable production model (Veleva et al., 2017), the direct link between green HRM initiatives —such as the role of organizational learning—, and circular economy principles is still underdeveloped (Chiappetta Jabbour et al., 2019; van Langen et al., 2021;

Subramanian & Suresh, 2022). This intersection has received insufficient attention, especially in non-western countries (Obeidat et al., 2023).

Furthermore, the environmental impact of reverse logistics activities is generally overlooked in the literature (Kazancoglu et al., 2021). This gap highlights the need for a more comprehensive evaluation that transcends traditional economic metrics to incorporate the multifaceted dimensions of sustainability advocated by the green economy. The analysis of green economy system indicators can guide the understanding of the intricate interplay between economic growth, environmental stewardship, and societal well-being (Bai & Li, 2023).

Although the technical aspects of circular economy have been addressed, the human dimension, particularly in terms of green HRM, needs further investigation (Chiappetta Jabbour et al., 2019). Current analyses have not adequately explored how green HRM practices affect sustainable performance, especially through potential mediating effects of circular economy (Obeidat et al., 2023). Similarly, the integration of the B Corps model within the context of circular economy requires a deeper analysis of the entrepreneurial ecosystems, given the numerous interconnections among various stakeholders, institutions, and organizations (Gazzola et al., 2023). Despite the recent proliferation of hybrid-purpose organizations like B Corps, their association with the entrepreneurial ecosystem and their relation to CE-related business practices remain poorly understood (Boffa et al., 2023).

To address these gaps, future research should focus on several key areas. Given the growing importance of environmental protection for both companies and governments (Testa et al., 2020), scholars should expand their efforts on topics such as green procurement, life-cycle assessment, and general management of environmental impacts (Daddi et al., 2021; De Giacomo et al., 2019; Marrucci et al., 2021). Despite the increasing variety of topics, areas such as employees' perceptions of green HRM still need further development (Marrucci et al., 2023).

From a theoretical perspective, exploring the nexus of green HRM and CE-based business models can be advanced by drawing on stakeholder theory and the resource-based view (Sodhi, 2015). In the same vein, a variety of methodological approaches, including qualitative, quantitative, mixed-methods, and case study or interview techniques, should be employed to gain deeper insights (Chiappetta Jabbour et al., 2019; Pham et al., 2019).

Likewise, future studies should enhance the explanatory power of existing models by investigating additional moderators and mediators, such as green teams and organizational ecological culture, which may influence the relationship between green HRM, circular economy, and sustainable performance (Obeidat et al., 2023). Comparative studies across different national contexts and industries (e.g., manufacturing and service sectors) will further enhance our understanding of green HRM applications (Pham et al., 2019).

Researchers should examine the role and commitment of top management in enhancing learning and implementing green HRM practices (Subramanian & Suresh, 2022). Additionally, the integration of green HRM practices, circular economy, green supply chain management, and sustainable consumption within organizations' development strategies warrants further investigation (Pham et al., 2019).

Lastly, there is a need for more robust approaches and techniques to properly measure environmental and social impacts. Policymakers should focus on developing interventions to support the adoption of these measures, as current approaches are not widely diffused (Ghisellini et al., 2024). By addressing these research gaps and following this future research agenda, we can advance both theoretical understanding and practical applications in the evolving domains of green HRM, circular economy and B Corps business models.

5. CONCLUSIONS, IMPLICATIONS AND MAIN LIMITATIONS.

This chapter has highlighted the growing importance of stakeholder pressure in driving the implementation of the circular economy. This approach, which aims to minimize waste through recycling and reusing, represents a significant shift from traditional economic models by focusing on maintaining the utility and value of materials, components, and products (World Economic Forum, 2022). While circular economy strategies are designed to accelerate sustainability, the role of green HRM in supporting these efforts has not been fully explored.

Green HRM is crucial for establishing effective organizational sustainability initiatives by fostering pro-environmental behavior among employees and enhancing environmental management practices. Despite its potential, green HRM is still a developing field and requires further research to fully understand its impact on sustainable development. In this context, Certified B Corps, with their commitment to sustainable practices, exemplify how integrating green HRM can facilitate the transition to a circular economy by promoting cleaner manufacturing practices and balancing profit with environmental responsibility.

5.1 Theoretical and Practical Implications

The findings of this study have significant implications for both theoretical advancements and practical applications in the realms of green HRM and the circular economy.

On a theoretical level, this research underscores the pivotal role of HRM in shaping the implementation of circular economy premises and B Corps' business models. By emphasizing the significance of human factors alongside technological innovations, the study highlights how integrating green HRM into circular economy models and B Corps' operations can provide a more comprehensive understanding of sustainability initiatives. Moreover, the study elucidates the synergies between green HRM practices, B Corps' business models, and circular economy principles. By delineating these interconnected relationships, the research provides a theoretical foundation for future investigations into how specific HRM practices—such as green recruitment, training, and performance management—align with B Corps' missions and directly contribute to achieving circular economy objectives.

Practically, the study underscores the circular economy's transformative potential, extracting value from waste materials and reshaping organizational dynamics with society, while also advancing sustainability efforts. It highlights the pivotal role of green HRM initiatives in enhancing employee well-being and driving forward green manufacturing practices, advocating for their integration into strategic decision-making processes. Moreover, the chapter emphasizes how the circular economy fosters business model innovation, enabling firms to adapt and thrive in the digital transformation era. Ultimately, the study aims to provide actionable insights for responsible and sustainable innovation practices, advocating for the emergence of B Corps as exemplary models for transitioning towards circularity in the entrepreneurial landscape.

5.2 Limitations

Certainly, while our research is comprehensive, it does have its limitations. Firstly, our systematic literature review relied solely on the Web of Science database, potentially excluding relevant studies from other sources and introducing a selection bias. However, it is worth noting that our inclusion criteria, which filtered by the quality impact of journals, ensured access to high-quality information. To address these limitations, future research could adopt a more comprehensive approach to literature review by incorporating multiple databases beyond just Web of Science, thus mitigating the risk of overlooking relevant studies and reducing selection bias.

Finally, although we employed the PRISMA model for reproducibility, its implementation may be subject to subjective interpretations during literature selection and data extraction. Additionally, while a double peer review process was conducted to enhance analytical rigor, the integration of Atlas.ti software served as a valuable complement in ensuring consistency and objectivity throughout our review process.

REFERENCES

Ahmad, S. (2015). Green Human Resource Management: Policies and practices. *Cogent Business & Management*, 2(1), 1030817. Advance online publication. DOI: 10.1080/23311975.2015.1030817

Batista, L., Gong, Y., Pereira, S., Jia, F., & Bittar, A. (2019). Circular supply chains in emerging economies – a comparative study of packaging recovery ecosystems in China and Brazil. *International Journal of Production Research*, 57(23), 7248–7268. DOI: 10.1080/00207543.2018.1558295

Boffa, D., Prencipe, A., Papa, A., Corsi, C., & Sorrentino, M. (2023). Boosting circular economy via the b-corporation roads. The effect of the entrepreneurial culture and exogenous factors on sustainability performance. *The International Entrepreneurship and Management Journal*, 19(2), 523–561. DOI: 10.1007/s11365-023-00835-8

Chaudhary, R. (2020). Green Human Resource Management and Employee Green Behavior: An Empirical Analysis. *Corporate Social Responsibility and Environmental Management*, 27(2), 630–641. DOI: 10.1002/csr.1827

Chiappetta Jabbour, C. J., Sarkis, J., Lopes de Sousa Jabbour, A. B., Scott Renwick, D. W., Singh, S. K., Grebinevych, O., Kruglianskas, I., & Filho, M. G. (2019). Who is in charge? A review and a research agenda on the 'human side' of the circular economy. *Journal of Cleaner Production*, 222, 793–801. DOI: 10.1016/j.jclepro.2019.03.038

Daddi, T., Heras-Saizarbitoria, I., Marrucci, L., Rizzi, F., & Testa, F. (2021). The effects of green supply chain management capability on the internalisation of environmental management systems and organisation performance. *Corporate Social Responsibility and Environmental Management*, 28(4), 1241–1253. DOI: 10.1002/csr.2144

Dai, J., Ahmed, Z., Sinha, A., Pata, U. K., & Alvarado, R. (2023). Sustainable green electricity, technological innovation, and ecological footprint: Does democratic accountability moderate the nexus? *Utilities Policy*, 82, 101541. DOI: 10.1016/j.jup.2023.101541

De Giacomo, M. R., Testa, F., Iraldo, F., & Formentini, M. (2019). Does Green Public Procurement lead to Life Cycle Costing (LCC) adoption? *Journal of Purchasing and Supply Management*, 25(3), 100500. DOI: 10.1016/j.pursup.2018.05.001

de Jesus, A., & Mendonça, S. (2018). Lost in Transition? Drivers and Barriers in the Eco-innovation Road to the Circular Economy. *Ecological Economics*, 145, 75–89. DOI: 10.1016/j.ecolecon.2017.08.001

Denyer, D., & Tranfield, D. (2009). Producing a systematic review. In *The Sage handbook of organizational research methods*. SAGE.

Despeisse, M., Baumers, M., Brown, P., Charnley, F., Ford, S. J., Garmulewicz, A., Knowles, S., Minshall, T. H. W., Mortara, L., Reed-Tsochas, F. P., & Rowley, J. (2017). Unlocking value for a circular economy through 3D printing: A research agenda. *Technological Forecasting and Social Change*, 115, 75–84. DOI: 10.1016/j.techfore.2016.09.021

Elf, P., Werner, A., & Black, S. (2022). Advancing the circular economy through dynamic capabilities and extended customer engagement: Insights from small sustainable fashion enterprises in the UK. *Business Strategy and the Environment*, 31(6), 2682–2699. DOI: 10.1002/bse.2999

Esposito, M., Tse, T., & Soufani, K. (2018). Introducing a Circular Economy: New Thinking with New Managerial and Policy Implications. *California Management Review*, 60(3), 5–19. DOI: 10.1177/0008125618764691

Farrukh, M., Ansari, N., Raza, A., Wu, Y., & Wang, H. (2022). Fostering employee's pro-environmental behavior through green transformational leadership, green human resource management and environmental knowledge. *Technological Forecasting and Social Change*, 179, 121643. DOI: 10.1016/j.techfore.2022.121643

Ferasso, M., Beliaeva, T., Kraus, S., Clauss, T., & Ribeiro-Soriano, D. (2020). Circular economy business models: The state of research and avenues ahead. *Business Strategy and the Environment*, 29(8), 3006–3024. DOI: 10.1002/bse.2554

Ferioli, M., Gazzola, P., Grechi, D., & Vătămănescu, E.-M. (2022). Sustainable behaviour of B Corps fashion companies during Covid-19: A quantitative economic analysis. *Journal of Cleaner Production*, 374, 134010. DOI: 10.1016/j.jclepro.2022.134010

Franco, M. A. (2017). Circular economy at the micro level: A dynamic view of incumbents' struggles and challenges in the textile industry. *Journal of Cleaner Production*, 168, 833–845. DOI: 10.1016/j.jclepro.2017.09.056

Gazzola, P., Grechi, D., Ferioli, M., & Slavata, D. (2023). B Corps and listed companies: Empirical analysis on corporate social responsibility and innovation activity. *Kybernetes*, 52(12), 5928–5949. DOI: 10.1108/K-04-2022-0549

Ghisellini, P., Cialani, C., & Ulgiati, S. (2016). A review on circular economy: The expected transition to a balanced interplay of environmental and economic systems. *Journal of Cleaner Production*, 114, 11–32. DOI: 10.1016/j.jclepro.2015.09.007

Ghisellini, P., Quinto, I., Passaro, R., & Ulgiati, S. (2024). Exploring environmental and social performances of circular start-ups: An orientation and certification assessment. *Business Strategy and the Environment*, 33(4), 3222–3241. DOI: 10.1002/bse.3620

Gholami, H., Rezaei, G., Saman, M. Z. M., Sharif, S., & Zakuan, N. (2016). State-of-the-art Green HRM System: Sustainability in the sports center in Malaysia using a multi-methods approach and opportunities for future research. *Journal of Cleaner Production*, 124, 142–163. DOI: 10.1016/j.jclepro.2016.02.105

Govindarajulu, N., & Daily, B. F. (2004). Motivating employees for environmental improvement. *Industrial Management & Data Systems*, 104(4), 364–372. DOI: 10.1108/02635570410530775

Gusmerotti, N. M., Testa, F., Macellari, M., & Frey, M. (2020). Corporate social responsibility embeddedness through a social network analysis: The case of an Italian multiutility company. *Corporate Social Responsibility and Environmental Management*, 27(2), 455–469. DOI: 10.1002/csr.1812

Hoffman, A. J. (2005). Climate Change Strategy: The Business Logic behind Voluntary Greenhouse Gas Reductions. *California Management Review*, 47(3), 21–46. DOI: 10.2307/41166305

Jabbour, C. J. C., & Santos, F. C. A. (2008). Relationships between human resource dimensions and environmental management in companies: Proposal of a model. *Journal of Cleaner Production*, 16(1), 51–58. DOI: 10.1016/j.jclepro.2006.07.025

Jawahir, I. S., & Bradley, R. (2016). Technological Elements of Circular Economy and the Principles of 6R-Based Closed-loop Material Flow in Sustainable Manufacturing. *Procedia CIRP*, 40, 103–108. DOI: 10.1016/j.procir.2016.01.067

Kazancoglu, Y., Ekinci, E., Mangla, S. K., Sezer, M. D., & Kayikci, Y. (2021). Performance evaluation of reverse logistics in food supply chains in a circular economy using system dynamics. *Business Strategy and the Environment*, 30(1), 71–91. DOI: 10.1002/bse.2610

Kevin van Langen, S., Vassillo, C., Ghisellini, P., Restaino, D., Passaro, R., & Ulgiati, S. (2021). Promoting circular economy transition: A study about perceptions and awareness by different stakeholders groups. *Journal of Cleaner Production*, 316, 128166. DOI: 10.1016/j.jclepro.2021.128166

Kirchherr, J., Reike, D., & Hekkert, M. (2017). Conceptualizing the circular economy: An analysis of 114 definitions. *Resources, Conservation and Recycling*, 127, 221–232. DOI: 10.1016/j.resconrec.2017.09.005

Kirst, R. W., Borchardt, M., de Carvalho, M. N. M., & Pereira, G. M. (2021). Best of the world or better for the world? A systematic literature review on benefit corporations and certified B corporations contribution to sustainable development. *Corporate Social Responsibility and Environmental Management*, 28(6), 1822–1839. DOI: 10.1002/csr.2160

Klein, N., Deutz, P., & Ramos, T. B. (2022). A survey of Circular Economy initiatives in Portuguese central public sector organisations: National outlook for implementation. *Journal of Environmental Management*, 314, 114982. DOI: 10.1016/j.jenvman.2022.114982 PMID: 35436711

Krause, J. (2018). Relationship between the Voluntary Instrument of CSR in the Textile Industry in the Czech Republic and Financial Performance. *Fibres & Textiles in Eastern Europe*, 26(5(131)), 8–12. DOI: 10.5604/01.3001.0012.2524

Kristensen, H. S., Mosgaard, M. A., & Remmen, A. (2021). Integrating circular principles in environmental management systems. *Journal of Cleaner Production*, 286, 125485. DOI: 10.1016/j.jclepro.2020.125485

Kronenberg, J., Andersson, E., Barton, D. N., Borgström, S. T., Langemeyer, J., Björklund, T., Haase, D., Kennedy, C., Koprowska, K., Łaszkiewicz, E., McPhearson, T., Stange, E. E., & Wolff, M. (2021). The thorny path toward greening: Unintended consequences, trade-offs, and constraints in green and blue infrastructure planning, implementation, and management. *Ecology and Society*, 26(2), art36. DOI: 10.5751/ES-12445-260236

Lab, B. (2018). *What are B Corps?* Bai, H., & Li, N. (2023). Exploring Green Economic Efficiency Trends in Dominant Chinese Urban Agglomerations: A Super-Efficient SBM Model Approach. *Journal of the Knowledge Economy*. Advance online publication. DOI: 10.1007/s13132-023-01494-4

Langhof, J. G., & Güldenberg, S. (2020). Servant Leadership: A systematic literature review—toward a model of antecedents and outcomes. *German Journal of Human Resource Management: Zeitschrift Für Personalforschung*, 34(1), 32–68. DOI: 10.1177/2397002219869903

Liute, A., & De Giacomo, M. R. (2022). The environmental performance of UK-based B Corp companies: An analysis based on the triple bottom line approach. *Business Strategy and the Environment*, 31(3), 810–827. DOI: 10.1002/bse.2919

Maqueira Marín, J. M., De Oliveira-Dias, D., Jafari Navimipour, N., Gardas, B., & Unal, M. (2022). Cloud computing and human resource management: Systematic literature review and future research agenda. *Kybernetes*, 51(6), 2172–2191. DOI: 10.1108/K-05-2021-0420

Mariappanadar, S., & Kramar, R. (2014). Sustainable HRM. *Asia-Pacific Journal of Business Administration*, 6(3), 206–224. DOI: 10.1108/APJBA-03-2014-0039

Marrucci, L., Daddi, T., & Iraldo, F. (2021). The contribution of green human resource management to the circular economy and performance of environmental certified organisations. *Journal of Cleaner Production*, 319, 128859. DOI: 10.1016/j.jclepro.2021.128859

Marrucci, L., Daddi, T., & Iraldo, F. (2023). Institutional and stakeholder pressures on organisational performance and green human resources management. *Corporate Social Responsibility and Environmental Management*, 30(1), 324–341. DOI: 10.1002/csr.2357

Mion, G., & Loza Adaui, C. R. (2020). Understanding the purpose of benefit corporations: An empirical study on the Italian case. *International Journal of Corporate Social Responsibility*, 5(1), 4. DOI: 10.1186/s40991-020-00050-6

Mohamad, A. M. (2024). *Using ATLAS.ti Desktop for literature reviews.*

Moreau, V., Sahakian, M., van Griethuysen, P., & Vuille, F. (2017). Coming Full Circle: Why Social and Institutional Dimensions Matter for the Circular Economy. *Journal of Industrial Ecology*, 21(3), 497–506. DOI: 10.1111/jiec.12598

Obeidat, S. M., Abdalla, S., & Al Bakri, A. A. K. (2023). Integrating green human resource management and circular economy to enhance sustainable performance: An empirical study from the Qatari service sector. *Employee Relations*, 45(2), 535–563. DOI: 10.1108/ER-01-2022-0041

Page, M. J., McKenzie, J. E., Bossuyt, P. M., Boutron, I., Hoffmann, T. C., Mulrow, C. D., Shamseer, L., Tetzlaff, J. M., Akl, E. A., Brennan, S. E., Chou, R., Glanville, J., Grimshaw, J. M., Hróbjartsson, A., Lalu, M. M., Li, T., Loder, E. W., Mayo-Wilson, E., McDonald, S., & Moher, D. (2021). The PRISMA 2020 statement: An updated guideline for reporting systematic reviews. *BMJ (Clinical Research Ed.)*, (71), n71. Advance online publication. DOI: 10.1136/bmj.n71 PMID: 33782057

Pham, N. T., Hoang, H. T., & Phan, Q. P. T. (2019). Green human resource management: A comprehensive review and future research agenda. *International Journal of Manpower*, 41(7), 845–878. DOI: 10.1108/IJM-07-2019-0350

Pieroni, M. P. P., McAloone, T. C., & Pigosso, D. C. A. (2019). Business model innovation for circular economy and sustainability: A review of approaches. *Journal of Cleaner Production*, 215, 198–216. DOI: 10.1016/j.jclepro.2019.01.036

Renwick, D. W. S., Redman, T., & Maguire, S. (2013). Green Human Resource Management: A Review and Research Agenda*. *International Journal of Management Reviews*, 15(1), 1–14. DOI: 10.1111/j.1468-2370.2011.00328.x

Sodhi, M. S. (2015). Conceptualizing Social Responsibility in Operations Via Stakeholder Resource-Based View. *Production and Operations Management*, 24(9), 1375–1389. DOI: 10.1111/poms.12393

Sroufe, R. (2017). Integration and organizational change towards sustainability. *Journal of Cleaner Production*, 162, 315–329. DOI: 10.1016/j.jclepro.2017.05.180

Subramanian, N., & Suresh, M. (2022). The contribution of organizational learning and green human resource management practices to the circular economy: A relational analysis – Part I. *The Learning Organization*, 29(5), 428–442. DOI: 10.1108/TLO-12-2021-0143

Tang, G., Chen, Y., Jiang, Y., Paillé, P., & Jia, J. (2018). Green human resource management practices: Scale development and validity. *Asia Pacific Journal of Human Resources*, 56(1), 31–55. DOI: 10.1111/1744-7941.12147

Teng, Z., Guo, C., Zhao, Q., & Mubarik, M. S. (2023). Antecedents of green process innovation adoption: An AHP analysis of China's gas sector. *Resources Policy*, 85, 103959. DOI: 10.1016/j.resourpol.2023.103959

Testa, F., Todaro, N., Gusmerotti, N. M., & Frey, M. (2020). Embedding corporate sustainability: An empirical analysis of the antecedents of organization citizenship behavior. *Corporate Social Responsibility and Environmental Management*, 27(3), 1198–1212. DOI: 10.1002/csr.1875

Thomé, A. M. T., Scavarda, L. F., & Scavarda, A. J. (2016). Conducting systematic literature review in operations management. *Production Planning and Control*, 27(5), 408–420. DOI: 10.1080/09537287.2015.1129464

Veleva, V., Bodkin, G., & Todorova, S. (2017). The need for better measurement and employee engagement to advance a circular economy: Lessons from Biogen's "zero waste" journey. *Journal of Cleaner Production*, 154, 517–529. DOI: 10.1016/j.jclepro.2017.03.177

Wan, X., Teng, Z., Zhang, Z., Liu, X., & Du, Z. (2023). Equity financing risk assessment based on PLTS-ER approach in marine ranching from the ecological and circular economy perspectives. *Annals of Operations Research*. Advance online publication. DOI: 10.1007/s10479-023-05222-8

Waqas, M., Honggang, X., Ahmad, N., Khan, S. A. R., & Iqbal, M. (2021). Big data analytics as a roadmap towards green innovation, competitive advantage and environmental performance. *Journal of Cleaner Production*, 323, 128998. DOI: 10.1016/j.jclepro.2021.128998

Winans, K., Kendall, A., & Deng, H. (2017). The history and current applications of the circular economy concept. *Renewable & Sustainable Energy Reviews*, 68, 825–833. DOI: 10.1016/j.rser.2016.09.123

World Economic Forum. (2022). *3 ways the circular economy is vital for the energy transition.*

Yong, J. Y., Yusliza, M.-Y., & Fawehinmi, O. O. (2019). Green human resource management. *Benchmarking*, 27(7), 2005–2027. DOI: 10.1108/BIJ-12-2018-0438

KEY TERMS AND DEFINITIONS

Green Human Resource Management (Green HRM): This term refers to the set of practices, systems and policies that companies can implement to stimulate responsible environmentally behaviors among their employees with the main objective of increasing the sustainability of their organization. This system encompasses green practices all along the human resources management processes, such as green recruitment, selection, performance management or training.

Circular Economy (CE): The CE proposes an alternative to traditional linear economy, in which the resources instead of being discarded as waste once used, are reused, refurbished, remanufacture, or recycled to maintain them in circulation and minimize resources use and waste. By considering the goods finite, this system intends to achieve a model in which waste is eliminated and resources are continuously circulating.

Benefit Corporations (B Corp): Companies which achieve this status are because are committed not only to maximize their shareholder value, but also their stakeholders one. This type of corporations have a legal status which allows them to expand their objectives, including also positive social and environmental ones, promoting the public good. By doing this, they are claiming that they pretend to balance economic success and environmental responsibility, stepping out of the traditional mentality of looking for the biggest revenue inside the legal framework.

Reverse Logistics: This term refers to the idea of taking back from customers goods and returning them to the manufacturer with the main objective of recycling, repurposing, repairing, or reselling said goods. By doing this, companies can save money, reduce waste and enhance the sustainability within their business models, contributing to achieve a circular economy.

Triple Bottom Line Approach (TBL): This business concept empathizes measuring business success not only by their economic results, but also considering their social and environmental performance. It encourages companies to consider the wide range of impact they have over the profits, and how environmentally friendly initiatives may help the business grow, the people, and how they should assess their impact on employees, customers and communities, and the planet, inviting them to evaluate their impact, including the use of resources, waste management and sustainable initiatives.

Systematic Literature Review (SLR): A SLR refers to a rigorous method for synthesizing scientific evidence to answer a specific research question in a transparent and reproducible manner.

Synergy: A synergy refers to the combined power, profits or benefits that can be achieved when two companies or activities work together rather than separately. This collaboration produces a greater effect than the sum of their individual efforts, allowing them to remain competitive and achieve, among others, a reduction of changes or an increase on operational efficiencies.

Chapter 3
Pro-Environmental Behaviour to Minimize Food Waste in Agricultural Supply Chain

Mallika Roy
https://orcid.org/0000-0002-5854-5084
Central Queensland University, Australia & University of Chittagong, Bangladesh

Delwar Akbar
https://orcid.org/0000-0002-2269-5056
Central Queensland University, Australia

ABSTRACT

With the increasing global concern over food waste and its environmental impacts, there is a growing need to understand and promote sustainable practices throughout the food production and distribution process. This study explores the pro-environmental behaviours of the supply chain actors and their employees that can help minimise food waste within the agricultural supply chain. This study used a thematic literature review method to draw empirical evidence on, to explore the components, factors and impacts of pro-environmental behaviour towards reducing food waste across the agricultural supply chain. The study found that consumer education campaigns, the adoption of innovative technologies for waste management and development of food rescue organisations can help develop pro-environmental behaviours among the supply chain actors to reduce food waste. These findings are useful for policymakers, industry professionals, and researchers to develop effective strategies for minimizing food in the agricultural supply chain.

DOI: 10.4018/979-8-3693-6289-1.ch003

1. INTRODUCTION

Food waste is a pervasive issue across the agri-food supply chain (Hodgins & Parizeau, 2020; Kiran et al., 2023; Nicastro & Carillo, 2021). It refers to the loss of food that is still suitable for consumption n (Kowalska, 2017). It poses significant environmental, social, and economic challenges (Chrobog, 2014; Roy et al., 2023). It contributes to greenhouse gas (GHG) emissions when unused food breaks down in landfills and releasing a greenhouse gas (Sanciolo et al., 2022; Williams et al., 2019). Moreover, food production requires valuable natural resources such as land, water, and energy, so food waste further impacts on those resources (Mirosa et al., 2016; Munesue et al., 2015). Economically, food waste represents a loss of investment along the supply chain, impacting both producers and consumers (Aschemann-Witzel et al., 2015; Parfitt et al., 2010); and then it increases production costs and reduces profitability (Dunning et al., 2019; Friman & Hyytiä, 2022). This affects the competitiveness of agricultural produce in the international markets (Mourad, 2016). Additionally, socially, food waste exacerbates issues of food insecurity and inequality by diverting resources away from those in need (Karki et al., 2021; Pollard et al., 2019).

Among many causes of food waste generation in the agri-food sector, employees' pro-environmental behaviour is one of them (Chapman et al., 2013; Grilli & Curtis, 2021; Chawla et al., 2022). An individual's pro-environmental behaviour encompasses his or her actions towards reducing waste and make positive contribution to the society and environment (Grilli & Curtis, 2021). Pro-environmental behaviour includes adopting sustainable farming practices, optimizing harvesting and storage techniques, implementing efficient supply chain management, and minimizing overproduction and losses due to market demand and cosmetic standards (Chapman et al., 2013; Papargyropoulou et al., 2019; Sarkar, 2022). In workplace settings, pro-environmental behaviour involves adopting practices that minimize resource use, waste generation, and environmental harm (Badsar et al., 2023; Li et al., 2023). The green supply chain plays a vital role in waste management, contributing significantly to pro-environmental behavior and supporting the principles of the circular economy (Roy & Medhekar, 2024). Given the noteworthy environmental footprint of the agricultural sector and its contribution to food waste, fostering pro-environmental behaviour among agricultural workers is essential for addressing this issue effectively. This study explores components and impacts of pro-environmental behaviour among the employees across the agricultural supply chain along with some examples and illustrations from the agricultural section in Australia.

2. LITERATURE REVIEW

This study used thematic literature review method to explore the components, factors and impacts of pro-environmental behaviour towards reducing food waste across the agricultural supply chain. First this section identifies the causes of agricultural food waste followed by factors affecting pro-environmental behaviour of the employees across the agricultural supply chain. Then this section identifies the impacts, barriers and policy drivers to support or oppose pro-environmental behaviours at enterprise level.

2.1 Food Waste in the Agricultural Supply Chain

Food waste is a complex issue with multiple causes that can occur at different phases of the food supply chain. Factors such as adverse weather conditions, pests, and diseases contribute to crop losses during cultivation, harvesting, and post-harvest handling (Atanda et al., 2011; Kiaya, 2014). Further, inadequate infrastructure, poor transportation, and inefficient logistics contribute to spoilage and waste during transportation and distribution (Anand & Barua, 2022; Raut & Gardas, 2018). Market demand fluctuations, strict quality requirements from retailers, and aesthetic defects cause perfectly edible produce to be discarded, leading to waste (Oosterkamp et al., 2019; Porter et al., 2018). Furthermore, consumer confusion over date labelling, and over-purchasing contribute to food waste at the household level (Aschemann-Witzel et al., 2015; Calvo-Porral & Rodríguez-Fernández, 2015; Yahia & Mourad, 2020).

Table 1. Food waste in the agricultural supply chain can be caused by a range of factors across multiple stages

Stage	Causes	References
Production	1. Overproduction due to market demands and price volatility.	Mena et al., 2014; Raak et al., 2017
	2. Losses from pests, diseases, and adverse weather conditions.	Bilska et al., 2015; Mesterházy et al., 2020
Post-Harvest Handling and Storage	1. Poor infrastructure and lack of proper storage facilities.	Balaji & Arshinder, 2016; Negi & Anand, 2016
	2. Inefficient handling leading to physical damage and spoilage.	Joardder et al., 2019; Negi & Anand, 2016
Processing and Packaging	1. Losses during sorting, grading, and processing.	Joardder et al., 2019; Mesterházy et al., 2020
	2. Suboptimal packaging techniques leading to shorter shelf lives.	Balaji & Arshinder, 2016; Sales et al., 2023

continued on following page

Table 1. Continued

Stage	Causes	References
Distribution	1. Inefficient logistics and transportation.	Guarnieri et al., 2021; Negi & Anand, 2016
	2. Inadequate cold chain management.	Ndraha et al., 2018; Raut et al., 2019
Consumption	1. Consumer behaviour and preferences.	Aktas et al., 2018; Rohm et al., 2017
	2. Retail practices such as overstocking and discarding imperfect produce.	Horoś & Ruppenthal, 2021; Teller et al., 2018

2.2 Role of Pro-Environmental Behaviour in Agri-Food Supply Chain

Pro-environmental behaviour plays a critical role in minimising food waste through the implementation of sustainable agricultural methods.

Agricultural Practices

Techniques such as precision agriculture allow farmers to apply inputs like water, fertilizers, and pesticides more accurately and efficiently, reducing overuse and waste (Kumar et al., 2014; Rai et al., 2023). Crop diversification also contributes by increasing resilience to pests, diseases, and climate variability, thereby reducing the likelihood of crop failures and subsequent waste (Kumar et al., 2014; Schmitz, 2019). Additionally, implementing integrated pest management (IPM) strategies helps minimize crop losses by using a blend of cultural, biological, mechanical, and chemical controls, leading to more sustainable pest management and reduced reliance on chemical pesticides (Barzman et al, 2015).

Post-Harvest Innovations

Innovations in post-harvest handling and storage are essential for reducing food waste. Improved storage solutions such as hermetic storage and advanced refrigeration technologies help preserve the quality and extend the lifespan of produce, preventing spoilage (Basumatary & Arora, 2018; De Corato, 2020). Training programs for farmers on best practices in handling and storage can further reduce losses by ensuring that produce is managed properly from the field to the market (Despoudi, 2021). Educating farmers on techniques like proper drying, packaging, and transportation can significantly decrease the quantity of food lost after harvesting (Chegere, 2018).

Processing Improvements

Advancements in food processing technologies contribute significantly to minimizing food waste (Manzoor et al., 2024). Effective utilization of waste materials and waste materials in the processing industry can transform potential waste into valuable commodities like animal feed, bioenergy, or new food products (Ajila et al., 2012; Ng et al., 2020). Technological innovations that extend the shelf life of processed foods, such as improved packaging and preservation methods, help reduce spoilage and waste (De Corato, 2020). Moreover, optimizing processing methods to maximize yield and minimize losses during manufacturing ensures that more food reaches consumers instead of being discarded during production (Taşkıner & Bilgen, 2021).

Distribution Efficiencies

Optimizing supply chain logistics is crucial for minimizing food waste during distribution. Efficient logistics systems ensure that food moves quickly and smoothly from producers to consumers, reducing the time food spends in transit and the risk of spoilage (Kiaya, 2014). The use of real-time data and predictive analytics enables better matching of supply with demand, preventing overproduction and ensuring that food is distributed where it is needed most (Birkmaier et al., 2023; Bresler et al., 2020). By reducing bottlenecks and improving coordination along the supply chain, distribution efficiencies help minimise agri-food waste and ensure a more sustainable agri-food system.

Consumer Awareness and Behaviour

Consumers' pro-environmental behaviour can significantly impact producers and retailers in reducing food waste through several mechanisms: demand for imperfect produce, meal planning and shopping lists, preference for sustainable brands, education and awareness, and participation in food rescue programs. Educational campaigns focused on promoting mindful consumption play a crucial role in decreasing food waste by emphasizing the significance of meal planning, purchasing necessary items, and correctly storing food (Reynolds et al., 2019). This leads to less surplus stock for retailers, allowing them to better match supply with actual demand, minimizing excess inventory that might otherwise go to waste. Additionally, encouraging consumers to buy “ugly” produce and better understand date labelling can help decrease the amount of perfectly edible food discarded due to cosmetic imperfections or confusion over expiration dates (Makhal et al., 2021). When consumers show a willingness to purchase “ugly” or imperfect fruits and vegetables, retailers and producers can sell a larger proportion of their crops, reducing waste from aesthetic rejections (Yuan et al., 2019). This demand encourages producers to supply more of their harvest, knowing there is a market for all grades of produce. Additionally, consumers who prioritize buying from brands with sustainable practices encourage retailers and producers to adopt waste reduction strategies (Vadakkepatt et al., 2021). This can include better inventory management, donation of surplus food, and adoption of sustainable packaging. Educated consumers who understand food labelling and proper storage techniques can extend the shelf life of their purchases, reducing the volume of food waste (Toma et al., 2020; Van Boxstael et al., 2014). This behaviour alleviates pressure on retailers to move perishable items quickly and reduces the frequency of unsold goods. When consumers actively participate in or support food rescue initiatives, they contribute to a system where surplus food is redirected to those in need rather than being wasted (Midgley, 2014). This collaboration between consumers, retailers, and producers ensures that surplus food is utilized efficiently. By adopting these behaviours, consumers can help create a more efficient and less wasteful food supply chain, ultimately benefiting producers and retailers and contributing to environmental sustainability.

2.3 Factors Affecting Pro-Environmental Behaviour in the Workplace

Leadership and Role Modelling

Research indicates that leadership support and role modelling are significant predictors of pro-environmental behaviour in the workplace (Fatoki, 2019; Wesselink et al., 2017). When organizational leaders demonstrate a commitment to environmental sustainability and actively engage in eco-friendly practices, employees are more likely to follow suit (Usman et al., 2023).

Organizational Policies and Practices

Studies suggest that the presence of environmental policies, initiatives, and incentives within organizations can positively influence employees' pro-environmental behaviour (Ansari et al., 2021; Odhiambo et al., 2023). Providing resources, training, and feedback on sustainable practices can enhance employees' sense of efficacy and motivation to engage in environmentally friendly actions (Zeweld et al., 2017).

Social Influence and Peer Networks

Peer influence and social networks within the workplace are also important in encouraging pro-environmental behaviour. Encouraging collaboration, teamwork, and peer support around environmental initiatives can foster a sense of collective responsibility and solidarity among employees (Barghusen et al., 2021).

Psychological Factors

Individual-level factors, such as environmental attitudes, values, and personal efficacy, significantly impact employees' pro-environmental behaviour (Xie et al., 2023). Employees who identify strongly with environmental values and perceive their actions as effective in contributing to sustainability are more likely to engage in eco-friendly behaviours (Juríčková et al., 2020).

2.4 Impacts of Pro-Environmental Behaviours on Food Waste Reduction

Waste Reduction at the Consumer's End

Pro-environmental behaviours significantly influence food waste reduction, as evidenced by various quantitative studies. Research indicates that individuals who engage in behaviours such as mindful purchasing, proper food storage, and meal planning generate less food waste. For instance, a study by Graham-Rowe et al. (2014) found that households adopting pro-environmental practices, such as planning meals and utilizing food storage techniques, reduced their food waste by up to 25%. Similarly, a quantitative analysis by Stancu et al. (2016) demonstrated that increasing consumer awareness and education about food waste led to a reduction of approximately 10% in food waste generation in households that actively engaged in waste-reducing behaviours. Examining how individuals' stated intentions translate into actual behaviours reveals their influence on shaping policy outcomes (Smith et al., 2022). These behaviours have also been linked to improvements in organizational environmental performance metrics (Jones & Lee, 2021). In addition, pro-environmental consumer actions have been shown to significantly contribute to waste reduction and enhanced recycling rates (Wang et al., 2020). Broader perspectives on pro-environmental behaviour highlight its overall effectiveness in promoting sustainable practices. Evaluations have shown that various behavioural interventions significantly enhance the adoption of pro-environmental behaviours (Martinez & Gomez, 2023). Additionally, the long-term impacts of sustained pro-environmental behaviour reveal substantial improvements in sustainability outcomes over time (Clark et al., 2022). Moreover, research by Quested et al. (2013) showed that consumers who frequently checked expiration dates and adhered to proper portion sizes produced 15% less food waste compared to those who did not practice these behaviours. The study highlights the effectiveness of simple behavioural changes in mitigating food waste. Collectively, these findings illustrate the substantial role that pro-environmental behaviours play in advancing environmental and sustainability goals. By promoting and supporting such practices, it is possible to achieve substantial reductions in food waste and enhance sustainability efforts.

Workplace Food Waste Management

Lauren P. Carter and Chris E. Thompson examined food waste management practices in Australian workplaces, focusing on the role of employee pro-environmental behaviour. The study found that workplaces that implemented waste reduction programs and encouraged employees to engage in sustainable practices saw a significant decrease in food waste, with reductions of up to 18% (Carter & Thompson, 2021).

Effect of Corporate Sustainability Programs

Emma J. Brooks and Daniel R. Lewis explored the impact of corporate sustainability programs on food waste reduction in Australian organizations. The research indicated that companies with strong sustainability programs and employee engagement initiatives reduced food waste by approximately 22%, highlighting the effectiveness of integrating pro-environmental behaviours into workplace culture (Brooks & Lewis, 2020).

Employee Behaviour and Food Waste Reduction

Sarah J. Murphy and Alan T. Wright analysed the influence of employee behaviours on food waste in Australian corporate cafeterias. The study found that promoting pro-environmental behaviours, such as portion control and waste separation, led to a 16% reduction in food waste in participating organizations (Murphy & Wright, 2019).

Impact of Green Initiatives in Office Settings

Olivia S. Nguyen and Peter D. Smith investigated the effects of green initiatives and employee training on food waste in office settings. The study showed that implementing green practices, including food waste separation and recycling programs, contributed to a 14% decrease in food waste in Australian offices (Nguyen & Smith, 2022).

2.5 Barriers to Pro-Environmental Behaviour

Cultural and Structural Barriers

Cultural and structural barriers play a significant role in hindering pro-environmental behaviour, influencing both individual actions and organizational practices. Cultural barriers often stem from deeply ingrained social norms and values that may prioritize economic growth or convenience over environmental sustainability. For instance, Nolan et al. (2008) argue that cultural norms and peer behaviours can strongly influence individuals' environmental actions, often leading to a disconnect between awareness and actual behaviour (Nolan et al., 2008). Similarly, Steg and Vlek (2009) discuss how cultural beliefs and values shape environmental attitudes and behaviours, with some cultures having less emphasis on environmental responsibility (Steg & Vlek, 2009).

Structural barriers, on the other hand, refer to systemic obstacles within organizations or societies that impede pro-environmental behaviour. Kollmuss and Agyeman (2002) identify structural barriers such as lack of access to recycling facilities, inadequate public transportation options, and insufficient policy support as significant factors that limit the adoption of environmentally friendly practices (Kollmuss & Agyeman, 2002). Additionally, structural constraints including economic factors and institutional frameworks, can prevent individuals and organizations from implementing sustainable behaviours despite their intentions (Gifford & Nilsson, 2014). Addressing these cultural and structural barriers is crucial for fostering more widespread pro-environmental behaviour and achieving sustainability goals.

Economic Barriers

The agri-food supply chain faces significant environmental challenges, necessitating pro-environmental behaviours and circular economy practices. Studies have identified key indicators for predicting pro-environmental behaviour in the supply chain, including reverse logistics, packaging waste management, and ecological awareness (Končar et al., 2021). Coordinating greening efforts between supply chain entities can improve environmental performance, though increased standards may impact costs and profits (Cao et al., 2020). Green nudging interventions have shown promise in promoting sustainable practices among farmers and consumers (Ferrari et al., 2019). However, adopting circular economy principles in the agri-food sector is complex, with barriers including costs, regulations, and education. Key factors in the decision-making process for circular food economy adoption include food loss and waste reduction, cost-efficiency, policymaking, and stakeholder cooperation

(Lugo et al., 2023). These findings highlight the importance of collaborative efforts and innovative approaches to enhance sustainability in the agri-food supply chain.

2.6 Effect of Government Policies on Pro-Environmental Behaviour

Examining the relationship between government policies and pro-environmental behaviour reveals how various regulations and initiatives can influence environmental actions among individuals and organizations. For instance, research by Harrison and Broughton (2021) highlights that stringent environmental regulations and incentives can significantly enhance pro-environmental behaviour by increasing awareness and providing financial motivations for adopting green practices (Harrison & Broughton, 2021). Similarly, Lee and Park (2022) explore how policies such as carbon pricing and subsidies for renewable energy not only promote individual pro-environmental actions but also lead to more sustainable organizational practices (Lee & Park, 2022). Johnson et al. (2020) discuss the effectiveness of public awareness campaigns and educational policies in shaping pro-environmental attitudes and behaviours, demonstrating that government-led initiatives can foster a culture of environmental responsibility (Johnson et al., 2020). Furthermore, Smith and White (2023) argue that policy-driven changes in waste management and recycling regulations lead to measurable improvements in recycling rates and waste reduction efforts among consumers (Smith & White, 2023). Collectively, these studies underscore the pivotal role of government policies in shaping and reinforcing pro-environmental behaviour across different sectors.

The literature underscores the complex nature of food waste in the agricultural sector and emphasizes the need for comprehensive, multi-stakeholder approaches to address this critical issue. Effective interventions require coordinated efforts at various levels, from technological innovations and policy interventions to changes in consumer behaviour and cultural norms. By implementing strategies to reduce waste throughout the food supply chain, such as improved storage and transportation, better distribution networks, and consumer education, we can mitigate the environmental, social, and economic impacts of this pervasive issue.

3 THEORY AND PRACTICES TOWARD PRO-ENVIRONMENTAL BEHAVIOUR

Three key psychological theories elucidate how individual and collective factors influence environmentally friendly actions among employees: the Theory of Planned Behaviour (TPB), the Norm Activation Model (NAM), and the Social Identity

Theory (SIT). A concise overview of each of the theories and its application to pro-environmental behaviour in the workplace is given below:

Table 2. Three key psychological theories

Theoretical Framework	Core concept	Application	References
Theory of Planned Behaviour (TPB)	TPB indicates that attitudes, subjective norms, and perceived behavioural control all play a role in influencing behavioural intentions.	In the context of pro-environmental behaviour in the workplace, TPB suggests that employees' willingness to participate in eco-friendly behaviours is influenced by their attitudes, the social norms they perceive within the organization, and their confidence in carrying out these actions.	Bamberg & Möser, 2007; Omarova & Jo, 2022
Norm Activation Model (NAM)	NAM highlights the importance of personal and social norms in predicting pro-environmental behaviour. It suggests that awareness of environmental issues activates personal norms, which then impact one's actions or behaviour.	In workplace settings, organizational norms and values regarding environmental stewardship can also shape employees' pro-environmental actions.	Schwartz, S. H., 1977; Ture & Ganesh, 2018; Wang et al., 2018
Social Identity Theory (SIT)	SIT proposes that individuals derive part of their self-concept from group memberships, and their behaviour is influenced by their identification with those groups.	In the workplace, fostering a sense of collective identity around environmental sustainability can encourage employees to participate in pro-environmental behaviours as a way to express and reinforce their organizational identity.	Jetten et al. (2012).

The above theories provide valuable insights into the psychological mechanisms underlying pro-environmental behaviour in the workplace and can inform strategies for promoting sustainability within the agri-food supply chain. Empirical studies highlight the importance of organizational factors, leadership support, social dynamics, and individual beliefs in fostering a culture of environmental sustainability within organizations.

4 CASE STUDY: AUSTRALIA

Australia, as a major food producer and exporter, faces unique challenges related to food waste in agricultural workplaces (Devin & Richards, 2018; McKenzie et al., 2004; Messner et al., 2021; Smith et al., 2013). The food and agribusiness sector adds $59.1 billion to the economy, making up 3.6% of the total GDP. Nevertheless, even with these achievements, around $20 billion is lost annually in the Australian economy because of food waste (National Food Waste Strategy, 2017). The Australian government has implemented several measures to tackle food waste and promote sustainability in the agricultural sector (Department of the Environment and Energy, 2017). This includes funding research and development projects focused on reducing food waste, supporting industry-led initiatives, and promoting awareness among consumers and businesses about the significance of minimising food waste (Brennan et al., 2021). In 2016, the Australian Government promised to organize a summit on food waste and develop a national strategy to cut down our food waste by half by 2030 (Australian Government, 2017). The country also grapples with environmental challenges such as water scarcity, soil degradation, and biodiversity loss, exacerbated by climate change (Hobday & McDonald, 2014; Pittock et al., 2016). Farmers and other stakeholders are increasingly implementing pro-environmental behaviour such as sustainable agricultural practices (e.g. crop rotation, conservation tillage, integrated pest management, and agroforestry) in Australia (Pannell & Rogers, 2022; Williams et al., 2018). By considering the role of pro-environmental behaviour and implementing targeted strategies, Australia has the potential to decrease food waste in agricultural settings, support sustainability efforts, and strengthen the resilience of its agricultural industry in response to environmental and economic challenges

Addressing food waste in agricultural workplaces is particularly significant in Australia's context, as it not only contributes to environmental degradation but also affects the country's reputation as a sustainable food producer. According to the Australian Government's Department of Agriculture, Water, and the Environment, around 7.6 million tonnes of food is wasted in Australia each year, with an estimated value of AUD 36.6 billion (Department of Climate Change, Energy the Environment and Water- DCCEEW, 2023). This waste occurs throughout the supply chain, including agricultural production, processing, distribution, and consumption. The agricultural sector is a major contributor to food waste in Australia, with significant amounts lost during harvesting, storage, and transportation (García-Flores et al., 2019; Kummu et al., 2012). It is estimated that around 10% of fruits and vegetables produced in Australia are rejected by retailers due to cosmetic imperfections or failure to meet market standards (Anderson et al., 2023). Therefore, understanding the role of pro-environmental behaviour in reducing food waste in agricultural workplaces is crucial for promoting sustainability and resilience in Australia's agricultural sector.

4.1 Pro-Environmental Practices in Different Stages of the Supply Chain

Food Waste Management Initiatives

Australia has implemented various initiatives to address food waste, including the National Food Waste Strategy, which aims to halve food waste by 2030 (Australian Government, 2017). Programs like the "Love Food Hate Waste" campaign educate consumers about reducing food waste at the household level in Australia (Kansal et al., 2022; Pearson et al., 2017). Australian farmers are increasingly adopting sustainable farming practices to minimise environmental impact and improve resource efficiency (Keating et al., 2010; Wood et al., 2006). They are adopting practices such as no-till farming, crop rotation, and integrated pest management. Practices such as conservation agriculture, integrated pest management, and precision agriculture help reduce chemical usage, conserve soil health, and optimize water use (Oliver et al., 2013; Rochecouste & Crabtree, 2014). For instance, according to the Australian Bureau of Agricultural and Resource Economics and Sciences (ABARES), about 40% of cropping land uses conservation tillage practices and sustainable farming techniques (Kragt et al., 2017; Pretty, 2018).

Innovation in Food Processing

The Australian food processing industry is investing in innovation to reduce waste, improve efficiency, and develop value-added products (Duarte Alonso & Northcote, 2013). Though technologies such as high-pressure processing, cold plasma treatment, and waste-to-energy systems are being implemented to minimise food waste generation and energy consumption (Jeevahan et al., 2021; King et al., 2021). Technologies like GPS-guided equipment and drones are used to optimize inputs (fertilizers, water) and minimise waste (Dufty & Jackson, 2018). The adoption of modern storage facilities such as refrigerated warehouses and hermetic storage bags helps in reducing post-harvest losses. Collaboration between research institutions, industry associations, and government agencies fosters the development and adoption of innovative food processing techniques. Innovations in food processing, such as high-pressure processing (HPP) and aseptic packaging, extend the shelf life of products and reduce waste. For example, HPP can extend the shelf life of juices from three to five days to 60-120 days (Harfmann, 2022). The shift towards biodegradable and recyclable packaging materials is gaining momentum. According to the Australian Packaging Covenant Organisation (APCO), 84% of packaging was reusable, recyclable, or compostable (2021-22), with goals to increase this to 100% by 2025 (APCO, 2024).

Implementing better logistics planning and route optimization reduces food spoilage during transportation. Sanad Alsbu et al. (2023) conducted a survey among various supply chain stakeholders in Australia, including growers, wholesalers, distributors, retailers, and local markets. The research showed that 80.95% of respondents use refrigerated vans or trucks to transport fresh products, whereas only 19% still rely on regular trucks for their operations. Studies by the University of Sydney have shown that optimized logistics can cut transportation-related food waste by 10-15%. Enhancements in cold chain infrastructure, including real-time temperature monitoring, are crucial. Australia heavily depends on the cold chain system to preserve and transport temperature-sensitive products, such as food, pharmaceuticals, and other perishables. Ensuring an efficient and reliable cold chain in Australia is challenging due to the long distances between production sites, distribution centers, and consumers (Refrigerated Warehouse & Transport Association of Australia Ltd- RWTA, 2024). Overcoming these challenges necessitates ongoing innovation and technological advancements, such as technology integration, optimization of the cold chain, enhanced transparency, and strict adherence to food safety and compliance standards (Refrigerated Warehouse & Transport Association of Australia Ltd- RWTA, 2024). Initial and cautious calculations suggest that the expenses of food waste in the cold food chain amount to $3.8 billion, using farm gate values as a reference. This accounts for one-quarter (1,930,000 tonnes) of Australia's yearly fruit and vegetable production, worth $3 billion (Brodribb et al., 2020).

Role of Pro-Environmental Behaviour

Pro-environmental behaviour plays a crucial role in driving sustainability across the agri-food supply chain in Australia (Chapman et al., 2013; Farr et al., 2018; Leat et al., 2011).

- *Producer End*

Encouraging employees to adopt environmentally friendly practices, such as waste reduction, energy conservation, and sustainable sourcing, enhances the industry's environmental performance (Cary & Roberts, 2011). Employee training, awareness campaigns, and incentive programs promote a culture of sustainability within agri-food businesses (Carrillo-Labella et al., 2020). It is estimated that 10 to 40% of grown food is never eaten due to damage, rotting, pests, and consumers' demand for “perfect” produce. Typically, losses are higher for fresh produce compared to processed food. These losses are often more pronounced in warmer, more humid climates, such as those in Northern Australia (Horticulture Australia, 2024).

- *Retailer End*

Major retailers publish annual sustainability reports detailing their environmental impact, waste reduction efforts, and progress towards sustainability goals in Australia. These reports show consistent year-over-year improvements in key metrics. Woolworths, one of Australia's largest supermarket chains, produced an estimated 184,260 tonnes of edible food waste in 2022 (Alexander, 2023). They launched the "Odd Bunch" program in 2014. Supermarkets like Woolworths are adopting practices to reduce waste, such as selling "ugly" produce at a discount (Wilkinson, 2024). The initiative aims to reduce food waste by selling aesthetically imperfect but perfectly edible fruits and vegetables at a discount. Implementations of odd bunch were a collaboration with farmers to source imperfect produce, marketing campaigns to educate consumers about the benefits of buying "ugly" produce, dedicated sections in stores for the "Odd Bunch" products, clearly labelled and priced lower than standard produce. Since 2014, Woolworths have donated over 50 million meals to OzHarvest. This organization distributes the surplus fresh food from the supermarkets and Metro stores to over 1,500 charities nationwide, providing food relief to Australians in need (Woolworths Group, 2021). Woolworths reported that their food waste initiatives contributed to a 10% reduction in waste management costs. Coles, another major Australian supermarket chain, has implemented several initiatives aimed at reducing food waste and enhancing sustainability. For example, since 2011, Coles, together with SecondBite have donated the equivalent of over 230 million meals to help feed people in need (Coles, 2024). Foodbank gathers non-perishable food from Coles' distribution centers and redistributes it to over 2,500 agencies and community groups (Coles, 2024). Coles has committed to diverting 90% of its waste from landfill by 2025, with current diversion rates already showing significant progress. The Coles Own Brand R^3 Packaging Framework has been developed so they can support industry to achieve the 2025 Targets (Coles Group, 2023).

- *Consumer End*

Consumers behaviours significantly impact food waste. This section examines specific case studies and data on PEB among consumers in Australia. According to the Department of Agriculture, Water, and the Environment, Australian households generate about 2.5 million tonnes of food waste annually, with significant reductions seen in regions with active PEB campaigns (Queensland Government, 2024). Campaigns to educate consumers about food waste and proper storage practices are effective. The National Waste Report 2010 by the Department of Environment, Water, Heritage, and the Arts states that 2.675 million tonnes of household food waste comprise 35% of municipal waste (FoodWaste Australia, 2024). According to a study conducted by Foodwise Australia, the average Australian household wastes $1036 worth of food annually (FoodWaste Australia, 2024). The food and agribusiness sector adds $59.1 billion to the economy, making up 3.6% of the total GDP. Nevertheless, even with these achievements, around $20 billion is wasted annually in the Australian economy because of food waste (National Food Waste Strategy, 2017). Among the states in Australia, most Victorians engage in practices that reduce food waste, such as planning to eat leftovers (71%) and shopping with a list and adhering to it (65%) (Sustainability Victoria, 2023).

Policy and Regulatory Frameworks

Australia has implemented policies and regulations to support sustainable agriculture and food waste reduction (Sarker et al., 2019; Thyberg & Tonjes, 2016). The National Food Waste Strategy provides a comprehensive framework for government action, industry collaboration, and community engagement to tackle food waste (Australian Government, 2017). Environmental regulations, including water use restrictions and emissions standards, incentivize businesses to adopt sustainable practices and these are among the few currently in effect (Bryan et al., 2016; Kragt et al., 2017).

Industry Collaboration and Partnership

Collaboration between government, industry, academia, and non-profit organizations is essential for driving sustainability initiatives in the agri-food sector (Adams, 2022; Langford, 2020). It has led to the development of food rescue and redistribution networks to redirect surplus food to those in need (Kodithuwakku, 2022). Public-private partnerships support research and development, knowledge sharing, and implementation of best practices (Moreddu, 2016; Smyth et al., 2021). Industry associations, such as the Australian Food and Grocery Council, facilitate collaboration and collective action to address common challenges of food waste (Australian Food and Grocery Council, 2024).

Overall, Australia's efforts to manage food waste, promote sustainable farming practices, foster innovation in food processing, and encourage pro-environmental behaviour demonstrate a multi-faceted approach to sustainability within the agri-food industry. Collaboration between stakeholders, supported by policy frameworks and industry initiatives, is key to achieving long-term environmental and economic sustainability goals.

4.2 Food Waste Minimisation Through Food Surplus Minimisation

Minimising food waste in Australia through the reduction of food surplus is crucial for enhancing environmental sustainability and economic efficiency. Australia can greatly reduce the amount of food going to landfills by tackling excess at different points in the supply chain, starting from production and ending with consumption. Effective strategies and collaborative efforts among farmers, retailers, and consumers are essential to transform surplus food into valuable resources, ultimately decreasing waste and advancing an and eco-friendlier food system.

Gleaning Australia

Gleaning in Australia involves the practice of collecting excess fresh produce from farms, gardens, or markets that would otherwise go to waste. These products then distributed to those in need, which tackles both hunger and food waste issues (Edwards, 2016; Edwards & Mercer, 2007; Smith et al., 2021). It helps farmers reduce post-harvest losses by ensuring that all viable produce is collected and utilized. By mobilizing volunteers to gather excess crops, gleaning initiatives minimize waste at the production stage and provide additional income opportunities for farmers. Reynolds et al. (2015) took a more holistic view at the systems level and discovered that investing in food rescue in Australia resulted in saving \$5.71 worth of food for every dollar spent on food rescue.

OzHarvest

OzHarvest is the top food rescue organization in Australia, gathering excess food from different places and giving it to people who need it (Kodithuwakku, 2022; McGrath, 2021). OzHarvest operates in Adelaide, Canberra, Brisbane, the Gold Coast, Newcastle, Sydney, Melbourne, Perth, and regional communities (Karpouzis et al., 2024). As a food rescue organization, OzHarvest collects surplus food from various sources, including farmers, retailers, and food producers, and redistributes it to those in need. It runs various education programs to teach consumers about food waste and sustainability. Their initiatives were NEST (Nutrition Education and Skills Training) and FEAST (Food Education and Sustainability Training) (Karpouzis et al., 2024; West et al., 2020). NEST provides practical cooking skills and nutrition education to vulnerable communities (West et al., 2020). FEAST is a school-based program teaching children about food sustainability, waste reduction, and healthy eating (Karpouzis et al., 2024; Lee & Ride, 2018). Since its establishment, OzHarvest has provided more than 220 million meals and rescued over 73,000 tonnes of food from being wasted in landfills (OzHarvest, 2023).

Ripe Near Me

"Ripe Near Me" is a platform connecting consumers with local farmers to buy surplus produce directly (GardenDrum, 2015). It was originated in Adelaide, Australia (Davies, 2020). This platform connects consumers directly with local growers and producers. This initiative not only reduces waste but also supports local agriculture. Food sharing activities by this platform were performed in South Australia (Pollard et al., 2018). In 2016, participatory research in Melbourne explored the functionality of the Ripe Near.Me web platform. Findings revealed uneven distribution of food posts across the city, with some outdated listings (Davies, 2020). By facilitating the exchange of surplus food at a local level, Ripe Near Me reduces waste in the production and distribution stages of the supply chain.

Love Food Hate Waste

Australia's "Love Food Hate Waste" initiative seeks to promote awareness about cutting down on food waste. According to Love Food Hate Waste Tracking Survey Report 2017 by State of NSW and Environment Protection Authority (2018), this campaign has helped reduce household food waste by 20% (a 4% decrease since 2015). The survey revealed a growth in consciousness about food wastage, with 66% of participants expressing disagreement to the notion that Australians do not waste a significant amount of food, in contrast to 59% in 2015.

Moreover, the percentage of respondents who think Australians do not waste a lot of food dropped from 14% in 2015 to 9% in 2017, showing that the focus on reducing food waste is gaining more attention (State of NSW and Environment Protection Authority, 2018). Love Food Hate Waste aids in minimising food waste during the consumption phase of the supply chain by spreading awareness and encouraging changes in behaviour.

4.3 Challenges and Opportunities Related to Food Waste in Australia

Food waste is a significant issue in Australia, driven by a range of factors that affect both the supply and demand sides of the food system. The country's vast geographic size and dispersed population present logistical challenges in transportation and distribution, leading to substantial food waste during transit. In Australia, there are several challenges and opportunities in decreasing food waste within the agri-food supply chain:

Table 3. Challenges and opportunities related to food waste

Theme	Challenges	Opportunities
Infrastructure and Logistics	- Australia's vast size and dispersed population create challenges in efficient transportation and distribution, leading to higher food waste during transit (Ridoutt et al., 2010).	- Investing in technology like smart packaging and cold chain management can optimize supply chain efficiency and minimize losses (Lockie et al., 2020).
Market Demand and Supply Dynamics	- Fluctuations in market demand, consumer preferences for perfect produce, and rigid quality standards contribute to surplus and wasted food, especially for perishable goods (Devin & Richards, 2018; Imports, 2001).	- Implementing supportive policies and incentives, such as tax incentives for food donations and standardized date labelling, can reduce waste (Zatyko et al., 2023).
Seasonal Variability and Climate Change	- Seasonal variability and extreme weather events impact agricultural productivity and exacerbate food waste due to crop losses and supply chain disruptions (Edwards et al., 2011).	- Exploring opportunities to create value-added products from surplus produce and by-products can minimize waste and generate revenue (McCarthy et al., 2020).
Behavioural and Cultural Factors	- Addressing consumer behaviours like over-purchasing and reluctance to buy imperfect produce requires sustained education and behaviour change campaigns (Porat et al., 2018; Verghese et al., 2015).	- Educating consumers about food waste effects and offering advice for reduction can minimize wastage from the demand side (Benyam, 2019).
Resource Constraints	- Limited resources, such as water and arable land, challenge sustainable agriculture and require efficient management to minimize waste (Chartres & Noble, 2015; McKenzie & Williams, 2015).	- Strengthening collaboration between government, industry, and research institutions can help tackle food waste at various stages (Godrich et al., 2022; Soosay, 2013).
Economic Barriers	- High initial investments for sustainable technologies and practices can be a barrier; financial incentives from the government could help (McKenzie & Williams, 2015).	- Finding alternative uses for by-products and surplus produce can generate additional revenue streams (McCarthy et al., 2020).
Policy and Regulation	- Overly stringent food safety regulations can hinder the redistribution of surplus food and necessitate more robust policies to encourage sustainable practices (Smith & Jones, 2022).	- Implementing waste diversion targets and supportive policies can create an enabling environment for waste reduction efforts (Zatyko et al., 2023).
Pro-Environmental Behaviour	- Changing ingrained consumer behaviours, such as over-purchasing and improper food storage, is challenging due to entrenched habits and lack of awareness (Porat & Efrat, 2018).	- Implementing behaviour change campaigns and educational programs to promote practices such as mindful purchasing and proper storage can reduce food waste (Verghese & Lewis, 2015).

Addressing these challenges and capitalizing on opportunities to reduce food waste in the agri-food supply chain in Australia will require a coordinated and multi-stakeholder approach, incorporating technological innovation, policy support, consumer education, and industry collaboration.

5. CONCLUSION

Agricultural workplaces can have a significant impact on reducing food waste and its environmental effects by promoting efficient resource use, minimizing waste, and practicing responsible consumption. This study endeavours to shed light on the pervasive issue of food waste within Australia's agricultural sector while also exploring avenues to foster pro-environmental behaviour among agricultural workers. Addressing food waste and promoting sustainability within the agricultural sector in Australia is a complex but crucial endeavour with significant implications for environmental conservation, economic efficiency, and social well-being. This study aims to help reduce food waste and promote sustainability by looking at how common it is, what causes it in agricultural settings, learning about the attitudes and actions of farmers, and finding effective ways to encourage environmentally friendly behaviour through targeted interventions and policies. Addressing sustainability in agriculture involves a detailed examination of life cycle stages across the supply chain, global initiatives, and the integration of advanced digital technologies. Each stage of the agricultural life cycle, from production to consumption, plays a critical role in minimizing environmental impact and ensuring efficient resource use (Finkbeiner et al., 2019). International programs such as the United Nations Sustainable Development Goals (SDGs) advocates for improved agricultural practices and the reduction of food waste, reflecting a global commitment to sustainability (United Nations, 2021).

To bridge these global initiatives with practical implementation, digitally enabled technologies like big data and artificial intelligence (AI) are crucial. These technologies enhance the efficiency of the food system by optimizing agricultural processes and reducing waste. Big data analytics provides real-time insights and predictive capabilities that improve supply chain management and minimize food spoilage (Garg et al., 2021). Meanwhile, AI-driven technologies facilitate precision farming, enabling targeted resource use and boosting crop yields while reducing waste (Kumar et al., 2022; Baker et al., 2020). Together, these technological advancements and global programs form a comprehensive approach to creating a sustainable and efficient food system from farm to fork. The adoption of pro-environmental behaviour in the agri-food supply chain in Australia is gaining traction, driven by technological innovations, consumer awareness, and supportive policies. While significant progress has been made, ongoing efforts are required to overcome economic, behavioural, and regulatory barriers. Pro-environmental behaviour among consumers in Australia is gaining momentum, driven by targeted campaigns and education programs. Initiatives like the "Love Food Hate Waste" campaign and OzHarvest's educational programs have demonstrated significant impacts in reducing food waste and fostering sustainable consumption patterns. Continued efforts to address behavioural and practical challenges, supported by robust policies and partnerships, will be crucial in further enhancing consumer PEB and achieving broader sustainability goals. Enhanced collaboration among stakeholders and continuous education and innovation will play a crucial role in further decreasing food waste and improving sustainability in the agricultural sector.

REFERENCES

Adams, D. J. (2022). *An investigation into the sustainability practices of large food manufacturers with operations in Australia and their supply chains* (Doctoral dissertation, Swinburne University of Technology).

Ajila, C. M., Brar, S. K., Verma, M., Tyagi, R. D., Godbout, S., & Valéro, J. R. (2012). Bio-processing of agro-byproducts to animal feed. *Critical Reviews in Biotechnology*, 32(4), 382–400. DOI: 10.3109/07388551.2012.659172 PMID: 22380921

Aktas, E., Sahin, H., Topaloglu, Z., Oledinma, A., Huda, A. K. S., Irani, Z., Sharif, A. M., van't Wout, T., & Kamrava, M. (2018). A consumer behavioural approach to food waste. *Journal of Enterprise Information Management*, 31(5), 658–673. DOI: 10.1108/JEIM-03-2018-0051

Alexander, A. (2023). In 2022, Woolworths generated an estimated 184,260 tonnes of edible food waste. Accessed from https://app.impaakt.com/analyses/in-2022-woolworths-generated-an-estimated-184260-tonnes-of-edible-food-waste-136837

Anand, S., & Barua, M. K. (2022). Modeling the key factors leading to post-harvest loss and waste of fruits and vegetables in the agri-fresh produce supply chain. *Computers and Electronics in Agriculture*, 198, 106936. DOI: 10.1016/j.compag.2022.106936

Anderson, L., Grudnoff, M., Hawking, T., & Campbell, R. (2023). Food waste in Australia and how supermarkets profit from it. In a *Discussion Paper*. The Australian Institute. Accessed from https://apo.org.au/node/324366

APCO. (2024). Australia's 2025 National Packaging Targets. Accessed from https://apco.org.au/national-packaging-targets

Aschemann-Witzel, J., De Hooge, I., Amani, P., Bech-Larsen, T., & Oostindjer, M. (2015). Consumer-related food waste: Causes and potential for action. *Sustainability (Basel)*, 7(6), 6457–6477. DOI: 10.3390/su7066457

Atanda, S. A., Pessu, P. O., Agoda, S., Isong, I. U., & Ikotun, I. (2011). The concepts and problems of post–harvest food losses in perishable crops. *African Journal of Food Science*, 5(11), 603–613.

Australian Food and Grocery Council. (2024). How We help. https://www.afgc.org.au/about-afgc/how-we-help

Australian Government. (2017). National Food Waste Strategy: Halving Australia's Food Waste by 2030. Accessed from https://www.agriculture.gov.au/sites/default/files/documents/national-food-waste-strategy.pdf

Badsar, M., Moghim, M., & Ghasemi, M. (2023). Analysis of factors influencing farmers' sustainable environmental behavior in agriculture activities: Integration of the planned behavior and the protection motivation theories. *Environment, Development and Sustainability*, 25(9), 9903–9934. DOI: 10.1007/s10668-022-02468-3

Baker, J., Nelson, T., & Liu, H. (2020). Artificial intelligence in precision agriculture: A review. *Computers and Electronics in Agriculture*, 179, 105–123.

Balaji, M., & Arshinder, K. (2016). Modeling the causes of food wastage in Indian perishable food supply chain. *Resources, Conservation and Recycling*, 114, 153–167. DOI: 10.1016/j.resconrec.2016.07.016

Bamberg, S., & Möser, G. (2007). Twenty years after Hines, Hungerford, and Tomera: A new meta-analysis of psycho-social determinants of pro-environmental behaviour. *Journal of Environmental Psychology*, 27(1), 14–25. DOI: 10.1016/j.jenvp.2006.12.002

Barghusen, R., Sattler, C., Deijl, L., Weebers, C., & Matzdorf, B. (2021). Motivations of farmers to participate in collective agri-environmental schemes: The case of Dutch agricultural collectives. *Ecosystems and People (Abingdon, England)*, 17(1), 539–555. DOI: 10.1080/26395916.2021.1979098

Barzman, M., Bàrberi, P., Birch, A. N. E., Boonekamp, P., Dachbrodt-Saaydeh, S., Graf, B., Hommel, B., Jensen, J. E., Kiss, J., Kudsk, P., Lamichhane, J. R., Messéan, A., Moonen, A.-C., Ratnadass, A., Ricci, P., Sarah, J.-L., & Sattin, M. (2015). Eight principles of integrated pest management. *Agronomy for Sustainable Development*, 35(4), 1199–1215. DOI: 10.1007/s13593-015-0327-9

Basumatary, R., & Arora, V. K. (2018). Review on the storage structure for longer shelf-life of vegetables. *Progressive Agriculture*, 18(2), 145–161. DOI: 10.5958/0976-4615.2018.00028.5

Benyam, A. (2019). *An interdisciplinary examination of behaviours and policy preferences for domestic food waste reduction: The case of households in Central Queensland, Australia* (Doctoral dissertation, CQUniversity).

Bilska, B., Wrzosek, M., Kołożyn-Krajewska, D., & Krajewski, K. (2015). Food losses and food waste in the context of sustainable development of the food sector. *The China Business Review*, 14(9), 452–462. DOI: 10.17265/1537-1506/2015.09.005

Birkmaier, A., Imeri, A., Riester, M., & Reiner, G. (2023). Preventing waste in food supply networks-a platform architecture for AI-driven forecasting based on heterogeneous big data. *Procedia CIRP*, 120, 708–713. DOI: 10.1016/j.procir.2023.09.063

Brennan, L., Parker, L., Lockrey, S., Verghese, K., Chin, S., Langley, S., ... & Alessi, N. (2021). The wicked problem of packaging and consumers: Innovative approaches for sustainability research. *Sustainable Packaging,* 137-176.

Bresler, M., Romsdal, A., Strandhagen, J. O., & Oluyisola, O. E. (2020). Principles and research agenda for sustainable, data-driven food production planning and control. In *Advances in Production Management Systems. The Path to Digital Transformation and Innovation of Production Management Systems: IFIP WG 5.7 International Conference, APMS 2020, Novi Sad, Serbia,August 30–September 3, 2020,Proceedings, Part I* (pp. 634-641). Springer International Publishing. DOI: 10.1007/978-3-030-57993-7_72

Brodribb, P., McCann, M., & Motavallia, J. (2020). *A study of waste in the cold food chain and opportunities for improvement.* Expert Group and Thinkwell Australia Pty Ltd for Department of Agriculture, Water and the Environment and Refrigerants Australia.

Brooks, E. J., & Lewis, D. R. (2020). Impact of corporate sustainability programs on workplace food waste reduction in Australia. *Journal of Environmental Management*, 258, 110034.

Bryan, B. A., Nolan, M., McKellar, L., Connor, J. D., Newth, D., Harwood, T., King, D., Navarro, J., Cai, Y., Gao, L., Grundy, M., Graham, P., Ernst, A., Dunstall, S., Stock, F., Brinsmead, T., Harman, I., Grigg, N. J., Battaglia, M., & Hatfield-Dodds, S. (2016). Land-use and sustainability under intersecting global change and domestic policy scenarios: Trajectories for Australia to 2050. *Global Environmental Change*, 38, 130–152. DOI: 10.1016/j.gloenvcha.2016.03.002

Calvo-Porral, C., & Rodríguez-Fernández, M. (2015). Food for thought: The food waste global issue. In *Experiencias en la modelación de la toma de decisiones en la salud humana, medio ambiente y desarrollo humano: Tomo 1* (pp. 1-23). Universidad de Granada.

Cao, Y., Tao, L., Wu, K., & Wan, G. (2020). Coordinating joint greening efforts in an agri-food supply chain with environmentally sensitive demand. *Journal of Cleaner Production*, 277, 123883. DOI: 10.1016/j.jclepro.2020.123883

Carrillo-Labella, R., Fort, F., & Parras-Rosa, M. (2020). Motives, barriers, and expected benefits of ISO 14001 in the agri-food sector. *Sustainability (Basel)*, 12(5), 1724. DOI: 10.3390/su12051724

Carter, L. P., & Thompson, C. E. (2021). Workplace food waste management: The role of pro-environmental behavior. *Resources, Conservation and Recycling*, 168, 105302.

Cary, J., & Roberts, A. (2011). The limitations of environmental management systems in Australian agriculture. *Journal of Environmental Management*, 92(3), 878–885. DOI: 10.1016/j.jenvman.2010.10.055 PMID: 21084146

Chapman, J., Skinner, N., & Seale, S. (2013). Working towards sustainability: Exploring the workplace as a site for pro-environmental behaviour change. In *Motivating change: sustainable design and behaviour in the built environment* (pp. 56–70). Routledge.

Chartres, C. J., & Noble, A. (2015). Sustainable intensification: Overcoming land and water constraints on food production. *Food Security*, 7(2), 235–245. DOI: 10.1007/s12571-015-0425-1

Chawla, G., Lugosi, P., & Hawkins, R. (2022). Factors influencing hospitality employees' pro-environmental behaviours toward food waste. *Sustainability (Basel)*, 14(15), 9015. DOI: 10.3390/su14159015

Chegere, M. J. (2018). Post-harvest losses reduction by small-scale maize farmers: The role of handling practices. *Food Policy*, 77, 103–115. DOI: 10.1016/j.foodpol.2018.05.001

Chrobog, C. K. (2014). *Wasted: understanding the economic and social impact of food waste* (Doctoral dissertation).

Clark, P., Anderson, H., & Mitchell, R. (2022). Assessing the direct impact of pro-environmental behavior on sustainability outcomes: Evidence from longitudinal studies. *Journal of Environmental Management*, 290(1), 112–128.

Coles (2024). Charity and community partners. *Accessed from*https://www.coles.com.au/about/our-partners/community/partnerships

Coles group. (2023). Together to zero waste. *Accessed from*https://www.colesgroup.com.au/sustainability/?page=environment

Davies, A. (2020). Food sharing. In *Routledge handbook of sustainable and regenerative food systems* (pp. 204–217). Routledge. DOI: 10.4324/9780429466823-15

De Corato, U. (2020). Improving the shelf-life and quality of fresh and minimally processed fruits and vegetables for a modern food industry: A comprehensive critical review from the traditional technologies into the most promising advancements. *Critical Reviews in Food Science and Nutrition*, 60(6), 940–975. DOI: 10.1080/10408398.2018.1553025 PMID: 30614263

Department of Climate Change. Energy the Environment and Water- DCCEEW. (2023). Reducing Australia's food waste. *Waste and Recycling.* Accessed from https://www.dcceew.gov.au/environment/protection/waste/food-waste

Department of the Environment and Energy. (2017). Working together to reduce food waste in Australia. In *a factsheet by DCCEEW.* Accessed from https://www.dcceew.gov.au/sites/default/files/documents/food-waste-fact-sheet.pdf

Despoudi, S. (2021). Challenges in reducing food losses at producers' level: The case of Greek agricultural supply chain producers. *Industrial Marketing Management*, 93, 520–532. DOI: 10.1016/j.indmarman.2020.09.022

Devin, B., & Richards, C. (2018). Food waste, power, and corporate social responsibility in the Australian food supply chain. *Journal of Business Ethics*, 150(1), 199–210. DOI: 10.1007/s10551-016-3181-z

Duarte Alonso, A., & Northcote, J. (2013). Investigating farmers' involvement in value-added activities: A preliminary study from Australia. *British Food Journal*, 115(10), 1407–1427. DOI: 10.1108/BFJ-04-2011-0104

Dufty, N., & Jackson, T. (2018). Information and communication technology use in Australian agriculture. Accessed from https://www.agriculture.gov.au/sites/default/files/sitecollectiondocuments/abares/ict-use-australian-agriculture.pdf

Dunning, R. D., Johnson, L. K., & Boys, K. A. (2019). Putting Dollars to Waste. *Choices*, 34(1), 1–9.

Edwards, F., Dixon, J., Friel, S., Hall, G., Hannigan, I., Hattersley, L., Hogan, A., Larsen, K., Lawrence, M., Lockie, S., Lopata, A., Wilson, A., & Wood, B. 2011, *Food systems, climate change adaptation and human health in Australia* [NCCARF National Climate Change Adaptation Research Facility], [Canbera, A.C.T.]. Accessed from http://hdl.handle.net/10536/DRO/DU:30042087

Edwards, F., & Mercer, D. (2007). Gleaning from Gluttony: An Australian youth subculture confronts the ethics of waste. *The Australian Geographer*, 38(3), 279–296. DOI: 10.1080/00049180701639174

Farr, M., Eagle, L., & Hay, R. (2018). *Key determinants of pro-environmental behaviour of land managers in the agricultural sector: literature review.*

Fatoki, O. (2019). Hotel employees' pro-environmental behaviour: Effect of leadership behaviour, institutional support and workplace spirituality. *Sustainability (Basel)*, 11(15), 4135. DOI: 10.3390/su11154135

Ferrari, L., Cavaliere, A., De Marchi, E., & Banterle, A. (2019). Can nudging improve the environmental impact of food supply chain? A systematic review. *Trends in Food Science & Technology*, 91, 184–192. DOI: 10.1016/j.tifs.2019.07.004

Finkbeiner, M., Inaba, A., & Schau, E. (2019). Life cycle assessment in agriculture: A review. *Agricultural Systems, 172,* 1-12. Foodwise Australia (2024). Fast facts on food waste. *Accessed from*https://www.foodwise.com.au/foodwaste/food-waste-fast-facts/

Friman, A., & Hyytiä, N. (2022). The economic and welfare effects of food waste reduction on a food-production-driven rural region. *Sustainability (Basel)*, 14(6), 3632. DOI: 10.3390/su14063632

García-Flores, R., Juliano, P., & Petkovic, K. (2019). Handling food waste and losses: Criticalities and methodologies. In *Sustainable Food Supply Chains* (pp. 261–276). Academic Press. DOI: 10.1016/B978-0-12-813411-5.00018-1

GardenDrum. (2015). Ripe Near Me website connects food growers with consumers. *Accessed from*https://gardendrum.com/2015/08/28/ripe-near-me-website-connects-food-growers-with-consumers/

Garg, R., Kumar, A., & Sharma, S. (2021). Big data analytics for sustainable agriculture: Opportunities and challenges. *Journal of Cleaner Production*, 292, 125–137.

Gifford, R., & Nilsson, A. (2014). Personal and social factors that influence pro-environmental concern and behaviour. *International Journal of Psychology*, 49(3), 278–290. DOI: 10.1002/ijop.12034 PMID: 24821503

Godrich, S. L., Macau, F., Kent, K., Lo, J., & Devine, A. (2022). Food supply impacts and solutions associated with the COVID-19 pandemic: A regional Australian case study. *International Journal of Environmental Research and Public Health*, 19(7), 4116. DOI: 10.3390/ijerph19074116 PMID: 35409797

Graham-Rowe, E., Jessop, D. C., & Sparks, P. (2014). Identifying motivations and barriers to minimizing household food waste. *Resources, Conservation and Recycling*, 84, 15–23. DOI: 10.1016/j.resconrec.2013.12.005

Grilli, G., & Curtis, J. (2021). Encouraging pro-environmental behaviours: A review of methods and approaches. *Renewable & Sustainable Energy Reviews*, 135, 110039. DOI: 10.1016/j.rser.2020.110039

Guarnieri, P., de Aguiar, R. C., Thomé, K. M., & Watanabe, E. A. D. M. (2021). The role of logistics in food waste reduction in wholesalers and small retailers of fruits and vegetables: A multiple case study. *Logistics (Basel)*, 5(4), 77. DOI: 10.3390/logistics5040077

Harfmann, B. (2022). High-pressure processing enhances food safety, extends shelf life. Accessed from https://www.bevindustry.com/articles/94807-high-pressure-processing-enhances-food-safety-extends-shelf-life

Harrison, R., & Broughton, A. (2021). The impact of environmental regulations on pro-environmental behavior: Evidence from a longitudinal study. *Environmental Policy and Governance*, 31(4), 345–359.

Hobday, A. J., & McDonald, J. (2014). Environmental issues in Australia. *Annual Review of Environment and Resources*, 39(1), 1–28. DOI: 10.1146/annurev-environ-012113-111451

Hodgins, K., & Parizeau, K. (2020). Farm-to-fork… and beyond? A call to incorporate food waste into food systems research. *Food & Foodways*, 28(1), 43–60. DOI: 10.1080/07409710.2020.1718280

Horoś, I. K., & Ruppenthal, T. (2021). Avoidance of food waste from a grocery retail store owner's perspective. *Sustainability (Basel)*, 13(2), 550. DOI: 10.3390/su13020550

Horticulture Australia. (2024). Vegetable Industry Development Program. *Accessed from*https://ausveg.com.au/app/data/technical-insights/docs/PostHarvestManagementforVegetables.pdf

Imports, J. (2001). *The Australian Apple Industry Squeeze.* Current Practice versus Best Practice. Economic Impacts of Apple. Accessed from https://citeseerx.ist.psu.edu/document?repid=rep1&type=pdf&doi=d017e0d9bc8a8ffa2b28ef2a619972f23c714455

Jeevahan, J., Anderson, A., Sriram, V., Durairaj, R. B., Britto Joseph, G., & Mageshwaran, G. (2021). Waste into energy conversion technologies and conversion of food wastes into the potential products: A review. *International Journal of Ambient Energy*, 42(9), 1083–1101. DOI: 10.1080/01430750.2018.1537939

Jetten, J., Haslam, C., & Haslam, S. A. (2012). *The social cure: Identity, health and well-being*. Psychology Press. DOI: 10.4324/9780203813195

Joardder, M. U., Hasan Masud, M., Joardder, M. U., & Masud, M. H. (2019). Causes of food waste. *Food preservation in developing countries: Challenges and solutions*, 27-55.

Johnson, M., Patel, R., & Turner, L. (2020). The role of public awareness campaigns in promoting pro-environmental behavior: A review of recent policies. *Journal of Environmental Psychology*, 65, 101–113.

Jones, T., & Lee, K. (2021). Quantifying the impact of pro-environmental behavior on organizational environmental performance. *Business Strategy and the Environment*, 30(3), 567–580.

Juríčková, Z., Lušňáková, Z., Hallová, M., Horská, E., & Hudáková, M. (2020). Environmental impacts and attitudes of agricultural enterprises for environmental protection and sustainable development. *Agriculture*, 10(10), 440. DOI: 10.3390/agriculture10100440

Kansal, M., Mitsis, A., Ananda, J., & Pearson, D. (2022). Challenges for food waste reduction campaigns: Requirements for Asian consumers in Australia. *Australasian Journal of Environmental Management*, 29(4), 368–385. DOI: 10.1080/14486563.2022.2143917

Karki, S. T., Bennett, A. C., & Mishra, J. L. (2021). Reducing food waste and food insecurity in the UK: The architecture of surplus food distribution supply chain in addressing the sustainable development goals (Goal 2 and Goal 12.3) at a city level. *Industrial Marketing Management*, 93, 563–577. DOI: 10.1016/j.indmarman.2020.09.019

Karpouzis, F., Lindberg, R., Walsh, A., Shah, S., Abbott, G., & Ball, K. (2024). Impact and process evaluation of a primary-school Food Education and Sustainability Training (FEAST) program in 10-12-year-old children in Australia: Pragmatic cluster non-randomized controlled trial. *BMC Public Health*, 24(1), 657. DOI: 10.1186/s12889-024-18079-8 PMID: 38429629

Keating, B. A., Carberry, P. S., Bindraban, P. S., Asseng, S., Meinke, H., & Dixon, J. (2010). Eco-efficient agriculture: Concepts, challenges, and opportunities. *Crop Science*, 50(S1), S-109. DOI: 10.2135/cropsci2009.10.0594

Kiaya, V. (2014). Post-harvest losses and strategies to reduce them. *Technical Paper on Postharvest Losses* [ACF]. *Action Contre la Faim*, 25(3), 1–25.

King, S., Hutchinson, S. A., & Boxall, N. J. (2021). *Advanced recycling technologies to address Australia's plastic waste*. Commonwealth Scientific and Industrial Research Organisation.

Kiran, B. R., Prasad, M. N. V., & Mohan, S. V. (2023). Farm to fork: sustainable agrifood systems. In *Sustainable and Circular Management of Resources and Waste Towards a Green Deal* (pp. 25–38). Elsevier. DOI: 10.1016/B978-0-323-95278-1.00012-7

Kodithuwakku, N. (2022). *Importance of food waste reporting for collaboration between Australian retail, farming, and food rescue organisations* (Doctoral dissertation, CQUniversity).

Kollmuss, A., & Agyeman, J. (2002). Mind the gap: Why do people act environmentally and what are the barriers to pro-environmental behavior? *Environmental Education Research*, 8(3), 239–260. DOI: 10.1080/13504620220145401

Končar, J., Marić, R., & Vučenović, S. (2021). Exploring pro-environmental behaviour in FMCG supply chain. *Tehnicki Vjesnik (Strojarski Fakultet)*, 28(6), 2060–2071.

Kowalska, A. (2017). The issue of food losses and waste and its determinants. *LogForum, 13*(1).

Kragt, M. E., Dumbrell, N. P., & Blackmore, L. (2017). Motivations and barriers for Western Australian broad-acre farmers to adopt carbon farming. *Environmental Science & Policy*, 73, 115–123. DOI: 10.1016/j.envsci.2017.04.009

Kumar, P., Raj, A., & Kumar, V. A. (2024). Approach to Reduce Agricultural Waste via Sustainable Agricultural Practices. In *Valorization of Biomass Wastes for Environmental Sustainability: Green Practices for the Rural Circular Economy* (pp. 21–50). Springer Nature Switzerland. DOI: 10.1007/978-3-031-52485-1_2

Kumar, S., Jha, M., & Sharma, A. (2022). AI-based approaches for precision agriculture and their impact on sustainability. *AI & Society*, 37(1), 35–48.

Kummu, M., De Moel, H., Porkka, M., Siebert, S., Varis, O., & Ward, P. J. (2012). Lost food, wasted resources: Global food supply chain losses and their impacts on freshwater, cropland, and fertiliser use. *The Science of the Total Environment*, 438, 477–489. DOI: 10.1016/j.scitotenv.2012.08.092 PMID: 23032564

Langford, A. (2020). *Agri-food transformations in Northern Australia* (Doctoral dissertation, The University of Queensland).

Leat, P. M., Lamprinopoulou-Kranis, C., Revoredo-Giha, C., & Kupiec-Teahan, B. (2011). *Agri-food supply chains and sustainability-related issues: evidence from across the Scottish agri-food economy.*

Lee, A., & Ride, K. (2018). Review of nutrition among Aboriginal and Torres Strait Islander people. *Australian Indigenous Health Reviews*, 20, 1–48.

Lee, J., & Park, S. (2022). Government incentives and their effects on organizational pro-environmental practices: A policy analysis. *Business Strategy and the Environment*, 31(2), 184–198.

Li, X., Cifuentes-Faura, J., & Tan, Y. (2023). Analyzing the low carbon and pro-environment behavior of agricultural enterprises based on organizational commitment and role models' guidance. *Environmental Science and Pollution Research International*, •••, 1–13. DOI: 10.1007/s11356-023-31302-0 PMID: 38079039

Lockie, S., Fairley-Grenot, K., Ankeny, R., Botterill, L., Howlett, B., Mcbratney, A., ... & Woodhead, I. (2020). *The future of agricultural technologies*. Australian Council of Learned Academies (ACOLA).

Lugo, S. D. R., Kimita, K., & Nishino, N. (2023). Characteristics of decision process towards circular food economy: A review. *Cleaner Logistics and Supply Chain*, 7, 100104. DOI: 10.1016/j.clscn.2023.100104

Makhal, A., Robertson, K., Thyne, M., & Mirosa, M. (2021). Normalising the "ugly" to reduce food waste: Exploring the socialisations that form appearance preferences for fresh fruits and vegetables. *Journal of Consumer Behaviour*, 20(5), 1025–1039. DOI: 10.1002/cb.1908

Manzoor, S., Fayaz, U., Dar, A. H., Dash, K. K., Shams, R., Bashir, I., Pandey, V. K., & Abdi, G. (2024). Sustainable Development Goals Through Reducing Food Loss and Food Waste: A Comprehensive Review. *Future Foods : a Dedicated Journal for Sustainability in Food Science*, 9, 100362. DOI: 10.1016/j.fufo.2024.100362

Martinez, A., & Gomez, M. (2023). Measuring the effectiveness of behavioral interventions in promoting pro-environmental behaviors: A meta-analysis. *Environmental Psychology Review*, 45(4), 302–318.

McCarthy, B., Kapetanaki, A. B., & Wang, P. (2020). Completing the food waste management loop: Is there market potential for value-added surplus products (VASP)? *Journal of Cleaner Production*, 256, 120435. DOI: 10.1016/j.jclepro.2020.120435

McGrath, D. (2021). *Watch my waste: how self-auditing affected Australian food-service food waste* (Doctoral dissertation, RMIT University).

McKenzie, F. C., & Williams, J. (2015). Sustainable food production: Constraints, challenges and choices by 2050. *Food Security*, 7(2), 221–233. DOI: 10.1007/s12571-015-0441-1

McKenzie, N. N., Jacquier, D. D., Isbell, R. R., & Brown, K. K. (2004). *Australian soils and landscapes: an illustrated compendium*. CSIRO publishing. DOI: 10.1071/9780643100732

Mena, C., Terry, L. A., Williams, A., & Ellram, L. (2014). Causes of waste across multi-tier supply networks: Cases in the UK food sector. *International Journal of Production Economics*, 152, 144–158. DOI: 10.1016/j.ijpe.2014.03.012

Messner, R., Johnson, H., & Richards, C. (2021). From surplus-to-waste: A study of systemic overproduction, surplus and food waste in horticultural supply chains. *Journal of Cleaner Production*, 278, 123952. DOI: 10.1016/j.jclepro.2020.123952

Mesterházy, Á., Oláh, J., & Popp, J. (2020). Losses in the grain supply chain: Causes and solutions. *Sustainability (Basel)*, 12(6), 2342. DOI: 10.3390/su12062342

Midgley, J. L. (2014). The logics of surplus food redistribution. *Journal of Environmental Planning and Management*, 57(12), 1872–1892. DOI: 10.1080/09640568.2013.848192

Mirosa, M., Pearson, D., & Pearson, R. (2016). Ethics of food waste. In *The Routledge Handbook of Food Ethics* (pp. 400–408). Routledge.

Moreddu, C. (2016). *Public-Private Partnerships for Agricultural Innovation: Lessons From Recent Experiences", OECD Food, Agriculture and Fisheries Papers, No. 92*. OECD Publishing., DOI: 10.1787/5jm55j9p9rmx-

Mourad, M. (2016). Recycling, recovering and preventing "food waste": Competing solutions for food systems sustainability in the United States and France. *Journal of Cleaner Production*, 126, 461–477. DOI: 10.1016/j.jclepro.2016.03.084

Munesue, Y., Masui, T., & Fushima, T. (2015). The effects of reducing food losses and food waste on global food insecurity, natural resources, and greenhouse gas emissions. *Environmental Economics and Policy Studies*, 17(1), 43–77. DOI: 10.1007/s10018-014-0083-0

Murphy, S. J., & Wright, A. T. (2019). Employee behavior and food waste reduction in Australian corporate cafeterias. *Waste Management (New York, N.Y.)*, 92, 55–62.

National Food Waste Strategy. (2017). Halving Australia's Food Waste By 2030. Accessed from https://www.agriculture.gov.au/sites/default/files/documents/national-food-waste-strategy.pdf

Ndraha, N., Hsiao, H. I., Vlajic, J., Yang, M. F., & Lin, H. T. V. (2018). Time-temperature abuse in the food cold chain: Review of issues, challenges, and recommendations. *Food Control*, 89, 12–21. DOI: 10.1016/j.foodcont.2018.01.027

Negi, S., & Anand, N. (2016). Factors leading to losses and wastage in the supply chain of fruits and vegetables sector in India. *Energy, Infrastructure.Transport Challenges: Way Forward*, 1, 80–105.

Ng, H. S., Kee, P. E., Yim, H. S., Chen, P. T., Wei, Y. H., & Lan, J. C. W. (2020). Recent advances on the sustainable approaches for conversion and reutilization of food wastes to valuable bioproducts. *Bioresource Technology*, 302, 122889. DOI: 10.1016/j.biortech.2020.122889 PMID: 32033841

Nguyen, O. S., & Smith, P. D. (2022). Green initiatives and their impact on food waste in office settings. *Sustainability*, 14(5), 2900.

Nicastro, R., & Carillo, P. (2021). Food loss and waste prevention strategies from farm to fork. *Sustainability (Basel)*, 13(10), 5443. DOI: 10.3390/su13105443

Nolan, J. M., Schultz, P. W., Cialdini, R. B., Goldstein, N. J., & Griskevicius, V. (2008). Normative social influence is under-detected. *Personality and Social Psychology Bulletin*, 34(7), 913–924. DOI: 10.1177/0146167208316691 PMID: 18550863

Odhiambo, G. M., Waiganjo, E., & Simiyu, A. N. (2023). Incentivizing Employee Pro-Environmental Behaviour: Harnessing the Potential of Green Rewards. *African Journal of Empirical Research*, 4(2), 601–611. DOI: 10.51867/ajernet.4.2.60

Oliver, M. A., Bishop, T. F., & Marchant, B. P. (Eds.). (2013). *Precision agriculture for sustainability and environmental protection* (pp. 1–283). Routledge. DOI: 10.4324/9780203128329

Omarova, L., & Jo, S. J. (2022). Employee pro-environmental behavior: The impact of environmental transformational leadership and GHRM. *Sustainability (Basel)*, 14(4), 2046. DOI: 10.3390/su14042046

Oosterkamp, E., van der Sluis, A., van Geffen, L., Aramyan, L., & Bos-Brouwers, H. (2019). *Cosmetic aspects in specific marketing standards for fruit and vegetables: removing cosmetic aspects from the EU marketing standards: implications for the market and impact on food waste* (No. 2019-014). Wageningen Economic Research.

OzHarvest. (2023). Inquiry into food security in Australia. *Accessed from*https://www.ozharvest.org/app/uploads/2023/03/221209-Inquiry-into-Food-Security-in-Australia-OzHarvest-submission-v2.pdf

Pannell, D., & Rogers, A. (2022). Agriculture and the environment: Policy approaches in Australia and New Zealand. *Review of Environmental Economics and Policy*, 16(1), 126–145. DOI: 10.1086/718053

Papargyropoulou, E., Steinberger, J. K., Wright, N., Lozano, R., Padfield, R., & Ujang, Z. (2019). Patterns and causes of food waste in the hospitality and food service sector: Food waste prevention insights from Malaysia. *Sustainability (Basel)*, 11(21), 6016. DOI: 10.3390/su11216016

Parfitt, J., Barthel, M., & Macnaughton, S. (2010). Food waste within food supply chains: Quantification and potential for change to 2050. *Philosophical Transactions of the Royal Society of London. Series B, Biological Sciences*, 365(1554), 3065–3081. DOI: 10.1098/rstb.2010.0126 PMID: 20713403

Pearson, D., Mirosa, M., Andrews, L., & Kerr, G. (2017). Reframing communications that encourage individuals to reduce food waste. *Communication Research and Practice*, 3(2), 137–154. DOI: 10.1080/22041451.2016.1209274

Pittock, J., Hussey, K., & Stone, A. (2016). Groundwater management under global change: Sustaining biodiversity, energy and food supplies. *Integrated groundwater management: Concepts, approaches and challenges,* 75-96.

Pollard, C. M., & Booth, S. (2019). Food insecurity and hunger in rich countries—It is time for action against inequality. *International Journal of Environmental Research and Public Health*, 16(10), 1804. DOI: 10.3390/ijerph16101804 PMID: 31117216

Pollard, G., Roetman, P., Ward, J., Chiera, B., & Mantzioris, E. (2018). Beyond productivity: Considering the health, social value and happiness of home and community food gardens. *Urban Science (Basel, Switzerland)*, 2(4), 97. DOI: 10.3390/urbansci2040097

Porat, M., & Efrat, A. (2018). Consumer behavior and food waste: A review of recent research. *Food Policy*, 82, 32–40.

Porat, R., Lichter, A., Terry, L. A., Harker, R., & Buzby, J. (2018). Postharvest losses of fruit and vegetables during retail and in consumers' homes: Quantifications, causes, and means of prevention. *Postharvest Biology and Technology*, 139, 135–149. DOI: 10.1016/j.postharvbio.2017.11.019

Porter, S. D., Reay, D. S., Bomberg, E., & Higgins, P. (2018). Avoidable food losses and associated production-phase greenhouse gas emissions arising from application of cosmetic standards to fresh fruit and vegetables in Europe and the UK. *Journal of Cleaner Production*, 201, 869–878. DOI: 10.1016/j.jclepro.2018.08.079

Pretty, J. (2018). Intensification for redesigned and sustainable agricultural systems. *Science*, 362(6417), eaav0294. DOI: 10.1126/science.aav0294 PMID: 30467142

Queensland Government. (2024). Food waste facts. *Accessed from*https://www.qld.gov.au/environment/circular-economy-waste-reduction/reduction/reduce-food-waste/facts

Quested, T. E., Ingle, R., & Parry, A. D. (2013). *Household food and drink waste in the UK: Quantification and analysis.* WRAP Report.

Raak, N., Symmank, C., Zahn, S., Aschemann-Witzel, J., & Rohm, H. (2017). Processing-and product-related causes for food waste and implications for the food supply chain. *Waste Management (New York, N.Y.)*, 61, 461–472. DOI: 10.1016/j.wasman.2016.12.027 PMID: 28038904

Rai, A. K., Bana, S. R., Sachan, D. S., & Singh, B. (2023). Advancing sustainable agriculture: A comprehensive review for optimizing food production and environmental conservation. *International Journal of Plant and Soil Science*, 35(16), 417–425. DOI: 10.9734/ijpss/2023/v35i163169

Raut, R., & Gardas, B. B. (2018). Sustainable logistics barriers of fruits and vegetables: An interpretive structural modeling approach. *Benchmarking*, 25(8), 2589–2610. DOI: 10.1108/BIJ-07-2017-0166

Raut, R. D., Gardas, B. B., Narwane, V. S., & Narkhede, B. E. (2019). Improvement in the food losses in fruits and vegetable supply chain-a perspective of cold third-party logistics approach. *Operations research perspectives, 6,* 100117.

Refrigerated Warehouse & Transport Association of Australia Ltd-RWTA. (2023). The Australian Cold Chain: Confidence in Food Quality, Every Day. *Accessed from*https://www.rwta.com.au/australian-cold-chain-summary

Reynolds, C., Goucher, L., Quested, T., Bromley, S., Gillick, S., Wells, V. K., Evans, D., Koh, L., Carlsson Kanyama, A., Katzeff, C., Svenfelt, Å., & Jackson, P. (2019). Consumption-stage food waste reduction interventions–What works and how to design better interventions. *Food Policy*, 83, 7–27. DOI: 10.1016/j.foodpol.2019.01.009

Reynolds, C. J., Piantadosi, J., & Boland, J. (2015). Rescuing food from the organics waste stream to feed the food insecure: An economic and environmental assessment of Australian food rescue operations using environmentally extended waste input-output analysis. *Sustainability (Basel)*, 7(4), 4707–4726. DOI: 10.3390/su7044707

Ridoutt, B. G., Juliano, P., Sanguansri, P., & Sellahewa, J. (2010). The water footprint of food waste: Case study of fresh mango in Australia. *Journal of Cleaner Production*, 18(16-17), 1714–1721. DOI: 10.1016/j.jclepro.2010.07.011

Rochecouste, J., & Crabtree, B. (2014). *Conservation agriculture in Australian dryland cropping*. Conservation agriculture: global prospects and challenges.

Rohm, H., Oostindjer, M., Aschemann-Witzel, J., Symmank, C., & Almli, L., V., De Hooge, I. E., ... & Karantininis, K. (. (2017). Consumers in a sustainable food supply chain (COSUS): Understanding consumer behavior to encourage food waste reduction. *Foods*, 6(12), 104. DOI: 10.3390/foods6120104 PMID: 29186883

Roy, P., Mohanty, A. K., Dick, P., & Misra, M. (2023). A review on the challenges and choices for food waste valorization: Environmental and economic impacts. *ACS Environmental Au*, 3(2), 58–75. DOI: 10.1021/acsenvironau.2c00050 PMID: 36941850

Roy, M., & Medhekar, A. (2024). Green Supply Chain, Circular Economy, and Technological Innovation: Challenges and Opportunities for Developing Countries. Green Supply Chain Management Practice and Principles, 102-124.

Sales, F. C. V., De Souza, M., Trento, L. R., Pereira, G. M., Borchardt, M., & Milan, G. S. (2023). Food Waste in Distribution: Causes and Gaps to Be Filled. *Sustainability (Basel)*, 15(4), 3598. DOI: 10.3390/su15043598

Sanad Alsbu, R. A., Yarlagadda, P., & Karim, A. (2023). Investigation of the factors that contribute to fresh fruit and vegetable losses in the Australian fresh food supply Chain. *Processes (Basel, Switzerland)*, 11(4), 1154. DOI: 10.3390/pr11041154

Sanciolo, P., Rivera, E., Navaratna, D., & Duke, M. C. (2022). Food Waste Diversion from Landfills: A Cost–Benefit Analysis of Existing Technological Solutions Based on Greenhouse Gas Emissions. *Sustainability (Basel)*, 14(11), 6753. DOI: 10.3390/su14116753

Sarkar, A. (2022). Minimalonomics: A novel economic model to address environmental sustainability and earth's carrying capacity. *Journal of Cleaner Production*, 371, 133663. DOI: 10.1016/j.jclepro.2022.133663

Sarker, A. H., Bornman, J. F., & Marinova, D. (2019). A framework for integrating agriculture in urban sustainability in Australia. *Urban Science (Basel, Switzerland)*, 3(2), 50. DOI: 10.3390/urbansci3020050

Schwartz, S. H. (1977). Normative influences on altruism. *Advances in Experimental Social Psychology*, 10, 221–279. DOI: 10.1016/S0065-2601(08)60358-5

Smith, F. P., Prober, S. M., House, A. P., & McIntyre, S. (2013). Maximizing retention of native biodiversity in Australian agricultural landscapes—The 10: 20: 40: 30 guidelines. *Agriculture, Ecosystems & Environment*, 166, 35–45. DOI: 10.1016/j.agee.2012.01.014

Smith, J., Brown, R., & White, A. (2021). *Food Recovery and Redistribution: Addressing Hunger and Waste in Australia*. Environmental Sustainability Publications.

Smith, K., & White, A. (2023). The effects of waste management policies on recycling behavior: A quantitative assessment. *Waste Management (New York, N.Y.)*, 114, 62–74.

Smith, L., & Jones, R. (2022). The impact of food safety regulations on surplus food redistribution: Balancing safety and sustainability. *Journal of Food Policy*, 92, 104–116.

Smith, R., Johnson, L., & Brown, A. (2022). The influence of pro-environmental behavior on environmental policy outcomes: An empirical analysis. *Policy Studies Journal: the Journal of the Policy Studies Organization*, 50(2), 225–244.

Smyth, S. J., Webb, S. R., & Phillips, P. W. (2021). The role of public-private partnerships in improving global food security. *Global Food Security*, 31, 100588. DOI: 10.1016/j.gfs.2021.100588

Soosay, C. (2013). Improving Sustainable Development in Australia's Agrifood Supply Chains. *Sustainability and Collaboration in Supply Chain Management: A Comprehensive Insight into Current Management Approaches, 43.*

Stancu, V., Haugaard, P., & Lähteenmäki, L. (2016). Determinants of consumer food waste behavior: A review. *Sustainability*, 8(6), 1377.

State of NSW and Environment Protection Authority (2018). Love Food Hate Waste Tracking Survey Report 2017.

Steg, L., & Vlek, C. (2009). Encouraging pro-environmental behaviour: An integrative review and research agenda. *Journal of Environmental Psychology*, 29(3), 309–317. DOI: 10.1016/j.jenvp.2008.10.004

Sustainability Victoria. (2023). SV's State of Sustainability Report 2023: Are Victorians living sustainably? *Accessed from*https://assets.sustainability.vic.gov.au/susvic/Document-SV-State-of-Sustainability-Report.pdf

Taşkıner, T., & Bilgen, B. (2021). Optimization models for harvest and production planning in agri-food supply chain: A systematic review. *Logistics (Basel)*, 5(3), 52. DOI: 10.3390/logistics5030052

Teller, C., Holweg, C., Reiner, G., & Kotzab, H. (2018). Retail store operations and food waste. *Journal of Cleaner Production*, 185, 981–997. DOI: 10.1016/j.jclepro.2018.02.280

Thyberg, K. L., & Tonjes, D. J. (2016). Drivers of food waste and their implications for sustainable policy development. *Resources, Conservation and Recycling*, 106, 110–123. DOI: 10.1016/j.resconrec.2015.11.016

Toma, L., Costa Font, M., & Thompson, B. (2020). Impact of consumers' understanding of date labelling on food waste behaviour. *Operations Research*, 20(2), 543–560. DOI: 10.1007/s12351-017-0352-3

Ture, R. S., & Ganesh, M. P. (2018). Pro-environmental behaviours at workplace: An empirical study in Indian manufacturing organizations. *Benchmarking*, 25(9), 3743–3766. DOI: 10.1108/BIJ-07-2017-0193

United Nations. (2021). The 17 Goals. Retrieved from https://sdgs.un.org/goalsUsman, M., Rofcanin, Y., Ali, M., Ogbonnaya, C., & Babalola, M. T. (2023). Toward a more sustainable environment: Understanding why and when green training promotes employees' eco-friendly behaviors outside of work. *Human Resource Management, 62*(3), 355-371.

Van Boxstael, S., Devlieghere, F., Berkvens, D., Vermeulen, A., & Uyttendaele, M. (2014). Understanding and attitude regarding the shelf life labels and dates on pre-packed food products by Belgian consumers. *Food Control*, 37, 85–92. DOI: 10.1016/j.foodcont.2013.08.043

Verghese, K., & Lewis, H. (2015). Promoting sustainable food practices through consumer behavior change. *Sustainability*, 7(6), 7910–7927.

Verghese, K., Lewis, H., Lockrey, S., & Williams, H. (2015). Packaging's role in minimizing food loss and waste across the supply chain. *Packaging Technology & Science*, 28(7), 603–620. DOI: 10.1002/pts.2127

Wang, B., Wang, X., Guo, D., Zhang, B., & Wang, Z. (2018). Analysis of factors influencing residents' habitual energy-saving behaviour based on NAM and TPB models: Egoism or altruism? *Energy Policy*, 116, 68–77. DOI: 10.1016/j.enpol.2018.01.055

Wang, Y., Zhang, L., & Chen, J. (2020). The effect of pro-environmental consumer behavior on waste reduction: A quantitative approach. *Waste Management (New York, N.Y.)*, 102, 45–56.

Wesselink, R., Blok, V., & Ringersma, J. (2017). Pro-environmental behaviour in the workplace and the role of managers and organisation. *Journal of Cleaner Production*, 168, 1679–1687. DOI: 10.1016/j.jclepro.2017.08.214

West, E. G., Lindberg, R., Ball, K., & McNaughton, S. A. (2020). The role of a food literacy intervention in promoting food security and food literacy—OzHarvest's NEST Program. *Nutrients*, 12(8), 2197. DOI: 10.3390/nu12082197 PMID: 32718054

Wilkinson (2024). Ugly fruit and vegetables sold at discount prices in Odd Bunch campaign by Woolworths. *Accessed from*https://www.news.com.au/lifestyle/food/ugly-fruit-and-vegetables-sold-at-discount-prices-in-odd-bunch-campaign-by-woolworths/news-story/e9a9d2527fbba38dd92ad7db1a8e4f1b

Williams, J., Alter, T., & Shrivastava, P. (2018). Systemic governance of sustainable agriculture: Implementing sustainable development goals and climate-friendly farming. *Outlook on Agriculture*, 47(3), 192–195. DOI: 10.1177/0030727018795907

Williams, S. R., Zhu-Barker, X., Lew, S., Croze, B. J., Fallan, K. R., & Horwath, W. R. (2019). Impact of composting food waste with green waste on greenhouse gas emissions from compost windrows. *Compost Science & Utilization*, 27(1), 35–45. DOI: 10.1080/1065657X.2018.1550023

Wood, R., Lenzen, M., Dey, C., & Lundie, S. (2006). A comparative study of some environmental impacts of conventional and organic farming in Australia. *Agricultural Systems*, 89(2-3), 324–348. DOI: 10.1016/j.agsy.2005.09.007

Woolworths Group. (2021). Reducing hunger and food waste. *Accessed from*https:// www.woolworthsgroup.com.au/au/en/sustainability/Planet/food-waste.html

Xie, Y., Chen, Z., Tang, H., Boadu, F., & Yang, Y. (2023). Effects of executives' pro-environmental education and knowledge sharing activities on eco-friendly agricultural production: Evidence from China. *Journal of Cleaner Production*, 395, 136469. DOI: 10.1016/j.jclepro.2023.136469

Yahia, E. M., & Mourad, M. (2020). Food waste at the consumer level. In *Preventing food losses and waste to achieve food security and sustainability* (pp. 341–366). Burleigh Dodds Science Publishing. DOI: 10.19103/AS.2019.0053.14

Yuan, J. J., Yi, S., Williams, H. A., & Park, O. H. (2019). US consumers' perceptions of imperfect "ugly" produce. *British Food Journal*, 121(11), 2666–2682. DOI: 10.1108/BFJ-03-2019-0206

Zatyko, N., Caldera, S., & Desha, C. (2023, July). Closing the Loop on Food Waste: Stakeholder Views and Experiences from Southeast Queensland, Australia. In *Waste* (Vol. 1, No. 3, pp. 640-653). MDPI.

Zeweld, W., Van Huylenbroeck, G., Tesfay, G., & Speelman, S. (2017). Smallholder farmers' behavioural intentions towards sustainable agricultural practices. *Journal of Environmental Management*, 187, 71–81. DOI: 10.1016/j.jenvman.2016.11.014 PMID: 27883941

KEY TERMS AND DEFINITIONS

Pro-environmental behaviour: Pro-environmental behaviour refers to actions and practices undertaken by individuals or groups that are intended to minimize negative impacts on the environment and promote sustainability. This behaviour is characterized by efforts to reduce resource consumption, waste generation, and pollution, as well as to support activities that conserve natural resources and enhance environmental quality. Pro-environmental behaviours can include a wide range of activities, such as reducing energy consumption, minimising waste, sustainable consumption, conserving water and engaging in environmental advocacy.

Agricultural Supply chain: The agricultural supply chain refers to the entire system involved in the production, processing, distribution, and consumption of agricultural products. It encompasses all stages from the initial production of raw agricultural commodities to their final delivery to consumers. The key components of the agricultural supply chain include production, processing, packaging, distribution, retailing, consumption, waste management, logistics and transportation.

Sustainability: Sustainability refers to the ability to maintain or improve systems, practices, and processes in a way that meets current needs without compromising the ability of future generations to meet their own needs. Sustainability is often represented by the triple bottom line approach, which seeks to balance these three pillars—environmental, social, and economic—ensuring that efforts to promote one aspect do not undermine the others. This holistic approach aims to create a stable, healthy, and equitable future for all.

Food waste management: Food waste management refers to the strategies and practices implemented to reduce, manage, and mitigate the environmental, economic, and social impacts of food waste. Effective food waste management involves several key components: prevention, reduction, reuse, recycling, disposal, regulatory and policy support, and technological innovations. Effective food waste management aims to minimize the environmental impact of waste, conserve resources, reduce costs, and support social well-being by addressing the issue from multiple angles.

Industry collaboration: Industry collaboration involves different organizations within a sector working together to achieve common goals, address shared challenges, or leverage complementary strengths. In the context of food waste management and sustainability, industry collaboration can take several forms: public-private partnerships, supply chain partnerships, industry associations and networks, collaborative research and innovation, shared resources and facilities, consumer and industry engagement, standardization and certification, collaborative policy advocacy. By fostering industry collaboration, organizations can drive significant progress in food waste management and sustainability, ultimately contributing to a more efficient and environmentally responsible food system.

Chapter 4
Blockchain Technology and the Future of Smart and Safe Workplaces

Medina Ayta Mohammed
https://orcid.org/0000-0003-3766-206X
Universidad Rey Juan Carlos, Spain

Carmen De Pablos-Heredero
https://orcid.org/0000-0003-0457-3730
Universidad Rey Juan Carlos, Spain

José Luis Montes Botella
https://orcid.org/0000-0001-9024-6167
Universidad Rey Juan Carlos, Spain

ABSTRACT

This chapter presents the applications of blockchain technology within workplace settings and guides future research and organizational adoption. This is achieved through a bibliometric analysis of literature sourced from Scopus and Web of Science between the years 2017-2024. The findings indicate a significant increase in publications on blockchain applications in workplaces since 2019, indicating the technology's rising relevance and potential in workplace contexts. The thematic analysis identifies key areas where blockchain technology is expected to have a substantial impact, including knowledge management, smart workstations, human resource management, confidential information sharing and storage, and optimized workplace communication. This study proposes five key areas for future research: testing existing prototypes in various workplace applications, evaluating regulatory and ethical compliance, and investigating the social and environmental impacts of

DOI: 10.4018/979-8-3693-6289-1.ch004

blockchain technology in the workplace.

1. INTRODUCTION

The concept of Industry 4.0 is evolving toward Industry 5.0, where the human aspect is at its core (Gutiérrez et al., 2022). Today's work environment is characterized by a mix of individuals with varied backgrounds and long-term aspirations, the expansion of the gig economy, adaptable workspaces, and changing priorities (Pandey, Grima, Pandey, & Balusamy, 2023). To succeed in this rapidly changing digital environment, continuous innovation and a focus on human needs are vital (Avanzo, 2021). Moreover, the evolving nature of work necessitates a strategic shift towards an innovation-driven, human-centric economy, requiring restructuring and forward-thinking approaches. In recent years, blockchain technology has emerged as a disruptive force with transformative potential across various sectors, including workplaces. Various research works highlight and propose several applications of blockchain technology in workplaces, revealing both direct and indirect implications for employees and companies (Kaswan, Dhanda, Dhatterwal, & Balusamy, 2023; Kok & Palaniappan, 2023; Rahman, Azam, & Sanjida Chowdhury, 2022). Blockchain is a decentralized, distributed ledger technology that securely records and verifies transactions across a network of computers. Unlike traditional centralized databases controlled by a single entity, blockchain operates on a network where each participant (node) maintains a copy of the entire record (Dwivedi et al., 2024). Moreover, transactions recorded on the blockchain are time-stamped forming an unalterable series of transaction records. This decentralization and immutability enhance security (Kayikci & Khoshgoftaar, 2024), reduce the risk of data manipulation (Duan et al., 2020), and prevent fraud (Le et al., 2019), Positioning blockchain as a practical solution for diverse workplace applications, including communication (Li, Su, Li, Zhang, & Wang, 2020), knowledge transfer (Selvi A, B, Rajan Y, & Geetha, 2023), monitoring health-related issues (Bandi & Fellah, 2022a; Kendzierskyj, Jahankhani, & Ndumbe, 2021), human resource management (Ramachandran, Babu, & Murugesan, 2023; Wang et al., 2017), and more.

This has led to a few studies reviewing the research on the role of blockchain in workplace operations. Nevertheless, these reviews have primarily focused on the impact of blockchain on workplace outcomes rather than examining the workplace environment itself. This review represents the first attempt to examine blockchain technology within workplaces by considering the workplace as a central focus (to the best of our knowledge). It is important to acknowledge that prior research has explored blockchain's role in specific workplace benefits such as change management (Tiron-Tudor, Deliu, Farcane, & Dontu, 2021), employee performance management

(Godavarthi et al., 2023), employee engagement (Bommisetti et al., 2024), and complaint management (Shetye, Morwadkar, Chavan, Rajole, & Kulkarni, 2024). This study explores the role of blockchain technology in workplace settings using a bibliometric approach based on data from the Web of Science (WOS) and Scopus databases. The main objectives of this study are to examine the current state of research on blockchain technology in workplace environments, to identify emerging trends, and to propose potential future areas of exploration in its application within workplaces that may assist in improving the adoption and integration of blockchain technology in these settings. Considering this, the following research questions will be addressed.

1. What are the primary themes addressed in the study of blockchain technology within workplace settings?
2. What is the relative relevance and development of each theme in the current research on blockchain technology's application within workplaces?
3. In which specific areas should future research concentrate?

The findings from this study hold significant implications for organizations, managers, and researchers. There are several implications for researchers from these findings. Researchers may find it useful to understand the main topics and their relative significance in terms of advancement and relevance inside the field. It also lays the foundation for future investigations on the workplace uses of blockchain technology. Building upon the groundwork this study laid, they can then investigate particular issues, confirm new trends, and create creative solutions that deal with the ever-changing demands and challenges that businesses encounter. The findings derived from this study will also help organizations and managers understand blockchain technology and its applications in workplaces. This understanding therefore contributes to the development of innovative solutions and strategies for organizational success. Following this introduction, the methodology section will elaborate on the specific approaches utilized in this study, detailing data collection methods, analysis techniques, and procedures. Subsequently, the results section will present the findings derived from the analysis, discussing the key themes and trends identified. Following the results, the section on future research lines proposition will offer recommendations for potential areas of further investigation. Finally, the conclusion section addresses the research questions posed, discusses their implications, and offers concluding remarks on the study's contributions to the field.

2. THEORETICAL BACKGROUND

The rapid evolution of digital technologies, including smart technology, artificial intelligence, and automation, is fundamentally transforming the nature of work. Among these technologies, blockchain is projected to make a significant impact on the future of workplaces and workforces. Blockchain, conceptualized by Satoshi Nakamoto in 2008, functions as a decentralized ledger system that securely and transparently records transactions across a peer-to-peer network (Faustino, Faria, & Marques, 2022). Blockchain technology has an impact on how we manage transactions and data because of its capabilities that provide benefits such as transparency, security, and efficiency. Consider a system in which every transaction is recorded on a public record that is visible and available to all network participants. This kind of transparency helps to reduce fraud and corruption because the complete transaction history is exposed to everyone. Furthermore, Blockchain uses complex cryptographic methods to secure data, making it incredibly difficult to change or tamper with after it has been introduced into the system (Rahman et al., 2022). This ensures that the data is dependable and secure against cyber threats. Furthermore, blockchain's decentralized structure implies there is no single point of failure, which eliminates the need for middlemen and reduces the chance of system breakdowns, resulting in a more dependable and cooperative environment.

As firms seek new methods to innovate and enhance processes, blockchain provides a solution across multiple industries. Its implementation in the workplace has sparked widespread interest due to its potential to improve transparency, security, and operational efficiency. Blockchain, for example, can help with supply chain transparency and traceability. Every transaction or movement of products may be tracked on a blockchain, resulting in an immutable trail from the product's origin to its final destination (Dobrovnik, Herold, Fürst, & Kummer, 2018). This level of visibility can reduce the risk of fraud and counterfeiting, improve inventory management, and increase trust among all parties involved. In addition, companies can trace back the source of any product issues, facilitating faster and more effective recalls and ensuring compliance with regulatory requirements (Dobrovnik et al., 2018). Blockchain enhances efficiency by utilizing smart contracts—self-executing agreements with terms directly embedded into the system (Maden & Alptekin, 2020). These contracts enable faster transactions and reduce costs by removing the need for intermediaries. In a trustless environment, participants do not need to rely on each other or a central authority to verify transactions. Moreover, it also cuts operational costs by streamlining processes and maintaining a transparency system (Maden & Alptekin, 2020). These features collectively establish blockchain as a groundbreaking technology capable of addressing many shortcomings of traditional systems and driving advancements in numerous workplace applications. This includes but not limited to workplace communication (Li et al., 2020), knowledge transfer (Selvi A et al., 2023), monitoring health-related issues (Bandi & Fellah, 2022a; Kendzierskyj et al., 2021), human resource management (Ramachandran et al., 2023; Wang et al., 2017), among others.

3. METHODOLOGY

This study used the databases Scopus and WOS following Ammirato et al. (2023) as these databases provide access to scholarly documents that cover a broad range of scholarly literature (Gomes, Coelho, & Ribeiro, 2024). The following identical searches were used in both databases using the search terms ("blockchain technology" OR "blockchain") AND ("workplace" OR "workforce") in April 2024. The initial search results retrieved 26 documents from WOS and 105 documents from Scopus. Subsequently, the selection process, along with the inclusion and exclusion criteria for papers, was guided by the PRISMA model (Page et al., 2021), as outlined in Figure 1. Following the screening process, the documents were transformed into a consistent and readable format, combined, and any duplicate entries were removed. R Studio was utilized to streamline and ensure accuracy in the data preparation phase. Ultimately, a total of 59 documents were chosen for analysis. The conceptual structure of the research was analyzed using two advanced bibliometric tools: VOSviewer (van Eck & Waltman, 2010) and Bibliometrix (Aria & Cuccurullo, 2017). VOSviewer was used to visualize and map the relationships between key terms and concepts and Bibliometrix was used to assess the development and significance of these themes. These two tools were chosen for several reasons. VOSviewer is preferred by many researchers due to its capability to facilitate easy data importation and its ability to produce high-quality visualizations (Donthu, Kumar, Mukherjee, Pandey, & Lim, 2021). Bibliometrix, on the other hand, was selected for its high customizability, allowing users to tailor their analyses and visualizations to specific needs. In this study, Bibliometrix was particularly used as it enabled the reduction of duplications and facilitated data importation.

Figure 1. Search and screening process

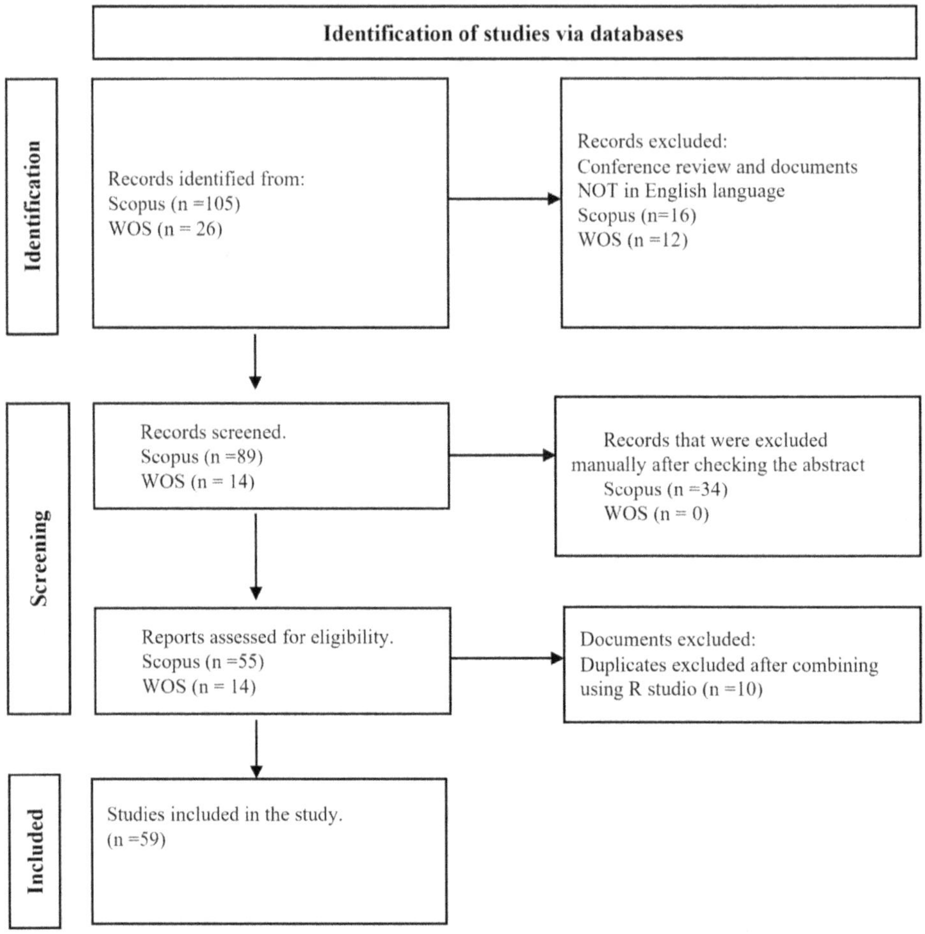

4. RESULTS

4.1. General Information on the Documents

Figure 2 presents data on articles published about blockchain for workplaces from 2017 to 2024. It shows a trend of growing interest and research in this field. Although it started with minimal publications in 2017 and 2018, the number of articles significantly increased in 2019 and 2020. This indicates a rising recognition of blockchain's potential for workplaces.

Figure 2. Evolution of studies

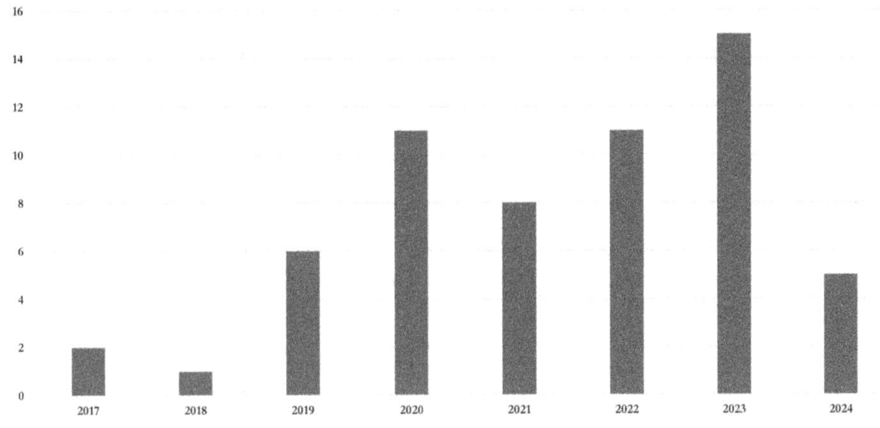

Moreover, the growth reflects advancements in technology, increased funding, and a response to global events such as the COVID-19 pandemic as organizations sought secure, remote, and decentralized solutions (Al-Habaibeh, Watkins, Waried, & Javareshk, 2021). The drop in 2021 indicates that some initial enthusiasm from the pandemic might have waned due to the normalization of working style, practical challenges, and limitations stemming from Blockchain technology. The production growth continues in 2022 and 2023 with 11 and 15 articles respectively. This shows that the evolving regulations around blockchain technology and data privacy may have driven research to address compliance and implementation challenges.

4.2. Conceptual Structure

Several scientific mapping techniques, such as citation analysis, co-word analysis, co-citation analysis, bibliographic coupling, and co-authorship analysis, help in understanding the bibliometric and intellectual structures of a research field (Aria & Cuccurullo, 2017; Donthu et al., 2021). In this study, we utilize co-word analysis to explore the conceptual interactions and structural connections among research components. Initially, the software Vosviewer was used to perform co-word analysis and understand the thematic structure of the data, allowing the identification and categorization of the main themes in the research. Subsequently, "Bibliometrix" was used to evaluate the development and significance of each theme.

4.2.1. Co-Word Analysis

Co-word analysis is a method that directly examines the content of publications. Typically, this involves extracting words from author keywords. If author keywords are unavailable, the keywords can be sourced from article titles, abstracts, and full texts for analysis (Donthu et al., 2021). Similar to co-citation analysis, co-word analysis operates on the premise that words frequently appearing together have a thematic relationship. Co-citation analysis or bibliographic coupling relies on existing citation networks to identify related documents and hence may not be suitable for emerging fields due to insufficient citations. Unlike co-citation analysis or bibliographic coupling, co-word analysis is particularly suitable for new fields (Donthu et al., 2021). As shown in Figure 3, the co-word analysis reveals the intellectual structure by forming six distinct clusters, each representing a group of keywords with thematic similarities.

Figure 3. Co-word network.

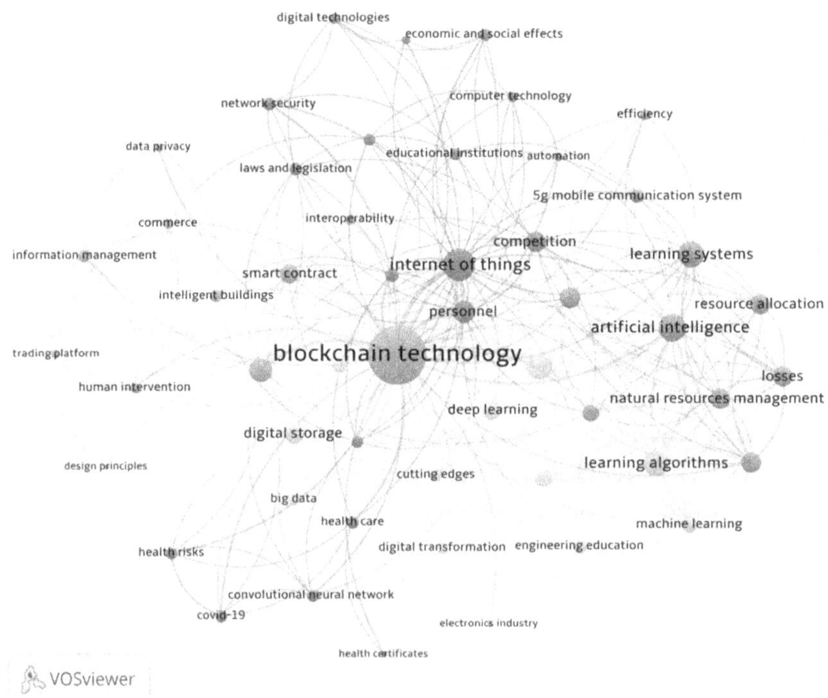

Blockchain-Based Anti-Forgery Solution (Red)

Cluster 1 comprises 13 keywords, such as Automation, Educational institutions, Industry 4, Knowledge management, Personnel, and Supply chain. This cluster focuses on research conducted on Blockchain-based anti-forgery mechanisms. Companies are shifting towards being more employee-centric and data-driven, acknowledging the importance of employee satisfaction (Liu, Han, Zhou, Parizi, & Korayem, 2020). The HR sector faces numerous challenges, with departments dedicating significant time to applicant screening and credential verification to reduce faulty hiring (Wei & Pokrovskaia, 2017). In modern workplaces activities such as searching, selecting, managing employees, and recruiting, retaining, and integrating new staff are increasingly dependent on technology (Kaswan et al., 2023). The key tasks in this process include hiring the right personnel and mitigating hiring liabilities such as workplace violence. To improve efficiency and professionalism, many companies outsource background screening to third parties rather than relying on traditional in-house checks (Liu et al. 2020). However, background screening remains challenging, particularly in verifying employment, education, and skills, with these difficulties being further complicated by information asymmetry in overseas recruitment (Liu et al. 2020). Khaleelullah et al. (2023) reports that numerous cases of academic certificate fraud have been documented due to the absence of an effective anti-forgery system. Khaleelullah et al. (2023) further highlights this deficiency could lead to frequent occurrences of fake academic certificates.

According to Roopa et al. (2020), the primary challenge in certificate verification in the workplace stems from a lack of a unified system to securely store, retrieve, and access data. Consequently, the need for reliable methods of educational credential verification and authentication is increasingly critical. Blockchain technology is a promising solution for establishing a secure, transparent, and unchangeable system for storing and verifying academic records. Few papers proposed different blockchain-based systems for verifying academic records (Binbusayyis & Vaiyapuri, 2023; Cheng, Lee, Chi, & Chen, 2018; Khaleelullah et al., 2023). For instance, Khaleelullah et al. (2023) proposed a permissioned blockchain-based system for verifying academic records, utilizing Hyperledger Fabric and InterPlanetary File System (IPFS). Academic institutions issue digital certificates to graduates, stored on IPFS with their hashes recorded on the Hyperledger Fabric blockchain. Khaleelullah et al. (2023) contend this model effectively addresses current document verification challenges, satisfying all system requirements. Binbusayyis and Vaiyapuri (2023) also proposed a framework using blockchain, IPFS, smart contracts, and session management for creating and sharing e-portfolios securely across organizations. Binbusayyis and Vaiyapuri (2023) further assert that the system is cost-effective and secure, making it a promising solution for implementing e-portfolios and enhancing professionals' competitiveness in the global job market. Cheng et al. (2018)

noted that a blockchain-based anti-forgery system not only boosts the credibility of certificates but also electronically mitigates the risk of loss associated with various types of certificates.

Blockchain for Secure and Smart Workstations (Green)

The keywords in Cluster 2 encompass various themes relevant to smart and secure work environments. Some of the keywords include Blockchain technology, Data privacy, Intelligent buildings, Human intervention, Information management, Interoperability, and Smart contract among others. The rapid urbanization worldwide has brought forth numerous economic, social, and environmental challenges. This has led to the concept of smart cities, aimed at making the best use of resources (Abella, Ortiz-de-Urbina-Criado, & De-Pablos-Heredero, 2019). As highlighted by various sources, such as González-Mendes et al. (2023); and Xie et al. (2019), blockchain technology plays a crucial role in the implementation of smart city initiatives. The concept of smart shared spaces in smart buildings represents a rapidly growing concept. Smart shared spaces refer to areas within a building that are equipped with advanced technology to enhance their functionality, efficiency, and user experience (Glaeser, Kourtit, & Nijkamp, 2021). These spaces can include conference rooms, coworking spaces, common areas, and other shared facilities. Smart shared spaces integrate numerous sensors that continuously generate valuable data (Neu, Gibson, Lunardi, Leesakul, & Morisset, 2023). This data is used to enhance automation processes, making the buildings more responsive and adaptable to the needs of their occupants. Likewise, smart shared spaces pose significant privacy challenges due to the extensive use of sensors that can potentially gather sensitive data about occupants (Neu et al., 2023). These sensors, while essential for enhancing automation and efficiency, can track and record various aspects of individuals' daily activities (Gilman et al., 2020). For instance, they can monitor detailed information about occupants' daily routines, such as their arrival and departure times, movement patterns within the building, and usage of different facilities. This level of surveillance can lead to concerns about privacy, as occupants may feel uncomfortable with the idea of their behaviors and movements being constantly monitored and recorded.

Research has proposed and projected blockchain as a viable solution. Neu et al. (2023) proposed a decentralized blockchain-based privacy model that provides occupants of shared spaces a way to specify and manage their privacy preferences anonymously. This ensures the users have full control of these records thus allowing traceability over the user's preferences for data usage. The literature also highlights the potential of blockchain technology to enhance IoT security within the context of smart workstations (Honar Pajooh, Rashid, Alam, & Demidenko, 2021; Mohammad Azahari, Ahmad, & Rahayu, 2021). Blockchain technology has the potential to enhance IoT systems by facilitating storage, retrieval, and secured data encryption

(Tang et al., 2019). For instance, Tang et al. (2019) introduced a blockchain-based IoT system known as the Internet of Responsibilities designed to facilitate a secured automatic reminder and assignment mechanism, ensuring responsibilities (i.e. tasks, obligations, roles, and duties) are managed and accountability is enforced without human intervention. By leveraging blockchain's decentralized and immutable nature, the system ensures that data transmitted and stored by IoT devices is protected against tampering and unauthorized access. This advancement offers enterprises the opportunity to achieve highly secure and safe workplaces (Tang et al., 2019).

Optimizing Workplace Communication with Blockchain Technology (Blue)

This cluster highlights the intersection of advanced technologies such as 5G mobile communication and artificial intelligence with blockchain to enhance workplace efficiency and management. The integration of 5G ensures faster and more reliable connectivity, vital for real-time data processing and decentralized applications of blockchain (Dwivedi et al., 2024). Artificial intelligence, when combined with blockchain, can optimize workflows, analyze large datasets, and improve decision-making processes, impacting employee performance and overall efficiency (Azzaoui, Singh, Pan, & Park, 2020). In sectors like manufacturing and logistics, blockchain also aids in natural resource management by providing transparent records of resource usage (Samadhiya, Agrawal, Kumar, & Garza-Reyes, 2023). In addition to its efficiency benefits, the research emphasizes the significant potential of blockchain technology in enhancing secure communication within workplace environments. According to Ellewala et al. (2020) ensuring the security of critical business communication, which involves the exchange of trade secrets, making business referrals, and strategic decision-making, presents a significant challenge. By leveraging blockchain's security features, such as encryption and decentralized data storage, organizations can establish robust communication channels that ensure the confidentiality, integrity, and authenticity of sensitive information exchanged among employees (Li et al., 2020). This enhanced security fosters a greater sense of trust and confidence among workers, knowing that their communications are protected from unauthorized access, tampering, or interception. Considering this, Ellewala et al. (2020) developed a blockchain-based chat application aimed at enhancing the security, confidentiality, and integrity of shared messages and enterprise-level communication channels.

Blockchain's transparency and immutability can facilitate the tracking and auditing of communication activities, providing stakeholders with a clear and verifiable record of interactions. Moreover, blockchain technology facilitates knowledge transfer in the workplace and enables the establishment of secure learning systems by preserving authenticated records of various aspects such as training, certifications, performance metrics, and employee data. According to Selvi et al. (2023), organizations can significantly improve performance and productivity by addressing knowledge concealment through the implementation of a blockchain-based knowledge transfer database. Consequently, organizations can harness the full potential of their workforce and drive innovation and growth. The keyword "Losses" in this cluster signifies the potential of Blockchain technology in mitigating financial and data losses through its tamper-proof ledger which is essential for preventing fraud and maintaining the integrity of transactions and sensitive information. Gupta et al. (2020) emphasize that blockchain technology ensures that auditors are effectively verifying accounts and financial records in compliance with international accounting standards.

Blockchain-Driven Confidential Information Storage and Sharing (Purple)

This cluster focuses on the utilization of blockchain technology to supervise health-related concerns within workplaces, covering aspects such as psychological well-being and the administration of health data. The keywords include health care, health certificates, health risk, sustainable development, convolutional neural networks, and COVID-19. The literature outlines blockchain technology holds promise in enabling secure and confidential information sharing both within the workplace and throughout the hiring process (Bandi & Fellah, 2022b; Kok & Palaniappan, 2023; Obu et al., 2023; Rahman et al., 2022). There are certain sensitive aspects that employees may be hesitant to share either from fear of potential discrimination, judgment, or negative repercussions in the workplace. These aspects include sharing information about workplace harassment, mental health issues, cognitive function, and physical well-being. Employees may seek assurance that their privacy will be respected and that disclosing such information will not hinder their career advancement or opportunities for growth within the organization (McMahon, 2000; Sheffey & Tindale, 1992). This challenge is especially pronounced during the recruitment phase, where the need for confidentiality and fair treatment of candidates is important.

Considering these challenges, organizations may adopt different measures to safeguard the privacy and integrity of the recruitment process. For instance, Obu et al. (2023) designed a blockchain-based hiring platform that is discreet and deliberately skewed to hinder hiring based on any discriminatory factors. This creates trust between employers and applicants in the recruitment process contributing to more accurate candidate assessments and better hiring decisions. In addition to its use in recruitment processes, blockchain technology possesses significant potential for enhancing the confidence and safety of workers during workplace harassment. Harassment in the workplace is a serious issue that can create a hostile and unproductive environment. Victims often face challenges when complaining, such as fear of retaliation, lack of support from management, and concerns about job security (McMahon, 2000). The reporting process can be intimidating, leading to underreporting and unresolved issues. Additionally, there can be skepticism about the effectiveness of the complaint mechanisms, further discouraging employees from coming forward. To resolve this problem, a few surveys present blockchain-based solutions. For instance, Rahman et al. (2022) present a blockchain-based anonymous, transparent, and secure platform where victims can easily complain against their harasser. This way, the proposed platform ensures workers a healthy work environment and the necessary support. Blockchain can also streamline processes by maintaining immutable records of employee health information, facilitating efficient and confidential access to medical histories. Kok and Palaniappan (2023) assert that workplace safety records, including detailed information on major accidents, minor accidents, near misses, and occupational health issues, can be securely stored in a decentralized manner through blockchain technology.

The COVID-19 crisis has highlighted the importance of efficiently collecting, storing, analyzing, and disseminating health data (Dagliati, Malovini, Tibollo, & Bellazzi, 2021). Blockchain can be instrumental by offering secure and verifiable records of health status and vaccination certificates. For example, convolutional neural networks, a deep learning network architecture that learns directly from data, can be integrated with blockchain to securely analyze medical imaging and health data, ensuring accurate health assessments of employees. Bandi and Fellah (2022) proposed a secure digital health passport using blockchain technology. The issuer has read-write access to upload test results, while holders and verifiers have read-only access to guarantee tamper-free results. Holders can share test results using QR codes with verifiers. This guarantees the authenticity of employees' health credentials while also enhancing employees' sense of security and trust. The empirical study by Kendzierskyj et al. (2021) affirms this, demonstrating that users recognize the positive outcomes of a blockchain system that consolidates and secures patient health information into a single repository.

Blockchain for Data and Information Management (Yellow)

This cluster focuses on the potential of blockchain technology to revolutionize various aspects of workplace data and information management. The keywords in the cluster include big data, data analytics, digital storage, digital transformation, human resource management, and real-time systems. As information technology continues to progress, enterprises, universities, and governments are frequently investing in electronic personnel information management systems (Chen, Lv, & Song, 2019). These systems gather and store data on hundreds of thousands, or even millions, of individuals, creating a critical foundation for big data development (Chen & Zhang, 2014). Blockchain technology can securely store and manage large volumes of data generated by organizations, ensuring data integrity and accessibility, which is vital for big data applications. By integrating blockchain with data analytics, organizations can also ensure the accuracy and security of analyzed data, leading to better decision-making and insights. Chen et al. (2019) explored the potential for integrating blockchain with big data. They propose a blockchain-based personnel management system utilizing on-chain and off-chain data storage models to address data redundancy and storage challenges. The keyword "human resource management" in this cluster emphasizes the transformative role of blockchain in HR processes and data management. Various models have been proposed and developed such as by Fachrunnisa & Hussain (2020) who developed a blockchain-based prototype to gather valid information on required skills, aiming to enhance workforce competency within organizations. Other models include a human resource information management model designed to reduce the risk of authenticity issues in HR data (Wang et al., 2017). The literature also explores how blockchain technology can improve decision-making in HR. Ramachandran et al. (2023) contend by implementing ledger technology, managerial functions can become more efficient, reducing the time, money, and effort needed by recruiters and HR professionals to verify and sort potential candidates. Additionally, for Hewage et al. (2020) blockchain technology has the potential to significantly enhance and enable smart human resource management systems by streamlining processes such as recruitment, credential verification, and payroll management.

Advanced Technologies Integration in Workplace Systems (Cyan)

This cluster explores how cutting-edge technologies such as deep learning, machine learning, and learning algorithms can be integrated with blockchain to enhance various workplace operations. Deep learning and machine learning rely on vast amounts of data to train models and make predictions (Janiesch, Zschech, & Heinrich, 2021; Shinde & Shah, 2018). Blockchain can provide a secure, transparent, and immutable ledger for storing this data, ensuring its integrity and verifiability (Kayikci & Khoshgoftaar, 2024). This means that the data used in these models is trustworthy and has not been tampered with, which is crucial for making accurate predictions and decisions. Pan et al. (2022) observed that integrating blockchain and deep learning technologies ensures data authenticity and protects data from tampering. Moreover, smart lighting and smart parking systems can leverage deep learning machine learning algorithms, and blockchain to improve their functionality. For instance, deep learning can be used to analyze patterns in lighting usage and optimize energy consumption (Mololoth, Saguna, & Åhlund, 2023). Similarly, machine learning can predict parking space availability and improve traffic flow within workplace parking lots. Blockchain can ensure the integrity of data collected from smart lighting sensors and parking systems, preventing tampering and ensuring reliable operation (Thomas & Robinson, 2020). Furthermore, learning algorithms can benefit from the integration of blockchain by ensuring that the data they process is accurate and up-to-date (Tanwar et al., 2020). This is essential for real-time applications in the workplace where decisions need to be based on the most current information available. For instance, in workplaces that require identifying employees' social behavior, physiological data linked to productivity, and emotional states (Nappi & de Campos Ribeiro, 2020). Blockchain's capability to provide real-time data processing and transaction verification supports these requirements, enabling more efficient and reliable workplace systems.

4.2.2. Thematic Map

The thematic map charts two important metrics the development degree (density) and the relevance degree (centrality). In this map, the position of topics or themes illustrates their relative significance and the overall progression of a research field (Aria & Cuccurullo, 2017). The development degree, or density, indicates how thoroughly a specific theme has been investigated in the literature (Aria & Cuccurullo, 2017). A higher development degree means there is a greater concentration of research output, indicating that the topic has attracted substantial attention and study. The relevance degree, or centrality, shown on the x-axis, measures the importance of a topic within the broader network of literature (Aria & Cuccurullo, 2017). A higher relevance degree suggests that the theme comprises highly cited or influential works, indicating the theme's importance as a key focus within the literature. Regarding centrality and density, centrality measures a theme's significance or impact within the overall framework of the research area by indicating how closely linked it is to other topics in the network. Conversely, density measures how closely related the keywords within a topic are to one another, indicating the internal coherence of a subject.

With this understanding, the thematic map categorizes topics into several types. For example, niche themes are characterized by low centrality but high density. These subjects show focused study or application, but they are not extensively discussed in the larger conversation. They may be heavily researched and given attention in their specialized field, but they do not yet have the same broad influence or integration. On the other hand, key topics are established domains that exhibit high density and high centrality. These subjects are fundamental to the area and are frequently discussed and referenced. Topics on the periphery are distinct because of their low centrality and density. These subjects are less central to the main discussions since they are at the edge of the field and have less connected research. subjects that are gaining popularity but are not yet well-established are considered emergent topics. Typically found in the peripheral regions of the diagram where centrality is low but density might be high, emerging topics have significant potential for growth and development. Their centrality remains low because they are not yet fully integrated into the core of the field, but their density is high due to the concentrated interest and activity within this area. As seen in Figure 2, research on blockchain for workplaces covers a wide range of topics at different phases of development and significance.

Figure 4. Thematic map

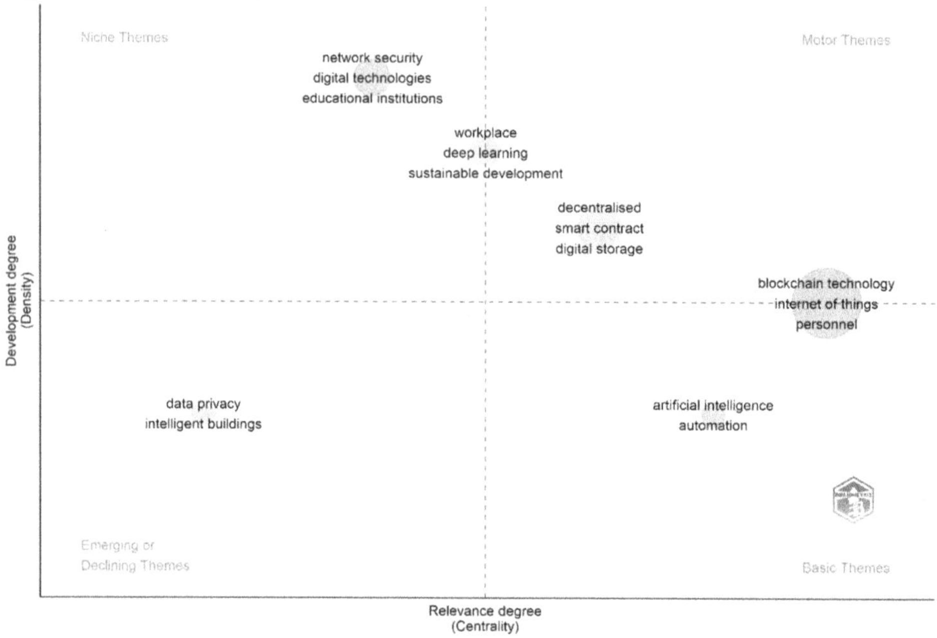

The niche themes are about specialized or narrowly focused topics within blockchain for workplaces. These themes often require specialized knowledge, targeted research, or specific solutions. At the niche level, themes such as network security, digital technologies, and educational institutions emphasize the role of blockchain in increasing transparency and security in academic certification (Cheng et al., 2018; Khaleelullah et al., 2023), as well as in knowledge sharing and workforce training (Selvi et al., 2023) In the intersection between niche and motor themes are topics related to workplace practices, deep learning, and sustainable development. As discussed in the co-word analysis in cluster 4, blockchain enables confidential information storage and sharing, minimizing bias during hiring and addressing issues such as workplace harassment. Consequently, blockchain contributes significantly to sustainable development, aligning with UN Sustainable Development Goal 11, which aims to make human settlements inclusive and safe (UN, 2015). Additionally, cluster 6 highlights that deep learning can be used in the workplace to analyze patterns in energy usage and optimize energy consumption. These topics relate to how blockchain can revolutionize business operations by improving efficiency and fostering sustainable development.

The motor themes encompass decentralization, smart contracts, and digital storage, emphasizing the technical aspects of blockchain technology and its diverse applications within the workplace such as in data management and safeguarding critical business communication. These are themes that are highly developed and highly relevant. As highlighted in cluster 5 previously, blockchain ensures the secure storage and management of organizational data, thereby preserving its integrity and accessibility. The emerging or declining themes include data privacy and intelligent buildings. As discussed in cluster 2, various models are being proposed for a decentralized blockchain-based privacy model in smart buildings. As these are proposals it indicates the themes are emerging. Some of the emerging topics include the role blockchain plays in intelligent buildings with renewable energy sources, such as solar panels. Blockchain can facilitate secure and transparent trading of excess energy between neighboring buildings, optimizing energy use and promoting sustainability (AlSkaif, Crespo-Vazquez, Sekuloski, van Leeuwen, & Catalao, 2022; W.-J. Liu, Chiu, & Hua, 2024). Additionally, blockchain can automate various processes within intelligent buildings. Smart contracts can manage rental agreements, maintenance schedules, and even automate payments for utilities, thereby reducing administrative overhead and enhancing operational efficiency (Jain, Gangwar, Kumari, & Mehra, 2024; Oke & Stephen, 2024). The basic themes in the thematic map "artificial intelligence" and "automation" represent technologies that, when integrated with blockchain have the potential to revolutionize workplace operations. As highlighted earlier in cluster 1, research emphasizes blockchain and AI's role in tasks such as personnel selection during applicant screening and credential verification. The themes that are positioned between basic and motor themes, blockchain technology along with the IoT and personnel management, highlight the central role of blockchain in driving efficiency in workplaces. As discussed above in the previous section, cluster 2 discussed blockchain technology's potential to secure IoT systems and facilitate a secured automatic reminder and assignment mechanism, ensuring tasks, obligations, roles, and duties are managed and accountability is enforced without human intervention.

5. DISCUSSION OF POTENTIAL CHALLENGES AND FUTURE PERSPECTIVES

5.1. Potential Challenges

While the literature and numerous investigations have emphasized the potential benefits and applications of blockchain technology in various workplace settings, its long-term value remains uncertain. Most projects have been tested on a limited scale and are still in the early stages of development, leaving the broader impact and sustainability of blockchain in the workplace largely unproven. Consequently, several critical questions must be resolved before blockchain can achieve widespread adoption in workplace environments. The integration of blockchain technology across different industries has already encountered several challenges, which may affect its implementation in the workplace as well. Integrating blockchain technology in its current state presents a range of challenges that must be addressed before its full potential can be realized. The literature emphasizes that these challenges span multiple dimensions, including technical, organizational, and legal aspects. According to Kok & Palaniappan (2023), scalability is one of the major technical hurdles that blockchain faces. They explain that as blockchain networks grow, handling large volumes of transactions per second becomes increasingly difficult. Belchior, Vasconcelos, Guerreiro, & Correia (2022) highlight the issue of interoperability, noting that integrating blockchain with existing systems requires complex interfaces, which can complicate its adoption. Additionally, the verification and validation of transactions can cause operational delays, and the high energy consumption of certain blockchain networks, particularly those using proof-of-work mechanisms, increases operational costs and raises environmental concerns (Sai, Buckley, Fitzgerald, & Gear, 2021). There are also security challenges including vulnerabilities in smart contracts that can be exploited by malicious actors and the difficulty of maintaining data privacy while ensuring transparency and immutability (Habsi, Nair, Sulti, & Adarsh, 2021).

A major organizational challenge noted in the literature is the resistance to change (Koster & Borgman, 2020). Employees and management may be hesitant to adopt blockchain technology due to a lack of understanding or fear of disrupting established workflows. This resistance is compounded by a significant skill gap; the expertise required to implement and maintain blockchain systems is scarce, making it difficult for organizations to find qualified personnel (Rana, Dwivedi, & Hughes, 2022). Additionally, considering the initial investment required for blockchain integration is substantial, organizations must allocate significant financial resources to develop infrastructure, train staff, and transition from legacy systems, which can hinder adoption (Casino, Dasaklis, & Patsakis, 2019). Many organizations rely on traditional databases and systems that are not designed to work seamlessly with blockchain technology. Ensuring data integrity across these disparate systems is both complex and costly. Moreover, as previously mentioned, blockchain networks frequently encounter scalability issues, with processing a high volume of transactions per second being a significant challenge. This limitation can result in operational delays, particularly in workplaces that handle high volumes of transactions. (Khan, Jung, & Hashmani, 2021).

The regulatory environment for blockchain is still evolving, and uncertainties regarding compliance with local and international laws can deter organizations from adopting the technology. Moreover, in many jurisdictions, blockchain transactions and smart contracts are not yet recognized as legally binding, creating significant barriers to their use in formal agreements and contracts (Lohmer & Lasch, 2020). These regulatory and legal uncertainties need to be addressed to foster confidence and facilitate broader adoption of blockchain technology. Beyond technical organizational, and legal issues, ethical and social challenges also play a critical role. One major concern is balancing the transparency inherent in blockchain technology with the need for privacy when handling sensitive workplace information (Kok & Palaniappan, 2023). While blockchain's transparency is one of its key advantages, it can conflict with privacy requirements, especially in contexts involving personal or confidential data (Tatar, Gokce, & Nussbaum, 2020). Additionally, the decentralized nature of blockchain technology can clash with traditional centralized control structures within organizations. Managing this tension requires careful consideration of governance models and the potential impacts on organizational hierarchy and decision-making processes.

To address these challenges several steps need to be taken such as a strategic approach that includes technical innovation, regulatory cooperation, workforce training, and effective change management. Continued research and development can lead to more efficient blockchain protocols and solutions tailored to the needs of different industries. Furthermore, regulatory cooperation is also crucial; working with regulators to establish clear guidelines and frameworks can provide the legal certainty needed for blockchain adoption. Moreover, organizations must invest in developing the skills and knowledge required to implement and maintain blockchain systems. This can be achieved through targeted training programs, partnerships with educational institutions, and ongoing professional development initiatives. Organizations should also engage stakeholders at all levels, communicate the benefits and implications of blockchain adoption, and provide support throughout the transition process. This approach can help mitigate resistance to change and foster a culture of innovation and continuous improvement.

5.2. Future Research Lines

Based on the co-word analysis and thematic clusters, it is evident that prior research has proposed several blockchain-based models, primarily focusing on the opportunities this technology offers within workplaces. Given the novelty of blockchain applications in this domain, it is understandable that the emphasis lies on exploring its potential. However, to further advance the field and expedite the adoption of this technology, it is imperative to address additional crucial aspects.

We propose that addressing the following aspects will perhaps assist in the field's development and the accelerated implementation of blockchain technology.

Proposition 1: Future research may address the various challenges mainly technical challenges such as scalability and interoperability challenges inherent in blockchain platforms as it is an issue that is been discussed in other applications (Khan, Jung, & Hashmani, 2021), particularly regarding the management of large volumes of academic records generated by educational institutions worldwide (cluster 1 in the co-word analysis). Moreover, efforts should be directed toward establishing interoperability standards to facilitate seamless data exchange between different blockchain platforms (Belchior, Vasconcelos, Guerreiro, & Correia, 2022) such as educational databases. This would ensure data consistency and accessibility across diverse systems, enhancing the efficiency of verification processes. Additionally, based on the cluster 2 blockchain for secure and smart workstations, a promising direction for future research lies in investigating privacy-preserving solutions tailored to smart shared spaces within smart buildings. Future research works could assess the development and evaluation of decentralized blockchain-based privacy models specifically designed for smart shared spaces. Furthermore, as discussed in cluster 3, the potential of blockchain technology in mitigating financial and data losses was highlighted. Subsequent research could investigate the efficacy of blockchain-based solutions in preventing fraud, preserving transaction integrity, and adhering to international accounting standards.

Proposition 2: The success of blockchain-based verification systems may depend on crucial factors such as usability and adoption. Therefore, these prototypes and propositions must transition from theory to practice, undergoing testing or piloting within various workplace applications. This step is crucial for assessing the diffusion, acceptance, and functionality of such systems, as well as promoting widespread adoption among stakeholders. For instance, cluster 3 highlights the intersection of advanced technologies such as 5G mobile communication and artificial intelligence with blockchain to enhance workplace efficiency and management. Future research could involve user-centered studies and feedback mechanisms to identify usability challenges and acceptance of blockchain-based communication solutions in diverse workplace environments. Likewise, in other contexts, applying this proposition can provide insight into how managers, employees, and other stakeholders perceive the technology and the dissemination levels at different stages and within different groups.

Proposition 3: Regulatory and ethical compliance need to be assessed and frameworks need to be developed to ensure adherence to data privacy regulations. Cluster 4 discussed the utilization of blockchain technology to supervise health-related concerns within workplaces, covering aspects such as psychological well-being and the administration of health data. Future investigations need to investigate the regulatory frameworks and legal implications surrounding the use of blockchain technology in managing confidential workplace information, especially health data. Research could focus on understanding compliance requirements such as HIPAA (Health Insurance Portability and Accountability), GDPR, and other data protection regulations in various countries, and explore how blockchain solutions can align with these standards while ensuring data security and privacy (Bolívar et al., 2021). Furthermore, researchers can assess the ethical implications of blockchain-enabled data sharing in the workplace, particularly concerning informed consent, transparency, and accountability. Research could investigate ethical guidelines and best practices for collecting, storing, and sharing sensitive employee information.

Proposition 4: Examine the social impact of blockchain-driven solutions on workplace dynamics, employee well-being, and organizational culture. Research could assess how blockchain technology influences trust, transparency, and fairness in the workplace, and explore their potential to promote diversity, equity, and inclusion initiatives. Prior research has emphasized the social impact of blockchain-driven solutions i.e. in higher education (Son-Turan, 2022) and general social impact (Semenzin, 2023). However, further investigations may particularly focus on their role in the workplace. Moreover, future analysis may explore how blockchain technologies can empower communities and promote decentralization in the workplace. For instance, future research could examine the role of blockchain-based governance mechanisms, decentralized autonomous organizations (DAOs), and digital tokens in redistributing power, resources, and decision-making authority among stakeholders, and participation in organizational processes. Specifically, there is a need to examine the practicality and effectiveness of digital tokens in rewarding contributors with voting rights in organizational decisions. Additionally, research might explore how these tokens incentivize stakeholder engagement and participation in resource management and decision-making processes.

Proposition 5: Subsequent research can evaluate the environmental footprint of blockchain technologies and their implications for sustainability in the workplace (Savelyeva & Park, 2022; Shakhbulatov, Arora, Dong, & Rojas-Cessa, 2019). Research could investigate the impact of blockchain on energy consumption, carbon emissions, and other environmental factors associated with blockchain infrastructure for workplaces. For instance, research in cluster 6 explored how smart lighting and smart parking systems can leverage deep learning machine learning algorithms in conjunction with blockchain technology to enhance their functionality and optimize energy consumption effectively (Mololoth et al., 2023). However, the extent of the impact on sustainability, the potential for improvement, and the overall environmental impact remain underexplored. Further research is needed to quantify the environmental benefits and drawbacks of such integrated systems, as well as to identify opportunities for enhancing their eco-friendliness.

6. CONCLUSION

This study used data from the WOS and Scopus databases and used a bibliometric method to understand the potential of blockchain technology in workplace settings through keyword analysis. The study reveals a growing interest in blockchain applications for workplaces, evident in the publication trend over the past five years, depicting significant growth. The first objective of the study was to identify the primary themes explored in the study of blockchain technology within workplace settings. The thematic structure and recent progressions in the sample papers pinpoint key domains such as blockchain's potential in knowledge management, enabling smart and secure work environments, enhancing workplace efficiency and management, overseeing health-related concerns, and managing workplace data and information. The common thread across these areas indicates the opportunities and promise of blockchain technology for workplaces.

The second objective of the study was to assess the relative relevance and development of each theme in the current research. The thematic mapping indicates niche themes such as the role of blockchain in enhancing transparency and security in academic certification, knowledge sharing, and workforce training. Themes at the intersection of niche and motor themes are topics related to workplace practices and sustainable development, which have matured and are gaining prominence. As the literature highlighted blockchain facilitates secure storage and sharing of confidential information, mitigating biases in hiring processes and addressing workplace harassment concerns. Consequently, blockchain contributes substantially to sustainable development, aligning with UN Sustainable Development Goal 11, aiming for inclusive and safe human settlements. These themes are gaining high attention. Motor themes are blockchain's diverse applications within workplaces, particularly in data management and safeguarding critical business communications. Meanwhile, emerging or diminishing themes include data privacy and intelligent buildings. The concept of smart shared spaces in smart buildings represents a rapidly growing concept as highlighted and discussed in the literature various studies propose decentralized blockchain-based privacy frameworks for smart buildings, indicating the theme is emerging rather than declining.

The final objective of the study was to determine the specific areas where future research should be focused. This study presented five propositions for future research focus. These include focussing on the diverse challenges, particularly the technical ones inherent in blockchain platforms, evaluating previously developed prototypes, and subjecting them to testing or piloting across various workplace applications. The study also proposes assessing regulatory and ethical compliance, as well as exploring the social and environmental impacts. The findings from this study hold significant implications for organizations, managers, and researchers. There are several implications for researchers from these findings. Researchers may find it useful to understand the main topics and their relative significance in terms of advancement and relevance inside the field. It also lays the foundation for future surveys on the workplace uses of blockchain technology. Building upon the groundwork this study laid, they can then investigate particular issues, confirm new trends, and create creative solutions that deal with the ever-changing demands and challenges that businesses encounter. Furthermore, as indicated by the research direction suggestion, a solid understanding of the legal, social, economic, technological, and other challenges posed by blockchain technology is needed in some crucial areas, such as knowledge management, data management, smart work environments, workplace productivity, and health-related applications. The findings derived from this study will also help organizations and managers understand blockchain technology and its applications in workplaces. This understanding therefore contributes to the development of innovative solutions and strategies for organizational success. For instance, understanding the potential applications of blockchain within the workplace environment such as how blockchain can strategically enhance aspects such as knowledge management, data security, and operational efficiency enables strategy leaders to advise on optimal adoption and implementation strategies. Moreover, insights into blockchain's potential to enhance organizational resilience against data breaches and fraud can help managers devise strategies for fortifying organizational defenses. Additionally, the study's findings can inspire innovation and collaboration within organizations by highlighting opportunities for leveraging blockchain in areas such as knowledge sharing, workforce training, and sustainable development practices.

One of the limitations of this review stems from the criteria used to select articles. While we included all documents related to the specified key terms, articles from non-indexed journals, books, and those written in languages other than English were excluded. This exclusion may have led to the omission of relevant papers. To address this limitation, a future study could aim to conduct a more comprehensive review, encompassing papers from non-indexed journals, books, emerging journals, and publications in languages other than English. Moreover, future work can offer a more tangible knowledge of how the clusters in this study materialize in real-world circumstances using practical case studies and empirical inquiries. Another limitation is that this study exclusively relies on co-word analysis to identify primary knowledge areas and associated topics. However, incorporating additional bibliometric techniques such as co-citation analysis or bibliographic coupling could yield intriguing insights. Furthermore, future research may explore prominent authors, publishers, journal sources, and countries to gain a deeper understanding of the field.

REFERENCES

Abella, A., Ortiz-de-Urbina-Criado, M., & De-Pablos-Heredero, C. (2019). A methodology to design and redesign services in smart cities based on the citizen experience. *Information Polity*, 24(2), 183–197. DOI: 10.3233/IP-180116

Al-Habaibeh, A., Watkins, M., Waried, K., & Javareshk, M. B. (2021). Challenges and opportunities of remotely working from home during Covid-19 pandemic. *Global Transitions*, 3, 99–108. DOI: 10.1016/j.glt.2021.11.001 PMID: 34870136

AlSkaif, T., Crespo-Vazquez, J. L., Sekuloski, M., van Leeuwen, G., & Catalao, J. P. S. (2022). Blockchain-Based Fully Peer-to-Peer Energy Trading Strategies for Residential Energy Systems. *IEEE Transactions on Industrial Informatics*, 18(1), 231–241. DOI: 10.1109/TII.2021.3077008

Ammirato, S., Felicetti, A. M., Linzalone, R., Corvello, V., & Kumar, S. (2023). Still our most important asset: A systematic review on human resource management in the midst of the fourth industrial revolution. *Journal of Innovation & Knowledge*, 8(3), 100403. DOI: 10.1016/j.jik.2023.100403

Aria, M., & Cuccurullo, C. (2017). bibliometrix : An R-tool for comprehensive science mapping analysis. *Journal of Informetrics*, 11(4), 959–975. DOI: 10.1016/j.joi.2017.08.007

Arun Sampaul Thomas, G., & Harold Robinson, Y. (2020). *IoT*. Big Data, Blockchain and Machine Learning Besides Its Transmutation with Modern Technological Applications., DOI: 10.1007/978-3-030-39119-5_4

Ávila-Gutiérrez, M. J., Suarez-Fernandez de Miranda, S., & Aguayo-González, F. (2022). Occupational Safety and Health 5.0—A Model for Multilevel Strategic Deployment Aligned with the Sustainable Development Goals of Agenda 2030. *Sustainability (Basel)*, 14(11), 6741. DOI: 10.3390/su14116741

Bandi, A., & Fellah, A. (2022a). An Implementation and Evaluation of Blockchain-based Digital Health Passports. *2022 International Conference on Inventive Computation Technologies (ICICT)*, 476–482. IEEE. DOI: 10.1109/ICICT54344.2022.9850724

Bandi, A., & Fellah, A. (2022b). An Implementation and Evaluation of Blockchain-based Digital Health Passports. *2022 International Conference on Inventive Computation Technologies (ICICT)*, 476–482. DOI: 10.1109/ICICT54344.2022.9850724

Belchior, R., Vasconcelos, A., Guerreiro, S., & Correia, M. (2022). A Survey on Blockchain Interoperability: Past, Present, and Future Trends. *ACM Computing Surveys*, 54(8), 1–41. DOI: 10.1145/3471140

Binbusayyis, A., & Vaiyapuri, T. (2023). A professional-driven blockchain framework for sharing E-Portfolio in the context of Industry 4.0. *ICT Express*, 9(2), 140–149. DOI: 10.1016/j.icte.2022.03.010

Bommisetti, R. K., Syed, S. M., Verma, M., Charugulla, S., Subbalakshmi, A. V. V. S., & Emani, S. (2024). Development of HR Metrics and Plans for Employee Engagement in Banking Sector Using Blockchain Technology. *2024 5th International Conference on Intelligent Communication Technologies and Virtual Mobile Networks (ICICV)*, 837–842. IEEE. DOI: 10.1109/ICICV62344.2024.00138

Chen, J., Lv, Z., & Song, H. (2019). Design of personnel big data management system based on blockchain. *Future Generation Computer Systems*, 101, 1122–1129. DOI: 10.1016/j.future.2019.07.037

Cheng, J.-C., Lee, N.-Y., Chi, C., & Chen, Y.-H. (2018). Blockchain and smart contract for digital certificate. *2018 IEEE International Conference on Applied System Invention (ICASI)*, 1046–1051. IEEE. DOI: 10.1109/ICASI.2018.8394455

D'Avanzo, W. (2021). *Italian Smart Working*. An Innovative Approach to Improve Productivity in Public Administration., DOI: 10.1007/978-3-030-85304-4_19

Dagliati, A., Malovini, A., Tibollo, V., & Bellazzi, R. (2021). Health informatics and EHR to support clinical research in the COVID-19 pandemic: An overview. *Briefings in Bioinformatics*, 22(2), 812–822. DOI: 10.1093/bib/bbaa418 PMID: 33454728

Dhar Dwivedi, A., Singh, R., Kaushik, K., Rao Mukkamala, R., & Alnumay, W. S. (2024). Blockchain and artificial intelligence for 5G-enabled Internet of Things: Challenges, opportunities, and solutions. *Transactions on Emerging Telecommunications Technologies*, 35(4), e4329. Advance online publication. DOI: 10.1002/ett.4329

Dobrovnik, M., Herold, D., Fürst, E., & Kummer, S. (2018). Blockchain for and in Logistics: What to Adopt and Where to Start. *Logistics (Basel)*, 2(3), 18. DOI: 10.3390/logistics2030018

Donthu, N., Kumar, S., Mukherjee, D., Pandey, N., & Lim, W. M. (2021). How to conduct a bibliometric analysis: An overview and guidelines. *Journal of Business Research*, 133, 285–296. DOI: 10.1016/j.jbusres.2021.04.070

Duan, J., Zhang, C., Gong, Y., Brown, S., of, Z. L.-I. J., & undefined 2020. (2020). A content-analysis based literature review in blockchain adoption within food supply chain. *Mdpi.Com*. DOI: 10.3390/ijerph17051784

El Azzaoui, A., Singh, S. K., Pan, Y., & Park, J. H. (2020). Block5GIntell: Blockchain for AI-Enabled 5G Networks. *IEEE Access : Practical Innovations, Open Solutions*, 8, 145918–145935. DOI: 10.1109/ACCESS.2020.3014356

Ellewala, U. P., Amarasena, W. D. H., Lakmali, H. S., Senanayaka, L. M., & Senarathne, A. N. (2020). Secure Messaging Platform Based on Blockchain. *2020 2nd International Conference on Advancements in Computing (ICAC)*, 317–322. IEEE. DOI: 10.1109/ICAC51239.2020.9357306

Fachrunnisa, O., & Hussain, F. K. (2020). Blockchain-based human resource management practices for mitigating skills and competencies gap in workforce. *International Journal of Engineering Business Management*, 12, 184797902096640. DOI: 10.1177/1847979020966400

Faustino, S., Faria, I., & Marques, R. (2022). The myths and legends of king Satoshi and the knights of blockchain. *Journal of Cultural Economics*, 15(1), 67–80. DOI: 10.1080/17530350.2021.1921830

Gilman, E., Tamminen, S., Yasmin, R., Ristimella, E., Peltonen, E., Harju, M., Lovén, L., Riekki, J., & Pirttikangas, S. (2020). Internet of Things for Smart Spaces: A University Campus Case Study. *Sensors (Basel)*, 20(13), 3716. DOI: 10.3390/s20133716 PMID: 32630833

Glaeser, E., Kourtit, K., & Nijkamp, P. (2021). New urban challenges: Shared spaces in smart places – Overview and positioning. *Land Use Policy*, 111, 105672. DOI: 10.1016/j.landusepol.2021.105672

Godavarthi, B., Dhar, M., Devi, S. A., Raju, S. S., Balaram, A., & Srilakshmi, G. (2023). Blockchain integration with the internet of things for the employee performance management. *The Journal of High Technology Management Research*, 34(2), 100468. DOI: 10.1016/j.hitech.2023.100468

Gomes, G. P., Coelho, A., & Ribeiro, N. (2024). A systematic literature review on sustainable HRM and its relations with employees' attitudes: state of art and future research agenda. *Journal of Organizational Effectiveness: People and Performance*. DOI: 10.1108/JOEPP-11-2023-0497

González-Mendes, S., González-Sánchez, R., Costa, C. J., & García-Muiña, F. (2023). Analysing the state of the art of Blockchain application in Smart Cities: A bibliometric study. *2023 18th Iberian Conference on Information Systems and Technologies (CISTI)*, 1–6. IEEE. DOI: 10.23919/CISTI58278.2023.10211371

Gupta, R., Shukla, V. K., Rao, S. S., Anwar, S., Sharma, P., & Bathla, R. (2020). Enhancing Privacy through "Smart Contract" using Blockchain-based Dynamic Access Control. *2020 International Conference on Computation, Automation and Knowledge Management (ICCAKM)*, 338–343. IEEE. DOI: 10.1109/ICCAKM46823.2020.9051521

Hewage, H. A. S., K.U, H., K.M.J.B, J., K.P.C., H., Senarathne, A. N., & Wijekoon, J. (2020). Smart Human Resource Management System to Maximize Productivity. *2020 International Computer Symposium (ICS)*, 479–484. IEEE. DOI: 10.1109/ICS51289.2020.00100

Honar Pajooh, H., Rashid, M., Alam, F., & Demidenko, S. (2021). Multi-Layer Blockchain-Based Security Architecture for Internet of Things. *Sensors (Basel)*, 21(3), 772. DOI: 10.3390/s21030772 PMID: 33498860

Jain, A., Gangwar, A., Kumari, C., & Mehra, P. S. (2024). A Survey on Blockchain for Rental Lease Management. *2024 11th International Conference on Reliability, Infocom Technologies and Optimization (Trends and Future Directions) (ICRITO)*, 1–5. IEEE. DOI: 10.1109/ICRITO61523.2024.10522110

Janiesch, C., Zschech, P., & Heinrich, K. (2021). Machine learning and deep learning. *Electronic Markets*, 31(3), 685–695. DOI: 10.1007/s12525-021-00475-2

Kaswan, K. S., Dhanda, S. K., Dhatterwal, J. S., & Balusamy, B. (2023). Blockchain Technology in HR Processes. In *The Role of HR in the Transforming Workplace* (pp. 104–116). Productivity Press., DOI: 10.4324/9781003372622-8

Kayikci, S., & Khoshgoftaar, T. M. (2024). Blockchain meets machine learning: A survey. *Journal of Big Data*, 11(1), 9. DOI: 10.1186/s40537-023-00852-y

Kendzierskyj, S., Jahankhani, H., & Ndumbe, S. I. (2021). Blockchain for Strengthening the Privacy of Healthcare Data. In *Research Anthology on Blockchain Technology in Business, Healthcare, Education, and Government* (pp. 672–688). IGI Global. DOI: 10.4018/978-1-7998-5351-0.ch039

Khaleelullah, S., Vangapalli, S. T., Gaddam, M., Hanumakonda, V. S., & Goud Gangapuram, U. K. (2023). Verifcation of Academic Records Using Hyperledger Fabric and IPFS. *2023 3rd International Conference on Pervasive Computing and Social Networking (ICPCSN)*, 210–217. IEEE. DOI: 10.1109/ICPCSN58827.2023.00040

Khan, D., Jung, L. T., & Hashmani, M. A. (2021). Systematic Literature Review of Challenges in Blockchain Scalability. *Applied Sciences (Basel, Switzerland)*, 11(20), 9372. DOI: 10.3390/app11209372

Kok, C. L., & Palaniappan, K. (2023). A futuristic approach to decentralize and authenticate workplace safety records leveraging on blockchain distributed ledger network. In *Distributed Computing to Blockchain* (pp. 425–431). Elsevier., DOI: 10.1016/B978-0-323-96146-2.00002-4

Le, N. T. T., Nguyen, Q. N., Phien, N. N., Duong-Trung, N., Huynh, T. T., Nguyen, T. P., & Son, H. X. (2019). Assuring non-fraudulent transactions in cash on delivery by introducing double smart contracts. *International Journal of Advanced Computer Science and Applications*, 10(5). Advance online publication. DOI: 10.14569/IJACSA.2019.0100584

Li, W., Su, Z., Li, R., Zhang, K., & Wang, Y. (2020). Blockchain-Based Data Security for Artificial Intelligence Applications in 6G Networks. *IEEE Network*, 34(6), 31–37. DOI: 10.1109/MNET.021.1900629

Liu, L., Han, M., Zhou, Y., Parizi, R. M., & Korayem, M. (2020). *Blockchain-Based Certification for Education*. Employment, and Skill with Incentive Mechanism., DOI: 10.1007/978-3-030-38181-3_14

Liu, W.-J., Chiu, W.-Y., & Hua, W. (2024). Blockchain-enabled renewable energy certificate trading: A secure and privacy-preserving approach. *Energy*, 290, 130110. DOI: 10.1016/j.energy.2023.130110

Lohmer, J., & Lasch, R. (2020). Blockchain in operations management and manufacturing: Potential and barriers. *Computers & Industrial Engineering*, 149, 106789. Advance online publication. DOI: 10.1016/j.cie.2020.106789

Maden, A., & Alptekin, E. (2020). Evaluation of factors affecting the decision to adopt blockchain technology: A logistics company case study using Fuzzy DEMATEL. *Journal of Intelligent & Fuzzy Systems*, 39(5), 6279–6291. Advance online publication. DOI: 10.3233/JIFS-189096

McMahon, L. (2000). Bullying and harassment in the workplace. *International Journal of Contemporary Hospitality Management*, 12(6), 384–387. DOI: 10.1108/09596110010343666

Mohammad Azahari, A., Ahmad, A., & Rahayu, S. B. (2021). *Contactless Attendance Method with Face Recognition*. Body Temperature Measurement and GPS System Using Blockchain Technology., DOI: 10.1007/978-981-33-6490-5_8

Mololoth, V. K., Saguna, S., & Åhlund, C. (2023). Blockchain and Machine Learning for Future Smart Grids: A Review. *Energies*, 16(1), 528. DOI: 10.3390/en16010528

Nappi, I., & de Campos Ribeiro, G. (2020). Internet of Things technology applications in the workplace environment: A critical review. *Journal of Corporate Real Estate*, 22(1), 71–90. DOI: 10.1108/JCRE-06-2019-0028

Neu, C. V., Gibson, J., Lunardi, R. C., Leesakul, N., & Morisset, C. (2023). *A Blockchain-Based Architecture to Manage User Privacy Preferences on Smart Shared Spaces Privately*. DOI: 10.1007/978-3-031-25734-6_9

Obu, U., Ambekar, Y., Lingam, R., Borikar, Y., Yadav, R., & Dongre, S. (2023). Blockchain System Against Gender Bias and Other Discriminatory Practices in Workplaces. *2023 IEEE 3rd International Conference on Technology, Engineering, Management for Societal Impact Using Marketing, Entrepreneurship and Talent (TEMSMET)*, 1–6. IEEE. DOI: 10.1109/TEMSMET56707.2023.10150193

Oke, A. E., & Stephen, S. S. (2024). Smart Contract for Sustainable Infrastructure Management. In *A Digital Path to Sustainable Infrastructure Management* (pp. 75–83). Emerald Publishing Limited., DOI: 10.1108/978-1-83797-703-120241008

Page, M. J., McKenzie, J. E., Bossuyt, P. M., Boutron, I., Hoffmann, T. C., Mulrow, C. D., Shamseer, L., Tetzlaff, J. M., Akl, E. A., Brennan, S. E., Chou, R., Glanville, J., Grimshaw, J. M., Hróbjartsson, A., Lalu, M. M., Li, T., Loder, E. W., Mayo-Wilson, E., McDonald, S., & Moher, D. (2021). The PRISMA 2020 statement: An updated guideline for reporting systematic reviews. *BMJ (Clinical Research Ed.)*, (71), n71. Advance online publication. DOI: 10.1136/bmj.n71 PMID: 33782057

Pan, X., Zhong, B., Sheng, D., Yuan, X., & Wang, Y. (2022). Blockchain and deep learning technologies for construction equipment security information management. *Automation in Construction*, 136, 104186. DOI: 10.1016/j.autcon.2022.104186

Pandey, A., Grima, S., Pandey, S., & Balusamy, B. (2023). *The Role of HR in the Transforming Workplace*. Productivity Press., DOI: 10.4324/9781003372622

Philip Chen, C. L., & Zhang, C.-Y. (2014). Data-intensive applications, challenges, techniques and technologies: A survey on Big Data. *Information Sciences*, 275, 314–347. DOI: 10.1016/j.ins.2014.01.015

Rahman, M. M., Azam, M. M., & Sanjida Chowdhury, F. (2022). Secure Complaint Management System against Women Harassment at Workplace Using Blockchain Technology. *International Journal of Electrical and Computer Engineering Systems*, 13(3), 209–217. DOI: 10.32985/ijeces.13.3.6

Ramachandran, R., Babu, V., & Murugesan, V. P. (2023). The role of blockchain technology in the process of decision-making in human resource management: A review and future research agenda. *Business Process Management Journal*, 29(1), 116–139. DOI: 10.1108/BPMJ-07-2022-0351

Rodríguez Bolívar, M. P., Scholl, H. J., & Pomeshchikov, R. (2021). *Stakeholders' Perspectives on Benefits and Challenges in Blockchain Regulatory Frameworks*. DOI: 10.1007/978-3-030-55746-1_1

Roopa, C., Suganthe, R. C., & Shanthi, N. (2020). Blockchain based certificate verification using ethereum and smart contract. *Journal of Critical Reviews*, 7(09). Advance online publication. DOI: 10.31838/jcr.07.09.71

Samadhiya, A., Agrawal, R., Kumar, A., & Garza-Reyes, J. A. (2023). Blockchain technology and circular economy in the environment of total productive maintenance: A natural resource-based view perspective. *Journal of Manufacturing Technology Management*, 34(2), 293–314. DOI: 10.1108/JMTM-08-2022-0299

Savelyeva, T., & Park, J. (2022). Blockchain technology for sustainable education. *British Journal of Educational Technology*, 53(6), 1591–1604. DOI: 10.1111/bjet.13273

Selvi A, J. A., Rajan Y, P., & Geetha, M. (2023). The mask of hidden knowledge behind advanced technologies: A case of distress, unlearning and knowledge transfer. Journal of Information Technology Teaching Cases, 20438869231210577.

Semenzin, S. (2023). 'Blockchain for good': Exploring the notion of social good inside the blockchain scene. *Big Data & Society*, 10(2), 20539517231205479. Advance online publication. DOI: 10.1177/20539517231205479

Shakhbulatov, D., Arora, A., Dong, Z., & Rojas-Cessa, R. (2019). Blockchain Implementation for Analysis of Carbon Footprint across Food Supply Chain. *2019 IEEE International Conference on Blockchain (Blockchain)*, 546–551. IEEE. DOI: 10.1109/Blockchain.2019.00079

Sheffey, S., & Tindale, R. S. (1992). Perceptions of Sexual Harassment in the Workplace. *Journal of Applied Social Psychology*, 22(19), 1502–1520. DOI: 10.1111/j.1559-1816.1992.tb00963.x

Shetye, I., Morwadkar, S., Chavan, B., Rajole, S., & Kulkarni, S. (2024). *Literature Survey: Complaint Management System Using Blockchain Technology*. DOI: 10.1007/978-981-97-1313-4_29

Shinde, P. P., & Shah, S. (2018). A Review of Machine Learning and Deep Learning Applications. *2018 Fourth International Conference on Computing Communication Control and Automation (ICCUBEA)*, 1–6. IEEE. DOI: 10.1109/ICCUBEA.2018.8697857

Son-Turan, S. (2022). Fostering Equality in Education: The Blockchain Business Model for Higher Education (BBM-HE). *Sustainability (Basel)*, 14(5), 2955. DOI: 10.3390/su14052955

Tang, X., Qiu, J., Zhang, W., Toure, I., Zhang, M., Messina, E., & Yu, S. (2019). The Internet of Responsibilities - Connecting Human Responsibilities using Big Data and Blockchain. *2019 IEEE International Conference on Big Data (Big Data)*, 6226–6228. IEEE. DOI: 10.1109/BigData47090.2019.9006521

Tanwar, S., Bhatia, Q., Patel, P., Kumari, A., Singh, P. K., & Hong, W.-C. (2020). Machine Learning Adoption in Blockchain-Based Smart Applications: The Challenges, and a Way Forward. *IEEE Access : Practical Innovations, Open Solutions*, 8, 474–488. DOI: 10.1109/ACCESS.2019.2961372

Tatar, U., Gokce, Y., & Nussbaum, B. (2020). Law versus technology: Blockchain, GDPR, and tough tradeoffs. *Computer Law & Security Report*, 38, 105454. DOI: 10.1016/j.clsr.2020.105454

Tiron-Tudor, A., Deliu, D., Farcane, N., & Dontu, A. (2021). Managing change with and through blockchain in accountancy organizations: A systematic literature review. *Journal of Organizational Change Management*, 34(2), 477–506. DOI: 10.1108/JOCM-10-2020-0302

UN. (2015). *Transforming Our World: The 2030 Agenda for Sustainable Development. Resolution Adopted by the General Assembly on 25 September 2015.*

van Eck, N. J., & Waltman, L. (2010). Software survey: VOSviewer, a computer program for bibliometric mapping. *Scientometrics*, 84(2), 523–538. DOI: 10.1007/s11192-009-0146-3 PMID: 20585380

Wang, X., Feng, L., Zhang, H., Lyu, C., Wang, L., & You, Y. (2017). Human Resource Information Management Model based on Blockchain Technology. *2017 IEEE Symposium on Service-Oriented System Engineering (SOSE)*, 168–173. IEEE. DOI: 10.1109/SOSE.2017.34

Wei, F., & Pokrovskaia, N. N. (2017). Digitizing of regulative mechanisms on the masterchain platform for the individualized competence portfolio. *2017 IEEE VI Forum Strategic Partnership of Universities and Enterprises of Hi-Tech Branches (Science. Education. Innovations) (SPUE)*, 73–76. IEEE. DOI: 10.1109/IVForum.2017.8246055

Xie, J., Tang, H., Huang, T., Yu, F. R., Xie, R., Liu, J., & Liu, Y. (2019). A Survey of Blockchain Technology Applied to Smart Cities: Research Issues and Challenges. *IEEE Communications Surveys and Tutorials*, 21(3), 2794–2830. DOI: 10.1109/COMST.2019.2899617

KEY TERMS AND DEFINITIONS

Industry 5.0: It refers to the next phase of industrial development wherein humans and machines work together. It also emphasizes human-technology collaboration to enhance worker productivity, creativity, and satisfaction while maximizing technological advancements.

Smart Workstations: These are technology-enabled work environments that utilize interconnected devices, sensors, and software to optimize the efficiency, productivity, and safety of employees. These workstations integrate various data analytics and Internet of Things (IoT) devices to provide personalized and adaptive workspaces that cater to the individual needs of workers.

Safe Workplaces: Safe workplaces are environments where the health, safety, and well-being of employees are prioritized through the implementation of safety protocols, advanced monitoring systems, and preventive measures.

Anti-forgery: Anti-forgery refers to the use of advanced technologies and methodologies to prevent the creation and distribution of counterfeit documents, or information.

Workplace Harassment: Workplace harassment is any unwelcome behavior, conduct, or communication that creates a hostile, intimidating, or offensive work environment for an individual or group of employees. This can include actions such as bullying, discrimination, sexual harassment, and other forms of mistreatment.

Chapter 5

Global Challenges and Opportunities of New Technologies for Workplace Conflict Resolution Through ADR

Marta Gonzalo Quiroga
https://orcid.org/0000-0002-6553-3268
Rey Juan Carlos University, Spain

ABSTRACT

This paper aims to provide a scientific analysis of the scarce existing academic and practical work on the global challenges and benefits of New Technologies and Artificial Intelligence (AI) in Alternative Dispute Resolution (ADR) and Online Dispute Resolution (ODR) applied to the workplace. Its innovative and unprecedented approach provides an in-depth and structured understanding of the integration of emerging technologies into ADR mechanisms in the workplace. At the same time, it includes a comprehensive analysis of technological and AI developments in ADR, the impact of these on the efficiency and accessibility of ADR in the workplace.

DOI: 10.4018/979-8-3693-6289-1.ch005

I. INTRODUCTION AND OBJECTIVES

This work addresses the issue of AI in the field of the so-called Alternative – Appropriate or Adequate- Dispute Resolution (ADR) Methods in the workplace, an area in which the production of conflicts is inherent to work and business activity itself in a universal manner (Losada Crespo & Briz Clariget, 2024).

With this principal goal in mind, the present research work will be completed by four other objectives methodologically differentiated into their corresponding sections, including four Tables and four Figures on the subject of the research.

The first section is a delimitation of the subject of study & Statistical Data. The ADRs that are applied globally in the workplace and their main characteristics are specified and compared with each other and with Universal Justice, by means of four illustrative research tables. It also provides a Flow Chart with the steps for dealing with a workplace conflict using an ADR Protocol and a proposal is made. A conceptual Hybrid Model is proposed to be applied in the workplace. In addition, in the absence of global statistics on the subject, it will provide statistical data on Conciliations, Mediations, and Arbitrations in Spain in the workplace.

The second section deals with digitalized conflict management and resolution mechanism in the workplace. It is analyzed the *Online Dispute Resolution* (ODR). It also provides a study on New Technologies & AI in ADRs beyond hot topic and established conceptions (AA. VV., 2022-2023). It specifies the AI programs applied to the different ADRs, and how AI can be applied in specific areas in the workplace, such us Human Resources (HR), Procurement and After-sales service. Extensive research is carried out on the different AI programs applied to the different ADRs. In turn it is provides the first case study of the use of AI in ADR (mediation) to resolve a workplace dispute.

The third section focuses on specifying the most relevant points on the advantages and disadvantages (benefits and challenges) of applying AI in ADR in the workplace. In particular, in those most commonly used in the worksite, such as conciliation, arbitration and mediation. It is precisely the ability to prevent, manage and resolve conflicts appropriately that, in a global context, is an essential indicator for measuring professional and business success or failure. For this reason, this paper includes a section aimed at addressing how the application of AI in certain alternative methods of conflict resolution, such as negotiation, mediation, arbitration, and conciliation, can benefit the proper management and the result in the handling of conflicts in certain functional areas of organizations (HR, Purchasing, After-sales Service, etc.) in the workplace. Furthermore, at the end, a table has been produced highlighting the *pros* and *cons* of applying AI in extra-judicial methods of conflict management and resolution in the workplace.

Finally, the last section summarises the main conclusions and proposals made in this scientific work. Adding, at the end, the main doctrinal, legislative, jurisprudential, case studies, statistics and other references used in the research.

This paper is relevant because it is innovative and aims to contribute to the scarce existing academic and practical work on the global challenges and opportunities of new technologies in extrajudicial justice systems applied to resolve disputes in the workplace through ADR. Its unprecedented approach explores the legal benefits and challenges of integrating new technologies and AI into ADR and ODR in the workplace. It aims to provide an in-depth and structured understanding of the integration of emerging technologies in ADR mechanisms.

II. DELIMITATION OF THE SUBJECT OF STUDY AND STATISTICAL DATA

1. What are the ADRs Applied to the Workplace?

The types of ADR that can be applied to the workplace are many and varied, including different types such as Negotiation (Fisher, Ury, & Patton, 2011; & Lewicki, Saunders & Barry, 2015), Settlement, Mediation (Moore, 2014), Conciliation, *Mini-Trial*, *Executive Hearing*, Neutral or Expert Evaluation, *Fact Finding*, Arbitration, Hybrids: *Multi-Tiered* or Multi-Step, or *Eskalationsklauseln* or *Mdr-Clauses*, Collaborative Law, etc. (Gonzalo, 2023). They are all global and part of the extrajudicial or alternative systems of justice in the vast majority of countries and legal cultures around the world.

The following figure summarizes the main differences between the most commonly used ADRs in the workplace.

Figure 1. Summary Descriptions of the most commonly used ADRs in the workplace.

ADR	SUMMARY DESCRIPTION
Negotiation	➢ The purpose of negotiation is to reach an agreement or solution to a conflict in the workplace, directly between the workers themselves or those involved in the dispute, by mutual agreement of the parties and giving priority to their interests. ➢ It is a process of interrelation that takes place without the need for conflict. It can be the origin of a relationship. ➢ It is a communication process that takes place between the parties.
Mediation	➢ A third party (the mediator) intervenes to help the parties. ➢ The mediator does not have the power to make proposals, but only brings the parties together and facilitates communication in order to solve the conflict. ➢ The solution of the conflict depends exclusively on the parties. ➢ It can be judicial or extrajudicial. ➢ Requires training or qualification of the mediator.
Conciliation	➢ Similar to mediation, where the third party (the conciliator) actively promotes the achievement of a solution to the conflict, having the power to generate options and proposals that are submitted for consideration by the parties, who can accept them or continue arguing. ➢ The conciliator makes proposals, but his or her proposals are not binding. ➢ The act of conciliation is exclusively judicial (usually prior to the trial). ➢ No specific training is required.
Arbitration	➢ The parties delegate to a third party (the arbitrator), who may be a sole or uneven collegiate arbitrator, the final settlement of the dispute by means of an award, which is binding on the parties. ➢ No specific training is required, but in practice it is usually executed by specialised arbitrators in conflicts at the workplace.

Source: Own elaboration based on the work published in AA.VV., Collantes, 2023, pp. 78-79.

In general, among all ADR, arbitration and mediation respectively, are the systems most used and preferred by the users of out-of-court justice systems, according to data from the *Queen Mary University & Pinset Masons Energy Arbitration Survey* in the energy sector (January 2023). Although this will obviously vary according to the availability of the material field (commercial, civil, family, etc.) and whether it is domestic or international.

Specifically, in the workplace, it can be stated that, globally, mediation is the most widely used ADR. In the sense that mediation has an 80% success rate because it is the people involved who participate in resolving the own conflict (Data from the *Human Resources Observatory of Spain,* 2022/2023).

2. Comparative of the Main Characteristics Between ADRs and Justice Applied to the Workplace

Irrespective of their specific application to the workplace, each of the ADRs has its own idiosyncrasies and characteristics - whose opportunities and challenges in relation to new technologies and AI could be dealt with in a specific way in each of them separately, as has been done in the specific field of arbitration (Gonzalo Quiroga, 2023) and in mediation (Ordelin Font, 2021). However, in view of the common characteristics of all of them, this research has made a unifying effort to focus on the generic universal particularities of ADRs and their basic principles and features that define their advantages over traditional justice systems (courts, tribunals, and jurisdictional orders) in the workplace.

Advantages of ADR are voluntariness and freedom of choice, confidentiality, speed and cost reduction, efficiency, flexibility, absence of reputational risk, specialty, continuity of relations, modernity, etc., more extensively developed by Gonzalo (2023). These properties have contributed in practice to favoring the dissemination of ADR and to ensuring its improvement and consolidation as an alternative system for the settlement of disputes. In the following table, a survey has been carried out on the main characteristics between ADRs and Justice applied to the workplace.

Table 1. Comparative table of the main characteristics between ADRs and Justice applied to the workplace

Adres CRITERIA	NEGOTIATION	CONCILIATION/ MEDIATION	ARBITRATION	JUDICIAL PROCESS
Economy/ Cost	Economical. Usually guaranteed. In principle, there are no costs at the workplace. Just the time and effort its take.	It is economical. There is a single fee to pay to the mediator. In labour conciliation, for example in Spain in 2024, it is possible to find fees for drafting and attending conciliation proceedings from €100 to €200.	It is not cheap, but less expensive than court proceedings. Practically all arbitration institutions have a calculator to find out the costs of arbitration. For example, in the calculator of the Chamber of Commerce of Madrid, 2024, https://www.arbitramadrid.com/calculadora/, the total cost with VAT of a labour arbitration with a single arbitrator (€1000 of fees) is €3.025.	It is not economical. Expenses for lawyers, solicitors, experts, and the high cost (economic and personal: wear and tear for the parties) of the time it takes to obtain a judgement. For instance, in Spain in 2024, the simple drafting of a claim and attendance at a labour trial can cost between €250 and more than €500. Just for starting. The total proceeding is around €3000. But in addition to this, the case can take between two to six years to be resolved (sometimes longer with appeals), so the time and financial cost is a clear disadvantage.
Time/ Speed	Depends on the parties, usually fast (in practice, from one day to three or four months at the latest to resolve a workplace dispute).	Depends on the parties, usually fast (in practice, from one day to three or four months at the latest to resolve a workplace dispute).	Depends on the Arbitrator, usually fast (in practice, no more than six/eight months at the latest - depending on the legislation of the country. In most countries the maximum time for arbitration is six months- to resolve a workplace dispute).	It depends on third parties (judges and justice systems) and is usually very slow in most judicial systems in the world.

continued on following page

Table 1. Continued

Adres CRITERIA	NEGOTIATION	CONCILIATION/ MEDIATION	ARBITRATION	JUDICIAL PROCESS
Formality	As agreed by the parties. No specific formality. No structure.	It does not exist. Although it should be noted that, depending on the legal systems, conciliation follows certain administrative procedures and mediation does have to follow certain stages.	There is some formality in that there are stages of compliance.	Fully formalistic structured.
Submission at the beginning	Voluntary	Voluntary	Voluntary	Mandatory
Binding of the result	Only if there is an agreement and the parties undertake to comply with it voluntarily. The result of the negotiation is a contract and is binding as such.	In conciliation, if the parties reach a consensus, this means the end of the conflict, thus avoiding the judicial process. The labour conciliation act issued by the legal counsel has legal force, without the need for a judge to intervene. In mediation, the mediation agreement must be complied with. However, both agreements do not have the same legal force as an arbitration award or a court judgement.	Compulsory. An arbitration award is obtained which is equivalent to a final court judgement.	Compulsory.
Participation of Third Parties	No	Yes, the conciliator, who will be the legal counsel, and the mediator, who may be chosen by the parties or by the Mediation Centre or Institution.	Yes, whether it is a single arbitrator or an arbitration panel (3 or 5 arbitrators) they are chosen by the parties at the workplace. In the absence of agreement on the choice of arbitrators, they could be chosen by a competent court.	Yes, provided by the State in accordance with the relevant domestic and international procedural rules.
Confidentiality	Yes, it is held by the parties.	Yes, it is a prior agreement between the parties.	Yes, unless an application is made to set aside the judgment.	It does not exist. The judicial process is public.

continued on following page

Table 1. Continued

Adres CRITERIA	NEGOTIATION	CONCILIATION/ MEDIATION	ARBITRATION	JUDICIAL PROCESS
Satisfaction of The Parties	Win/Win. A mutually satisfactory agreement is sought.	Win/Win. A mutually satisfactory agreement is sought.	The award is based on arbitral law or case law or on opinions founded in equity.	The court judgment is based on law and jurisprudence (principle of legality: Roman Law systems) or on legal cases (Common Law).
Control of the Parties to the procedure to be followed	High control.	High control.	Less control.	No control.

Source: Own elaboration based on the work published in AA.VV., Collantes, 2023, pp. 79-80. Adapted to the workplace (July 2024)

It is precisely the aforementioned advantages that are increasingly convincing individuals and companies to include in their contracts clauses whereby they voluntarily refer to ADRs (negotiation, mediation, arbitration, etc.) for the resolution of their conflicts in the workplace. This, together with the inadequacies of a congested and worn-out public justice system that was unable to respond to the needs of litigants in times of crisis and pandemic, calling into question *Effective Judicial Protection* itself, has had a considerable influence on judicial systems around the world causing them to pay more attention to ADR and new technologies in the workplace.

3. Proposals for a Protocol: Flow Chart With the Steps for Dealing With a Workplace Conflict Using an ADR Protocol

In the following, it has been considered illustrative to make an original proposal in the form of a flow chart on which visualizes the steps of ADR in the workplace, using an ADR Protocol

Figure 2. Flow chart with the steps for dealing with a workplace conflict using an ADR Protocol: Hybrid proposal.

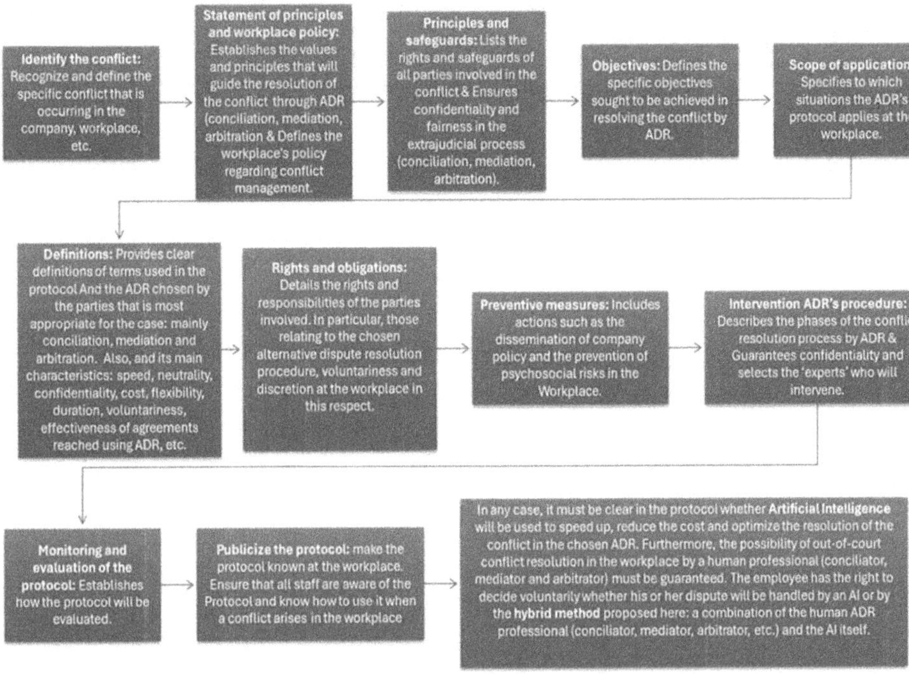

Source: Own elaboration and proposal (July 2024)

4. Statistical Data on Conciliations, Mediations, and Arbitrations in Spain in the Workplace

The Ministry of Labour and Social Economy publishes monthly in its Bulletin of Labour Statistics and annually in its Mediation, Arbitration and Conciliation Statistics, from which the data presented here have been extracted. Section I of this publication includes data on individual conciliations. Table 4 shows the main figures of the use of the ADRs in the Spanish labor market since 2010, classified by resolution unit and type and Figure 1 summarizes the main features of the evolution of conciliations, mediations, and arbitrations in the last decade.

Table 2. Mediation, arbitration, and conciliation in the labor market. Spain. Series 2010 – 2023. Completed conciliations and mediations, by resolution unit and type.

	2023	2022	2021	2020	2019	2018	2017	2016	2015	2014	2013	2012	2011	2010
TOTAL	**472454**	**407325**	**337581**	**313247**	**482797**	**449521**	**432564**	**422156**	**426389**	**475383**	**551421**	**523471**	**481516**	**492770**
Resolved by the administrative units of mediation, arbitration, and conciliation	**453149**	**385468**	**315.057** (1)	**294.354** (1)	**461.077** (1)	**428.893** (1)	**397.554** (4)	**392.731** (4)	**397.719** (4)	**442.579** (4)	**513.406** (4)	**488.185** (4)	**448.823** (4)	**459.802** (4)
Individual conciliations	**452521**	**384891**	**314477**	**293878**	**460421**	**428228**	**397093**	**392294**	**397281**	**441934**	**512421**	**487331**	**447321**	**458479**
With agreement	159656	135284	112109	100863	147403	135590	117556	115555	111420	113095	120831	88850	52383	56044
Without agreement	143659	124617	104607	90759	155778	134810	132973	139377	147260	167937	188897	192054	145080	135265
Attempted without effect and others (2)	149206	124990	97761	102256	157240	157828	146564	137362	138601	160902	202693	206427	249858	267170
Collective conciliations and mediations*	**628**	**577**	**580**	**476**	**656**	**665**	**432**	**391**	**396**	**554**	**796**	**806**	**1448**	**1275**
With agreement	79	59	70	41	69	100	27	12	12	32	36	119	87	103
Without agreement	453	421	431	342	461	450	304	287	304	389	539	563	483	479
Attempted without effect and others (2)	96	97	79	93	126	115	101	92	80	133	220	124	878	693
Mediations*							**29**	**46**	**42**	**170**	**189**	**48**	**54**	**48**
Resolved by the regional bodies of extrajudicial conflict resolution	**19305**	**21857**	**22671**	**18893**	**21720**	**17445**	**35010**	**29425**	**28670**	**32804**	**38015**	**35286**	**32693**	**33291**
Individual conciliations	**15129**	**17597**	**17947**	**14765**	**16678**	**12552**	**29894**	**24321**	**23789**	**27479**	**30405**	**29932**	**27164**	**27845**
Collective conciliations and mediations	**4151**	**4236**	**4711**	**4109**	**5016**	**4850**	**5073**	**5062**	**4832**	**5283**	**7541**	**5308**	**5529**	**5446**
With agreement	1314	1317	1390	1033	1511	1511	1555 (3)	1493	1450	1665	1997	1858	1803	1768
Without agreement	2265	2321	2591	2193	2527	2565	2708 (3)	2711	2538	2734	4060	2808	2649	2555
Attempted without effect and others (2)	572	598	730	884	978	774	810	858	844	884	1484	642	1077	1123
Arbitrations	**25**	**24**	**13**	**19**	**26**	**43**	**43**	**42**	**49**	**42**	**69**	**46**	**-**	**-**

* From the year 2018, mediations are not listed individually but are integrated along with collective conciliations.

(1) Includes the collective and individual conciliations resolved by the Regional Bodies of Extrajudicial Resolution of Baleares (TAMIB) and Cantabria (ORECLA).

(2) Includes attempted without effect, those deemed not presented, withdrawn, and other reasons.

((3) Does not include information from Baleares and Navarra.

((3) Does not include information from Baleares and Navarra.

Source: Estadística de Mediación Arbitraje y conciliación. Ministerio de Trabajo y Economía Social. España. https://www.poderjudicial.es/cgpj/es/Temas/Estadistica-Judicial/Estadistica-por-temas/Medios-alternativos-de-resolucion-de-conflictos/Mediacion--Arbitraje-y-Conciliacion-laborales/

Figure 3. Mediation, arbitration, and conciliation in Spain. Series 2010 – 2023

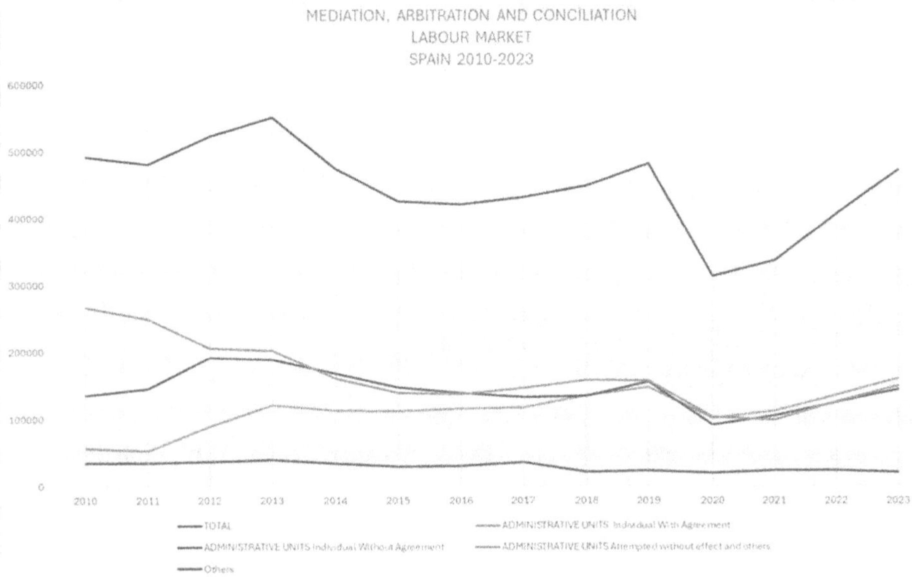

Source: Estadística de Mediación Arbitraje y conciliación. Ministerio de Trabajo y Economía Social. España. https://www.poderjudicial.es/cgpj/es/Temas/Estadistica-Judicial/Estadistica-por-temas/Medios-alternativos-de-resolucion-de-conflictos/Mediacion--Arbitraje-y-Conciliacion-laborales/

The global figures are stable, once recovered from the pandemics´ shock (using digital ADR u ODR for resolving conflicts in the workplace) close to half a million a year, being the individual conciliations performed by the administrative units the bulk of it (more than 95% of the total).

The pandemic caused by the SARS-CoV-2 virus underscored the urgent need for appropriate technology and secure, guaranteed, and confidential platforms for out-of-court dispute resolution, emphasizing the importance of AI (Sánchez García, 2024). This digitization of ADR, known as ODR, has become crucial. ADR/ODR methods are currently favored due to their proven effectiveness in conflict management and resolution across various legal systems and cultures, promoting reconciliation, cooperation, and strengthening interpersonal and social relations. They also ensure the improvement and adaptation of alternative justice systems in the current digital era in the workplace.

III. DIGITALIZED CONFLICT MANAGEMENT AND RESOLUTION MECHANISM

1. Online Dispute Resolution (ODR): Should There be Hybrid in the Workplace?

Originally, ODR emerged from ADR as a natural by-product of the creation of cyberspace (Ballesteros, 2021). However, in recent years, thanks in part to the pandemic, ODR has itself become an independent entity with its own legal autonomy due to the growth of *online* activities and the consequent conflicts arising from them.

ODR are in essence digitalized conflict management and resolution mechanisms that make it possible to carry out *online* dispute management and resolution procedures regardless of distance, pandemics, location, or any other barrier preventing the parties involved to meet in person (Alzate y Vázquez, 2014). Although they were originally designed for parties located in different countries or other workplaces and had their heyday at the time of the pandemic caused by the COVID-19 virus (Gonzalo, 2022), it was soon realized that they were extremely useful for many unique cases, like ODR and disability, whether physical or intellectual (Pérez Tortosa, 2022). Or, in the context of our research, in an international world of work, ODRs are very useful for managing conflicts arising between different workplaces.

Thus, ODR manages and resolves disputes in whole or in part with the help of electronic or digital tools (Gómez Valenzuela, 2023). These instruments range from web-based communication platforms that connect the relevant parties to AI that replaces the role of different professionals and traditional practices of the most commonly used classic ADR such as mediation and arbitration in the workplaces. However, a third clarification is urgently needed. A clear distinction must be made between ODR, delivered through different platforms, and AI exclusively applied in the procedures of some ADR procedures such as arbitration and mediation.

Finally, a difference must also be made between ODR, which carry out the entire extrajudicial procedure digitally, and online hybrids, HDR, that only carry out part of the procedure online, for example, taking evidence or a videoconference (Conforti, 2020). With the obligation to ensure their wider dissemination and availability to all interested parties, they must be digitized and updated, which requires a significant financial investment procuring the electronic equipment and subsequently comprehensive training of their proper use.

2. New Technologies and AI in ADRs

2.1. Beyond Hot Topic and Established Conceptions

There is no doubt that in the modern digital age AI is a hot topic also in the field of research (Cárdenas, 2024). The dizzying and revolutionary advances of AI are a source of both opportunities and challenges. Opportunities, because we see AI as a tool with which we can find solutions and resolve conflicts and problems of the most varied types in different fields, like here in the workplace (Gonzalez García, 2024).

The challenges arise because the introduction of AI in the legal and specifically extrajudicial sphere produces obvious reasons for mistrust and suspicion, along with interesting challenges to be faced. The full potential of AI and how far it will take us is unknown. here are fears that the most popular and currently fashionable variant of AI, machine learning, will degrade our science, debase our values, and undermine our justice systems—whether traditional or extrajudicially applied—and our ethics by incorporating a misconception of language and knowledge into our technology (Gonzalo, 2023). What seemed abstract and even science fiction suddenly became tangible and accessible to all and there is no standard that regulates or indicates the way forward for AI in general, let alone for ADR/ODR specifically (García San José, 2021).

Contradictions between the opportunities and challenges awakened by AI, loaded with prejudices and fears, are inappropriate in the scientific sphere. Technology is neither inherently good nor bad; the problem lies in how we use it (Antón Juárez, 2021). We choose when to use new technologies and when to refrain from using them. Hence, as a starting point, these fears must be overcome by stressing that AI is nothing more than a tool. From a scientific point of view, we must deal with AI by focusing on understanding how it works, preventing the risks of its misuse, and promoting its opportunities and benefits, particularly in ADR (Gonzalo & Suñez, 2024/2025).

2.2. Specific Areas in the Workplace Where AI Can Be Used

The application of AI to internal conflict management and resolution methods, such as mediation or arbitration, within organizations and in the workplace, offers significant advantages for conflict resolution in key functional areas. In this context, AI can benefit Human Resources (HR), Procurement and After Sales Service departments, improving efficiency, fairness, and quality of solutions. Of all the ADRs used in the workplace, mediation is essential for resolving internal disputes in organizations. AI, with its ability to process data, analyze patterns and facilitate communication, has become a valuable tool in this field. AI can be applied in specific areas in the workplace, such us:

Figure 4. Specific areas in the workplace where AI can be used

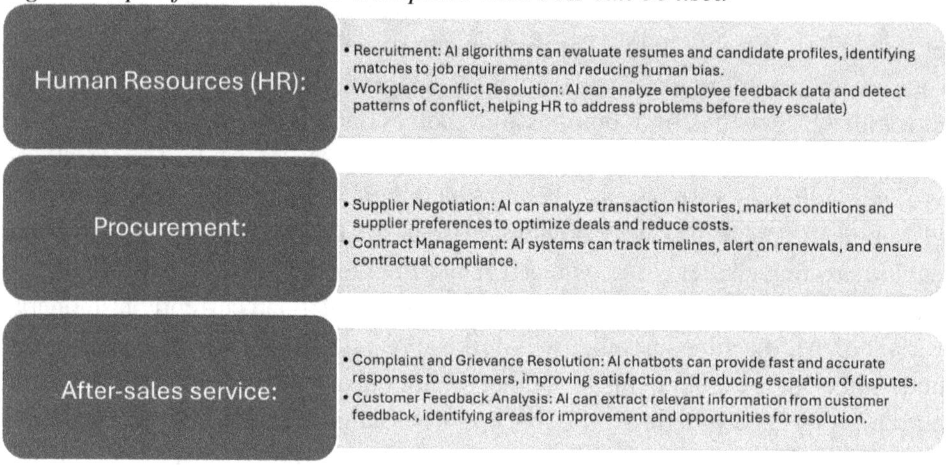

Note: Own elaboration based on the work carried out in the research project: "ODS, ADR and ODR: Justice, Human Rights and Culture of Peace", King Juan Carlos University, 2021-24.

2.3. AI Programs Applied to the Different ADRs

There are various AI programs applied to the different ADRs. Two of the most widely used are *Arbitrator Intelligence*, for the appointment of arbitrators (Rogers, 2019), and *Dispute Resolution Data, a* program of great utility and application in any extrajudicial method of conflict resolution, especially arbitration and mediation. There are also other more general legal tools that are also very useful in ADR procedures, such as *Luminance, eBrevia, Jurimetria, Arbilex*, etc. (Data on all of them in the final references, section: *AI programs applied to the different ADRs*)

There are also AI programs that allow us to choose - from among all the ADRs - which is the best one to apply to a specific case. These programs are of great help and utility in the procedures of the different ADRs, both domestic and international, processing the information so quickly that they save a great deal of time and work. Instruments which, when applied to ADR, where speed is one of the main advantages over traditional justice, greatly increase the prerogatives attributed to ADR- lower cost and greater speed, among others.

2.4. Case Study: First Case Study of the Use of AI in ADR (Mediation) to Resolve a Workplace Dispute

As early as 2019, an AI platform was used for the first time in an ADR case to reach a settlement (Hilborne, 2019). The parties had attempted a court-derived mediation in a case where a personal trainer was claiming £2,000 from a client for services rendered. Following a failed attempt at telephone mediation, professional mediator *Graham Ross*, an ODR expert, proposed using an AI platform to the parties involved in order to settle their dispute as quickly and efficiently as possible.

To do so, they used the *Smartsettle ONE* program, invented by *Ernest Thiessen* and developed by *ICan Systems* in *British Columbia*, based on an AI that, through algorithms that feed it, proposes a system of offers and counter-offers - identified by green and yellow flags - that prevents each party from sending proposals that will not be accepted by the other party, thus helping them to reach an agreement without "angering" or making the other party leave the negotiation platform and without revealing their secret proposals.

Thanks to this "robot ADR" or "robot mediator" (although in this case we would not call it a mediator because technically the mediator was still *Graham Ross*, who recommended it and controlled the procedure at all times) the parties were able to resolve a conflict that had not been resolved either by the court or by the previous mediation attempt and in record time, resolving a three-month conflict in less than an hour.

2.5. Hybrid Model Proposal

It is true that, as stated above, it is tempting for some to accept fully automated ADR procedures (carried out entirely by an AI) in & out the workplace. This is attractive and could be considered a good strategic option due to the novelty, speed, and cost reduction it represents, but, in our opinion, this would not be a genuine ADR. It would be more like a copy or a simulacrum of ADR. However, it should not be called ADR in the strict sense of the word, because it would lack the essential characteristics of Alternative Justice and the added value that it implies. AI is an invaluable and useful tool in ADR, but the humanity and integrity of an alternative justice procedure cannot be sacrificed in the name of efficiency. Being faster does not always mean being more efficient.

In order to guarantee that the use of AI in ADR is both legal and ethical, rules and control mechanisms are once again demanded which, for the moment, can only come from a human (the mediator, arbitrator, etc.), but also from extrajudicial conflict resolution bodies and institutions that must do everything to become more involved, and we call for this to be the case. Hence the importance of "human review" systems. AI control in ADR should be neutral, guaranteed, and permanent. Thus, the digital future of ADR is likely to move towards a "*Hybrid model*", in which AI and ADR professionals work in full collaboration (Gonzalo & Suñez, 2024)). This will require ensuring, firstly, that there is no digital divide between the parties and, secondly, respect for the essential principles of ADR, in particular, the acceptance by the parties of AI: autonomy of will and freedom of agreement.

IV. ADVANTAGES AND DISADVANTAGES OF USING AI IN ADRS APPLIED TO THE WORKPLACE

ADR/ODR are used today because experience with them has amply demonstrated their effectiveness as methods of conflict management. In other words, they are used for a purely practical reason: because they work (Brand, 2003). They are good in and of themselves; essentially, they offer a series of advantages that make them effective and practical as key tools for conflict management and resolution in all available matters, according to the different legal systems and cultures, promoting reconciliation, cooperation, and the strengthening of interpersonal and social relations; They also ensure the improvement and adaptation of alternative justice systems also in the new and current digital era (AA.VV., Palao *et al,* 2024). Can AI enhance the conflict management and resolution benefits of ADR in the workplace, or might its use otherwise be counterproductive?

This section aims to specify the most relevant points on the advantages and disadvantages of applying AI in ADR. In particular, in those most commonly used in the workplace, such as conciliation, arbitration and mediation. In fact, the application of AI in mediation (Ordelin Font, 2021) can work particularly well in developing and applying it in internal company functions, such as conflicts arising from labour relations (collective bargaining, etc.), conflicts with suppliers and customers, etc.

1. Advantages

AI offers great advantages, benefits, and opportunities, illuminating the ADR process through increased efficiency, cost reduction, and time savings. By automating repetitive tasks and administrative processes, AI frees up professionals involved in ADR to focus on more complex tasks, enhancing the overall efficiency and effectiveness of the ADR process (Delenz Lorieto, 2020). AI applied in ADRs provides important advantages in the management and resolution of conflicts in the workplace:

- **Efficiency:** AI streamlines and improves the efficiency of conflict management and resolution in the workplace, for example, through the automation of routine tasks and the analysis of large volumes of data in ADR. Thus, firstly, it has become clear how AI enhances the very advantages and essential characteristics of ADR, even turning them, thanks to the use of the aforementioned technology and AI, into faster dispute management and resolution procedures than they already are in comparison with traditional justice. In this sense, thanks to advances in AI, programmes have been developed to process large amounts of information, allowing data to be accessed, sorted, and systematized in such a way that they can be decisive for the development of legal and juridical strategies in ADR applied to the workplace.

- **Time (Speed):** In this way, new technologies, led by AI, by processing large volumes of information in record time, further accelerate the extrajudicial process of conflict management and resolution, enhancing one of the essential characteristics of ADR such as speed and, consequently, its efficiency. Hence, on the one hand, AI benefits and enhances everything that has to do with the essential temporal characteristics of ADR: speed, economy and time saving, generating even greater efficiency, cost reduction and considerable time savings.
- **Economy and global accessibility:** In addition, AI has the potential to ensure that, in the available areas of workplace disputes - with everything being done online and ODR being faster and cheaper (See table 2: comparison of costs between different ADRs and with Justice) - ADR/ODR itself is more accessible and affordable for those involved, allowing parties with more limited resources to participate in justice, in this case alternative justice, through ODR, and to obtain a fair and equitable resolution to their disputes.
- **Advanced data analytics:** In this way, the use of new technologies and assistive AI in ADR/ODR is of great help in accessing, analyzing, and obtaining data that can be decisive in ADR procedures to determine the strategy to follow in each case and to speed up the management and resolution of the conflict in the most appropriate and effective way for the parties.
- **Strategic reasons for conflicts resolutions:** AI is of great use in all kinds of strategic issues in every ADR: from the presentation and presentation of cases, the carrying out of predictive searches of what is to be found (conflict management and the design of strategies through predictive justice); the practice of tests or simulations of great utility in mediations and arbitrations through AI; its successful use in the different phases of alternative justice procedures (choice of the most appropriate ADR for the specific conflict raised in the workplace) In practice, AI is already being used in *Legal Research* or *search engines,* where AI has been providing invaluable support for some time now, both in the academic and research fields, advice and consultancy, practice, negotiations, mediations, arbitration, etc. Additionally, in the management

of conflicts and the design of strategies through the aforementioned *predictive justice* with platforms such as *Arbilex, Jurimetria,* among others and, in particular, the AI programs that assist in the selection of arbitrators, for example, *Intelligence Dispute Resolution Data, Arbitrator,* etc. (mentioned *above*, section II.). If AI can assist us here, any expenditure or investment in AI would be fully justified. So welcome AI and technology in ADR. We are still at a very early stage, but it will evolve as we move forward and, with the necessary control and guarantees, it can become a very beneficial tool for the extrajudicial practice of conflict management and resolution.

- **Small claims in the workplace:** In fact, in the near future it is expected to be quite common that, for small claims in the workplace itself, as a case strategy and for the purpose of reducing costs, an AI will be used to resolve a conflict rather than a procedure, institutional or ad hoc; or extrajudicial conflict management: conciliation, arbitration, mediation, etc. The current understanding from international perspectives is that technological assistance can be optimized when used for small claims (Ballesteros, 2021, 115). Resolving larger disputes over the internet is largely considered to be more challenging and that ODR is more beneficial for handling small repetitive claims. So, it is reasonable, possible and would be entirely appropriate depending on the strategy and legal advice applied to the case, provided, of course, that the parties are aware that they are using a pseudo ADR (it has become legally clear here that, at present -in accordance with international and domestic arbitration and mediation laws- it is far from possible to legally designate as ADR that which is carried out entirely by an AI (Gonzalo & Suñez, 2024) but they give their explicit consent to it. Consent and autonomy of will in ADR, and those out-of-court dispute resolution mechanisms that use its name, which remains the cornerstone also with new technologies and AI.

In conclusion, there is no doubt that the integration of AI in ADR applied to the workplace offers significant advantages in terms of efficiency, speed, sustainability, and facilitation of the work of ADR professionals and of the workers and users themselves who use these alternative mechanisms to manage and resolve their conflicts. However, as will be discussed below, it then goes on to show how in parallel it also projects disadvantages related to the lack of humanization, transparency, truthfulness, accountability, confidentiality, legality, possible bias in the algorithms used, in particular by AI, which could affect the impartiality of the ADR/ODR employed, along with various legal, ethical and privacy issues.

2. Disadvantages

The development of AI in different ADR systems also casts a number of challenges that need to be clarified applied in the workplace. Many of these relate to AI education and training, regulation, data privacy, data veracity and biases, transparency, and the complicated balance that this has to combine with the confidentiality of ADR, whose secrecy and reserved nature is one of the inherent characteristics of its institution.

- **Education & Liability:** as a starting point, the biggest challenge of AI in ADR is that everyone involved in ADR/ODR, from professionals to programmers to users, must understand how AI & the technology works, so they can determine whether to use it as a tool in a process ADR in the workplace. Education in AI and new technologies is a challenge for everyone, outside and inside the workplace, in the new era of AI in which we are immersed (AA.VV., *Inteligencia Artificial y Educación Superior,* 2024)
- **Costs barrier:** It cannot be ignored the fact that AI requires a significant financial investment: the purchase of equipment and materials, *software* licensing, servers, maintenance, etc. In this sense, as there is a disparity between the parties (users, mediators, arbitrators, etc.) in access to dispute resolution processes based on AI, it could give rise to an insurmountable issue of inequality, which has been called the digital divide (Alonso, Kothari & Rehman, 2018).
- **Sustainability and Environment.** AI imposes a paradigm shift in ADR practices, advocating for more sustainable and environmentally friendly methods. Practices such as electronic document use, reduced travel, and videoconferencing, supported by AI, contribute to greener ADR. In 2019, an important step was taken towards greener arbitration through the *Green Pledge*. In 2020, the *Campaign for Greener Arbitrations* proposed six action protocols - the Green Protocols- aimed at reducing the carbon footprint in arbitration by following good practices: requesting electronic documents instead of paper documents, avoiding unnecessary travel, maintaining electronic communications with the parties, and considering the possibility of holding private hearings via videoconferencing. These are practices and protocols that we advocate should be transferred to the rest of ADR. Depending on whether or not we make good use of ADR in out-of-court procedures, it can help us to achieve greener and more planet-friendly ADR, in line with the requirements of the SDGs, agenda 2030. All of this is in line with recent times where concern about the state of the environment and the consequences of climate

change has spread to the most responsible and committed ADR circles (AA. VV., 2020).

- **Acceptance of the use of AI in each chosen ADR/ODR in the workplace:** All of the above - training and education in new technologies and AI, understanding how they work, acquiring specialized AI equipment for use in ADR, sustainable and environmentally responsible ADR, etc. - would be of no use without the acceptance of the parties. Compliance with the use of AI in ADR procedures, at this point in time, may meet some resistance due to the lack of trust in AI by the parties involved in ADR/ODR. It is still relatively new, unregulated, and uncontrolled, and this poses a key obstacle- the acceptance and trust necessary for the adoption of AI in ADR in the workplace. Under the rule of the autonomy of will, agreement and pact that governs all *ADR* and *ODR*, it is possible, even advisable, to agree in each specific case on the use of the AI tools that we want to use in each procedure, how and when to do so, and even the prohibition of AI in the procedure. In conclusion, wherever ADR goes, with or without AI, we cannot afford to forget its origins. And the origin of ADR is none other than free will and freedom of agreement (Gonzalo & Suñez, 2024)
- **Data:** Data is the foundation on which AI is built. The use of data in ADR raises questions about consent, transparency, reliability, privacy, and data protection (Gastón Marcen, 2021). The right to work is particularly protected, not only by law (like *General Data Protection Regulation*, 2015), but also by the very discretion required in dealing with workplace conflicts. Have the data subjects given their conscious consent? Is it transparent? Where does the data the AI is fed come from and is it reliable? What is the minimum volume and variety of data for an AI to function efficiently and effectively? Ensuring the privacy and security of data in ADR proceedings is crucial to avoid breaches and protect sensitive information. Questions, too, about transparency and neutrality in ADR/ODR around the algorithms that underpin it: How can we ensure that the algorithms used in ADR/ODR for decision-making are neutral and unbiased? How can transparency in AI decision-making processes be ensured? From this, further questions arise about liability for decision-making in an AI-based ADR/ODR procedure: Who is responsible for planning procured by an AI algorithm? How are errors or incorrect decisions dealt with? How is legal liability determined in cases where AI decisions cause damage or harm? (Gonzalo & Suñez, 2024) In almost all ADR there is a lack of structured data. To effectively train and use AI algorithms, a sufficient amount of systematized and relevant data is required. However, in most ADRs, data can be scattered, disorganized and in different formats, making it difficult for AI systems to utilize it effectively. This is compounded by the lack of context

and human judgement. Given that, despite AI's analytical capabilities, lacking human judgement and contextual and cultural knowledge often required in ADR, its responses are far from being able to fill these critical gaps in dispute resolution (AA. VV., Ibañez, 2024). Hence, some decisions will require a broader assessment and a more flexible approach which AI may struggle to provide.

- **Privacy:** The use of AI involves the processing of large amounts of data that may be confidential, which may raise concerns about the privacy and confidentiality of sensitive information used in ADR proceedings, especially those relating to the workplace. It is crucial to ensure the privacy and security of this data to avoid breaches and to protect the confidentiality of the parties involved in appropriate ADR methods (Gonzalo & Barriga, 2016) Data privacy becomes a crucial concern, as the exchange of sensitive information in the context of ADR may expose parties to risks of privacy violations. It is essential to put in place robust data protection measures to ensure that confidential information is not misused or accessed by unauthorized third parties. There is a risk of data leakage, both their own and that of third parties, and the user may be unaware of it because they do not know how the *software,* they are using works. In reality, this risk exists and can occur with any technological system, but AI systems are even more opaque and obscure (García San José, 2021). They also provide a false sense of security in which the user may have the impression that no information is getting through or that information cannot get out of the system, but it does get out.
- **Neutrality and Bias:** Bias is inherent in everyone - humans and AI. Therefore, it is very likely that data can contain biases, errors, and omissions (deliberate or not). Certain data can be silenced while others overrepresented, leading to a consciously or unconsciously self-interested point of view prevailing. With such data, the responses of these AI systems will also contain these biases, these errors and, consequently, this discrimination (Gerards & Xenidis, 2020). These errors can sometimes be detected hence the importance of "human review and control" systems. A control which we insist should be neutral, guaranteed, and permanent. The need for permanent control and review "by a human party" to which Altman alluded in the speech to the US Congress in May 2023. Some examples of algorithmic biases have been detected by companies such as *Amazon,* which used an algorithm to hire employees and found that due to certain biases in its database, it tended to favor men, thus harming the hiring of women and aggravating inequality by introducing

this gender bias. Interestingly, gender bias is one of the most prevalent biases in operating systems, but isn't it in society? Similarly, racial bias has also led to several situations of discrimination caused by AI. Another example, of racial bias, comes from the US *hardware* system itself, which had an algorithm it used in hospitals to predict which patients would need more technical assistance. Here too, it was found to be biased and heavily favored the white population. In conclusion, there are multiple examples of bias in human - natural - intelligence being transferred, consciously or unconsciously, to AI (Rivas Vallejo, 2022).

Moreover, there is an additional risk in the case of algorithms, which is that if the data is biased, algorithms tend to magnify it. This is true by the very mechanism of algorithms as they end up learning from their own decisions. Then, if they learn solutions that are biased, that bias feeds back and is magnified in the operating system itself. This is obviously a challenge for the veracity of the data. There is a certain risk, then, if there is no control, not only of silencing data, but also of enhancing and magnifying biases because AI systems are alive. Intelligence- or natural language-based media have already shared biased, false, and outdated information, but they do so with such authority that it appears to be true. Therefore, one must be very skeptical of the answers they give us.

- **Confidentiality:** Confidentiality is one of the most important reasons why parties choose ADRs in the workplace. Users of ADR methods primarily do so because of the advantages it offers over the court system, with confidentiality being a key benefit (Gonzalo and Barriga, 2016). Thus, the opacity of *ADR* and *ODR,* stemming from their confidential nature, presents a significant challenge for AI. It should not be forgotten that the foundation of AI is data. However, what would confidentiality—and therefore the absence of data—mean for the generation of reliable AI in ADR, whose essence and *raison d'être*, for many practitioners, is confidentiality? This raises critical questions: Where does the data that has fed the AI come from? Why is this data considered more valid than other data that has been ignored or overlooked? These are fundamental issues that need to be addressed to ensure the integrity and reliability of AI in the context of confidential dispute resolution processes. There are several reasons to be cautious here, many of which (noted by Gonzalo & Suñez, 2024) are beyond the scope of this study but could initiate another line of research.
- **Legal Accountability:** Determining who is responsible when IA makes mistakes can be a challenge, especially if a clear allocation of responsibility has

not been established in prior agreements. This raises a number of questions about liability arising from the use of new technologies and AI in ADR. Who is liable in case of mistakes or incorrect decisions made by AI systems? How is liability allocated in an environment where both humans and AI algorithms are involved? The new technologies and AI sector is likely to be one of the sectors that will see the most changes and discussions regarding liability issues. Legal liability in case of errors or malfunctions of AI has to be considered in alternative dispute management and resolution procedures. In fact, we already have examples of this with other technologies. In 2016, in Colombia, the taxi company *Cotech S.A.* filed a lawsuit against *Uber Technologies Inc. and Uber Colombia S.A.S.* for acts of unfair competition (UBER case, 2016). The process ended on 20 December 2019, with a judgement declaring that the defendant companies had committed acts of unfair competition by diverting customers and ordering the immediate cessation of the *Uber* application and its services in the Colombian territory. However, just ten days later, *Uber* sent the Colombian state a *Notice of Dispute*, invoking the application of the dispute resolution clause included in the *Free Trade Agreement* (FTA) between Colombia and the US, to try to reach an amicable agreement with the Colombian government. If a mutually satisfactory agreement was not reached within six months, *Uber* threatened to initiate investment arbitration to claim the estimated US$250 million in damages. In the end, the deal was concluded in record time, allowing *Uber* to continue operating (*Global Arbitration Review*, 2020). We will need to pay close attention to normative regulations on digital risk prevention, civil liability, and data protection, as well as to the specialized doctrine in this field (Gastón, 2021).

- **Flexibility** is another key principle of ADR. This flexibility can be compromised by the rigidity of IA & new technologies. Combining the efficiency of AI with human sensitivity, creativity, and intrinsic values can lead to higher, safer, more sophisticated, faster, and more effective conflict management and resolution. We must not lag behind in this respect. We are talking about justice, alternative justice, but justice, nonetheless. It is not about machines replacing humans, but about them cooperating and collaborating with each other. The collaboration between humans and AI, leveraging the strengths of both, can elevate conflict management and resolution to an unprecedented level of effectiveness, security, reliability, and success (Antón, 2022).

3. Pros and Cons of Applying AI in Extra-Judicial Methods of Conflict Management and Resolution in the Workplace

Table 3. Pros and cons of applying AI in extra-judicial methods of conflict management and resolution in the workplace.

Benefits of AI applied to ADR (essentially mediation) in the workplace.	Efficiency: AI systems can process large amounts of data quickly, which speeds up the ADR process even more. In this case, AI applied to ADR enhances ADR's own characteristics: making it even faster than it already is.
	Time: If disputes handled by ADR are already much faster than those handled by a court of law, the speed is further increased by the use of AI (Data: See Table 2). Speed which is highly desirable to prevent conflict or pre-conflict situations from escalating and to resolve conflicts in the workplace,
	Economy: ADRs is less expensive than court proceedings in all countries around the world. Economy which also translates into considerable cost and time savings through ADR in the workplace (See Table 1)
	Global accessibility: AI-supported mediation can be accessible anytime and anywhere for workers, regardless of whether they are in an international environment (distant and different countries or workplaces) or simply in the same workplace but prefer to resolve their differences as quickly as possible. Ultimately, workplace conflict management and resolution through ADR, especially conciliation and mediation, facilitates conflict resolution without the need for physical meetings.
	Advanced data analytics: AI can help identify patterns and trends in disputes, enabling informed decision-making in the workplace.
	Strategic reasons: the systematization, analysis and understanding of all the data and documents related to an ADR in order to develop better strategies for each case in the workplace. systematizing, generating ideas and assisting in the preparation of the ADR, analyzing texts, assisting, and helping with the presentation of evidence, anticipating and drafting agreements, etc.).
	IA for the small claims in the workplace: The current understanding from international perspectives is that technological assistance can be optimized when used for small claims

continued on following page

Table 3. Continued

Disadvantages of AI applied to ADR (essentially mediation) in the workplace.	**Lack of personal contact:** e-mediation lacks direct human contact, which can affect empathy and understanding between the parties. **Education & Liability:** All parties involved in the resolution of the conflict (parties, professionals, and company) must understand how AI works, so they can determine whether to use it as a tool in a process ADR in the workplace. **Costs barrier:** Digital divide. **Sustainability and Environment.** AI needs a lot of energy to be generated and is expensive for the environment. It advocates for ADRs more sustainable and environmentally friendly methods in the workplace. **Specific acceptance of the use of AI in each chosen ADR/ODR in the workplace:** AI still relatively new, unregulated, and uncontrolled, and this poses a key obstacle- the acceptance and trust necessary for the adoption of AI in ADR in the workplace. **Data &Technical issues:** we rely on technology, and any technical glitches can hinder the mediation process in the workplace. **Privacy concerns/Confidentiality:** AI handles confidential data, which raises privacy and security issues. **Legal Accountability:** Determining who is responsible when IA makes mistakes can be a challenge, especially if a clear allocation of responsibility has not been established in prior agreements or specifics protocols in the workplace. **Flexibility**, as another key principle of ADR, which makes it the most flexible and tailored dispute management and resolution mechanism in the workplace, may be compromised in the face of the robotic rigidity of new technologies and AI. However, combining the efficiency of new technologies with the sensitivity, creativity, and intrinsically human values of ADR can lead to higher, safer, more sophisticated, faster, and more effective rates of alternative dispute management and resolution in the workplace.

Note: Own elaboration (May/July 2024)

V. CONCLUSION

The strategic application of AI in ADR/ODR to resolve workplace disputes can transform the way organizations deal with internal conflicts. In order to do this, it is crucial to balance IA automation with human empathy and to ensure transparency in ADR procedures (especially negotiation, conciliation, arbitration, and mediation, which are the most commonly used extra-judicial conflict resolution systems in the workplace, especially mediation). AI does not replace professional negotiators, conciliators, mediators and arbitrators specialized in workplace disputes, but rather empowers them to achieve more effective and fair solutions.

The convergence between AI and out-of-court dispute management and resolution systems has cast both benefits and disadvantages applied in the workplace. On the one hand, there is no doubt that the integration of AI in ADR applied to the workplace offers significant advantages in terms of efficiency, speed, sustainability, and facilitation of the work of ADR professionals and of the workers and users themselves who use these alternative mechanisms to manage and resolve their conflicts. However, on the other hand, it then goes on to show how in parallel it also projects disadvantages related to the lack of humanization, transparency, truthfulness, accountability, confidentiality, legality, possible bias in the algorithms used, in particular by AI, which could affect the impartiality of the ADR/ODR employed, along with various legal, ethical and privacy issues.

The responsible implementation of AI in ADR requires a continued balance between technological efficiency and the preservation of the fundamental principles of the ADR Institutions themselves: voluntariness, neutrality, confidentiality, speed, appropriateness, security, fairness, and equity. The critical analysis here of the intersection between AI and ADR raises the need for clear regulatory frameworks to address these issues, ensuring fairness and transparency in the process of conflict management and resolution, as well as the protection of the rights of the parties involved in AI-based ADR processes, ensuring that AI is used appropriately, fairly, and equitably in the workplace. A combination of continuous regulatory developments and best practices in this area will be essential to make the most of the opportunities of AI and minimizing its challenges in the quest for a more accessible and effective alternative justice.

The digital future of ADR in the workplace is expected to evolve towards a *Hybrid Model* in which AI and ADR professionals work in full collaboration. This requires ensuring, firstly, that there is no digital divide between the parties, and secondly, that the essential principles of ADR are respected, particularly the parties' acceptance of AI, the autonomy of will, and the freedom of contract. Thus, the hybrid approach combining human and artificial intelligence is a winning strategy in ADR, provided that equality in access, use, and training in new technologies is guaranteed and unequivocally accepted by the parties in the workplace. In conclusion, AI should not operate alone in ADR. The human factor is essential to ensure that new technologies benefit alternative, and often more appropriate, systems of justice, especially in its application in the workplace.

REFERENCES

Acevedo Rehbein, A. (19/02/2019), Inteligencia artificial en el arbitraje internacional: de la predicción legal a los laudos emitidos por robots | Garrigues.

Alonso, C., Kothari, S., & Rehman, S. (2020). How artificial intelligence could widen the gap between rich and poor nations. IMF Blog, 2.

Alzate, R., & Vázquez, E. (2014). *Resolución de disputas en línea (RDL). Las claves de la mediación en línea*. Reus S.A.

Antón Juárez, I. (2021, March). *Marketplaces* que personalizan precios a través del Big Data y de los Algoritmos: ¿Esta práctica es legal en atención al Derecho de la Competencia Europeo? *Cuadernos de Derecho Transnacional*, 13(1), 42. DOI: 10.20318/cdt.2021.5951

Ballesteros, T. (2021). International Perspectives on Online Dispute Resolution in the E-Commerce Landscape. *International Journal of Online Dispute Resolution*, 2(2), 87. DOI: 10.5553/IJODR/235250022021008002002

Brand, N. (2003). *How ADR works*. American Bar Association Committee on Alternative Dispute Resolution.

Cárdenas Herrera, J. (2024), El impacto de la Inteligencia Artificial en la investigación, https://vertice.cpd.ua.es/290670|http://hdl.handle.net/10045/141247

Conforti, F. (2020), "A vueltas con las diferencias entre una videoconferencia y una mediación online", *Revista Jurídica SEPIN*.https://blog.sepin.es/2020/11/videoconferencia-mediacion-online-diferencias/5 de noviembre de 2020

Delenz Lorieto, N. (7 de octubre de 2020), "La inteligencia artificial en el arbitraje internacional", available at La inteligencia artificial en el arbitraje internacional — Guardiana.

Fisher, R., Ury, W., & Patton, B. (2011). *Getting to Yes: Negotiating Agreement Without Giving In*. Penguin.

García San José, D. (2021, March). Implicaciones jurídicas y bioéticas de la Inteligencia Artificial (IA). Especial consideración al marco normativo internacional. *Cuadernos de Derecho Transnacional*, 13(1), 255–276. DOI: 10.20318/cdt.2021.5959

Gastón Marcen, A. (2021, October). El Reglamento general de Protección de Datos como modelo de las recientes propuestas de legislación digital europea. *Cuadernos de Derecho Transnacional*, 13(2), 209–232. DOI: 10.20318/cdt.2021.6256

Gerards & Xenidis. (3 December 2020), "Algorithmic discrimination in Europe: Challenges and Opportunities for EU equality law", *European Futures.* Available at: https://www.europeanfutures.ed.ac.uk/algorithmic-discrimination-in-europe-challenges-and-opportunities-for-eu-equa

Gómez Valenzuela, E. (20/02/2023). *Resolución Judicial y Extrajudicial de controversias en la contratación electrónica,* Colex, A Coruña, pp. 208.

Gonzalo, M., & Barriga, K. (2016). "El acuerdo de confidencialidad en el arbitraje", y "El acuerdo de confidencialidad en la mediación". In *Sánchez García, A. et al. (coord.), Tipología contractual de los mecanismos alternativos de solución de conflictos* (pp. 113–137). Tirant lo Blanch.

Gonzalo Quiroga, M. (2022), "Covid-19, innovación y tecnología en la e-justicia alternativa: ¿algo hemos aprendido?", en Fariña Rivera, F. *et al.* (coord.), *Reflexiones mediadoras en la post pandemia*, Santiago de Compostela, ed. CUEMYC/USC, pp. 184-206.

Gonzalo Quiroga, M. (2023). La inteligencia artificial en el arbitraje internacional 2.0. Oportunidades y desafíos en un futuro que ya es presente. *Cuadernos de Derecho Transnacional*, 15(2), 516–550. DOI: 10.20318/cdt.2023.8067

Gonzalo Quiroga, M., & Suñez Tejera, Y. (2024). *Innovación y resolución de conflictos: La intersección entre las nuevas tecnologías, la Inteligencia Artificial y los Métodos Alternativos.* Ediciones ONBC.

Hilborne, N. (febrero 2019), Robot mediator settles first ever court case - Legal Futures

Lewicki, R. J., Saunders, D. M., & Barry, B. (2015). *Negotiation: Readings, Exercises, and Cases.* McGraw-Hill Education.

Losada Crespo, B., & Briz Clariget, M.J. (2024), "La gestión de conflictos laborales. Habilidades necesarias para el mediador laboral". *Revista de Derecho (Universidad Católica Dámaso A. Larrañaga, Facultad de Derecho)*, (29), e3694. Epub 01 de junio de 2024.https://doi.org/DOI: 10.22235/rd29.3694

Méndez Zamora, E. (13/06/2019), "La inteligencia artificial en el arbitraje internacional", available at LexLatin | La inteligencia artificial en el arbitraje internacional

Moore, C. W. (2014). *The Mediation Process: Practical Strategies for Resolving Conflict.* Jossey-Bass.

Ordelin Font, J. L. (diciembre de 2021) "El uso de la inteligencia artificial en la mediación: ¿Quimera o realidad?", *Revista IUS,* Vol. 15, pp. 357-382.

Pérez Tortosa, F. (2022), "Personas con discapacidad intelectual y mediación: especial referencia a la mediación electrónica", available at https://riuma.uma.es/xmlui/handle/10630/24516?show=full

Rogers, C. A. (2019), "*Arbitrator Intelligence: From Intuition to Data in Arbitrator Appointments*", *New York Dispute Resolution Lawyer,* vol. 11 No.2, available at https://papers.ssrn.com/sol3/papers.cfm?abstract_id=3113800

Vida Fernández, J. (2022, March). La gobernanza de los riesgos digitales: Desafíos y avances en la regulación de la inteligencia artificial. *Cuadernos de Derecho Transnacional*, 14(1), 489–503. DOI: 10.20318/cdt.2022.6695

ADDITIONAL READING

AI mediation case study: (March 2019). https://metodosderesoluciondeconflictos.wordpress.com/2019/03/29/se-resuelve-un-caso-de-mediacion-usando-inteligencia-artificial-por-primera-vez/#

Data from the Observatorio de Recursos Humanos de España. (2022/2023) https://www.observatoriorh.com/orh-posts/la-mediacion

Data from web analytics company Similarweb, available at https://www.reuters.com/technology/chatgpt-sets-record-fastest-growing-user-base-analyst-note-2023-02-01/

Energy Arbitration Survey (2022), available at 2022 Energy Arbitration Survey - School of International Arbitration (qmul.ac.uk); https://arbitration.qmul.ac.uk/media/arbitration/docs/Future-of-International-Energy-Arbitration-Survey-Report.pdf

APPENDIX

- Arbitrator Intelligence: for the appointment of arbitrators: https://arbitratorintelligence.com/.
- Dispute Resolution Data: software for application in any out-of-court dispute resolution method, especially arbitration and mediation: Available at https://www.disputeresolutiondata.com/. For further information, see https://datadog.nationbuilder.com/drd_wins_gar.
- NextLevel Mediation: a company that uses AI and new technologies to mediate disputes for clients: https://nextlevelmediation.com/
- Finboot: blockchain company partnering with LCAM (London Chamber of Arbitration and Mediation) to create a mediation platform using blockchain technology: https://www.finboot.com/.
- Other more general legal instruments that are also very useful in ADR/ADR proceedings, such as:
  - Jurimetria: https://jurimetria.laleynext.es/content/Inicio.aspx.
  - Luminance: Available at https://www.luminance.com/.
  - Arbilex: https://www.arbilex.co/.
  - eBrevia: https://www.dfinsolutions.com/products/ebrevia.

Chapter 6
Emerging Psychosocial Risks in the Digital Age:
Education in Its Dual Role as an Affected Sector and Control Tool

Jesus Barrena-Martinez
https://orcid.org/0000-0002-5501-742X
Universidad de Cadiz, Spain

Maria-Jose Foncubierta-Rodriguez
https://orcid.org/0000-0003-3231-5261
Universidad de Cadiz, Spain

José Luis Gilabert Villard
https://orcid.org/0000-0001-9323-8138
Universidad de Cadiz, Spain

ABSTRACT

The process of digital transformation in which we live has generated a significant number of efficiency-related advantages, but, at the same time, has brought with it the emergence of different psychosocial risks that affect people's health in the workplace context. The purpose of this chapter is dual. On the one hand, to reflect and structure these emerging risks of a psychosocial nature, which are being experienced by workers; on the other, to provide training measures at the micro level to assist the managers of the organizations in the control of these risks, with a view to their elimination or maximum possible reduction.

DOI: 10.4018/979-8-3693-6289-1.ch006

1. INTRODUCTION

In the digital age, technological transformation has permeated all aspects of society, including the workplace and educational dynamics (Hashim et al. 2022). This process, although it has brought multiple benefits, has also led to a number of emerging psychosocial risks affecting both individuals and organizations. In this context, education plays a twofold crucial role: it is a sector significantly affected by these risks and, in turn, a potentially powerful tool for mitigating them.

This work addresses the issue of emerging psychosocial risks in the digital age, focusing on education as a vulnerable sector to these risks as a possible solution to address them. The first section contextualizes the importance of this study within the global sustainability goals, specifically in relation to the United Nations Sustainable Development Goals (SDGs), such as SDG-3 (Health and Welfare) and SDG-8 (Dignity Work and Economic Growth). Macroeconomic data are analysed and the call for action by supranational bodies is emphasized to address these challenges.

The second section explores the emerging psychosocial risks arising from digitization, highlighting the pressure and stress that workers suffer, in the educational sector. This part of the work disaggregates how digitization affects the working environment, generating new fears and challenges for teachers, a collective especially vulnerable to these changes.

The third section focuses on the promotion of a healthy working environment, with an emphasis on the psychosocial and mental health of workers. It is argued that a happier and healthier teacher is not only more productive, but also contributes positively to the educational environment and student development.

In the fourth section, several preventive measures for psychosocial risks applicable to organizations are presented, regardless of the sector of activity. These measures are designed to address and mitigate various factors that can affect employees' mental health and well-being, thereby contributing to the creation of healthier and more productive work environments.

The fifth section of the work presents concrete proposals for using education as a solution to these psychosocial risks. Strategies are proposed to implement support and training programmes to help teachers better manage the stress and pressure associated with digitization.

Finally, the last section proposes a conceptual model for a future research agenda. Key areas where deeper study of psychosocial risks in the digital age is needed are suggested and the importance of developing evidence-based policies and practices for improving the psycho-social health of workers in the educational sector is highlighted.

This work is relevant because it not only identifies and analyzes emerging psychosocial risks in the digital age, but also provides practical solutions and a framework for future research, thereby contributing to the well-being of workers and the advancement of global sustainability goals.

2. SUSTAINABILITY AS A GLOBAL GOAL. UN SDGS: SDG-3 AND SDG-8. ECONOMIC DATA

2.1. The Call of Supranational Agencies

Promoting the health and well-being of enterprise workers and inclusive and sustainable economic growth, employment and decent work for all are goals pursued by the UN in Agenda 2030, specifically addressed in the SDGs 3 and 8 (United Nations, 2023), and supported by other supranational agencies such as the ILO and the EU.

All of them are concerned about the crisis that the world is experiencing and which is causing the deterioration of the economic conditions of many territories, dragging their workers to informal employment, as inequalities between developed and developing countries increase.

With regard to people's health, the United Nations continues to have an important challenge, in fulfilling SDG-3, to alleviate financial difficulties that reduce the possibilities of health protection and guarantees. In this regard, it is highlighted that a high percentage of workers spend much of their family budget on direct health payments, reaching 10% of the family budget by 2023, pushing many of them into extreme poverty (Department of Economic and Social Affairs, UN, 2023, p. 19).

The ILO and WHO guidelines emphasize that safe and healthy working environments can contribute to improving the physical and mental health of workers. In many cases, mental health is underestimated, lacks resources and is left with interest in physical health (International Labour Organization ILO, 2023). There are psychosocial risk factors in working environments with decent work deficits, as well as in decent jobs. For this reason, companies must be alert to changes in the world of work that may create new risks of a psychosocial nature or increase existing ones.

Health and safety at work are relevantly covered in the Action Plan of the European Pillar of Social Rights, adopted at the 2021 Lisbon Social Summit. As part of it, the Commission presented a new EU strategic framework for health and safety at work 2021-2027, which focuses on anticipating and managing changes in the new world of work, improving the prevention of accidents and diseases at work and increasing preparedness for possible future health crises. The Commission will also review the Directives on the workplace and on equipment that includes display displays (European Parliament, 2023).

The European Parliament believes that employment should be adapted to the capacities and needs of people, and not vice versa, and that work environments should pay greater attention to the specific needs of vulnerable workers. In addition, it has requested the Commission to investigate emerging risks that are not yet covered by current legislation, such as exposure to nanoparticles, stress, occupational exhaustion and violence and harassment in the workplace (European Parliament, 2023).

With regard to the use of digital technologies, on 5 July 2022, the European Parliament adopted a resolution on mental health in the digital working environment, recognizing the impact of the COVID-19 pandemic on the organization of work and on the mental health of employees. In this resolution, Parliament calls on the Commission to propose legislative initiatives to manage psychosocial risks and promote well-being at work, as well as to present a mental health strategy for the Union and a European care strategy. (European Parliament, 2023).

Also, on 13 March 2024, the European Parliament has ratified the first law on artificial intelligence (AI), which will try to limit the dangers of this technology without jeopardising innovation and guaranteeing the fundamental rights of all people, including women workers. AI systems may contain elements and techniques that enhance the socio-economic benefits for companies, reduce their negative outsourcing and increase the well-being of workers, but can also lead to new risks or negative health and safety consequences for workers.

The European Agency for Safety and Health at Work (EU-OSHA), through its European Risk Observatory, continues to monitor and forecast new and emerging risks with a view to enabling companies to take preventive measures. The 2023-2025 campaign is about raising awareness, in particular, about the impact of new technologies on work and the challenges and opportunities that arise in relation to health and safety at work (EU-OSHA, 2018).

In this regard, public health systems can play an important role as allies and through proper management of human resources. They can increase their investment in preventive actions, including by reviewing occupational risk management policies, including psychosocial ones, protecting and promoting standards aimed at workers to detect risks, supporting the reintegration of people discharged from work due to illness, and tackling discrimination. The involvement of workers and social actors, leadership, funding, rights, integration and inclusion are some of the key factors in creating an enabling environment for addressing health and safety at work.

According to The Conference Board (2023), based on 2023 data from the International Labour Organization (2024), as can be seen in Figure 1, low levels of productivity persist in many territories, which are leading to the existence of so-called "poor workers", with the need for governments, and supranational agencies to place their emphasis on improving it in order to increase wages and be able to fight hunger, promote decent work and drive sustainable economic growth, as set out by the UN in SDG-8.

Figure 1. Growth of GDP, total hours worked, and GDP per hour worked by major region, 2011–2023 (percent change)

	Mature Economies	United States	Japan	Germany	United Kingdom	France	EU-14	EU-13	EU-27
				Growth of GDP per Hour Worked					
2000-2007	2.1	2.2	1.5	1.5	1.9	1.5	1.2	5.0	1.8
2011-2019	1.0	0.6	0.9	1.0	0.5	0.8	0.7	2.8	1.1
2020	2.0	4.0	-1.4	1.0	-0.6	0.5	1.5	0.4	1.0
2021	1.4	1.4	2.0	0.9	0.9	-1.5	-0.4	2.1	0.1
2022	-0.1	-1.1	0.8	0.4	0.4	-1.6	-0.1	2.7	0.6
2023 (Forecast)	0.4	-0.7	2.3	-0.3	-0.1	-0.1	-0.2	0.5	0.0
				Growth of Total Hours Worked					
2000-2007	0.6	0.5	-0.1	0.0	0.7	0.6	1.0	-0.2	0.7
2011-2019	0.8	1.6	0.0	0.7	1.5	0.5	0.5	0.4	0.5
2020	-6.1	-6.5	-3.0	-4.6	-10.5	-8.2	-7.9	-3.8	-6.9
2021	4.0	4.5	0.2	1.7	6.6	8.4	5.5	4.1	5.2
2022	2.8	3.2	0.3	1.4	3.6	4.3	3.4	1.4	2.9
2023 (Forecast)	0.4	1.4	-1.6	0.4	-0.1	0.6	0.7	-0.2	0.5
				Growth of Real GDP					
2000-2007	2.7	2.7	1.4	1.5	2.6	2.1	2.2	4.8	2.5
2011-2019	1.9	2.2	0.9	1.7	2.0	1.4	1.2	3.2	1.5
2020	-4.3	-2.8	-4.3	-3.7	-11.0	-7.8	-6.5	-3.4	-6.0
2021	5.4	5.9	2.1	2.6	7.6	6.8	5.1	6.3	5.3
2022	2.7	2.1	1.0	1.8	4.1	2.6	3.3	4.2	3.4
2023 (Forecast)	0.7	0.7	0.7	0.1	-0.2	0.5	0.5	0.3	0.5

Note. From Total Economy Database™ Summary Tables & Charts April 2023 (p. 6), in Global Productivity Brief 2023, by The Conference Board, March 2023. Copyright 2023 by The Conference Board.

Among the causes of low productivity are the problems of inequality, diversity and inclusion in the labour market (particularly with regard to the gender pay gap), temporality and informality in employment. Another source of low productivity is poor working conditions, as well as the existence of unsafe working environments.

It has been observed that the average total number of hours worked has increased in countries following the COVID-19 pandemic, owing to the shortage of skilled labour in some sectors. Workers who have returned to their jobs work longer hours, in some cases due to the increased duration of sick leave, which has a negative impact on productivity levels.

Similarly, the reversal of the population pyramid, the shortage of skilled labour or the low wages in certain sectors, the difficulties of finding housing for the working population, which hampers geographical mobility, are also causing imbalances in the labour market. Some of these imbalances could be corrected by improved working conditions and increased productivity, as well as by a more equitable distribution of employment opportunities among areas with a severe surplus labour force.

There is a slowing process of growth in aggregate labour productivity, despite technological advances, especially in areas such as data aggregation and artificial intelligence.

Technologies can help to a more just, peaceful and equitable world, through new forms and models of work, by supporting and accelerating the achievement of the SDGs, the 3rd and 8th, by ensuring a healthy life and promoting well-being for all at all ages, as well as promoting inclusive and sustainable economic growth, employment and decent work for all.

However, technologies are also having negative effects in many areas. The loss of jobs due to process automation and robotization is being confirmed, especially significant in low- and middle-skilled jobs, which are the majority in the Western labour markets (Acemoglu & Restrepo, 2017; Brynjolfsson & McAfee, 2011).

According to PwC's report (2024) of the 27th Global Annual Survey of CEOs, one in four surveyed CEOs expects to reduce their company's staffing by 5% or more over the next year, as seen in Figure 2, attributing this reduction to the implementation of Generative Artificial Intelligence.

Figure 2. Question: To what extent will generative AI impact headcount in your company in the next 12 months?

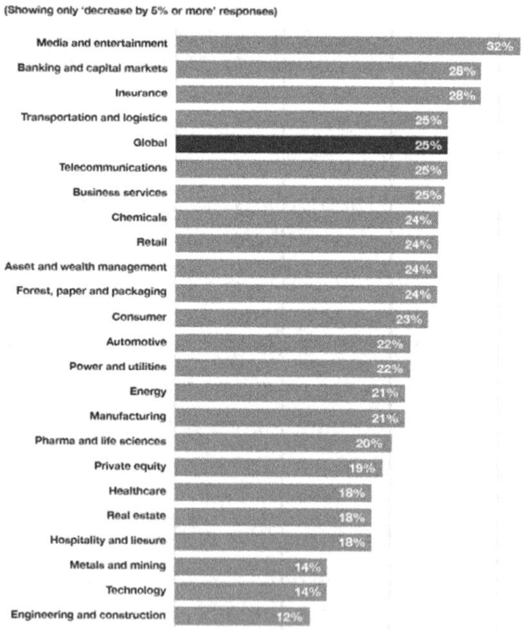

Note. From PwC's 27th Annual Global CEO Survey: Thriving in an age of continuous reinvention (p. 13), by PwC, 2024. Copyright 2024 by PwC.

According to the World Economic Forum's Future of Labour Report (2023), digitization is projected to eliminate around 85 million jobs worldwide between 2020 and 2025. At the same time, however, approximately 97 million new jobs will be created, as a result of the new division of work between humans, machines and algorithms.

Research by the US consultancy McKinsey Global Institute predicts that by 2030, 11.8 million workers in the United States will have to change jobs, as can be seen in Figure 3; not because they want to, but because they will be forced to do so; nine million people will need to completely reinvent themselves and look for a new job in a new sector.

Employees with lower wages are expected to be the most affected by these changes. According to McKinsey analysis, people with lower wages are up to 14 times more likely to have to change jobs before 2030 (McKinsey Global Institute, 2023). As can be seen in Figure 3, researchers point out that artificial intelligence could improve health care, STEM, and construction roles, while demand for office support and customer service roles could decrease. Artificial intelligence could relocate low-wage workers to better-paid jobs, depending on the capacity of states and companies to train the most vulnerable workers.

Figure 3. Estimated future US job growth by occupational category.

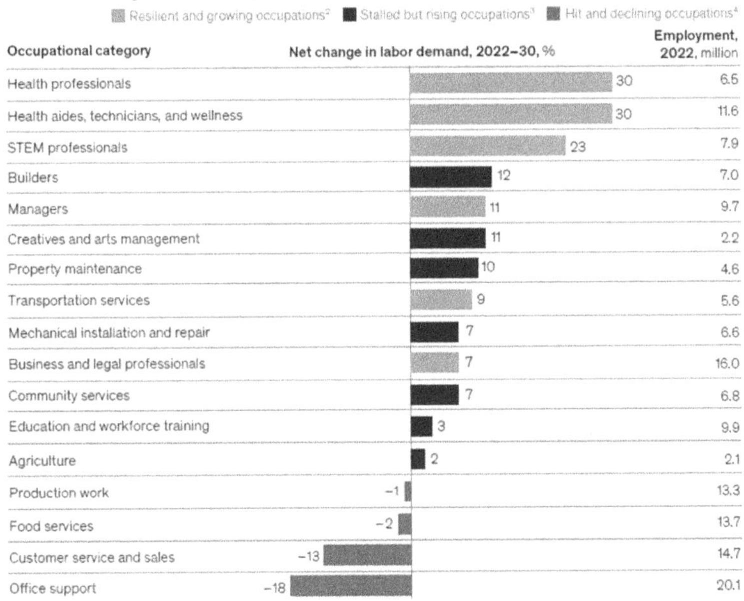

Note. From Generative AI and the future of work (p. 9), by McKinsey Global Institute, July 2023. Copyright 2023 by McKinsey Global Institute.

Based on ILO employment statistics and the report of the "Future of Employment Survey 2023" by the World Economic Forum (2023, p.31), 83 million jobs will be destroyed, with jobs mostly affected by those whose tasks are likely to be automated, not only by robots, but by AI, such as bank boxes, postal services, administrative secretaries, officers, accounting, statistics, archives and documentation, etc., as shown in Figure 4.

This new context will lead to a more skill-based labour market, in which companies will have to place greater emphasis on recruitment and human resources selection processes, valuing workers' technological skills as much or more than their academic level.

Another factor that hinders the achievement of SDG-8 is the so-called "digital divide," an inherent issue in the information society that continues to require an in-depth analysis to detect the elements that hinder and exclude certain people and/or groups from ICT (Pérez Alonso & Gadea Peiró, 2021, p. 4). The concept of the "digital divide" is not entirely new; we refer to "digital divide" when we talk about inequalities in the use of digital technologies. The terms "information rich" and "information poor" were popular in the late 1980s and early 1990s.

Figure 4 Top roles ordered by the largest net jobs reduction, calculated based on ILO Occupation Employment statistics and growth reported by organizations surveyed

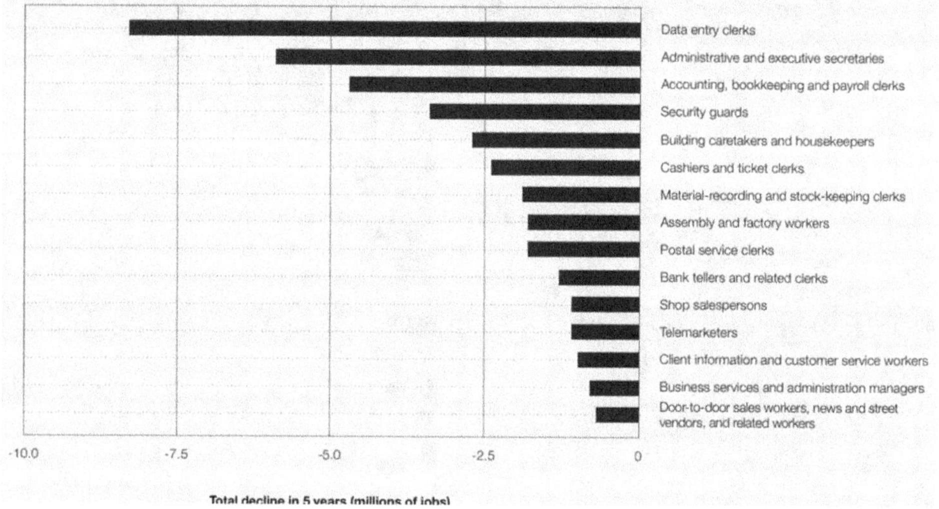

Note. From Future of Jobs Survey 2023 (p. 31), by World Economic Forum, May 2023. Copyright 2023 by the World Economic Forum.

In the European context, studies have shown that the digital divide is influenced by various socio-demographic factors. Digitalization can be considered a new form of social exclusion and is clearly related to factors such as education, economic level, region, age, and is notably marked by gender. This analysis is crucial for developing policies and measures that promote digital inclusion and reduce existing disparities.

Digital inequalities are changing, moving from being an issue of access to also encompassing the intensity, frequency, and purpose of Internet use (Elena-Bucea et al., 2021). In the European Union, the key factors driving the digital divide in e-services are mainly education and age, while in the use of social networks, the main factor is age (Elena-Bucea et al., 2021).

While the use of information and communication technologies (ICT) in households has increased worldwide in recent years, a digital divide still persists between those who use them and those who do not, which is more pronounced in developing countries. Some of the reasons justifying social stratification both nationally and internationally are motivated by differences in (Afzal et al., 2023; INE, 2023; ITU, 2023; Thompson, 2024):

- Ownership of digital tools (computers, mobiles, etc.).
- Access to information technology - in terms of infrastructure and Internet connectivity (including broadband penetration), especially in rural areas.
- Mobile phone subscriptions and ICT affordability (service prices).
- Computer skills and knowledge needed to participate in the information society.
- Interest in what the information society can offer (resistance to adapting to technological changes).

Providing widespread Internet connectivity helps certain populations thrive by helping them acquire the essential technological knowledge needed to succeed in the digital economy (Pearson, 2002). According to the ITU (2023), Internet use remains closely linked to a country's level of development. In 2020, nine out of ten people in high-income countries used the Internet. In 2023, the proportion increased to 93 percent, nearing universality. In low-income countries, 27 percent of the population uses the Internet, compared to 24 percent in 2022. This gap of 66 percentage points reflects the breadth of the digital divide between high- and low-income countries and regions.

The "Digital 2024 Global Overview Report", published in partnership between We Are Social and Meltwater based on the latest data from the ITU, GSMA Intelligence, Eurostat, and various local government agencies, indicates that Internet users grew by 1.8 percent in 2023, with 97 million new users bringing the global total to 5.35 billion at the start of 2024. However, more than 2.7 billion people remain unconnected worldwide, with more than 680 million of the world's "unconnected" living in India alone, as shown in Figure 5 (Thompson, 2024).

Figure 5. Unconnected populations. Countries and territories with the largest unconnected populations and lowest levels of Internet adoption in January 2024.

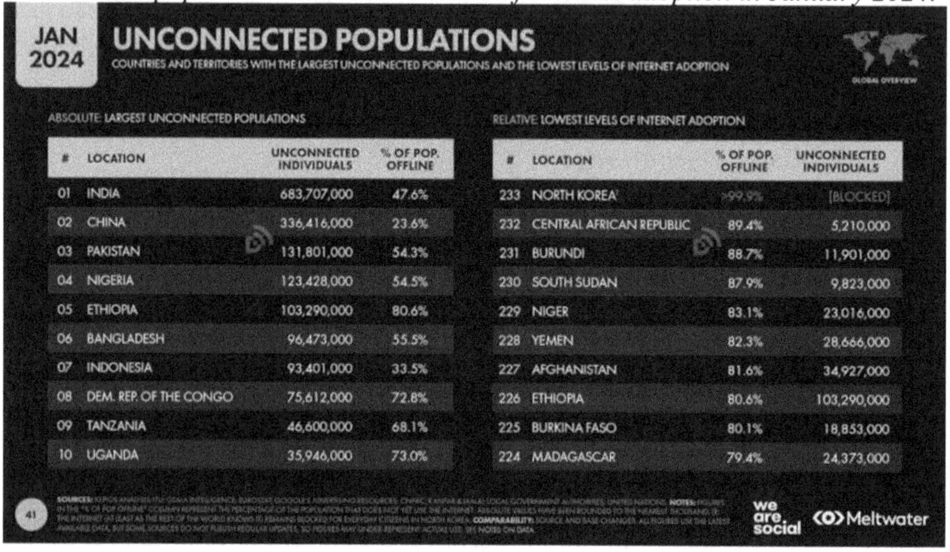
JAN 2024

UNCONNECTED POPULATIONS

COUNTRIES AND TERRITORIES WITH THE LARGEST UNCONNECTED POPULATIONS AND THE LOWEST LEVELS OF INTERNET ADOPTION

ABSOLUTE: LARGEST UNCONNECTED POPULATIONS

#	LOCATION	UNCONNECTED INDIVIDUALS	% OF POP. OFFLINE
01	INDIA	683,707,000	47.6%
02	CHINA	336,416,000	23.6%
03	PAKISTAN	131,801,000	54.3%
04	NIGERIA	123,428,000	54.5%
05	ETHIOPIA	103,290,000	80.6%
06	BANGLADESH	96,473,000	55.5%
07	INDONESIA	93,401,000	33.5%
08	DEM. REP. OF THE CONGO	75,612,000	72.8%
09	TANZANIA	46,600,000	68.1%
10	UGANDA	35,946,000	73.0%

RELATIVE: LOWEST LEVELS OF INTERNET ADOPTION

#	LOCATION	% OF POP. OFFLINE	UNCONNECTED INDIVIDUALS
233	NORTH KOREA	>99.9%	[BLOCKED]
232	CENTRAL AFRICAN REPUBLIC	89.4%	5,210,000
231	BURUNDI	88.7%	11,901,000
230	SOUTH SUDAN	87.9%	9,823,000
229	NIGER	83.1%	23,016,000
228	YEMEN	82.3%	28,666,000
227	AFGHANISTAN	81.6%	34,927,000
226	ETHIOPIA	80.6%	103,290,000
225	BURKINA FASO	80.1%	18,853,000
224	MADAGASCAR	79.4%	24,373,000

Note. From Digital 2024: 5 billion social media users (p. 41), by We Are Social, January 2024. Copyright 2024 by We Are Social Media.

According to the ITU (2023), globally, 79 percent of people aged 15 to 24 use the Internet, 14 percentage points higher than the rest of the population (65 percent), as shown in Figure 6. This generational gap has remained stable over the past four years and is observed in all regions. Universality, which is considered reached when at least 95 percent of people use the Internet, has already been achieved by this age group in high- and upper-middle-income economies. In low-income countries, people aged 15 to 24 are almost twice as likely to use the Internet as other people in those countries, in relative terms. While this is the largest usage gap of any income group, it has narrowed since 2019, when young people aged 15 to 24 were 2.5 times more likely to use the Internet than the rest of the population in low-income countries.

Figure 6. Percentage of individuals using the Internet by age group (2023)

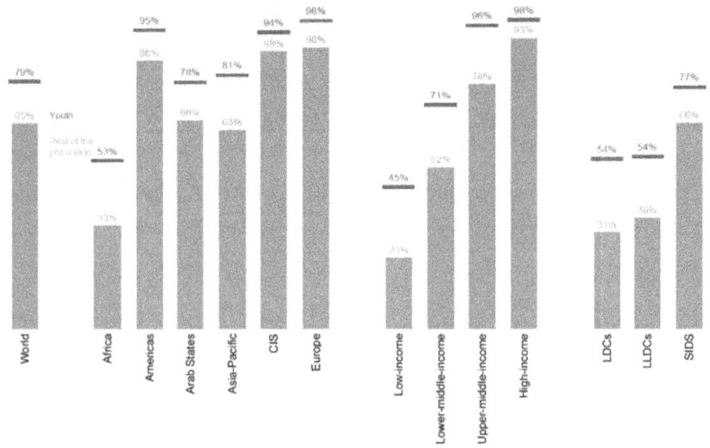

Note. From Measuring digital development Facts and Figures (p. 5), by ITU, 2023. Copyright 2023 by International Telecommunication Union.

The lower use of the internet by older adults and their resistance to adapting to and learning about information and communication technologies (ICT) can be attributed to a range of psychological, social, and technical factors. Here are some reasons why older adults may not easily adopt technological changes:

- Lack of familiarity and previous experience (Beier, 2015).
- Lack of confidence in new technologies (Venkatesh & Bala, 2008).
- Cognitive and physical difficulties (Rogers & Fisk, 2010).
- Prejudices and stereotypes (North & Fiske, 2012).
- Change can be perceived as a threat to established routines and existing skills (Oreg, 2006).

The lack of technological skills among older employees can decrease productivity and organizational efficiency and limit companies' ability to adapt to new technologies and processes. The technological gap can create barriers to intergenerational communication and limit older adults' access to online services and resources that could improve their quality of life (LaMonica et al., 2021). Resistance to ICT among older adults can affect access to government and social services increasingly managed online, exacerbating the digital divide and limiting social inclusion (Digital Economy and Society Index 2018).

The growing digitalization has made technological capabilities essential in many jobs, a trend that has been intensified by the COVID-19 pandemic's impact on work models; the digital divide has become more visible as a result. According to Picatoste et al. (2023), the pandemic increased inequality in several areas, including gender disparities and the digital divide (which accelerated with the pandemic), particularly for women and young people, whose unemployment rates increased. In terms of the pandemic's impacts on the global labor market, young women were among the most affected. According to the ITU (2023), globally, 70% of men use the internet, compared to 65% of women, as shown in Figure 7. This indicates a significant gender digital divide, which is more pronounced in lower-income countries. Globally, there are 244 million more men than women using the internet.

Figure 7. Digital gender parity is still a distant prospect in regions with low Internet use, 2023

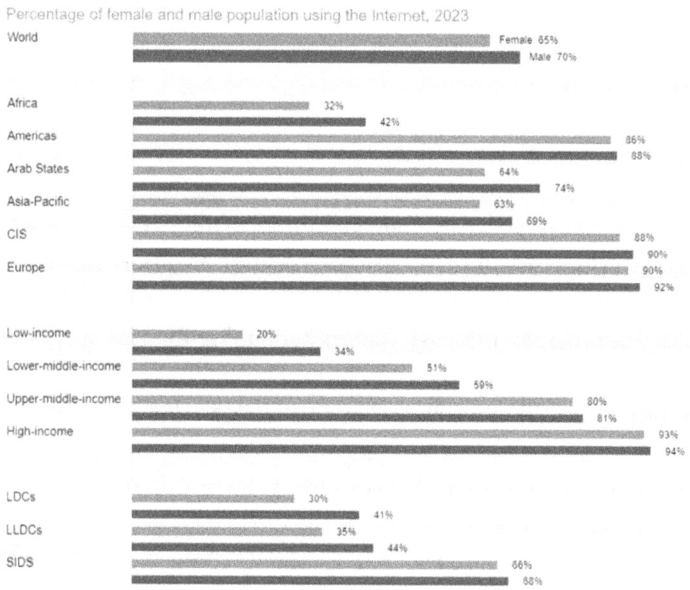

Note. From Measuring digital development Facts and Figures (p. 3), by ITU, 2023. Copyright 2023 by International Telecommunication Union.

In Spain, the gender digital division continues to affect half of the population, placing women at a disadvantage in accessing technological opportunities, which negatively impacts society. Measures have been implemented to reduce this gap by promoting female talent in the technological and entrepreneurial sectors and contributing to improving women's digital skills, specifically increasing the number of female digital specialists. Programs such as ENISA Digital Entrepreneurs, Digital Generation Change Agents, NEOTEC Women Entrepreneurs, and The Break: Attracting Female Talent have been launched to foster digital entrepreneurship, integrate female digital specialists into SMEs, and attract female talent. In Europe, efforts are also being made to reduce the gender gap. The Digital Decade Strategic Program for 2030 aims to promote opportunities and develop digital skills in both educational and work contexts, with the goal of balancing gender presence among sector professionals and facilitating women's access to digital specialist roles (National Observatory of Technology and Society, 2024).

Despite the importance of digital skills for leveraging ICT in economic prosperity and social well-being, the available global data is very limited. According to the ITU (2023), only 83 countries submitted data, and they rarely cover all skill areas. ICT skills self-assessment is subjective, measured by whether a person has recently engaged in certain activities requiring various skills. These activities are grouped into five areas of digital skills: communication/collaboration; problem solving; safety; content creation; and information/data literacy. Data indicate that information/data literacy skills are the most common, with a median of 56% and an average ranging between 33% and 69% in most countries. Communication/collaboration is the second most frequent (median of 51%), followed by problem-solving (36%), safety (34%), and content creation (25%). Among the 70 countries that reported data to the ITU in at least three skill areas, 58 reported averages of at least 25% in multiple areas, 32 reported averages of over 50%, and only two exceeded 75%. The relatively low skill levels in countries providing data contrast with their high average internet usage rate of 87 percent. This gap between people using the internet and those with digital skills shows that many might be using the internet without fully benefiting from it or avoiding its dangers.

The COVID-19 pandemic exacerbated the educational gap driven by the digital divide, affecting students from less resourceful families. Not all students could access the internet to continue their schooling, and not all who did had equal conditions.

There are many proposals from the educational world aimed at eliminating this digital division. UN has issued an urgent call for both workers and businesses to overcome their resistance to change and adapt to new information and communication technologies (ICT), artificial intelligence (AI), robotics, and so on. This adaptation is crucial for achieving Sustainable Development Goals (SDGs) 8 and 3, which promote inclusive economic growth and global health and well-being, respectively.

SDG 8, which aims to stimulate sustainable, inclusive, and continuous economic growth, faces significant challenges in a constantly evolving technological world. Digital transformation through the effective incorporation of ICT, AI, robotics, the Internet of Things, and other technologies has the potential to revolutionize production processes, improve efficiency, and generate new employment opportunities.

However, resistance to change from workers and businesses can hinder these benefits. According to the United Nations Conference on Trade and Development (UNCTAD, 2020) report, it is crucial for businesses and workers to adapt to new technological environments and acquire the necessary skills to meet current labor market demands. Employees may be reluctant to adopt new technologies due to fear of the unknown or concerns about job security. To overcome this resistance, strong leadership and a clear vision of the future are essential. Additionally, effective communication and training programs must be implemented to help employees understand the benefits of digital transformation and develop the skills needed to use new technologies efficiently. Organizations must also tackle technical challenges related to integrating various digital technologies into their existing systems, which often requires substantial investment and meticulous planning (Reynolds, 2024).

In parallel, SDG 3, which focuses on ensuring healthy lives and promoting well-being for all, can also be affected by this resistance. The adoption of emerging technologies in the healthcare sector, such as the Internet of Things, virtual assistance, remote monitoring, artificial intelligence, data analytics, blockchain, and smart devices, can enhance medical services and expand access to care in remote areas. These technologies facilitate more accurate diagnoses, data-driven therapeutic decisions, digital therapies, clinical trials, self-care, and person-centered care (WHO, 2021). Additionally, they broaden evidence-based knowledge and improve the skills of healthcare professionals. However, resistance to these new technologies may limit the effectiveness of medical interventions and perpetuate inequalities in access to healthcare.

To achieve SDGs 8 and 3, it is crucial for both workers and businesses to overcome their resistance to change and adopt new technologies that are redefining the nature of work in the digital age. Educational institutions (universities, institutes, colleges, and training centers) are particularly attuned to this adaptation to change, even more so after the COVID-19 pandemic, as they had to transform traditional teaching methods and in-person courses into online programs based on their resource availability.

2.2. Psychosocial Risks Emerging from the Digitization Process

Digitization and remote work, among other causes, have made work increasingly sedentary, thereby increasing the risk of overweight, obesity and other chronic diseases (Foncubierta-Rodriguez et al. 2024). For this reason, the 2018-2030 Global Action Plan on Physical Activity (WHO, 2019) identifies the workplace as key to promoting physical activity through the introduction of active rest, healthy physical activity and urban mobility. In the case of many adults, the workplace is crucial for being physically active (on the way to and from work and during working hours), reducing sedentary habits and thus increasing productivity and preventing trauma and absenteeism. Companies that provide their employees with physical bicycle parking spaces contribute to regular daily physical activity. Furthermore, companies that adapt part of their facilities for sports practice help reduce the stress and anxiety of their employees, while encouraging their creativity. These measures are part of the so-called emotional salary and boost the well-being of workers (Gallup, 2023).

Numerous studies are demonstrating the potential benefits of measures such as physical activity at work, which contribute to the prevention of physical diseases, disorders and mental illnesses, increase worker well-being, improve productivity and reduce absence in organizations, and reduce public health spending (Grimani et al. 2019; McEachan et al., 2011; Foncubierta-Rodriguez et al. 2024).

These problems are reflected in manifestations of techno-stress and anxiety. On the other hand, the overuse and misuse of digital tools in communications between members of organizations, teleworking, etc., are favoring the proliferation of toxic working environments, increasing cases of burnout (burned worker syndrome), frequent job changes (job hopping), the great resignation), observed after the COVID-19 pandemic, or the silent renunciation attitude observed in recent times. (quiet quitting). The misuse of technologies is also having a negative impact on the increase in bullying and cyberbullying, and improvements in regulation by States are needed in everything related to the use of digital technologies. For this reason, must implement a comprehensive approach that includes, inter alia, preventive measures on violence and harassment, in accordance with ILO Convention 190 on Violence and Harassment in the World of Work.

The new forms of corporate control allow the manager to know in detail the behaviour of his employees during the working day. Examples of this are the use of geolocalizers, timetable control, video surveillance and programs that allow access to the worker's computer. This comprehensive surveillance can generate psychosocial risks, which are sought to be limited by appropriate regulation.

The application of artificial intelligence to employment management and its impact on current employment relationships represents a new form of corporate control over employee performance. However, continuous monitoring of work through algorithms, enabling managers to make management decisions based on production levels, working rhythms and the quality of the products and services provided by workers, can lead them to increase their working pace and extend their working days to meet the standards required by artificial intelligence and avoid negative observations. This situation can cause stress in workers, who feel constantly watched and increasing their self-exigence, which can also cause errors and work accidents due to lack of proper attention in each task performed. Additionally, negative leadership - and even that self-exigency - is causing problems due to the breach of the right to digital disconnection recognized for workers. Accordingly, one of the main psychosocial risk factors is the stress generated by permanent or potential control through artificial intelligence technologies.

According to the World Economic Forum (2023), the world population continues to suffer from shortages in science, technology, engineering and mathematics-related training or skills (STEM). Lack of interpersonal skills and resilience, which foster the emergence of multifaceted, flexible and innovative professional profiles that promote people's adaptation to the VUCA (Volatility + Uncertainly + Complexity + Ambiguity) environments in which companies develop, which represents a significant challenge for the future of work (World Bank, 2020; McKinsey & Company, 2019; National Academies of Sciences, Engineering, and Medicine, 2014; National Science Board, 2020); OECD, 2019, 2021). Increased involvement by public administrations and is needed to ensure that people acquire skills that improve their employability, thereby achieving the goals set out in SDG-8 by the United Nations.

3. TOWARDS A HEALTHY ENTERPRISE, INCLUDING WITH REGARD TO THE PSYCHOSOCIAL AND MENTAL HEALTH OF THE WORKER

For WHO, a healthy workplace is one in which workers and senior staff collaborate in implementing a process of continuous improvement to protect and promote the health, safety and well-being of all workers and the sustainability of the workplace, taking into account the following considerations established on the basis of previously determined needs. These needs include aspects related to health and safety in the physical work environment; safety and well-being in the psychosocial work environment, including work organisation and work culture; personal health resources in the workplace, and ways to participate in the community to improve the health of workers, their families and other members of the community (World Health Organization, 2019).

Therefore, a healthy company is one that not only cares about the physical health of its employees, but also focuses on the psychosocial and mental well-being of its workers. This comprehensive approach aims to create a working environment that promotes health and well-being in all its aspects.

According to the European Agency for Safety and Health at Work (EU-OSHA, 2024), psychosocial risks arise from deficiencies in the design, organization and management of work, as well as from a scarce social context at work, and can result in psychological, physical and social harm to workers' health, such as work stress, exhaustion or depression. Psychosocial factors include, among other things, excessive labor demands, lack of clarity in functions, low autonomy, insufficient social support, inadequate management of change and job insecurity.

Psychosocial risks relate to SDG-3, which focuses on "Health and well-being", also covering the working environment. Aspects such as job demands, interpersonal relationships at work, clarity in functions, organizational culture, role in the organization, work autonomy, fostering the innovative and creative spirit, social support, change management, and job stability are factors that, if not properly managed, can generate stress, conflict, fear, injustice, and consequently psychosocial risks (Leka and Houdmont, 2010; Näswall et al., 2008), thereby reducing safety, health and job satisfaction. In addition, resilience, commitment, healthy and service leadership, quality of employment and organizational justice act as mitigating factors of psychosocial risks. These elements contribute to well-being, happiness and satisfaction at work, which are positive results of their implementation and fundamental pillars of truly decent work, as proposed in SDG-3 (Foncubierta-Rodriguez et al., 2022).

Healthy organizations prioritize occupational risk prevention and the promotion of healthy living habits, and are currently paying special attention to the following aspects: occupational stress, gender equality and inclusion, and workplace harassment.

These problems, as outlined above, not only affect the individual welfare of workers, but also negatively affect the productivity and health of the organization, as well as society as a whole.

3.1. New Environment in the Digital Age: Emerging Psychosocial Fears and Risks

In the digital age, emerging or digital risks appear (ESENER, EU-OSHA, 2024). The adoption of ICTs has introduced unprecedented factors and working conditions that can generate employee dissatisfaction if they are not properly managed: cybersecurity problems, attacks on privacy and intellectual property, automation that replaces the person with the machine, among others (Foncubierta-Rodriguez and Sánchez-Montero, 2019). This has been accompanied by the situation generated by the COVID-19 pandemic, the restrictions experienced in relationships and proximity, forced telework, etc., which have affected the level of perceived well-being; and that have generated new ways of working.

Various psychosocial factors previously not considered are directly affecting the well-being of workers, highlighting mainly the uneven physical spaces for remote work, low privacy, the choice of work, the increased uncertainty and the difficulty to telework in houses with relatives and household mates, adding to this, the low level of training and training in remote working, evidence of low effectiveness and productivity, and in the welfare of employees (Jain, 2021).

Among the professions that suffer especially from psychosocial risks is the teaching profession, which is one of the main causes of illnesses and accidents at work. The teaching profession requires high labour demands, in which the integration of new information and communication technologies in an increasingly competitive global market has been growing. Moreover, since the COVID-19 pandemic, during which the educational process was forced toward emergency remote education, teaching has evolved toward remote work. As a result, teachers have had to invest and organize their time to acquire the necessary skills, with the need to increase overtime work outside their usual place (college, institute or university), and thus sacrificing hours of their free time (time to take care of their family, leisure, etc.) in which they not only devote time to preparing material, reviewing papers, etc. but also to addressing matters using digital means -instant messaging applications, email, virtual platforms, etc.-

Also, the irruption and misuse of mobile and other digital media in the classrooms generate problems of distraction, performance in the pupils and in general of coexistence, being a source of conflicts in the educational centres, in such a way that a growing global trend towards the prohibition of their use in classroom is observed in recent times (OECD, 2022). All these changes have generated a psychosocial risk factor in the teacher's work that can affect his/her performance, health and safety, as well as the teaching-learning process, having direct consequences on the center of attention of the teacher, the student, and negative effects on the rest of the educational community and society (Farley & Doyle, 2014; Huang & Leung 2020; UNESCO, 2019).

Teachers are vulnerable to burnout, a risk that has increased in recent years due to the increase in remote work. Faced with this risk, resilience presents itself as a key human capacity to recover from adversities. In addition, the latest trends in the study of burnout have focused on the analysis of engagement, considered a positive and optimal aspect of professional development. Among the main causes of engagement are personal resources. The increase in remote work involves for many teachers an excess of tasks to be carried out, time pressures and overload of work due to the demands of the managers of educational centres to adapt to the new environment, the inadequacy of schedules, to which we have to join the increase of bureaucracy and "paperwork" that involves adapting to the continuous reforms of the educational systems and the norms that they carry coupled, all this has caused negative effects, such as techno-stress, the deterioration of interpersonal relations, sickness losses, abandonments of the teaching profession, etc.

During recent years, three problems in educational centres are increasing, ciberbullying, grooming and sexting, due among other factors, to the substantial use of the Internet and social networks, these practices can have serious consequences for students, from the loss of quality of life and interference in academic, social and family life, to depression and even suicide. The increase in these cases concerns the entire educational community and society, and implies an increase in the tasks of the teachers in their daily tasks, since they must be alert to identify them in an accurate and early manner, in this sense, the educational centres and families have a decisive task to protect the well-being and health of the students, and it is essential that they work in a coordinated way to mitigate and/or curb these threats (European Parliament, 2023).

At present, it is crucial to consider Internet addiction and the misuse of ICTs by all generations, especially young people, to prevent future occupational risks when integrated into the labour market. Teachers are not alien to these addictions, since many spend many hours searching for information on the Internet or immersed in social networks, especially the professionals, and work with a collective, the young people, who spend a lot of hours connected to the network.

Social networks are one of the pillars of the development of new information technologies, the interaction through them is easy, simple, instantaneous and globalized, configuring a number of behaviors in today's society offering many positive, but also negative aspects, which carry coupled many psychosocial risks.

There are many studies that demonstrate the existence of important links between excessive use of social networks and increased chances of suffering from diseases such as depression, anxiety, impulsiveness, Attention Deficit and Hyperactivity Disorder (ADHD), eating disorders (Bernstein et al., 2022; Homewood Health, 2022); the youth collective being the most affected.

Other psychosocial risks that may appear in educational environments are those that arise with the development of artificial intelligence and virtual reality, the accessibility to applications, such as the popularized ChatGPT and the generalization in the use by students and teachers of its broad functionalities.

The new digital age creates uncertainty about the working models that will be implemented in the future, generating some discontent among workers. However, it is providing tools that can mean a great step forward towards increasing workers' productivity and happiness. The development of new technologies and the rapid advancement of AI contribute to the improvement and enrichment of teaching and learning. Likewise, technology has the potential to be a very useful tool for equality, as well as to close the gaps between the least-earned (Hashim et al., 2022). These utilities contribute to reducing errors, saving time, improving productivity and the quality of services provided by both teaching and non-teaching staff and increasing the satisfaction of workers, students and families.

3.2 A Happier Teacher is a More Productive Worker

Managers and leaders of organizations should implement measures to mitigate these risks, in which employees play a crucial role. These actions increase employee satisfaction and happiness in their work, resulting in higher performance and productivity for the organization. Furthermore, this satisfaction improves the user experience of the organizations, thus benefiting society as a whole.

A happier teacher can be a more productive worker for several key reasons that relate to their emotional well-being, motivation, and ability to perform their functions efficiently. The society of the twenty-first century has created new demands and challenges for both educational centres and teachers who have deeply questioned the existing educational principles and objectives. Among them is the conquest of happiness. Some aspects that explain how a teacher's happiness can be translated into greater productivity:

- *Increased motivation and commitment.* A happy teacher is more motivated and committed to his/her work. This motivation translates into a greater willingness to plan creative learning situations, devote extra time to preparing materials and constantly search for ways to improve their teaching. A motivated teacher is also more likely to engage in extracurricular or complementary activities, which can enrich the student's educational experience.
- *Stress reduction.* Happiness is related to lower levels of stress. A less stressed teacher has a greater ability to concentrate and make effective decisions. Chronic stress can lead to exhaustion and decreased performance, even to illness or abandoning educational practice. Hence, a positive working environment that promotes happiness can help prevent these negative effects.
- *Improving interpersonal relationships and the working climate.* Happy teachers tend to have better relationships with the educational community (their peers, students, and parents/mothers/tutors), creating a more harmonious and collaborative working environment. Emotional intelligence facilitates good communication and positive relationships with others, helping to solve problems and improve teamwork, which can increase efficiency and effectiveness in teaching. The managers of educational centres should try to promote working environments and a climate of coexistence that generate happiness, as well as manage and resolve conflict situations in order to optimize the performance in the teaching work and the achievement of the objectives of the students. In this sense, interpersonal relationships between all members of the educational community, organizational culture and communication on performance assessment are determining variables for creating a good working climate.
- *Creativity and Innovation.* Happiness and emotional well-being foster creativity and innovation, and in turn, the design of physical environments and types of leadership can foster interdisciplinary work facilitating creativity, and driving innovation (Amabile, 1996). Large companies such as Pixar, Virgin, Lego, Google, as well as prestigious universities, resort to strate-

gies to inspire creativity and teamwork. A happy teacher is more inclined to experiment with new teaching methodologies, integrate technology into the classroom and seek innovative solutions to educational challenges; ultimately, he is more prone to intra-entrepreneurship. Creativity in teaching can make learning more attractive and effective for students.

- *Increased resilience.* Happy teachers tend to be more resilient and able to handle challenges and downtime more effectively. Resilience allows them to recover quickly from difficult situations, maintain a positive attitude and continue to work with enthusiasm (Foncubierta-Rodriguez, 2023). This contributes to a more stable and predictable learning environment for students.
- *Improved physical and mental health.* Happiness is associated with improved mental and physical health. Teachers who are in good health are less likely to leave due to illness and have more energy to devote to their work responsibilities. Positive mental health also helps teachers to maintain an optimistic and proactive attitude at work. Practice of healthy physical activity enables the ability to express, regulate and understand emotions, as well as is essential for the treatment and prevention of signs of Burnout syndrome.
- *Increased job satisfaction.* Numerous studies understand that teachers who feel satisfied in their duties, are more motivated with regard to their activity and professional development. Satisfaction encourages a greater interest in achieving educational objectives, the teachers being more inclined to experimentation and more committed to their work and training, which in turn improves their skills and competences. A competent and constantly improving teacher is more efficient and effective in his work. It is important to know the employment satisfaction of teachers for their relationship with the implications it has with professional abandonment, stress, commitment, educational goals, work performance and academic performance of students (Ainley & Cartens, 2018). Work satisfaction is perceived as an attitude, an emotion, a feeling and related to the climate, mental health and personal balance. There are studies that try to analyze what are the factors that are positively related to the employment satisfaction of teachers, some of them are the following: the discipline of the pupils and the cooperation of the teachers (Sims, 2017), the size of the educational centres, to smaller size, greater satisfaction (Gil-Robles, 2017).

Teacher job satisfaction can contribute to the improvement of the personal and professional well-being of teachers and to the quality of teaching. Promoting a positive working environment, supporting professional development and recognizing teachers' achievements are key strategies for increasing happiness and, consequently, productivity in education.

4. GENERAL PREVENTIVE MEASURES FOR PSYCHOSOCIAL RISKS

To address psychosocial risks in the workplace, it is essential to implement a series of general preventive measures that are applicable regardless of the organization's sector of activity. By adopting these measures, companies not only improve the quality of life for their employees but also optimize their performance and long-term stability.

These measures include:

- *Regular Risk Assessments:* Periodically evaluating psychosocial risks allows for the identification and mitigation of stress factors before they escalate into serious issues.
- *Clear Job Organization and Effective Communication:* Clearly defining job roles and tasks, and emphasizing the importance of each position within the organization, enhances staff understanding and commitment.
- *Management of Workload and Work Hours:* Properly managing workload and schedules to prevent stress and burnout is crucial for maintaining the mental and physical health of employees.
- *Work-Life Balance Measures:* Implementing policies that support work-life balance, such as flexible working hours and promoting digital disconnection outside of work hours, helps reduce stress and improves employees' quality of life.
- *Protocols for Violence and Harassment:* Designing and communicating clear protocols to address situations of violence, harassment, racism, and other forms of aggression in the workplace ensures a safe and supportive environment for employees.
- *Career Development Policies*: Encouraging professional development within the organization fosters employee motivation and commitment, reducing the risk of professional burnout.
- *Training Policies to Prevent Psychosocial Risks*: Implementing training programs tailored to emerging psychosocial risks equips employees with the skills needed to handle stressful situations and prevent psychosocial problems.

5. EDUCATION AS A SOLUTION: PROPOSALS

From the diagnosis and identification of the emerging psychosocial risks that are emerging in the digital age, it is observed that Education is configured as a key strategic instrument to prevent and mitigate its negative effects, both now and in the future.

In the case of Spain, the current state educational regulation obliges educational centres to offer students subjects that enable them to foster the critical, responsible and sustainable use of technology, the valuation of the contributions and the impact of technology on society, on environmental sustainability and health, respect for the standards and protocols established for participation in the network, as well as the acquisition of values that promote equality and respect for others and for their own work (Ministry of Education and Vocational Training, 2022).

Public and private educational institutions, through managers, play a crucial role in the prevention and management of psychosocial risks in both educational environments and in future organizations and. Education is a transformative tool for societies, and it is the leaders of educational centres, directors and administrators who must lead this transformation by implementing effective measures to mitigate these emerging psychosocial risks.

The results of many studies suggest designing training programmes for teachers and families oriented towards the identification and intervention of these problems, and designing prevention programs for primary and secondary school students.

The following are a series of proposals for measures at the micro level, consisting of educational programmes that can be designed and implemented by the managers of the organizations to prevent and manage emerging psychosocial risks:

- *Training in cybersecurity*. Cyber security is critical to protecting sensitive information and preventing vulnerabilities that could be exploited. In an increasingly digitized world, both students and workers must be trained to recognize and manage cyber threats. This not only protects individuals, but also ensures the integrity of organizations.
- *Training for management teams of educational centres in leadership and conflict management*. Educational leaders must be equipped with leadership skills that promote a safe and healthy environment. Training in appropriate leadership styles and conflict management techniques ensures that they can effectively address and mitigate emerging psychosocial risks, inspiring confidence and security in their team.
- *Training for the correct use of digital tools*. Digital tools such as computers, tablets, mobile phones, etc., if not used properly, can be a source of physical risks (such as vision and posture problems) and psychosocial risks, such as

addiction and stress. Training individuals in the proper use of these tools ensures that they benefit from their advantages without exposing themselves to their potential disadvantages, promoting a healthier working and study environment.

- *Specific training to prevent sexting and grooming*. These are serious risks that can seriously affect young people. Education on the dangers of sexting and grooming, and how to prevent them, is vital to protecting students from potentially traumatic and harmful situations.
- *Training to prevent addiction to video games and online gambling*. Pathological gambling is a multicausal disorder, involving environmental risk factors (gender, age, socio-economic level, studies, availability and offer of gambling, etc.), psychological factors (impulsiveness and search for sensations, deficits in tackling and conflict resolution strategies, deficit and neuropsychological disturbances) and biological factors (Silence Pandemic, 2021).
- *Training plan to promote healthy physical practices among all the staff of the educational centre (teacher and non-teacher), the students and their families*. Encouraging regular physical activity contributes to overall well-being, improves physical and mental health, creates long-term healthy lifestyle habits, increases participation in regular physical activities and creates a more dynamic and positive environment for the entire educational community, reducing the negative consequences of psychosocial risks. For teaching and non-teaching staff, actions could include: functional training sessions, active breaks, physical education and health workshops. For students: Improved physical education classes, active recreation, organization of sports competition tournaments (with an inclusive perspective), extracurricular programmes of dance classes, martial arts, yoga, dances, and group sports (adapting the offer to the characteristics of the environment). For families actions could include Healthy living workshops (chats on nutrition, the importance of physical activity, etc.), family sports (sports competitions, games and recreational activities in the family), hiking routes, etc.

6. FUTURE RESEARCH AGENDA

The managers of educational institutions (colleges, institutes, universities) have the responsibility to implement measures to create safe and healthy environments. Their leadership and commitment are crucial to transforming education and preparing future generations to face and overcome emerging psychosocial risks.

It is, as mentioned at the beginning of this chapter, to help educational organizations to move closer to the achievement of the "healthy educational centre", especially, because of its power of affecting the collective, in the psychosocial. By doing so, both schools and teachers will benefit, and society will, too, because happier teachers better educate the generations that will manage the future.

The fourth industrial revolution, whose psychosocial effects have already been widely discussed, will bring with it an unprecedented educational transformation. This revolution will affect both formal education and continuing training, equipping workers with greater skills and resilience to face the emerging challenges seen in companies.

Among the expected results of this reflection and theoretical chapter, it is intended to carry out a quantitative and qualitative study aimed at identifying these risks, to measure at different stages how the training carried out to the different agents (teachers and students) and stakeholders involved contributes to mitigating these psychosocial risks.

The study would help to:

1) Obtain various points of view on an international and interdisciplinary scale, enriching the understanding of psychosocial risks in different educational contexts.
2) Apply this type of analysis in future research to other work sectors, providing in-depth case studies and exploring various disciplinary approaches. This would include considering cultural and regional variability to offer a more comprehensive and global perspective.
3) Progress by providing concrete examples of successful educational programs on mental health and resilience in the workplace, either in a later phase of the study or in a new proposal.

REFERENCES

Acemoglu, D., & Restrepo, P. (2017). Robots and Jobs. Evidence from U.S. Labor Markets. *National Bureau of Economic Research, Working Paper* 23285.

Afzal, A., Khan, S., Daud, S., Ahmad, Z., & Butt, A. (2023). Addressing the digital divide: Access and use of technology in education. *Journal of Social Sciences Review*, 3(2), 883–895. DOI: 10.54183/jssr.v3i2.326

Ainley, J., & Carstens, R. (2018). *Teaching and Learning International Survey (TALIS) 2018 Conceptual Framework OECD*. Education Working Papers, 187, OECD Publishing, Paris. https://doi.org/DOI: 10.1787/19939019

Amabile, T. M. (1996). *Creativity in context: Update to "The Social Psychology of Creativity"*. Westview Press.

Beier, M. E. (2015). *Facing the challenges of a multi-age workforce: A use-inspired approach* (Finkelstein, L. M., Truxillo, D. M., Fraccaroli, F., & Kanfer, R., Eds.). Taylor & Francis Group.

Bernstein, A., Diamond, R., McQuade, T., & Pousada, B. (2022). Housing market spillovers: Evidence from the end of rent control in Cambridge, Massachusetts. *The American Economic Review*, 112(10), 3235–3270. DOI: 10.1257/aer.20211218

Brynjolfsson, E., & McAfee, A. (2011). *Race Against the Machine: How the Digital Revolution is Accelerating Innovation, Driving Productivity, and Irreversibly Transforming Employment and the Economy*. Digital Frontier Press.

Digital Economy and Society Index (DESI) (2018) Senior Citizens.

Elena-Bucea, A., Oliveira, T., Simões Coelho, P., & Cruz-Jesus, F. (2021). Assessing the role of age, education, gender, and income on the digital divide: Evidence for the EU-28. *Information Systems Frontiers*, 23(4), 1007–1021. DOI: 10.1007/s10796-020-10012-9

EU-OSHA. (2018). *Foresight on new and emerging occupational safety and health risks associated with digitalisation by 2025*. https://osha.europa.eu/sites/default/files/documents/Foresight_Flyer_ES.pdf

EU-OSHA. (2024). *Psychosocial risks and stress at work. European Agency for Safety and Health at Work*. https://osha.europa.eu/en/themes/psychosocial-risks-and-mental-health/research

Eurofound (2024). *COVID-19 and digitalisation*. https://www.eurofound.europa.eu/en/covid-19-and-digitalisation

European Parliament. (2023). Health and Safety at work https://www.europarl.europa.eu/factsheets/es/sheet/56/la-salud-y-la-seguridad-en-el-trabajo

Falcón, J. L. (2020). *Teacher job satisfaction: A qualitative cases study examining the perceptions of job satisfaction of teachers at a secondary school setting*. (Doctoral dissertation). Texas State University, Texas, USA. https://repository.library.northeastern.edu/files/neu:cj82r812t/fulltext.pdf

Farley, A., & Doyle, K. (2014). Classroom distractions: The impact of mobile phones on teacher stress. *Journal of Educational Psychology*, 106(3), 765–776.

Foncubierta Rodríguez, M. J., Popescu, C. R. G., & Ravina Ripoll, R. (2022). A New Leadership for a New Era: Effects of Association of Socio-Demographic Variables on the Leader's Competencies. In Popescu, C. R. G. (Ed.), *Handbook of research on building inclusive global knowledge societies for sustainable development*. IGI Global. DOI: 10.4018/978-1-6684-5109-0.ch001

Foncubierta-Rodríguez, M. J., Poza-Méndez, M., & Holgado-Herrero, M. (2024). Workplace health promotion programs: The role of compliance with workers' expectations, the reputation and the productivity of the company. *Journal of Safety Research*, 89, 56–63. DOI: 10.1016/j.jsr.2024.02.008 PMID: 38858063

Foncubierta-Rodríguez, M. J., & Sánchez-Montero, J. M. (2019). Towards happiness in workplace: Taking care of motivations and eliminating "digital fears", *Challenges.Revista de Ciencias de la Administración y Economía*, 9(18), 239–257. DOI: 10.17163/ret.n18.2019.04

Gallup (2023). *State of the global workplace*. Recuperado el 10 de junio de 2024, de https://www.2468group.com/wp-content/uploads/2023/07/state-of-the-global-workplace-2023-download.pdf

Geraldine, D. (2020). *Perveived effects of black female principales´servant leadership on teacher job satisfaction*. Doctoral dissertation. Grand Canyon University. ProQuest Dissertations Publishing. (202028029674). *Getting ready for digital transformation: Change your culture, workforce, and technology*. (s/f). EDUCAUSE Review. https://er.educause.edu/articles/2019/7/getting-ready-for-digital-transformation-change-your-culture-workforce-and-technology

Gil-Flores, J. (2017). The role of personal characteristics and school characteristics in explaining teacher job satisfaction. [English Ed]. *Revista de Psicodidáctica*, 22(1), 16–22. DOI: 10.1016/S1136-1034(17)30039-4

Grimani, A., Aboagye, E., & Kwak, L. (2019). The effectiveness of workplace nutrition and physical activity interventions in improving productivity, work performance and workability: A systematic review. *BMC Public Health*, 19(1), 1676. DOI: 10.1186/s12889-019-8033-1 PMID: 31830955

Hashim, S., Omar, M. K., Ab Jalil, H., & Mohd Sharef, N. (2022). Trends on technologies and artificial intelligence in education for personalized learning: Systematic literature review. *International Journal of Academic Research in Progressive Education and Development*, 11(1). Advance online publication. DOI: 10.6007/IJARPED/v11-i1/12230

Hinson, J. D. (2018). *Transformational leadership, perceived principal support, and collective efficacy: Predictors of teacher job satisfaction*. Doctoral dissertation. The University of Alabama, Tuscaloosa, AL. https://ir.ua.edu/handle/123456789/5411

Homewood Health. (2022, febrero). *The Impact of Social Media on Body Image & Mental Health*. https://image.mkt.homewoodhealth.com/lib/fe3911717164047d7d1672/m/2/ab2c0a6a-aa5b-4a92-881d-fd56493b60c0.pdf

Huang, C., & Leung, L. (2020). Mobile phone usage and teacher stress in the classroom. *The Journal of Educational Research*, 113(2), 148–158.

Instituto Nacional de Estadística. (2023). *Tecnologías de la información y la comunicación en los hogares*https://www.ine.es/prensa/tich_2023.pdf

International Labour Organization. (2019). *Convention 190: Convention concerning the elimination of violence and harassment in the world of work, adopted by the conference at its one hundred and eighth session, Geneva, 21 June 2019*. Geneva: International Labour Organization.

International Telecommunication Union. (2023, October 10). *Facts and Figures 2023: The Gender Digital Divide*. ITU. https://www.itu.int/itu-d/reports/statistics/2023/10/10/ff23-the-gender-digital-divide/

Jain, A. (2021). *Impact of digitalization and artificial intelligence as causes and enablers of organizational change*. Nottingham University Business School.

LaMonica, H. M., Davenport, T. A., Roberts, A. E., & Hickie, I. B. (2021). Understanding technology preferences and requirements for health information technologies designed to improve and maintain the mental health and well-being of older adults: Participatory design study. *JMIR Aging*, 4(1), e21461. DOI: 10.2196/21461 PMID: 33404509

Leka, S., & Houdmont, J. (Eds.). (2010). *Occupational health psychology*. Wiley Blackwell.

Liu, Y., & Whatson, S. (2020). Whose leadership role is more substantial for teacher professional collaboration, job satisfaction and organizational commitment: A lens of distributed leadership. *International Journal of Leadership in Education*. Advance online publication. DOI: 10.1080/13603124.2020.1820580

McEachan, R. R. C., Lawton, R. J., Jackson, C., Conner, M., Meads, D. M., & West, R. M. (2011). Testing a workplace physical activity intervention: A cluster randomized controlled trial. *The International Journal of Behavioral Nutrition and Physical Activity*, 8(1), 1–12. http://www.ijbnpa.org/content/8/1/29. DOI: 10.1186/1479-5868-8-29 PMID: 21481265

McKinsey & Company. (2020). *The future of work in Europe: Automation, workforce transitions, and the shifting geography of employment*. https://www.mckinsey.com/featured-insights/future-of-work/the-future-of-work-in-europe

McKinsey Global Institute. (2023). *Generative AI and the future of work in America* (Informe). Recuperado el 10 de junio de 2024, de https://www.mckinsey.com/~/media/mckinsey/mckinsey%20global%20institute/our%20research/generative%20ai%20and%20the%20future%20of%20work%20in%20america/generative-ai-and-the-future-of-work-in-america-vf1.pdf

Measuring digital development - Facts and Figures 2023. (2023, noviembre 27). ITU; ITU/UN tech agency. https://www.itu.int/hub/publication/d-ind-ict_mdd-2023-1/

Näswall, K., Hellgren, M., & Sverke, M. (2008). *The individual in the changing working life*. Cambridge University Press. DOI: 10.1017/CBO9780511490064

National Academies of Sciences, Engineering, and Medicine. (2014). *Revisiting the STEM workforce: A companion to science and engineering indicators 2014*. National Academies Press. https://www.nap.edu/catalog/18953/revisiting-the-stem-workforce-a-companion-to-science-and-engineering

National Science Board. (2020). *Science and engineering indicators 2020: The state of U.S. science and engineering*. Recuperado el 10 de junio de 2024, de https://ncses.nsf.gov/pubs/nsb20201

North, M. S., & Fiske, S. T. (2012). An obstacle race: Ageism and its impact on older adults. *Perspectives on Psychological Science*, 7(3), 264–269. PMID: 26168463

OECD. (2019). *Skills outlook 2019: Thriving in a digital world.*https://www.oecd.org/education/skills-outlook-2019/

OECD. (2021). *Skills outlook 2021: Learning for life.*https://www.oecd.org/education/skills-outlook-2021-learning-for-life.htm

OECD. (2022). *PISA 2022 Results*. OECD Publishing. https://www.oecd.org/pisa/publications/pisa-2022-results.htm

Olsen, A., & Huang, F. (2019). Teacher job satisfaction by principal support and teacher cooperation: Results from the Schools and Staffing Survey. *Education Policy Analysis Archives*, 27, 11. DOI: 10.14507/epaa.27.4174

Oreg, S. (2006). Personality, context, and resistance to organizational change. *European Journal of Work and Organizational Psychology*, 15(1), 73–101. DOI: 10.1080/13594320500451247

Pearson, T. (2002). Falling Behind: A Technology Crisis Facing Minority Students. *TechTrends*, 46(2), 15–20. https://www.learntechlib.org/p/95168/. DOI: 10.1007/BF02772070

Pérez Alonso, Y., & Gadea Peiró, I. (2021). *Bretxa digital de gènere en la Comunitat Valenciana – Informe 2021*. Universitat de València., DOI: 10.7203/10550.82251

Picatoste, X., Mesquita, A., & González-Laxe, F. (2023). Gender wage gap, quality of earnings and gender digital divide in the European context. *Empirica*, 50(2), 301–321. DOI: 10.1007/s10663-022-09555-8 PMID: 36471732

PwC. (2024). *27th Annual Global CEO Survey: Thriving in an age of continuous reinvention*. Recuperado el 10 de junio de 2024, de https://www.pwc.com/gx/en/ceo-survey/2024/download/27th-ceo-survey.pdf

Reynolds, S. (2024). Adapting to technological change: A qualitative investigation of digital transformation in supply chain operations. En *Preprints*. https://doi.org/ DOI: 10.20944/preprints202406.1115.v1

Rogers, W. A., & Fisk, A. D. (2010). Human factors for engineers and designers: The role of age and ability. En *Handbook of Human Factors and Ergonomics*.

Sims, S. (2017). TALIS 2013: Working conditions, teacher job satisfaction and retention. *Department for Education Statistical Working Paper*. Londres: Department for Education. Recuperado el 10 de junio de 2024, de https://eric.ed.gov/?id=ED604491

The Conference Board (2023). *TED: Summary tables and charts*https://www.conference-board.org/retrievefile.cfm?filename=TED_SummaryTables_Charts_april20231.pdf&type=subsite

Thompson, A. (2024). *Digital 2024: 5 billion social media users*. We Are Social UK; We Are Social. https://wearesocial.com/uk/blog/2024/01/digital-2024-5-billion-social-media-users/

UNCTAD. (2020). Report about digital economy. https://unctad.org/webflyer/digital-economy-report-2020

UNESCO. (2019). *Teaching and Learning in the Digital Age*. UNESCO Publishing.

UNESCO. (2022). *Transforming Technical and Vocational Education and Training for successful and just transitions: UNESCO strategy 2022-2029*. UNESCO Publishing.

United Nations. (2023). Department of Economics and Social Affairs.

Venkatesh, V., & Bala, H. (2008). Technology acceptance model 3 and a research agenda on interventions. *Decision Sciences*, 39(2), 273–315. DOI: 10.1111/j.1540-5915.2008.00192.x

World Bank. (2019). *World development report 2019: The changing nature of work*. https://www.worldbank.org/en/publication/wdr2019

World Economic Forum. (2023). *The future of jobs report 2023*. https://www3.weforum.org/docs/WEF_Future_of_Jobs_2023.pdf

World Health Organization. (2019). *Global action plan on physical activity 2018-2030: More active people for a healthier world*. World Health Organization. https://iris.who.int/handle/10665/272722

World Health Organization. (2021). Global strategy on digital health 2020–2025. World Health Organization. https://iris.who.int/handle/10665/344251

Yavuzkurt, T., & Kiral, E. (2020). The Relationship Between Workplace Friendship and Job Satisfaction in Educational Organizations. *International Journal of Progressive Education*, 16(5), 404–425. DOI: 10.29329/ijpe.2020.277.25

Chapter 7
Perspectives and Trends Relating to a Bibliometric Analysis of Hot-Desking Using VOSviewer

Belen Maria Moreno-Cabezali
https://orcid.org/0000-0002-6013-3310
Rey Juan Carlos University, Spain

Cristina Carrasco-Garrido
https://orcid.org/0000-0003-4234-1519
Rey Juan Carlos University, Spain

Antonio Martínez Raya
https://orcid.org/0000-0002-4878-396X
Universidad Politécnica de Madrid, Spain

ABSTRACT

This chapter examines hot desks, a workspace strategy in which employees use available workstations instead of assigned desks. This has gained importance due to its potential for cost savings and flexibility. The chapter uses VOSviewer to analyze literature on hotdesking from 2010 to 2024. It highlights a peak in publications between 2016 and 2018, followed by a decline during the COVID-19 pandemic. Key contributors include researchers from England, the United States, and New Zealand, which demonstrate significant international collaboration and high impact. The chapter explores key issues such as employee reactions, communication, job satisfaction, open-plan offices, and office design. It emphasizes the need for strategic implementation to maximize benefits and address hot-desk challenges.

DOI: 10.4018/979-8-3693-6289-1.ch007

This bibliometric analysis provides a foundation for future research and practical applications in workspace management, highlighting the importance of international collaboration and adaptation to emerging challenges.

1. INTRODUCTION

Hot-desking represents a strategic approach to office resource management that gained importance in the 1990s. This methodology has fundamentally redesigned organizational practices in the use of workspaces. In a hot-desking system, employees do not have designated desks; instead, they use any available desk within the office. The main objective behind implementing hot-desking is to facilitate reductions in real estate expenditures for organizations (Fulton, 2005; Maraslis et al., 2016; Selwyn-Rowland, 2021). Although hot desks offer notable advantages in terms of workspace flexibility and efficient utilization, they also introduce specific challenges that require strategic planning and adaptation by both organizations and employees.

The literature review of hotlines predominantly includes three primary research areas. First, there is a substantial body of research that examines the influence of hot desk practices on employee health and overall well-being. Some studies have indicated that the transition to shared workspaces can have significant implications for employee physical and psychological health, highlighting the importance of careful design and implementation of such environments. Berelson et al. (2018) promote a system that facilitates the temporary allocation of desks to employees, considering individual preferences, spatial constraints, and temporal dynamics, to optimize both well-being and productivity. Similarly, Maraslis et al. (2016) introduce an intelligent hot-desking model that uses occupancy sensor data to facilitate real-time desk assignments, to improve working conditions and productivity.

Second, the evolution of organizational workspaces over time, its impact on employee teams, and organizational identification have been the subject of academic investigation. Research has shown that employees with designated desks tend to place greater value on face-to-face communication and exhibit stronger identification with their immediate team, while those without assigned desks tend to prioritize electronic communication methods and identify more closely with the broader organization (Millward et al., 2007).

Lastly, the importance of physical workspace in influencing employee productivity, mindset, and team cohesion has been a focal point of academic investigation. Despite the inherent benefits of hot desks, such as increased flexibility, they also present challenges, including spatial restrictions, feelings of marginalization among employees, and potential disruptions to social processes (Selwyn-Rowland, 2021). Fulton (2005) further emphasizes that mobile workers, commonly referred to as e-workers, rely extensively on electronic resources and mobile technologies to navigate the complexities of hot-desking. However, challenges such as restricted access to information, the need for an enhanced technological infrastructure, and limited storage capacities remain pertinent issues that require innovative solutions.

In conclusion, hot-desking continues to be a pertinent and evolving subject within the space of office resource management. As organizations strive to optimize workspace use, cultivate flexible and collaborative work environments and improve employee well-being and productivity, a detailed understanding of the multifaceted benefits, challenges, and opportunities of hot desks is imperative. The present bibliometric analysis offers a comprehensive synthesis of the extant literature on hot-desking, interpreting its diverse dimensions and contributing to academic discourse and practical applications in this emergent field.

This research aims to identify the current state of knowledge on hot-desking. The section dedicated to findings examines emerging trends related to this topic, highlighting the most influential authors, institutions, countries, and sources. In addition, the most relevant areas in the field of hot-desking have been identified. The research concludes with the main findings and conclusions derived from the bibliometric analysis. Additionally, the limitations of the study, such as data availability and accessibility, are addressed, and a future research agenda is proposed, suggesting promising areas for exploration.

This work explores the following research questions (RQ) related to hot-desking:

- RQ1: What has been the growth trend of hot-desking research from 2010 to May 2024?
- RQ2: Who are the most influential authors, institutions, countries, and journals in the field of hot-desking?
- RQ3: What are the topics that are the most frequently studied within hot desk research?
- RQ4: Which documents are more prominent in hot desk research?

2. FRAMEWORK

The workspace is undergoing more and more changes. New issues in the modern world, such as digitization, the Coronavirus Disease 2019 (hereafter, COVID-19) pandemic, teleworking, and flexible work arrangements are some of the practices driving the various changes in the workplace where employees perform their jobs (Egorova et al., 2021; Pan et al., 2023).

Telework has experienced remarkable growth in its implementation after the COVID-19 pandemic. Until then, few companies had implemented these practices despite their multiple benefits, due to the false belief that teleworking was not a practice that could be applied to most jobs. After the pandemic, this perception changed, and companies and workers saw telework as a great option. Especially hybrid telework, an option mostly chosen and preferred by employees and companies, leaving full telework as a secondary option (Carrasco-Garrido et al., 2023).

Due to the practice of hybrid telework, numerous changes in organizational culture and interpersonal relationships between workers and workplaces have begun to be experienced (Millward et al., 2007).

The workplace is a space that belongs to and identifies the worker, and therefore many elements personalize that space. A plant, a photo of a relative, or any symbol that represents us is usually present at that place.

Hybrid teleworking has many advantages that employees and companies can exploit. On the employee side, teleworking generates greater flexibility in task and time organization, better work-life balance, time savings, and financial savings by avoiding commuting. On the companies' side, savings on office costs and greater employee satisfaction lead to higher productivity and more possibilities to choose their employees without the barrier of the place of residence. Here, a distinction should be made between hybrid and full telework. In the case of full telework, employees can afford to have a residence in another country or in a town or small city where the cost of living is lower. In the case of hybrid teleworking, it requires some face-to-face presence; employees cannot obtain the same advantage. It all depends on the type of hybrid teleworking that is established. It is not the same to work three days a week remotely and two days in person, as it is to establish a type of hybrid teleworking by weeks, where the employee's freedom to set up his or her home is greater, and the constraints are more extensive (Groen et al., 2018; Pérez et al., 2005; Teleoacă Vartolomei, 2020; Vinezuela-Cabezas et al., 2022).

Although teleworking also has its disadvantages, on the worker side, the one that stands out the most is the isolation they suffer, as sometimes they may not even leave home all day. On the company's side, the lack of control over their employees can sometimes lead to a refusal to implement these practices. If tasks performed by employees at home cannot be monitored, companies do not want to take the risk (Wieser & Abraham, 2024). Therefore, among all the advantages, savings come from both perspectives, worker and employer (Carrasco-Garrido et al., 2023; Golden et al., 2008; Kucera et al., 2021).

Hybrid teleworking has numerous advantages that can be taken advantage of on the employees' and companies' sides. Savings are one of them. On the part of the workers because it avoids displacements and on the part of the companies because it saves them to have offices for the total of the personnel (Carrasco-Garrido et al., 2023; Ipsen et al., 2021).

With full telework, companies can eliminate the expense of workspaces. With hybrid telework, companies can rotate workstations (Hopkins & Bardoel, 2023; Stanford University, 2021). Something that has already been experienced after the confinements of the COVID-19 outbreak (Chua et al., 2023). Despite lifting certain restrictions, some were still present, such as respecting a minimum distance between people. This forced companies to combine face-to-face and nonface-to-face shifts among their employees (Ipsen et al., 2023).

Once all restrictions were over and companies became aware of the possibility for their employees to telework, the reduction of office space became a fixed cost saving and hot-desking began to emerge (Chua et al., 2023). Despite the disadvantages of hot-desking, its main advantage is not only in terms of cost savings for companies but also for employees due to the high level of depersonalization suffered in the workplace (Morrison & Macky, 2017).

As with teleworking, the practice of hot-desking will depend on the type of tasks performed by the employee to ensure the success or failure of its implementation. For example, a study carried out in England (Alshehri et al., 2021) established that almost half of the pharmacists surveyed (45%) worked in a shared office or hot-desking environment. Part of the success can also be ensured by adding Artificial Intelligence tools, as (Fukumura et al., 2021) propose, where health and safety aspects in the workplace are usually considered on that matter. For example, lighting, temperature, or adopting the correct posture in the chair while working. With new practices, new challenges also arise. Here, the question arises as to how employees develop that sense of community when hot-desking. This tries to address this question in their research (Arnold et al., 2019). This is also a challenge that can also be applied to offices that perform hybrid or full teleworking.

3. METHODOLOGY

3.1. Research Design

This study used a bibliometric approach to investigate publications related to hot-desking in workplace environments. This method facilitated a thorough analysis of the structure and trends of the research, as well as the interrelationship between different key aspects, which is essential to understanding the dynamics and impact of hot desks in the workplace. These data were analyzed and visualized using VOSviewer software, revealing the evolution of hot desks in the workplace over time.

3.2. Database Selection and Research Protocol

The bibliographic data used as input for this bibliometric and scientometric analysis were extracted from the Web of Science (WoS) database. Bibliographic databases, particularly the WoS database, are crucial for bibliometric and scientometric studies, as they allow for comprehensive coverage and reliable data (Zupic & Cater, 2015). However, limitations of these databases, such as content discrepancies, should be considered in the design of such studies. Despite these limitations, the correlation between WoS and Scopus bibliographic indicators is high, indicating the reliability of these databases (Salvador-Oliván, 2015). The global analysis, in terms of scientometric or bibliometric, of various disciplines further underscores the importance and impact of these studies (Wei, 2019).

Concerning the study, one of the weaknesses could be the fact that only the WoS database is used; therefore, any related research available in other databases, such as Scopus, is not considered. This greatly reduces the scope of this study and excludes data collected from other related databases.

An exhaustive search strategy was implemented to include as many relevant publications as possible on the topic of hot-desking. The search protocol followed was 'hot-desking' or 'hot desking' to capture all possible variants of the expression used in the literature. This methodology allowed for a more comprehensive and precise search of related documents. As a result, a total of 24 documents covering a variety of formats were retrieved, including articles, conference papers, book chapters, and review articles. These publications were collected from January 1, 2010, to May 1, 2024, to include the most recent research on the topic. The relatively low number of documents included in the bibliometric analysis may be primarily due to the novelty of the subject and the impact of COVID-19, which redirected some lines of research toward teleworking, thus relegating hot-desking to a secondary position.

3.3. Data Pre-Processing

According to Murillo-Ramos et al. (2022) and Carrasco-Garrido et al. (2023), the Preferred Reporting Items for Systematic Reviews and Meta-Analyses (PRISMA) checklist was applied to obtain the final bibliographic sample (see Figure 1). This guideline focuses on the clarity, transparency, and coherence of the results, thus contributing to reducing biases in processes (Figueiredo et al., 2024). The initial search identified 24 documents. Due to the low number, each of them underwent a full reading to avoid duplicates or irrelevant entries. Once each document on the bibliometric topics was verified, a final sample of 24 documents was selected for the study.

Figure 1. PRISMA 2020 flow diagram

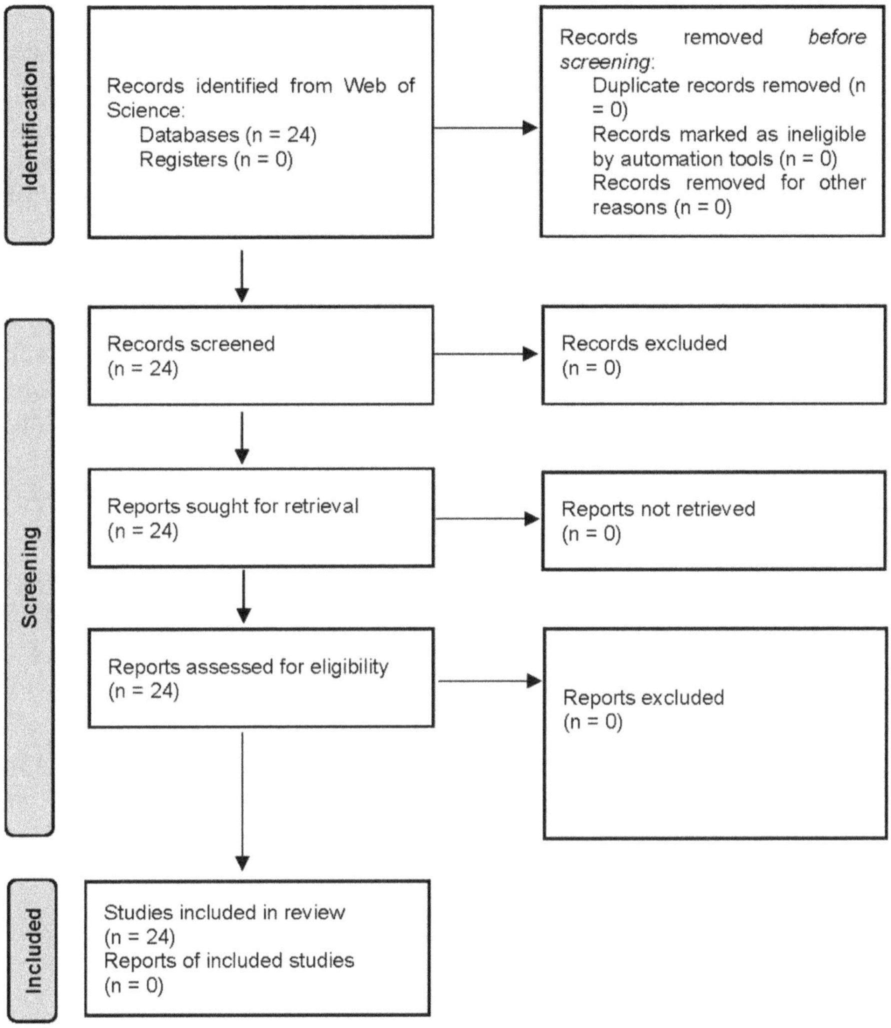

Due to the novelty of the topic, it has been necessary to include all available references, including original research articles, conference proceedings, and book chapters. This inclusion is justified by the need to leverage all existing and relevant information on the subject, thus ensuring a comprehensive and up-to-date review. Additionally, by encompassing different types of documents indexed in the WoS database, the analysis is enriched, providing a more complete view of the state of research in the field of hot-desking.

3.4. Data Analysis

For the analysis of bibliographic data, VOSviewer was chosen, widely recognized, and used in bibliometric studies because of its effectiveness and versatility. This software played a crucial role in conducting detailed visualization analyses and creating bibliometric maps that provided a graphical representation of document structure and relationships (Van Eck & Waltman, 2010). Specifically, a keyword co-occurrence analysis was performed, involving the identification of the most frequent terms present in the selected documents, enabling the identification of the most relevant and current topics in the field of study. Furthermore, a co-authorship, citation, and co-citation analysis was performed, helping to understand the collaboration networks among authors, organizations, and countries, as well as the influence of previous work on current research. This combination of analyzes provided a comprehensive and detailed view of the bibliographic landscape related to the topic under investigation.

4. FINDINGS

4.1. Analysis of Annual Publication Volume (RQ1)

A total of 24 publications related to hot-desking were identified within the WoS database spanning the years 2010 to 2024. Among these, 19 (79.18%) were classified as original research articles, 5 (20.83%) as conference proceedings, and 2 (8.33%) as book chapters. All articles were authored in English and indexed within the primary WoS database.

Figure 2. Annual evolution of publications related to hot-desking

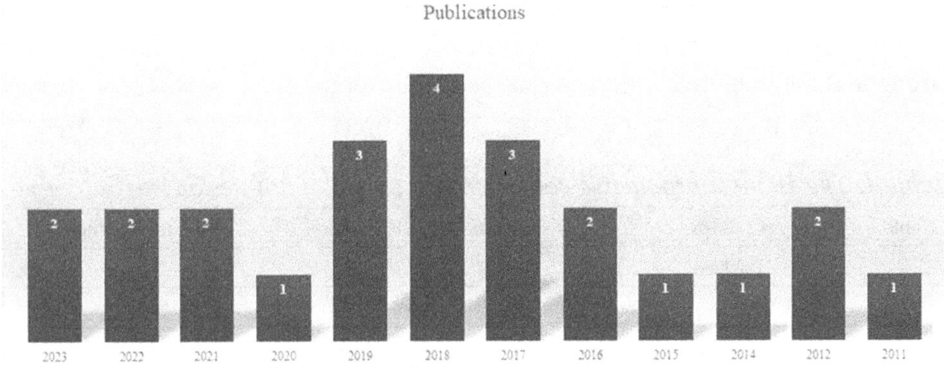

Source: Own elaboration from WoS database.

Figure 2 shows the annual volume of publications on hot topics from 2011 to 2023, revealing an initially modest start followed by an uptick in 2012. Publications were sparse between 2013 and 2015, followed by a notable increase between 2016 and 2018, peaking at four publications in 2018. Subsequently, there was a decline in 2019 and 2020, with a recovery of three publications in 2021. In 2022 and 2023, the number of publications stabilized at two per year, indicative of sustained on the topic, although not escalating.

The lack of publications on hot desks can be partially attributed to its recent inclusion in labor research and the onset of the COVID-19 pandemic, further complicating research efforts in this area. With workplaces around the world facing unprecedented challenges, such as the need for social distancing and remote work arrangements, there has been a shift in research focus toward immediate pandemic-related concerns, particularly toward teleworking. As a result, there has been limited academic attention and availability of data on the implementation and effectiveness of hot services in the context of workplace adaptations to COVID-19. These combined factors likely contribute to the limited number of studies available on this topic.

4.2. Country and Institutional Analysis (RQ2)

4.2.1. Country Analysis

The bibliometric analysis of hot-desking reveals a diverse geographical distribution in academic production on the subject. This section presents a detailed examination of the most productive countries and their impact on academic literature.

4.2.1.1 Productivity by Country

Table 1 lists the ten most productive countries in the field of hot-desking, classified by the number of published documents, the citations received, and the total strength of the link, indicating international collaboration.

Table 1. The 10 most productive countries in the field of hot-desking

Rank	Country	Documents	Citations	Total link strength
1	England	9	153	6
2	USA	4	14	1
3	New Zealand	3	120	3
4	Germany	2	73	2
5	Malaysia	2	13	0
6	Austria	1	72	2
7	Sweden	1	33	2
8	The Netherlands	1	121	0
9	Italy	1	18	0
10	Switzerland	1	16	0

Source: own elaboration based on data collected from the WoS database.

Analysis of the most productive countries in hot-desking research reveals that England leads by a considerable margin. It can be observed that England has produced not only the highest number of documents, but also a high number of citations and a notable total link strength, reflecting strong international collaboration and the high impact of its publications. Specifically, England has produced nine documents, received 153 citations, and had a total link strength of six. The United States follows with four documents, 14 citations, and a total link strength of 1. New Zealand has contributed three documents, 120 citations, and a total link strength of three, while Germany has produced two documents, received 73 citations, and had a total link strength of two. Malaysia has two documents and 13 citations, but no links. Other countries like Austria, Sweden, the Netherlands, Italy, and Switzerland also contribute, but with a smaller number of documents and citations. This distribution indicates a strong presence of research in English-speaking countries, especially in England and the United States, as well as a significant impact from New Zealand in terms of citations received.

4.2.1.2. Co-Authorship Analysis

Co-authorship analysis provides a more detailed view of international collaborations in hot-desking research. England leads by a considerable margin, producing not only the highest number of documents but also receiving the most citations. This reflects its influential academic production and strong presence in international collaborations, consolidating its position as a central hub in hot-desking research.

The United States, although producing fewer documents than England, maintains a significant presence in co-authorships. Its inclusion as a major node in international collaborations indicates active and relevant participation in global research. New Zealand, despite producing fewer documents, was surprised with a high number of citations, highlighting the quality and impact of its academic production. Its presence in the co-authorship analysis demonstrates its considerable influence on international hot-desking research.

Germany, while contributing fewer documents and citations compared to England, New Zealand, and the USA, still plays a notable role. The number of citations for German documents indicates a respectable impact in the field. However, its total link strength of zero suggests that there is a lack of co-authorship connections in the analysis. This indicates that German researchers might benefit from increased international collaboration to enhance their visibility and impact in the hot-desking research network.

Together, England, the United States, New Zealand, and Germany represent key contributors to the hot-desking research landscape. England, the United States, and New Zealand are the most productive and connected countries in terms of international collaboration, playing a central role in the hot-desking research network. Meanwhile, Germany's contributions are impactful, but there is potential for greater collaboration to integrate more effectively into the global research community.

Figure 3. Co-authorship analysis by country

Source: own elaboration from VOSviewer.

4.2.2. Institutional Analysis

Bibliometric analysis of research on hot-desking can be broken down not only by countries but also by academic and research institutions that contribute significantly to this field. This section provides a detailed examination of the most productive institutions and their impact on the academic literature.

4.2.2.1. Institution Productivity

Table 2 lists the top ten most productive institutions in the field of hot-desking, ranked by the number of published documents, the citations received, and the total strength of the linkage, indicating institutional collaboration.

Table 2. Top 10 most productive institutions in the field of hot-desking

Rank	Organization	Documents	Citations	Total link strength
1	Lancaster University	3	4	9
2	The University of Auckland	2	76	8
3	University of Birmingham	2	0	8
4	University of Bristol	2	0	1
5	University of Nottingham	2	0	8
6	Northumbria University	2	9	5
7	University of Bedfordshire	1	1	4
8	University of Münster	1	4	1
9	University of Vienna	1	8	1
10	Arup University	1	9	2

Source: own elaboration based on data collected from the WoS database.

The analysis reveals that Lancaster University leads both in production and collaboration, with three documents and high linkage strength. The University of Auckland stands out for its high impact, with 76 citations in two documents. The University of Birmingham and the University of Nottingham demonstrate strong collaboration, although without significant citations. Northumbria University combines a good number of citations with collaboration. Other institutions, such as the University of Bristol, the University of Bedfordshire, the University of Münster, the University of Vienna, and Arup University, contribute less to quantity, but some with high quality, such as Arup University with nine citations.

4.2.2.2. Institutional Co-Authorship Analysis

The co-authorship analysis provides a more detailed insight into collaborations between institutions in hot-desking research. Figure 4 shows an institutional co-authorship analysis that highlights key collaborations and research networks.

Lancaster University, the University of Auckland, the University of Birmingham and the University of Nottingham are prominent institutions in hot-desking research. Lancaster University leads in both production and collaboration, while The University of Auckland stands out for its high citation impact. Some prestigious universities, such as Birmingham and Nottingham, though with fewer citations, exhibit strong international collaboration. These institutions form a robust and interconnected research network, essential for the advancement and dissemination of knowledge in this field.

Figure 4. Institutional co-authorship analysis

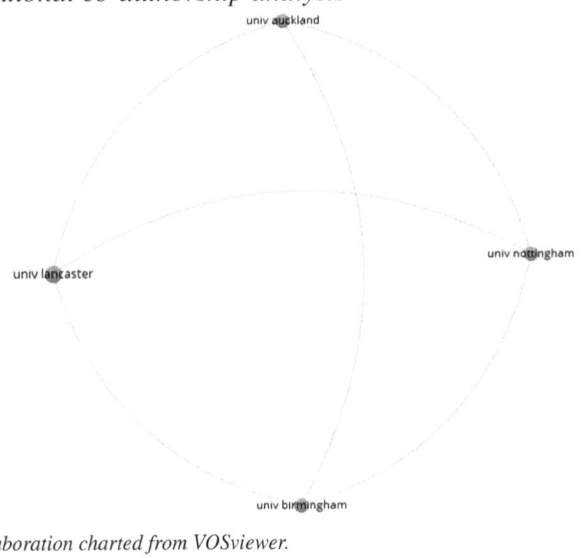

Source: Own elaboration charted from VOSviewer.

4.3. Author Analysis (RQ2)

The bibliometric analysis of the most productive authors in hot desk research provides valuable insight into individual contributions and their impact on the field. The following is a detailed examination of the most productive authors and their relevance in the previous literature.

4.3.1. Author Productivity

Table 3 shows the top ten most productive authors in the field of hot-desking, ranked by the number of published documents, the citations received, and the total strength of the linkage, indicating collaboration between authors.

Table 3. Top 10 most productive authors in the field of hot-desking

Authors	Documents	Citations	Total link strength
Beddoe L	2	44	11
Cooner TS	2	44	11
Disney T	2	44	11
Ferguson H	2	44	11
Leigh J.	2	44	11
Warwick L	2	44	11
Tryfonas T	2	13	6
Alavi H	1	16	0
Abdullah SMB	1	8	0
Arnold D.	1	0	0

Source: own elaboration based on data collected from the WoS database.

Beddoe L, Cooner TS, Disney T, Ferguson H, Leigh J, and Warwick L lead with two documents each, 44 citations, and strong linkage strength (11), indicating significant impact and effective collaboration in hot-desking research. Tryfonas T, with two documents, 13 citations, and a link strength of six, remains an important contributor. Alavi H, despite publishing only one document, stands out with 16 citations, highlighting the high quality and impact of his work, although without significant collaboration (linkage strength zero). Abdullah SMB and Arnold D each published one document, with eight and zero citations, respectively, and without linkage strength, indicating more isolated contributions.

4.3.2. Co-Authorship Analysis

Co-authorship analysis among the authors reveals that those with higher linkage strength, such as Beddoe L and their collaborators, form a strong and well-connected core in the hot-desking research network.

As shown in Figure 5, the bibliometric analysis of the authors in the hot desk field indicates that collaboration is a key factor in the production of influential research. Authors like Beddoe L, Cooner TS, and others in their group lead in terms of productivity and citation, while others like Alavi H stand out for the individual impact of their publications. The co-authorship network demonstrates a strong core of researchers whose collaboration has been essential in advancing knowledge in this field.

Figure 5. Analysis of the networks of co-authorship

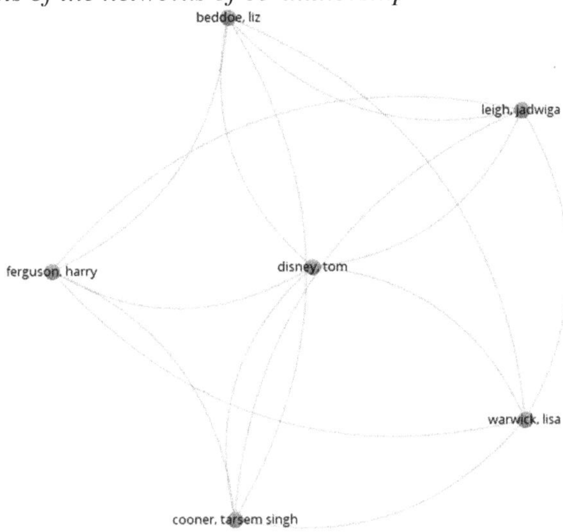

Source: own elaboration charted from VOSviewer.

4.4. Journal Analysis (RQ2)

The bibliographic analysis of the most productive journals in hot desk research provides a detailed overview of the primary academic sources that contribute to this field. The following is a detailed examination of the most productive journals and their impact on academic literature related to hot-desking.

4.4.1. Journal Productivity

Table 4. Top 10 most productive journals in the field of hot-desking

Rank	Journal	Documents	Citations	Total link strength
1	Environment and Behavior	2	105	1
2	Journal of Corporate Real Estate	2	42	0
3	European Management Journal	1	121	0
4	Applied Ergonomics	1	76	1
5	Child & family social work	1	27	1
6	European Journal of Social Work	1	17	1
7	Asean Conference on Environment-Behavior Studies (ace-bs)	1	8	0
8	Dtuc'18: proceedings of the first international conference on digital transformation	1	4	0
9	Architectural Review	1	0	0
10	ASHRAE Transactions 2023, vol. 129, pt. 1	1	0	0

Source: own elaboration based on data collected from the WoS database.

Table 4 presents a bibliometric analysis of the ten most productive journals in the field of hot desks, ranked by the number of published documents, the number of citations received, and the total strength of the links, indicating institutional collaboration. The Environment and Behavior list is topped with two documents and 105 citations, demonstrating notable influence and academic relevance, followed by the 'Corporation Real Estate Journal' with two documents and 42 citations, although lacking collaboration. The European Management Journal stands out with one document and 121 citations, indicating high relevance but no institutional collaboration. Applied Ergonomics has one document with 76 citations and a link strength of one, highlighting the importance of ergonomic studies in hot desks. Child & Family Social Work and the European Journal of Social Work show the integration of hot-desking into social work, each with one document and 27 and 17 citations, respectively, both with a link strength of one.

The ASEAN Conference on Environment-Behavior Studies (ACE-BS) includes one document with eight citations and no collaboration, similar to DTUC18: Proceedings of the First International Conference on Digital" with one document and four citations. The Architectural Review and ASHRAE Transactions have each published one document without receiving citations or showing institutional collaboration. In summary, Environment and Behavior and the European Management Journal stand out for their high number of citations, indicating a significant impact in hot desk research, while other journals like Applied Ergonomics and Child & Family Social Work also show relevance with a good number of citations and collaboration. However, some journals, such as Architectural Review and ASHRAE Transactions, have not yet achieved significant visibility.

4.4.2. Journal Co-Citation Analysis

Journal co-citation analysis provides insight into how different journals are interconnected through their shared citations, revealing relationships and patterns in the literature on hot-desking. Figure 6 illustrates the analysis of journal co-citation, highlighting the connections between key academic sources in this field.

This co-citation analysis reveals that journals such as Applied Ergonomics, Journal of Environmental Psychology, Journal of Environmental and Behavior, Journal of Corporate Real Estate, and Journal of Facilities are the ones with the strongest connections. These journals span a wide range of disciplines, from ergonomics to environmental psychology and facility management, reflecting the interdisciplinary nature of hot desks and their impact on various aspects of the workplace environment.

The inclusion of these journals in the co-citation analysis suggests that they are valuable sources of research to understand the ergonomic, psychological, and facility management aspects related to hot-desking. Furthermore, it underscores the importance of approaching this topic from multiple disciplinary perspectives to gain a comprehensive understanding of its implications. As organizations seek to adapt to more flexible and dynamic work environments, research published in these journals plays a crucial role in the formation of best practices and strategies to implement and manage hot-desking effectively.

In summary, bibliometric and journal co-citation analysis offers a deeper understanding of how hot-desking research is distributed and interconnected across different disciplines and publications, facilitating the identification of the most influential and relevant sources for future studies.

Figure 6. Co-citation analysis of the journal

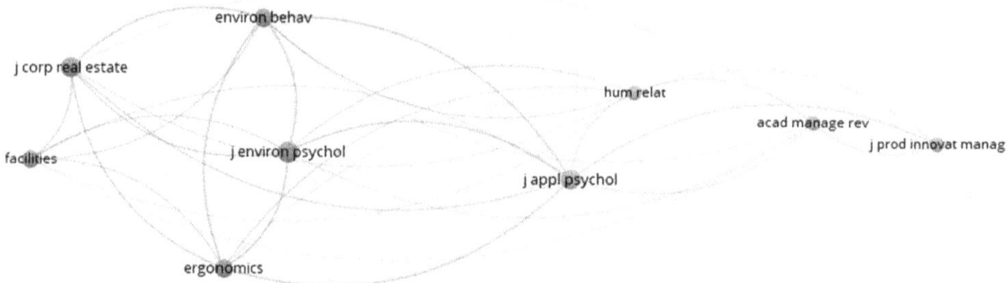

Source: own elaboration charted from VOSviewer.

4.5. Keyword Analysis (RQ3)

Keyword analysis in hot-desking research provides a detailed insight into the topics and trends most frequently explored in this field. Below is a table listing the top 10 most recurrent keywords and their respective total linkage strength, offering a guide to the areas of highest interest and relevance in the academic literature on hot-desking.

Table 5. Top 10 most frequent keywords in the field of hot-desking

Rank	Keywords	Occurrences	Total link strength
1	Hot-desking	8	24
2	Impact	4	7
3	Job Satisfaction	3	19
4	Physical Environment	3	20
5	Work	3	20
6	Behavior	2	6
7	Child protection	2	3
8	Comfort	2	5
9	Communication	2	9
10	Employee reactions	2	14

Source: own elaboration based on data collected from the WoS database.

The term 'hot desk' appears more frequently, reflecting its centrality in research on the topic. It is followed by keywords such as impact and job satisfaction, indicating significant interest in how hot desks affect employees and their levels of job satisfaction. The terms 'physical environment' and 'work' are also recurring terms, highlighting the importance of the physical environment and work dynamics in hot-desking studies.

Other relevant terms include behavior, comfort, and communication, suggesting that behavioral aspects, user comfort, and workplace communication are key areas of research. Keywords such as 'employee reactions' and 'method bias' highlight attention to employee responses and potential methodological biases in studies.

4.4.1. Keyword Co-Occurrence Analysis

Figure 7. Keyword co-occurrence analysis

Source: Own elaboration charted from VOSviewer.

Figure 7 illustrates the interconnectedness of various concepts associated with hot-desking through a keyword co-occurrence analysis. Each node, depicted with a distinctive size and color, symbolizes a keyword and its significance within the study. The lines connecting these nodes reflect the relationships between terms, with the 'hot-desking' as the central core of the network. This node is closely linked to other key terms such as 'physical environment', 'employee reactions', 'communication', 'workplace', and 'work'.

This is because it is likely that the physical environment, employee reactions, communication in the workplace, and work itself are discussed, as all these aspects are related to the implementation and experience of hot-desking. Therefore, it is common for these terms to appear together in discussions of hot-desking.

This representation is of great value for understanding the dynamics and correlations among the different elements that make up the concept of hot-desking, offering a comprehensive perspective that facilitates the identification of areas of interest and trends in the field of labor research.

5. PROMINENT ACADEMIC WORKS IN HOT DESKING RESEARCH (RQ4)

This section highlights and analyzes certain key academic works that have contributed significantly to hot desk research. These works have provided important information exploring various dimensions of hot desks and their impact on organizations, employees, and social dynamics within the workplace. By presenting these contributions, the objective is to improve the reader's understanding of the complexity and importance of hot desks in the contemporary workplace. This emphasis on specific works is justified by the need to strengthen bibliometric analysis given the relative novelty of the topic and the limited number of available references. Furthermore, the pandemic has shifted research focus to other fields such as telecommuting, further underscoring the importance of highlighting existing work on hot-desking.

The emergence of hot-desking as a workspace management approach has sparked a multifaceted discussion within the related literature, exploring its implications across various dimensions. Hot desks, characterized by the absence of assigned desks and the utilization of shared workspaces, present challenges and opportunities for organizations and employees alike.

Karlsson (2012) demonstrates in his research how hot-desking involves a conflict between individuality and organizational standardization. The case study illustrates how employees strive to maintain a sense of identity and dignity in a dynamic workspace where personalization is restricted, sparking debates on autonomy and identity expression.

From a sociological point of view, Hirst (2011) provides a sociological analysis of emerging socio-spatial structures in hot-desking office environments, where space is used interchangeably. This matter highlights the emergence of a social structure that distinguishes between employees who settle in one place and those who must constantly move. It is noted that this movement generates additional work and feelings of marginalization. Additionally, it contextualizes hot-desking within the broader framework of capitalism, where space is used interchangeably to maximize economic returns. Instead of using the popular metaphor of 'nomad,' it employs the metaphor of 'vagrancy' to underscore the consequences of loss of space ownership.

On the managerial front, Cooper et al. (2017) and Morrison and Macky (2017) examine resource management and ergonomic implications of hot desks. Although advances in technology offer avenues for intelligent desk allocation, concerns regarding privacy, productivity, and employee well-being persist, necessitating a nuanced approach to implementation and regulation.

Endrejat and Burnes (2024) take a theoretical approach to navigate the complexities of organizational change associated with hot-desking. Drawing on Kurt Lewin's topology, the study illuminates the psychological barriers and resistance encountered during implementation, highlighting the need for comprehensive change management strategies.

On the contrary, studies by Ferguson et al. (2020) and Chadburn et al. (2017) offer critical reflections on the impact of hot-desking within specific professional domains. The adverse effects on social work culture and knowledge workers' productivity underscore the importance of contextualizing workspace design within professional practices and organizational cultures.

While the debates surrounding hot-desking continue to evolve, it is evident that its implications extend beyond mere spatial arrangements. The discourse underscores the need for a nuanced understanding of organizational dynamics, individual experiences, and social norms to shape the future of workspaces. As organizations navigate the complexities of modern work environments, embracing diversity, equity, and inclusivity in workspace design remains paramount to fostering innovation, collaboration, and employee well-being.

6. FUTURE RESEARCH DIRECTIONS

Hot-desking has been proven to be a very little explored topic given its scarce publications in 14 years. Therefore, although in such a case some proposals for the future agenda have been commented on above, it is worthy of note that the topic has been scarcely studied in the earlier literature, so there are many gaps to be filled. In this case and after this research, the following points are proposed for future studies. First, the use of more databases, taking special care to avoid duplication of documents. Second, the proposal is to carry out the same study through a methodology that includes and combines two bibliographic tools, such as SciMAT and VOSviewer. Therefore, it can favor a broader view of research topics for future work. Third, the findings suggest the introduction of more variables related to the research topic from which further analyses could be drawn. Indeed, it has previously been argued that limitations in the investigation of the topic are related to the difficulty in raising sufficient knowledge for economic development later in the future workforce.

8. CONCLUSIONS

Among the conclusions obtained from the study, it should be noted that the topic has been identified as a key issue that was scarcely studied in the previous literature, in addition to being booming with the growth of teleworking practices. The results identified in this study with only 24 articles between 2010 and 2024 show that it is a topic that attracts interest and that there is still much to explore. However, the lack of sufficient literature referring to hot desks in coworking spaces forces researchers interested in the subject of the study toward primary data to conduct quantitative research with a database of the highest quality. This also inhibits public efforts to promote emerging trends in the area. However, the discussion of the findings is a broad generalization and does not yet allow conclusions on economic costs.

As a result of the findings, the scope of the study initially focused on teleworking should be expanded beyond their core areas to identify additional needs in the business field. Consequently, the challenges and benefits of hot-desking seem to be intimately linked to hybrid works. In total practical terms, it is foreseeable that this labor matter will increase what companies do in the coming years, thus providing better practices to embrace new ways of working.

REFERENCES

Alshehri, A. A., Cheema, E., Yahyouche, A., Haque, M. S., & Jalal, Z. (2021). Evaluating the role and integration of general practice pharmacists in England: A cross-sectional study. *International Journal of Clinical Pharmacy*, 43(6), 1609–1618. DOI: 10.1007/s11096-021-01291-6 PMID: 34080088

Arnold, W., Arnold, D., Neher, A., & Miles, M. P. (2019). Developing a contemporary measure of employee perceptions of their work unit's psychological sense of community. *Journal of Workplace Learning*, 32(1), 16–34. DOI: 10.1108/JWL-03-2019-0040

Berelson, K., Simini, F., Tryfonas, T., & Cooper, P. (2018). Smart sensor-based hot searching to improve office well-being. Proceedings of the First International Conference on Digital Tools & Uses Congress - DTUC & 18. https://doi.org/ DOI: 10.1145/3240117.3240131

Carrasco-Garrido, C., De-Pablos-Heredero, C., & Rodríguez-Sánchez, J.-L. (2023). Exploring hybrid telework: A bibliometric analysis. *Heliyon*, 9(12), e22472. DOI: 10.1016/j.heliyon.2023.e22472 PMID: 38076145

Chadburn, A., Smith, J., & Milan, J. (2017). Productivity drivers of knowledge workers in the central London office environment. *Journal of Corporate Real Estate*, 19(2), 66–79. DOI: 10.1108/JCRE-12-2015-0047

Chua, S. J. L., Myeda, N. E., & Teo, Y. X. (2023). Facilities management: Toward implementation of flexible work arrangements (FWA) during COVID-19. *Journal of Facilities Management*, 21(5), 697–716. DOI: 10.1108/JFM-09-2021-0101

Cooper, P. B., Maraslis, K., Tryfonas, T., & Oikonomou, G. (2017). An intelligent hot-desking model harnessing the power of occupancy sensing data. *Facilities*, 35(13/14), 766–786. DOI: 10.1108/F-01-2016-0014

Egorova, M., D'Aponte, M., Ponomareva, D., & Minbaleev, A. (2021). The Impact of Digitalization on the Enterprise System: Russia and Italy and the discipline of smart working between constraints and opportunities. *Lexonomica*, 13(2), 151–166. DOI: 10.18690/lexonomica.13.2.151-166.2021

Endrejat, P. C., & Burnes, B. (2022). Draw it, check it, and change it: Reviving Lewin's topology to facilitate organisational change theory and practice. *The Journal of Applied Behavioral Science*, 60(1), 87–112. DOI: 10.1177/00218863221122875

Ferguson, H., Warwick, L., Cooner, T. S., Leigh, J., Beddoe, L., Disney, T., & Plumridge, G. (2020). The nature and culture of social work with children and families in long-term casework: Findings of a qualitative longitudinal study. Child & Family Social Work, 25(3), 694–703. Portico. https://doi.org/DOI: 10.1111/cfs.12746

Figueiredo, E., Margaça, C., Hernández-Sánchez, B., & Sánchez-García, J. C. (2024). Teleworking Effects on Mental Health—A Systematic Review and a Research Agenda. *International Journal of Environmental Research and Public Health*, 21(3), 243. DOI: 10.3390/ijerph21030243 PMID: 38541245

Fukumura, Y. E., Gray, J. M., Lucas, G. M., Becerik-Gerber, B., & Roll, S. C. (2021). Worker Perspectives on Incorporating Artificial Intelligence into Office Workspaces: Implications for the Future of Office Work. *International Journal of Environmental Research and Public Health*, 18(4), 1690. DOI: 10.3390/ijerph18041690 PMID: 33578736

Fulton, C. (2005). Hotdesking. *Mobile Information Systems*, II, 163–170. DOI: 10.1007/0-387-31166-1_12

Golden, T. D., Veiga, J. F., & Dino, R. N. (2008). The Impact of Professional Isolation on Teleworker Job Performance and Turnover Intentions: Does Time Spent Teleworking, Interacting Face-to-Face, or Having Access to Communication-Enhancing Technology Matter? *The Journal of Applied Psychology*, 93(6), 1412–1421. DOI: 10.1037/a0012722 PMID: 19025257

Groen, B. A. C., van Triest, S. P., Coers, M., & Wtenweerde, N. (2018). Managing flexible work arrangements: Teleworking and output controls. *European Management Journal*, 36(6), 727–735. DOI: 10.1016/j.emj.2018.01.007

Hirst, A. (2011). Settlers, vagrants and mutual indifference: Unintended consequences of hot-desking. *Journal of Organizational Change Management*, 24(6), 767–788. DOI: 10.1108/09534811111175742

Hopkins, J., & Bardoel, A. (2023). The Future Is Hybrid: How Organisations Are Designing and Supporting Sustainable Hybrid Work Models in Post-Pandemic Australia. Sustainability 2023, Vol. 15, Page 3086, 15(4), 3086. https://doi.org/ DOI: 10.3390/su15043086

Ipsen, C., Kirchner, K., Bolisani, E., & Scarso, E. (2023). In a digitalising Europe: Unfolding knowledge of working from home during the COVID-19 pandemic in Italy and Denmark. *Work (Reading, Mass.)*, 74(1), 59–74. DOI: 10.3233/WOR-220137 PMID: 36189522

Ipsen, C., van Veldhoven, M., Kirchner, K., & Hansen, J. P. (2021). Six Key Advantages and Disadvantages of Working from Home in Europe during COVID-19. International Journal of Environmental Research and Public Health 2021, Vol. 18, Page 1826, 18(4), 1826. https://doi.org/DOI: 10.3390/ijerph18041826

Karlsson, J. Ch. (2012). Hot-Desking and Family Photos. Organizational Misbehaviour in the Workplace, 144–144. https://doi.org/DOI: 10.1057/9780230354630_64

Kucera, J., Krulicky, T., & Navratilova, P. (2021). The trend of work from home and its advantages and disvantages during the COVID-19 pandemic: A comparative study. *Ad Alta-Journal of Interdisciplinary Research*, 11(2), 140–150. DOI: 10.33543/1102145150

Maraslis, K., Cooper, P., Tryfonas, T., & Oikonomou, G. (2016). An Intelligent Hot-Desking Model Based on Occupancy Sensor Data and Its Potential for Social Impact. *Lecture Notes in Computer Science*, 9860, 142–158. DOI: 10.1007/978-3-662-53416-8_9

Millward, L. J., Haslam, S. A., & Postmes, T. (2007). Putting Employees in Their Place: The Impact of Hot Desking on Organizational and Team Identification. *Organization Science*, 18(4), 547–559. DOI: 10.1287/orsc.1070.0265

Morrison, R. L., & Macky, K. A. (2017). The demands and resources arising from shared office spaces. *Applied Ergonomics*, 60, 103–115. DOI: 10.1016/j.apergo.2016.11.007 PMID: 28166868

Murillo-Ramos, L., Huertas-Valdivia, I., & García-Muiña, F. E. (2022). Exploring the cornerstones of green, sustainable and socially responsible human resource management. *International Journal of Manpower*, 44(3), 524–542. DOI: 10.1108/IJM-12-2021-0696

Pan, J., Cho, T. Y., Sun, M., Debnath, R., Lonsdale, N., Wilcox, C., & Bardhan, R. (2023). Future workspace needs flexibility and diversity: A machine learning-driven behavioural analysis of coworking space. PLoS ONE, 18(10 October). https://doi.org/DOI: 10.1371/journal.pone.0292370

Pérez, M. P., Sánchez, A. M., De Luis Carnicer, P., & Vela Jiménez, M. J. (2005). The differences of firm resources and the adoption of teleworking. *Technovation*, 25(12), 1476–1483. DOI: 10.1016/j.technovation.2005.04.002

Salvador-Oliván, J. A., & Agustín-Lacruz, C. (2015). Correlación entre indicadores bibliométricos en revistas de Web of Science y Scopus. *Revista General de Información y Documentación*, 25(2). Advance online publication. DOI: 10.5209/rev_RGID.2015.v25.n2.51241

Selwyn-Rowland, T. (2021). Impact of Hotdesking on team cohesion. *Journal of Asia Entrepreneurship and Sustainability*, 17(5), 123–152.

Stanford University. (2021). Bloom, N. Hybrid in the future work. Available at: https://drive.google.com/file/d/1U8NeVFONOHO0rHQq6A4hytlm3I1wio0T/view (URL date accessed on 31 July 2023). Publication based on the Working Paper https://www.nber.org/papers/w28731

Teleoacă Vartolomei, B. O. (2020). Considerations Regarding Work from Home and Telework. *Proceedings of the International Conference on Business Excellence*, 14(1), 1217–1221. https://doi.org/DOI: 10.2478/picbe-2020-0115

van Eck, N. J., & Waltman, L. (2009). Software survey: VOSviewer, a computer program for bibliometric mapping. *Scientometrics*, 84(2), 523–538. DOI: 10.1007/s11192-009-0146-3 PMID: 20585380

Vinezuela-Cabezas, A., Osejo-Taco, G., Unda-López, A., Paz, C., & Hidalgo-Andrade, P. (2022). A Comparison of Working Conditions and Workers' Perceptions among On-Site, Telework, and Hybrid Workers in Ecuador during the COVID-19 Pandemic. *International Journal of Environmental Research and Public Health*, 19(21), 14337. DOI: 10.3390/ijerph192114337 PMID: 36361220

Wei, G. (2019). A Map of Bibliometrics and Scientometrics in Journals of Various Disciplines Excluding Library and Information Science From 2009 to 2018. SSRN Electronic Journal. https://doi.org/DOI: 10.2139/ssrn.3557950

Wieser, L., & Abraham, M. (2024). Employee acceptance of digital monitoring systems while working from home. *New Technology, Work and Employment*, 39(1), 109–142. DOI: 10.1111/ntwe.12280

Zupic, I., & Čater, T. (2014). Bibliometric Methods in Management and Organization. *Organizational Research Methods*, 18(3), 429–472. DOI: 10.1177/1094428114562629

KEY TERMS AND DEFINITIONS

Hot-desking: Workplace strategy where employees do not have permanently assigned desks. Instead, they select from available workstations each day on a first-come, first-served basis. This approach promotes flexibility, optimizes the use of office space, and encourages interaction among employees from different departments. While it can enhance collaboration and reduce costs, it may also present challenges related to personal space and privacy.

VOSviewer: Sophisticated software application specifically designed to construct, visualize, and explore bibliographic networks. These networks can encompass various elements, such as journals, researchers, and individual publications, and can be based on different types of relationship, including citation, bibliographic coupling, cocitation, or coauthorship. One of the key features of VOSviewer is its advanced text mining capabilities, which enable the creation and visualization of co-occurrence networks of significant terms extracted from large bodies of scientific literature. This tool is widely used in academic research to map and analyze the structure, development, and interconnections within scientific fields. VOSviewer supports the analysis of large-scale data and offers user-friendly graphical representations, making it easier to interpret complex bibliometric data. Researchers use VOSviewer to identify research trends, detect emerging topics, and explore the intellectual landscape of various academic disciplines.

Telework: Telecommuting, or teleworking, refers to a work arrangement in which employees perform their tasks and responsibilities from a location other than the employer's premises, using information and communication technologies (ICT) to maintain communication and collaboration with colleagues and supervisors. This type of work allows greater flexibility in terms of work hours and location and typically involves the use of tools such as email, video conferencing, project management systems, and other digital platforms. Telework is studied from various perspectives, including its impact on productivity, work-life balance, mental health, and employee well-being, as well as its influence on organizational structure and team dynamics.

Open-plan office: Workplace layout that features large open spaces without or with minimal partitions between desks or workstations. This design encourages collaboration and communication between employees by reducing physical barriers and promoting a more fluid and interactive environment. Open-plan offices often include shared areas such as meeting rooms, break areas, and collaborative spaces to facilitate teamwork and creative exchange. This layout is intended to enhance flexibility, efficiency in space use, and a sense of organizational transparency, although its effectiveness and impact on employee productivity and privacy have been the subject of ongoing debate and research in workplace design.

Chapter 8
Teleworking and the Deployment of Dynamic Capabilities

Cristina Gallego-Gomez
https://orcid.org/0000-0002-7477-520X
Universidad Rey Juan Carlos, Spain

Carmen De-Pablos Heredero
https://orcid.org/0000-0003-0457-3730
Universidad Rey Juan Carlos, Spain

José Luis Montes
https://orcid.org/0000-0001-9024-6167
Universidad Rey Juan Carlos, Spain

ABSTRACT

Teleworking was just an option for many companies up to mid-2020. (1)This study examines the acceptance of teleworking practices by employees because of the covid-19 scenario from the dynamic capabilities' framework. Although this study is based on whether telework promotes dynamic capabilities within organizations, specifically absorption and adaptation capabilities, it includes other factors, such as quality of life and productivity. (2)A questionnaire has been built and distributed to 1000 Spanish workers. Data were processed by using the structural equation modeling analysis (SEM). (3) Results confirm that the model built provides a sound theoretical framework to understand and explain the practice of teleworking in a work environment, providing workers with a longer time to rest, an increase in their quality of life (4) This work can help companies understand the need to redesign telework processes based on the deployment of dynamic capabilities to achieve bet-

DOI: 10.4018/979-8-3693-6289-1.ch008

ter results from this practice, which is no longer an option in pandemic scenarios.

1 INTRODUCTION

Technological advances play a fundamental role in the way we communicate and in today's work systems. As a result of digitization, COVID 19 and new trends, a change has taken place in the new ways of consuming information, both in work and learning environments (Morrar, et al., 2017; Paiola y Gebauer, 2020). The technological advance and the threats caused by the COVID-19 pandemic made the organizational challenges increase and require an effort of adaptation by companies and workers in circumstances not yet known, since Spanish society, due to having a consolidated primary and services sector, had not experienced massive teleworking actions before COVID-19.

In this context, companies that have to adapt their work processes during the health alarm are opting for a remote working model, i.e. teleworking. teleworking has been the most common working practice during the pandemic. Initially, it was a result of the necessary processes to adapt jobs to the new Covid-19 scenario, but it has been accepted by both companies and workers over time, maintained beyond the health alarm (Metallo, et al., 2022) to this day, giving rise to a mixed model, where workers combine remote work with office attendance as dictated by the regulations that emerged to regulate this situation in Spain, Law 10/2021 of July 9, on Remote Work.

Based on these two modalities, it should be noted that according to Vartiainen (2021), there is a difference between teleworking and remote work. It is mainly because remote work uses personal electronic devices in addition to physically be working remotely from a place other than an office or company, while teleworking does not require visits to the main office, workplace, or use of personal electronic devices. In addition, there is the category of "remote and mobile phone workers" who use places other than home to work, and digital online telework is flexible both in time and place, which is the main characteristic.

Although there are particularities in each modality, both present generalized advantages in the adoption of new work models. According to Metallo, et al., (2022) it is not a reality that organizations can introduce changes them quickly and without problems. Teleworking is not based on accurately replicating the traditional way of working, but rather requires rethinking the work process to achieve success. The literature affirms that it *is essential to activate communication mechanisms, and social exchanges increase 'employees' feelings of connection with and trust in their colleagues, leading to greater satisfaction and motivation* (Shipman, et al., 2021).

Therefore, it is necessary to address telework from a systemic approach, since its successful implementation does not simply respond to the sum of the factors that compose it. There are elements that have emerged as a result of mixed work patterns, and that is why hybrid work models, platform innovation and new business opportunities focused on sustainability and increased digitization are components to be managed from the organizational point of view to maintain and increase the productivity of teams, which has been one of the main concerns and determinants of resistance to change in work models (Stoian et al., 2022).

In fact, hybrid work emerges as a combination of face-to-face work and teleworking. Following the pandemic, companies have opted to introduce "flexible hybrid work programs" as a commitment to the welfare of their employees by offering them the flexibility they value so much, especially young people, who are choosing to work in companies that offer this benefit. Based on this, the National Observatory of Technology and Society [ONTSI], (2022) points to a direct relationship between talent retention and hybrid work. The institution states that from 2020 to 2022, Spain has gone from being the European country with the lowest implementation of teleworking to the third with the highest preference for this modality to the return to normality, where workers ask to extend the days of teleworking in those places where it is limited. This is why Spain becomes an opportunity for study to explore how companies are approaching this process, since organizations that respond best to this request from employees will have more opportunities to attract talent. From an organizational point of view, this modality allows redesigning jobs to better adjust to the levels of teleworking expectations of its employees, through an efficient planning of tasks by management (Urién, 2023). According to Carrasco-Garrido et al., (2023) this telework modality is more beneficial than other telework alternatives for both workers and organizations.

In this sense, according to Jacquenet (2021), the virus is not the only reason to rethink the current design of organizations but the potential of technology itself too. Today we count on infrastructures that enable teleworking. For example, greater speed through 5G is among the technologies of networking that promote the spread of new services, such as immersive services based on Augmented Reality/Virtual Reality techniques, among other uses, and providing the speed and new mechanisms necessary to redefine the way we work.

Because the demands in the markets, the available elements must be reconfigured and adapted to give optimal responses. In this context, the theory of dynamic capabilities arises, which is defined as organizational and strategic routines developed through organizational learning and molded by path dependencies, complementary assets, and industry opportunities (Teece et al., 1997). This is possible, thanks to the recombination of the required resources to develop value creation strategies that allow companies to remain competitive and continue to perform their work in the market effectively (Hernández-Linares, et al., 2018; Polo, et al., 2020). In fact, according to Ali, et al., (2022), based on Teece et al. (1997) and Teece (2007), the following is stated: *Prior research suggests that cultivation of dynamic capabilities becomes crucial for firms to respond to external shocks, and it is in such a context that scholars have highlighted their role in enhancing firm's performance. Companies can mitigate external impacts by leveraging their key resources and effectively deploying key capabilities* (Ali et al,2022:2).

In fact, from the RBV perspective, in organizations that are already mature in the adoption of digitization and have technical expertise, ease of use is emerging as a resource for the adoption of Industry 4.0 technologies, these tools that enable the automation of organizational processes are found with an intention to reconfigure their technological competencies (Rodriguez, et al., 2022).

Based on this theory, this study examines whether dynamic capabilities are developed in organizations that accept teleworking as a new input to reach greater efficiency within the company due to the covid-19 scenario. This context causes companies to continue to maintain the development of their competitive advantages, and the theory holds that in the face of new or adverse circumstances, a positive impact occurs in the competitiveness of companies through dynamic capabilities, which play a crucial role in pursuing it (Teece, 2014). This study is based on a dynamic capabilities' framework, specifically absorption and adaptation, both of which are relevant because they are determining factors in the acquisition of new knowledge and how the companies apply them. However, it includes more variables linked to purely business such as employee satisfaction, productivity, and improved quality of life. This research constitutes the first approach to the application of dynamic capabilities theory to teleworking practices and is framed by workers from the different Autonomous Communities of Spain.

According to previous explanations, this work analyzes how the active Spanish population senses the telework situation concerning their personal situation. Teleworking was perceived during the pandemic as a unique alternative to work. However, the reality is that keeping it when the pandemic situation improves seems not to be as viable as advertised (Gala Durán, 2021).

Therefore, this work is oriented to answer the following three research questions:

- RH1: Is there influence of adaptive capacity on the absorptive capacity?
- RH2: Is there an influence of absorptive capacity on the productivity resulting capability?
- RH3: Is there an influence of the adaptation capability on the productivity resulting capability?

This research specifically analyzes: (1) The influence between variables such as work-life balance, autonomy and trust in relation to attendance, absenteeism, learning, innovation and internal promotion; (2) The influence between variables such as attendance, absenteeism, learning, innovation and internal promotion in relation to productivity, rest and quality of life, and; (3) The influence between variables such as work-life balance, autonomy and trust in relation to productivity, rest and quality of life. Accordingly, this article contributes to the literature in several ways. First, it will demonstrate the influence between selected dynamic capabilities and how telework is reconfigured by those organizational capabilities, which will help scholars choose the most relevant literature on the topic and identify possible gaps in the research base. Second, it provides a descriptive contribution on this specific area of research and the state of the art offering relevant studies related to the topic under study.

Results of this research can help companies where teleworking is possible to understand how workers in different situations adopt changes in the way they work and if this really helps increase the 'company's productivity and adds value to "worker's quality of life".

This research is structured as follows: After an introduction that addresses the topic of telework, the theoretical framework is presented to go in deep on dynamic capabilities and present the hypotheses. The methodology section describes how the research has been carried out. Afterwards, the results are explained. After a discussion, the paper shows the conclusions.

2 THEORETICAL FRAMEWORK

2.1. Dynamic Capabilities in the Context of Organizations

It is a fact that the digital transformation within the company has gained momentum and not only in the high technology industry, where teleworking was cautiously introduced, but in diverse fields such as training or self-learning. This is an opportunity for leaders who manage companies, as they can create long-term competitive advantages based on digital innovation (Kamning, 2021)

In this research, we turn to the theory of dynamic capabilities (Teece, et al.,1990) to explain the adoption and absorption of these new routines through the internal perspective of the firm (modifying the design of resources since they had to be reconfigured due to the pandemic) and by considering the external perspective (oriented to adapt and follow a dynamically changing environment) (Cyfert et al., 2021; Dovbischuk, 2022). In this sense, knowledge is created within companies derived from internal and external learning transformed into new forms of work management.

The concept of dynamic capabilities emphasizes the critical importance of firms adapting to changes coming from the environment. In the management of processes, a company can identify and prevent harmful forms of dependence on the road, avoid blockages and maintain levels of development of skills and appropriate organizational changes in terms of market evolution or management (Cyfert, et al., 2021; Hermano, et al., 2022).

Hermano, et al., (2022) affirm that dynamic capabilities have the objective to help the organization to address environmental changes using a collection of routines. Also, Hermano, et al., (2022), confirmed that adaptive and absorptive capabilities have an effect in the medium and short term in the improvement of the services offered. In this sense, adaptive capability is especially useful to detect opportunities in new markets, where gaps still exist, which indicates they are not saturated (Chakravarthy, 1982, Hooley et al., 1992, Miles & Snow, 1978, Wang & Ahmed, 2007, Biedenbach & Müller, 2012). These authors show that market surveillance leads to the opening of new products to new markets, as can be detected by monitoring trends over short periods of time, when the idea is still incipient.

Critical elements of adaptive capabilities are the ability to respond in a short space of time to market changes and develop products that meet the imminent demand (Chakravarthy, 1982). Furthermore, research suggests that adaptability should lead to an improved performance. In other words, it is necessary for companies to be aware of their current market situation in order to provide qualified people to manage the business cycle and enable growth. These decisions have a risk and a direct impact on the business due to the need for change and reconfiguration for organizational prosperity, since the company is a dynamic entity by nature.

2.2. Absorption and Adaptative Capabilities

In fact, the capacity to adapt is linked to organizational resilience (Napier et al.,2024), because it is emerging as a mandatory capacity that companies must have to face times in which that changes happen very quickly due to great technological advances, pandemics, etc. Therefore, flexible resources that adapt to adversities are needed.

According to Zahra and Hayton (2008), absorptive capability is defined as a dynamic capability to deliberately create, expand, and modify a firm's resource base (Zahra y George 2002), and a higher-order capacity to develop skills and capabilities (Eisenhardt y Martin 2000). In fact, absorption capability consists of identifying knowledge and incorporating it for commercial purposes and thus maximizing value creation in the firm (Bastanchury-López et al.,2020; Gallego-Gómez

& De-Pablos-Heredero, 2013). These dimensions are interrelated, allowing us to study the development and interaction of telework skills and competencies. In fact, innovation and development are increased by the influence of the environment to improve learning capability in companies, as they develop absorptive capabilities through this process (Biedenbach & Müller, 2012).

Absorption and adaptation are related, according to Dovbischuk (2022), because of the ability to absorb the impact of disruptive events related to COVID-19 by resisting change. According to Shipman et al., (2021), the unexpected change from face-to-face work to remote work in 2020, meant that organizations could not comply with the new working conditions since they had neither the means nor the knowledge to do so, due to the speed of implementation. The companies that adopted this form of work for the first time were mostly unaware of the dynamics of communication, expectations, responsibilities, policies, implementation strategies, tasks to be handled with this modality. Among them, it involves managing priority issues such as reconciling life and mental health and employee welfare.

Precisely, according to the definition of Cyfert et al.,(2021), the capability of adaptation is what promotes the following organizational benefits: 1) transformation of the business model, 2) managing the organizational boundaries, which transforms the dimensions of efficiency, power, competence and organizational culture 3) ensuring an adequate level of dynamism in the strategic management process, taking into account the need to influence the organization by means of an appropriate level of coordination with the environment by maintaining the identity. 4) improvement of the organization to ensure a higher level of adaptation to the environment 5) Adaptation and implementation of best management practices 6) guarantor of the flexibility of the organizational structure according to the implementation of modern solutions based on the organization's networks.

The organizations that have deployed dynamic capabilities have better adapted to the crisis caused by the pandemic. They refer to this situation as agility. It is precisely this agility that gives rise to theories dealing with adaptability, perception, and reaction to change, and the associated competitive advantages (Heidt et al., 2023).

Changing to a work strategy can help companies locate opportunities for their clients and be successful in their innovation process (Christensen et al.,2016). Companies can improve their growth and profitability in the short term through R&D strategies that promote, for example, internationalization to achieve this. However, they will not be able to achieve it in a short time horizon unless they improve their absorptive capability (Zahra & Hayton, 2008). However, the company's organizational innovation continues in the background, prioritizing technological innovation. Furthermore, organizational innovation is essential for the correct development of good business practices, the organization of the workspace and encourages both external collaboration and coworking (Fernandes et al.,2018).

The absorptive capability links the knowledge generated outside the company with the knowledge generated within the company to quote (Tengjian et al.,2018). That is why we chose this capability to explain individual and organizational learning, which has led to the new ways of working that have been promoted both internally and through interorganizational processes, since this capacity is directly related to organizational learning (Zahra & George 2002; Todorova & Durisin, 2007), Additionally, according to Tengjian et al., (2018) this capability is influenced in its development by the size of the company, stating that large companies are in a better position to build their absorptive capability by having more resources. However, it is not the only variable, the age of the company also influences to develop this capability, since it is based on previously accumulated knowledge (Cohen y Levinthal, 1990) and they absorb more external knowledge.

Cui et al. (2020) based their research on the absorption capability, concluded that this capability produced three other knowledge abilities: 1) knowledge exploitation capacity 2) knowledge exploration capacity, 3) Capacity for social integration between companies in an environment of collaborative innovation. These capabilities are hampered by the lack of physical contact/shared physical space and by a significant decrease in informal conversations and contacts in professional networks outside the organization are reduced.

According to Neuber et al., (2021) the results of work engagement depend on three facets (vigor, dedication, and absorption). Yalabik et al., (2017) defined these facets. Vitality refers to the energy used to achieve the objectives, the mental resistance that requires resilience at work and the effort for continuous improvement. Dedication means being inspired, sharing the values of the company, and very committed to your work. The final dimension, immersion, refers to a greater sense of concentration and immersion in work and a lack of awareness about the time spent at work (Extremera et al., 2018).

Several studies have emphasized the importance of absorptive capacity for increasing a 'company' productivity (Acevedo & Díaz-Molina, 2021; Zhou et al., 2020).

Porter and Lawler (1968) are committed to worker satisfaction. The authors suggest that the way to achieve this is to generate a work environment based on both internal and external rewards. The strategy of organizations in recent times focuses on offering challenges, motivations and benefits to make the employee feel "happy" and thus achieve a committed and lasting relationship with the company, which is associated with greater productivity and success in organizational management (Fogaça & Júnior, 2016).

Having into consideration previous arguments, the following hypothesis is proposed:

- H1: The adaptation capability influences the absorption capability.

2.3. Productivity Result Capability

Burrell (2020) identifies a need for middle management to help employees be productive by using technology platforms and communication tools to facilitate relationships and collaboration between co-workers, through appropriate technical assistance.

In addition, decision makers must ensure that the rules of transparency are observed among all of them for the proper performance of functions. The duties and work to be performed must be perfectly defined to reduce confusion and stress of employees. Providing technical resources and training for remote work is a good practice that employees need to increase their productivity.

Participants found it difficult to maintain their pre-pandemic productivity levels because of the lack of available technological resources, such as printers, photocopiers, or home scanners. Participants also reported difficulties in maintaining a stable Internet connection while working remotely (Shipman et al., 2021).

In addition, the adaptation capability is the ability to combine existing internal and external knowledge and create new and improve the productivity of knowledge workers (Khaksar et al.,2020). The knowledge technology is very dynamic because it is defined as an industry that evolves rapidly in its knowledge and involves the effort of organizations to be updated so as not to fall into obsolescence in order to maintain their capacity for innovation. This is why organizations need to learn before implementing new solutions to be more efficient.

However, workers must also redefine the resources they have and the capabilities associated with their knowledge to maintain their results, in terms of productivity. This adaptation is called adaptive performance (Bieńkowska & Tworek, 2020) and is based on the ability to transfer training/learning from one task to another within the organizational culture, maintaining satisfaction, personal and work motivation, and engagement towards the task. organization.

There are employees who face changes as challenges and are proactive in including changes in their routines as part of continuous improvement or adverse situations. This behavior helps the company maintain its efficiency. These are employees with high skills and knowledge, who are valuable assets for the company and therefore, it must maintain their satisfaction as part of its challenges. That is, the human resources department plays a fundamental role in the adoption of changes, and must guide CEOs as part of their job, so that the company remains attractive to maintain and attract the best talent as part of its success business (Lopez-Cabrales et al., 2017).

Based on the above arguments, the following assumptions are made:

- H2: The absorption capability influences the productivity of the company
- H3: The adaptation capability influences the productivity of workers.

2.4. Hypothetical Model

After the foundation of the research hypotheses, a research model is proposed in Figure 1.

In the model, the capacity for productivity results is identified as the dependent variable, since it is the main variable of the object of study and its value depends on how independent variables are measured, which in this case are the absorption and adaptation capacities.

Figure 1. The model research

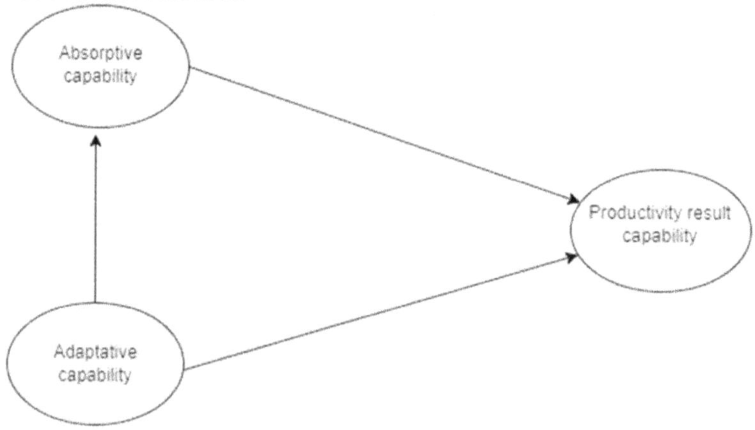

Own Elaborated, 2024

3 METHODOLOGY

3.1. Instrument and Analysis

Structural equation modeling (SEM) was used in this study. Latent variables (constructs) represent concepts and indicators are input data. SEM looks for causal relationships between latent variables and assumes complex relationships (with direct and indirect effects) (Ringle, Wende, & Will, 2005).

The method was applied to data obtained from the responses of "workers" to the afore mentioned online questionnaire (n = 1000). Analyze data using structural equation modeling (SEM) to estimate and test causal relationships between multiple dependent and independent constructs in a single analysis.

3.2. Sample

Regarding the selection of the sample, it has been considered that all age groups participate, including people with and without children who have different levels of education, situations and who work in different sectors.

In Spain, office work is predominant in Madrid and Barcelona, but all of rest regions of the country are represented, as this is a study at the Spanish level. This questionnaire survey has been distributed throughout Spain in its seventeen Autonomous Communities, although the response rate is not entirely homogeneous. The highest responses come from Andalusia, 18.1%, Catalonia, 15.9%, the Community of Madrid, 14%, and the Valencian Community, 10.7%. The communities with the minor representation are La Rioja, 0.8%, Navarra, and Cantabria, with 1.4% of responses.

By age groups, all of them in active age are represented, from 20 to 29 years old (12.7%), from 30 to 39 years old (26.5%), from 40 to 49 years old (35.6%), and 50 to 65 (25.2%). Of the total of those surveyed, 54.5% have children, to have the perspective of conciliation, and 45.5% of those surveyed do not have children.

The investigation was performed on a sample of 1000 workers from June (2021/06/29) to July (2021/07/15). During this time, the online survey was sent to them.

3.3. Questionnaire Design

Regarding the procedure, we conducted an online survey among people working in Spanish organizations to test the hypothesized relationships. The online survey was conducted using the Google Forms platform, and the link distribution time for completing the survey was half a month. This study received the support of an agency that distributed it through its subscribers. After defining the target audience with them, nineteen filter questions allow a detailed analysis.

3.4. Measurement Scales

The dependent variable refers to the measurement that organizations that telework manage to increase their dynamic capabilities.

The measurement scale is on a 5-point Likert-type scale, anchored in totally disagree (1) and totally agree (5). This is intended to measure the items that help to know the willingness of workers to accept telework as a possibility that allows them a higher quality of life, productivity, and rest. Through this scale respondents were asked if they thought teleworking was here to stay and how it has helped them in their personal and professional development.

The following figure (Table. 1) shows the measurement indicators of each of the variables.

Table 1. Questionnaire, variables, & authors. own elaborated, 2021

Questionnaire	Variable	Meaning	Inspiring Authors
Do you think teleworking has helped you reconcile your personal, work and family life?	ADAP_CONC	Adaptation	Cyfert et al.(2021); Shipman et al. (2021)
Do you think that teleworking increases your autonomy?	ADAP_AUTO		
Do you think your boss trusts employees when they telework?	ADAP_CONF		
Do you think that telework allows you increasing your presence in front of the computer?	ABS_PRESE	Absorption	Kamning (2021), Neuber, et al. (2021); Dovbischuk (2022)
Do you think that teleworking helps reduce absenteeism?	ABS_ABSE		
Do you think that teleworking can be a promoter of learning within the company?	ABS_LEAR		
Do you consider that teleworking can be a driver for innovation within the company?	ABS_INNO		
Do you think that teleworking can be a stimulus for internal promotion within the company?	ABS_PROMO		
Do you think teleworking has increased your productivity?	RESUL_PROD	Result	Adamovic (2022); Rodríguez-Modroño & López-Igual, (2021); Niu, et al. (2021); Acevedo y Díaz-Molina (2021)
Do you think that you can disconnect to rest despite teleworking?	RESUL _DESC		
Do you consider that your quality of life has increased with teleworking?	RESUL_QUAL		

4 RESULTS

4.1. Model Measurements

In order to establish the relationships between the hypotheses, a model based on structural equations is proposed. This type of model is selected because it allows for graphical representation, which implies a visualization of the variables and relationships under study. Based on this, this procedure has the possibility of analyzing causal effects between variables, allowing the concatenation of effects between variables and allowing reciprocal relationships between them.

To do this, the model was estimated by applying the Partial Least Squares (PLS) procedure using the Smart PLS 3.3.9 software program (Ringle et al., 2005). The reasons that have motivated its choice are based on the following criteria: (1) the phenomenon investigated is relatively new, (2) its modelling is in an emerging stage, so the minimum recommendations of PLS regarding sample size are followed, (3) Prediction accuracy and comparatively low demands regarding multinormality of the data are required (Jöreskog and Wold, 1982; Henseler & Chin, 2010).

To evaluate the model, we proceeded in two phases: first, we evaluated the measurement model; then, the measurement model. Structural model. Considering the external (measurement) model, the factor loadings are above the thresholds of 0.600. The reliability of internal consistency was measured by Cronbach's alpha (Cronbach, 1951) and by the composite reliability (Dillon-Goldstein rho). Both measurements exceed the minimum threshold values proposed for exploratory research, the threshold of 0.600. Convergent validity was verified by the average variance extracted (AVE), taking values greater than 0.5 except for the ABS construct. Regarding discriminant validity, the Fornell-Larcker and cross-loading criteria were met.

4.3. Model Results

We built a structural equation model (SEM) to test the relationships between indicators and latent constructs and the structural relationships between the latent constructs. The model is based on three latent variables. Two of them, corresponding to dynamic capabilities, i.e. the capacity for absorption and adaptation, are measured through the factors detected in the questionnaire. These latent variables cannot be observed directly, so the coefficients by which they are measured are provided.

On the other hand, the result variable is a latent variable, which does not correspond to the theory of dynamic capabilities, but when these capabilities are implemented in companies, they have a positive influence on rest, productivity and quality of life, which are the three factors that define the productivity result variable (figure.2).

Figure 2. The model

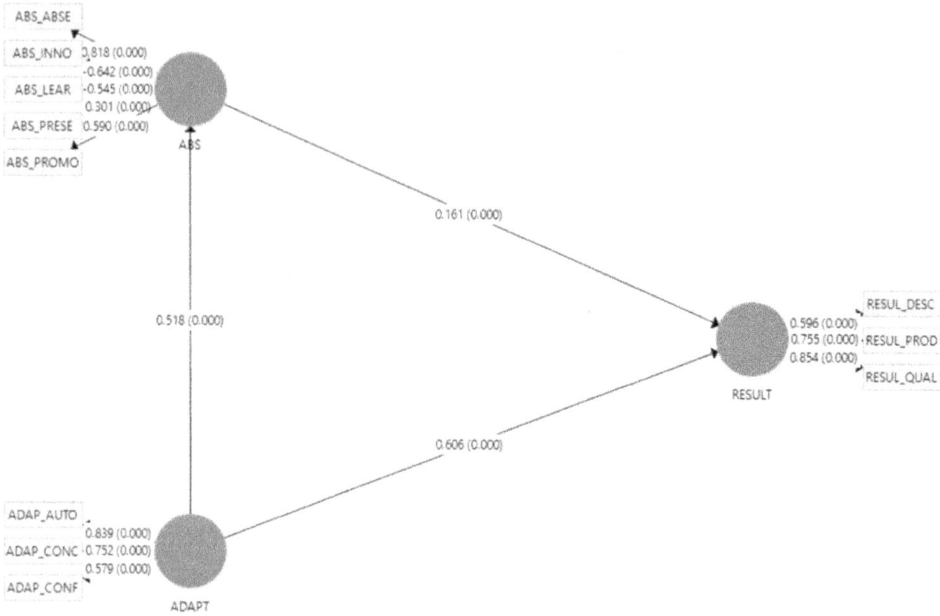

Own Elaborated, 2021

All the path values are significant (p<0.000).Results show a significant positive relationship between adaptive capability and absorptive capability (H1: β= 0.518, p <.000), absorptive capability and results capability (H2: β= 0.161, p <.0.000), adaptive capability and productivity results capability (H3: β= 0.606, p <.0.000), which confirms the three hypotheses raised

As descriptive results, it should be noted that all 1000 individuals were workers, 501 of whom (50,1%) were men, and 499 (49,9%) were women. All of them have worked, but the current situation is that 74.5% are working, of which 88.9% are employed, and 11.1% are self-employed. 5.0% are retired, 10.5% are without work, and 3% combine it with their studies. Of the total, 54.5% have children, while 45.5% do not.

Regarding the level of studies, 36.4% have second-cycle studies, followed by 33.6% who have third-degree studies of more than four years of career, followed by 21.7% who have third-degree studies, equivalent to a three-year career. To a lesser extent, only 7.0% contain studies related to primary/secondary school, and 1.1% the school certificate.

DISCUSSION

The research findings confirm that teleworking needs of the deployment of a variety of organizational capabilities to be effective inside the firm. Factors such as productivity, rest and increased quality of life make workers have accepted the model imposed in pandemic scenario positively.

In this sense, adaptive and absorptive capabilities exhibit a direct impact on final firm's performance. Both capabilities demands a reorganization of existing resources like personnel, facilities, and production machinery (Valtonen et al.,2022). And as previously found by Dovbischuk (2022), the result of our research finds a relationship between absorption and adaptation capabilities. The ability to absorb the impact of disruptive events related to COVID-19 has forced companies to develop adaptation capabilities by developing organizational mechanisms to resist change at a fast speed.

Concerning to absorptive capability, according to Shipman, Burrell, and Huff (2021), at the beginning of 2020, the rapid and unexpected shift from face-to-face to remote work left many organizations underpowered to meet the new working conditions. Our results also show that the absorptive capability promotes higher degrees in terms of employee productivity as Acevedo & Díaz-Molina, 2021; Zhou et al., (2020) have previously found.

According to Cyfert et al., (2021), adaptative capability promotes benefits at organizations, such as transforming and adapting the existing business model. The adaptative capability also influences worker's productivity in view of our results. This is aligned with results derived from previous analyses as the one from Khaksar et al., (2020).

However, today there is reluctance on the part of companies to keep on with practices, even though temporarily, they adapted their processes to new forms of work enhancing the use of technology (Woiceshyn, 2005; Christensen et al., 2016; Alves et al., 2018). Further research should be focused on the analysis of variables that may provide a deep explanation of this reality.

5 CONCLUSION

According to the results, we can affirm that:

- RH1: The adaptive capability influences the absorption capability.
- RH2: The absorption capability influences the productivity resulting capability.
- RH3: The adaptation capability influences the productivity resulting capability.

Therefore, the research questions have been solved through the validation of the proposed model.

These results confirm that the model with dynamic capabilities built provides a sound theoretical model to help understand and explain the practice of teleworking in a work environment, providing insight in the relationship between the capabilities analyzed and the results of indicators.

The relationship that adaptability exerts on absorption capability is one of the main contributions of this work from the theoretical perspective.

This model helps in the transformation process to new ways of working at organizations. It contributes to understand the importance of increasing dynamic capabilities in organizations and understand better their relationships which can result in less absenteeism and greater learning abilities by employees and therefore, enhance improvements in organizational innovation and promotions of workers.

These results are particularly relevant at a time when companies have already learned lessons in managing new environments in practical terms, labor regulations and have new technological systems in place for collaboration that allow them to embrace change and evolve.

Finally, this paper entails some theoretical and practical contributions. From the theoretical perspective, it implies an advance in the application of the dynamic capabilities' theory to remote work environments. From the practical perspective, this research can help companies understand the need to redesign telework processes based on the deployment of dynamic capabilities. In an unforeseen and crisis scenario as the covid-19 one, teleworking practices have become essential for firms to continue being operative.

The limitations of this work may be related to the bias of active workers who have little experience in the work modalities mentioned when answering the survey. Currently, society is more mature in this subject, being more aware of the implications.

Therefore, a longitudinal study that would lead to comparative work is a future line of thought.

As second line of research, this study could be conducted focusing not only on employees but also on company managers, analyzing the inputs analyzed in the post-covid era and the effectiveness of business results by adopting different work models. Additionally, the challenges of the hybrid work model can be studied for small and medium-sized companies, where their needs are different in terms of management and there is little literature focused on this (Benedic, 2023). Also, the dynamic capabilities model can focus on the necessary capabilities to be adopted by workers within a company to determine the factors necessary to reconfigure to achieve personal success in terms of productivity, satisfaction and work-life balance.

CONFLICT OF INTEREST

On behalf of all authors, the corresponding author states that there is no conflict of interest.

DATA AVAILABLE

The datasets generated during and/or analysed during the current study are available from the corresponding author on reasonable request.

REFERENCES

Adamovic, M. (2022). How does employee cultural background influence the effects of telework on job stress? The roles of power distance, individualism, and beliefs about telework. *International Journal of Information Management*, 62, 102437. DOI: 10.1016/j.ijinfomgt.2021.102437

Ali, I., Arslan, A., Chowdhury, M., Khan, Z., & Tarba, S. Y. (2022). Reimagining global food value chains through effective resilience to COVID-19 shocks and similar future events: A dynamic capability perspective. *Journal of Business Research*, 141, 1–12. DOI: 10.1016/j.jbusres.2021.12.006 PMID: 34908632

Ayuso, L., Requena, F., Jiménez-Rodriguez, O., & Khamis, N. (2020). The effects of COVID-19 confinement on the Spanish family: Adaptation or change? *Journal of Comparative Family Studies*, 51(3-4), 274–287. DOI: 10.3138/jcfs.51.3-4.004

Bastanchury-López, M. T., De-Pablos-Heredero, C., Montes-Botella, J. L., Martin-Romo-Romero, S., & Garcia, A. (2020). Impact of dynamic capabilities on performance in dairy sheep farms in Spain. *Sustainability (Basel)*, 12(8), 3368. DOI: 10.3390/su12083368

Benedic, M. (2023). Hybrid work for small businesses: Strategies for reaping benefits. *The Journal of Business Strategy*. Advance online publication. DOI: 10.1108/JBS-09-2022-0163

Biedenbach, T., & Müller, R. (2012). Absorptive, innovative and adaptive capabilities and their impact on project and project portfolio performance. *International Journal of Project Management*, 30(5), 621–635. DOI: 10.1016/j.ijproman.2012.01.016

Bieńkowska, A., Koszela, A., & Tworek, K. (2021). Verification of the Job Performance Model based on 'Employees' Dynamic Capabilities in organisations under the COVID-19 pandemic crisis. *Engineering Management in Production and Services*, 13(3), 66–85. DOI: 10.2478/emj-2021-0022

Bieńkowska, A., & Tworek, K. (2020). Job performance model based on Employees' Dynamic Capabilities (EDC). *Sustainability (Basel)*, 12(6), 2250. DOI: 10.3390/su12062250

Carrasco-Garrido, C., De-Pablos-Heredero, C., & Rodríguez-Sánchez, J. L. (2023). Exploring hybrid telework: A bibliometric analysis. *Heliyon*, 9(12), e22472. Advance online publication. DOI: 10.1016/j.heliyon.2023.e22472 PMID: 38076145

Chakravarthy, B. S. (1982). Adaptation: A promising metaphor for strategic management. *Academy of Management Review*, 7(1), 35–44. DOI: 10.2307/257246

Christensen, C. M., Hall, T., Dillon, K., & Duncan, D. S. (2016). Know your customers' jobs to be done. *Harvard Business Review*, 94(9), 54–62.

Christopoulos, K., Eleftheriou, K., & Nijkamp, P. (2021). The role of pre-pandemic teleworking and E-commerce culture in the COVID-19 dispersion in Europe. *Letters in Spatial and Resource Sciences*, 15(1), 1–16. DOI: 10.1007/s12076-021-00286-1 PMID: 34745370

Cohen, W. M., & Levinthal, D. A. (1990). Absorptive capacity: A new perspective on learning and innovation. *Administrative Science Quarterly*, 35(1), 128–152. DOI: 10.2307/2393553

Cyfert, S., Chwiłkowska-Kubala, A., Szumowski, W., & Miśkiewicz, R. (2021). The process of developing dynamic capabilities: The conceptualization attempt and the results of empirical studies. *PLoS One*, 16(4), e0249724. DOI: 10.1371/journal.pone.0249724 PMID: 33914761

Dovbischuk, I. (2022). Innovation-oriented dynamic capabilities of logistics service providers, dynamic resilience and firm performance during the COVID-19 pandemic. *International Journal of Logistics Management*, 33(2), 499–519. Advance online publication. DOI: 10.1108/IJLM-01-2021-0059

Eisenhardt, K. M., & Martin, J. A. (2000). Dynamic capabilities: What are they? *Strategic Management Journal*, 21(10-11), 1105–1121. DOI: 10.1002/1097-0266(200010/11)21:10/11<1105::AID-SMJ133>3.0.CO;2-E

Extremera, N., Mérida-López, S., Sánchez-Álvarez, N., & Quintana-Orts, C. (2018). How does emotional intelligence make one feel better at work? The mediational role of work engagement. *International Journal of Environmental Research and Public Health*, 15(9), 1909. DOI: 10.3390/ijerph15091909 PMID: 30200548

Fernandes Rodrigues Alves, M., Vasconcelos Ribeiro Galina, S., & Dobelin, S. (2018). Literature on organizational innovation: Past and future. *Innovation & Management Review*, 15(1), 2–19. DOI: 10.1108/INMR-01-2018-001

Fogaça, N., & Junior, F. A. C. (2016). Is 'happy worker' more productive. *Management*, 4(4), 149–160.

Gala Durán, C. (2021). El teletrabajo en las Administraciones Públicas. *Trabajo, Persona, Derecho. Mercado*, (3), 69–94. DOI: 10.12795/TPDM.2021.i3.06

Gallego Gómez, C., & De Pablos Heredero, C. (2013). La gamificación y el enriquecimiento de las prácticas de innovación en la empresa: Un análisis de experiencias. *Intangible Capital*, 9(3), 800–822. DOI: 10.3926/ic.377

Heidt, L., Gauger, F., & Pfnür, A. (2023). Work from Home Success: Agile work characteristics and the Mediating Effect of supportive HRM. *Review of Managerial Science*, 17(6), 2139–2164. DOI: 10.1007/s11846-022-00545-5

Henseler, J., and Chin, W.W. (2010). A Comparison of Approaches for the Analysis of Interaction Effects Between Latent Variables Using Partial Least Squares Path Modeling. Structural Equation Modeling, (17:1), 82–109. https://doi.org/DOI: 10.1080/10705510903439003

Hermano, V., Martin-Cruz, N., & Pajares, J. (2022). The effect of project management dynamic capabilities on firm performance. *Baltic Journal of Management*, 17(2), 266–284. Advance online publication. DOI: 10.1108/BJM-06-2021-0218

Hernández-Linares, R., Kellermanns, F. W., & López-Fernández, M. C. (2018). A note on the relationships between learning, market, and entrepreneurial orientations in family and nonfamily firms. *Journal of Family Business Strategy*, 9(3), 192–204. DOI: 10.1016/j.jfbs.2018.08.001

Jacquenet, C. (2021). Optimized, automated, and protective: An operator's view on future networks. *IEEE Transactions on Network and Service Management*, 18(2), 1350–1359. DOI: 10.1109/TNSM.2021.3076293

Jöreskog, K. G., & Wold, H. The ML and PLS technique for modeling with latent variables: Historical and comparative aspects. In Jöreskog. K.G., and Would, H. (Eds.). Systems Under Indirect Observation. Part I. Amsterdam: North Holland, 1982, 1263-1270.

Kamning, D. L. (2021). Exploring the impact of the COVID-19 pandemic on approaches to innovation in the consulting industry: A grounded theory pilot study. *Innovation & Management Review*. Advance online publication. DOI: 10.1108/INMR-05-2021-0076

Khaksar, S. M. S., Chu, M.-T., Rozario, S., & Slade, B. (2020). Knowledge-based dynamic capabilities and knowledge worker productivity in professional service firms. The moderating role of organisational culture. *Knowledge Management Research and Practice*, 21(2), 241–258. DOI: 10.1080/14778238.2020.1794992

Lawler, E. E., Porter, L. W., & Tennenbaum, A. (1968). 'Managers' attitudes toward interaction episodes. *Journal of Applied Psychology*, 52(6p1), 432. https://doi.org/DOI: 10.1037/h0026504

Lopez-Cabrales, A., Bornay-Barrachina, M., & Diaz-Fernandez, M. (2017). Leadership and dynamic capabilities: The role of HR systems. *Personnel Review*, 46(2), 255–276. DOI: 10.1108/PR-05-2015-0146

Metallo, C., Agrifoglio, R., & Maria, F. (2021). Effective Management of a Remote Workforce for Covid-19: A Proposed Research Model Toward Smart Working Adoption Within Organizations. *HR Analytics and Digital HR Practices*, 101–126. https://doi.org/DOI: 10.1007/978-981-16-7099-2_5

Mondal, S. R., Di Virgilio, F., & Das, S. (Eds.), *HR Analytics and Digital HR Practices*. Palgrave Macmillan., DOI: 10.1007/978-981-16-7099-2

Morrar, R., Arman, H., & Mousa, S. (2017). The fourth industrial revolution (Industry 4.0): A social innovation perspective. *Technology Innovation Management Review*, 7(11), 12–20. DOI: 10.22215/timreview/1117

Napier, E., Liu, S. Y., & Liu, J. (2024). Adaptive strength: Unveiling a multilevel dynamic process model for organizational resilience. *Journal of Business Research*, 171, 114334. DOI: 10.1016/j.jbusres.2023.114334

Neuber, L., Englitz, C., Schulte, N., Forthmann, B., & Holling, H. (2022, March 04). Colinda Englitz, Niklas Schulte, Boris Forthmann & Heinz Holling (2021) How work engagement relates to performance and absenteeism: A meta-analysis. *European Journal of Work and Organizational Psychology*, 31(2), 292–315. Advance online publication. DOI: 10.1080/1359432X.2021.1953989

Niu, Q., Nagata, T., Fukutani, N., Tezuka, M., Shimoura, K., Nagai-Tanima, M., & Aoyama, T. (2021). Health effects of immediate telework introduction during the COVID-19 era in Japan: A cross-sectional study. *PLoS One*, 16(10), e0256530. DOI: 10.1371/journal.pone.0256530 PMID: 34624027

Okano, M. T., & Santos, H. de C. L. dos, Honorato, W. J., Viana, A. M., &; Ursini, E. L. (. (2020). Impacts of the Covid-19 pandemic on large companies: Evaluation of changes in technology infrastructure for telework under the optics of theories of dynamic capacity and adaptive structure. *Research. Social Development*, 9(9), e756997852. DOI: 10.33448/rsd-v9i9.7852

ONTSI. (2022) El teletrabajo en España antes, durante y después de la pandemia. https://www.ontsi.es/sites/ontsi/files/2022-06/teletrabajoenespana.pdf

Paiola, M., & Gebauer, H. (2020). Internet of things technologies, digital servitization and business model innovation in BtoB manufacturing firms. *Industrial Marketing Management*, 89, 245–264. DOI: 10.1016/j.indmarman.2020.03.009

Polo García-Ochoa, C., De Pablos Heredero, C., & Blanco Jiménez, F. J. (2020). How business accelerators impact startup's performance: Empirical insights from the dynamic capabilities approach. *Intangible Capital*, 16(3), 107–125. DOI: 10.3926/ic.1669

Ringle. C. M. Wende. S. and Will A. SmartPLS 3.0 M3, 2005.

Rodríguez-Espíndola, O., Chowdhury, S., Dey, P. K., Albores, P., & Emrouznejad, A. (2022). Analysis of the adoption of emergent technologies for risk management in the era of digital manufacturing. *Technological Forecasting and Social Change*, 178, 121562. DOI: 10.1016/j.techfore.2022.121562

Rodríguez-Modroño, P., & López-Igual, P. (2021). Job Quality and Work-Life Balance of Teleworkers. *International Journal of Environmental Research and Public Health*, 18(6), 3239. DOI: 10.3390/ijerph18063239 PMID: 33800995

Shipman, K., Burrell, D. N., & Huff Mac Pherson, A. (2021). An organizational analysis of how managers must understand the mental health impact of teleworking during COVID-19 on employees. *The International Journal of Organizational Analysis*. Advance online publication. DOI: 10.1108/IJOA-03-2021-2685

Stoian, C.-A., Caraiani, C., Anica-Popa, I. F., Dascălu, C., & Lungu, C. I. S. (2022). Telework Systematic Model Design for the Future of Work. *Sustainability (Basel)*, 14(12), 7146. DOI: 10.3390/su14127146

Teece D, Pisano G, Shuen A. Capacidades, recursos y concepto de estrategia de la empresa: cuatro paradigmas de la gestión estratégica. Documento de trabajo de la CCC. Universidad de California en Berkeley, Centro de Investigación en Gestión, Consorcio sobre Competitividad y Cooperación; 1990.

Teece, D. J. (2007). Explicating dynamic capabilities: The nature and microfoundations of (sustainable) enterprise performance. *Strategic Management Journal*, 28(13), 1319–1350. DOI: 10.1002/smj.640

Teece, D. J. (2014). A dynamic capabilities-based entrepreneurial theory of the multinational enterprise. *Journal of International Business Studies*, 45(1), 8–37. DOI: 10.1057/jibs.2013.54

Teece, D. J., Pisano, G., & Shuen, A. (1997). Dynamic capabilities and strategic management. *Strategic Management Journal*, 18(7), 509–533. DOI: 10.1002/(SICI)1097-0266(199708)18:7<509::AID-SMJ882>3.0.CO;2-Z

Tengjian, Z., Gokhan, E., & Gerard, G. (2018). The capacity to innovate: A meta-analysis of absorptive capacity. *Innovation (North Sydney, N.S.W.)*, 20(2), 87–121. DOI: 10.1080/14479338.2018.1428105

Todorova, G., & Durisin, B. (2007). Absorptive capacity: Valuing a reconceptualization. *Academy of Management Review*, 32(3), 774–786. DOI: 10.5465/amr.2007.25275513

Tokarchuk, O., Gabriele, R., & Neglia, G. (2021). Teleworking during the Covid-19 Crisis in Italy: Evidence and Tentative Interpretations. *Sustainability (Basel)*, 13(4), 2147. DOI: 10.3390/su13042147

Urien, B. (2023). Teleworkability, Preferences for Telework, and Well-Being: A Systematic Review. *Sustainability (Basel)*, 15(13), 10631. DOI: 10.3390/su151310631

Vartiainen, M. Telework and Remote Work. Oxford Research Encyclopedia of Psychology. Retrieved 7 Jan. 2022, from https://oxfordre.com/psychology/view/10.1093/acrefore/9780190236557.001.0001/acrefore-9780190236557-e-850

Vidmar, M., Rosiello, A., & Golra, O. (2020). Resilience of New Space Firms in the United Kingdom During the Early Stages of COVID-19 Crisis: The Case for Strategic Agility. *New Space*, 8(4), 172–178. DOI: 10.1089/space.2020.0057

Woiceshyn, J. (2005). Integrative capability and technology adoption: Evidence from oil firms. *Industrial and Corporate Change*, 14(2), 307–342. DOI: 10.1093/icc/dth053

Yalabik, Z. Y., Rayton, B. A., & Rapti, A. (2017). Facets of job satisfaction and work engagement. *Evidence-based HRM*, 5(3), 248–265. DOI: 10.1108/EBHRM-08-2015-0036

Zahra, S. A., & George, G. (2002). Absorptive capacity: A review, reconceptualization, and extension. *Academy of Management Review*, 27(2), 185–203. DOI: 10.2307/4134351

Zahra, S. A., & Hayton, J. C. (2008). The effect of international venturing on firm performance: The moderating influence of absorptive capacity. *Journal of Business Venturing*, 23(2), 195–220. DOI: 10.1016/j.jbusvent.2007.01.001

Zhou, A. J., Fey, C., & Yildiz, H. E. (2020). Fostering integration through HRM practices: An empirical examination of absorptive capacity and knowledge transfer in cross-border M&As. *Journal of World Business*, 55(2), 100947. DOI: 10.1016/j.jwb.2018.05.005

Chapter 9
Main Topics in Workplace Recycling Behavior Studies: A Bibliometric Analysis

Marta Villatoro-Borque
Universidad Rey Juan Carlos, Spain

ABSTRACT

There is an extensive body of literature on the factors that condition waste separation behaviors in households; however, the same is not true when analyzing research on the behavior in the workplace. In this study we have carried out a bibliometric analysis of the scientific publications about individual waste separation behavior in their workplaces. The aim is to identify the main issues affecting such behavior, as well as the current state of research on the subject. Given the serious negative impact that waste has on the environment, knowing the reasons that lead individuals to make the effort to separate waste will be a key factor in designing any environmental policy.

INTRODUCTION

Today's consumer society is generating enormous quantities of waste that have undesirable effects on the environment. The separation of waste at its source allows its selective collection and subsequent recycling. Recycling allows the recovery of raw materials, minimizing the plundering of natural resources. It also minimizes the volume of waste to be treated in landfills or incineration plants, reducing pollution and the emission of greenhouse gases into the atmosphere, including carbon diox-

DOI: 10.4018/979-8-3693-6289-1.ch009

ide (Lian et al., 2020). Increasing recycling volumes should be an objective when designing any environmental policy. To increase waste separation at source, it is necessary that individuals carry out such separation at the source of waste generation, either in their homes or in their workplaces, so the collaboration of individuals is essential to improving the rates of separation at source and recycling. Knowing the reasons why individuals separate waste at source is essential for designing any environmental policy. Although waste separation and recycling are different concepts, in literature, both are used indistinctly to define the action of separating the waste when it is generated. So, in this text, both concepts will be used that way.

There are many studies that analyze waste separation behaviors within households and there are also studies that analyze recycling behavior in a generic way without considering the place where waste separation is taking place, to cite some relevant articles: (Fiorillo, 2013; Sidique et al., 2010; Vassanadumrongdee & Kittipongvises, 2018). There have also been a wide range of literature reviews on recycling behavior, among them, we can highlight some important titles like: (Fogt Jacobsen et al., 2022; Knickmeyer, 2020; Schultz et al., 1995). In the articles about household recycling behavior, a variety of variables that influence the recycling behavior of individuals have been found. These variables are usually related to political actions or to personal variables. Among the political factors, there is scientific evidence that certain government actions influence recycling levels. For example, a positive relationship was found between waste separation rates and compulsory recycling policies (Chen et al., 2018) incentive programs to increase recycling had positive effects (Allen et al., 1993) and the existence of curbside recycling also improved the source separation rates (Abbott et al., 2011). A positive relationship was also found between waste separation and the existence of recycling facilities and services so that they are closer and more convenient to citizens (Bernstad, 2014). Within the individual factors, there are psychological and sociodemographic factors that have been shown to influence waste separation behavior. Several psychological theories have studied these behaviors, the most common of which are the Theory of Planned Behavior (TPB) (Ajzen, 1985) and the Theory of Norm Activation (TNA) (Schwartz, 1973). Among sociodemographic factors, there is scientific evidence that some of them are relevant in determining pro-environmental behaviors. The most frequently studied are income level, education, age, and gender (Saphores et al., 2006) *Income level* is a variable that has proved to be significant in predicting waste separation. In some studies, a positive relation has been found between income level and increased source separation rates (Fiorillo, 2013; Li et al., 2023; Nencková et al., 2020). However, in other studies, this relationship has been negative, arguably due to the lack of time available to people with higher incomes and the higher opportunity cost they bear for separating waste (Alhassan et al., 2020). Other studies have not found a relationship between these two factors (Saphores et al., 2006, 2012). *Age* is a factor that does not show homogeneous results in waste separation. There is a positive relationship between age and waste separation in the 31 to 70-year-old age group (Fiorillo, 2013). According to other research the age group most likely to engage in recycling-related activities was between 36 and 65 (Saphores et al., 2006). These results differ from those of the study conducted in the Czech Republic, where age had a negative influence on textile recycling (Nencková et al., 2020). *Educational* level, which is also a frequently used variable to assess recycling, is generally related to income levels. A positive relationship between educational level and recycling was found in studies performed by Li et al. (2023) and Nencková et al. (2020). On the other hand, *gender*, normally has significance in conditioning pro-recycling behavior. Women were more likely to be involved in source separation of waste in (Fan et al., 2022; Li et al., 2023; Nencková et al., 2020), among others.

However, there are fewer studies that analyze the factors that motivate individuals to recycle at workplaces. There are differences between the waste separation behavior of individuals at homes and at workplaces. The variables that have been shown to influence the recycling of waste generated in households do not coincide with the factors that influence individuals recycling behavior at workplaces. In a study conducted among office and laboratory workers in the UK an inconsistency between recycling behavior at home and at work was found, being the recycling rates far superior at home than at work (Whitmarsh et al., 2018). In a study carried out among employees of six UK northern companies was found that waste separation behavior at home was unrelated to the behavior of those same workers at their workplaces (Heidrich & Harvey, 2018) Factors such as supervisory support (Paillé et al., 2019) the commitment of the superiors to environmental protection, or the existence of facilities that help green behaviors (Lo et al., 2012) are predictors of waste separation behavior at workplaces. Given the importance of the subject, it was decided to delve deeper into the behavior of individuals at workplaces by conducting an analysis of the existing scientific literature and a bibliometric analysis to learn about the main topics covered in these investigations.

The main objective of this study is to perform an analysis of the scientific production and a bibliometric analysis to identify the most relevant literature in this field, group the main topics addressed in this area, and answer the following research questions:

1. What are the most prolific authors, articles, and journals on the topic on workplace recycling behavior?
2. What are the main topics in these articles?

Answering these questions will be a contribution to scientific literature, mainly for three reasons. First, it will reveal if recycling behavior at workplaces is deeply studied. Second, it will serve as a guideline for researchers conducting future studies in this field. And third, it can be a reference for the development of any policy aimed at encouraging recycling behavior at workplaces. The first research question will be answered through a descriptive analysis of the scientific production and the second through a bibliometric analysis of co-words.

MATHERIALS AND METHODS

Given that the objective is to know scientific production the conceptual structure and to elaborate a science mapping of the field of study, the analysis has been carried out through the co-word method. With this, key concepts are analyzed, on the understanding that when they are frequently repeated together, these topics are closely related and form the knowledge base of the subject under research. The analysis was carried out following the following steps: research design, compilation of data, analysis of the information, visualization of the results and interpretation (Zupic & Čater, 2015).

Step 1: Research Design

The research questions were posed to know the most prolific authors in this area, the most cited articles and journals that deal with aspects related to workplace recycling behavior, and what the main topics in this area are. Through descriptive analysis, the most relevant authors, articles, and journals will be found. Through bibliometric analysis, a conceptual structure, and a scientific mapping of the field of study will be drawn. Bibliometric analysis is a method used to analyze the nuances of a particular field of study by designing scientific maps, or a bibliometric map. A scientific map is a tool that depicts the relationship between authors, journals, articles, or concepts (Donthu et al., 2021). To construct the scientific map the co-word method analysis has been used, in this method the scientific maps include clusters that represent the main research topics (Cobo et al., 2011).

Step 2: Compilation of Bibliometric Data

The data were downloaded from the Web of Science (WoS) which is a database developed by Thomsom Reuters Scientific that comprises a wide range of scientific journals and is compatible with SciMat, the software tool used to perform the bibliometric analysis.

After previous research on the concepts that appeared most frequently in the articles related to the topic of study, a research string was designed. It included in the topic the concepts "RECYCL*" OR "WASTE SEPARATION" and "WORKPLACE*" OR "OFFICE*". The download was performed on May 22, 2024, without including date limits to cover as much literature as possible. The initial results were 1.054 records, including articles (777), proceeding paper (242), review articles (50), book chapters (12), early access (5), editorial material (4), meeting abstracts (4), data paper (1), and notes (1). Of these, articles, review articles and early Access were selected as they were considered rigorous documents given their peer review process, and they are more reliable than other types of documents (Si et al., 2019). After this filter, a total of 827 titles remained, 778 in English, 18 in German, 9 in Portuguese, 7 in Spanish, 4 in French, 3 in Turkish, 2 in Chinese, 2 in Polish, 2 in Russian, 1 in Italian and 1 in Multiple Languages. All articles that were not written in English were discarded. Thus, the search was narrowed down to 778 articles. Of the 778 documents selected, titles and abstracts were reviewed and articles that were not directly related to the topic of study were discarded. It was not possible to access one of the titles.

Articles dealing with waste separation behavior or with pro-environmental behavior in general terms were selected when these behaviors were framed within the workplaces. Those that analyzed other types of environmental behaviors not related to waste, such as green purchase, energy reduction or water saving were excluded. Studies that characterized waste from corporations as a collective without considering individual aspects were also excluded. Moreover, articles that were not related to the topic were discarded. In this group there were articles dealing with aspects such as recycling techniques, the use of recycled materials, or the medical risk of recycling workers, among others. Finally, the search was reduced to 48 documents.

The resulting small number of articles demonstrates the scarcity of this type of study and reflects a gap in research. However, with 40-50 or more relevant articles, this is enough articles for the purpose of carrying out an analysis(Paul & Criado, 2020) because it reflects that although the number of references is small, there exist a maturity in the field of analysis that can be analyzed (Paul et al., 2021).

Step 3: Analysis of the Information

The analysis was divided into two parts: on the one hand, a descriptive analysis of the scientific production was carried out to analyze the so-called "intellectual base" of the area of knowledge and, on the other hand, a bibliometric analysis of co-words was carried out to determine its "conceptual structure".

To conduct bibliometric analysis, we chose SciMAT software. It is a tool developed by researchers at the University of Granada (Spain) which has various visualization techniques, such as clusters or strategy maps, and is compatible with data downloaded from WoS(Moral-Muñoz et al., 2020). For all these reasons, it was considered an ideal tool for the study.

RESULTS: VISUALIZATION AND INTERPRETATION

Step 4. Part I. Scientific Production (Research Question Number 1)

The selected articles cover a time range from 1990 to 2024. It is highly probable that the interest on the topic was triggered in 1987 when the World Commission on Environment and Development presented to the General Assembly of the United Nations (WCED) the report *Our Common Future*, also known as the *Brundtland Report*, where the concept sustainable development was first defined(WCED, 1987). As can be seen in Figure 1, since then, although the number of publications is small, they have quadrupled in number, from 1 article in 1990 to 4 publications in 2023. The publications of the year 2024 have not been considered since the figures for the full year were not available at the date of publication of this chapter. However, the evolution is not constant throughout the entire period. There were seven publications between 1900 and 1995 followed by a gap of research between 1996 and 2011, during this period there were no publications on the topic. We have no explanation for the lack of research during this period, so we believe it should be considered as a future research topic. In 2012, interest in the topic recovered and since then, a minimum of two articles per year are published. In 2021 it reached a high with six publications.

Figure 1. number of articles of the analyzed topic published per year

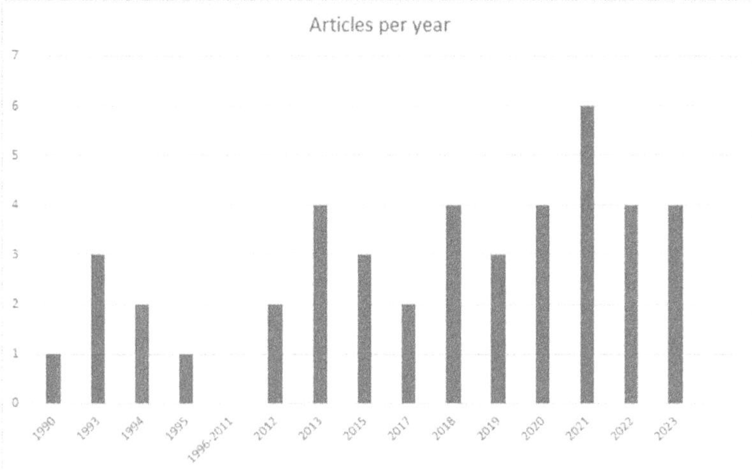

Source: Drawn up by author with data from WoS database

The 48 selected articles were written by 125 authors, 107 of whom participated in one article (85.60%), 14 in two (11.20%) and four authors participated in three articles (3.20%). In particular, Lee, YJ; has been involved in the authorship of:(Marans & Lee, 1993), (Lee & De Young, 1994) and (Lee et al., 1995). Oke, A. in: (Oke, 2015), (Oke, McDonald, & Korobilis-Magas, 2021) y (Oke, McDonald, Korobilis-Magas, et al., 2021). Han, H. in: (Saleem et al., 2020), (Saleem et al., 2021) and (Yu et al., 2021),and Ariza-Montes, A. in: (Saleem et al., 2020), (Saleem et al., 2021), y (Yu et al., 2021).

As can be seen in table 1, according to the author's affiliation, these articles come from 29 different countries, the most prolific one is the United Kingdom, with 15 articles (England ten, Scotland four and Wales one) followed by the United States of America, with nine articles. China has participated in four publications and Chile, Pakistan, South Korea, Spain, and Taiwan have contributed three articles each. Finland, France, The Netherlands, and Portugal have two articles each, and the rest of the countries have one article each.

Table 1. Number of articles by authors' country of affiliation

Authors affiliation	Number of Articles
United Kingdom	15
USA	9
China	5

continued on following page

Table 1. Continued

Authors affiliation	Number of Articles
Australia	4
Canadá	4
Chile	3
Pakistan	3
South Korea	3
Spain	3
Taiwan	3
Finland	2
France	2
Netherlands	2
Portugal	2
India	1
Ethiopia	1
Greece	1
Italy	1
Malasya	1
Norway	1
Oman	1
Peru	1
Russia	1
Singapore	1
South Africa	1
Sweeden	1
Switzerland	1
Thailand	1
Turkey	1
TOTAL	**75**

Source: Drawn up by author with data from WoS database

Regarding the more relevant articles, Table 2 shows the ten articles with the higher number of citations on the Web of Science Core Collection. The Authors, the date of publication and its DOI are also shown.

Table 2. Ten most cited articles

Authors	Article Title	Times Cited WoS Core Collection	Publication Year	DOI
Greaves, M; Zibarras, LD; Stride, C	Using the theory of planned behavior to explore environmental behavioral intentions in the workplace	421	2013	10.1016/j.jenvp.2013.02.003
Norton, TA; Parker, SL; Zacher, H; Ashkanasy, NM	Employee Green Behavior: A Theoretical Framework, Multilevel Review, and Future Research Agenda	404	2015	10.1177/1086026615575773
Yuriev, A; Boiral, O; Francoeur, V; Paillé, P	Overcoming the barriers to pro-environmental behaviors in the workplace: A systematic review	136	2018	10.1016/j.jclepro.2018.02.041
Austin, J; Hatfield, DB; Grindle, AC; Bailey, JS	Increasing Recycling in Office Environments - The Effects of Specific, Informative Cues.	110	1993	10.1901/jaba.1993.26-247
Lo, SH; Peters, GJY; Kok, G	A Review of Determinants of and Interventions for Proenvironmental Behaviors in Organizations	103	2012	10.1111/j.1559-1816.2012.00969.x
Lee, YJ; DeYoung, R; Marans, RW	Factors Influencing Individual Recycling Behavior in Office Settings - A Study of Office Workers in Taiwan	80	1995	10.1177/0013916595273006
Manika, D; Wells, VK; Gregory-Smith, D; Gentry, M	The Impact of Individual Attitudinal and Organisational Variables on Workplace Environmentally Friendly Behaviours	78	2015	10.1007/s10551-013-1978-6

continued on following page

Table 2. Continued

Authors	Article Title	Times Cited WoS Core Collection	Publication Year	DOI
Ofstad, SP; Tobolova, M; Nayum, A; Klöckner, CA	Understanding the Mechanisms behind Changing People's Recycling Behavior at Work by Applying a Comprehensive Action Determination Model	72	2017	10.3390/su9020204
Saleem, M; Qadeer, F; Mahmood, F; Ariza-Montes, A; Han, H	Ethical Leadership and Employee Green Behavior: A Multilevel Moderated Mediation Analysis	69	2020	10.3390/su12083314
Brothers, KJ; Krantz, PJ; McClannahan, LE	Office Paper Recycling - A Function of Container Proximity	57	1994	10.1901/jaba.1994.27-153

Source: Drawn up by author with data from WoS database

The most cited article (Greaves et al., 2013), conducted a study of employees' environmental behavioral intentions. The analysis was done through questionnaires using the TPB (Ajzen, 1991) and analyzed three different behaviors: the switching down of computers when they are not in use, the utilization of videoconferences instead of traveling to do them in person, and waste recycling. Norton et al. (2015) conducted a review of the factors related to employee green behavior distinguishing between the behavior required by the organization and that performed voluntarily by employees. Yuriev et al. (2018) reviewed the empirical studies that analyze pro-environmental behaviors in the workplace and the barriers or obstacles they find when performing them. Austin et al. (1993) analyzed how posting signs with information on how to dispose of waste correctly influenced waste separation rates. Lo et al. (2012) analyzed 21 empirical studies on green behaviors within different organizations. Lee et al. (1995) conducted a survey of 1,788 respondents investigating recycling behaviors in offices and households. Manika et al. (2015) conducted an analysis of the behavior of workers in different types of organizations, both from an individual and organizational point of view, and with respect to three types of environmental behaviors: recycling, energy saving and print reduction. Ofstad et al. (2017) approaches waste separation behaviors in the workplace from a psychological point of view, applying variables from different psychological theories, those of the Ajzen´s TPB (Ajzen, 1985, 1991) among others. (Saleem et al., 2020) studied how ethical leadership can influence employees' environmental behavior. Brothers et al. (1994) analyzed the relationship between the increase in the number of office paper recycling garbage cans and the increase in their separation at source.

Table 3 shows the journals with the highest number of articles published, and its Publisher. There are a wide range of journal publishing about the topic of analysis. The journal with the highest number of publications is Sustainability, with nine titles published. There are six journals with two publications each: Frontiers in Psychology; International Journal of Environmental Research and Public Health; Journal of Applied Behavior Analysis; Journal of Business Ethics; Journal of Cleaner Production and Waste Management. The rest of the journals have only one publication.

Table 3. Articles published by journals

Source Title	**Number of articles**
SUSTAINABILITY	9
FRONTIERS IN PSYCHOLOGY	2
INTERNATIONAL JOURNAL OF ENVIRONMENTAL RESEARCH AND PUBLIC HEALTH	2
JOURNAL OF APPLIED BEHAVIOR ANALYSIS	2
JOURNAL OF BUSINESS ETHICS	2
JOURNAL OF CLEANER PRODUCTION	2
WASTE MANAGEMENT	2
BIOCYCLE	1
BUSINESS ETHICS-A EUROPEAN REVIEW	1
CANADIAN JOURNAL OF PUBLIC HEALTH-REVUE CANADIENNE DE SANTE PUBLIQUE	1
CUREUS JOURNAL OF MEDICAL SCIENCE	1
ENVIRONMENT AND BEHAVIOR	1
ENVIRONMENTAL COMMUNICATION-A JOURNAL OF NATURE AND CULTURE	1
ENVIRONMENTAL ENGINEERING AND MANAGEMENT JOURNAL	1
ETHNOS	1
EUROPEAN MANAGEMENT REVIEW	1
INDOOR AND BUILT ENVIRONMENT	1
INTERNATIONAL JOURNAL OF ENVIRONMENTAL HEALTH RESEARCH	1
INTERNATIONAL JOURNAL OF SUSTAINABILITY IN HIGHER EDUCATION	1

continued on following page

Table 3. Continued

Source Title	Number of articles
JOURNAL OF APPLIED SOCIAL PSYCHOLOGY	1
JOURNAL OF ASIA BUSINESS STUDIES	1
JOURNAL OF ENVIRONMENTAL PSYCHOLOGY	1
JOURNAL OF ORGANIZATIONAL CHANGE MANAGEMENT	1
JOURNAL OF PHARMACY PRACTICE AND RESEARCH	1
LANDSCAPE AND URBAN PLANNING	1
LARYNGOSCOPE	1
ORGANIZATION & ENVIRONMENT	1
PERTANIKA JOURNAL OF SOCIAL SCIENCE AND HUMANITIES	1
PLOS ONE	1
SOCIAL INDICATORS RESEARCH	1
SOCIAL SCIENCE JOURNAL	1
SUSTAINABLE CITIES AND SOCIETY	1
TURKISH JOURNAL OF ANAESTHESIOLOGY AND REANIMATION	1
WORKPLACE HEALTH & SAFETY	1
TOTAL	**48**

Source: Drawn up by author with data from WoS database

These journals are published by 24 editorials, table 4 shows the editorials sorted by number of published articles. The publisher with the highest number of publications is MDPI with 11 articles which represents 22.92% of the total publications. It is followed by Willey with four published articles which represents 8.33% of the total articles. Emeral Group Publishing LTD, Routledge Journals Taylor & Francis LTD and Sage Publications INC, have three articles, representing 6.25% of the total published articles each. The other publishers have published two or one article each.

Table 4. Articles published by editorials

Publisher	Number of articles
MDPI	11
WILEY	4
EMERALD GROUP PUBLISHING LTD	3
ROUTLEDGE JOURNALS, TAYLOR & FRANCIS LTD	3
SAGE PUBLICATIONS INC	3

continued on following page

Table 4. Continued

Publisher	Number of articles
ELSEVIER SCIENCE BV	2
ELSEVIER SCI LTD	2
FRONTIERS MEDIA SA	2
JOURNAL APPL BEHAV ANAL	2
PERGAMON-ELSEVIER SCIENCE LTD	2
SPRINGER	2
ACADEMIC PRESS LTD- ELSEVIER SCIENCE LTD	1
AVES	1
CANADIAN PUBL HEALTH ASSN	1
GH ASACHI TECHNICAL UNIV IASI	1
JG PRESS, INC	1
KLUWER ACADEMIC PUBL	1
PUBLIC LIBRARY SCIENCE	1
SAGE PUBLICATIONS LTD	1
SPRINGERNATURE	1
TAYLOR & FRANCIS LTD	1
UNIV PUTRA MALAYSIA PRESS	1
WILEY PERIODICALS, INC	1
TOTAL	**48**

Source: Drawn up by author with data from WoS database

Step 4. Part II. Co-Word Analysis (Research Question Number 2)

The second purpose of this study is to identify the different thematic areas studied in the articles related to workplaces recycling behavior. To answer this research question, a bibliometric analysis of co-words has been performed. Through bibliometric analysis, the conceptual structure of a scientific field can be studied. Co-word analysis shows the most important topic in this field by connecting concepts that appear in the same title, abstract or keyword list (Zupic & Čater, 2015). The SciMat software tool helps to identify these areas of knowledge. The use of co-word analysis has two important drawbacks, some words are used in multiple contexts and others may be very generic (Donthu et al., 2021). To avoid this, an exhaustive review of all the words was carried out and groups were made with those that had the same meaning. No words were eliminated.

When the information was entered in the software tool, a total of 328 words were shown. Words with similar meanings were grouped by hand. The results were 287 words. The most repeated concepts are *pro-environmental behavior; sustainability; recycling; planned behavior; determinants;* and *workplace*. They represent the core of the analysis related to recycling. It was decided not to divide the analysis into periods, since the aim was to analyze scientific production and not its evolution.

When co-word analysis is applied it generates clusters considered themes, each theme has two characteristics: density and centrality. According to this characteristic the themes can be represented in a strategic diagram and classified into different groups (Callon et al., 1991). The visualization of the results through a strategic diagram, enables us to know the information according to its density and centrality. Density measures the degree of development of a topic and its centrality measures its importance among the research area (Murillo-Ramos et al., 2023). In contrast to the highly developed and isolated themes, which are peripheral themes, motor themes are those that are of great importance in the research area. The basic and transversal themes are relevant themes that are not yet fully developed. Finally, emerging or declining themes are those that are not very developed and are not central to the research area. Within the strategy diagram, each sphere represents a key term, and its size is proportional to the number of articles cited. Figure 2: shows the explanation of the quadrants of the strategy diagram (Cobo et al., 2011).

Figure 2. Explanation of the quadrants of the strategy diagram

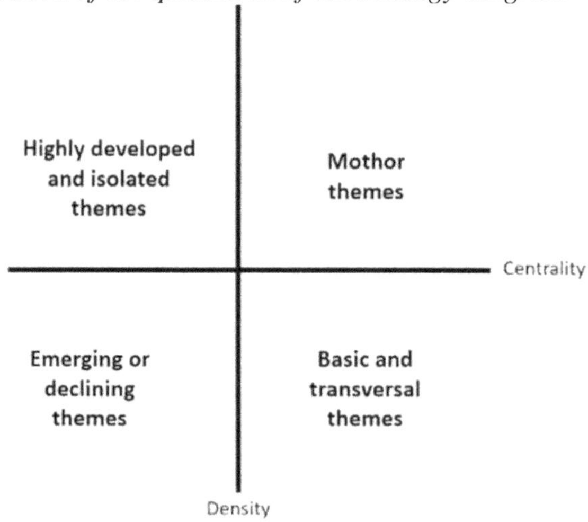

Source: (Cobo et al., 2011)

Figure 3 shows the strategic diagram of the research area. Through the cluster analysis we can find the relationship that exists between the different terms and with others of lesser relevance or subtopics.

Figure 3. Strategic diagram

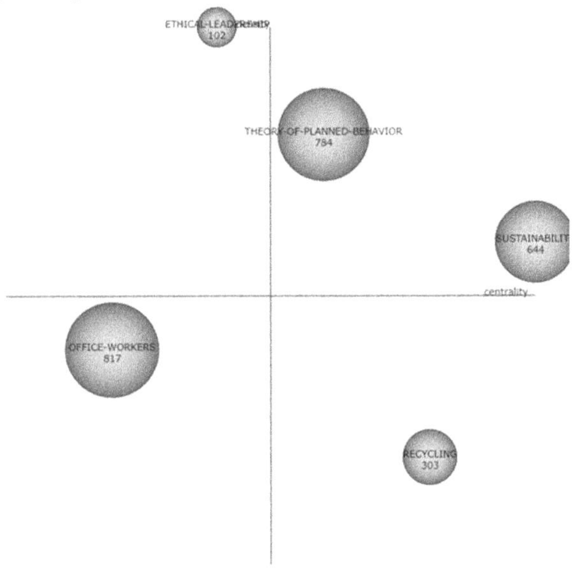

Source: SciMat

Once the strategic diagram has been obtained, research question number 2 will be answered by analyzing each area and the most relevant clusters.

MOTOR THEMES: SUSTAINABILITY AND THEORY OF PLANNED BEHAVIOR

Within the articles on workplace recycling behavior *sustainability and Theory of Planned Behavior* are considered motor themes. *Sustainability* is the pilar of any kind of study related to pro-environmental behavior. Furthermore, the main goal when analyzing any kind of environmental behavior is to achieve high levels of sustainability. TPB is the most used theory to explain environmental behaviors, such as recycling, saving water, energy reduction or environmentally responsible consumption patterns. It is based on the premise that individuals have good intentions and tend to care about the environment; however, when engaging in pro-environmental behaviors that require effort, the attitude does not always turn into behavior. This depends on three main variables: attitudes, subjective norms, and perceived behavioral control (Ajzen, 1991).

Cluster´s Network of Theory of Planned Behavior

Figure 4 shows the cluster's network of the TPB. Several psychological theories have studied pro-environmental behaviors, the most common of which are the Theory of Reasoned Action (TRA) (Fishbein & Ajzen, 1977), the TPB (Ajzen, 1991),and the Theory of Norm Activation (TNA) (Schwartz, 1973) . TPB is an extension of TRA and is the most widely applied theory to explain pro-environmental behaviors, including recycling. There are three constructs that determine the way from intentions to actions: *attitudes* towards such behavior, depending on whether the individual considers it positive or negative; *subjective norms*, which depend on the social pressure that the individual has to behave in a certain way; and *perceived behavioral control*, which is the feeling that individuals have about the ease or difficulty of performing a certain behavior (Ajzen, 1985). For its part, the TNA developed by Schwartz (1973) considers that there are three main variables to predict behavior with the environment: *moral norms*, which reflect the commitment of individuals to ethical or moral values and cause individuals to behave in a certain way, the preconception that individuals have about the consequences of their actions *(consequence awareness)* and how they attribute responsibility for these actions *(attribution of responsibility)* (Schwartz, 1973).

According to these studies, there exists scientific evidence that confirms the validity of the TPB constructs to explain pro-environmental behaviors. And it is demonstrated that it is a solid base for studying environmental behaviors at work (Greaves et al., 2013).

Using the TPB in a study conducted in Portugal, a positive relationship was found between workers perceived green organizational climate and their attitudes, their subjective norms, and their perceived behavioral control for recycling. In addition, it was found that supervisors could be facilitators of social norms that serve as an example for employees to perform pro-environmental actions (Costa et al., 2022). It was also found in a reseach carried out in the UK that the central constructs of the TPB explained 53% of the variation in recycling behavior intentions (Greaves et al., 2013). In another study conducted in the UK among office and laboratory workers, the TPB explained approximately twice as much variation between recycling at home compared to recycling at work. But, the conclusion of the study was that TBP does not provide a good explanation for recycling because it is influenced by different factors and maybe the actual models, among which is the TPB, are not able to reflect this diversity (Whitmarsh et al., 2018).

Within this cluster network we can observe that there is a close relationship between the studies of domestic recycling and workplace recycling. At the same time, there is a significant difference between the number of articles on domestic recycling and on workplace recycling, with a reduced number of articles on workplace recycling. This is a topic mentioned in most of the studies analyzed, along with the need to carry out more research on workplace recycling behavior. The relationship between concepts also derives from the existence of several articles that made comparisons between the recycling behavior of individuals at home and at the workplace(Ng, 2023; Whitmarsh et al., 2018). These analyses were not limited to waste behavior, but there is also analysis of different pro-environmental behaviors in households and workplaces(Paillé et al., 2019).

Regarding the cluster on social norms, these are framed within the different types of norms that condition the behavior of individuals. There are different types of norms: social, organizational and personal (Janmaimool, 2017). Social norms encompass those behaviors that are generally understood by society to be appropriate (Thøgersen, 2006). Within this group, we find subjective social norms, which are those created by people with personal relationships with individuals, and are one of the constructs that are applied to explain the intentions of performing pro-environmental behaviors within the TPB (Ajzen, 1991). In a study conducted among Thai workers, all three types of norms were found to be related to the performance of positive waste management behaviors within organizations. The most influential one was the group of organizational norms, followed by personal norms at almost the same level of significance (Janmaimool, 2017).

Figure 4. Cluster's network of theory of planned behavior

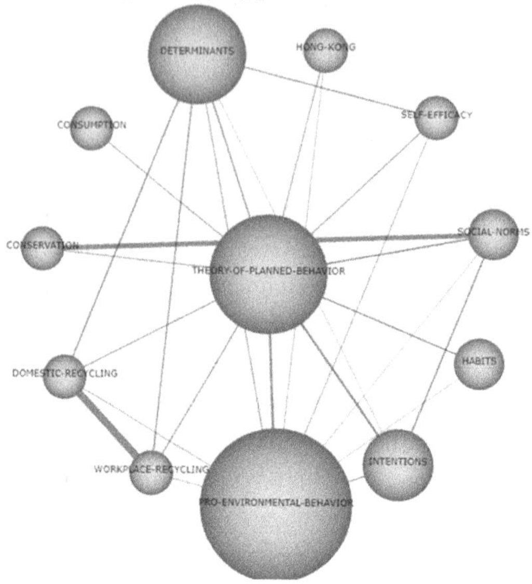

Source: SciMat

Cluster´s Network of Sustainability

Figure 5 shows the cluster's network of Sustainability. It is coherent that the concept of sustainability is one of the most repeated when analyzing recycling or pro-environmental behaviors. Sustainability or sustainable development are concepts associated with human activity and economic development, so any citizen or company that aspires to behave in an environmentally friendly manner must be based on the criteria of environmental sustainability. Brundtland report defined sustainable development as that which *allows economic development that meets the needs of present generations without compromising the resources needed by future generations* (WCED, 1987).

Sustainability is related to different aspects, and it has different facets. In the clusters we can see how it is related to issues such as behavior or recycling behavior. We also see how it can occur at work or in workplaces, when entities are able to develop environmental behaviors both in their organization and in the transmission of these values to their workers.

Within the field of financial performance, the concepts of sustainability, recycling and behavior are intrinsically associated with Corporate Social Responsibility. There is no single definition of CSR and it varies according to the areas in which it is applied (Dahlsrud, 2008). CSR from a social point of view refers to the relations between companies and the people who are affected, both directly and indirectly, by their activities. CSR from an environmental point of view, however, refers to the behavior of companies towards the environment. All actions aimed at promoting recycling by organizations will fall within the latter facet of CSR. The study of CSR has focused on the behavior of companies as a collective; however, there are few articles that analyze this behavior from the point of view of individuals. An analysis carried out in China in different small and medium-sized companies, found that when CSR programs focused on workers are applied, they perform environmentally friendly behaviors, which also results in improvements in the environmental impact of companies on the environment. In addition, the promotion of pro-environmental behaviors by individuals leads to a lower consumption of resources, which facilitates improvements in the financial performance of companies (Yu et al., 2021). Another study conducted among employees of 51 organizations in the United States of America, analyzed the relationship between the environmental orientation of the company and how this affects the environmental behavior of the employees. It was found that there was a positive relationship between the environmental orientation of the company and the recycling behavior of the employees (Salvador & Burciaga, 2020).

Sustainability, therefore, is a concept that can be achieved by acting at different levels, and it is possible for individuals to contribute to sustainability by adopting pro-environmental behaviors in their homes and workplaces. However, in view of the results analyzed so far, individuals do not behave in the same way in their homes as they do in their workplaces. Getting individuals to behave in a pro-environmental manner in the workplace can be largely achieved, thanks to the environmental behaviors and policies of companies.

Figure 5. Cluster´s network of sustainability

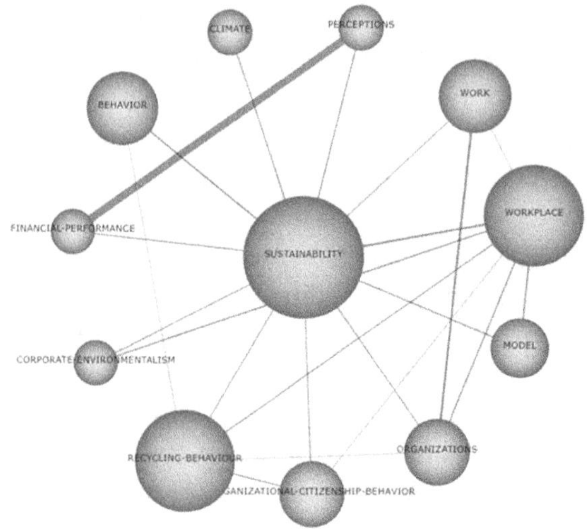

Source: SciMat

Basic Themes: Recycling

Cluster´s Network of Recycling

Figure 6: shows the cluster's network of *Recycling*. Recycling is a type of pro-environmental behavior. Although there is no single classification of pro-environmental behaviors, they are usually classified into three categories: those related to water and energy use, consumption behavior and waste management. Among the behaviors related to the use of water and energy, we find all those responsible for saving energy or the use of means of transport, such as the use of public transport or environmentally friendly vehicles. Responsible consumption includes behaviors in which individuals make their purchasing decisions based on environmental criteria including the avoiding of plastic packaging, the purchase of local products to avoid transportation costs, and the acquisition of products made from recycled materials or that can be easily recycled. Within the behavior of individuals with regard to waste, the so-called three R's are included. The first R refers to the behavior of waste reduction, in order to avoid the existence of waste. Normally this type of behavior is associated with the reduction of the consumption of goods. The second R corresponds to the concept of reuse; once the item being discarded exists, another use is sought for it. Finally, recycling means that once the item exists and is to be discarded, it is not sent to landfills or incineration plants, but is recycled, resulting in less pollution and the generation of new raw materials, avoiding the need to extract new materials from the environment and avoiding climate change (Lian et al., 2020).

Recycling, or the sustainable treatment of waste, is the central theme of this analysis and is considered the basic theme of the study. The concepts of waste minimization and waste separation are closely related to it, and even, as previously mentioned, despite being different concepts, waste separation and recycling are often used interchangeably when referring to WMB. In the articles analyzed, recycling is not the only objective of the analysis, but is often analyzed in conjunction with other environmental behaviors, such as the appropriate use of energy (Ozkan et al., 2024; Rojas-Perez et al., 2024), consumption patterns (Oke, et al., 2021b) or the use of videoconferencing instead of public transportation in (Greaves et al., 2013).

Figure 6. Cluster's network of recycling

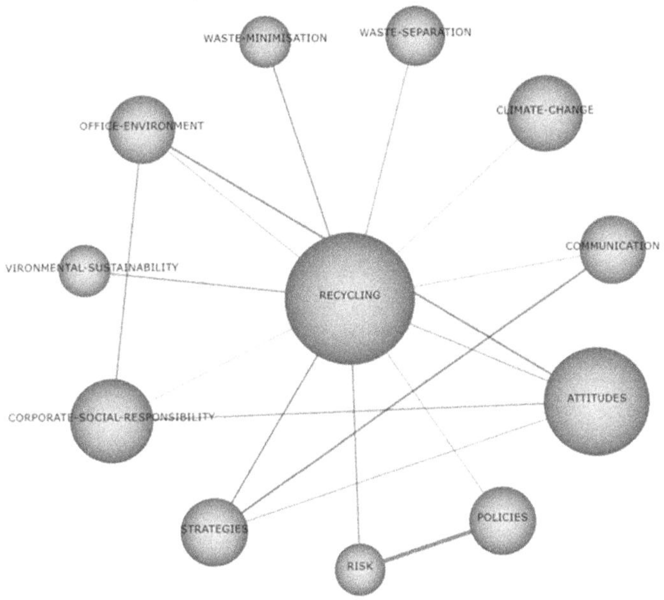

Source: SciMat

Emerging or Declining Themes: Office-Workers

Cluster´s Network of Office-Workers

Figure 7 shows the cluster's network of office-workers. As the search criteria were based on office-workers or employees' behavior at workplaces, this cluster shows the relationship between employees and their waste management practices. Workers are an emerging issue in the analysis of recycling behavior. As we have seen previously, they are a key element in achieving environmental performance in companies and reducing their environmental footprint. The participation of workers in waste management in the construction sector to achieve improved sustainability was studied in Hao et al. (2022) and the spillover effect of waste separation behavior from home to workplaces has been analyzed in(Ng, 2023). A relationship between knowledge about waste management, intention of recycling and waste separation behavior was found at home, but this relation did not exist when it was analyzed at workplaces.

Figure 7. Cluster's network of office-workers

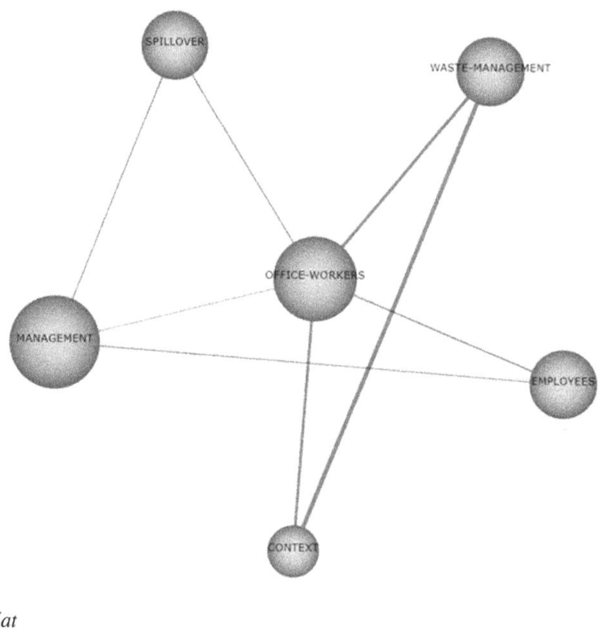

Source: SciMat

Highly Developed and Isolated Themes: Ethical Leadership

Cluster´s Network of Ethical Leadership

Figure 8 shows the cluster's network of ethical leadership. Ethical leadership is a highly developed but isolated theme. It is the central topic in (Saleem et al., 2020, 2021). These articles explore how leaders with ethical values and positive attitudes towards the environment can influence employee environmental behavior. The way to transmit these behaviors is through the creation of a green psychological climate in the workplace and through environmental passion (Saleem et al., 2021). These behaviors are based on the Social Learning theory. It considers that individuals can learn from the observation of people with ethical behavior, and from the perception of a green psychological climate (Bandura & Walters, 1977). This transmission of behaviors could also be carried out through so-called workplace spirituality, whereby, through a spiritual type of leadership different types of values are generated and that encourage greater commitment of workers to the company and better levels of productivity (Fry, 2003).

Figure 8. Cluster's network of ethical leadership

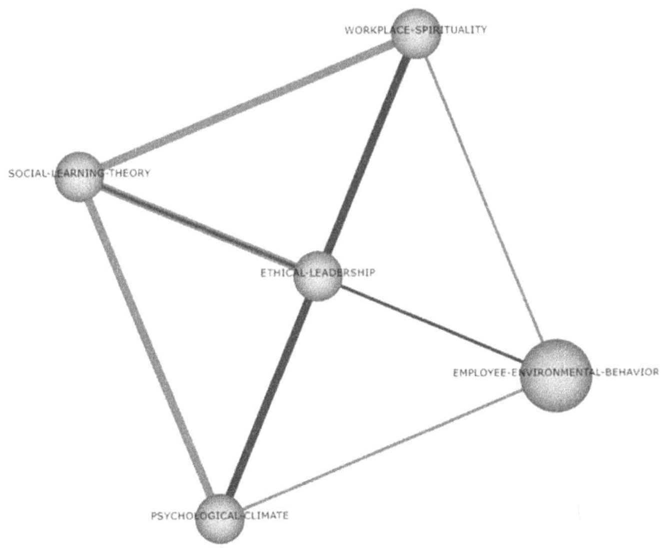

Source: SciMat

DISCUSSION: GAPS, CURRENT CHALLENGES, AND FUTURE RESEARCH AGENDA

Limitations

The results obtained in this study were generated by analyzing only documents indexed on the Web of Science, without considering those from other databases. Furthermore, only articles, review articles and early access were taken into account, without including the information contained in book chapters, proceeding papers and other complementary materials that could provide more information. A future line of research will be to complete this analysis in two ways, the first by adding material from other document types and the second by adding bibliography from other databases to provide a larger sample for analysis. This study should also be completed by carrying out a meta-analysis that includes the results obtained in the empirical analyses contained in the articles used for the bibliometric analysis.

Current Challenges

Waste separation at source for subsequent recycling is an activity that must be extended to all levels if environmental deterioration is to be avoided. Getting individuals involved in this task should be an objective of government programs at all levels. Knowing the aspects of recycling behavior is a challenge facing researchers in all areas of knowledge.

Future Research Agenda

As has become evident throughout this analysis, recycling behavior within workplaces is not sufficiently studied; it is necessary to carry out research aimed at knowing the factors that determine the behavior of individuals regarding recycling at their workplaces. This analysis could be done either from a quantitative point of view, through surveys and measurements of the waste generated, or from a qualitative point of view to understand the workers' discourse when they refer to their behavior regarding recycling. In addition, a reasonable explanation should be sought for the lack of studies on this topic during the years 1996 to 2011.

CONCLUSIONS

The descriptive analysis of scientific production allows us to know which are the most relevant articles within a subject, the journals, and publishers with a major number of publications and the most prolific authors. Through bibliometric analysis, we can know the most important topics within a field of study. In this analysis we have found that TPB and sustainability are the driving themes of these areas and, as expected, recycling is the central theme in this type of study. It has also become clear that there are few articles that analyze the recycling behavior of individuals in their workplaces, especially analyzing it individually and not in conjunction with other types of pro-environmental behaviors. This highlights the need to carry out more studies on this topic so that it will be possible to know the factors and motivations for which individuals recycle in their workplaces. That will serve as the basis for the design of policies to minimize the negative impact of waste on the environment.

REFERENCES

Abbott, A., Nandeibam, S., & O'Shea, L. (2011). Explaining the variation in household recycling rates across the UK. *Ecological Economics*, 70(11), 2214–2223. DOI: 10.1016/j.ecolecon.2011.06.028

Ajzen, I. (1985). From Intentions to Actions: A Theory of Planned Behavior. *Action Control*, 11–39. DOI: 10.1007/978-3-642-69746-3_2

Ajzen, I. (1991). The theory of planned behavior. *Organizational Behavior and Human Decision Processes*, 50(2), 179–211. DOI: 10.1016/0749-5978(91)90020-T

Alhassan, H., Kwakwa, P. A., & Owusu-Sekyere, E. (2020). Households' source separation behaviour and solid waste disposal options in Ghana's Millennium City. *Journal of Environmental Management*, 259, 110055. DOI: 10.1016/j.jenvman.2019.110055 PMID: 31929038

Allen, J., Davis, D., & Soskin, M. (1993). Using Coupon Incentives in Recycling Aluminum: A Market Approach to Energy Conservation Policy. *The Journal of Consumer Affairs*, 27(2), 300–318. DOI: 10.1111/j.1745-6606.1993.tb00750.x

Austin, J., Hatfield, D. B., Grindle, A. C., & Bailey, J. S. (1993). INCREASING RECYCLING IN OFFICE ENVIRONMENTS: THE EFFECTS OF SPECIFIC, INFORMATIVE CUES. *Journal of Applied Behavior Analysis*, 26(2), 247–253. DOI: 10.1901/jaba.1993.26-247 PMID: 16795793

Bandura, A., & Walters, R. (1977). *Social learning theory*. Prentice Hall., https://www.asecib.ase.ro/mps/Bandura_SocialLearningTheory.pdf

Bernstad, A. (2014). Household food waste separation behavior and the importance of convenience. *Waste Management (New York, N.Y.)*, 34(7), 1317–1323. DOI: 10.1016/j.wasman.2014.03.013 PMID: 24780762

Brothers, K. J., Krantz, P. J., & McClannahan, L. E. (1994). OFFICE PAPER RECYCLING: A FUNCTION OF CONTAINER PROXIMITY. *Journal of Applied Behavior Analysis*, 27(1), 153–160. DOI: 10.1901/jaba.1994.27-153 PMID: 16795821

Callon, M., Courtial, J. P., & Laville, F. (1991). Co-word analysis as a tool for describing the network of interactions between basic and technological research: The case of polymer chemsitry. *Scientometrics*, 22(1), 155–205. DOI: 10.1007/BF02019280

Chen, F., Li, X., Ma, J., Yang, Y., & Liu, G. J. (2018). An Exploration of the Impacts of Compulsory Source-Separated Policy in Improving Household Solid Waste-Sorting in Pilot Megacities, China: A Case Study of Nanjing. *Sustainability 2018, Vol. 10, Page 1327, 10*(5), 1327. DOI: 10.3390/su10051327

Cobo, M. J., López-Herrera, A. G., Herrera-Viedma, E., & Herrera, F. (2011). An approach for detecting, quantifying, and visualizing the evolution of a research field: A practical application to the Fuzzy Sets Theory field. *Journal of Informetrics*, 5(1), 146–166. DOI: 10.1016/j.joi.2010.10.002

Costa, A., Mouro, C., & Duarte, A. P. (2022). Waste separation—Who cares? Organizational climate and supervisor support's role in promoting pro-environmental behaviors in the workplace. *Frontiers in Psychology*, 13, 1082155. Advance online publication. DOI: 10.3389/fpsyg.2022.1082155 PMID: 36619029

Dahlsrud, A. (2008). How corporate social responsibility is defined: An analysis of 37 definitions. *Corporate Social Responsibility and Environmental Management*, 15(1), 1–13. DOI: 10.1002/csr.132

Donthu, N., Kumar, S., Mukherjee, D., Pandey, N., & Lim, W. M. (2021). How to conduct a bibliometric analysis: An overview and guidelines. *Journal of Business Research*, 133, 285–296. DOI: 10.1016/j.jbusres.2021.04.070

Fan, M., Khalique, A., Qalati, S. A., Gillal, F. G., & Gillal, R. G. (2022). Antecedents of sustainable e-waste disposal behavior: The moderating role of gender. *Environmental Science and Pollution Research International*, 29(14), 20878–20891. DOI: 10.1007/s11356-021-17275-y PMID: 34741741

Fiorillo, D. (2013). Household waste recycling: National survey evidence from Italy. *Journal of Environmental Planning and Management*, 56(8), 1125–1151. DOI: 10.1080/09640568.2012.709180

Fishbein, M., & Ajzen, I. (1977). Belief, Attitude, Intention, and Behavior: An Introduction to Theory and Research. In *Philosophy and Rhetoric*. https://philpapers.org/rec/FISBAI?all_versions=1

Fogt Jacobsen, L., Pedersen, S., & Thøgersen, J. (2022). Drivers of and barriers to consumers' plastic packaging waste avoidance and recycling – A systematic literature review. *Waste Management (New York, N.Y.)*, 141, 63–78. DOI: 10.1016/j.wasman.2022.01.021 PMID: 35093857

Fry, L. W. (2003). Toward a theory of spiritual leadership. *The Leadership Quarterly*, 14(6), 693–727. DOI: 10.1016/j.leaqua.2003.09.001

Greaves, M., Zibarras, L. D., & Stride, C. (2013). Using the theory of planned behavior to explore environmental behavioral intentions in the workplace. *Journal of Environmental Psychology*, 34, 109–120. DOI: 10.1016/j.jenvp.2013.02.003

Hao, J. L., Yu, S., Tang, X., & Wu, W. (2022). Determinants of workers' pro-environmental behaviour towards enhancing construction waste management: Contributing to China's circular economy. *Journal of Cleaner Production*, 369, 133265. DOI: 10.1016/j.jclepro.2022.133265

Heidrich, O., & Harvey, J. (2018). An examination into recycling and waste management attitudes and behaviors by UK employees. *Environmental Engineering and Management Journal*, 17(1), 71–81. DOI: 10.30638/eemj.2018.009

Janmaimool, P. (2017). The role of descriptive social norms, organisational norms and personal norms in explaining solid waste management behaviours in workplaces. *Journal of Organizational Change Management*, 30(2), 184–198. DOI: 10.1108/JOCM-12-2016-0265

Knickmeyer, D. (2020). Social factors influencing household waste separation: A literature review on good practices to improve the recycling performance of urban areas. *Journal of Cleaner Production*, 245, 118605. DOI: 10.1016/j.jclepro.2019.118605

Lee, Y. J., & De Young, R. (1994). Intrinsic satisfaction derived from office recycling behavior: A case study in Taiwan. *Social Indicators Research*, 31(1), 63–76. DOI: 10.1007/BF01086514

Lee, Y. J., de Young, R., & Marans, R. W. (1995). Factors Influencing Individual Recycling Behavior in Office Settings: A Study of Office Workers in Taiwan. *Environment and Behavior*, 27(3), 380–403. DOI: 10.1177/0013916595273006

Li, W., Sun, K., Liu, X., Wang, Z., & Li, G. (2023). What attributes of mandatory waste management policy can enhance the separation intention of residents in China? A behaviour choice experiment. *Journal of Material Cycles and Waste Management*, 25(4), 2365–2380. DOI: 10.1007/s10163-023-01695-8

Lian, H., Wang, D., & Li, H. (2020). Waste sorting and its effects on carbon emission reduction: Evidence from China. *Zhongguo Renkou Ziyuan Yu Huanjing*, 18(1), 26–34. DOI: 10.1016/j.cjpre.2021.04.027

Lo, S. H., Peters, G. J. Y., & Kok, G. (2012). A Review of Determinants of and Interventions for Proenvironmental Behaviors in Organizations. *Journal of Applied Social Psychology*, 42(12), 2933–2967. DOI: 10.1111/j.1559-1816.2012.00969.x

Manika, D., Wells, V. K., Gregory-Smith, D., & Gentry, M. (2015). The Impact of Individual Attitudinal and Organisational Variables on Workplace Environmentally Friendly Behaviours. *Journal of Business Ethics*, 126(4), 663–684. DOI: 10.1007/s10551-013-1978-6

Marans, R. W., & Lee, Y. J. (1993). Linking recycling behavior to waste management planning: A case study of office workers in Taiwan. *Landscape and Urban Planning*, 26(1–4), 203–214. DOI: 10.1016/0169-2046(93)90017-8

Moral-Muñoz, J. A., Herrera-Viedma, E., Santisteban-Espejo, A., & Cobo, M. J. (2020). Software tools for conducting bibliometric analysis in science: An up-to-date review. *El Profesional de la Información*, 29(1). Advance online publication. DOI: 10.3145/epi.2020.ene.03

Murillo-Ramos, L., Huertas-Valdivia, I., & García-Muiña, F. E. (2023). Exploring the cornerstones of green, sustainable and socially responsible human resource management. *International Journal of Manpower*, 44(3), 524–542. DOI: 10.1108/IJM-12-2021-0696

Nencková, L., Pecáková, I., & Šauer, P. (2020). Disposal behaviour of Czech consumers towards textile products. *Waste Management (New York, N.Y.)*, 106, 71–76. DOI: 10.1016/j.wasman.2020.03.001 PMID: 32222682

Ng, S. L. (2023). Knowledge–intention–behavior associations and spillovers of domestic and workplace recycling. *The Social Science Journal*, 60(2), 254–273. DOI: 10.1080/03623319.2020.1735857

Norton, T. A., Parker, S. L., Zacher, H., & Ashkanasy, N. M. (2015). Employee Green Behavior: A Theoretical Framework, Multilevel Review, and Future Research Agenda. *Organization & Environment*, 28(1), 103–125. DOI: 10.1177/1086026615575773

Ofstad, S. P., Tobolova, M., Nayum, A., & Klöckner, C. A. (2017). Understanding the Mechanisms behind Changing People's Recycling Behavior at Work by Applying a Comprehensive Action Determination Model. *Sustainability 2017, Vol. 9, Page 204, 9*(2), 204. DOI: 10.3390/su9020204

Oke, A. (2015). Workplace Waste Recycling Behaviour: A Meta-Analytical Review. *Sustainability 2015, Vol. 7, Pages 7175-7194, 7*(6), 7175–7194. DOI: 10.3390/su7067175

Oke, A., McDonald, S., & Korobilis-Magas, E. (2021). Demystifying the complexity and heterogeneity of recycling behavior in organizational settings: A mixed-methods approach. *Waste Management (New York, N.Y.)*, 136, 337–347. DOI: 10.1016/j.wasman.2021.10.020 PMID: 34752973

Oke, A., McDonald, S., Korobilis-Magas, E., Osobajo, O. A., & Awuzie, B. O. (2021). Reframing Recycling Behaviour through Consumers' Perceptions: An Exploratory Investigation. *Sustainability 2021, Vol. 13, Page 13849, 13*(24), 13849. DOI: 10.3390/su132413849

Ozkan, S., Tari Selcuk, K., & Kan, Z. E. (2024). Is green behaviors of health professionals related to green practices in the workplace? Multicenter study in Turkey. *International Journal of Environmental Health Research*, 34(2), 898–910. DOI: 10.1080/09603123.2023.2185209 PMID: 36854645

Paillé, P., Raineri, N., & Boiral, O. (2019). Environmental Behavior On and Off the Job: A Configurational Approach. *Journal of Business Ethics*, 158(1), 253–268. DOI: 10.1007/s10551-017-3758-1

Paul, J., & Criado, A. R. (2020). The art of writing literature review: What do we know and what do we need to know? *International Business Review*, 29(4), 101717. DOI: 10.1016/j.ibusrev.2020.101717

Paul, J., Lim, W. M., O'Cass, A., Hao, A. W., & Bresciani, S. (2021). Scientific procedures and rationales for systematic literature reviews (SPAR-4-SLR). *International Journal of Consumer Studies*, 45(4). Advance online publication. DOI: 10.1111/ijcs.12695

Rojas-Perez, H. L., Díaz-Vásquez, M. A., Díaz-Manchay, R. J., Zeña-Ñañez, S., Failoc-Rojas, V. E., & Smith, D. (2024). Nurses' Environmental Practices in Northern Peruvian Hospitals. *Workplace Health & Safety*, 72(2), 68–74. DOI: 10.1177/21650799231163130 PMID: 37016802

Saleem, M., Qadeer, F., Mahmood, F., Ariza-Montes, A., & Han, H. (2020). Ethical Leadership and Employee Green Behavior: A Multilevel Moderated Mediation Analysis. *Sustainability 2020, Vol. 12, Page 3314, 12*(8), 3314. DOI: 10.3390/su12083314

Saleem, M., Qadeer, F., Mahmood, F., Han, H., Giorgi, G., & Ariza-Montes, A. (2021). Inculcation of Green Behavior in Employees: A Multilevel Moderated Mediation Approach. *International Journal of Environmental Research and Public Health 2021, Vol. 18, Page 331, 18*(1), 331. DOI: 10.3390/ijerph18010331

Salvador, R. O., & Burciaga, A. (2020). Organizational environmental orientation and employee environmental in-role behaviors: A cross-level study. *Business Ethics (Oxford, England)*, 29(1), 98–113. DOI: 10.1111/beer.12241

Saphores, J. D. M., Nixon, H., Ogunseitan, O. A., & Shapiro, A. A. (2006). Household willingness to recycle electronic waste: An application to California. *Environment and Behavior*, 38(2), 183–208. DOI: 10.1177/0013916505279045

Saphores, J. D. M., Ogunseitan, O. A., & Shapiro, A. A. (2012). Willingness to engage in a pro-environmental behavior: An analysis of e-waste recycling based on a national survey of U.S. households. *Resources, Conservation and Recycling*, 60, 49–63. DOI: 10.1016/j.resconrec.2011.12.003

Schultz, P. W., Oskamp, S., & Mainieri, T. (1995). Who recycles and when? A review of personal and situational factors. *Journal of Environmental Psychology*, 15(2), 105–121. DOI: 10.1016/0272-4944(95)90019-5

Schwartz, S. H. (1973). Normative explanations of helping behavior: A critique, proposal, and empirical test. *Journal of Experimental Social Psychology*, 9(4), 349–364. DOI: 10.1016/0022-1031(73)90071-1

Si, H., Shi, J. G., Tang, D., Wen, S., Miao, W., & Duan, K. (2019). Application of the Theory of Planned Behavior in Environmental Science: A Comprehensive Bibliometric Analysis. *International Journal of Environmental Research and Public Health 2019, Vol. 16, Page 2788, 16*(15), 2788. DOI: 10.3390/ijerph16152788

Sidique, S. F., Joshi, S. V., & Lupi, F. (2010). Factors influencing the rate of recycling: An analysis of Minnesota counties. *Resources, Conservation and Recycling*, 54(4), 242–249. DOI: 10.1016/j.resconrec.2009.08.006

Thøgersen, J. (2006). Norms for environmentally responsible behaviour: An extended taxonomy. *Journal of Environmental Psychology*, 26(4), 247–261. DOI: 10.1016/j.jenvp.2006.09.004

Vassanadumrongdee, S., & Kittipongvises, S. (2018). Factors influencing source separation intention and willingness to pay for improving waste management in Bangkok, Thailand. *Sustainable Environment Research*, 28(2), 90–99. DOI: 10.1016/j.serj.2017.11.003

WCED. (1987). Our common future. World commission on environment and development. *Sustainable Development*, 154, 1–374.

Whitmarsh, L. E., Haggar, P., & Thomas, M. (2018). Waste reduction behaviors at home, at work, and on holiday: What influences behavioral consistency across contexts? *Frontiers in Psychology*, 9(DEC), 417854. DOI: 10.3389/fpsyg.2018.02447 PMID: 30574111

Yu, H., Salman Shabbir, M., Ahmad, N., Ariza-Montes, A., Vega-Muñoz, A., Han, H., Scholz, M., & Safdar Sial, M. (2021). A Contemporary Issue of Micro-Foundation of CSR, Employee Pro-Environmental Behavior, and Environmental Performance toward Energy Saving, Carbon Emission Reduction, and Recycling. *International Journal of Environmental Research and Public Health*, 18(10), 5380. DOI: 10.3390/ijerph18105380 PMID: 34070088

Yuriev, A., Boiral, O., Francoeur, V., & Paillé, P. (2018). Overcoming the barriers to pro-environmental behaviors in the workplace: A systematic review. *Journal of Cleaner Production*, 182, 379–394. DOI: 10.1016/j.jclepro.2018.02.041

Zupic, I., & Čater, T. (2015). Bibliometric Methods in Management and Organization. *Organizational Research Methods*, 18(3), 429–472. DOI: 10.1177/1094428114562629

KEY TERMS AND DEFINITIONS

Environmental sustainability: Is a way of acting in which it is intended that the impact of the actions of individuals or companies does not affect the environment or affects it as little as possible.

Greenhouse gasses: There are gases that exist in the atmosphere and serve to maintain the heat emitted by the sun; when they are emitted in excess, they cause the so-called greenhouse effect.

Pro-environmental behavior: Is a kind of behavior aimed to protect the environment.

Theory of Planned Behavior: It is one of the main theories that explains how pro-environmental intentions are transformed into pro-environmental behaviors.

Waste recycling: Is the process by which waste is treated in such a way that it can give rise to new products.

Waste reutilization: It is a pro-environmental behavior in which waste is given a new use, instead of being discarded.

Waste separation: Is the act of separating waste when it is generated. It is usually carried out in homes, industries, or offices. Although it is not the same, the term recycling is sometimes used colloquially to refer to this behavior.

Chapter 10
Factors for the Effective Training of Young Entrepreneurs:
An Experience in Southeastern Mexico

Francisco Gerardo Barroso-Tanoira
https://orcid.org/0000-0002-2035-2113
Universidad Autónoma de Yucatán, Mexico

Raul Alberto Santos-Valencia
Instituto Tecnológico de Mérida, Mexico

Jorge Ramón Salazar-Cantón
Universidad Autónoma de Yucatán, Mexico

Valentín Alonso-Novelo
https://orcid.org/0000-0002-1970-6594
Universidad Autónoma de Yucatán, Mexico

ABSTRACT

This paper aims to verify whether there is a relationship between creative thinking and the entrepreneurial skills of young entrepreneurs to determine the factors that should be included in effective programs to train them as entrepreneurs. For this, a creative thinking test was designed that includes mathematical reasoning, inference and logical-deductive thinking, with software specially designed for this purpose. For entrepreneurial competencies, a validated questionnaire was used, which also served to detect the factors in the training of young entrepreneurs, design and implement

DOI: 10.4018/979-8-3693-6289-1.ch010

a course based on these factors, so that it is confirmed if they are decisive or not. Undergraduate students from a private university in the city of Mérida, Yucatán, in southeastern Mexico, participated in this course, both for the diagnostic study (phase 1) and for the course (phase 2), but it is expected to replicate the study in other groups and companies in the future.

INTRODUCTION

Given the current unemployment rate of 2.6% of the economically active population (EAP) (Rodríguez, 2024), which is about half the rate in 2013 (El Economista, 2013), but with a growth of only 2% of the gross domestic product (GDP), which is insufficient compared to the expected goal of 4.5% per year, symptoms of economic stagnation are felt (Mexico, How are we doing?, 2024). If the effects of the new reforms due to the changes in the Federal Government are considered, the future for companies, especially the new ones, is uncertain and difficult.

Mexico is in second place, as a member of the OECD (Organization for Economic Co-operation and Development), in terms of levels of income inequality, with 57% of the country's wealth in the hands of just 10% of the population (El Economista, 2023). For this reason, it is not possible to continue depending on the possibility that only large companies or the Government generate more jobs. Access to financing sources, the procedure for starting a business and business education must improve (Meza-Rodríguez, 2023). Therefore, it is necessary to encourage the creation of new companies able to adapt fast and effectively to their respective environments, creating jobs and improving the quality of life of people and communities.

Mexicans are known for their high entrepreneurial spirit, but the education system for entrepreneurs is deficient (Domínguez-Sagols, 2024). The main strengths for innovation in Mexico are centered in infrastructure, market sophistication, institutions and human capital (Estudio Global, 2023). However, although the country is ranked 44 among the countries with the best entrepreneurship ecosystems (it was 30th in 2021), 64% of Mexican entrepreneurs do not receive governmental support, and 57% do not know about public support programs for business (Meza-Rodríguez, 2023). Unfortunately, 76% of entrepreneurs go out of business in the first three years of operation due to lack of financing and delays in paying suppliers (Asociación de Emprendedores de México, 2023). According to Meza-Rodríguez (2023), 13% of adults are starting a business, but most of them are informal.

On the other hand, it is neither possible nor desirable for higher education institutions (HEIs) to educate students just with an employee mentality, who will passively wait to find someone to hire them at the end of their university studies. Entrepreneurship must go beyond the simple idea of starting a business, since it consists of skills and attitudes to prepare people to face challenges through vision, innovation and teamwork for achieving common objectives (Domínguez-Sagols, 2024). The best places for starting a business, in terms of public policy, macroeconomic factors and access to financing sources, are the United Arab Emirates, Saudi Arabia and Taiwan (Meza-Rodríguez, 2023).

A solution for economic development and poverty reduction is increasing the number of entrepreneurs, this is, people who have the capacity and will to create businesses and innovate. However, although current study programs include entrepreneurial capacity training for future professionals, there is no guarantee that those students will effectively have the will to create businesses, so it is necessary to encourage them to realize that it is not only about finishing university studies to be somebody´s employee, but that there is also the possibility of starting their own path in business. It's not bad to work for someone else if that's what they want... the bad thing is to think that it is the only option for students when they get their bachelor's degree.

For De Bono (1996), as well as for Clegg and Birch (2001), insufficient quality in teaching is largely responsible for poor education aimed at helping students to be creative, since education systems in different countries can inhibit creativity because they have been designed to pass exams and provide the answers teachers expect to hear, without necessarily being the most original or the most creative (Clegg & Birch, 2001). On the other hand, since creative thinking seems to require neither logic nor experience, there are those who assume that anyone can be a creativity, critical thinking and innovation "expert" in a short time just by learning a few techniques, or that this education is just a passing fashion, dedicating more time to rational thinking (Gámez, 1998). It is important to educate for creativity and critical thinking development, improving teacher attitude and didactic strategies for making creativity and critical thinking cultural values (Cárdenas-Martínez, 2019). For Domínguez-Sagols (2024), resilience, adaptation to change, teamwork, problem solution, leadership and creative thinking are essential skills to be taught not only for becoming entrepreneurs, but for life. Entrepreneurship intention must be also enhanced because it affects entrepreneurship behavior (Yi, 2021).

It has been observed that, at the end of their undergraduate studies, there are students who start their own business, while others join an existing company or organization, despite the fact that all of them have been educated in their institutions with programs that include the development of critical and creative thinking, entrepreneurship and innovation through courses, seminars, workshops and curricular subjects. However, one problem is that even if a student has the ability to start a business, there may be personal or contextual factors that become barriers to do so. Assuming that those who want to do things could achieve more than those who just can, there have been attempts to stimulate creativity and critical thinking in HEIs as a basis for innovation and the desire for entrepreneurship.

Although there are studies on entrepreneurial skills and creative thinking, it is desirable to verify if they are related to entrepreneurial competencies. For this, there are some research questions: (1) Is the development of creative and critical thinking significantly associated with entrepreneurial skills? (2) Is the better performance score in creative thinking expected to result in a better score in entrepreneurship competencies tests? (3) Which are the determining factors for educating undergraduate students to orient themselves to entrepreneurship, becoming agents that trigger the economic development of a region?

For all of the above, the objectives of this study are: (1) to verify whether there is a relationship between creative and critical thinking skills with entrepreneurial competencies; (2) to determine the factors that must be included in the study programs to motivate students to become entrepreneurs, and (3) to determine the relevance of these factors by evaluating the effectiveness of an entrepreneur training program designed and implemented according to the information obtained in this study. It is worth mentioning that this study was carried out during 2012 and that the participating students have been followed up to date.

The results will generate pertinent and relevant information to evaluate the study programs of HEIs in relation to creative thinking and entrepreneurship, as well as to open education and training opportunities linking academic institutions with companies, financial agencies, and the Government, allowing teachers, consultants and students learn from real experiences. In addition, the methodology can be used, with the corresponding adaptations, to verify the entrepreneurial competencies of business workers and help them improve their capacity for creative and critical thinking, so that they could react favorably to challenges and be more sensitive to environmental needs, detecting opportunity areas to improve their working methods and innovate in their products and services, making investment in human capital more effective.

The information generated in this study could guide more young undergraduate students towards entrepreneurship, increasing the possibility of increasing productive employment rates and reducing the dependence from other countries. Financial institutions such as banks and investment groups could find an opportunity for increasing profitability in a win-win scheme: entrepreneurs, investors and, of course, the country.

The chapter presents a literature review regarding creativity, critical thinking and innovation, as well as the concepts of competencies and skills needed by entrepreneurs. The methodology presents the diagnose, its instruments and procedure, as well as the designed course results. Then, there is the discussion, conclusions, and future studies section.

LITERATURE REVIEW

Creativity, critical thinking, and innovation

Creativity

Creativity consists of generating new ideas and communicating them (De la Torre, 1997). It is the ability to create, produce, form, give birth, give origin, or representing something for the first time (Gámez, 1998). For Robbins and Judge (2009), it is the ability to combine new and useful ideas, different from what has been done before, but appropriate to the problem or opportunity that is presented. For these authors, creativity development consists of three components: (a) competency, this is, knowledge and skills about what is going to be done or what is going to be acted upon; (b) creative thinking skills, which include thinking skills, mental calculation, inference and logical deduction, and (c) intrinsic task motivation, which is the attitudinal part of creativity and is related to creating challenges in the system and makes the individual creative.

Critical thinking

Critical thinking is understood as an intellectual attitude for questioning, analyzing or evaluating the structure and consistency of reasoning, particularly beliefs or statements that are normally considered true, through knowledge and intelligence (Carroll, 2000). In this way, it is intended to arrive at a more reasoned and justified position on an issue. Fobler and LeBlanc (1995) suggest implementing actions leading to ideas evaluation, avoiding their acceptance just as they come. For Caroll (2000), evaluation can be based on observation, experience, reasoning or through scientific methods because the important is going beyond mere subjective perceptions, impressions and particular opinions.

Critical thinking seeks clarity, accuracy, precision, evidence, and fairness, so it has an analytical and an evaluative aspect, seeking to provide the individual with intellectual tools to distinguish the reasonable from the unreasonable, as well as the true from the false. On the other hand, creative thinking seeks to generate new ideas. Good critical thinkers tend to be better prepared and equipped for decision making and problem solving, compared to those who do not use critical thinking. Problem solving orientation is fundamental for the development of creativity, as indicated by Clegg and Birch (2001), and Gámez (1998), so the development of critical thinking helps to develop creativity.

For Altman, creator of OpenAI and ChatGPT, cited by Rodríguez (2024), creativity and critical thinking will be the great differentiators to offer value in organizations, since the ability to generate new ideas and a deep understanding of human desires will be the most valuable skills. The ideas exchange, as well as their fair and constructive evaluation through critical thinking, makes creativity learning meaningful (CESUMA University, 2023).

Innovation

Innovation is only possible if creativity is an ally (De la Torre, 1997). Innovation requires the individual to see change as an opportunity, since success is only achieved when change is enhanced, rather than trying to force it (Drucker, 1993).

Gupta (2012) indicates that, in order to innovate, it is important for individuals to master the following areas: (1) time management; (2) logical reasoning processes (*process thinking*); (3) statistical thinking, and (4) innovative thinking. Learning within innovation is not merely accumulating knowledge, but getting the best out of that knowledge. The goal of education for innovation is to prepare and empower individuals for faster innovation by applying creativity to deliver value to the customer. For an innovation to be meaningful, it must be accepted by users, and when it comes to commercial or business environments, it must be profitable, which means to be accepted by the market. From this point of view, an innovation is such only if it produces profits.

In simple words, creativity is an idea. Invention is to make this idea work for the first time, and innovation is to reproduce the creative solution so customers or users could acquire it, concludes Gupta (2012). Then, the entrepreneur comes for making profits. For his part, Zavala (2012) suggests that the latter is very important for both personal and business success, since successful companies follow innovative behavior according to the acronym KING: K (*knowledge*); I (*innovation*); N (*National*), and G (*Global*). Innovation is the only way to maintain the prosperity of any organization, no matter if it is a community, a company, or a country. However, innovation without entrepreneurship is void and could be reduced just to invention or creativity, which are worth, but without producing benefits.

Competencies

Traditionally, competencies are defined as the combination of knowledge, skills, and attitudes that people use in various real work situations, according to established performance standards. However, a competency is a capacity that can be measured and is necessary for performing a task successfully, which means to produce the results desired by the organization (Marelli, 2000, cited by Vargas, 2006). For

SRHM (2022), a competency is a group of highly interrelated knowledge, skills, abilities and other characteristics that give rise to the behaviors needed to perform a given job effectively.

The objective of competency analysis is to identify the knowledge, skills, abilities and enabling behaviors that individuals must demonstrate the organization to achieve its goals and objectives, which implies: (1) a degree of effectiveness and efficiency in achieving these objectives; (2) a degree in which a program has used resources appropriately and completed the activities in a timely manner, and (3) a set of tasks, functions, and responsibilities that must be taken by the person who performs these activities to satisfy the characteristics of each professional area (Méndez, 2006).

According to the International Labour Organization (2002), competencies can be classified into three groups: (1) *general human competencies* (oriented to the development of the person himself/herself and his/her relationship with reality); (2) *business competencies* (ability to influence and motivate the will of employees), and (c) *technical competencies* (ability of the individual to perform his/her trade or function according to the requirements defined and recognized by the labor market). And although the meaning of competencies is very broad, it could be summarized as the ability people have to successfully carry out the activities entrusted to them, which implies that these activities are in the required time and with the expected quality.

Competencies Needed by Entrepreneurs

De la Vega (2004) suggests that for a business project to be successful, it is necessary to know the person's or people's entrepreneurial competencies. According to this author, it has been frequently proven that the same business idea could be successful or a failure depending on the entrepreneur who launches it, thus it is worth finding people who can make successful almost any project they start. For some authors, the entrepreneur "is born, not made", and therefore, anyone who meets the right characteristics is practically predestined to be an entrepreneur and, in the long run, a business owner (Bull & Winter, 1991). This is difficult to achieve since being an entrepreneur and a businessman or businesswoman is a function of the context and influence of cultural, economic, sociological, and psychological factors (Landström & Winborg, 1996).

Entrepreneurship can grow and develop only in a society in which cultural norms allow variability in the choice of paths of life (Kumar & Kumra, 2023). Factors such as behavioral control, attitudes, start-up self-efficacy, technical knowledge and subjective norms have a significant effect on the intention to create new start-ups (Njoku et al., 2024). Aggressive behavior is not strongly related to entrepreneurial intention (Al-Mamary et al., 2022).

Filión and Roy (1996) made a synthesis of the main characteristics of entrepreneurs, result of the analysis of hundreds of studies they reviewed: (1) self-confidence; (2) perseverance, determination, long-term commitment; (3) energy; (4) talent; (5) ability to take calculated risks; (6) need for self-realization; (7) creativity; (8) initiative; (9) flexibility; (10) liability; (11) independence; (12) forecasting; (13) dynamism; (14) versatility, knowledge of the product, market, equipment, technology; (15) ability to deal with people; (16) adaptation to critical moments; (17) profit orientation; (18) optimism: (19) internalization; (20) tolerance for facing ambiguity and uncertainty; (21) nonconformism, and (22) leadership. On the other hand, Palacios (1999) implemented a methodology of entrepreneurial competencies that has been systematically observed in entrepreneurs based on their behaviors, practices and strategies implemented by them, which are the following:

1. ***Entrepreneurial spirit***. It refers to characteristics such as "having a business nose", having an idea between "eyebrows and eyebrows" and carrying out an idea against "all odds".
2. ***Necessity of existence***. It involves feeling a great need to do the business. It includes a willingness to sacrifice initial gains for long-term permanence. It also refers to the desire for having a business.
3. ***Previous technical experience***. Knowledge about the business, processes and the product are important parts for company success. It is desirable that to achieve business success, the person connects with the business for a period of no less than five years.
4. ***Risk tolerance***. It is the ability to face calculated risks, this is, the ability to assume risks based on a previously established study or plan.
5. ***Hard work***. Willingness to dedicate effort and many hours of work, often without immediate rewards. It is also known as liability.
6. ***Ability to recover and learn***. It also implies tenacity and perseverance. Not to feel defeated by failure and learning from mistakes.
7. ***Tolerant society***. It is the ability to know how to understand each other, to choose the most suitable and know how to work as a team.
8. ***Credibility.*** It has to do with offering quality products, respecting customers, showing appreciation to workers. In short, it is doing things well, having integrity and acting according to their principles.
9. ***Prioritize***. Be skilled enough to set priorities and follow them.
10. ***Family culture***. Since many of the new businesses are family-owned, much of the business success is achieved through the proper management of family relationships, the importance of introducing professional management and the ability to prepare the company for succession. It is also known as "family and business"

11. ***Professionalism of the entrepreneur***. It involves having the ability to develop internal skills and capabilities, as well as the necessary practices and strategies to ensure survival and company growth. It is also known as "entrepreneur qualities".

For Palacios (1999), as well as for Bilbao and Pachano (2002), the entrepreneur faces innumerable obstacles such as lack of entrepreneurial culture, family impediments, lack of knowledge, and consequently, insecurity in the business field and lack of resources, among others. It is a constant challenge for entrepreneurs, but they can turn to various organizations for support for procedures, financing, tax and labor education, as well as for promoting a strong link with the Government. The main thing is that they have the capacity and will for entrepreneurship. Entrepreneurial intention has also a strong relation with autonomy, innovativeness, risk-taking, and proactiveness (Al-Mamary et al., 2022).

It is important for entrepreneurship programs to enhance the growth of mindset training, since it leads to improve self-efficacy for trainees and leads them to action, complementing technical based training (Shad et al., 2023). However, other factors must be considered when designing entrepreneurship programs, such as religious, socio-economic, and structural forces of society, since they could play a significant role in suppressing social and cultural capital, especially in rural areas (Kumar & Kumra, 2023).

METHODOLOGY

The study has two phases: The first (1) is to verify if there is a statistical relationship between creative thinking and entrepreneurial skills, which was done through the administration of a creative and critical thinking test, followed by a questionnaire of entrepreneurial skills. This was also for determining the factors that must be included in the study programs for the training of young entrepreneurs. The second (2) was to evaluate the effectiveness of an entrepreneur training course designed and implemented according to the information generated in phase 1 and the literature review.

Phase 1

The study was descriptive and evolved into correlational, with a quantitative approach and a cross-sectional non-experimental design (Hernández et al., 2014). The survey was used as the information gathering technique, also using a test and a questionnaire as instruments. During the first semester of 2012, 33 students of

International Business, Marketing and Administration from a private university in the Southeast of Mexico participated. Those students belong to the medium-high socioeconomic segment and are from different cities, but mostly from Mérida. In the participant group, 39.3% work in the family business, 21.2% in companies outside the family and the rest were not working at the time of the study. About gender, 60.6% of the total participants are women. The test and quiz were administered during the last week of classes of the mentioned semester.

It is worth mentioning that this study was the beginning of a series consisting of applying the same procedure to other groups later. In the future, with pertinent adjustments, it will be replicated in business companies for helping managers detect opportunity areas for improving their workers' creative and critical thinking, identifying and increasing their entrepreneurial competencies.

Phase 2

In this second phase, the study was descriptive and evolved to correlational, with a quantitative approach and pre-experimental design (Hernández et al., 2014), using the survey as the information gathering technique. 56 undergraduate students from the same university, disciplines, semester, and socioeconomic level participated, but those students were different from those who participated in phase 1. It is worth mentioning that 35 are women (62.5%) and that the entrepreneurial skills questionnaire was administered at the beginning and at the end of an entrepreneurship and innovation course designed according to the findings of phase 1 and the literature review, implemented in the second semester of 2012. It was intensive and included sessions with topics, practices, simulations, and project development. The students accepted to participate voluntarily.

Instruments

Creative and Critical Thinking Test

The first author of this work designed a test adhering to the guidelines of Robbins and Judge (2009) regarding the components for the development of creative and creative thinking exposed in the literature review, which alludes to the capacity for mental calculation, as well as the concepts established by Gupta (2012) regarding that to be innovative, statistical thinking is required, suggesting numerical ability. This test was used only in phase 1.

The first section of the instrument consists of 30 items, which are additions, subtractions, multiplications, and divisions of three quantities, with a value of one point each (e.g.: 6 x 9 – 4=), to verify agility in mental calculation. The second section comprises twenty items composed of series of figures in which one item is missing to complete the sequence, verifying the way in which the student can infer, predict and extrapolate, with a value of two points each item. It was based on subsection (b) of the components of creativity by Robbins and Judge (2009) presented in the literature review. Finally, the third section includes ten puzzle-type problems of logical-deductive thinking, of three points each, to verify the orientation to problem solving indicated by Caroll (2000) in terms of the fact that through critical thinking it is possible to provide individuals with tools for creativity, since these puzzles combine critical and creative thinking, leading the students to use both brain hemispheres (De Bono, 1996). This last section also complies with what is suggested for the three components of creativity according to Robbins and Judge (2009), since they involve knowledge, capacity for induction and deduction, as well as intrinsic motivation. Students were given a maximum of one hour to respond, setting the maximum grade at 100 points (Barroso & Santos, 2012).

To answer this test and get the results for immediate feedback, an electronic version was developed in a computer application called "Creative Thinking Test" developed by Murillo and Barroso (2012) in php and Java Script language, published on an Apache HTTP Server 2.2 with databases in MySQL version 5.5. The Apache server was used for the system publication with access through an internal Web browser in the institution, but prepared for access via Internet by any browser (Internet Explorer, Firefox, Google Chrome, and others). It is free licensed, modular, cross-platform and there is a lot of documentation on its website to develop any relevant application or modification.

The php language was selected because it is object-oriented for the development of Web applications with access to information stored in databases, in addition to being freely licensed, easily accessible to any developer, and with the ability to connect with most database engines. Finally, MySQL was selected as the database manager because of its wide availability in a large number of platforms and systems, as well as its ability to select storage mechanisms that offer different speeds of operation, in addition to secure connectivity, replication, search and indexing of text fields.

Questionnaire on Entrepreneurial Competencies

For the questionnaire elaboration, Palacio´s (1999) eleven categories model, mentioned in the literature review, was used. It was modified by Barroso and Santos (2012) for adapting it to undergraduate students. This instrument was selected because it was already validated and considered reliable, in addition to the fact that it had to be adapted to students at this level. It is worth mentioning that a pilot test was performed with 10 students only to verify reliability by calculating Cronbach's alpha, which was 0.81, and then proceeding with its administration to the remaining 23 participants, following the methodology used by Santos (2011). In addition to being used in phase 1, this same questionnaire was administered to the students participating in phase 2, both before (pre-test) and after (post-test) the course. Some intention oriented items were included in this questionnaire, as well as open-ended questions.

Procedure

Phase 1

The 33 students solved the creative and critical thinking test at the university computer center in the same session, with immediate feedback for their results. At the end of this test, the entrepreneurial competencies test was distributed to the students to be returned with the answers the next day. Subsequently, the correlations between the scores of the three parts of the creative and critical thinking test with the eleven categories of the questionnaire of entrepreneurial qualities, were calculated to verify if there was any significant outcome.

With the results of the entrepreneurial competencies instrument, a factor analysis was calculated using the main components method and varimax rotation, to identify the critical factors according to their explained variance.

Phase 2

According to the results obtained in phase 1, the experience of this work authors and the literature review, a course was designed and implemented for the participating institution students during December 2012, as indicated above. This course covered 40 intensive hours plus 16 hours of work outside the classroom. It was taught by entrepreneurship experts in the city of Mérida, Yucatán, assisted by the authors of this study.

The course was predominantly practical and aimed at motivating students to be entrepreneurs, emphasizing the constructive use of failure, resilience, behavioral control attitudes, self-efficacy, risk prevention and family-work balance, reinforcing teamwork. Their orientation to goals and decision-making was also enhanced. The course was during December 2012 vacations, although it counted for students as an optional subject in their university studies, getting the corresponding academic credits.

Information Analysis Plan

SPSS and Excel tools were used for data management, but some spaces were left in the diagnostic questionnaire for open responses. The results, due to the type of variable and result generation, met the scale and normality requirements to use Pearson's correlation since they are not spurious and represent distinct and differentiable data. In the correlations, (*) means 95% significance, which means that the "p" significance value must be smaller than 0.05. The double asterisk (**) means 99% significance, which means that the "p" significance value is less than 0.01.

To interpret the quantitative data, the following interval scale (own prepared) was used:

1.0 to 1.49 = Strongly Disagree
1.5 to 2.49 = Disagree
2.5 to 3.49 = Indifferent (neutral)
3.5 to 4.49 =Agree
4.5 to 5.00 =Strongly agree

The open-ended responses were classified according, to the mention frequency, into key ideas and defined categories, assigning the key ideas the corresponding repetition response percentage.

RESULTS

Phase 1

Regarding the results for the 33 participating students, both for the Creative and Critical Thinking Test and the category average for the Entrepreneurship Questionnaire, the highest scores in terms of the Entrepreneurial Competency Questionnaire, were for Desire to have a business" (4.4, Agree), Ability to recover and learn (4.4, Agree), and Family and business (4.5, Strongly agree), while the lowest were for Previous technical experience and Qualities of the entrepreneur, both with 4 (Agree).

Regarding correlations, only significant ones, equal to or greater than 0.4, were taken. It was found that the only significant correlation among the Creative and Critical Thinking Test, with the questionnaire of entrepreneurial competencies, was the Inference section and Ability to recover and learn (-0.486**, $p<0.01$). However, significant correlations were observed among some of the competencies in the questionnaire, since Risk tolerance correlates positively with Responsibility (0.403*, $p<0.05$), as well as the Ability to recover and learn (0.430*, $p<0.05$) and Prioritize (0.504**, $p<0.01$).

Tenacity, reflected in the Ability to recover and learn, correlates with the Ability to work with others (0.479**, p<0.01), Prioritize (0.503**, p<0.01), and the Proper family relationships management (0.572**, p<0.01). The Ability to work with others correlated significantly with adequate Family relationships (0.481**, p<0.01) and Responsibility with the Ability to recover and learn (0.606**, p<0.01), being the strongest correlation. Entrepreneur qualities correlated with Responsibility (0.404*, p<0.05), Credibility (0.556**, p<0.01), and Prioritizing (0.427*, p<0.05).

Within the open ended questions, it is important to say that 33.3% of the participants would dedicate to production activities, 6.06% to banks, 69.7% to service organizations, 9.09% would be interested in dedicating to teaching, 63.6% would opt for commerce as an activity to become entrepreneurs, and 27.3% would be linked to Government projects. These answers are not mutually exclusive, as more than 50% of students considered more than one possibility. Although 96.9% felt competent to start a business, only 72.7% considered themselves ready to do it.

From the factor analysis results, it was obtained that the most critical factors corresponded to Entrepreneurial spirit, this is, the desire to have a business, as established by Palacios (1999), followed by Risk prevention, Persuasion capacity and Sense of belonging. The lowest explained variances are associated with factors that the population uniformly presents, such as initiative and the experience needed for work, which must be reinforced. These eleven factors constituted 68.7% of the total explained variance, as can be seen in Table 1.

Table 1. Explained variance per factor. Research data.

Factor	%
Risk prevention	**7.9**
Persuasion Skills	**6.8**
Sense of belonging	**6.0**
Perfectionism	**5.2**
Search for opportunities	4.6
Practical approach to action	3.7
Ability to work with others	3.6
Business orientation	3.4
On-the-job experience	3.0
Initiative	2.8
Total explained variance	68.7

In the answers to open questions (qualitative), it was reported that the main causes for not being an entrepreneur and affecting the entrepreneurial spirit are the lack of experience in entrepreneurship (51.5% of the mentions), not knowing the market (30.3%) and the lack of knowledge of financing options (18.2%).

Phase 2

When administering the questionnaire before the course, a mean of 4.15 (Agree) was obtained, with a standard deviation of 0.31. After the course, the mean was 4.43 (Agree), with a standard deviation of 0.21. The difference between the results after and before the course was significant ($t= -11.786$, $p< 0.01$**). The correlation between the result averages before and after the course was 0.78 ($p<0.01$**), which is significant.

DISCUSSION, CONCLUSIONS AND FUTURE STUDIES

Discussion

The highest scores for the entrepreneurial competencies questionnaire is related to the Desire to own a business, Tenacity, and Balance with family, which relates more to the individual's vision than to their creative thinking skills. Risk tolerance, a fundamental factor as entrepreneurial competence (Palacios, 1999, Barroso & Santos, 2012), increases when the Ability to recover and learn (Tenacity, Perseverance, and constructive management of failure) increases, which is desirable in the entrepreneur behavior, as well as the ability to set priorities, which is a purely administrative competence. Factors such as Responsibility and Credibility are fundamental in leadership (Aragón & Séveri, 2004; Bull & Winter, 1991), and are related to each other, as well as the ability to work as a team with good family relationships.

The negative correlation of the inference section results of the Creative and Critical Thinking test with Tenacity (-0.486**, $p<0.01$) may indicate that the greater the capacity for inference, the less tenacity there is on the individual behalf, which suggests that there are brilliant individuals for making inferences who are too confident on their ability, so they are less perseverant. They miss opportunities and do not learn from their mistakes. However, this correlation could also indicate that the teaching means do not motivate them to become entrepreneurs, which coincides with De Bono (1994) and Clegg and Birch (2001), in that an inadequate educational system can inhibit creativity, in this case, the creativity related to inferential or inductive thinking. Therefore, for the students to be oriented towards innovation, it is not enough to teach them courses in critical and creative thinking skills, but it is necessary to reinforce entrepreneurial skills by emphasizing vision, leadership, teamwork, resilience, self-efficacy, family-work balance, attitudes, technical knowledge and subjective norms, as well as perseverance and tolerance to risk. This is consistent with Al-Mamary et al. (2024), Kumar and Kumra (2023) and Morris et al. (2023). And since entrepreneurial competencies include attitudes towards entrepreneurship, the best way to teach an attitude is through the example and testimonies of successful people in business, as well as case study analysis and life stories creation.

It is not enough to talk to students about how to become entrepreneurs. It is necessary to help them lose their fear of failure and learn from their own practice and the experience of others in an inclusive and meaningful environment to make entrepreneurial activities attractive, so everyone wants to be in them instead of running away from them. The entrepreneurial spirit is formed by attitudes, and although the family influences the student, the school must provide the conditions for talent and opportunity to come together. This was corroborated by the participation in the entrepreneurship course, in which after the entrepreneurship experience, the corresponding scores to entrepreneurial competencies improved significantly.

The course designed and implemented improved the skills the students already had. Therefore, it is possible to significantly improve entrepreneurship (desire to be an entrepreneur), the constructive use of failure and other entrepreneurial skills through effective training allowing students improve their attitudes towards entrepreneurship rather than with a traditional courses, where they just learn about how to start a business with theoretical exercises or traditional simulations.

The fact that almost all students felt competent for entrepreneurship without considering themselves prepared to do so, suggests that they lacked experience, knowledge of the market and opportunities to get financial resources, which coincides with the lowest scores in the questionnaire by Palacios (1999) and in the qualitative responses. As well as their entrepreneurial spirit and their tolerance to risk, they had entrepreneurial qualities to be improved. In addition to their ability to learn, students were willing to work with others, so it was not surprising that most of them chose to be in commerce, service, productive activities or even activities related to the Government. More structured activities such as working in schools, or more administrative activities such as banks, were not the most considered by them at that moment. This could change if the students reorient their vision towards entrepreneurship related to education and banking.

It is worth mentioning that twelve years after teaching the course, 32 students have started their own business (9 in production, 15 in commerce and 8 in service), and that all the others are already working in the private sector, but with the intention for starting a business in the near future. All of them agreed, in a follow-up activity, that this course helped them to reflect, detect and solve their opportunity areas to start a business, especially in terms of the desire to be an entrepreneur, lose the fear for starting a business, the ability to persuade and to combine their work with the family. They recommend other people to participate in this experience (diagnostic tests and course) because of the relevance and importance of entrepreneurship in their lives.

CONCLUSION

Answering the first objective, activities for intellectual development, mental agility, as well as the ability to infer and deduce, are important for developing creative and critical thinking. However, although necessary in entrepreneurial education, these skills are not predictors of entrepreneurial competencies development, according to the results of this study.

For answering the second objective, although in the traditional curriculum there are subjects for students in terms of intellectual knowledge, skills and critical and creative thinking, only through training in entrepreneurship competencies will be possible to awaken in them the desire to create new sources of business, so necessary for the development of the country. Subjects that focus on the areas proposed by Gupta (2012), Kumar and Kumra (2023), Njoku et al. (2024) and Al-Mamary et al. (2023), must also be included in the curricula, as well as activities for reinforcing the students' orientation towards innovation, as it was done in the course reported in this study. These competencies must enhance the development of self-discipline and entrepreneurial competencies, especially those related to the desire to own a business, tolerance to risk, self-efficacy, technical knowledge, and work-family life balance. Entrepreneurial spirit, constructive management of failure, persuasion skills and teamwork are also determining factors to be included in the training of young people, as well as fostering sensitivity to environmental problems, increasing knowledge and experience, also enhancing a personal vision. For answering objective 3, the course designed and implemented was effective for all of this.

For making entrepreneurship sustainable, it´s important for the Government, private companies, non-governmental organizations, and the academic sector, working together for creating an entrepreneurship ecosystem. Otherwise, projects will be running independently and disconnected, limiting their potential to increase value for society.

Among the activities to promote entrepreneurship, HEIs could organize groups of entrepreneurs to share their experiences with each other, including the testimony of successful entrepreneurs. Mentoring internships could also be organized, in which experts in entrepreneurial activities guide young people in their projects and help them in activities to get the necessary funds, so these young people gain experience as entrepreneurs. Attendance to forums and innovation fairs are important, as well as approaching business incubators. There is talent in young people, but they need to see the benefits of entrepreneurship to lose their fear for starting a business and properly combine their family and business priorities.

Entrepreneurship is a pertinent, viable and necessary solution to increase jobs, increase the number of taxpayers and take advantage of human capital because with more and better companies that generate value for consumers, it will be possible to detonate the country's economy and improve the quality of life for its people, reducing dependence on large companies and lowering the rate of migration to urban centers or abroad. It is about entrepreneurship education now or depending forever of external agents. It´s necessary to educate young students to start a business today!

Future Studies

A point to highlight in this work is the support provided by information and communication technologies (ICTs), since the processing of information proved to be fast, accurate and immediately available for the Creative and Critical Thinking Test, opening the possibility of joint programs among HEIs and the environment that surrounds them.

Although creative and critical thinking competencies are not predictive of entrepreneurial competencies at the student level, it would be desirable to verify this point in other organizations in the field. Therefore, the next step will be to perform the same procedure in companies and the public sector to help those organizations adept better to their environment through improving their human capital. Only through entrepreneurship and innovation will every country move forward, with the consequent improvement in the quality of life of its citizens.

REFERENCES

Al-Mamary, Y. H., & Alshallaqi, M. (2022, October-December). Impact of autonomy, innovativeness, risk-taking, proactiveness, and competitive aggressiveness on students' intention to start a new venture. *Journal of Innovation & Knowledge*, 7(4), 1–10. DOI: 10.1016/j.jik.2022.100239

Aragón, F., & Severi, M. (2004). *Personal characteristics of entrepreneurs. Differences with corporate executives*. Universidad del CEMA.

Asociación de Emprendedores de México (ASEM). (2023, 10 de noviembre). El 64 por ciento de emprendedores mexicanos no reciben apoyo gubernamental: ASEM [64% of Mexican entrepreneurs do not receive governmental support: ASEM]. CONCANACO SERVYTUR México. *El Financiero*. https://www.concanaco.com.mx/prensa/tepuedeinteresar/el-64-por-ciento-de-emprendedores-mexicanos-no-reciben-apoyo-gubernamental-asem-

Barroso, F., & Santos, R. (2012). *Proposal of a methodology supported by ICTs to determine the relationship between critical thinking and entrepreneurial competencies of undergraduate students. Research progress. Proceedings of the Joint Ibero-American Conference on Learning Technologies (Ccita)*. Technological Institute of Mérida. Mérida, Yucatán, Mexico.

Bilbao, A., & Pachano, S. (2002). *Traits and attitudes of entrepreneurs*. Venezuela, Andean Development Corporation – CAF.

Bull, I., & Winter, F. (1991). Community differences in business birth and business growths. *Journal of Business Venturing*, 6(1), 29–43. DOI: 10.1016/0883-9026(91)90004-W

Cárdenas-Martínez, L. D. (2019). Creativity and education in the twenty-first century. Inter-*American Journal of Research. Education and Pedagogy*, 12(2), 211–224. DOI: 10.15332/25005421.5014

Caroll, R. T. (2000). *Becoming a critical thinker. A guide for the new millennium*. Pearson Publishing.

CESUMA University. (2023). *What is meaningful learning?*https://www.cesuma.mx/blog/que-es-el-aprendizaje-significativo.html

Clegg, B., & Birch, P. (2001). *Instant creativity*. Granica.

De Bono, E. (1996). *Creative thinking*. Editorial Paidós Mexicana.

De la Torre, S. (1997). *Creativity and training: identification, design and evaluation*. Trillas.

De la Vega, M. (2004). *Self-employment manual*. Youth Council of Castile.

Domínguez-Sagols, A. (2024, 3 de marzo). Transformando México a través del emprendimiento educativo [Transforming Mexico through educational entrepreneurship]. *El Economista*. https://www.eleconomista.com.mx/opinion/Transformando-Mexico-a-traves-del-Emprendimiento-Educativo-20240303-0037.html

Drucker, P. (1993). *Management for the future. The 90s and beyond*. Grupo Editorial Norma.

El Economista. (2013, October 30). *Unemployment rises to 4.92% in September: INEGI*. https://eleconomista.com.mx/industrias/2013/10/18/tasa-desempleo-se-ubica-492-inegi [REMOVED HYPERLINK FIELD]

El Economista. (2023, November 24). *Costa Rica and Mexico are among the OECD countries with the most inequality*. https://www.eleconomista.com.mx/economia/Costa-Rica-y-Mexico-estan-entre-los-paises-de-la-OCDE-con-mas-desigualdad-20231124-0019.html

Estudio Global. (2023, 27 de septiembre). México es el tercer país con mayor innovación en Latinoamérica [Mexico is the third country with most innovation in Latin America]. CONCANACO SERVYTUR México. https://www.concanaco.com.mx/comercio/interesdecomercio/mexico-es-el-tercer-pais-con-mayor-innovacion-en-latinoamerica-senala-estudio-global-septiembre-27-2023#:~:text=13%3A35%3A48-,M%C3%A9xico%20es%20el%20tercer%20pa%C3%ADs%20con%20mayor%20innovaci%C3%B3n%20en%20Latinoam%C3%A9rica,mercado%2C%20instituciones%20y%20capital%20humano

Expansión, C. N. N. (2013, October 30). *The Mexican economy grew only 1.5%*. https://www.cnnexpansion.com/economia/2013/08/20/mexico-crecimiento-pib-economia

Filion, J. & Roy, G. (1996). *Didactic document*. School of Higher Commercial Studies (HEC). Québec, Montreal, Copec University Bookstore.

Gámez, G. (1998). *Todos somos creatives* [We are all creative]. Ediciones Urano.

Gupta, P. (2012). *The innovation solution. Making innovation more pervasive, predictable and profitable*. Accelper Consulting.

Hernández, R., Fernández, C., & Baptista, P. (2014). *Metodología de la investigación* [Methodology of Research]. 6th ed.). Mc Graw Hill.

International Labour Organization. (2002). *Certification of professional skills*. Author.

International Labour Organization (2002). *Certification of professional skills.*

Kumar, P., & Kumra, R. (2023) Problems of entrepreneurs in India – case of rural self-employment training institutes' trainees'. *International Journal of Entrepreneurship and Small Business*, 48(3), 231–244. ttps://www.researchgate.net/publication/368857512_Problems_of_entrepreneurs_in_India_-_case_of_rural_self-employment_training_institutes'_trainees

Landström, H., & Winborg, J. (1996). *Financial bootstrapping in small businesses-a resource-based view on small business finance*. Scandinavian Institute for Research in Entrepreneurship. Universidad Halmstad

Mendez, J. (2006), *Approaches and models for the development of competence*.https://www.icam.com.mx/canales6/rrhh/gestion-y-desarrollo-de-competencias.htm (2006).

Mexico, how are we doing? (2024, April 30). *National and state growth of the Mexican economy.* https://mexicocomovamos.mx/publicaciones/2021/08/crecimiento-nacional-y-estatal-de-la-economia-mexicana/#:~:text=La%20econom%C3%ADa%20mexicana%20tuvo%20un,4.5%25%20anual%20de%20forma%20sostenida

Meza-Rodríguez, E. (2023, 22 de marzo). Emprender es más difícil: México baja en el índice de creación de negocios [Entrepreneurship is more difficult: Mexico descends in the business creation index]. *El Economista*. https://www.eleconomista.com.mx/el-empresario/Emprender-es-mas-dificil-Mexicobaja-en-el-indice-de-creacion-de-negocios-20230321-0098.html

Murillo, G., & Barroso, F. (2012). *Design of a test for critical thinking* [Software]. Unpublished work. Universidad Anáhuac Mayab, Mérida, Yucatán, Mexico.

Njoku, A., Mouloudj, K., Bouarar, A. C., Evans, M. A., Asanza, D. M., Mouloudj, S., & Bouarar, A. (2024). Intentions to Create Green Start-Ups for Collection of Unwanted Drugs: An Empirical Study. *Sustainability (Basel)*, 16(2797), 1–19. DOI: 10.3390/su16072797

Palacios, L. (1999). *Popular wisdom in Venezuelan business*. Universidad Católica Andrés Bello.

Robbins, S., & Judge, T. (2009). *Comportamiento Organizacional* [Organizational Behavior]. 13th ed.). (Brito, J. L., Trans.). Pearson-Prentice Hall.

Rodríguez, E. (2024). Critical thinking and creativity, indispensable skills in the era of Artificial Intelligence. *ISDI Digitalent Group*. https://www.isdi.education/mx/blog/pensamiento-critico-y-creatividad-las-skills-indispensables-en-la-era-de-inteligencia-artificial

Rodríguez, S. (2024, May 30). Unemployment decreases. It reaches a rate of 2.6% of the EAP in April 2024. *Forbes*. https://www.forbes.com.mx/disminuye-desempleo-alcanza-tasa-de-2-6-de-la-pea-en-abril-de-2024/#:~:text=En%20abril%20de%202024%2C%201.6,Poblaci%C3%B3n%20Econ%C3%B3micamente%20Activa%20(PEA)

Santos, R. (2011). *Entrepreneurial skills of young people and opportunities for job development in their region. The case of the Mayan area called Camino Real de Campeche*. Unpublished doctoral thesis. Universidad Anáhuac Mayab, Mérida, Yucatán, México.

SRHM. (2022). *SHRM Body of Applied Skills and Knowledge*. https://www.shrm.org/content/dam/en/shrm/credentials/shrm-certification/shrm-bask.pdf

Vargas, F. (2006). Competencies in training and human talent management. *Annals of common education.Third Century*, 2(5), 147–163.

Yi, G. (2021). From green entrepreneurial intentions to green entrepreneurial behaviors: The role of university entrepreneurial support and external institutional support. *The International Entrepreneurship and Management Journal*, 17(2), 963–979. DOI: 10.1007/s11365-020-00649-y

Zavala, J. (2012). *Think like Silicon Valley being anywhere*.

KEY TERMS AND DEFINITIONS

Competencies: It is adding knowledge plus ability plus attitude to do things in the correct way, with the correct standards and the correct time.

Creativity: It is solving problems with value, generating ideas to create and produce, result of combining new and different ideas, appropriate for the problem to be solved.

Critical thinking: Competence for organizing information to give it a meaning, fostering reasoning and going beyond subjective perceptions and particular opinions.

Culture: Set of shared values and symbols that identify a social group and help with the cohesion of its members. It could also be understood as a collective mental programming for a social group.

Entrepreneurial spirit: It is "smelling" a business opportunity or any chance for improving, willing to be in action despite all barriers.

Entrepreneurship Taking: the risk for starting a new venture, company, or any other action. Doing things for the first time. Creativity and innovation are necessary for entrepreneurship.

Innovation Result of creativity: It is placing creativity at any human reach. Making money for solving a problem with value.

Chapter 11
Tourism Marketing: Perspective of Visual Behavior in Adventure Sports

Juan Carlos Castro
https://orcid.org/0000-0002-5371-9727
Universidad Tecnica de Ambato, Ecuador

ABSTRACT

People visiting different destinations around the world demand that tourist attractions be showcased before being visited. This drives us to study which types of adventure tourist attractions arouse greater interest among potential visitors, with the aim of optimizing communication in the city of Baños de Agua Santa in Ecuador. An eye-tracking-based design was used with 42 male and female participants, who were shown adventure images according to visual path-oriented pairings. Among all fixations, it is men who prevail in visual scanning, focusing on action elements, while women contribute with greater peripheral fluency in visual elements and their processing. There is a marked coincidence in the visual attraction of rafting between both sexes, as a group activity within the set of sports considered adventure sports. Thus, the data set shows a certain dominance by the male target in fixations on adventure images, probably rooted in competitive culture, defined by the covert action around the practice of these sports, which involves adventure and nature.

1. INTRODUCTION

Undoubtedly, visual stimuli are leading us to a visual culture (Burri, 2012) that has been exploited by tourism marketing for the promotion of destinations and their attractions in different regions of the world (Jiang et al., 2024; Wisnujati et al., 2024). This has increased the visibility of many destinations and, in the same way,

DOI: 10.4018/979-8-3693-6289-1.ch011

has increased competition among them, aiming to enhance their image with visual resources used in tourism marketing strategies.

In this way, tourism marketing becomes a driver for the use of images or photographs (Li et al., 2024) of recreational activities, landscapes, adventure sports, and other attractions, as visual means for the promotion and commercialization of destinations. This is based on tourist attractions that establish a competitive position (González et al., 2023; Navarro et al., 2023; Saqib, 2019), playing a key role in developing a positive image in target markets. Thus, tourism marketing emphasizes the use of images as a means of communication, incorporating people to enhance realism (Zhang et al., 2023), interpreted and influenced by potential visitors in various media to become factors that affect their purchasing decisions and behaviors.

From the above, it is clear the importance of images of adventure sports as tourist attractions (Mihai et al.2023) for the promotion and marketing of destinations, as elements that capture attention and enhance social presence, as well as the attractiveness and intention of viewers to visit the destination (Filieri et al., 2021; Roy et al., 2021). Undoubtedly, the effect that images provoke when exposed to potential visitors in various media is a topic that is receiving increasing attention within tourism marketing research.

Despite its importance, greater effort is still needed to study the phenomenon of images of adventure sports as attractions of a destination (Hunter, 2012; Ye & Tussyadiah, 2011). In this way, through the analysis of images of adventure sports and their representation in human visual signals, measured through eye tracking, it is expected to find which images related to the practice of adventure sports (rafting, bungee jumping, canyoning, paragliding) are more attractive to the male target audience compared to the female audience (Calderón et al., 2024; Wang & Sparks, 2016).

2. CONCEPTUAL FRAMEWORK

2.1. A Glance at the Tourism Sector

Tourism has emerged as one of the primary sectors contributing to the economic development of countries worldwide (Díaz, 2012; Holik, 2016; Moral, 2016; Mihalič, 2014; Orgaz &. In 2015, there was an increase of 52 million tourists, representing a 4.6% rise compared to 2014. This resulted in revenues of $1.186 millions, marking the sixth consecutive year of growth since the 2009 crisis, despite the influx of visitors, currency fluctuations, oil prices falling, and insecurity during that period (World Tourism Organization, 2016; World Travel & Tourism Council, 2017. Thus, international visitors movements worldwide has been steadily increasing, rising from 25 million in 1950 to approximately 1.2 billion in 2015. This growth has reflected into global destination revenues, which increased from $2 billion in 1950 to $1.26 trillion in 2015. In 2018, according to the UNWTO Barometer, international tourist arrivals grew by 6% in the first half of the year following a record year of growth in 2017. From January to June 2018, all regions of the world experienced solid growth in arrivals, this effect fostered an increasing demand for outbound travel to major source markets, driven by the global economy recovery (Sofronov, 2017; World Travel & Tourism Council, 2017).

This sector's increase in the first half of 2018 is supported by better job opportunities, higher profits, and opportunities for sustainable destinations and livelihoods (Matiku et al., 2020; Roxas et al., 2020; Liu et al., 2020), acting as a catalyst for the local, national, and global economy. Europe, Asia, and the Pacific lead in arrivals with 7%. Southern and Mediterranean Europe, along with Southeast Asia, show the best results with 9%. In the Middle East and Africa, there was growth of 5% and 4% respectively. While America achieved a growth of 3%, South America saw a 7% increase and North America a 5% increase. The United States is largely responsible for the growth in the region. Tourist demand in France, the United Kingdom, and Russia recorded double-digit increases in outbound spending from Europe. India and Korea led growth in Asia and the Pacific, while the world's largest source market, China, achieved spending levels similar to the same period last year (Barómetro OMT del Turismo Mundial y anexo estadístico Junio 2018).

The prominence of tourism became more evident in 2022, with nearly 965 million international tourist arrivals worldwide. While this figure shows improvement compared to the previous year, it still far from the figures recorded before the start of the COVID-19 pandemic (Herrero et al., 2022). Nevertheless, the global importance of the sector remains quite encouraging, as it is responsible for creating over 290 million jobs, both directly and indirectly.

2.2 Tourism Before and After the Pandemic

The COVID-19 pandemic has had a massive impact on tourism worldwide, affecting sectors that play an important role in various economies. Various research and analyses conducted by experts reveal significant changes in the number of tourists before and after the epidemic. In 2019, there were 1.5 billion international tourist arrivals, marking the tenth consecutive year of growth. However, in 2020, international arrivals fell by 74%, resulting in a loss of $1.3 trillion in tourism export revenues (World Tourism Organization, 2020).

Research on the impact of COVID-19 on tourism shows a similar pattern across all regions. In 2020, there was a sharp decline, followed by a gradual recovery due to the easing of restrictions and the implementation of stimulus measures. Studies emphasize the importance of technological innovations, the convenience of visas, and public-private partnerships to increase tourism (Jamal & Budke, 2020).

However, in 2023, encouraging data was observed, with an estimated 975 million tourists between January and September, representing an 87% recovery of pre-pandemic levels. Some regions, such as the Middle East, even surpassed 2019 levels with a 22% increase in arrivals (World Tourism Organization, 2023), while others, like Asia and the Pacific, are still in the process of reaching those numbers. Europe has shown notable resilience, supported by strong intraregional and the United States demand. In contrast, the United States and China have experienced a slower recovery in terms of international tourist spending (World Travel & Tourism Council, 2023).

2.3. Job Opportunities in the Tourism Industry

In the last decade, tourism has experienced significant growth in terms of global employment, this sector has generated approximately 319 million jobs, accounting for around 10% of global employment. This increase is largely due to the expansion of emerging markets and the growing demand for personalized experiences (Gossling, 2021; Juvan & Dolnicar, 2022; Popp & D'Angelo, 2021). Furthermore, it is projected to be one of the sectors with the highest potential for job growth, driven by the rise in international travel and sustainable tourism (Baum et al., 2022).

The impact of tourism on employment can vary between regions. In developing countries, it represents a source of income and employment in rural and coastal areas. A study by Wang & Hsu (2022) reveals that, in rural regions of Asia and Africa, it has contributed to the creation of approximately 10 million jobs in the last five years. Undoubtedly, the diversification of tourism offerings and infrastructure development have facilitated this growth, creating opportunities in sectors such as hospitality, transportation and recreational activities (Pérez & Kwortnik, 2021; Zhao et al., 2021).

The COVID-19 pandemic had a devastating impact on tourism employment, with a loss of approximately 62 million jobs by 2020 (World Tourism Organization, 2021). However, recovery is underway, with employment expected to recover to previous levels by 2024. Studies reveal that adaptation to new technologies and business models, such as digital tourism and sustainability, will be key to this recovery (Evers et al., 2021; Gossling, 2021). Investment in training and the development of digital skills are essential to take advantage of the new job opportunities emerging in the sector (Jovanovic & Rajh, 2022).'

2.4. Visual Attention as Seen From the Field or Spatial Attention

The relationship between attention and eye movements has been the subject of much debate over the years (Hunt et al., 2019; Yüksel, 2023). Two main aspects dominate this discussion: the first defines spatial attention as a neuronal mechanism associated with the eye movement system and characterizes attention as a planned but not executed eye movement. The second suggestion is based on observations that focus attention on saccadic targets, rapid, jerky movements of the eyes between fixation points (Duc et al., 2008; Hoffman, 1998).

In this sense, the definition of visual attention gains prominence as a process through which individuals select a subset of available spatial information to recognize and understand objects in their environment. Thus, our visual system processes the most important information by changing the focus in the image, paying more attention to significant parts and ignoring irrelevant ones (Reingold et al., 2016). In this case, attention provides the first integrated description of the most important area. With this direct view, it is easy to guide the viewer without the need for a connection; rather, attention can focus on the same line while also paying attention to what happens in other parts of the field. In James' words "*we can pay attention to something around the visible field and we cannot look away*" (James, 1890).

Among all these contributions, spatial attention and eye movements stand out, pointing to the existence of two interconnected but separate systems. These visual attention mechanisms seek to establish a connection between attention and saccadic movements; some theories show a close relationship, while others see them as completely independent systems. These differences can likely be resolved by distinguishing between sustained attention and attentional shifts (Sheremata & Silver, 2015).

2.5. Adventure Sports Photography and Eye-Tracking of a Tourist Destination

The recreation of adventure images can be highlighted for its range within the destination image; its visual evocation can express impressions, prejudices, imaginations, and thoughts that a visitor or group may have about a particular place. The prominence of images and their level of attention are closely related to discrimination processes and activation based on field theory or spatial attention, where it is distinguished as a selectively distributed limited capacity across the visual field. This can recreate images of tourist attractions in a destination in the minds of potential visitors (Yang et al., 2022).

This visual field is not filtered, but rather visual attention has a spatial focus, viewed from the subconscious mind as mental processes that can influence our thoughts, emotions, and behaviors. This means that when recognizing tourism advertising, they shape our experiences (Schoner et al., 2021). In this context, the processing of attentional focus is discussed, and two theoretically valuable models are presented: the spotlight model and the zoom model, which proved useful for synchronizing images of adventure sports with visual movements

2.6. Photographic Adventure Images Sase Don the Light and Lens Focus Models

Since tourism is an intangible phenomenon, tourism marketing specialists heavily rely on visual elements such as photographic images. It is important to choose stimuli that attract the audience's attention. In this context, evaluating stimuli from the spotlight model promotes automatic movements guided by internal forces that create a reality produced as a focus, allowing for the analysis of information driven by human behavior, characterized by faster and more focused processing. However, processing takes longer when the stimulus is outside the focus of attention (LaBerge, 1983; Vidyasagar, 1999). Undoubtedly, this model promotes an implicit automatic action of fixations when observing stimuli that represents the image of a destination, depicted in activities of high or low excitement in natural or constructed environments. It relies on the mental representation of beliefs, feelings, and global visions about the nature of the destination and its components presented as images, particularly decisive because consumers face larger amounts of information that cannot be processed in detail.

To compensate for the weaknesses of the focus model, the stance of the lens or zoom model was adopted, characterized not only by taking information within the focus but also from other points. That is, the attentional focus can be adjusted to illuminate small regions of space as well as broader areas (Eriksen & Yeh, 1985). This means that the attentional focus does not have a fixed size, and information outside of it is not completely unnoticed, as attentional facilitation is inversely proportional to the size of the focus and attention can operate in other areas, although attention is greater the closer it is to the focus.

2.7. Adventure Images within the Framework of Fixation and Heat Maps

Studies on human elements in tourism communication or promotion have revealed the impact of human image attributes on the perception of tourism advertisements (Deng & Liu, 2021; Schoner et al., 2021). Certain areas can be limited by the aesthetics of photographs; spontaneous ones capture natural moments, whereas posed photographs are often staged to create an image directed by the photographer (Berger & Barasch, 2018). This difference in adventure photographs significantly influences destination marketing campaigns, with the simple fact that we are what we pay attention to. While destinations evoke a set of information units through tourism promotion, their attention has been limited in terms of activation and possibly appeal. These effects make potential visitors more likely to engage with and comment on spontaneous photographs shared on social media rather than generated images (Farace et al., 2017).

These images, from the dynamics of gaze mapping and the way of representing the visual world through a static image of a tourist destination, campaigns are supposed to incorporate appropriate human elements to shape the personality of the destination, along with the feelings of potential visitors towards the place (Feighey, 2003).

These feelings can be translated into levels of attention processed through fixations, which sometimes may not fully reveal what the person is thinking. However, this dynamic information can be converted into heat maps, where the visual representation shows the overall distribution of objects and gaze points. This color overlapping foundation on the images represents the ascending and descending order of the number of gaze points directed towards the information units in the destination's adventure images (Shen et al., 2020; Sparks & Wang, 2014)

3. RESEARCH OBJECTIVE AND INITIAL HYPOTHESIS

From the framework presented, adventure tourism emerges as an activity that receives significant attention in outlining the guidelines for alternative tourism. This serves as a catalytic phenomenon between rural areas and nature, featuring numerous activities on land, air, and water (Stipanović et al., 2019). This multi-dimensional relationship prompts a large number of people to travel to different places and spend substantial amounts of money to experience emotions and sensations that they find challenging (Štefko et al., 2021).

In line with this objective, this study aims to analyze which types of adventure tourism attractions generate the most interest among potential visitors, in order to optimize the communication strategy for the city of Baños de Agua Santa in Ecuador. Maintaining attention is critical, especially when consumers are faced with increasing amounts of information that they are potentially unable to process in detail. Models of attention as information processing emphasize the physical properties of advertisements to attract consumers' attention (Rosbergen et al., 1997). For researchers such as Wedel & Pieters (2008) there is high attention in photographic images.

Tourism in its context is a good ally to understand visual attention, its intangibility makes its products require the use of images to shape the market's perception of a destination (Feighey, 2003; Rakić & Chambers, 2010). The tourism market has been increasingly gaining popularity, adventure tourism could not be the exception it has a growing following for its ability to provide relatively high levels of sensory stimulation and challenging physical experiences encompassing a variety of aerial, land, water activities.

During participation, adventure tourists experience contrasting emotions, a central element of the adventure, occasionally influenced by motivation and personality. Motivation suggests that complex motives trigger the pursuit of risk and challenges. Meanwhile, personality reveals traits of sensation-seeking and the desire for varied, novel, complex, and intense experiences, along with a willingness to take physical and social risks for unique experiences (Pomfret, 2006; Ye & Tussyadiah, 2011).

Despite advances in forms of outdoor recreation, it seems that men have dominated these activities. However, there are findings that contradict this dominance in physical activities, showing that women have made advances in other areas of outdoor sports. This suggests that these activities are not perceived in the same way and may have particular meanings for women that discourage their participation (Boniface, 2006). This reinforces the notion of gender regarding outdoor recreation, determined by structural constraints such as cultural beliefs about places, which can lead to a gender bias that limits some women's participation in these activities. Undoubtedly, gender in relation to participation in adventure sports tourism remains higher among men, who have traditionally dominated this market niche. However, in recent years, the number of women participating in these activities has increased (Apollo et al., 2023; Fraiz & Araújo, 2020; Kruger et al., 2016)

Individuals who engage in extreme sports are predominantly those who take risks, seek sensations, and have a connection with the natural world. In this context, selecting visual stimuli that capture the attention of the target audience is crucial. Thus, this article aims to focus on testing the following hypothesis: H1. Images related to adventure sports (rafting, bungee jumping, canyoning, paragliding) are perceived as more attractive to the male target audience compared to the female target audience.

4. METHODOLOGY

This research in Neuromarketing, particularly in eye tracking, involved a study of measurements using eye movements (Wang & Sparks, 2016), a technique for mapping tourists' visual interests and routes as an advantage for studying the process of attention to images of adventure sports in a tourist destination (Kim, J. Y. & Kim, M. J., 2023; Shen et al., 2020). Another advantage that eye tracking allowed us was to capture objective, real-time data on what elements of a specific stimulus people were attending to, each scene within the stimulus that the participant fixates on is referred to as fixation that reflected the participant's specific areas of interest within the stimulus (Deng et al., 2021; Guo et al., 2021; Pan et al., 2014). These visual attention processes reflect commonly used eye tracking measures: duration of the first fixation, count of fixations, and saccadic patterns, which provide information on the underlying cognitive processes supporting tourist experiences (Liu et al., 2024; Lourenção et al., 2020).

The tourist destination referenced in this research is Baños de Agua Santa in Ecuador due to its geophysical characteristics, capabilities, and overall population dynamics, it has become a popular destination for both national and international tourists seeking to connect with nature and engage in adventure sports (Ruiz et al., 2017; Herrera & Rodríguez, 2017). It has an average temperature of 20°C, throughout the year, due to its position is a strategic place that offers a variety of tourist attractions, highlights, adventure sports (rafting, bungee jumping, canyoning, paragliding). It receives the largest number of visitors in the Sierra region of Ecuador, establishing itself as a tourist city (Díaz, 2012; Instituto Nacional de Estadísticas, Censos 2001). According to the National Institute of Statistics, Census of Ecuador (2016), the number of foreign tourist arrivals to Ecuador is 80,000, with Baños receiving 23% of these, amounting to 18,400 foreign tourists annually. The growing demand requires meeting visitors' needs, which has driven the city's economic development and promotes making Baños a competitive tourist destination in the region.

4.1. Participants

For the study, university students (22 women, 22 men) aged between 22 and 24 years (M = 23.5) were recruited; they were non-residents of the city of Baños (Guo et al., 2021; Kim, J. Y. & Kim, M. J., 2023; Wang & Sparks, 2016). The study adhered to the current regulations of the Sciencia & Business Association (NMSBA). According to Miellet et al. (2010) and Wedel & Pieters (2008), small samples are common in eye-tracking studies and are not intended to be statistically significant.

4.2. Stimuli

Specifically, four tourist adventure images were selected, experimental images such as Canyoning or canyoning is practiced in the Chamana, Rio Blanco and Cashaurco waterfalls. For those who like adrenaline, there are two places to practice this activity, especially the Rio Blanco and San Francisco bridges (Castro & Calle, 2023). In the second case, Paragliding, due to the geographical location and the presence of the Andes Mountains, the irregular terrain and a favorable climate allows the practice of flying down from a mountain by means of a parachute. Finally, rafting is practiced on the Pastaza River and allows a trip in the middle of the Sangay and Llanganates National Park. These sports reveal a true spectacle of adventure in each of the destination's natural environments (Morgan et al. 2005). The number of stimuli was sourced from the tourism website of the city of Baños in Ecuador, available for free on the Internet. All the images feature people engaged in various adventure activities. The presence of individuals in the images adds significance as a means of communication in tourism marketing (Li & Wan (2025); Zhang et al., 2023).

For the predictive tests, categories of adventure images (a, b, c, d) were formed and presented in pairs across six different trials (ab, ac, ad, bc, bd, and cd), according to the following pairings: bungee-jumping-rafting, canyoning-rafting, paragliding-rafting, canyoning-bungee-jumping, paragliding-bungee-jumping, canyoning-paragliding (Deng et al., 2021). The pairings included human elements, which enhanced perceived social presence and the intention of potential visitors (Roy et al., 2021). Although categorical pairings may not be strictly independent, appropriate representation of human cues in advertisements is particularly important for products with hedonic qualities, such as adventure tourism (Sparks & Wang, 2014).

Figure 1. The six different trials ab, ac, ad, bc, bd and cd are shown according to the following pairings: canyoning-rafting, canyoning-rafting, paragliding-rafting, canyoning-rafting, paragliding-rafting, canyoning-paragliding

Source: The photographic material was taken from the Baños Ecuador website. (2022). Explora Baños de Agua Santa: Actividades, naturaleza y turismo. Reproduced [or adapted] with permission, By Buen Trip Travel Ecuador. © Copyright – 2022 – Baños de Agua Santa | Guía Oficial de Turismo. https://banos-ecuador.com/.

4.3. Evaluation of Adventure Stimuli Based on Eye-Tracking

Due to the intangibility of tourism, visual elements such as photographic images were used (Deng et al., 2021; Wang & Sparks, 2016). Each participant rated the pairings through visual tracking: a) first fixation (engagement), total duration of the first fixation (engagement), and average fixation duration (areas focused on more than others). The Standard Allowed Minutes (SAM) procedure was employed. Participants viewed two images on a 40-inch VA Direct LED television screen with a resolution of 1920 x 1080 pixels and viewing angles (H/V) of 178°/178°. The screen had a brightness of 250 cd/m², static contrast ratio of 3400:1, and a refresh rate of 50 Hz / 60 Hz with 240 XR interpolation (Motionflow XR). The screen was paired with a Tobii Pro Spectrum eye tracker, which sampled eye movements at up to 600 Hz per camera with an accuracy between 0.06° and 0.04°. Participants were positioned at a recording distance ranging from 55 to 75 cm from the eye tracker's reference point. For fixation and saccade detection parameters, a maximum speed threshold of 30° and a minimum fixation duration of 150 ms were utilized.

Figure 2. Visual tracking system presented according to pairings

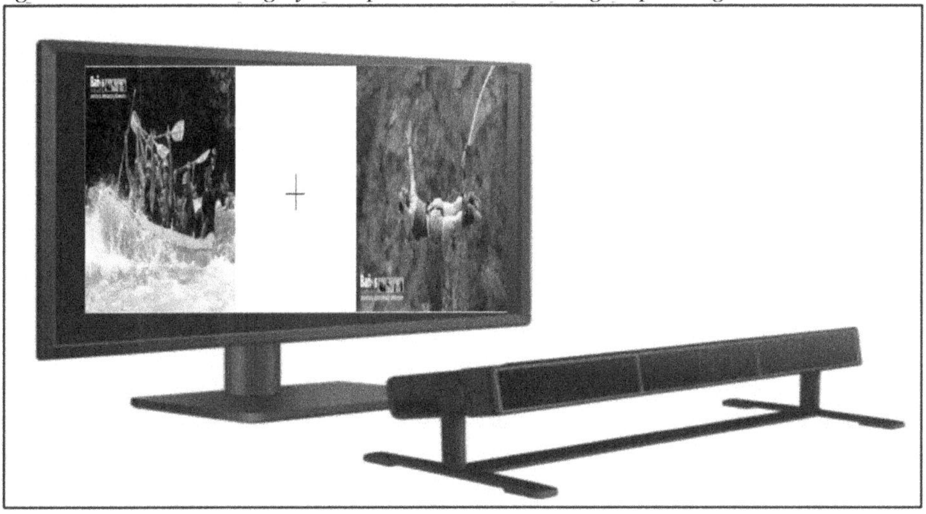

The 3D eye model made it possible to collect high-resolution data, including the angles of the gazes in all corners of the screen. The two eye-tracking cameras were able to take up to 1200 images per second of both eyes. The illumination of the light and dark pupils generated quality regarding displayed images. Based on the assumption of luminance and perceptual saliency of the images that can influence attention (Torralba et al., 2006; Underwood & Foulsham, 2006) physical properties were meticulously controlled, including adjusting luminance across trials until images within each pair were nearly identical. Additionally, low-level image properties such as contrast, asymmetry, and signal-to-noise ratio (SNR) were evaluated. The visual prominence of each scene within every pair was computed using the Tobii Pro Lab toolkit.

4.4. Procedure

The sample was collected based on the convenience sampling method, selecting university students from the city of Ambato-Ecuador, who where personally contacted. There were 22 women and 22 men who participated in the study (Garczarek et al., 2021; Vozzi et al., 2021). Four images were selected from the city's tourism department website to set up the unconscious evaluation scenario.

The participants were explained the objective of the study and the instructions for the evaluation, which consisted of looking at a cross that would appear in the center of the screen, then two images would be shown on either side of the cross, for free-form observation. they were informed that a gray resting image would appear before starting the next trial.

Once the images were selected, they were edited using Adobe Photoshop for retouching. Subsequently, the trials were calibrated and prepared with the equipment in the NEUROLAB laboratory for testing with the Tobii Pro Spectrum. The 44 participants remained in the waiting room to begin the evaluation of the images (rafting, bungee jumping, canyoning, paragliding), with each image displayed on either side (fixed images of adventure tourism attractions) for three minutes (Wedel & Pieters, 2008). Each participant then entered a second room isolated from external noise, with ambient lighting of 190 lumens, creating a comfortable environment, to begin the trial tests.

Each participant was asked to take a seat in a chair, and then a 40-inch screen presented the visual field of adventure images (fixation at the center of the screen). Each gaze mapping scene was combined as measured by fixations as a measure of attention, which occurred when the participants' eye paused to examine the components of the images (Marcos & Gonzalez, 2010).

In each trial, two paired images (bungee-rafting, canyoning-rafting, paragliding-rafting, canyoning-rafting, canyoning-rafting, paragliding-rafting, canyoning-paragliding) were displayed simultaneously, one on each side of the screen, with a peripheral view of 50 according to the visual angle between the central cross that they previously observed, as well as the inner edges of the images. Each image reached a height of 10 cm by 12 cm wide at a viewing distance of 50 cm. The sequence of events for each trial, was treated according to the procedure adapted by Deng et al., (2021); Fernández et al., (2017); Wang & Sparks (2016) in ocular follow-up studies.

Figure 3. Sequence of events in each trial exposed to participants

In particular, eye movements were recorded using an eye tracker (Pro Spectrum) with a maximum frequency of 600 Hz (accuracy: spatial resolution: 0.3°; gaze position precision: 0.06°). For fixation and saccade detection parameters, a maximum speed threshold of 30° and duration threshold of 150 ms were used. This setup allowed for measuring orientation: elapsed time of the first fixation, total duration of the first fixation, and total fixations in each trial (Calderón et al., 2024; Guo et al., 2021).

5. RESULTS

In this study, it was aimed to analyze which types of adventure tourism attractions generated the greatest interest among potential visitors to a tourist destination, leading us to formulate the research hypothesis that guides this analysis: which images related to adventure sports are more attractive to men compared to women. To address these hypotheses, the average fixation duration was initially used as a preliminary exploration, followed by more extensive statistical tests. First, the Wilcoxon test was employed to compare fixation times of the same participant across different pairs of adventure images. Second, the Kruskal-Wallis test was used to compare fixation times between men and women for each specific sport. Finally, heat maps were analyzed to visualize areas of greatest interest in each image, offering a graphical representation of the most common fixation points.

5.1. Average Fixations According to Adventure Attractions

Measuring where someone looks or how they visually scan their environment is an automatic observation process. This allowed us to leverage the non-conscious processes governing potential visitors.

Table 1. Experiments with adventure images according to eye-tracking metrics

Trials (Matching)	Gender	First fixation time (FFT)		Duration of firt fixation (DFF)		Average duration fixation (ADF)	
		FFT Average (seconds)	Most significant Adventure Sport	DFF Average (seconds)	Most significant Adventure Sport	ADF Average (seconds)	Most significant Adventure Sport
	H	1.25	Rafting	1.25	Rafting	0,82	Rafting
(ab)	M	1.29	Bungee jumping	0,25	Puenting	0,82	Bungee jumping
	H	0.26	Rafting	0,19	Canyoning	1,33	Rafting
(ac)	M	0.55	Canyoning	0,27	Rafting	0,78	Canyoning
	H	0,25	Paragliding	0,36	Rafting	1,30	Paragliding
(ad)	M	0.51	Rafting	0,23	Parapente	0,93	Rafting
	H	1.26	Canyoning	0,23	Puenting	1,02	Canyoning
(bc)	M	0.33	Bungee jumping	0,29	Canyoning	0,84	Bungee jumping
	H	0.47	Paragliding	0,38	Parapente	1,16	Paragliding
(bd)	M	0.35	Paragliding	0,21	Puenting	0,86	Paragliding
	H	0.39	Paragliding	0,20	Parapente	0,75	Paragliding
(cd)	M	0.50	Canyoning	0,48	Canyoning	1,09	Canyoning

Source: Author's elaboration

In the structure of the first fixation time, it is noted that the adventure sport Paragliding (0.25) was observed for the shortest duration in the Paragliding-Rafting trial. Meanwhile, for the total duration of the first fixation, the longest duration was observed for Rafting (1.25). Finally, in the total duration of fixations, Rafting (1.33) was the most significant in the Canyoning-Rafting trial.

5.2. Fixations for the Same Participant in Different Pairs of Images

For comparing the first fixation times of the same participant across different pairs of images, the Wilcoxon test was used. This non-parametric test is employed to compare related samples when normal distributions in reaction times or preference measures are not assumed.

Table 2. Fixation for the same participant in different pairs of images

Tests Ranks		N	Average rank	Sum of Ranks
Rafting – Bungee Jumping	Negative Ranks	20[a]	23,60	472,00
	Positive Ranks	18[b]	14,94	269,00
	Ties	6[c]		
	Total	44		
Rafting - Canyoning	Negative Ranks	25[d]	23,52	588,00
	Positive Ranks	14[e]	13,71	192,00
	Ties	5[f]		
	Total	44		
Rafting - Paragliding	Negative Ranks	16[g]	14,88	238,00
	Positive Ranks	24[h]	24,25	582,00
	Ties	4[i]		
	Total	44		
Bungee Jumping- Canyoning	Negative Ranks	21[j]	26,64	559,50
	Positive Ranks	19[k]	13,71	260,50
	Ties	4[l]		
	Total	44		
Bungee Jumping - Paragliding	Negative Ranks	19[m]	16,76	318,50
	Positive Ranks	21[n]	23,88	501,50
	Ties	3[o]		
	Total	43		
Paragliding - Canyoning	Negative Ranks	25[p]	17,22	430,50
	Positive Ranks	15[q]	25,97	389,50
	Ties	4[r]		
	Total	44		

Source: Author's own elaboration

Table 3. Wilcoxon signed-rank test

Test statistics[a]	Rafting – Bungee Jumping	Rafting - Canyoning	Rafting - Paragliding	Bungee Jumping- Canyoning	Bungee Jumping - Paragliding	Paragliding - Canyoning
Z	-1,472[b]	-2,763[b]	-2,312[c]	-2,010[b]	-1,230[c]	-,276[b]
Asymptotic sign (bilateral)	0,141	0,006	0,021	0,044	0,219	0,783

Source: Author's elaboration

In the context of eye tracking in the first fixation during the minimum period of time, the comparison by pairs of images is shown where Rafting - Canyoning (p=0.006), Rafting-Paragliding (p=0.021), Canyoning - Canyoning (p=0.044) have statistically significant difference in the fixation times between these images and the participants. While, the images such as Rafting - Canyoning, Rafting - Paragliding, Paragliding - Canyoning have values greater than 0.05, finding that participants spent more time looking at a particular image of that pair, indicating less interest or attraction and no significant difference was found.

5.3. Fixation Between Men and Women for a Specific Sport

To compare the first fixation times between men and women for a specific adventure sport we used the non-parametric Kruskal-Wallis test. With this test we determine if there are significant differences in fixation times between independent groups when observing the images, which in turn indicates different visual preferences between both sexes.

Table 4. Fixation between men and women for a specific sport

Adventure attractions	Sex	N	Average rank	Sum of ranks
Bungee jumping	women	22	23,93	526,50
	men	22	21,07	463,50
	Total	44		
Rafting	women	22	25,05	551,00
	men	22	19,95	439,00
	Total	44		
Canyoning	women	22	21,05	463,00
	men	22	23,95	527,00
	Total	44		
Rafting	women	22	23,89	525,50
	men	22	21,11	464,50
	Total	44		
Paragliding	women	22	23,86	525,00
	men	22	21,14	465,00
	Total	44		
Rafting	women	22	21,27	468,00
	men	22	23,73	522,00
	Total	44		

continued on following page

Table 4. Continued

Adventure attractions	Sex	N	Average rank	Sum of ranks
Canyoning	women	22	24,23	533,00
	men	22	20,77	457,00
	Total	44		
Bungee jumping	women	22	21,36	470,00
	men	22	23,64	520,00
	Total	44		
Paragliding	women	22	20,64	454,00
	men	22	24,36	536,00
	Total	44		
Bungee jumping	women	22	24,24	509,00
	men	22	19,86	437,00
	Total	44		
Canyoning	women	22	22,80	501,50
	men	22	22,20	488,50
	Total	44		
Paragliding	women	22	22,61	497,50
	men	22	22,39	492,50
	Total	44		

Source: Author's elaboration

Table 5. Mann-Whitney U-test

Test statistics[a]	a	b	a	c	a	d	b	c	b	d	c	d
Mann-Whitney U	210,5	186,0	210,0	211,5	212,0	215,0	204,0	217,0	201,0	184,0	235,5	239,5
Wilcoxon X	463,5	439,0	463,0	464,5	465,0	468,0	457,0	470,0	454,0	437,0	488,5	492,5
Z	-0,7	-1,4	-0,8	-0,8	-0,8	-0,7	-0,9	-0,6	-1,0	-1,2	-0,2	-0,1
Asymptotic sign (bilateral)	0,5	0,2	0,4	0,5	0,4	0,5	0,4	0,6	0,3	0,2	0,9	0,9

Source: Own elaboration

In the results for each sport, it is observed that no significant differences were found, for most sports, the p-value is greater than 0.05, indicating that there is no significant difference in fixation times between men and women. In some cases, women tend to have slightly higher average ranges, this could mean greater attention in general, but this is not statistically significant.

5.4. Eye-Tracking Maps in Adventure Attraction Images

The heat maps created fixation positioning according to viewing time in the images of adventure attractions. By visualizing all points of the total duration of fixations of the 44 participants, six heat maps were obtained. In the analysis, the classical method of difference analysis was applied to evaluate the total duration of fixations in order to test the visual behavior of the six pairings or trials.

Figure 4. Heat maps of adventure images

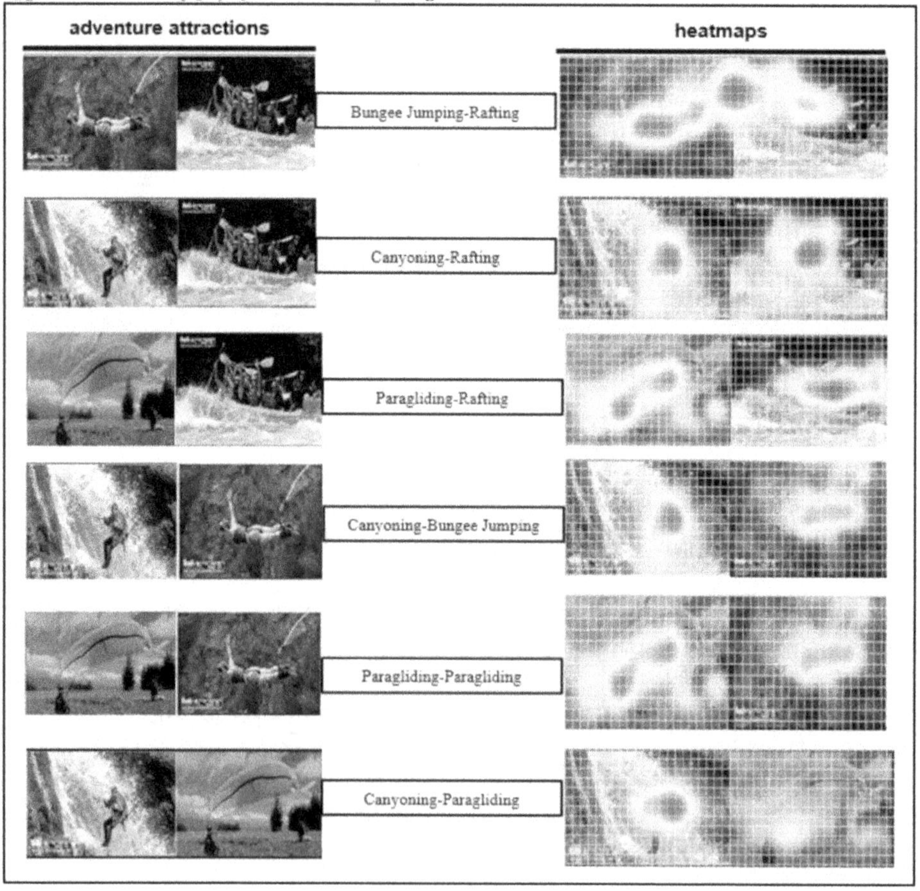

The heat maps provided offer a visualization of the areas of greatest visual interest in each image pair. Areas in red indicate a high concentration of fixations or areas where participants focused their attention most frequently. Areas in yellow represent a medium level of attention, while areas in green indicate a low concentration of fixations. In the analysis by pair of images (bungee jumping-rafting), in bungee jumping the attention is mainly focused on the person, especially on the limbs and facial expression of the person performing this activity. This interest in action and risk would be associated with this sport. In Rafting, attention is divided between the face of the participants in the raft and the natural environment (river, mountains). This indicates an interest in both social interaction and the natural environment. In the case of (Canyoning-Rafting), Canyoning the attention is concentrated on the person descending the canyon, especially on the hands and feet interacting with the environment, the interest is concentrated on the technique and skill required to practice this sport. In rafting, this is similar to the previous pair. However, in this trial, the focus on the environment is slightly greater, possibly due to the wilder and more rugged nature of the canyon. In trial three (Paragliding-Rafting) in Paragliding the attention is focused on the person who is going to initiate the activity, especially on the wing and body position. This indicates an interest in the sensation of freedom and the aerial perspective of this sport. In Rafting, the focus remains similar to the previous pairs, with a balance between the participants and the environment.

For the following cases (Canyoning-Puenting) in Canyoning the attention is concentrated on the person descending the canyon, similar to the previous pair. In Bungee Jumping attention is focused on the person performing this activity, but in this case, there is a greater proportion of attention on the surrounding environment, possibly due to the contrast between the natural environment and the action of jumping. In the fifth trial (Paragliding-Puenting), in Paragliding attention is similar to previous pairs. Whereas, in Bungee Jumping the focus is on the person, with an emphasis on facial expression and body position. Finally, in Canyoning-Paragliding (Canyoning-Paragliding), the focus is on the person descending the canyon and, in Paragliding, the focus is on elements similar to previous pairs.

5.4. Hyphothesis Verification

In relation to the hypothesis, it was expected to find that images related to the practice of adventure sports (rafting, bungee jumping, canyoning, paragliding) were more attractive to the target men than women. To test this hypothesis, ANOVA analysis of variance was performed (Guo et al., 2021).

Table 6. Anova analysis according to relative images in the practice of adventure sports

Sports		Sum of squars	d.f.	Root mean square	F-test	Sig.
Canyoning	Between groups	0,362	1,000	0,362	0,643	0,427
	Within groups	23,624	42,000	0,562		
	Total	23,986	43,000			
Paragliding	Between groups	0,369	1,000	0,369	0,382	0,540
	Within groups	40,622	42,000	0,967		
	Total	40,991	43,000			
Bungee Jumping	Between groups	0,161	1,000	0,161	0,341	0,562
	Within groups	19,794	42,000	0,471		
	Total	19,955	43,000			
Rafting	Between groups	0,000	1,000	0,000	0,000	0,983
	Within groups	12,612	42,000	0,300		
	Total	12,612	43,000			

Source: Author's elaboration

The ANOVA analysis of variance shows that there is a significant difference between men and women in rafting ($p < 0.001$). In adventure sports such as canyoning, paragliding and bungee jumping no significant differences were found between the two sexes ($p > 0.05$). In the case of rafting the mean square between groups (12.612) shows that the variability between men and women is significantly higher than the variability within each group. This means that the differences in attraction to rafting between males and females are greater than the differences between individuals of the same sex.

5. DISCUSSION

Given the intangible characteristics of tourism experiences that cannot be experienced beforehand, photographs are important tools used by marketers to promote ideas about the experience and identity that a tourism destination can convey to potential visitors and evoke an image formation of the place (Li et al., 2024; Pan et al., 2014). This evocation is channeled in this study in general, at the time that participants showed significant preferences for certain images of adventure sports over others. This leads us to believe that the type of image influences fixation time.

However, this cannot be generalized to all comparisons, although some show significant differences and others do not.

Undoubtedly, the type of photographs or images can vary the perception of those who observe this type of material, hence, the visual attraction can be modified by certain characteristics such as design, color, movement and composition of the images that can be presented with small changes and make a difference in fixation times depending on the specific images being compared (Al-Maqbali et al., 2022). Existing research has shown that images with artificial elements can be equally consistent with their natural environment (Guo et al., 2021). However, the more visually sensitive the environment is, the more visual pollution will occur and the more inharmonious the area of interest of adventure sports is intended to be shown.

Research on the adventure tourist attractions that arouse greater interest in men and women has provided us with valuable insight into these activities, but our study found no conclusive evidence to support the contrasts in fixation times between men and women. Both sexes show similar interest in adventure imagery. While there are no significant differences between the sexes in most adventure sports, it is important to note that fixation times and level of visual attention may vary between the different sports themselves. These findings mark some difference with Rojo et al. (2023) who show that women tend to value more the connection to nature and men focus more on the thrill and adrenaline of the activity; these patterns connect with underlying cognitive processes in tourism experiences (Li & Wan, 2025; Liu et al., 2024) inferring that the artificial elements of the images project greater visual sensitivity in early perception due to the level of commitment, risk and enthusiasm (engagement) that this type of sport awakens in potential tourists (Deng et al., 2021). In addition, the content is an indicator of a natural environment that can evoke a pleasurable and exciting experience at the moment of contact with the natural environment, embedded in the destination (Nong & Fong, 2021; Wang & Sparks, 2016).

The heat maps are projected on the elements of the photographs to highlight the observed areas, marking great interest in the actions of people who are practicing adventure sports, especially in the limbs and facial expression, to this is added, the interest when impressive environments such as canyons or mountains are shown, demonstrating the importance of natural environments as a visual attraction. However, there is a certain tendency in visual preferences in individual variability due to the implications of action, emotion and connection with nature as effective axes to capture the attention of potential adventure tourists (Burns et al., 1993). Undoubtedly, visual appeal compares the perception of physical appearance (people) as the result of interactions between human beings, where pleasurable experiences are projected in natural environments, which means a greater impact on people's experience (Hadinejad et al., 2018; Marder et al., 2021). Artificial elements (sports equipment) aesthetically are shown as elements of care against risk in the practice of these sports and as prerequisites for visual capture (Deng et al., 2021; Guo et al., 2021). This concordance is evidenced in our study in the attention on four heat maps, positioning fixation points in Paragliding adventure photography in males and females. This scanning path in both sexes shows a wider visual range in the artificial elements (wings). While, in Bungee Jumping women focus on the body of the character and the natural environment (mountain), men in Rafting focused mainly on people and, especially limited to a relative area of the faces.

7. CONCLUSION

Based on the results of our study the preferences are clear for certain adventure images, revealing significant differences in the times of fixations for different pairs of images that have impact and attract more attention of potential tourists, for certain visual characteristics that play an important role in the optimization of visual communication in adventure tourism. The visual display of the six trials shown to potential tourists of both sexes, revealed similar interest in adventure images, these findings provide greater knowledge for the promotion of the destination, under the preference involving adventure action and contact with nature.

The manifesto of nature attracts potential tourists in a special way, the different components in natural environments evoke positive visual paths in the images, with certain differences in the attention of men and women. This positive evocation can become a strategic element in tourism marketing campaigns, under the main components action and nature, which means, not only the impulse in adventure sports, but also, in the natural resources of the destination, which will act as anchors of projection in the brain to project a reality of Baños, as a place in the affective and unique plane during the process of choice as a tourist destination of adventure.

The analysis of heat maps provides a rich and detailed view of how participants visually interact with adventure images. The results suggest that both the action and the natural environment are key factors in capturing attention. Additionally, participants are more attracted to activities that involve higher levels of risk and excitement, such as Bungee Jumping and Paragliding.

These findings could be useful in designing more effective tourism promotion materials by focusing on images that generate greater interest. This type of visual communication in adventure tourism sets the emotional tone for creating more appealing tourist experiences based on visitor preferences. Although no significant differences were found between men and women, the results are valuable for developing attractive marketing materials for all adventure sports, presenting a variety of images that showcase different aspects of each sport to capture the attention of a broader audience. Finally, clear and concise messaging could be used for both genders, as they respond similarly to adventure images, highlighting the benefits and unique experiences offered by each sport.

This study has several limitations. First, the small sample size for eye tracking is primarily due to experimental conditions and costs. Second, the visual aesthetics involve an analysis of this nature which was not explored in our study. Additionally, other factors that could influence visual attention, such as prior experience with adventure sports, personal interest in each sport, or individual characteristics related to adventure tourism, were not considered. Furthermore, the limited variety of information regarding the specific characteristics of the images adds to these limitations. Regarding future research, it is advisable to broaden the scope beyond just men and women to include larger segments of the tourism population. This can be complemented by incorporating new experimental designs, such as presenting images in a random order or using different types of visual stimuli. Additionally, combining qualitative and quantitative designs through interviews and surveys could enhance sample size, leading to more robust and generalizable results.

REFERENCES

Al-Maqbali, H., Kader, A., Albalushi, J., Luimula, M., & Calbureanu-Popescu, C. (2022). Impact of image features on visual attention: An eye-tracking study. En T. Ahram & C. Falcão (Eds.), *Usability and User Experience* (Vol. 39). AHFE International Conference. AHFE Open Access. AHFE International, USA. http://doi.org/DOI: 10.54941/ahfe1001732

Apollo, M., Mostowska, J., Legut, A., Maciuk, K., & Timothy, D. J. (2023). Gender differences in competitive adventure sports tourism. *Journal of Outdoor Recreation and Tourism*, 42, 100604. DOI: 10.1016/j.jort.2022.100604

Baum, T., Mooney, K., & Roberts, C. (2022). *Tourism employment and economic recovery in a post-pandemic world*. Routledge., DOI: 10.4324/9780367334056

Berger, J., & Barasch, A. (2018). A Candid Advantage? The Social Benefits of Candid Photos. *Social Psychological & Personality Science*, 9(8), 1010–1016. DOI: 10.1177/1948550617732390

Boniface, M. (2006). The meaning of adventurous activities for 'women in the outdoors.'. *Journal of Adventure Education and Outdoor Learning*, 6(1), 9–24. DOI: 10.1080/14729670685200711

Burns, A. C., Biswas, A., & Babin, L. A. (1993). The Operation of Visual Imagery as a Mediator of Advertising Effects. *Journal of Advertising*, 22(2), 71–85. DOI: 10.1080/00913367.1993.10673405

Burri, R. V. (2012). Visual rationalities: Towards a sociology of images. *Current Sociology*, 60(1), 45–60. DOI: 10.1177/0011392111426647

Calderón-Fajardo, V., Anaya-Sánchez, R., Rejón-Guardia, F., & Molinillo, S. (2024). Neurotourism Insights: Eye Tracking and Galvanic Analysis of Tourism Destination Brand Logos and AI Visuals. *Tourism & Management Studies*, 20(3), 53–78. DOI: 10.18089/tms.20240305

Castro Salcedo, J. P., & Calle Lituma, N. S. (2023). Survival as a strategy for increasing adventure tourism in Ecuador.

Deng, N., & Liu, J. (2021). Where did you take those photos? Tourists' preference clustering based on facial and background recognition. *Journal of Destination Marketing & Management*, 21, 100632. DOI: 10.1016/j.jdmm.2021.100632

Deng, W., Lin, Y., & Chen, L. (2021). Exploring Destination Choice Intention by Using the Tourism Photographic: From the Perspectives of Visual Esthetic Processing. *Frontiers in Psychology*, 12, 713739. DOI: 10.3389/fpsyg.2021.713739 PMID: 34867592

Díaz Carrión, I. A. (2012). Turismo de aventura y participación de las mujeres en Jalcomulco (México). *Pasos (El Sauzal)*, 10(5), 531–542. DOI: 10.25145/j.pasos.2012.10.068

Duc, A. H., Bays, P., & Husain, M. (2008). Eye movements as a probe of attention. *Progress in Brain Research*, 171, 403–411. DOI: 10.1016/S0079-6123(08)00659-6 PMID: 18718333

Eriksen, C. W., & Yeh, Y. Y. (1985). Allocation of attention in the visual field. *Journal of Experimental Psychology. Human Perception and Performance*, 11(5), 583–597. DOI: 10.1037/0096-1523.11.5.583 PMID: 2932532

Evers, T., Li, G., & Zhang, H. (2021). The impact of COVID-19 on global tourism employment: A review and future perspectives. *Tourism Management Perspectives*, 39, 100–110. DOI: 10.1016/j.tmp.2021.100110

Farace, S., van Laer, T., de Ruyter, K., & Wetzels, M. (2017). Assessing the effect of narrative transportation, portrayed action, and photographic style on the likelihood to comment on posted selfies. *European Journal of Marketing*, 51(11/12), 1961–1979. DOI: 10.1108/EJM-03-2016-0158

Feighey, W. (2003). Negative Image? Developing the Visual in Tourism Research. *Current Issues in Tourism*, 6(1), 76–85. DOI: 10.1080/13683500308667945

Fernández-Martín, A., Gutiérrez-García, A., Capafons, J., & Calvo, M. G. (2017). Adaptive attunement of selective covert attention to evolutionary-relevant emotional visual scenes. *Consciousness and Cognition*, 51, 223–235. DOI: 10.1016/j.concog.2017.03.011 PMID: 28411473

Filieri, R., Lin, Z., Pino, G., Alguezaui, S., & Inversini, A. (2021). The role of visual cues in eWOM on consumers' behavioral intention and decisions. *Journal of Business Research*, 135, 663–675. DOI: 10.1016/j.jbusres.2021.06.055

Fraiz, J. A., de Carlos, P., & Araújo, N. (2020). Disclosing homogeneity within heterogeneity: A segmentation of Spanish active tourism based on motivational pull factors. *Journal of Outdoor Recreation and Tourism*, 30, 100294. DOI: 10.1016/j.jort.2020.100294

Garczarek-Bąk, U., Szymkowiak, A., Gaczek, P., & Disterheft, A. (2021). A comparative analysis of neuromarketing methods for brand purchasing predictions among young adults. *Journal of Brand Management*, 28(2), 171–185. DOI: 10.1057/s41262-020-00221-7

González-Rodríguez, M. R., Díaz-Fernández, M. C., & Pulido-Pavón, N. (2023). Tourist destination competitiveness: An international approach through the travel and tourism competitiveness index. *Tourism Management Perspectives*, 47, 101127. DOI: 10.1016/j.tmp.2023.101127

Gossling, S. (2021). Tourism employment and the impact of COVID-19: A global perspective. *Journal of Sustainable Tourism*, 29(5), 741–758. DOI: 10.1080/09669582.2021.1898717

Guo, S., Sun, W., Chen, W., Zhang, J., & Liu, P. (2021). Impact of artificial elements on mountain landscape perception: An eye-tracking study. *Land (Basel)*, 10(10), 1102. DOI: 10.3390/land10101102

Hadinejad, A., Moyle, B. D., Scott, N., & Kralj, A. (2018). Emotional responses to tourism advertisements: The application of FaceReader™. *Tourism Recreation Research*, 44(1), 131–135. DOI: 10.1080/02508281.2018.1505228

Herrera Enríquez, G., & Rodríguez Rodríguez, G. (2017). Turismo y Sistemas Empresariales Resilientes: Factores Críticos de Adaptabilidad en Baños de Agua Santa – Ecuador. *Revista De Gestão E Secretariado, 8*(1), 01–25. https://doi.org/DOI: 10.7769/gesec.v8i1.606

Herrero, C. C., Laso, J., Cristóbal, J., Fullana-i-Palmer, P., Albertí, J., Fullana, M., Herrero, Á., Margallo, M., & Aldaco, R. (2022). Tourism under a life cycle thinking approach: A review of perspectives and new challenges for the tourism sector in the last decades. *The Science of the Total Environment*, 845, 157261. DOI: 10.1016/j.scitotenv.2022.157261 PMID: 35835187

Hoffman, J. E. (1998). Visual attention and eye movements. In H. Pashler (Ed.), *Attention* (pp. 119–153). Psychology Press/Erlbaum (UK) Taylor & Francis. https://psycnet.apa.org/record/1998-07791-003

Holik, A. (2016). Relationship of economic growth with tourism sector. *JEJAK: Jurnal Ekonomi dan Kebijakan, 9*(1), 16-33. https://doi.org/DOI: 10.15294/jejak.v9i1.7184

Hunt, A. R., Reuther, J., Hilchey, M. D., & Klein, R. M. (2019). The Relationship Between Spatial Attention and Eye Movements. In Hodgson, T. (Ed.), *Processes of Visuospatial Attention and Working Memory* (pp. 255–278). Springer International Publishing., DOI: 10.1007/7854_2019_95

Hunter, W. C. (2012). Projected destination image: A visual analysis of Seoul. *Tourism Geographies*, 14(3), 419–443. DOI: 10.1080/14616688.2011.613407

Instituto Nacional de Estadísticas. Censos. (25 de noviembre de 2001). *Fascículo Censal del Catón Baños*. https://www.ecuadorencifras.gob.ec/documentos/web-inec/Bibliotecas/Fasciculos_Censales/Fasc_Cantonales/Tungurahua/Fasciculo_Banos.pdf

Instituto Nacional de Estadísticas. Censos. (22 de junio de 2016). *Índice de Precios al Productor de Disponibilidad Nacional*. https://anda.inec.gob.ec/anda/index.php/catalog/562/overview

Jamal, T., & Budke, C. (2020). Tourism in a world with pandemics: Local-global responsibility and action. *Journal of Tourism Futures*, 6(2), 181–188. DOI: 10.1108/JTF-02-2020-0014

James, W. (1890). *The principles of psychology* (Vol. 2). Henry Holt and Company., DOI: 10.1037/11059-000

Jiang, X., Mohamed, A. E. B., & Affifudin, A. H. B. (2024). Unveiling the Drivers of Chinese Tourists' Visit Intentions Regarding Malaysia. *Sustainability (Basel)*, 16(8), 3406. DOI: 10.3390/su16083406

Jovanovic, S., & Rajh, E. (2022). Future of work in tourism: Digital skills and employment prospects. *International Journal of Hospitality Management*, 94, 102835. DOI: 10.1016/j.ijhm.2021.102835

Juvan, E., & Dolnicar, S. (2022). How the COVID-19 pandemic has reshaped tourism employment: A comparative analysis. *Tourism Economics*, 28(1), 15–32. DOI: 10.1177/21684890211063367

Kim, J. Y., & Kim, M. J. (2023). Identifying customer preferences through the eye-tracking in travel websites focusing on neuromarketing. *Journal of Asian Architecture and Building Engineering*, 23(2), 515–527. DOI: 10.1080/13467581.2023.2244566

Kruger, M., Viljoen, A., & Saayman, M. (2016). Who visits the Kruger National Park, and why? identifying target markets. *Journal of Travel & Tourism Marketing*, 34(3), 312–340. DOI: 10.1080/10548408.2016.1156618

LaBerge, D. (1983). Spatial extent of attention to letters and words. *Journal of Experimental Psychology. Human Perception and Performance*, 9(3), 371–379. DOI: 10.1037/0096-1523.9.3.371 PMID: 6223977

Li, S., Huang, H., Liu, X., & Chen, Z. (2024). The power of visuals in destination advertising. *Annals of Tourism Research*, 107, 103790. DOI: 10.1016/j.annals.2024.103790

Li, Y. W., & Wan, L. C. (2025). Inspiring tourists' imagination: How and when human presence in photographs enhances travel mental simulation and destination attractiveness. *Tourism Management*, 106, 104969. DOI: 10.1016/j.tourman.2024.104969

Liu, B., Moyle, B., Kralj, A., & Li, Y. (2023). Celebrity endorsement in tourism: Attention, emotional arousal and familiarity. *Tourism Management*, 98, 104750. DOI: 10.1016/j.tourman.2023.104750

Liu, B., Moyle, B., Kralj, A., & Li, Y. (2024). *Eye-Tracking in Tourism, Cognitive Psychology and Tourism* (Vol. 27). Tourism Social Science Series. Emerald Publishing Limited., DOI: 10.1108/S1571-504320240000027020

Liu-Lastres, B., Mariska, D., Tan, X., & Ying, T. (2020). Can post-disaster tourism development improve destination livelihoods? A case study of Aceh, Indonesia. *Journal of Destination Marketing & Management*, 18, 100510. DOI: 10.1016/j.jdmm.2020.100510

Lourenção, M., de Moura Engracia Giraldi, J., & de Oliveira, J. H. C. (2020). Destination advertisement semiotic signs: Analysing tourists' visual attention and perceived ad effectiveness. *Annals of Tourism Research*, 84, 103001. DOI: 10.1016/j.annals.2020.103001

Marcos, M.-C., & González-Caro, C. (2010). Comportamiento de los usuarios en la página de resultados de los buscadores. Un estudio basado en eye tracking. *El Profesional de la Información*, 19(4), 348–358. DOI: 10.3145/epi.2010.jul.03

Marder, B., Erz, A., Angell, R., & Plangger, K. (2021). The Role of Photograph Aesthetics on Online Review Sites: Effects of Management- versus Traveler-Generated Photos on Tourists' Decision Making. *Journal of Travel Research*, 60(1), 31–46. DOI: 10.1177/0047287519895125

Matiku, S. M., Zuwarimwe, J., & Tshipala, N. (2020). Sustainable tourism planning and management for sustainable livelihoods. *Development Southern Africa*, 38(4), 524–538. DOI: 10.1080/0376835X.2020.1801386

Miellet, S., Zhou, X., He, L., Rodger, H., & Caldara, R. (2010). Investigating cultural diversity for extrafoveal information use in visual scenes. *Journal of Vision (Charlottesville, Va.)*, 10(6), 21–21. DOI: 10.1167/10.6.21 PMID: 20884570

Mihalič, T. (2014). 3. Tourism and Economic Development Issues. In R. Sharpley & D. Telfer (Ed.), *Tourism and Development: Concepts and Issues* (pp. 77-117). Bristol, Blue Ridge Summit: Channel View Publications. https://doi.org/DOI: 10.21832/9781845414740-005

Morgan, D., Moore, K., & Mansell, R. (2005). Adventure tourists on water: Linking expectations, affect, achievement and enjoyment to the sports tourism adventure. *Journal of Sport & Tourism*, 10(1), 73–88. DOI: 10.1080/14775080500101593

Navarro-Navarro, J., Juárez-Tárraga, F., Ramón-Rodríguez, A. B., & Perles-Ribes, J. F. (2023). The life cycle and competitive position of tourism destinations: A global empirical approach. *Current Issues in Tourism*, •••, 1–17. DOI: 10.1080/13683500.2023.2280161

Nong, S. Z., & Fong, L. H. N. (2021). Eye tracking in tourism. *Information Technology & Tourism*, 23(4), 633–635. DOI: 10.1007/s40558-021-00210-9

Orgaz Agüera, F., & Moral Cuadra, S. (2016). El turismo como motor potencial para el desarrollo económico de zonas fronterizas en vías de desarrollo. Un estudio de caso. *El Periplo Sustentable*, (31). https://www.redalyc.org/articulo.oa?id=193449985009

Pan, S., Lee, J., & Tsai, H. (2014). Travel photos: Motivations, image dimensions, and affective qualities of places. *Tourism Management*, 40, 59–69. DOI: 10.1016/j.tourman.2013.05.007

Pérez, M. A., & Kwortnik, K. J. (2021). Tourism development and employment: Evidence from emerging markets. *Journal of Destination Marketing & Management*, 19, 100–112. DOI: 10.1016/j.jdmm.2021.100112

Pomfret, G. (2006). Mountaineering adventure tourists: A conceptual framework for research. *Tourism Management*, 27(1), 113–123. DOI: 10.1016/j.tourman.2004.08.003

Popp, M., & D'Angelo, R. (2021). The evolving landscape of tourism employment: Opportunities and challenges. *Journal of Hospitality and Tourism Management*, 49, 251–263. DOI: 10.1016/j.jhtm.2021.07.012

Rakić, T., & Chambers, D. (2010). Innovative techniques in tourism research: An exploration of visual methods and academic filmmaking. *International Journal of Tourism Research*, 12(4), 379–389. DOI: 10.1002/jtr.761

Reingold, E. M., Sheridan, H., Meadmore, K. L., Drieghe, D., & Liversedge, S. P. (2016). Attention and eye-movement control in reading: The selective reading paradigm. *Journal of Experimental Psychology. Human Perception and Performance*, 42(12), 2003–2020. DOI: 10.1037/xhp0000291 PMID: 27643527

Rojo-Ramos, J., Gómez-Paniagua, S., Guevara-Pérez, J. C., & García-Unanue, J. (2023). Gender Differences in Adventure Tourists Who Practice Kayaking in Extremadura. *International Journal of Environmental Research and Public Health*, 20(5), 3889. DOI: 10.3390/ijerph20053889 PMID: 36900899

Rosbergen, E., Pieters, R., & Wedel, M. (1997). Visual attention to advertising: A segment-level analysis. *The Journal of Consumer Research*, 24(3), 305–314. DOI: 10.1086/209512

Roxas, F. M. Y., Rivera, J. P. R., & Gutierrez, E. L. M. (2020). Mapping stakeholders' roles in governing sustainable tourism destinations. *Journal of Hospitality and Tourism Management*, 45, 387–398. DOI: 10.1016/j.jhtm.2020.09.005

Roy, S., Dryl, W., & de Araujo Gil, L. (2021). Celebrity endorsements in destination marketing: A three country investigation. *Tourism Management*, 83, 104213. DOI: 10.1016/j.tourman.2020.104213

Ruiz, G., García, C., & Covarrubias, R. (2017) Environmental Assessment for Health Tourism in Baños de Agua Santa, Ecuador. *Journal of Environmental Protection*, 8, 799-809. https://doiDOI: 10.4236/jep.2017.87050

Saqib, N. (2019). A positioning strategy for a tourist destination, based on analysis of customers' perceptions and satisfactions: A case of Kashmir, India. *Journal of Tourism Analysis*, 26(2), 131–151. DOI: 10.1108/JTA-05-2019-0019

Schoner-Schatz, L., Hofmann, V., & Stokburger-Sauer, N. E. (2021). Destination's social media communication and emotions: An investigation of visit intentions, word-of-mouth and travelers' facially expressed emotions. *Journal of Destination Marketing & Management*, 22, 100661. DOI: 10.1016/j.jdmm.2021.100661

Shen, Y., Lever, M., & Joppe, M. (2020). Investigating the appeal of a *visitor guide: A triangulated approach. International Journal of Contemporary Hospitality Management*, 32(4), 1539–1562. DOI: 10.1108/IJCHM-03-2019-0281

Sheremata, S. L., & Silver, M. A. (2015). Hemisphere-Dependent Attentional Modulation of Human Parietal Visual Field Representations. *The Journal of Neuroscience : The Official Journal of the Society for Neuroscience*, 35(2), 508–517. DOI: 10.1523/JNEUROSCI.2378-14.2015 PMID: 25589746

Sofronov, B. (2017). The economic impact on global tourism. Annals of Spiru Haret University. Economic Series, 17(2), 127-139. https://www.ceeol.com/search/article-detail?id=561416

Sparks, B. A., & Wang, Y. (2014). Natural and Built Photographic Images: Preference, Complexity, and Recall. *Journal of Travel & Tourism Marketing*, 31(7), 868–883. DOI: 10.1080/10548408.2014.890155

Štefko, R., Šambronská, K., Matušíková, D., Šenková, A., & Tumpach, M. (2021). Analytical study on adventure tourism destination management concerning expenditure on adventure activities. *Polish Journal of Management Studies*, 24(1), 373–391. Advance online publication. DOI: 10.17512/pjms.2021.24.1.22

Stipanović, C., Rudan, E., & Zubović, V. (2019). Development concept of adventure tourism for the purposes of destination competitiveness. In *Proceedings of the International Scientific Conference* (p. 163). https://fet.unipu.hr/images/50033564/Conference_Proceedings_2020.pdf

Torralba, A., Oliva, A., Castelhano, M. S., & Henderson, J. M. (2006). Contextual guidance of eye movements and attention in real-world scenes: The role of global features in object search. *Psychological Review*, 113(4), 766–786. DOI: 10.1037/0033-295X.113.4.766 PMID: 17014302

Underwood, G., & Foulsham, T. (2006). Visual saliency and semantic incongruency influence eye movements when inspecting pictures. *Quarterly Journal of Experimental Psychology*, 59(11), 1931–1949. DOI: 10.1080/17470210500416342 PMID: 16987782

Vidyasagar, T. R. (1999). A neuronal model of attentional spotlight: Parietal guiding the temporal. *Brain Research. Brain Research Reviews*, 30(1), 66–76. DOI: 10.1016/S0165-0173(99)00005-3 PMID: 10407126

Vozzi, A., Ronca, V., Aricò, P., Borghini, G., Sciaraffa, N., Cherubino, P., Trettel, A., Babiloni, F., & Di Flumeri, G. (2021). The sample size matters: To what extent the participant reduction affects the outcomes of a neuroscientific research. A case-study in neuromarketing field. *Sensors (Basel)*, 21(18), 6088. DOI: 10.3390/s21186088 PMID: 34577294

Wang, Y., & Hsu, C. H. C. (2022). The effect of tourism on rural employment: A comparative study of Asia and Africa. *Journal of Rural Studies*, 89, 88–98. DOI: 10.1016/j.jrurstud.2022.02.012

Wang, Y., & Sparks, B. A. (2016). An Eye-Tracking Study of Tourism Photo Stimuli: Image Characteristics and Ethnicity. *Journal of Travel Research*, 55(5), 588–602. DOI: 10.1177/0047287514564598

Wedel, M., & Pieters, R. (Eds.). (2007). *Visual marketing: From attention to action* (1st ed.). Psychology Press., DOI: 10.4324/9780203809617

Wedel, M., & Pieters, R. (2008). Eye Tracking for Visual Marketing. *Foundations and Trends® in Marketing, 1*(4), 231-320. https://doi.org/DOI: 10.1561/1700000011

Wisnujati, N. S., Sangadji, S. S., & Handriana, T. (2024). Assessing the Role of Marketing Communication in Shaping Tourist Intentions to Morotai Island. *International Journal of Sustainable Development and Planning*, 19(5), 1845–1854. DOI: 10.18280/ijsdp.190522

World Tourism Organization. (2016). *Panorama OMT del turismo internacional, Edición 2016*. UNWTO., DOI: 10.18111/9789284418152

World Tourism Organization. (2020). *UN Tourism | Bringing the world closer*. UNWTO. https://www.unwto.org

World Tourism Organization. (2021). *Impact assessment of COVID-19 on tourism employment*. United Nations World Tourism Organization. https://www.unwto.org/resources/impact-assessment-covid-19-tourism-employment

World Tourism Organization. (2023). *International Tourism to End 2023 Close to 90% of Pre-Pandemic Levels*. https://www.unwto.org/

World Travel & Tourism Council. (2023). *Travel & Tourism set to Break All Records in 2024*. https://wttc.org/news-article/travel-and-tourism-set-to-break-all-records-in-2024-reveals-wttc

World Travel and Tourism Council (WTTC). (2017) Travel and Tourism Economic Impact Caribbean. World Travel and Tourism Council, London. https://www.slovenia.info/uploads/dokumenti/raziskave/world2017.pdf

Yang, W., Chen, Q., Huang, X., Xie, J., Xie, M., & Shi, J. (2022). Image and text presentation forms in destination marketing: An eye-tracking analysis and a laboratory experiment. *Frontiers in Psychology*, 13, 1024991. DOI: 10.3389/fpsyg.2022.1024991 PMID: 36536866

Ye, H., & Tussyadiah, I. P. (2011). Destination visual image and expectation of experiences. *Journal of Travel & Tourism Marketing*, 28(2), 129–144. DOI: 10.1080/10548408.2011.545743

Yüksel, D. (2023). Investigation of web-based eye-tracking system performance under different lighting conditions for neuromarketing. *Journal of Theoretical and Applied Electronic Commerce Research*, 18(4), 2092–2106. DOI: 10.3390/jtaer18040105

Zhang, K., Zhang, J., & Yang, J. (2023). The influence of human elements in photographs on tourists' destination perceptions and intentions. *Tourism Management*, 95, 104684. DOI: 10.1016/j.tourman.2022.104684

Zhao, X., Zhang, X., & Zhang, Y. (2021). Employment trends in the tourism industry post-pandemic: An analysis of recovery patterns. *Tourism Management*, 83, 104219. DOI: 10.1016/j.tourman.2020.104219

Chapter 12
Digital Corporate Identity in the Healthcare Sector: Cross-National Analysis of the HR Marketing of Hospitals

Henning Tirrel
https://orcid.org/0000-0002-4610-3158
FOM University of Applied Sciences, Germany

Stefanie Hohenhorst
FOM University of Applied Sciences, Germany

Lothar Winnen
Fachhochschule Südwestfalen, Germany

ABSTRACT

German, Austrian and Swiss hospitals operate in a highly competitive labor market. Therefore, companies have to present themselves in a highly professional manner in the digital environment and shape their digital corporate identity. Therefore, the aim of this study is to analyze the digital corporate identity of international hospitals in order to uncover differences and to generate implications. To achieve this goal, the largest 20 hospitals of each country were analyzed by using unobtrusive measures. Accordingly, publicly available data has been generated without informing the participants, so as not to influence the sample. The findings show that none of the 60 hospitals analyzed achieved very good results. In contrast, for most of the hospitals there is room for improvement in relation to their digital corporate identities, which is surprising as the War for Talent is still ongoing. This is the first analysis of its kind, underlining the originality of our work.

DOI: 10.4018/979-8-3693-6289-1.ch012

INTRODUCTION

The shortage of skilled workers and the War for Talent have affected the healthcare sector which raises concerns around the globe (Haryanto, 2019; Weidinger et al., 2022). In addition, the COVID-19 pandemic revealed that many healthcare institutions are already at the limit of their workload capacity (Schneiders & Schönauer, 2022; Roland Berger Krankenhausstudie, 2022). Thus, it is important for hospitals to employ personnel with appropriate qualifications (Matzke, 2018). However, the recent development in the employment market is contradictory as it is estimated that between 2018 and 2030 there will be a shortage of approximately eleven million healthcare employees in Europe (Boskovic, 2021). This is accompanied by a decrease in the working population, i.e., demographic change, while professionals are needed in the healthcare sector (Augurzky et al., 2018; Weidinger et al., 2022). Particularly affected are the professional groups of nursing, medical service, medical doctors and the administrative departments (Endemann, 2021; Matzke, 2018).

As a consequence, organizations have to have a professional digital corporate identity, i.e., unique representation of their attributes, especially related to the work conditions, corporate values and insights into everyday working life, in the digital environment (Tirrel & Winnen, 2024). This is beneficial for companies as it affects the digital employer brand(ing) and thus supports digital recruitment (Gruel & Tirrel, 2024) by sending positive signals to potential applicants, according to Spence's (1973) signaling theory.

The digital perspective is of paramount importance for companies since the internet is used by approximately 4.4 billion people worldwide, of which 4.2 billion of the users interact in social networks (Voigt, 2022). The relevance is also underlined by the statement from Coiné and Babbitt (2014, p. 22) that "companies that fail to adapt to the Social Age are losing control with yet another group coming into power: employees". Current studies underline that communication takes place digitally on a daily basis to people of all age groups (ARD/ZDF, 2023; Bitkom, 2023). Moreover, social networks stimulate the interest of potential employees and can enhance the number of applications (Panday et al., 2022) since organizational values as well as the possibility to interact with organizations in social media are related to the employer brand and the intention to apply (Bahri-Ammari et al., 2022). This, again, is in line with the signaling theory (Spence, 1973). Jeyaraman et al. (2022), highlight that social media recruiting is also of utmost importance for the healthcare sector. Thus, the healthcare sector is the focus of this analysis on the corporate digital identity.

Germany, Austria and Switzerland are neighboring countries. Moreover, German is an officially recognized language in all these countries. In Switzerland, French is also an official language, along with Italian and Romansh, although they did not affect our analysis. Thus, the labor market is not bound to a specific country, but is cross-national (Bachor & Susebeek, 2015). Despite being separated by borders, these three countries are competing for applicants/further employees. This leads to the following research question:

RQ: How do the digital corporate identities of selected hospitals in Germany, Austria and Switzerland differ referring to technology-driven HR marketing for talent attraction?

Therefore, the aim of this study is to analyze the digital corporate identity of hospitals, representing technology-driven HR marketing for talent attraction in Germany, Austria and Switzerland in order to uncover differences and to generate managerial as well as theoretical implications.

LITERATURE REVIEW

The importance of recruiting increases steadily due to the ongoing War for Talent. Two meta-analyses (Chapman et al., 2005; Uggerslev et al., 2012) highlight the relevance of employer attractiveness. This is linked to the recruiting process and affects the likelihood of candidates leaving the application process as well as their acceptance of job offers. In order to shape the employer brand and its attractiveness, companies have recognized that social media is critical to success (Petry et al. 2018; Weitzel et al., 2020). Approximately 4.2 billion global internet users are actively engaged in social networks, spending an average of around four and a half hours daily on these platforms (Voigt, 2022). El-Menawy and Saleh (2023) uncover that using social media platforms mediates the nexus between employer attractiveness as well as the intention to apply for a certain job positively among young people. Moreover, using social media and digital technologies to inform oneself about a job or a company are an essential for potential applicants (Zhang & Chen, 2024). These interactions between employers and potential candidates are known as the candidate journey (Beck & Stember, 2020; Ullah & Ullah, 2015). This journey shapes the perceived strength of the employer brand, capturing all the experiences, emotions, and impressions formed along the way (Rügner, 2021). Therefore, referring to Spence's signaling theory (1973), positive signals are sent into the (inter)national employment market in order to attract applicants. Since information asymmetry exists between employers and applicants, employers have to communicate positive characteristics of their jobs as well as their organization. So, applicants receive an inside view of the organization without yet being part of it. It is important that companies send reliable signals, otherwise, the early employee turnover is expected to be high since organizations promise something they cannot deliver. In this context, it is crucial for companies to promote transparency and to clearly and honestly communicate their identity (Jansen et al., 2023). However, professional social media marketing, which is understood as a positive signal, is statistically significantly related to recruitment success (Winnen et al., 2021). Mičík and Mičudová (2018), who also conducted an obtrusive measure, but in the Czech Republic, identified two main channels for talent attraction, i.e., social media platforms and career websites. This also applies to hospitals as engagement in social media provides inside views and affects employer branding, which ultimately supports employee recruiting (Loloi et al., 2023). Thus, it represents an innovative way of talent attraction as it improves the candidate experience (Gruel & Tirrel, 2024). The COVID-19 pandemic pushed digital developments in hospitals even further (Endemann, 2021). Therefore, hospitals nowadays have to embrace modern technology for employer branding and recruitment purposes. In general, social media plays a crucial role in information communication in recruitment processes (Si et al., 2023).

Cultural Comparison

As job markets are now global rather than being tied to a specific country (Ployhart, 2006), social media enables international recruiting (Koch et al., 2018). When recruiting internationally, organizations have to be aware of culture as it is statistically significantly related to social media recruitment ($\beta = .525; p < .01$) (Muduli et al., 2021). Furthermore, culture mediates the relationship between social media recruitment and hiring outcomes (Muduli et al., 2021).

Due to the relevance of culture, German, Austrian and Swiss culture were compared by using Hofstede's country comparison tool (Hofstede Insights, 2023). The culture comparison contains six cultural dimensions, which will be explained briefly in line with the results of the three countries. The cultural dimension scores have been summarized in table 1.

Table 1. Cultural comparison of Germany, Austria and Switzerland, own table, based on Hofstede Insights (2023)

Country / Cultural dimension	Germany	Austria	Switzerland
Power distance	35	11	34
Individualism	79	77	79
Motivation towards achievement and success	66	79	70
Uncertainty avoidance	65	70	58
Long term orientation	57	47	42
Indulgence	40	63	66

The results indicate that the cultures of Germany, Austria and Switzerland are roughly comparable. Individualism (i.e., the self-image of people identifying as we or I), motivation towards achievement and success (culture led by competition or success, striving to win) as well as long term orientation (association of a society with its past which is transferred into both the present as well as the future to help overcome challenges) (Hofstede Insights, 2023) are comparable in all three countries. Power distance describes how power is distributed unequally among people (Hofstede, 2011). When there is a small power distance, there has to be a legitimation of power, that distinguishes between "good and evil" while there is respect for the elderly rather than a fear (Hofstede, 2011, p. 9). Moreover, income distribution is more equitable (Hofstede, 2011). This dimension is rather low for all three countries, while it is particularly low for Austria.

Referring to Hofstede (2011), uncertainty avoidance is associated with inherent uncertainty in life when uncertainty avoidance is weak, while in cultures with strong uncertainty avoidance it is perceived as a threat in strong uncertainty avoidance cultures. Thus, uncertainty avoidance is an indicator for being (un)comfortable in situations which are unstructured. These values are also comparable, although uncertainty avoidance is slightly lower in Switzerland than in Austria and Germany.

Indulgence refers to the state of being happy, i.e., people describe themselves as being rather happy and they feel that they are in control of their lives (Hofstede, 2011). Freedom of speech is important and positive emotions are more likely remembered (Hofstede, 2011). Germany has a lower indulgence than Austria and Switzerland, so, German culture is rather restrained.

However, as the values for the cultural dimensions do not differ significantly, we interpret the cultures as being similar, so no constraints are expected when it comes to working in these countries. This underlines that there is a competitive international employment market in the geographical area of Germany, Austria and Switzerland. Therefore, it is expected that recruiting does not only focus on a particular country, but is geocentric, i.e., companies recruit the best possible employees globally (Perlmutter, 1969). As a result, a cross-national analysis of hospitals, focusing on the digital corporate identity, is conducted.

Healthcare Systems

The healthcare systems in Germany, Austria and Switzerland provide the institutional framework for the mode of operation of hospitals in their respective countries. These systems are comparable since, despite their own nuances, they pursue similar goals and have fundamental structural similarities.

All three countries are committed to providing high quality healthcare for their citizens (Brock, 2022; Greiling & Schneider, 2019; Hollat & Siebelt, 2019). The German healthcare system is characterized by its complex structures and high standards, based on five fundamental principles, including compulsory insurance, solidarity, and self-administration (Friesendorf & Lüttschwager, 2021). Approximately 87.7% of the population is covered by statutory health insurance, while private health insurance primarily serves self-employed individuals and higher earners (Simon, 2021). In Austria, the system is based on a social insurance model with nearly universal coverage, where about 99.9% of the population is insured, supported by a federal structure that includes the central government and the nine federal states (Habl & Bachner, 2010; Bachner et al., 2019). The Swiss healthcare system operates under a federal structure, with the cantons mainly responsible for healthcare provision. It includes mandatory insurance with the option to choose between private providers, ensuring universal access (Greiling, 2019; Egger, 2018).

In terms of financing, Germany relies on a combination of contributions from insured individuals and government subsidies, supported by a health fund that ensures fair distribution of resources (Friesendorf & Lüttschwager, 2021). Austria also finances its system through a mix of public funds and mandatory contributions, with a significant portion coming from general taxes (Bundesministerium für Arbeit, Soziales, Gesundheit und Konsumentenschutz, 2019; Bachner et al., 2019). In contrast, the financing of the Swiss system is primarily based on premiums paid to private insurers, covering about 60% of healthcare costs (Oggier, 2015). The health care structures in Germany, Austria, and Switzerland include a network of hospitals operated by public, non-profit or private entities that provide medical services ranging from primary care to specialization (Bachner et al. 2019; Brock, 2022; Minz et al., 2023).

Overall, all three healthcare systems play a crucial role in their countries' economies. This is not only due to the provision of healthcare services but also because the health sector creates numerous jobs. However, all hospitals in these three countries encounter comparable challenges in filling these numerous vacancies due to their similar cultural backgrounds and healthcare systems. Specifically, the War for Talent demands an adaptation of their digital corporate identity to ensure competitiveness in the international labor market. It is therefore particularly relevant to conduct a comparative analysis of their digital corporate identity.

METHODOLOGY

Measurement Instrument

In order to systematically analyze quantitative data of hospitals' online presences, a coding guideline was used. This coding guideline has been developed and validated via a Cohen's Kappa = .74 (Cohen, 1960) and 84% of agreement in earlier studies (Winnen et al., 2024). It contains eleven online channels with 181 items (Winnen et al., 2024). In order to finally generate data, unobtrusive measures were applied (Lee, 2019; Webb et al., 1966) which are part of social sciences (Bungard & Lück, 1974). This enables researchers to generate data which are publicly available, like from company websites or social media profiles without informing the participating institutions (Hill et al., 2014; Lee, 2019; Rasmussen & Thimm, 2015; Short et al., 2018). This is why the unobtrusive measures are currently experiencing a renaissance. Since the data should not be biased, only objectively assessable criteria were considered and analyzed in this study (Tirrel et al., 2022). The following channels were analyzed: Hospital career website, job advertisement, Google business profile, kununu (employer review platform), Facebook, Instagram, TikTok, LinkedIn, XING, YouTube, YouTube Shorts. The following table 2 provides an overview of sample items as well as information regarding the number of items per channel.

Table 2. Overview of channels including sample items, own table, based on Winnen et al. (2024)

Channel (number of items)	Sample items
Hospital career website (26 items)	Responsive design, use of image and video content, benefits (e.g., career development, salary, culture, HR development), using blog function, employee testimonials available, depiction of application process, short application opportunity, links to social media
Job advertisement (23 items)	Minimum description of the organization, working hours, tasks, requirements, mentioning relevant benefits, ways to contact the HR department, integration of photos and videos, online application, links to social media
Google business profile (11 items)	Amount of star ratings, reaction to ratings, up-to-date company information, use of image content, function to contribute used
kununu (employer review platform) (27 items)	kununu score, recommendation rate, rated information on culture, benefits, videos, contact person, FAQ, response to reviews
Facebook (24 items), Instagram (20 items), LinkedIn (17 items), TikTok (16 items)	Ratings, contact details to HR department, links from social media to career website, interaction rate, community management, relevant content on culture, everyday working life, benefits, career-related content

continued on following page

Table 2. Continued

Channel (number of items)	Sample items
XING (four items)	About us area maintained, posts per day
YouTube (five items)	Video use, use of playlists, channel information available
YouTube Shorts (eight items)	Interaction rate, relevant content (culture, everyday working life, benefits, presentation of employees)

Sampling

The sample for the study comprises the 20 largest hospitals in Germany, Austria and Switzerland, in total 60 hospitals. These were selected on the basis of their number of beds, based on data from official hospital directories of the respective countries Germany (Statistische Ämter des Bundes und der Länder, 2023), Austria (Bundesministerium für Soziales, Gesundheit, Pflege und Konsumentenschutz, 2023) and Switzerland (Bundesamt für Gesundheit b, 2023). The number of beds, i.e., the size of the hospitals in this study, vary from 2,988 to 332 beds. On average, the analyzed German hospitals have 1,782, Austrian hospitals have 968 and Swiss hospitals have 693 beds (Bundesamt für Gesundheit b, 2023; Bundesministerium für Soziales, Gesundheit, Pflege und Konsumentenschutz, 2023; Statistische Ämter des Bundes und der Länder, 2023). Thus, the sizes of the hospitals in the respective countries differ based on the official data of the respective countries.

The three countries were chosen since German is spoken in all three countries and they have a competitive cross-national labor market. However, in Switzerland French is a common language as well. Hospitals with French online presences were also analyzed, since the researchers are speaking French as well. As the data is available without any barrier, the sample was not informed about the study. However, in order to ensure anonymity, the names of the hospitals will not be published, but replaced by pseudonyms along with the country of origin.

Data Generation

The data generation took place between November 13 to 29, 2023. Each hospital was analyzed completely, i.e., data was generated, during one day by following the coding guideline. This prevented it from having an impact if the hospitals paid more attention to one channel on one day and more attention to another channel on another day. Of course, it was possible to analyze several hospitals per day.

So, 60 digital corporate identities of international hospitals were generated by applying the coding guideline. Every item was assessed by rating it with 1 = achieved or 0 = not achieved (Winnen et al., 2024), in order to generate objective results. This finally ended up in a total score value per hospital but also per channel, enabling differentiated analysis. This coding guideline has been developed and validated via a Cohen's Kappa = .74 (Cohen, 1960) and 84% of agreement in earlier studies (Winnen et al., 2024).

Presentation and Discussion of Results

In order to structure the results of the cross-national analysis, first, the maximum achievable score will be presented and discussed. Second, an international ranking will be presented and discussed as well.

Table 3. Overview of maximum achievable scores and average results per country

Channel	Maximum achievable score	Average German hospital:	Average Austrian hospital:	Average Swiss hospital:
Hospital career website	26.0	17.6	17.5	18.9
Job advertisement	23.0	14.1	13.2	12.9
Google business profile	11.0	3.7	4.1	5.6
kununu	27.0	14.2	13.2	11.3
Facebook	24.0	9.0	9.3	7.5
Instagram	20.0	8.7	9.3	6.3
LinkedIn	17.0	7.1	8.1	8.7
XING	4.0	2.4	1.3	2.2
YouTube	5.0	3.8	4.1	4.0
YouTube Shorts	8.0	0.5	0.1	0.1
TikTok	16.0	0.7	4.3	1.5

Table 3 as well as figure 1 provide an overview of the maximum score value per channel. Moreover, the generated average results per country as well as across the three countries are presented. An international comparison shows that the average use of the eleven channels is similarly professional in all three countries, although there are slight differences. The results show that no country on average was able to reach the maximum achievable score, with the channel YouTube scoring closest to the maximum achievable score.

However, certain country-specific results occur. The hospital career website, the Google business profile as well as LinkedIn are used mostly by Swiss hospitals. kununu and YouTube Shorts are predominantly used by German hospitals. However, Facebook, Instagram, YouTube and TikTok are mostly used by Austrian hospitals. This indicates that Austrian hospitals tend to have the best (on average) social media marketing of these three countries.

Figure 1. Graphical visualization of maximum achievable scores and average results per country

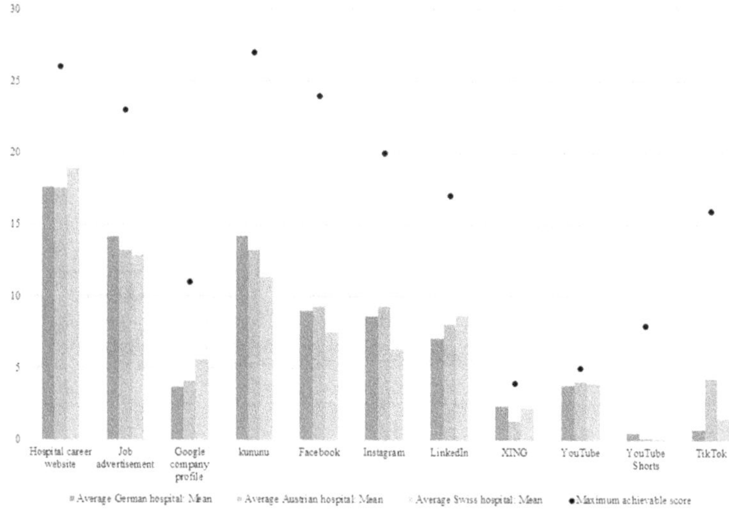

Nevertheless, as no country came close to reaching all maximum achievable scores per channel, there is plenty of room for improvement regarding the digital corporate identity throughout the 60 hospitals analyzed in the three countries. This indicates that the results across the countries have a similar trend across all countries: there is still a lot of untapped potential in the respective channels.

Now, the results will be presented per hospital. In order to structure the analysis and presentation of the results section, four quartiles have been derived out of the 60 hospitals.

Table 4. Leading group, own table, based on Tirrel and Winnen (2019)

Position	Country	Total score	Hospital career website	Job advertise-ment	Google business profile	kununu	Facebook	Instagram	LinkedIn	XING	YouTube	YouTube Shorts	TikTok
1	GER	**61.99%**	83.12%	76.81%	50.55%	77.43%	49.81%	54.88%	66.70%	75.00%	80.00%	25.11%	49.01%
2	AUT	**53.59%**	75.12%	48.55%	35.09%	80.68%	47.03%	54.39%	44.44%	75.00%	100.00%	0.00%	39.88%
3	SUI	**53.11%**	63.27%	56.52%	60.73%	74.41%	37.90%	42.60%	52.21%	75.00%	100.00%	0.00%	32.53%
4	SUI	**52.65%**	90.31%	64.49%	51.45%	72.18%	35.75%	29.07%	65.84%	75.00%	100.00%	0.00%	6.25%
5	AUT	**52.64%**	75.42%	59.29%	24.73%	80.68%	41.36%	49.46%	44.44%	75.00%	100.00%	0.00%	39.88%
6	SUI	**52.11%**	75.77%	73.04%	51.45%	27.93%	43.23%	40.99%	70.73%	75.00%	80.00%	14.77%	31.79%
7	SUI	**51.85%**	70.92%	65.22%	60.55%	40.42%	41.90%	43.30%	47.21%	85.71%	100.00%	0.00%	32.04%
8	SUI	**50.98%**	86.23%	56.52%	69.27%	39.64%	26.40%	29.35%	57.24%	75.00%	100.00%	13.51%	19.65%
9	AUT	**50.95%**	67.62%	52.17%	42.36%	45.49%	41.02%	37.13%	39.76%	75.00%	100.00%	31.01%	40.96%
10	SUI	**50.79%**	87.08%	52.80%	60.55%	44.11%	44.52%	45.38%	55.36%	75.00%	60.00%	0.00%	45.96%
11	AUT	**50.39%**	73.81%	71.74%	60.73%	79.67%	45.00%	45.16%	49.27%	75.00%	60.00%	0.00%	6.25%
12	SUI	**50.36%**	82.23%	60.14%	51.64%	40.73%	45.31%	46.86%	58.11%	75.00%	100.00%	0.00%	6.25%
13	GER	**50.33%**	75.88%	58.94%	42.00%	45.41%	48.22%	64.11%	50.16%	75.00%	100.00%	0.00%	6.25%
14	AUT	**49.93%**	71.50%	69.57%	33.82%	37.15%	47.37%	57.90%	64.04%	0.00%	100.00%	0.00%	42.95%
15	AUT	**49.52%**	67.31%	66.67%	41.27%	37.15%	47.85%	58.03%	63.16%	0.00%	100.00%	0.00%	38.47%

Notes: GER = Germany, AUT = Austria, SUI = Switzerland

The leading group, i.e., the fourth quartile (cf. table 4), contains hospitals from all three countries, while Swiss hospitals are disproportionately strongly represented. Furthermore, the leading hospital is located in northern Germany and reached 61.99% of the maximum achievable total score. Thus, the best hospital in our analysis is still 38.01 percentage points below the maximum score value. This raises concerns as even the best of the 60 hospitals are not using their potential in relation to their digital corporate identity. So, even the best hospital did not manage to use the channel efficiently. The results of the leading group show that the hospital career website, XING and YouTube have been used quite well. The best five hospitals also used kununu very well. Social media channels like Facebook, Instagram, TikTok and YouTube Shorts have not been used very professionally. Moreover, there is much room for improvement with the use of the business social network LinkedIn.

In the upper midfield (cf. table 5 in the appendix), the hospital career website, YouTube, XING as well as the job advertisements are, in general, handled professionally. Private social media channels tend to be neglected by the hospitals. TikTok, Facebook, Instagram and YouTube Shorts, in particular, are not being used efficiently, as shown by their rather low scores.

Furthermore, kununu and the Google business profile yielded rather low scores. LinkedIn, as a business social network, is also not used adequately by the hospitals.

Overall, the range of the scores in the upper midfield is small since the scores vary from 49.20% to 44.56%. This range is much smaller than the range in the leading group. However, all hospitals located in the upper midfield have achieved less than half of the achievable results. The average value, calculated on the basis of all 60 hospitals is 43.75%. Thus, the average value is located in the lower midfield.

The results of the lower midfield (cf. table 6 in the appendix) show that, again, the hospital career website, YouTube and XING reached the best results. YouTube Shorts has not been used by a single hospital. The other private social networks are also rarely used. Two hospitals are aware of the relevance of the Google business profile and used it appropriately. However, the majority of hospitals do not take advantage of the possibilities offered by the Google business profile. Most hospitals do not use kununu, with only two shown to be using it in a constructive manner. The same applies for LinkedIn, the business social network. Job advertisements include most of the relevant information, although there is also room for improvement.

The results of the closing group (cf. table 7 in the appendix) show that the hospital's career website is the most relevant channel for hospitals. This is followed by XING and YouTube. However, private or business social media are more or less neglected. Even the job advertisements are not of a good quality. This is very surprising, as job advertisements are often the first point of contact for applicants along the candidate journey. Hence, the hospitals themselves do not use this well-known medium adequately.

In more general terms, the best hospital in the closing group still achieved 38.05%. This means that 61.95% is missing the maximum. The hospital in last place achieved just 20.05%. This is only one fifth of the maximum achievable points. Thus, 79.95% are missing. The hospital in last place is a German hospital which, geographically speaking, is located roughly in the middle of Germany.

The range of the best hospital from the leading group and the worst hospital from the closing group ranges from 61.99% to 20.05%. We interpret this range as very wide, particularly in view of the ongoing War for Talent and the demographic developments as aforementioned.

The average scores per county account for Austria = 44.82%, Germany = 43.23% and Switzerland = 43.30%. So, there are only slight differences per country referring to the averages. Therefore, the results in general indicate that hospitals from Austria are at the forefront, while German hospitals are in the middle. Swiss hospitals tend to be rated last. Nevertheless, it is also important to emphasize that each channel makes its own contribution to achieving the goal.

DISCUSSION OF RESULTS

With regard to the signaling theory (Spence, 1973), it is of paramount importance to send positive signals into the labor market. These signals have to be sent via the analyzed channels, as those affect employer attractiveness as well as intention to apply (El-Menawy & Saleh, 2023), as they are regarded as innovative instruments for talent attraction (Gruel & Tirrel, 2024). In general, hospitals send positive signals, but they do so professionally only on a few of the available channels. This is counterproductive since, for instance, 52% of the Germans use social media, especially Instagram and Facebook but also TikTok, on a daily basis (ARD/ZDF, 2023). Thus, it is not clear why hospitals do not exploit this huge potential, i.e., target group. This is especially of interest since Zhang and Chen (2024) highlight that this is essential for potential applicants. Since culture and healthcare systems are roughly comparable, we expect the HR department within the hospitals to either not be aware of the available options in the respective channels or they are not able to use them due to being untrained or due to not having enough personnel resources or financial budget. This is surprising since digital recruiting is associated to reduced costs (Gruel & Tirrel, 2024).

By partly using the respective channels, the analyzed hospitals show that they have recognized the relevance of these channels. However, they do not seem to be aware of the consequences of poor use. Thus, it is interpreted as if they do not want to use digital media to sharpen their digital corporate identity, besides its positive association to recruitment success (Winnen et al., 2022). It remains unclear why the analyzed hospitals are so reluctant to use the available opportunities in the War for Talent. Moreover, they could positively influence employer attractiveness (El-Menawy & Saleh, 2023) by communicating their benefits like flexible work which is beneficial for employees and employers (Kamp et al., 2024) as it is associated with less absenteeism and employee turnover (Tirrel, 2023; Tirrel et al., 2021), but refuse improving it. However, the career website, which was besides social media, identified as one of the major channels (Mičík & Mičudová, 2018), is the best-used and therefore best-rated channel in this study.

Looking at a previous study that was conducted using the same methodology, Winnen et al. (2024) were able to reveal that there are numerous reasons for the lack of professionalization in digital communication. Based on a qualitative survey of participants from the German social economy, the following problems were identified that serve as explanations:

(1) Lack of sufficient competence on the part of those involved
(2) Lack of understanding of the relevance of digital HR marketing by the managers/ departments involved
(3) Lack of digital personnel marketing
(4) Lack of time
(5) Lack of financial resources
(6) Irregular social media postings
(7) Excessively long response times in digital communication
(8) Unclear, undefined processes and structures (e.g., with regard to approval in communication or in the recruiting process)
(9) Restrictions under data protection law
(10) High need for communication and coordination in large organizations with different departments and independently operating locations

In summary, we conclude that there is still great potential in appropriately shaping the digital corporate identity, which hospitals will probably have to exploit in the shortest possible time in order to attract and retain employees in the future and long term. The increase in digital developments in hospitals initiated by the COVID-19 pandemic (Endemann, 2021) is interpreted as a starting point rather than a completion. It seems that hospitals did not fully understand the crucial role of social media in information communication during recruitment processes, as underlined by Si et al. (2023).

Managerial Implications

Based on the results, managerial implications are drawn. Hospitals have to reconsider the use of certain online channels with all its possibilities for shaping their digital corporate identity in order that they can better tackle the War for Talent based on a very well-structured digital communication. This has to be led by their HR strategy. In addition, hospitals must have a look at social media channels which are not strategically steered by the hospitals. Employees, former employees, applicants or customers can, for example, create a Google business profile for a company and thus shape the digital corporate identity without the hospital being aware of it (Tirrel & Winnen, 2024).

Moreover, hospitals should either recruit or train their HR social media managers in order to enhance the performance referring to the digital corporate identities. Furthermore, hospitals have to set up an HR social media strategy. This strategy serves as a guide which hospitals should follow in order to get in touch with their target groups. In order to successfully do so, HR social media managers have to be trained, i.e., they have to know about the functions of the channels. Moreover, HR social media managers have to be knowledgeable via which channel they can get in touch with which target group(s), since young employees are often not aware of business social media channels like LinkedIn (Wübbelt & Tirrel, 2022).

Theoretical Implications

The unobtrusive measures are, in general, highly useable for analyzing publicly available data. However, data analysis has to be based on highly objective data, as in our case. Thus, the method should be further developed by including a mechanism which enables researchers to generate subjective data and to analyze it without being biased due to subjectivity. This has to be done in a very rigorous way, so data generation and analysis are useable and interpretable. Thereafter, also aspects like usability of websites could be included in further analysis.

Limitations and Avenues for Further Research

This study has some limitations. First, the study was conducted in German-speaking countries and consequently focuses on a specific geographic region. Thus, no conclusions can be drawn regarding other countries. However, the analysis was necessary since employees also change their job across national borders, since there is no language barrier. As a result, further research is required for analyzing the employment market in other countries or geographical areas.

Second, we focused on the 20 largest hospitals of each country. Therefore, there are no implications for small or medium-sized hospitals, representing another gap for further research as we expect them to have fewer resources for dealing with this issue. This might lead to worse results.

Third, this analysis was conducted as an unobtrusive measure, which aims to generate objective results. However, despite implementing mechanisms to prevent subjectivity, we cannot rule out the possibility that subjectivity might have biased our analysis. Therefore, we suggest conducting further studies by using different methods. This would also enable an inside view, e.g., via a survey, of how effective digital efforts have been. So, results are triangulated.

Fourth, only channels that are permanently visible and verifiable to the outside world were evaluated. The extent to which hospitals have used promising temporary paid digital recruiting campaigns, for example, could therefore not be recorded and evaluated.

CONCLUSION

The presented results show that out of the 60 largest hospitals in Germany, Austria and Switzerland, no hospital achieved a very good result with regard to their digital corporate identity. Although the signaling theory teaches HR social media managers to send attractive and desirable aspects of an employer, in this case hospitals, responsible managers seem to be unaware of this. Moreover, not all functions are used for most of the channels. It is anticipated that hospitals try to be present on some or even most of the channels. However, having a profile which provides old information, e.g., last update was posted several weeks ago, is probably counterproductive.

Thus, hospitals have to set up an HR social media strategy in which they define how to handle the various channels appropriately in order to form a professional digital corporate identity. Thereafter, hospitals have a better chance to recruit new employees in the highly competitive international labor market.

Referring back to the aim of this study, the digital corporate identity of 60 international hospitals was analyzed. Differences and similarities were identified and theoretical and practical implications were derived. In addition, further avenues for future research were presented on the basis of this analysis.

REFERENCES

ARD/ZDF. (2023). *ARD/ZDF-Onlinestudie 2023*. https://www.ard-zdf-onlinestudie.de/

Augurzky, B., & Kolodziej, I. (2018). *Fachkräftebedarf im Gesundheits- und Sozialwesen 2030*. RWI - Leibniz-Institut für Wirtschaftsforschung.

Bachner, F., Bobek, J., Habimana, K., Ladurner, J., Lepuschutz, L., Ostermann, H., Rainer, L., Schmidt, A., Zuba, M., Quentin, W., & Winkelmann, J. (2019). Das österreichische Gesundheitssystem. *European Observatory on Health Systems ans Policies*, 20(3), 1-288.

Bachor, N., & Susebeek, L. (2015). Personalsuche im Gesundheitswesen. In Naegler, H. (Ed.), *Personalmanagement im Krankenhaus* (pp. 174–179). MWV Medizinisch Wissenschaftliche Verlagsgesellschaft.

Bahri-Ammari, N., Soliman, M., & Ben Salah, O. (2022). The Impact of Employer Brand on Job Seekers' Attitudes and Intentions: The Moderating Role of Value Congruence and Social Media. *Corporate Reputation Review*. Advance online publication. DOI: 10.1057/s41299-022-00154-8

Beck, J., & Stember, J. (2020). *Der demographische Wandel: Zwischen Digitalisierung, Aufgabenwandel und neuem Personalmanagement*. Nomos. DOI: 10.5771/9783748902713

Bitkom (2023). *Wie die Deutschen Social Media nutzen*. https:// www.bitkom.org/sites/main/files/2023-02/BitkomChartsSocialMedia2023.pdf

Boskovic, S. (2021). *Health and longterm care workforce: Demographic challenges and potential contribution of migration and digital technology*. Publications Office of the European Union.

Brock, H. (2022). Das Gesundheitssystem der Schweiz. *ÖKZ*, 63(1), 22-24.

Bundesamt für Gesundheit b (BAG) (2023). *Kennzahlen der Schweizer Spitäler*. https://spitalstatistik.bagapps.ch/data/download/kzp21_publication.pdf?v=1679384362

Bundesministerium für Arbeit, Soziales, Gesundheit und Konsumentenschutz (2019). *Das österreichische Gesundheitssystem*. https://broschuerenservice.sozialministerium.at/Home/Download?publicationId=636

Bundesministerium für Soziales, Gesundheit, Pflege und Konsumentenschutz (2023). *Krankenanstalten in Österreich*. https://www.sozialministerium.at/dam/jcr:0a2c1fb9-68c3-4355-bf22-ff0d11c0186e/KA-Verzeich nis%202023-10-21.xlsx

Bungard, W., & Lück, H. E. (1974). *Forschungsartefakte und nicht-reaktive Meßverfahren*. Teubner. DOI: 10.1007/978-3-322-94911-0

Chapman, D. S., Uggerslev, K. L., Carroll, S. A., Piasentin, K. A., & Jones, D. A. (2005). Applicant attraction to organizations and job choice: A meta-analytic review of the correlates of recruiting outcomes. *The Journal of Applied Psychology*, 90(5), 928–944. DOI: 10.1037/0021-9010.90.5.928 PMID: 16162065

Cohen, J. (1960). A coefficient of agreement for nominal scales. *Educational and Psychological Measurement*, 20(1), 37–46. DOI: 10.1177/001316446002000104

Coiné, T., & Babbitt, M. (2014). *A world gone social*. Amacom.

Egger, M. (2018). Gesundheitssysteme im internationalen Vergleich. In Egger, M., Razum, O., & Rieder, A. (Eds.), *Public Health Kompakt* (pp. 117–159). De Gruyter.

El-Menawy, S. M. A., & Saleh, P. S. (2023). How does the mediating role of the use of social media platforms foster the relationship between employer attractiveness and generation Z intentions to apply for a job? *Future Business Journal*, 9(65), 1–13. DOI: 10.1186/s43093-023-00233-0

Endemann, M. (2021). Digitale Wege zum Personal, in: Das österreichische Gesundheitswesen. *ÖKZ, 62*(3-4), 59-60. DOI: 10.1007/s43830-021-0031-9

Friesendorf, C., & Lüttschwager, S. (2021). *Digitale Gesundheitsanwendungen*. Springer. DOI: 10.1007/978-3-658-33983-8

Greiling, D. (2019). Das österreichische Gesundheitswesen im internationalen Vergleich. In Fuchs, M., Greiling, D., & Rosenberger, M. (Eds.), *Gut versorgt? Ökonomie und Ethik im Gesundheits- und Pflegebereich* (pp. 23–43). Nomos.

Greiling, D., & Schneider, F. (2019). Zentralisierung von Gesundheitsleistungen. In Fuchs, M., Greiling, D., & Rosenberger, M. (Eds.), *Gut versorgt? Ökonomie und Ethik im Gesundheits- und Pflegebereich* (pp. 53–62). Nomos.

Gruel, M., & Tirrel, H. (2024). Digital recruiting. In *Reference Module in Social Sciences*. https://doi.org/DOI: 10.1016/B978-0-443-13701-3.00066-9

Habl, C., & Bachner, F. (2010). *Das österreichische Gesundheitssystem im internationalen Vergleich 2009*. Österreichisches Bundesinstitut für Gesundheitswesen.

Haryanto, M. (2019). Nursing Shortage: Myth or Fact. *Orthopedic Nursing*, 38(1), 1–2. DOI: 10.1097/NOR.0000000000000535 PMID: 30676566

Hill, A. D., White, M. A., & Wallace, J. C. (2014). Unobtrusive measurement of psychological constructs in organizational research. *Organizational Psychology Review*, 4(2), 148–174. DOI: 10.1177/2041386613505613

Hofstede, G. (2011). Dimensionalizing cultures: The Hofstede Model in context. *Online Readings in Psychology and Culture*, 2(1), 1–26. DOI: 10.9707/2307-0919.1014

Hofstede Insights. (2023). Country comparison tool. https://www.hofstede-insights.com/country-comparison-tool?countries=austria%2Cgermany%2Cswitzerland

Hollat, S., & Siebelt, P. (2019). Möglichkeiten und Grenzen des Dienstleistungsmarketings für Apotheken. In Matusiewicz, D., Stratmann, F., & Wimmer, J. (Eds.), *Marketing im Gesundheitswesen* (pp. 421–432). Springer. DOI: 10.1007/978-3-658-20279-8_31

Jansen, L. J., Diercks, J., & Kupka, K. (2023). *Recrutainment - Gamifcation in Employer Branding,* Personalmarketing und Personalauswahl. Springer.

Jeyaraman, M., Ramasubramanian, S., Kumar, S., Jeyaraman, N., Selvaraj, P., Nallakumarasamy, A., Bondili, S. K., & Yadav, S. (2023). Multifaceted Role of Social Media in Healthcare: Opportunities, Challenges, and the Need for Quality Control. *Cureus*, 15(5), 1–9. DOI: 10.7759/cureus.39111 PMID: 37332420

Kamp, L.-M., Tirrel, H., & Winnen, L. (2024). The paradox of flexibility: Unraveling the impact of flexible work arrangements on affective commitment during the Covid-19 pandemic. *Economics & Sociology (Ternopil)*, 17(2), 151–172. DOI: 10.14254/2071-789X.2024/17-2/7

Koch, T., Gerber, C., & De Klerk, J. J. (2018). The impact of social media on recruitment: Are you LinkedIn? *SA Journal of Human Resource Management/SA Tydskrif vir Menslikehulpbronbestuur*, 16(0), a861. DOI: 10.4102/sajhrm.v16i0.861

Lee, R. M. (2019). Unobtrusive Methods. In Liamputtong, P. (Ed.), *Handbook of Research Methods in Health Social Sciences* (pp. 491–507). Springer. DOI: 10.1007/978-981-10-5251-4_85

Loloi, J., Berstein, A., & Dubin, J. (2023). „Likes“ in Social Media: Does it carry any implications? *Société Internationale d'Urologie Journal : SIUJ*, 4(2), 105–111. DOI: 10.48083/KTOL8925

Matzke, U. (2018). Personalgewinnung und -bindung im Wandel. In Simon, A. (Ed.), *Akademisch ausgebildetes Pflegefachpersonal* (pp. 115–136). Springer. DOI: 10.1007/978-3-662-54887-5_9

Mičík, M., & Mičudová, K. (2018). Employer brand building: Using social media and career websites to attract generation Y. *Economia e Sociologia*, 11(3), 171–189.

Minz, R., Grüttner, D., & von Heusinger-Lender, M. (2023). Krankenhaus 2030 – Was sich ändern muss. *Gefässchirurgie*, 2(28), 98–107. DOI: 10.1007/s00772-023-00986-6 PMID: 36945660

Muduli, A., Trivedi, J., & Pingle, S. (2021). Social media recruitment and culture: An empirical study. *International Journal Indian Culture and Business Management*, 22(3), 364–382. DOI: 10.1504/IJICBM.2021.114085

Oggier, W. (2015). *Gesundheitswesen Schweiz*. Hogrefe.

Panday, R., Almira, S., & Navanti, D. (2022). Employer branding and social media as an attractive job seeker to e-commerce companies for Z generation. *American Journal of Humanities and Social Sciences Research*, 6(7), 141–150.

Perlmutter, H. V. (1969). The tortuous evolution of the multinational corporation. *The Columbia Journal of World Business*, 4(1), 9–18.

Petry, T. (2019). *Digital Leadership: Erfolgreiches Führen in Zeiten der Digital Economy*. Haufe.

Ployhart, R. E. (2006). Staffing in the 21st century: New challenges and strategic opportunities. *Journal of Management*, 32(6), 868–897. DOI: 10.1177/0149206306293625

Rasmussen, K. B., & Thimm, H. (2015). Circumventing nonresponse - upgrading traditional company survey data with unobtrusive data from company websites. *Bulletin of Sociological Methodology. Bulletin de Methodologie Sociologique*, 127(1), 85–96. DOI: 10.1177/0759106315582198

Roland Berger Krankenhausstudie. (2022). *Zeit für Lösungen. Warum der Umgang mit COVID, Fachkräftemangel und Ambulantisierung für deutsche Kliniken zur Existenzfrage wird*. Roland Berger.

Schneiders, K., & Schönauer, A.-L. (2022). Fachkräftemangel in der Sozialwirtschaft: Empirische Befunde zu Ursachen und Handlungsbedarfen. In Gehrlach, C., von Bergen, M., & Eiler, K. (Eds.), *Zwischen gesellschaftlichem Auftrag und Wettbewerb* (pp. 355–370). Springer. DOI: 10.1007/978-3-658-35381-0_21

Short, J. C., McKenny, A. F., & Reid, S. W. (2018). More than words? Computer-aided text analysis in organizational behavior and psychology research. *Annual Review of Organizational Psychology and Organizational Behavior*, 5(1), 415–435. DOI: 10.1146/annurev-orgpsych-032117-104622

Si, K., Jalees, T., Zaman, S. I., Alam, S. H., & Khan, S. (2023). The role of communication, informativeness, and social presence play in the social media recruitment context of an emerging economy. *Cogent Business & Management*, 10(3), 2251204. DOI: 10.1080/23311975.2023.2251204

Simon, M. (2021). *Das Gesundheitssystem in Deutschland.* Hogrefe. DOI: 10.1024/86147-000

Spence, M. (1973). Job Market Signaling. *The Quarterly Journal of Economics*, 87(3), 355–374. DOI: 10.2307/1882010

Statistische Ämter des Bundes und der Länder. (2023). *Verzeichnis der Krankenhäuser und Vorsorge- oder Rehabilitationseinrichtungen.* https://www.statistikportal.de/de/veroeffentlichungen/krankenhausverzeichnis

Tirrel, H. (2023). *Working flexibly: A study on German SMEs in relation to information and communication technology and leadership.* University of Nicosia.

Tirrel, H., Kaufmann, H. R., & Winnen, L. (2021). Why not to work in flexible workplaces? A systematic literature review and development of a conceptual framework for SMEs. *International Review of Entrepreneurship*, 19(4), 555–584.

Tirrel, H., & Winnen, L. (2019). Die digitale Identität der DAX-30-Unternehmen aus Sicht des Personalmarketings 2.0. In Winnen, L., Rühle, A., & Wrobel, A. (Eds.), *Innovativer Einsatz digitaler Medien im Marketing: Analysen, Strategien, Erfolgsfaktoren, Fallbeispiele* (pp. 29–46). Springer Gabler., DOI: 10.1007/978-3-658-16774-5_3

Tirrel, H., & Winnen, L. (2024). Digital Corporate Identity. In *Reference Modul in Social Sciences.* DOI: 10.1016/B978-0-443-13701-3.00068-2

Tirrel, H., Winnen, L., & Baumann, R. (2022). Durch Social Media Personal gewinnen. *Personalführung*, 55(5), 10–11.

Uggerslev, K. L., Fassina, N. E., & Kraichy, D. (2012). Recruiting through the stages: A meta-analytic test of predictors of applicant attraction at different stages of the recruiting process. *Personnel Psychology*, 65(3), 597–660. DOI: 10.1111/j.1744-6570.2012.01254.x

Ullah, M., & Ullah, R. (2015). *Erfolgsfaktor Candidate Experience: Der Perspektivwechsel im Recruiting*. Schäffer-Poeschel Verlag.

Voigt, D. (2022). *Digitalisierung im Sozial- und Gesundheitswesen*. Springer. DOI: 10.1007/978-3-658-38360-2

Webb, E., Campbell, D. T., Schwartz, R. D., & Sechrest, L. (1966). *Unobtrusive measures: Nonreactive research in the social sciences*. Rand McNally.

Weidinger, L., Löschnigg-Tausz, M., & Hausmann, D. (2022). Fachkräftemangel in der Pflege – ein Blick über Österreichs Grenzen hinaus. *Procare : das Forbildungsmagazin fur Pflegeberufe*, 27(3), 48–51. DOI: 10.1007/s00735-022-1540-9

Weitzel, T., Maier, C., Weinert, C., Pflügner, K., Oehlhorn, C., & Wirth, J. (2020). *Mobile Recruiting: Ausgewählte Ergebnisse der Recruiting Trends 2020, einer empirischen Unternehmens-Studie mit den Top-1.000-Unternehmen aus Deutschland sowie den Top-300-Unternehmen aus der Branche IT und der Bewerbungspraxis 2020, einer empirischen Kandidaten-Studie mit Antworten von über 3.500 Kandidaten.*https://www.uni-bamberg.de/fileadmin/uni/fakultaeten/wiai_lehrstuehle/isdl/Recruiting_Trends_2020/Studien_2020_02_Mobile_Recruiting_Web.pdf

Winnen, L., Schrader, S., & Tirrel, H. (2021). Der Einfluss von Social Media (im Employer Branding) auf den Stellenbesetzungserfolg: Eine quantitative Analyse. In Tirrel, H., Winnen, L., & Lanwehr, R. (Eds.), *Digitales Human Resource Management. Aktuelle Forschungserkenntnisse, Trends und Anwendungsbeispiele* (pp. 173–194). Springer., DOI: 10.1007/978-3-658-35590-6_11

Winnen, L., Tirrel, H., & Mertens, A. (2024). Digitale Identität ausgewählter Organisationen der Sozialwirtschaft: Eine quantitative Analyse des digitalen Personalmarketings. *PERSONALquarterly*, 76(2), 36–41.

Wübbelt, A., & Tirrel, H. (2022). Attracting members of generation Z to companies via social media recruiting in Germany. *Human Technology*, 18(3), 213–233. DOI: 10.14254/1795-6889.2022.18-3.2

Zhang, J., & Chen, Z. (2024). Exploring human resource management digital transformation in the digital age. *Journal of the Knowledge Economy*, 15(1), 1482–1498. DOI: 10.1007/s13132-023-01214-y

ADDITIONAL READING

Eger, L., Mičík, M., & Řehoř, P. (2018). Employer branding on social media and recruitment websites: Symbolic traits of an ideal employer. *E+M. Ekonomie a Management*, 21(1), 224–237. DOI: 10.15240/tul/001/2018-1-015

Melanthiou, Y., Pavlou, F., & Constantinou, E. (2015). The use of social network sites as an e-recruitment tool. *Journal of Transnational Management*, 20(1), 31–49. DOI: 10.1080/15475778.2015.998141

Mičík, M., & Mičudová, K. (2018). Employer brand building: Using social media and career websites to attract generation Y. *Economia e Sociologia*, 11(3), 171–189.

KEY TERMS AND DEFINITIONS

Digital corporate identity: Presenting unique company characteristics, especially with regard to their working environment, company values as well as day-to-day work insights, in the digital environment

Social media recruiting: Use of social media such as Instagram, LinkedIn, TikTok or Facebook to recruit and attract employees

Unobtrusive measures: Publicly freely accessible data, e.g. from websites, is gathered and analyzed on the basis of a priori defined criteria

Coding guideline: This is a catalog of criteria including instructions for data generation, in which anchor examples are also listed

Signaling: This involves setting the right accents. This article deals with positive aspects of employers in order to attract employees.

War for Talent: The War for Talent describes the competitive environment in which organizations today have to attract the best specialists and managers for their company. In the War for Talent, however, talented individuals can choose their jobs and their desired employers more or less at their own. So, talents decide where they work, not the organizations.

Culture: Culture describes how people in a company interact and work together, often based on values.

APPENDIX

Table 5. Upper midfield, own table, based on Tirrel and Winnen (2019)

Position	Country	Total score	Hospital career website	Job advertise-ment	Google business profile	kununu	Facebook	Instagram	LinkedIn	XING	YouTube	YouTube Shorts	TikTok
16	GER	**49.20%**	60.73%	62.32%	51.45%	59.15%	35.94%	36.61%	45.39%	75.00%	100.00%	27.56%	0.00%
17	AUT	**49.11%**	64.69%	72.73%	32.91%	37.15%	47.37%	58.26%	64.04%	0.00%	100.00%	0.00%	38.52%
18	GER	**49.05%**	78.77%	56.52%	43.09%	70.54%	37.17%	51.50%	48.32%	85.71%	80.00%	0.00%	6.25%
19	SUI	**48.98%**	79.08%	56.52%	60.91%	62.08%	35.47%	42.93%	52.28%	50.00%	100.00%	0.00%	0.00%
20	GER	**48.81%**	82.85%	75.78%	24.00%	44.05%	47.00%	43.15%	25.81%	75.00%	100.00%	26.16%	6.25%
21	AUT	**48.65%**	67.31%	66.30%	32.55%	37.15%	47.85%	58.03%	63.16%	0.00%	100.00%	0.00%	38.47%
22	AUT	**48.61%**	63.50%	68.70%	41.09%	33.44%	47.82%	53.21%	61.50%	0.00%	100.00%	0.00%	41.15%
23	AUT	**48.24%**	67.38%	62.32%	32.18%	37.15%	47.85%	58.03%	63.16%	0.00%	100.00%	0.00%	38.47%
24	GER	**47.93%**	63.15%	55.98%	42.55%	42.64%	46.53%	53.88%	40.52%	50.00%	100.00%	26.80%	6.25%
25	SUI	**47.75%**	67.69%	65.22%	51.45%	44.23%	44.27%	31.31%	59.69%	75.00%	100.00%	0.00%	0.00%
26	AUT	**47.24%**	51.35%	64.35%	60.00%	42.15%	42.02%	31.63%	49.96%	75.00%	80.00%	0.00%	37.05%
27	GER	**46.63%**	90.04%	55.07%	41.09%	65.20%	28.32%	44.59%	47.81%	75.00%	80.00%	0.00%	0.00%
28	GER	**45.42%**	83.00%	73.91%	42.18%	65.26%	12.50%	42.20%	37.72%	80.36%	80.00%	0.00%	0.00%
29	GER	**45.31%**	63.08%	68.60%	42.18%	43.90%	24.00%	38.04%	65.60%	75.00%	80.00%	12.82%	0.00%
30	GER	**44.56%**	75.42%	55.07%	33.09%	82.77%	39.09%	35.27%	55.75%	57.14%	60.00%	2.81%	0.00%

Notes: GER = Germany, AUT = Austria, SUI = Switzerland

Table 6. Lower midfield, own table, based on Tirrel and Winnen (2019)

Position	Country	Total score	Hospital career website	Job advertise-ment	Google business profile	kununu	Facebook	Instagram	LinkedIn	XING	YouTube	YouTube Shorts	TikTok
31	AUT	44.43%	67.04%	47.83%	49.64%	38.22%	37.21%	49.94%	47.83%	0.00%	100.00%	0.00%	28.76%
32	SUI	44.42%	66.73%	44.02%	70.18%	40.88%	47.36%	39.38%	54.11%	75.00%	60.00%	0.00%	6.25%
33	GER	43.77%	71.15%	67.93%	24.18%	42.95%	42.25%	48.95%	44.64%	75.00%	80.00%	0.00%	0.00%
34	AUT	43.72%	78.23%	36.23%	24.36%	49.50%	43.30%	43.59%	51.64%	0.00%	100.00%	0.00%	32.23%
35	AUT	43.57%	71.08%	56.52%	51.09%	74.26%	0.00%	45.37%	47.92%	50.00%	80.00%	0.00%	6.25%
36	GER	43.26%	54.96%	63.48%	69.27%	41.06%	40.39%	30.20%	37.31%	75.00%	80.00%	0.00%	0.00%
37	GER	41.80%	50.31%	69.57%	50.91%	40.85%	49.05%	36.35%	61.88%	0.00%	80.00%	0.00%	0.00%
38	AUT	41.78%	67.19%	52.17%	23.45%	32.07%	37.21%	49.91%	47.91%	0.00%	100.00%	0.00%	28.76%
39	GER	41.37%	63.35%	65.22%	5.27%	72.76%	40.23%	39.62%	24.13%	75.00%	80.00%	0.00%	6.25%
40	AUT	41.24%	84.88%	63.64%	24.18%	43.05%	38.93%	43.30%	55.01%	0.00%	80.00%	0.00%	0.00%
41	SUI	41.21%	71.31%	68.12%	42.36%	42.07%	32.21%	37.59%	59.01%	0.00%	80.00%	0.00%	0.00%
42	SUI	41.03%	78.62%	62.11%	51.27%	42.41%	0.00%	17.02%	35.59%	75.00%	100.00%	0.00%	6.25%
43	GER	39.67%	75.46%	71.47%	4.73%	45.19%	43.70%	51.23%	27.30%	75.00%	60.00%	0.00%	0.00%
44	SUI	38.85%	71.00%	54.66%	42.55%	37.67%	20.98%	41.22%	42.39%	75.00%	60.00%	0.00%	0.00%
45	SUI	38.27%	65.88%	41.55%	42.73%	0.00%	40.76%	28.73%	58.41%	75.00%	80.00%	0.00%	6.25%

Notes: GER = Germany, AUT = Austria, SUI = Switzerland

Table 7. Closing group, own table, based on Tirrel and Winnen (2019)

Position	Country	Total score	Hospital career website	Job advertise-ment	Google business profile	kununu	Facebook	Instagram	LinkedIn	XING	YouTube	YouTube Shorts	TikTok
46	GER	**38.05%**	69.46%	45.22%	0.00%	46.48%	37.80%	45.28%	31.48%	75.00%	80.00%	0.00%	6.25%
47	GER	**38.02%**	71.65%	52.17%	51.09%	44.93%	32.56%	34.54%	32.27%	0.00%	80.00%	0.00%	0.00%
48	AUT	**36.96%**	47.77%	47.83%	32.91%	71.39%	33.87%	27.20%	11.76%	75.00%	40.00%	0.00%	37.83%
49	SUI	**36.74%**	55.42%	51.09%	50.73%	29.56%	32.79%	42.25%	43.96%	0.00%	80.00%	0.00%	0.00%
50	AUT	**36.12%**	62.54%	56.52%	42.55%	40.89%	41.55%	40.07%	17.65%	75.00%	40.00%	0.00%	0.00%
51	GER	**36.09%**	62.58%	43.12%	41.09%	35.37%	28.42%	42.03%	40.07%	0.00%	80.00%	0.00%	6.25%
52	SUI	**35.86%**	70.85%	56.88%	31.82%	41.50%	24.19%	41.19%	52.58%	75.00%	20.00%	0.00%	0.00%
53	SUI	**33.85%**	63.08%	46.09%	33.64%	35.56%	27.40%	32.98%	36.72%	0.00%	80.00%	0.00%	0.00%
54	AUT	**33.42%**	59.04%	58.26%	25.09%	45.22%	36.62%	31.52%	17.65%	75.00%	40.00%	0.00%	0.00%
55	GER	**33.29%**	48.96%	60.43%	6.00%	41.26%	37.10%	46.51%	29.99%	78.57%	40.00%	0.00%	0.00%
56	SUI	**33.00%**	75.46%	54.35%	23.45%	56.15%	0.00%	0.00%	39.56%	75.00%	60.00%	0.00%	0.00%
57	SUI	**31.57%**	70.77%	51.09%	59.09%	35.69%	17.30%	0.00%	37.52%	0.00%	60.00%	0.00%	0.00%
58	SUI	**30.55%**	63.08%	41.50%	51.64%	31.78%	30.02%	0.00%	42.77%	0.00%	60.00%	0.00%	0.00%
59	AUT	**26.29%**	65.81%	30.43%	42.00%	38.00%	4.17%	40.47%	48.94%	0.00%	0.00%	0.00%	6.25%
60	GER	**20.05%**	31.92%	52.17%	5.64%	44.81%	32.00%	26.37%	17.65%	0.00%	0.00%	0.00%	0.00%

Notes: GER = Germany, AUT = Austria, SUI = Switzerland

Compilation of References

Abbott, A., Nandeibam, S., & O'Shea, L. (2011). Explaining the variation in household recycling rates across the UK. *Ecological Economics*, 70(11), 2214–2223. DOI: 10.1016/j.ecolecon.2011.06.028

Abella, A., Ortiz-de-Urbina-Criado, M., & De-Pablos-Heredero, C. (2019). A methodology to design and redesign services in smart cities based on the citizen experience. *Information Polity*, 24(2), 183–197. DOI: 10.3233/IP-180116

Aboueid, S., Beyene, M., & Nur, T. (2023). Barriers and enablers to implementing environmentally sustainable practices in healthcare: A scoping review and proposed roadmap. *Healthcare Management Forum*, 36(6), 405–413. DOI: 10.1177/08404704231183601 PMID: 37357691

Acemoglu, D., & Restrepo, P. (2017). Robots and Jobs. Evidence from U.S. Labor Markets. *National Bureau of Economic Research, Working Paper* 23285.

Acevedo Rehbein, A. (19/02/2019), Inteligencia artificial en el arbitraje internacional: de la predicción legal a los laudos emitidos por robots | Garrigues.

Adamovic, M. (2022). How does employee cultural background influence the effects of telework on job stress? The roles of power distance, individualism, and beliefs about telework. *International Journal of Information Management*, 62, 102437. DOI: 10.1016/j.ijinfomgt.2021.102437

Adams, D. J. (2022). *An investigation into the sustainability practices of large food manufacturers with operations in Australia and their supply chains* (Doctoral dissertation, Swinburne University of Technology).

Afzal, A., Khan, S., Daud, S., Ahmad, Z., & Butt, A. (2023). Addressing the digital divide: Access and use of technology in education. *Journal of Social Sciences Review*, 3(2), 883–895. DOI: 10.54183/jssr.v3i2.326

Ahmad, S. (2015). Green Human Resource Management: Policies and practices. *Cogent Business & Management*, 2(1), 1030817. Advance online publication. DOI: 10.1080/23311975.2015.1030817

Ainley, J., & Carstens, R. (2018). *Teaching and Learning International Survey (TALIS) 2018 Conceptual Framework OECD*. Education Working Papers, 187, OECD Publishing, Paris. https://doi.org/DOI: 10.1787/19939019

Ajila, C. M., Brar, S. K., Verma, M., Tyagi, R. D., Godbout, S., & Valéro, J. R. (2012). Bio-processing of agro-byproducts to animal feed. *Critical Reviews in Biotechnology*, 32(4), 382–400. DOI: 10.3109/07388551.2012.659172 PMID: 22380921

Ajzen, I. (1985). From Intentions to Actions: A Theory of Planned Behavior. *Action Control*, 11–39. DOI: 10.1007/978-3-642-69746-3_2

Ajzen, I. (1991). The theory of planned behavior. *Organizational Behavior and Human Decision Processes*, 50(2), 179–211. DOI: 10.1016/0749-5978(91)90020-T

Aktas, E., Sahin, H., Topaloglu, Z., Oledinma, A., Huda, A. K. S., Irani, Z., Sharif, A. M., van't Wout, T., & Kamrava, M. (2018). A consumer behavioural approach to food waste. *Journal of Enterprise Information Management*, 31(5), 658–673. DOI: 10.1108/JEIM-03-2018-0051

Alexander, A. (2023). In 2022, Woolworths generated an estimated 184,260 tonnes of edible food waste. Accessed from https://app.impaakt.com/analyses/in-2022-woolworths-generated-an-estimated-184260-tonnes-of-edible-food-waste-136837

Al-Habaibeh, A., Watkins, M., Waried, K., & Javareshk, M. B. (2021). Challenges and opportunities of remotely working from home during Covid-19 pandemic. *Global Transitions*, 3, 99–108. DOI: 10.1016/j.glt.2021.11.001 PMID: 34870136

Alhassan, H., Kwakwa, P. A., & Owusu-Sekyere, E. (2020). Households' source separation behaviour and solid waste disposal options in Ghana's Millennium City. *Journal of Environmental Management*, 259, 110055. DOI: 10.1016/j.jenvman.2019.110055 PMID: 31929038

Ali, I., Arslan, A., Chowdhury, M., Khan, Z., & Tarba, S. Y. (2022). Reimagining global food value chains through effective resilience to COVID-19 shocks and similar future events: A dynamic capability perspective. *Journal of Business Research*, 141, 1–12. DOI: 10.1016/j.jbusres.2021.12.006 PMID: 34908632

Allen, J., Davis, D., & Soskin, M. (1993). Using Coupon Incentives in Recycling Aluminum: A Market Approach to Energy Conservation Policy. *The Journal of Consumer Affairs*, 27(2), 300–318. DOI: 10.1111/j.1745-6606.1993.tb00750.x

Al-Mamary, Y. H., & Alshallaqi, M. (2022, October-December). Impact of autonomy, innovativeness, risk-taking, proactiveness, and competitive aggressiveness on students' intention to start a new venture. *Journal of Innovation & Knowledge*, 7(4), 1–10. DOI: 10.1016/j.jik.2022.100239

Al-Maqbali, H., Kader, A., Albalushi, J., Luimula, M., & Calbureanu-Popescu, C. (2022). Impact of image features on visual attention: An eye-tracking study. En T. Ahram & C. Falcão (Eds.), *Usability and User Experience* (Vol. 39). AHFE International Conference. AHFE Open Access. AHFE International, USA. http://doi.org/DOI: 10.54941/ahfe1001732

Alonso, C., Kothari, S., & Rehman, S. (2020). How artificial intelligence could widen the gap between rich and poor nations. IMF Blog, 2.

Alshehri, A. A., Cheema, E., Yahyouche, A., Haque, M. S., & Jalal, Z. (2021). Evaluating the role and integration of general practice pharmacists in England: A cross-sectional study. *International Journal of Clinical Pharmacy*, 43(6), 1609–1618. DOI: 10.1007/s11096-021-01291-6 PMID: 34080088

AlSkaif, T., Crespo-Vazquez, J. L., Sekuloski, M., van Leeuwen, G., & Catalao, J. P. S. (2022). Blockchain-Based Fully Peer-to-Peer Energy Trading Strategies for Residential Energy Systems. *IEEE Transactions on Industrial Informatics*, 18(1), 231–241. DOI: 10.1109/TII.2021.3077008

Al-Surf, M. (2023, August 15). Sustainable Healthcare: Green Practices in the Medical Industry. https://www.linkedin.com/pulse/sustainable-healthcare-green-practices-medical-industry-al-surf/

Alzate, R., & Vázquez, E. (2014). *Resolución de disputas en línea (RDL). Las claves de la mediación en línea*. Reus S.A.

Amabile, T. M. (1996). *Creativity in context: Update to "The Social Psychology of Creativity"*. Westview Press.

Ammirato, S., Felicetti, A. M., Linzalone, R., Corvello, V., & Kumar, S. (2023). Still our most important asset: A systematic review on human resource management in the midst of the fourth industrial revolution. *Journal of Innovation & Knowledge*, 8(3), 100403. DOI: 10.1016/j.jik.2023.100403

Anåker, A., & Elf, M. (2014). Sustainability in nursing: A concept analysis. *Scandinavian Journal of Caring Sciences*, 28(2), 381–389. DOI: 10.1111/scs.12121 PMID: 24602178

Anand, S., & Barua, M. K. (2022). Modeling the key factors leading to post-harvest loss and waste of fruits and vegetables in the agri-fresh produce supply chain. *Computers and Electronics in Agriculture*, 198, 106936. DOI: 10.1016/j.compag.2022.106936

Anderson, L., Grudnoff, M., Hawking, T., & Campbell, R. (2023). Food waste in Australia and how supermarkets profit from it. In a *Discussion Paper*. The Australian Institute. Accessed from https://apo.org.au/node/324366

Antón Juárez, I. (2021, March). *Marketplaces* que personalizan precios a través del Big Data y de los Algoritmos: ¿Esta práctica es legal en atención al Derecho de la Competencia Europeo? *Cuadernos de Derecho Transnacional*, 13(1), 42. DOI: 10.20318/cdt.2021.5951

APCO. (2024). Australia's 2025 National Packaging Targets. Accessed from https://apco.org.au/national-packaging-targets

Apollo, M., Mostowska, J., Legut, A., Maciuk, K., & Timothy, D. J. (2023). Gender differences in competitive adventure sports tourism. *Journal of Outdoor Recreation and Tourism*, 42, 100604. DOI: 10.1016/j.jort.2022.100604

Aragón, F., & Severi, M. (2004). *Personal characteristics of entrepreneurs. Differences with corporate executives*. Universidad del CEMA.

ARD/ZDF. (2023). *ARD/ZDF-Onlinestudie 2023*. https://www.ard-zdf-onlinestudie.de/

Aria, M., & Cuccurullo, C. (2017). bibliometrix : An R-tool for comprehensive science mapping analysis. *Journal of Informetrics*, 11(4), 959–975. DOI: 10.1016/j.joi.2017.08.007

Arnold, W., Arnold, D., Neher, A., & Miles, M. P. (2019). Developing a contemporary measure of employee perceptions of their work unit's psychological sense of community. *Journal of Workplace Learning*, 32(1), 16–34. DOI: 10.1108/JWL-03-2019-0040

Arun Sampaul Thomas, G., & Harold Robinson, Y. (2020). *IoT*. Big Data, Blockchain and Machine Learning Besides Its Transmutation with Modern Technological Applications., DOI: 10.1007/978-3-030-39119-5_4

Aschemann-Witzel, J., De Hooge, I., Amani, P., Bech-Larsen, T., & Oostindjer, M. (2015). Consumer-related food waste: Causes and potential for action. *Sustainability (Basel)*, 7(6), 6457–6477. DOI: 10.3390/su7066457

Asociación de Emprendedores de México (ASEM). (2023, 10 de noviembre). El 64 por ciento de emprendedores mexicanos no reciben apoyo gubernamental: ASEM [64% of Mexican entrepreneurs do not receive governmental support: ASEM]. CONCANACO SERVYTUR México. *El Financiero*. https://www.concanaco.com.mx/prensa/tepuedeinteresar/el-64-por-ciento-de-emprendedores-mexicanos-no-reciben-apoyo-gubernamental-asem-

Atanda, S. A., Pessu, P. O., Agoda, S., Isong, I. U., & Ikotun, I. (2011). The concepts and problems of post–harvest food losses in perishable crops. *African Journal of Food Science*, 5(11), 603–613.

Augurzky, B., & Kolodziej, I. (2018). *Fachkräftebedarf im Gesundheits- und Sozialwesen 2030*. RWI - Leibniz-Institut für Wirtschaftsforschung.

Austin, J., Hatfield, D. B., Grindle, A. C., & Bailey, J. S. (1993). INCREASING RECYCLING IN OFFICE ENVIRONMENTS: THE EFFECTS OF SPECIFIC, INFORMATIVE CUES. *Journal of Applied Behavior Analysis*, 26(2), 247–253. DOI: 10.1901/jaba.1993.26-247 PMID: 16795793

Australian Food and Grocery Council. (2024). How We help. https://www.afgc.org.au/about-afgc/how-we-help

Australian Government. (2017). National Food Waste Strategy: Halving Australia's Food Waste by 2030. Accessed from https://www.agriculture.gov.au/sites/default/files/documents/national-food-waste-strategy.pdf

Ávila-Gutiérrez, M. J., Suarez-Fernandez de Miranda, S., & Aguayo-González, F. (2022). Occupational Safety and Health 5.0—A Model for Multilevel Strategic Deployment Aligned with the Sustainable Development Goals of Agenda 2030. *Sustainability (Basel)*, 14(11), 6741. DOI: 10.3390/su14116741

Ayuso, L., Requena, F., Jiménez-Rodriguez, O., & Khamis, N. (2020). The effects of COVID-19 confinement on the Spanish family: Adaptation or change? *Journal of Comparative Family Studies*, 51(3-4), 274–287. DOI: 10.3138/jcfs.51.3-4.004

Bachner, F., Bobek, J., Habimana, K., Ladurner, J., Lepuschutz, L., Ostermann, H., Rainer, L., Schmidt, A., Zuba, M., Quentin, W., & Winkelmann, J. (2019). Das österreichische Gesundheitssystem. *European Observatory on Health Systems ans Policies*, 20(3), 1-288.

Bachor, N., & Susebeek, L. (2015). Personalsuche im Gesundheitswesen. In Naegler, H. (Ed.), *Personalmanagement im Krankenhaus* (pp. 174–179). MWV Medizinisch Wissenschaftliche Verlagsgesellschaft.

Badsar, M., Moghim, M., & Ghasemi, M. (2023). Analysis of factors influencing farmers' sustainable environmental behavior in agriculture activities: Integration of the planned behavior and the protection motivation theories. *Environment, Development and Sustainability*, 25(9), 9903–9934. DOI: 10.1007/s10668-022-02468-3

Bahri-Ammari, N., Soliman, M., & Ben Salah, O. (2022). The Impact of Employer Brand on Job Seekers' Attitudes and Intentions: The Moderating Role of Value Congruence and Social Media. *Corporate Reputation Review*. Advance online publication. DOI: 10.1057/s41299-022-00154-8

Baker, J., Nelson, T., & Liu, H. (2020). Artificial intelligence in precision agriculture: A review. *Computers and Electronics in Agriculture*, 179, 105–123.

Balaji, M., & Arshinder, K. (2016). Modeling the causes of food wastage in Indian perishable food supply chain. *Resources, Conservation and Recycling*, 114, 153–167. DOI: 10.1016/j.resconrec.2016.07.016

Ballesteros, T. (2021). International Perspectives on Online Dispute Resolution in the E-Commerce Landscape. *International Journal of Online Dispute Resolution*, 2(2), 87. DOI: 10.5553/IJODR/235250022021008002002

Bamberg, S., & Möser, G. (2007). Twenty years after Hines, Hungerford, and Tomera: A new meta-analysis of psycho-social determinants of pro-environmental behaviour. *Journal of Environmental Psychology*, 27(1), 14–25. DOI: 10.1016/j.jenvp.2006.12.002

Bandi, A., & Fellah, A. (2022a). An Implementation and Evaluation of Blockchain-based Digital Health Passports. *2022 International Conference on Inventive Computation Technologies (ICICT)*, 476–482. IEEE. DOI: 10.1109/ICICT54344.2022.9850724

Bandura, A., & Walters, R. (1977). *Social learning theory*. Prentice Hall., https://www.asecib.ase.ro/mps/Bandura_SocialLearningTheory.pdf

Barghusen, R., Sattler, C., Deijl, L., Weebers, C., & Matzdorf, B. (2021). Motivations of farmers to participate in collective agri-environmental schemes: The case of Dutch agricultural collectives. *Ecosystems and People (Abingdon, England)*, 17(1), 539–555. DOI: 10.1080/26395916.2021.1979098

Barroso, F., & Santos, R. (2012). *Proposal of a methodology supported by ICTs to determine the relationship between critical thinking and entrepreneurial competencies of undergraduate students. Research progress. Proceedings of the Joint Ibero-American Conference on Learning Technologies (Ccita)*. Technological Institute of Mérida. Mérida, Yucatán, Mexico.

Barzman, M., Bàrberi, P., Birch, A. N. E., Boonekamp, P., Dachbrodt-Saaydeh, S., Graf, B., Hommel, B., Jensen, J. E., Kiss, J., Kudsk, P., Lamichhane, J. R., Messéan, A., Moonen, A.-C., Ratnadass, A., Ricci, P., Sarah, J.-L., & Sattin, M. (2015). Eight principles of integrated pest management. *Agronomy for Sustainable Development*, 35(4), 1199–1215. DOI: 10.1007/s13593-015-0327-9

Bastanchury-López, M. T., De-Pablos-Heredero, C., Montes-Botella, J. L., Martin-Romo-Romero, S., & Garcia, A. (2020). Impact of dynamic capabilities on performance in dairy sheep farms in Spain. *Sustainability (Basel)*, 12(8), 3368. DOI: 10.3390/su12083368

Basumatary, R., & Arora, V. K. (2018). Review on the storage structure for longer shelf-life of vegetables. *Progressive Agriculture*, 18(2), 145–161. DOI: 10.5958/0976-4615.2018.00028.5

Batista, L., Gong, Y., Pereira, S., Jia, F., & Bittar, A. (2019). Circular supply chains in emerging economies – a comparative study of packaging recovery ecosystems in China and Brazil. *International Journal of Production Research*, 57(23), 7248–7268. DOI: 10.1080/00207543.2018.1558295

Baum, T., Mooney, K., & Roberts, C. (2022). *Tourism employment and economic recovery in a post-pandemic world*. Routledge., DOI: 10.4324/9780367334056

Beck, J., & Stember, J. (2020). *Der demographische Wandel: Zwischen Digitalisierung, Aufgabenwandel und neuem Personalmanagement*. Nomos. DOI: 10.5771/9783748902713

Beier, M. E. (2015). *Facing the challenges of a multi-age workforce: A use-inspired approach* (Finkelstein, L. M., Truxillo, D. M., Fraccaroli, F., & Kanfer, R., Eds.). Taylor & Francis Group.

Belchior, R., Vasconcelos, A., Guerreiro, S., & Correia, M. (2022). A Survey on Blockchain Interoperability: Past, Present, and Future Trends. *ACM Computing Surveys*, 54(8), 1–41. DOI: 10.1145/3471140

Benedic, M. (2023). Hybrid work for small businesses: Strategies for reaping benefits. *The Journal of Business Strategy*. Advance online publication. DOI: 10.1108/JBS-09-2022-0163

Benyam, A. (2019). *An interdisciplinary examination of behaviours and policy preferences for domestic food waste reduction: The case of households in Central Queensland, Australia* (Doctoral dissertation, CQUniversity).

Berelson, K., Simini, F., Tryfonas, T., & Cooper, P. (2018). Smart sensor-based hot searching to improve office well-being. Proceedings of the First International Conference on Digital Tools & Uses Congress - DTUC & 18. https://doi.org/ DOI: 10.1145/3240117.3240131

Berger, J., & Barasch, A. (2018). A Candid Advantage? The Social Benefits of Candid Photos. *Social Psychological & Personality Science*, 9(8), 1010–1016. DOI: 10.1177/1948550617732390

Berniak-Woźny, J., & Rataj, M. (2023). Towards Green and Sustainable Healthcare: A Literature Review and Research Agenda for Green Leadership in the Healthcare Sector. *International Journal of Environmental Research and Public Health*, 20(2), 908. DOI: 10.3390/ijerph20020908 PMID: 36673663

Bernstad, A. (2014). Household food waste separation behavior and the importance of convenience. *Waste Management (New York, N.Y.)*, 34(7), 1317–1323. DOI: 10.1016/j.wasman.2014.03.013 PMID: 24780762

Bernstein, A., Diamond, R., McQuade, T., & Pousada, B. (2022). Housing market spillovers: Evidence from the end of rent control in Cambridge, Massachusetts. *The American Economic Review*, 112(10), 3235–3270. DOI: 10.1257/aer.20211218

Biedenbach, T., & Müller, R. (2012). Absorptive, innovative and adaptive capabilities and their impact on project and project portfolio performance. *International Journal of Project Management*, 30(5), 621–635. DOI: 10.1016/j.ijproman.2012.01.016

Bieńkowska, A., Koszela, A., & Tworek, K. (2021). Verification of the Job Performance Model based on 'Employees' Dynamic Capabilities in organisations under the COVID-19 pandemic crisis. *Engineering Management in Production and Services*, 13(3), 66–85. DOI: 10.2478/emj-2021-0022

Bieńkowska, A., & Tworek, K. (2020). Job performance model based on Employees' Dynamic Capabilities (EDC). *Sustainability (Basel)*, 12(6), 2250. DOI: 10.3390/su12062250

Bilbao, A., & Pachano, S. (2002). *Traits and attitudes of entrepreneurs*. Venezuela, Andean Development Corporation – CAF.

Bilska, B., Wrzosek, M., Kołożyn-Krajewska, D., & Krajewski, K. (2015). Food losses and food waste in the context of sustainable development of the food sector. *The China Business Review*, 14(9), 452–462. DOI: 10.17265/1537-1506/2015.09.005

Binbusayyis, A., & Vaiyapuri, T. (2023). A professional-driven blockchain framework for sharing E-Portfolio in the context of Industry 4.0. *ICT Express*, 9(2), 140–149. DOI: 10.1016/j.icte.2022.03.010

Birkmaier, A., Imeri, A., Riester, M., & Reiner, G. (2023). Preventing waste in food supply networks-a platform architecture for AI-driven forecasting based on heterogeneous big data. *Procedia CIRP*, 120, 708–713. DOI: 10.1016/j.procir.2023.09.063

Bitkom (2023). *Wie die Deutschen Social Media nutzen*. https:// www.bitkom.org/sites/main/files/2023-02/BitkomChartsSocialMedia2023.pdf

Boffa, D., Prencipe, A., Papa, A., Corsi, C., & Sorrentino, M. (2023). Boosting circular economy via the b-corporation roads. The effect of the entrepreneurial culture and exogenous factors on sustainability performance. *The International Entrepreneurship and Management Journal*, 19(2), 523–561. DOI: 10.1007/s11365-023-00835-8

Bommisetti, R. K., Syed, S. M., Verma, M., Charugulla, S., Subbalakshmi, A. V. V. S., & Emani, S. (2024). Development of HR Metrics and Plans for Employee Engagement in Banking Sector Using Blockchain Technology. *2024 5th International Conference on Intelligent Communication Technologies and Virtual Mobile Networks (ICICV)*, 837–842. IEEE. DOI: 10.1109/ICICV62344.2024.00138

Boniface, M. (2006). The meaning of adventurous activities for 'women in the outdoors.'. *Journal of Adventure Education and Outdoor Learning*, 6(1), 9–24. DOI: 10.1080/14729670685200711

Boskovic, S. (2021). *Health and longterm care workforce: Demographic challenges and potential contribution of migration and digital technology*. Publications Office of the European Union.

Bouarar, A. C., Mouloudj, K., Makhlouf, A., & Mouloudj, S. (2023). Exploring Intention to Purchase Energy-Efficient Home Appliances: An Extension of the Theory of Planned Behavior. In Goel, R., & Baral, S. (Eds.), *Handbook of Research on Sustainable Consumption and Production for Greener Economies* (pp. 58–73). IGI Global., DOI: 10.4018/978-1-6684-8969-7.ch004

Brand, N. (2003). *How ADR works*. American Bar Association Committee on Alternative Dispute Resolution.

Brennan, L., Parker, L., Lockrey, S., Verghese, K., Chin, S., Langley, S., ... & Alessi, N. (2021). The wicked problem of packaging and consumers: Innovative approaches for sustainability research. *Sustainable Packaging*, 137-176.

Bresler, M., Romsdal, A., Strandhagen, J. O., & Oluyisola, O. E. (2020). Principles and research agenda for sustainable, data-driven food production planning and control. In *Advances in Production Management Systems. The Path to Digital Transformation and Innovation of Production Management Systems: IFIP WG 5.7 International Conference, APMS 2020, Novi Sad, Serbia,August 30–September 3, 2020,Proceedings, Part I* (pp. 634-641). Springer International Publishing. DOI: 10.1007/978-3-030-57993-7_72

Brock, H. (2022). Das Gesundheitssystem der Schweiz. *ÖKZ*, 63(1), 22-24.

Brodribb, P., McCann, M., & Motavallia, J. (2020). *A study of waste in the cold food chain and opportunities for improvement*. Expert Group and Thinkwell Australia Pty Ltd for Department of Agriculture, Water and the Environment and Refrigerants Australia.

Brooks, E. J., & Lewis, D. R. (2020). Impact of corporate sustainability programs on workplace food waste reduction in Australia. *Journal of Environmental Management*, 258, 110034.

Brothers, K. J., Krantz, P. J., & McClannahan, L. E. (1994). OFFICE PAPER RECYCLING: A FUNCTION OF CONTAINER PROXIMITY. *Journal of Applied Behavior Analysis*, 27(1), 153–160. DOI: 10.1901/jaba.1994.27-153 PMID: 16795821

Bryan, B. A., Nolan, M., McKellar, L., Connor, J. D., Newth, D., Harwood, T., King, D., Navarro, J., Cai, Y., Gao, L., Grundy, M., Graham, P., Ernst, A., Dunstall, S., Stock, F., Brinsmead, T., Harman, I., Grigg, N. J., Battaglia, M., & Hatfield-Dodds, S. (2016). Land-use and sustainability under intersecting global change and domestic policy scenarios: Trajectories for Australia to 2050. *Global Environmental Change*, 38, 130–152. DOI: 10.1016/j.gloenvcha.2016.03.002

Brynjolfsson, E., & McAfee, A. (2011). *Race Against the Machine: How the Digital Revolution is Accelerating Innovation, Driving Productivity, and Irreversibly Transforming Employment and the Economy*. Digital Frontier Press.

Bull, I., & Winter, F. (1991). Community differences in business birth and business growths. *Journal of Business Venturing*, 6(1), 29–43. DOI: 10.1016/0883-9026(91)90004-W

Bundesamt für Gesundheit b (BAG) (2023). *Kennzahlen der Schweizer Spitäler*. https://spitalstatistik.bagapps.ch/data/download/kzp21_publication.pdf?v=1679384362

Bundesministerium für Arbeit, Soziales, Gesundheit und Konsumentenschutz (2019). *Das österreichische Gesundheitssystem*. https://broschuerenservice.sozialministerium.at/Home/Download?publicationId=636

Bundesministerium für Soziales, Gesundheit, Pflege und Konsumentenschutz (2023). *Krankenanstalten in Österreich*. https://www.sozialministerium.at/dam/jcr:0a2c1fb9-68c3-4355-bf22-ff0d11c0186e/KA-Verzeich nis%202023-10-21.xlsx

Bungard, W., & Lück, H. E. (1974). *Forschungsartefakte und nicht-reaktive Meßverfahren*. Teubner. DOI: 10.1007/978-3-322-94911-0

Burns, A. C., Biswas, A., & Babin, L. A. (1993). The Operation of Visual Imagery as a Mediator of Advertising Effects. *Journal of Advertising*, 22(2), 71–85. DOI: 10.1080/00913367.1993.10673405

Burri, R. V. (2012). Visual rationalities: Towards a sociology of images. *Current Sociology*, 60(1), 45–60. DOI: 10.1177/0011392111426647

Calderón-Fajardo, V., Anaya-Sánchez, R., Rejón-Guardia, F., & Molinillo, S. (2024). Neurotourism Insights: Eye Tracking and Galvanic Analysis of Tourism Destination Brand Logos and AI Visuals. *Tourism & Management Studies*, 20(3), 53–78. DOI: 10.18089/tms.20240305

Callon, M., Courtial, J. P., & Laville, F. (1991). Co-word analysis as a tool for describing the network of interactions between basic and technological research: The case of polymer chemsitry. *Scientometrics*, 22(1), 155–205. DOI: 10.1007/BF02019280

Calvo-Porral, C., & Rodríguez-Fernández, M. (2015). Food for thought: The food waste global issue. In *Experiencias en la modelación de la toma de decisiones en la salud humana, medio ambiente y desarrollo humano: Tomo 1* (pp. 1-23). Universidad de Granada.

Cao, Y., Tao, L., Wu, K., & Wan, G. (2020). Coordinating joint greening efforts in an agri-food supply chain with environmentally sensitive demand. *Journal of Cleaner Production*, 277, 123883. DOI: 10.1016/j.jclepro.2020.123883

Cárdenas Herrera, J. (2024), El impacto de la Inteligencia Artificial en la investigación, https://vertice.cpd.ua.es/290670|http://hdl.handle.net/10045/141247

Cárdenas-Martínez, L. D. (2019). Creativity and education in the twenty-first century. Inter-*American Journal of Research. Education and Pedagogy*, 12(2), 211–224. DOI: 10.15332/25005421.5014

Caroll, R. T. (2000). *Becoming a critical thinker. A guide for the new millennium*. Pearson Publishing.

Carrasco-Garrido, C., De-Pablos-Heredero, C., & Rodríguez-Sánchez, J.-L. (2023). Exploring hybrid telework: A bibliometric analysis. *Heliyon*, 9(12), e22472. DOI: 10.1016/j.heliyon.2023.e22472 PMID: 38076145

Carrillo-Labella, R., Fort, F., & Parras-Rosa, M. (2020). Motives, barriers, and expected benefits of ISO 14001 in the agri-food sector. *Sustainability (Basel)*, 12(5), 1724. DOI: 10.3390/su12051724

Carter, L. P., & Thompson, C. E. (2021). Workplace food waste management: The role of pro-environmental behavior. *Resources, Conservation and Recycling*, 168, 105302.

Cary, J., & Roberts, A. (2011). The limitations of environmental management systems in Australian agriculture. *Journal of Environmental Management*, 92(3), 878–885. DOI: 10.1016/j.jenvman.2010.10.055 PMID: 21084146

Castro Salcedo, J. P., & Calle Lituma, N. S. (2023). Survival as a strategy for increasing adventure tourism in Ecuador.

CESUMA University. (2023). *What is meaningful learning?*https://www.cesuma.mx/blog/que-es-el-aprendizaje-significativo.html

Chadburn, A., Smith, J., & Milan, J. (2017). Productivity drivers of knowledge workers in the central London office environment. *Journal of Corporate Real Estate*, 19(2), 66–79. DOI: 10.1108/JCRE-12-2015-0047

Chakravarthy, B. S. (1982). Adaptation: A promising metaphor for strategic management. *Academy of Management Review*, 7(1), 35–44. DOI: 10.2307/257246

Chan, E. S., Hon, A. H., Chan, W., & Okumus, F. (2014). What drives employees' intentions to implement green practices in hotels? The role of knowledge, awareness, concern and ecological behaviour. *International Journal of Hospitality Management*, 40, 20–28. DOI: 10.1016/j.ijhm.2014.03.001

Chapman, D. S., Uggerslev, K. L., Carroll, S. A., Piasentin, K. A., & Jones, D. A. (2005). Applicant attraction to organizations and job choice: A meta-analytic review of the correlates of recruiting outcomes. *The Journal of Applied Psychology*, 90(5), 928–944. DOI: 10.1037/0021-9010.90.5.928 PMID: 16162065

Chapman, J., Skinner, N., & Seale, S. (2013). Working towards sustainability: Exploring the workplace as a site for pro-environmental behaviour change. In *Motivating change: sustainable design and behaviour in the built environment* (pp. 56–70). Routledge.

Chartres, C. J., & Noble, A. (2015). Sustainable intensification: Overcoming land and water constraints on food production. *Food Security*, 7(2), 235–245. DOI: 10.1007/s12571-015-0425-1

Chaudhary, R. (2020). Green Human Resource Management and Employee Green Behavior: An Empirical Analysis. *Corporate Social Responsibility and Environmental Management*, 27(2), 630–641. DOI: 10.1002/csr.1827

Chawla, G., Lugosi, P., & Hawkins, R. (2022). Factors influencing hospitality employees' pro-environmental behaviours toward food waste. *Sustainability (Basel)*, 14(15), 9015. DOI: 10.3390/su14159015

Chegere, M. J. (2018). Post-harvest losses reduction by small-scale maize farmers: The role of handling practices. *Food Policy*, 77, 103–115. DOI: 10.1016/j.foodpol.2018.05.001

Chen, F., Li, X., Ma, J., Yang, Y., & Liu, G. J. (2018). An Exploration of the Impacts of Compulsory Source-Separated Policy in Improving Household Solid Waste-Sorting in Pilot Megacities, China: A Case Study of Nanjing. *Sustainability 2018, Vol. 10, Page 1327, 10*(5), 1327. DOI: 10.3390/su10051327

Chen, C., Gregoire, M. B., Arendt, S., & Shelley, M. C. (2011). College and university dining services administrators' intention to adopt sustainable practices: Results from US institutions. *International Journal of Sustainability in Higher Education*, 12(2), 145–162. DOI: 10.1108/14676371111118200

Cheng, J.-C., Lee, N.-Y., Chi, C., & Chen, Y.-H. (2018). Blockchain and smart contract for digital certificate. *2018 IEEE International Conference on Applied System Invention (ICASI)*, 1046–1051. IEEE. DOI: 10.1109/ICASI.2018.8394455

Chen, J., Lv, Z., & Song, H. (2019). Design of personnel big data management system based on blockchain. *Future Generation Computer Systems*, 101, 1122–1129. DOI: 10.1016/j.future.2019.07.037

Chiappetta Jabbour, C. J., Sarkis, J., Lopes de Sousa Jabbour, A. B., Scott Renwick, D. W., Singh, S. K., Grebinevych, O., Kruglianskas, I., & Filho, M. G. (2019). Who is in charge? A review and a research agenda on the 'human side' of the circular economy. *Journal of Cleaner Production*, 222, 793–801. DOI: 10.1016/j.jclepro.2019.03.038

Christensen, C. M., Hall, T., Dillon, K., & Duncan, D. S. (2016). Know your customers' jobs to be done. *Harvard Business Review*, 94(9), 54–62.

Christopoulos, K., Eleftheriou, K., & Nijkamp, P. (2021). The role of pre-pandemic teleworking and E-commerce culture in the COVID-19 dispersion in Europe. *Letters in Spatial and Resource Sciences*, 15(1), 1–16. DOI: 10.1007/s12076-021-00286-1 PMID: 34745370

Chrobog, C. K. (2014). *Wasted: understanding the economic and social impact of food waste* (Doctoral dissertation).

Chua, S. J. L., Myeda, N. E., & Teo, Y. X. (2023). Facilities management: Toward implementation of flexible work arrangements (FWA) during COVID-19. *Journal of Facilities Management*, 21(5), 697–716. DOI: 10.1108/JFM-09-2021-0101

Clark, P., Anderson, H., & Mitchell, R. (2022). Assessing the direct impact of pro-environmental behavior on sustainability outcomes: Evidence from longitudinal studies. *Journal of Environmental Management*, 290(1), 112–128.

Clegg, B., & Birch, P. (2001). *Instant creativity*. Granica.

Cobo, M. J., López-Herrera, A. G., Herrera-Viedma, E., & Herrera, F. (2011). An approach for detecting, quantifying, and visualizing the evolution of a research field: A practical application to the Fuzzy Sets Theory field. *Journal of Informetrics*, 5(1), 146–166. DOI: 10.1016/j.joi.2010.10.002

Cohen, J. (1960). A coefficient of agreement for nominal scales. *Educational and Psychological Measurement*, 20(1), 37–46. DOI: 10.1177/001316446002000104

Cohen, W. M., & Levinthal, D. A. (1990). Absorptive capacity: A new perspective on learning and innovation. *Administrative Science Quarterly*, 35(1), 128–152. DOI: 10.2307/2393553

Coiné, T., & Babbitt, M. (2014). *A world gone social*. Amacom.

Coles (2024). Charity and community partners. *Accessed from*https://www.coles.com.au/about/our-partners/community/partnerships

Coles group. (2023). Together to zero waste. *Accessed from*https://www.colesgroup.com.au/sustainability/?page=environment

Conforti, F. (2020), "A vueltas con las diferencias entre una videoconferencia y una mediación online", *Revista Jurídica SEPIN*.https://blog.sepin.es/2020/11/videoconferencia-mediacion-online-diferencias/5 de noviembre de 2020

Cooper, P. B., Maraslis, K., Tryfonas, T., & Oikonomou, G. (2017). An intelligent hot-desking model harnessing the power of occupancy sensing data. *Facilities*, 35(13/14), 766–786. DOI: 10.1108/F-01-2016-0014

Costa, A., Mouro, C., & Duarte, A. P. (2022). Waste separation—Who cares? Organizational climate and supervisor support's role in promoting pro-environmental behaviors in the workplace. *Frontiers in Psychology*, 13, 1082155. Advance online publication. DOI: 10.3389/fpsyg.2022.1082155 PMID: 36619029

Cyfert, S., Chwiłkowska-Kubala, A., Szumowski, W., & Miśkiewicz, R. (2021). The process of developing dynamic capabilities: The conceptualization attempt and the results of empirical studies. *PLoS One*, 16(4), e0249724. DOI: 10.1371/journal.pone.0249724 PMID: 33914761

D'Avanzo, W. (2021). *Italian Smart Working*. An Innovative Approach to Improve Productivity in Public Administration., DOI: 10.1007/978-3-030-85304-4_19

Daddi, T., Heras-Saizarbitoria, I., Marrucci, L., Rizzi, F., & Testa, F. (2021). The effects of green supply chain management capability on the internalisation of environmental management systems and organisation performance. *Corporate Social Responsibility and Environmental Management*, 28(4), 1241–1253. DOI: 10.1002/csr.2144

Dagliati, A., Malovini, A., Tibollo, V., & Bellazzi, R. (2021). Health informatics and EHR to support clinical research in the COVID-19 pandemic: An overview. *Briefings in Bioinformatics*, 22(2), 812–822. DOI: 10.1093/bib/bbaa418 PMID: 33454728

Dahlsrud, A. (2008). How corporate social responsibility is defined: An analysis of 37 definitions. *Corporate Social Responsibility and Environmental Management*, 15(1), 1–13. DOI: 10.1002/csr.132

Dai, J., Ahmed, Z., Sinha, A., Pata, U. K., & Alvarado, R. (2023). Sustainable green electricity, technological innovation, and ecological footprint: Does democratic accountability moderate the nexus? *Utilities Policy*, 82, 101541. DOI: 10.1016/j.jup.2023.101541

Davies, A. (2020). Food sharing. In *Routledge handbook of sustainable and regenerative food systems* (pp. 204–217). Routledge. DOI: 10.4324/9780429466823-15

De Bono, E. (1996). *Creative thinking*. Editorial Paidós Mexicana.

De Corato, U. (2020). Improving the shelf-life and quality of fresh and minimally processed fruits and vegetables for a modern food industry: A comprehensive critical review from the traditional technologies into the most promising advancements. *Critical Reviews in Food Science and Nutrition*, 60(6), 940–975. DOI: 10.1080/10408398.2018.1553025 PMID: 30614263

De Giacomo, M. R., Testa, F., Iraldo, F., & Formentini, M. (2019). Does Green Public Procurement lead to Life Cycle Costing (LCC) adoption? *Journal of Purchasing and Supply Management*, 25(3), 100500. DOI: 10.1016/j.pursup.2018.05.001

de Jesus, A., & Mendonça, S. (2018). Lost in Transition? Drivers and Barriers in the Eco-innovation Road to the Circular Economy. *Ecological Economics*, 145, 75–89. DOI: 10.1016/j.ecolecon.2017.08.001

De la Torre, S. (1997). *Creativity and training: identification, design and evaluation*. Trillas.

De la Vega, M. (2004). *Self-employment manual*. Youth Council of Castile.

Delenz Lorieto, N. (7 de octubre de 2020), "La inteligencia artificial en el arbitraje internacional", available at La inteligencia artificial en el arbitraje internacional — Guardiana.

Deng, N., & Liu, J. (2021). Where did you take those photos? Tourists' preference clustering based on facial and background recognition. *Journal of Destination Marketing & Management*, 21, 100632. DOI: 10.1016/j.jdmm.2021.100632

Deng, W., Lin, Y., & Chen, L. (2021). Exploring Destination Choice Intention by Using the Tourism Photographic: From the Perspectives of Visual Esthetic Processing. *Frontiers in Psychology*, 12, 713739. DOI: 10.3389/fpsyg.2021.713739 PMID: 34867592

Denyer, D., & Tranfield, D. (2009). Producing a systematic review. In *The Sage handbook of organizational research methods*. SAGE.

Department of Climate Change. Energy the Environment and Water- DCCEEW. (2023). Reducing Australia's food waste. *Waste and Recycling*. Accessed from https://www.dcceew.gov.au/environment/protection/waste/food-waste

Department of the Environment and Energy. (2017). Working together to reduce food waste in Australia. In *a factsheet by DCCEEW*. Accessed from https://www.dcceew.gov.au/sites/default/files/documents/food-waste-fact-sheet.pdf

Despeisse, M., Baumers, M., Brown, P., Charnley, F., Ford, S. J., Garmulewicz, A., Knowles, S., Minshall, T. H. W., Mortara, L., Reed-Tsochas, F. P., & Rowley, J. (2017). Unlocking value for a circular economy through 3D printing: A research agenda. *Technological Forecasting and Social Change*, 115, 75–84. DOI: 10.1016/j.techfore.2016.09.021

Despoudi, S. (2021). Challenges in reducing food losses at producers' level: The case of Greek agricultural supply chain producers. *Industrial Marketing Management*, 93, 520–532. DOI: 10.1016/j.indmarman.2020.09.022

Devin, B., & Richards, C. (2018). Food waste, power, and corporate social responsibility in the Australian food supply chain. *Journal of Business Ethics*, 150(1), 199–210. DOI: 10.1007/s10551-016-3181-z

Dhar Dwivedi, A., Singh, R., Kaushik, K., Rao Mukkamala, R., & Alnumay, W. S. (2024). Blockchain and artificial intelligence for 5G-enabled Internet of Things: Challenges, opportunities, and solutions. *Transactions on Emerging Telecommunications Technologies*, 35(4), e4329. Advance online publication. DOI: 10.1002/ett.4329

Díaz Carrión, I. A. (2012). Turismo de aventura y participación de las mujeres en Jalcomulco (México). *Pasos (El Sauzal)*, 10(5), 531–542. DOI: 10.25145/j.pasos.2012.10.068

Digital Economy and Society Index (DESI) (2018) Senior Citizens.

Dobrovnik, M., Herold, D., Fürst, E., & Kummer, S. (2018). Blockchain for and in Logistics: What to Adopt and Where to Start. *Logistics (Basel)*, 2(3), 18. DOI: 10.3390/logistics2030018

Domínguez-Sagols, A. (2024, 3 de marzo). Transformando México a través del emprendimiento educativo [Transforming Mexico through educational entrepreneurship]. *El Economista*. https://www.eleconomista.com.mx/opinion/Transformando-Mexico-a-traves-del-Emprendimiento-Educativo-20240303-0037.html

Donthu, N., Kumar, S., Mukherjee, D., Pandey, N., & Lim, W. M. (2021). How to conduct a bibliometric analysis: An overview and guidelines. *Journal of Business Research*, 133, 285–296. DOI: 10.1016/j.jbusres.2021.04.070

Dovbischuk, I. (2022). Innovation-oriented dynamic capabilities of logistics service providers, dynamic resilience and firm performance during the COVID-19 pandemic. *International Journal of Logistics Management*, 33(2), 499–519. Advance online publication. DOI: 10.1108/IJLM-01-2021-0059

Drucker, P. (1993). *Management for the future. The 90s and beyond.* Grupo Editorial Norma.

Duan, J., Zhang, C., Gong, Y., Brown, S., of, Z. L.-I. J., & undefined 2020. (2020). A content-analysis based literature review in blockchain adoption within food supply chain. *Mdpi.Com*. DOI: 10.3390/ijerph17051784

Duarte Alonso, A., & Northcote, J. (2013). Investigating farmers' involvement in value-added activities: A preliminary study from Australia. *British Food Journal*, 115(10), 1407–1427. DOI: 10.1108/BFJ-04-2011-0104

Duarte, J., & Pinto-Gouveia, J. (2017). Mindfulness, self-compassion and psychological inflexibility mediate the effects of a mindfulness-based intervention in a sample of oncology nurses. *Journal of Contextual Behavioral Science*, 6(2), 125–133. DOI: 10.1016/j.jcbs.2017.03.002

Duc, A. H., Bays, P., & Husain, M. (2008). Eye movements as a probe of attention. *Progress in Brain Research*, 171, 403–411. DOI: 10.1016/S0079-6123(08)00659-6 PMID: 18718333

Dufty, N., & Jackson, T. (2018). Information and communication technology use in Australian agriculture. Accessed from https://www.agriculture.gov.au/sites/default/files/sitecollectiondocuments/abares/ict-use-australian-agriculture.pdf

Dunning, R. D., Johnson, L. K., & Boys, K. A. (2019). Putting Dollars to Waste. *Choices*, 34(1), 1–9.

Edwards, F., Dixon, J., Friel, S., Hall, G., Hannigan, I., Hattersley, L., Hogan, A., Larsen, K., Lawrence, M., Lockie, S., Lopata, A., Wilson, A., & Wood, B. 2011, *Food systems, climate change adaptation and human health in Australia* [NCCARF National Climate Change Adaptation Research Facility], [Canbera, A.C.T.]. Accessed from http://hdl.handle.net/10536/DRO/DU:30042087

Edwards, F., & Mercer, D. (2007). Gleaning from Gluttony: An Australian youth subculture confronts the ethics of waste. *The Australian Geographer*, 38(3), 279–296. DOI: 10.1080/00049180701639174

Egger, M. (2018). Gesundheitssysteme im internationalen Vergleich. In Egger, M., Razum, O., & Rieder, A. (Eds.), *Public Health Kompakt* (pp. 117–159). De Gruyter.

Egorova, M., D'Aponte, M., Ponomareva, D., & Minbaleev, A. (2021). The Impact of Digitalization on the Enterprise System: Russia and Italy and the discipline of smart working between constraints and opportunities. *Lexonomica*, 13(2), 151–166. DOI: 10.18690/lexonomica.13.2.151-166.2021

Eisenhardt, K. M., & Martin, J. A. (2000). Dynamic capabilities: What are they? *Strategic Management Journal*, 21(10-11), 1105–1121. DOI: 10.1002/1097-0266(200010/11)21:10/11<1105::AID-SMJ133>3.0.CO;2-E

El Azzaoui, A., Singh, S. K., Pan, Y., & Park, J. H. (2020). Block5GIntell: Blockchain for AI-Enabled 5G Networks. *IEEE Access : Practical Innovations, Open Solutions*, 8, 145918–145935. DOI: 10.1109/ACCESS.2020.3014356

El Economista. (2013, October 30). *Unemployment rises to 4.92% in September: INEGI.* https://eleconomista.com.mx/industrias/2013/10/18/tasa-desempleo-se-ubica-492-inegi [REMOVED HYPERLINK FIELD]

El Economista. (2023, November 24). *Costa Rica and Mexico are among the OECD countries with the most inequality.* https://www.eleconomista.com.mx/economia/Costa-Rica-y-Mexico-estan-entre-los-paises-de-la-OCDE-con-mas-desigualdad-20231124-0019.html

Elena-Bucea, A., Oliveira, T., Simões Coelho, P., & Cruz-Jesus, F. (2021). Assessing the role of age, education, gender, and income on the digital divide: Evidence for the EU-28. *Information Systems Frontiers*, 23(4), 1007–1021. DOI: 10.1007/s10796-020-10012-9

Elf, P., Werner, A., & Black, S. (2022). Advancing the circular economy through dynamic capabilities and extended customer engagement: Insights from small sustainable fashion enterprises in the UK. *Business Strategy and the Environment*, 31(6), 2682–2699. DOI: 10.1002/bse.2999

Ellewala, U. P., Amarasena, W. D. H., Lakmali, H. S., Senanayaka, L. M., & Senarathne, A. N. (2020). Secure Messaging Platform Based on Blockchain. *2020 2nd International Conference on Advancements in Computing (ICAC)*, 317–322. IEEE. DOI: 10.1109/ICAC51239.2020.9357306

El-Menawy, S. M. A., & Saleh, P. S. (2023). How does the mediating role of the use of social media platforms foster the relationship between employer attractiveness and generation Z intentions to apply for a job? *Future Business Journal*, 9(65), 1–13. DOI: 10.1186/s43093-023-00233-0

Endemann, M. (2021). Digitale Wege zum Personal, in: Das österreichische Gesundheitswesen. *ÖKZ, 62*(3-4), 59-60. DOI: 10.1007/s43830-021-0031-9

Endrejat, P. C., & Burnes, B. (2022). Draw it, check it, and change it: Reviving Lewin's topology to facilitate organisational change theory and practice. *The Journal of Applied Behavioral Science*, 60(1), 87–112. DOI: 10.1177/00218863221122875

Eriksen, C. W., & Yeh, Y. Y. (1985). Allocation of attention in the visual field. *Journal of Experimental Psychology. Human Perception and Performance*, 11(5), 583–597. DOI: 10.1037/0096-1523.11.5.583 PMID: 2932532

Erokhin, V., Mouloudj, K., Bouarar, A. C., Mouloudj, S., & Gao, T. (2024). Investigating farmers' intentions to reduce water waste through water-smart farming technologies. *Sustainability (Basel)*, 16(11), 4638. DOI: 10.3390/su16114638

Esposito, M., Tse, T., & Soufani, K. (2018). Introducing a Circular Economy: New Thinking with New Managerial and Policy Implications. *California Management Review*, 60(3), 5–19. DOI: 10.1177/0008125618764691

Estudio Global. (2023, 27 de septiembre). México es el tercer país con mayor innovación en Latinoamérica [Mexico is the third country with most innovation in Latin America]. CONCANACO SERVYTUR México. https://www.concanaco.com.mx/comercio/interesdecomercio/mexico-es-el-tercer-pais-con-mayor-innovacion-en-latinoamerica-senala-estudio-global-septiembre-27-2023#:~:text=13%3A35%3A48-,M%C3%A9xico%20es%20el%20tercer%20pa%C3%ADs%20con%20mayor%20innovaci%C3%B3n%20en%20Latinoam%C3%A9rica,mercado%2C%20instituciones%20y%20capital%20humano

EU-OSHA. (2018). *Foresight on new and emerging occupational safety and health risks associated with digitalisation by 2025.* https://osha.europa.eu/sites/default/files/documents/Foresight_Flyer_ES.pdf

EU-OSHA. (2024). *Psychosocial risks and stress at work. European Agency for Safety and Health at Work.* https://osha.europa.eu/en/themes/psychosocial-risks-and-mental-health/research

Eurofound (2024). *COVID-19 and digitalisation.* https://www.eurofound.europa.eu/en/covid-19-and-digitalisation

European Parliament. (2023). Health and Safety at work https://www.europarl.europa.eu/factsheets/es/sheet/56/la-salud-y-la-seguridad-en-el-trabajo

Evers, T., Li, G., & Zhang, H. (2021). The impact of COVID-19 on global tourism employment: A review and future perspectives. *Tourism Management Perspectives*, 39, 100–110. DOI: 10.1016/j.tmp.2021.100110

Expansión, C. N. N. (2013, October 30). *The Mexican economy grew only 1.5%.* https://www.cnnexpansion.com/economia/2013/08/20/mexico-crecimiento-pib-economia

Extremera, N., Mérida-López, S., Sánchez-Álvarez, N., & Quintana-Orts, C. (2018). How does emotional intelligence make one feel better at work? The mediational role of work engagement. *International Journal of Environmental Research and Public Health*, 15(9), 1909. DOI: 10.3390/ijerph15091909 PMID: 30200548

Fachrunnisa, O., & Hussain, F. K. (2020). Blockchain-based human resource management practices for mitigating skills and competencies gap in workforce. *International Journal of Engineering Business Management*, 12, 184797902096640. DOI: 10.1177/1847979020966400

Falcón, J. L. (2020). *Teacher job satisfaction: A qualitative cases study examining the perceptions of job satisfaction of teachers at a secondary school setting*. (Doctoral dissertation). Texas State University, Texas, USA. https://repository.library.northeastern.edu/files/neu:cj82r812t/fulltext.pdf

Fan, M., Khalique, A., Qalati, S. A., Gillal, F. G., & Gillal, R. G. (2022). Antecedents of sustainable e-waste disposal behavior: The moderating role of gender. *Environmental Science and Pollution Research International*, 29(14), 20878–20891. DOI: 10.1007/s11356-021-17275-y PMID: 34741741

Farace, S., van Laer, T., de Ruyter, K., & Wetzels, M. (2017). Assessing the effect of narrative transportation, portrayed action, and photographic style on the likelihood to comment on posted selfies. *European Journal of Marketing*, 51(11/12), 1961–1979. DOI: 10.1108/EJM-03-2016-0158

Farley, A., & Doyle, K. (2014). Classroom distractions: The impact of mobile phones on teacher stress. *Journal of Educational Psychology*, 106(3), 765–776.

Farr, M., Eagle, L., & Hay, R. (2018). *Key determinants of pro-environmental behaviour of land managers in the agricultural sector: literature review.*

Farrukh, M., Ansari, N., Raza, A., Wu, Y., & Wang, H. (2022). Fostering employee's pro-environmental behavior through green transformational leadership, green human resource management and environmental knowledge. *Technological Forecasting and Social Change*, 179, 121643. DOI: 10.1016/j.techfore.2022.121643

Fatoki, O. (2019). Hotel employees' pro-environmental behaviour: Effect of leadership behaviour, institutional support and workplace spirituality. *Sustainability (Basel)*, 11(15), 4135. DOI: 10.3390/su11154135

Faustino, S., Faria, I., & Marques, R. (2022). The myths and legends of king Satoshi and the knights of blockchain. *Journal of Cultural Economics*, 15(1), 67–80. DOI: 10.1080/17530350.2021.1921830

Feighey, W. (2003). Negative Image? Developing the Visual in Tourism Research. *Current Issues in Tourism*, 6(1), 76–85. DOI: 10.1080/13683500308667945

Ferasso, M., Beliaeva, T., Kraus, S., Clauss, T., & Ribeiro-Soriano, D. (2020). Circular economy business models: The state of research and avenues ahead. *Business Strategy and the Environment*, 29(8), 3006–3024. DOI: 10.1002/bse.2554

Ferguson, H., Warwick, L., Cooner, T. S., Leigh, J., Beddoe, L., Disney, T., & Plumridge, G. (2020). The nature and culture of social work with children and families in long-term casework: Findings of a qualitative longitudinal study. Child & Family Social Work, 25(3), 694–703. Portico. https://doi.org/DOI: 10.1111/cfs.12746

Ferioli, M., Gazzola, P., Grechi, D., & Vătămănescu, E.-M. (2022). Sustainable behaviour of B Corps fashion companies during Covid-19: A quantitative economic analysis. *Journal of Cleaner Production*, 374, 134010. DOI: 10.1016/j.jclepro.2022.134010

Fernandes Rodrigues Alves, M., Vasconcelos Ribeiro Galina, S., & Dobelin, S. (2018). Literature on organizational innovation: Past and future. *Innovation & Management Review*, 15(1), 2–19. DOI: 10.1108/INMR-01-2018-001

Fernández-Martín, A., Gutiérrez-García, A., Capafons, J., & Calvo, M. G. (2017). Adaptive attunement of selective covert attention to evolutionary-relevant emotional visual scenes. *Consciousness and Cognition*, 51, 223–235. DOI: 10.1016/j.concog.2017.03.011 PMID: 28411473

Ferrari, L., Cavaliere, A., De Marchi, E., & Banterle, A. (2019). Can nudging improve the environmental impact of food supply chain? A systematic review. *Trends in Food Science & Technology*, 91, 184–192. DOI: 10.1016/j.tifs.2019.07.004

Figueiredo, E., Margaça, C., Hernández-Sánchez, B., & Sánchez-García, J. C. (2024). Teleworking Effects on Mental Health—A Systematic Review and a Research Agenda. *International Journal of Environmental Research and Public Health*, 21(3), 243. DOI: 10.3390/ijerph21030243 PMID: 38541245

Filieri, R., Lin, Z., Pino, G., Alguezaui, S., & Inversini, A. (2021). The role of visual cues in eWOM on consumers' behavioral intention and decisions. *Journal of Business Research*, 135, 663–675. DOI: 10.1016/j.jbusres.2021.06.055

Filion, J. & Roy, G. (1996). *Didactic document.* School of Higher Commercial Studies (HEC). Québec, Montreal, Copec University Bookstore.

Finkbeiner, M., Inaba, A., & Schau, E. (2019). Life cycle assessment in agriculture: A review. *Agricultural Systems, 172,* 1-12. Foodwise Australia (2024). Fast facts on food waste. *Accessed from*https://www.foodwise.com.au/foodwaste/food-waste-fast-facts/

Fiorillo, D. (2013). Household waste recycling: National survey evidence from Italy. *Journal of Environmental Planning and Management*, 56(8), 1125–1151. DOI: 10.1080/09640568.2012.709180

Fishbein, M., & Ajzen, I. (1977). Belief, Attitude, Intention, and Behavior: An Introduction to Theory and Research. In *Philosophy and Rhetoric*. https://philpapers.org/rec/FISBAI?all_versions=1

Fisher, R., Ury, W., & Patton, B. (2011). *Getting to Yes: Negotiating Agreement Without Giving In*. Penguin.

Fletcher, L. (2023). The intersection of nursing and environmental health - A call to action for sustainable practices. *Journal of Advanced Practices in Nursing*, 8(6), 349.

Fogaça, N., & Junior, F. A. C. (2016). Is 'happy worker' more productive. *Management*, 4(4), 149–160.

Fogt Jacobsen, L., Pedersen, S., & Thøgersen, J. (2022). Drivers of and barriers to consumers' plastic packaging waste avoidance and recycling – A systematic literature review. *Waste Management (New York, N.Y.)*, 141, 63–78. DOI: 10.1016/j.wasman.2022.01.021 PMID: 35093857

Foncubierta Rodríguez, M. J., Popescu, C. R. G., & Ravina Ripoll, R. (2022). A New Leadership for a New Era: Effects of Association of Socio-Demographic Variables on the Leader's Competencies. In Popescu, C. R. G. (Ed.), *Handbook of research on building inclusive global knowledge societies for sustainable development*. IGI Global. DOI: 10.4018/978-1-6684-5109-0.ch001

Foncubierta-Rodríguez, M. J., Poza-Méndez, M., & Holgado-Herrero, M. (2024). Workplace health promotion programs: The role of compliance with workers' expectations, the reputation and the productivity of the company. *Journal of Safety Research*, 89, 56–63. DOI: 10.1016/j.jsr.2024.02.008 PMID: 38858063

Foncubierta-Rodríguez, M. J., & Sánchez-Montero, J. M. (2019). Towards happiness in workplace: Taking care of motivations and eliminating "digital fears", *Challenges.Revista de Ciencias de la Administración y Economía*, 9(18), 239–257. DOI: 10.17163/ret.n18.2019.04

Fraiz, J. A., de Carlos, P., & Araújo, N. (2020). Disclosing homogeneity within heterogeneity: A segmentation of Spanish active tourism based on motivational pull factors. *Journal of Outdoor Recreation and Tourism*, 30, 100294. DOI: 10.1016/j.jort.2020.100294

Franco, M. A. (2017). Circular economy at the micro level: A dynamic view of incumbents' struggles and challenges in the textile industry. *Journal of Cleaner Production*, 168, 833–845. DOI: 10.1016/j.jclepro.2017.09.056

Friesendorf, C., & Lüttschwager, S. (2021). *Digitale Gesundheitsanwendungen*. Springer. DOI: 10.1007/978-3-658-33983-8

Friman, A., & Hyytiä, N. (2022). The economic and welfare effects of food waste reduction on a food-production-driven rural region. *Sustainability (Basel)*, 14(6), 3632. DOI: 10.3390/su14063632

Fry, L. W. (2003). Toward a theory of spiritual leadership. *The Leadership Quarterly*, 14(6), 693–727. DOI: 10.1016/j.leaqua.2003.09.001

Fukumura, Y. E., Gray, J. M., Lucas, G. M., Becerik-Gerber, B., & Roll, S. C. (2021). Worker Perspectives on Incorporating Artificial Intelligence into Office Workspaces: Implications for the Future of Office Work. *International Journal of Environmental Research and Public Health*, 18(4), 1690. DOI: 10.3390/ijerph18041690 PMID: 33578736

Fulton, C. (2005). Hotdesking. *Mobile Information Systems*, II, 163–170. DOI: 10.1007/0-387-31166-1_12

Gala Durán, C. (2021). El teletrabajo en las Administraciones Públicas. *Trabajo, Persona, Derecho. Mercado*, (3), 69–94. DOI: 10.12795/TPDM.2021.i3.06

Gallego Gómez, C., & De Pablos Heredero, C. (2013). La gamificación y el enriquecimiento de las prácticas de innovación en la empresa: Un análisis de experiencias. *Intangible Capital*, 9(3), 800–822. DOI: 10.3926/ic.377

Gallup (2023). *State of the global workplace*. Recuperado el 10 de junio de 2024, de https://www.2468group.com/wp-content/uploads/2023/07/state-of-the-global-workplace-2023-download.pdf

Gámez, G. (1998). *Todos somos creatives* [We are all creative]. Ediciones Urano.

García San José, D. (2021, March). Implicaciones jurídicas y bioéticas de la Inteligencia Artificial (IA). Especial consideración al marco normativo internacional. *Cuadernos de Derecho Transnacional*, 13(1), 255–276. DOI: 10.20318/cdt.2021.5959

García-Flores, R., Juliano, P., & Petkovic, K. (2019). Handling food waste and losses: Criticalities and methodologies. In *Sustainable Food Supply Chains* (pp. 261–276). Academic Press. DOI: 10.1016/B978-0-12-813411-5.00018-1

Garczarek-Bąk, U., Szymkowiak, A., Gaczek, P., & Disterheft, A. (2021). A comparative analysis of neuromarketing methods for brand purchasing predictions among young adults. *Journal of Brand Management*, 28(2), 171–185. DOI: 10.1057/s41262-020-00221-7

GardenDrum. (2015). Ripe Near Me website connects food growers with consumers. *Accessed from*https://gardendrum.com/2015/08/28/ripe-near-me-website-connects-food-growers-with-consumers/

Garg, R., Kumar, A., & Sharma, S. (2021). Big data analytics for sustainable agriculture: Opportunities and challenges. *Journal of Cleaner Production*, 292, 125–137.

Gastón Marcen, A. (2021, October). El Reglamento general de Protección de Datos como modelo de las recientes propuestas de legislación digital europea. *Cuadernos de Derecho Transnacional*, 13(2), 209–232. DOI: 10.20318/cdt.2021.6256

Gaudreau, C., Guillaumie, L., Jobin, É., & Diallo, T. A. (2024). Nurses and climate change: A narrative review of nursing associations' recommendations for integrating Climate Change Mitigation Strategies. *Canadian Journal of Nursing Research*, 56(3), 193–203. DOI: 10.1177/08445621241229932 PMID: 38373438

Gazzola, P., Grechi, D., Ferioli, M., & Slavata, D. (2023). B Corps and listed companies: Empirical analysis on corporate social responsibility and innovation activity. *Kybernetes*, 52(12), 5928–5949. DOI: 10.1108/K-04-2022-0549

Geraldine, D. (2020). *Perveived effects of black female principales´servant leadership on teacher job satisfaction*. Doctoral dissertation. Grand Canyon University. ProQuest Dissertations Publishing. (202028029674). *Getting ready for digital transformation: Change your culture, workforce, and technology*. (s/f). EDUCAUSE Review. https://er.educause.edu/articles/2019/7/getting-ready-for-digital-transformation-change-your-culture-workforce-and-technology

Gerards & Xenidis. (3 December 2020), "Algorithmic discrimination in Europe: Challenges and Opportunities for EU equality law", *European Futures*. Available at: https://www.europeanfutures.ed.ac.uk/algorithmic-discrimination-in-europe-challenges-and-opportunities-for-eu-equa

Ghisellini, P., Cialani, C., & Ulgiati, S. (2016). A review on circular economy: The expected transition to a balanced interplay of environmental and economic systems. *Journal of Cleaner Production*, 114, 11–32. DOI: 10.1016/j.jclepro.2015.09.007

Ghisellini, P., Quinto, I., Passaro, R., & Ulgiati, S. (2024). Exploring environmental and social performances of circular start-ups: An orientation and certification assessment. *Business Strategy and the Environment*, 33(4), 3222–3241. DOI: 10.1002/bse.3620

Gholami, H., Rezaei, G., Saman, M. Z. M., Sharif, S., & Zakuan, N. (2016). State-of-the-art Green HRM System: Sustainability in the sports center in Malaysia using a multi-methods approach and opportunities for future research. *Journal of Cleaner Production*, 124, 142–163. DOI: 10.1016/j.jclepro.2016.02.105

Gifford, R., & Nilsson, A. (2014). Personal and social factors that influence pro-environmental concern and behaviour. *International Journal of Psychology*, 49(3), 278–290. DOI: 10.1002/ijop.12034 PMID: 24821503

Gil-Flores, J. (2017). The role of personal characteristics and school characteristics in explaining teacher job satisfaction. [English Ed]. *Revista de Psicodidáctica*, 22(1), 16–22. DOI: 10.1016/S1136-1034(17)30039-4

Gilman, E., Tamminen, S., Yasmin, R., Ristimella, E., Peltonen, E., Harju, M., Lovén, L., Riekki, J., & Pirttikangas, S. (2020). Internet of Things for Smart Spaces: A University Campus Case Study. *Sensors (Basel)*, 20(13), 3716. DOI: 10.3390/s20133716 PMID: 32630833

Glaeser, E., Kourtit, K., & Nijkamp, P. (2021). New urban challenges: Shared spaces in smart places – Overview and positioning. *Land Use Policy*, 111, 105672. DOI: 10.1016/j.landusepol.2021.105672

Godavarthi, B., Dhar, M., Devi, S. A., Raju, S. S., Balaram, A., & Srilakshmi, G. (2023). Blockchain integration with the internet of things for the employee performance management. *The Journal of High Technology Management Research*, 34(2), 100468. DOI: 10.1016/j.hitech.2023.100468

Godrich, S. L., Macau, F., Kent, K., Lo, J., & Devine, A. (2022). Food supply impacts and solutions associated with the COVID-19 pandemic: A regional Australian case study. *International Journal of Environmental Research and Public Health*, 19(7), 4116. DOI: 10.3390/ijerph19074116 PMID: 35409797

Golden, T. D., Veiga, J. F., & Dino, R. N. (2008). The Impact of Professional Isolation on Teleworker Job Performance and Turnover Intentions: Does Time Spent Teleworking, Interacting Face-to-Face, or Having Access to Communication-Enhancing Technology Matter? *The Journal of Applied Psychology*, 93(6), 1412–1421. DOI: 10.1037/a0012722 PMID: 19025257

Gomes, G. P., Coelho, A., & Ribeiro, N. (2024). A systematic literature review on sustainable HRM and its relations with employees' attitudes: state of art and future research agenda. *Journal of Organizational Effectiveness: People and Performance*. DOI: 10.1108/JOEPP-11-2023-0497

Gómez Valenzuela, E. (20/02/2023). *Resolución Judicial y Extrajudicial de controversias en la contratación electrónica,* Colex, A Coruña, pp. 208.

González-Mendes, S., González-Sánchez, R., Costa, C. J., & García-Muiña, F. (2023). Analysing the state of the art of Blockchain application in Smart Cities: A bibliometric study. *2023 18th Iberian Conference on Information Systems and Technologies (CISTI)*, 1–6. IEEE. DOI: 10.23919/CISTI58278.2023.10211371

González-Rodríguez, M. R., Díaz-Fernández, M. C., & Pulido-Pavón, N. (2023). Tourist destination competitiveness: An international approach through the travel and tourism competitiveness index. *Tourism Management Perspectives*, 47, 101127. DOI: 10.1016/j.tmp.2023.101127

Gonzalo Quiroga, M. (2022), "Covid-19, innovación y tecnología en la e-justicia alternativa: ¿algo hemos aprendido?", en Fariña Rivera, F. *et al.* (coord.), *Reflexiones mediadoras en la post pandemia*, Santiago de Compostela, ed. CUEMYC/ USC, pp. 184-206.

Gonzalo Quiroga, M. (2023). La inteligencia artificial en el arbitraje internacional 2.0. Oportunidades y desafíos en un futuro que ya es presente. *Cuadernos de Derecho Transnacional*, 15(2), 516–550. DOI: 10.20318/cdt.2023.8067

Gonzalo Quiroga, M., & Suñez Tejera, Y. (2024). *Innovación y resolución de conflictos: La intersección entre las nuevas tecnologías, la Inteligencia Artificial y los Métodos Alternativos*. Ediciones ONBC.

Gonzalo, M., & Barriga, K. (2016). "El acuerdo de confidencialidad en el arbitraje", y "El acuerdo de confidencialidad en la mediación". In *Sánchez García, A. et al. (coord.), Tipología contractual de los mecanismos alternativos de solución de conflictos* (pp. 113–137). Tirant lo Blanch.

Goodman, B. (2011). The need for a 'sustainability curriculum' in nurse education. *Nurse Education Today*, 31(8), 733–737. DOI: 10.1016/j.nedt.2010.12.010 PMID: 21232830

Gossling, S. (2021). Tourism employment and the impact of COVID-19: A global perspective. *Journal of Sustainable Tourism*, 29(5), 741–758. DOI: 10.1080/09669582.2021.1898717

Govindarajulu, N., & Daily, B. F. (2004). Motivating employees for environmental improvement. *Industrial Management & Data Systems*, 104(4), 364–372. DOI: 10.1108/02635570410530775

Graham-Rowe, E., Jessop, D. C., & Sparks, P. (2014). Identifying motivations and barriers to minimizing household food waste. *Resources, Conservation and Recycling*, 84, 15–23. DOI: 10.1016/j.resconrec.2013.12.005

Greaves, M., Zibarras, L. D., & Stride, C. (2013). Using the theory of planned behavior to explore environmental behavioral intentions in the workplace. *Journal of Environmental Psychology*, 34, 109–120. DOI: 10.1016/j.jenvp.2013.02.003

Greiling, D. (2019). Das österreichische Gesundheitswesen im internationalen Vergleich. In Fuchs, M., Greiling, D., & Rosenberger, M. (Eds.), *Gut versorgt? Ökonomie und Ethik im Gesundheits- und Pflegebereich* (pp. 23–43). Nomos.

Griggs, C., Fernandez, A., & Callanan, M. (2017). Nursing and the barriers to sustainable health care: A literature review. *British Journal of Nursing (Mark Allen Publishing)*, 26(22), 1230–1237. DOI: 10.12968/bjon.2017.26.22.1230 PMID: 29240479

Grilli, G., & Curtis, J. (2021). Encouraging pro-environmental behaviours: A review of methods and approaches. *Renewable & Sustainable Energy Reviews*, 135, 110039. DOI: 10.1016/j.rser.2020.110039

Grimani, A., Aboagye, E., & Kwak, L. (2019). The effectiveness of workplace nutrition and physical activity interventions in improving productivity, work performance and workability: A systematic review. *BMC Public Health*, 19(1), 1676. DOI: 10.1186/s12889-019-8033-1 PMID: 31830955

Groen, B. A. C., van Triest, S. P., Coers, M., & Wtenweerde, N. (2018). Managing flexible work arrangements: Teleworking and output controls. *European Management Journal*, 36(6), 727–735. DOI: 10.1016/j.emj.2018.01.007

Gruel, M., & Tirrel, H. (2024). Digital recruiting. In *Reference Module in Social Sciences*. https://doi.org/DOI: 10.1016/B978-0-443-13701-3.00066-9

Guarnieri, P., de Aguiar, R. C., Thomé, K. M., & Watanabe, E. A. D. M. (2021). The role of logistics in food waste reduction in wholesalers and small retailers of fruits and vegetables: A multiple case study. *Logistics (Basel)*, 5(4), 77. DOI: 10.3390/logistics5040077

Guo, S., Sun, W., Chen, W., Zhang, J., & Liu, P. (2021). Impact of artificial elements on mountain landscape perception: An eye-tracking study. *Land (Basel)*, 10(10), 1102. DOI: 10.3390/land10101102

Gupta, P. (2012). *The innovation solution. Making innovation more pervasive, predictable and profitable*. Accelper Consulting.

Gupta, R., Shukla, V. K., Rao, S. S., Anwar, S., Sharma, P., & Bathla, R. (2020). Enhancing Privacy through "Smart Contract" using Blockchain-based Dynamic Access Control. *2020 International Conference on Computation, Automation and Knowledge Management (ICCAKM)*, 338–343. IEEE. DOI: 10.1109/ICCAKM46823.2020.9051521

Gusmerotti, N. M., Testa, F., Macellari, M., & Frey, M. (2020). Corporate social responsibility embeddedness through a social network analysis: The case of an Italian multiutility company. *Corporate Social Responsibility and Environmental Management*, 27(2), 455–469. DOI: 10.1002/csr.1812

Habl, C., & Bachner, F. (2010). *Das österreichische Gesundheitssystem im internationalen Vergleich 2009*. Österreichisches Bundesinstitut für Gesundheitswesen.

Hadinejad, A., Moyle, B. D., Scott, N., & Kralj, A. (2018). Emotional responses to tourism advertisements: The application of FaceReader™. *Tourism Recreation Research*, 44(1), 131–135. DOI: 10.1080/02508281.2018.1505228

Haider, S., Fatima, F., Bakhsh, K., & Ahmed, M. (2019). Effect of intervention on employees' intentions to use environmentally sustainable work practices: A field experiment. *Journal of Environmental Management*, 248, 109334. DOI: 10.1016/j.jenvman.2019.109334 PMID: 31466182

Hao, J. L., Yu, S., Tang, X., & Wu, W. (2022). Determinants of workers' pro-environmental behaviour towards enhancing construction waste management: Contributing to China's circular economy. *Journal of Cleaner Production*, 369, 133265. DOI: 10.1016/j.jclepro.2022.133265

Harfmann, B. (2022). High-pressure processing enhances food safety, extends shelf life. Accessed from https://www.bevindustry.com/articles/94807-high-pressure-processing-enhances-food-safety-extends-shelf-life

Harrison, R., & Broughton, A. (2021). The impact of environmental regulations on pro-environmental behavior: Evidence from a longitudinal study. *Environmental Policy and Governance*, 31(4), 345–359.

Haryanto, M. (2019). Nursing Shortage: Myth or Fact. *Orthopedic Nursing*, 38(1), 1–2. DOI: 10.1097/NOR.0000000000000535 PMID: 30676566

Hashim, S., Omar, M. K., Ab Jalil, H., & Mohd Sharef, N. (2022). Trends on technologies and artificial intelligence in education for personalized learning: Systematic literature review. *International Journal of Academic Research in Progressive Education and Development*, 11(1). Advance online publication. DOI: 10.6007/IJARPED/v11-i1/12230

Heidrich, O., & Harvey, J. (2018). An examination into recycling and waste management attitudes and behaviors by UK employees. *Environmental Engineering and Management Journal*, 17(1), 71–81. DOI: 10.30638/eemj.2018.009

Heidt, L., Gauger, F., & Pfnür, A. (2023). Work from Home Success: Agile work characteristics and the Mediating Effect of supportive HRM. *Review of Managerial Science*, 17(6), 2139–2164. DOI: 10.1007/s11846-022-00545-5

Henseler, J., and Chin, W.W. (2010). A Comparison of Approaches for the Analysis of Interaction Effects Between Latent Variables Using Partial Least Squares Path Modeling. Structural Equation Modeling, (17:1), 82–109. https://doi.org/DOI: 10.1080/10705510903439003

Hermano, V., Martin-Cruz, N., & Pajares, J. (2022). The effect of project management dynamic capabilities on firm performance. *Baltic Journal of Management*, 17(2), 266–284. Advance online publication. DOI: 10.1108/BJM-06-2021-0218

Hernández-Linares, R., Kellermanns, F. W., & López-Fernández, M. C. (2018). A note on the relationships between learning, market, and entrepreneurial orientations in family and nonfamily firms. *Journal of Family Business Strategy*, 9(3), 192–204. DOI: 10.1016/j.jfbs.2018.08.001

Hernández, R., Fernández, C., & Baptista, P. (2014). *Metodología de la investigación* [Methodology of Research]. 6th ed.). Mc Graw Hill.

Herrera Enríquez, G., & Rodríguez Rodríguez, G. (2017). Turismo y Sistemas Empresariales Resilientes: Factores Críticos de Adaptabilidad en Baños de Agua Santa – Ecuador. *Revista De Gestão E Secretariado, 8*(1), 01–25. https://doi.org/DOI: 10.7769/gesec.v8i1.606

Herrero, C. C., Laso, J., Cristóbal, J., Fullana-i-Palmer, P., Albertí, J., Fullana, M., Herrero, Á., Margallo, M., & Aldaco, R. (2022). Tourism under a life cycle thinking approach: A review of perspectives and new challenges for the tourism sector in the last decades. *The Science of the Total Environment*, 845, 157261. DOI: 10.1016/j.scitotenv.2022.157261 PMID: 35835187

Hewage, H. A. S., K.U, H., K.M.J.B, J., K.P.C., H., Senarathne, A. N., & Wijekoon, J. (2020). Smart Human Resource Management System to Maximize Productivity. *2020 International Computer Symposium (ICS)*, 479–484. IEEE. DOI: 10.1109/ICS51289.2020.00100

Hilborne, N. (febrero 2019), Robot mediator settles first ever court case - Legal Futures

Hill, A. D., White, M. A., & Wallace, J. C. (2014). Unobtrusive measurement of psychological constructs in organizational research. *Organizational Psychology Review*, 4(2), 148–174. DOI: 10.1177/2041386613505613

Hinson, J. D. (2018). *Transformational leadership, perceived principal support, and collective efficacy: Predictors of teacher job satisfaction*. Doctoral dissertation. The University of Alabama, Tuscaloosa, AL. https://ir.ua.edu/handle/123456789/5411

Hirst, A. (2011). Settlers, vagrants and mutual indifference: Unintended consequences of hot-desking. *Journal of Organizational Change Management*, 24(6), 767–788. DOI: 10.1108/09534811111175742

Hobday, A. J., & McDonald, J. (2014). Environmental issues in Australia. *Annual Review of Environment and Resources*, 39(1), 1–28. DOI: 10.1146/annurev-environ-012113-111451

Hodgins, K., & Parizeau, K. (2020). Farm-to-fork… and beyond? A call to incorporate food waste into food systems research. *Food & Foodways*, 28(1), 43–60. DOI: 10.1080/07409710.2020.1718280

Hoffman, J. E. (1998). Visual attention and eye movements. In H. Pashler (Ed.), *Attention* (pp. 119–153). Psychology Press/Erlbaum (UK) Taylor & Francis. https://psycnet.apa.org/record/1998-07791-003

Hoffman, A. J. (2005). Climate Change Strategy: The Business Logic behind Voluntary Greenhouse Gas Reductions. *California Management Review*, 47(3), 21–46. DOI: 10.2307/41166305

Hofstede Insights. (2023). Country comparison tool. https://www.hofstede-insights.com/country-comparison-tool?countries=austria%2Cgermany%2Cswitzerland

Hofstede, G. (2011). Dimensionalizing cultures: The Hofstede Model in context. *Online Readings in Psychology and Culture*, 2(1), 1–26. DOI: 10.9707/2307-0919.1014

Holik, A. (2016). Relationship of economic growth with tourism sector. *JEJAK: Jurnal Ekonomi dan Kebijakan, 9*(1), 16-33. https://doi.org/DOI: 10.15294/jejak.v9i1.7184

Hollat, S., & Siebelt, P. (2019). Möglichkeiten und Grenzen des Dienstleistungsmarketings für Apotheken. In Matusiewicz, D., Stratmann, F., & Wimmer, J. (Eds.), *Marketing im Gesundheitswesen* (pp. 421–432). Springer. DOI: 10.1007/978-3-658-20279-8_31

Homewood Health. (2022, febrero). *The Impact of Social Media on Body Image & Mental Health*. https://image.mkt.homewoodhealth.com/lib/fe3911717164047d7d1672/m/2/ab2c0a6a-aa5b-4a92-881d-fd56493b60c0.pdf

Honar Pajooh, H., Rashid, M., Alam, F., & Demidenko, S. (2021). Multi-Layer Blockchain-Based Security Architecture for Internet of Things. *Sensors (Basel)*, 21(3), 772. DOI: 10.3390/s21030772 PMID: 33498860

Hopkins, J., & Bardoel, A. (2023). The Future Is Hybrid: How Organisations Are Designing and Supporting Sustainable Hybrid Work Models in Post-Pandemic Australia. Sustainability 2023, Vol. 15, Page 3086, 15(4), 3086. https://doi.org/ DOI: 10.3390/su15043086

Horoś, I. K., & Ruppenthal, T. (2021). Avoidance of food waste from a grocery retail store owner's perspective. *Sustainability (Basel)*, 13(2), 550. DOI: 10.3390/su13020550

Horticulture Australia. (2024). Vegetable Industry Development Program. *Accessed from*https://ausveg.com.au/app/data/technical-insights/docs/PostHarvestManagementforVegetables.pdf

Huang, C., & Leung, L. (2020). Mobile phone usage and teacher stress in the classroom. *The Journal of Educational Research*, 113(2), 148–158.

Hunt, A. R., Reuther, J., Hilchey, M. D., & Klein, R. M. (2019). The Relationship Between Spatial Attention and Eye Movements. In Hodgson, T. (Ed.), *Processes of Visuospatial Attention and Working Memory* (pp. 255–278). Springer International Publishing., DOI: 10.1007/7854_2019_95

Hunter, W. C. (2012). Projected destination image: A visual analysis of Seoul. *Tourism Geographies*, 14(3), 419–443. DOI: 10.1080/14616688.2011.613407

Imports, J. (2001). *The Australian Apple Industry Squeeze.* Current Practice versus Best Practice. Economic Impacts of Apple. Accessed from https://citeseerx.ist.psu.edu/document?repid=rep1&type=pdf&doi=d017e0d9bc8a8ffa2b28ef2a619972f23c714455

Instituto Nacional de Estadística. (2023). *Tecnologías de la información y la comunicación en los hogares*https://www.ine.es/prensa/tich_2023.pdf

Instituto Nacional de Estadísticas. Censos. (22 de junio de 2016). *Índice de Precios al Productor de Disponibilidad Nacional.* https://anda.inec.gob.ec/anda/index.php/catalog/562/overview

Instituto Nacional de Estadísticas. Censos. (25 de noviembre de 2001). *Fascículo Censal del Catón Baños.*https://www.ecuadorencifras.gob.ec/documentos/web-inec/Bibliotecas/Fasciculos_Censales/Fasc_Cantonales/Tungurahua/Fasciculo_Banos.pdf

International Labour Organization (2002). *Certification of professional skills.*

International Labour Organization. (2002). *Certification of professional skills.* Author.

International Labour Organization. (2019). *Convention 190: Convention concerning the elimination of violence and harassment in the world of work, adopted by the conference at its one hundred and eighth session, Geneva, 21 June 2019*. Geneva: International Labour Organization.

International Telecommunication Union. (2023, October 10). *Facts and Figures 2023: The Gender Digital Divide*. ITU. https://www.itu.int/itu-d/reports/statistics/2023/10/10/ff23-the-gender-digital-divide/

Ipsen, C., van Veldhoven, M., Kirchner, K., & Hansen, J. P. (2021). Six Key Advantages and Disadvantages of Working from Home in Europe during COVID-19. International Journal of Environmental Research and Public Health 2021, Vol. 18, Page 1826, 18(4), 1826. https://doi.org/DOI: 10.3390/ijerph18041826

Ipsen, C., Kirchner, K., Bolisani, E., & Scarso, E. (2023). In a digitalising Europe: Unfolding knowledge of working from home during the COVID-19 pandemic in Italy and Denmark. *Work (Reading, Mass.)*, 74(1), 59–74. DOI: 10.3233/WOR-220137 PMID: 36189522

Jabbour, C. J. C., & Santos, F. C. A. (2008). Relationships between human resource dimensions and environmental management in companies: Proposal of a model. *Journal of Cleaner Production*, 16(1), 51–58. DOI: 10.1016/j.jclepro.2006.07.025

Jacquenet, C. (2021). Optimized, automated, and protective: An operator's view on future networks. *IEEE Transactions on Network and Service Management*, 18(2), 1350–1359. DOI: 10.1109/TNSM.2021.3076293

Jain, A., Gangwar, A., Kumari, C., & Mehra, P. S. (2024). A Survey on Blockchain for Rental Lease Management. *2024 11th International Conference on Reliability, Infocom Technologies and Optimization (Trends and Future Directions) (ICRITO)*, 1–5. IEEE. DOI: 10.1109/ICRITO61523.2024.10522110

Jain, A. (2021). *Impact of digitalization and artificial intelligence as causes and enablers of organizational change*. Nottingham University Business School.

Jamal, T., & Budke, C. (2020). Tourism in a world with pandemics: Local-global responsibility and action. *Journal of Tourism Futures*, 6(2), 181–188. DOI: 10.1108/JTF-02-2020-0014

James, W. (1890). *The principles of psychology* (Vol. 2). Henry Holt and Company., DOI: 10.1037/11059-000

Janiesch, C., Zschech, P., & Heinrich, K. (2021). Machine learning and deep learning. *Electronic Markets*, 31(3), 685–695. DOI: 10.1007/s12525-021-00475-2

Janmaimool, P. (2017). The role of descriptive social norms, organisational norms and personal norms in explaining solid waste management behaviours in workplaces. *Journal of Organizational Change Management*, 30(2), 184–198. DOI: 10.1108/JOCM-12-2016-0265

Jansen, L. J., Diercks, J., & Kupka, K. (2023). *Recrutainment - Gamifcation in Employer Branding,* Personalmarketing und Personalauswahl. Springer.

Jawahir, I. S., & Bradley, R. (2016). Technological Elements of Circular Economy and the Principles of 6R-Based Closed-loop Material Flow in Sustainable Manufacturing. *Procedia CIRP*, 40, 103–108. DOI: 10.1016/j.procir.2016.01.067

Jeevahan, J., Anderson, A., Sriram, V., Durairaj, R. B., Britto Joseph, G., & Mageshwaran, G. (2021). Waste into energy conversion technologies and conversion of food wastes into the potential products: A review. *International Journal of Ambient Energy*, 42(9), 1083–1101. DOI: 10.1080/01430750.2018.1537939

Jetten, J., Haslam, C., & Haslam, S. A. (2012). *The social cure: Identity, health and well-being*. Psychology Press. DOI: 10.4324/9780203813195

Jeyaraman, M., Ramasubramanian, S., Kumar, S., Jeyaraman, N., Selvaraj, P., Nallakumarasamy, A., Bondili, S. K., & Yadav, S. (2023). Multifaceted Role of Social Media in Healthcare: Opportunities, Challenges, and the Need for Quality Control. *Cureus*, 15(5), 1–9. DOI: 10.7759/cureus.39111 PMID: 37332420

Jiang, X., Mohamed, A. E. B., & Affifudin, A. H. B. (2024). Unveiling the Drivers of Chinese Tourists' Visit Intentions Regarding Malaysia. *Sustainability (Basel)*, 16(8), 3406. DOI: 10.3390/su16083406

Joardder, M. U., Hasan Masud, M., Joardder, M. U., & Masud, M. H. (2019). Causes of food waste. *Food preservation in developing countries: Challenges and solutions*, 27-55.

Johnson, M., Patel, R., & Turner, L. (2020). The role of public awareness campaigns in promoting pro-environmental behavior: A review of recent policies. *Journal of Environmental Psychology*, 65, 101–113.

Jones, T., & Lee, K. (2021). Quantifying the impact of pro-environmental behavior on organizational environmental performance. *Business Strategy and the Environment*, 30(3), 567–580.

Jöreskog, K. G., & Wold, H. The ML and PLS technique for modeling with latent variables: Historical and comparative aspects. In Jöreskog. K.G., and Would, H. (Eds.). Systems Under Indirect Observation. Part I. Amsterdam: North Holland, 1982, 1263-1270.

Jovanovic, S., & Rajh, E. (2022). Future of work in tourism: Digital skills and employment prospects. *International Journal of Hospitality Management*, 94, 102835. DOI: 10.1016/j.ijhm.2021.102835

Juríčková, Z., Lušňáková, Z., Hallová, M., Horská, E., & Hudáková, M. (2020). Environmental impacts and attitudes of agricultural enterprises for environmental protection and sustainable development. *Agriculture*, 10(10), 440. DOI: 10.3390/agriculture10100440

Juvan, E., & Dolnicar, S. (2022). How the COVID-19 pandemic has reshaped tourism employment: A comparative analysis. *Tourism Economics*, 28(1), 15–32. DOI: 10.1177/21684890211063367

Kamning, D. L. (2021). Exploring the impact of the COVID-19 pandemic on approaches to innovation in the consulting industry: A grounded theory pilot study. *Innovation & Management Review*. Advance online publication. DOI: 10.1108/INMR-05-2021-0076

Kamp, L.-M., Tirrel, H., & Winnen, L. (2024). The paradox of flexibility: Unraveling the impact of flexible work arrangements on affective commitment during the Covid-19 pandemic. *Economics & Sociology (Ternopil)*, 17(2), 151–172. DOI: 10.14254/2071-789X.2024/17-2/7

Kansal, M., Mitsis, A., Ananda, J., & Pearson, D. (2022). Challenges for food waste reduction campaigns: Requirements for Asian consumers in Australia. *Australasian Journal of Environmental Management*, 29(4), 368–385. DOI: 10.1080/14486563.2022.2143917

Karki, S. T., Bennett, A. C., & Mishra, J. L. (2021). Reducing food waste and food insecurity in the UK: The architecture of surplus food distribution supply chain in addressing the sustainable development goals (Goal 2 and Goal 12.3) at a city level. *Industrial Marketing Management*, 93, 563–577. DOI: 10.1016/j.indmarman.2020.09.019

Karlsson, J. Ch. (2012). Hot-Desking and Family Photos. Organizational Misbehaviour in the Workplace, 144–144. https://doi.org/DOI: 10.1057/9780230354630_64

Karpouzis, F., Lindberg, R., Walsh, A., Shah, S., Abbott, G., & Ball, K. (2024). Impact and process evaluation of a primary-school Food Education and Sustainability Training (FEAST) program in 10-12-year-old children in Australia: Pragmatic cluster non-randomized controlled trial. *BMC Public Health*, 24(1), 657. DOI: 10.1186/s12889-024-18079-8 PMID: 38429629

Kaswan, K. S., Dhanda, S. K., Dhatterwal, J. S., & Balusamy, B. (2023). Blockchain Technology in HR Processes. In *The Role of HR in the Transforming Workplace* (pp. 104–116). Productivity Press., DOI: 10.4324/9781003372622-8

Kayikci, S., & Khoshgoftaar, T. M. (2024). Blockchain meets machine learning: A survey. *Journal of Big Data*, 11(1), 9. DOI: 10.1186/s40537-023-00852-y

Kazancoglu, Y., Ekinci, E., Mangla, S. K., Sezer, M. D., & Kayikci, Y. (2021). Performance evaluation of reverse logistics in food supply chains in a circular economy using system dynamics. *Business Strategy and the Environment*, 30(1), 71–91. DOI: 10.1002/bse.2610

Keating, B. A., Carberry, P. S., Bindraban, P. S., Asseng, S., Meinke, H., & Dixon, J. (2010). Eco-efficient agriculture: Concepts, challenges, and opportunities. *Crop Science*, 50(S1), S-109. DOI: 10.2135/cropsci2009.10.0594

Kendzierskyj, S., Jahankhani, H., & Ndumbe, S. I. (2021). Blockchain for Strengthening the Privacy of Healthcare Data. In *Research Anthology on Blockchain Technology in Business, Healthcare, Education, and Government* (pp. 672–688). IGI Global. DOI: 10.4018/978-1-7998-5351-0.ch039

Kevin van Langen, S., Vassillo, C., Ghisellini, P., Restaino, D., Passaro, R., & Ulgiati, S. (2021). Promoting circular economy transition: A study about perceptions and awareness by different stakeholders groups. *Journal of Cleaner Production*, 316, 128166. DOI: 10.1016/j.jclepro.2021.128166

Khaksar, S. M. S., Chu, M.-T., Rozario, S., & Slade, B. (2020). Knowledge-based dynamic capabilities and knowledge worker productivity in professional service firms. The moderating role of organisational culture. *Knowledge Management Research and Practice*, 21(2), 241–258. DOI: 10.1080/14778238.2020.1794992

Khaleelullah, S., Vangapalli, S. T., Gaddam, M., Hanumakonda, V. S., & Goud Gangapuram, U. K. (2023). Verifcation of Academic Records Using Hyperledger Fabric and IPFS. *2023 3rd International Conference on Pervasive Computing and Social Networking (ICPCSN)*, 210–217. IEEE. DOI: 10.1109/ICPCSN58827.2023.00040

Khan, D., Jung, L. T., & Hashmani, M. A. (2021). Systematic Literature Review of Challenges in Blockchain Scalability. *Applied Sciences (Basel, Switzerland)*, 11(20), 9372. DOI: 10.3390/app11209372

Kiaya, V. (2014). Post-harvest losses and strategies to reduce them. *Technical Paper on Postharvest Losses* [ACF]. *Action Contre la Faim*, 25(3), 1–25.

Kim, J. Y., & Kim, M. J. (2023). Identifying customer preferences through the eye-tracking in travel websites focusing on neuromarketing. *Journal of Asian Architecture and Building Engineering*, 23(2), 515–527. DOI: 10.1080/13467581.2023.2244566

King, S., Hutchinson, S. A., & Boxall, N. J. (2021). *Advanced recycling technologies to address Australia's plastic waste*. Commonwealth Scientific and Industrial Research Organisation.

Kiran, B. R., Prasad, M. N. V., & Mohan, S. V. (2023). Farm to fork: sustainable agrifood systems. In *Sustainable and Circular Management of Resources and Waste Towards a Green Deal* (pp. 25–38). Elsevier. DOI: 10.1016/B978-0-323-95278-1.00012-7

Kirchherr, J., Reike, D., & Hekkert, M. (2017). Conceptualizing the circular economy: An analysis of 114 definitions. *Resources, Conservation and Recycling*, 127, 221–232. DOI: 10.1016/j.resconrec.2017.09.005

Kirst, R. W., Borchardt, M., de Carvalho, M. N. M., & Pereira, G. M. (2021). Best of the world or better for the world? A systematic literature review on benefit corporations and certified B corporations contribution to sustainable development. *Corporate Social Responsibility and Environmental Management*, 28(6), 1822–1839. DOI: 10.1002/csr.2160

Klein, A., Taieb, O., Xavier, S., Baubet, T., & Reyre, A. (2020). The benefits of mindfulness-based interventions on burnout among health professionals: A systematic review. *Explore (New York, N.Y.)*, 16(1), 35–43. DOI: 10.1016/j.explore.2019.09.002 PMID: 31727578

Klein, N., Deutz, P., & Ramos, T. B. (2022). A survey of Circular Economy initiatives in Portuguese central public sector organisations: National outlook for implementation. *Journal of Environmental Management*, 314, 114982. DOI: 10.1016/j.jenvman.2022.114982 PMID: 35436711

Knickmeyer, D. (2020). Social factors influencing household waste separation: A literature review on good practices to improve the recycling performance of urban areas. *Journal of Cleaner Production*, 245, 118605. DOI: 10.1016/j.jclepro.2019.118605

Koch, T., Gerber, C., & De Klerk, J. J. (2018). The impact of social media on recruitment: Are you LinkedIn? *SA Journal of Human Resource Management/SA Tydskrif vir Menslikehulpbronbestuur*, 16(0), a861. DOI: 10.4102/sajhrm.v16i0.861

Kocoglu-Tanyer, D., Dengiz, K. S., & Sacikara, Z. (2024). Nursing students' conceptualization of environmental problems: A descriptive cross-sectional study. *Nurse Education Today*, 140, 106296. DOI: 10.1016/j.nedt.2024.106296 PMID: 38972168

Kodithuwakku, N. (2022). *Importance of food waste reporting for collaboration between Australian retail, farming, and food rescue organisations* (Doctoral dissertation, CQUniversity).

Kok, C. L., & Palaniappan, K. (2023). A futuristic approach to decentralize and authenticate workplace safety records leveraging on blockchain distributed ledger network. In *Distributed Computing to Blockchain* (pp. 425–431). Elsevier., DOI: 10.1016/B978-0-323-96146-2.00002-4

Kollmuss, A., & Agyeman, J. (2002). Mind the gap: Why do people act environmentally and what are the barriers to pro-environmental behavior? *Environmental Education Research*, 8(3), 239–260. DOI: 10.1080/13504620220145401

Končar, J., Marić, R., & Vučenović, S. (2021). Exploring pro-environmental behaviour in FMCG supply chain. *Tehnicki Vjesnik (Strojarski Fakultet)*, 28(6), 2060–2071.

Kowalska, A. (2017). The issue of food losses and waste and its determinants. *LogForum, 13*(1).

Kragt, M. E., Dumbrell, N. P., & Blackmore, L. (2017). Motivations and barriers for Western Australian broad-acre farmers to adopt carbon farming. *Environmental Science & Policy*, 73, 115–123. DOI: 10.1016/j.envsci.2017.04.009

Krause, J. (2018). Relationship between the Voluntary Instrument of CSR in the Textile Industry in the Czech Republic and Financial Performance. *Fibres & Textiles in Eastern Europe*, 26(5(131)), 8–12. DOI: 10.5604/01.3001.0012.2524

Kristensen, H. S., Mosgaard, M. A., & Remmen, A. (2021). Integrating circular principles in environmental management systems. *Journal of Cleaner Production*, 286, 125485. DOI: 10.1016/j.jclepro.2020.125485

Kronenberg, J., Andersson, E., Barton, D. N., Borgström, S. T., Langemeyer, J., Björklund, T., Haase, D., Kennedy, C., Koprowska, K., Łaszkiewicz, E., McPhearson, T., Stange, E. E., & Wolff, M. (2021). The thorny path toward greening: Unintended consequences, trade-offs, and constraints in green and blue infrastructure planning, implementation, and management. *Ecology and Society*, 26(2), art36. DOI: 10.5751/ES-12445-260236

Kruger, M., Viljoen, A., & Saayman, M. (2016). Who visits the Kruger National Park, and why? identifying target markets. *Journal of Travel & Tourism Marketing*, 34(3), 312–340. DOI: 10.1080/10548408.2016.1156618

Kucera, J., Krulicky, T., & Navratilova, P. (2021). The trend of work from home and its advantages and disvantages during the COVID-19 pandemic: A comparative study. *Ad Alta-Journal of Interdisciplinary Research*, 11(2), 140–150. DOI: 10.33543/1102145150

Kumar, P., & Kumra, R. (2023) Problems of entrepreneurs in India – case of rural self-employment training institutes' trainees'. *International Journal of Entrepreneurship and Small Business*, 48(3), 231–244. ttps://www.researchgate.net/publication/368857512_Problems_of_entrepreneurs_in_India_-_case_of_rural_self-employment_training_institutes'_trainees

Kumar, P., Raj, A., & Kumar, V. A. (2024). Approach to Reduce Agricultural Waste via Sustainable Agricultural Practices. In *Valorization of Biomass Wastes for Environmental Sustainability: Green Practices for the Rural Circular Economy* (pp. 21–50). Springer Nature Switzerland. DOI: 10.1007/978-3-031-52485-1_2

Kumar, S., Jha, M., & Sharma, A. (2022). AI-based approaches for precision agriculture and their impact on sustainability. *AI & Society*, 37(1), 35–48.

Kummu, M., De Moel, H., Porkka, M., Siebert, S., Varis, O., & Ward, P. J. (2012). Lost food, wasted resources: Global food supply chain losses and their impacts on freshwater, cropland, and fertiliser use. *The Science of the Total Environment*, 438, 477–489. DOI: 10.1016/j.scitotenv.2012.08.092 PMID: 23032564

Lab, B. (2018). *What are B Corps?* Bai, H., & Li, N. (2023). Exploring Green Economic Efficiency Trends in Dominant Chinese Urban Agglomerations: A Super-Efficient SBM Model Approach. *Journal of the Knowledge Economy*. Advance online publication. DOI: 10.1007/s13132-023-01494-4

LaBerge, D. (1983). Spatial extent of attention to letters and words. *Journal of Experimental Psychology. Human Perception and Performance*, 9(3), 371–379. DOI: 10.1037/0096-1523.9.3.371 PMID: 6223977

LaMonica, H. M., Davenport, T. A., Roberts, A. E., & Hickie, I. B. (2021). Understanding technology preferences and requirements for health information technologies designed to improve and maintain the mental health and well-being of older adults: Participatory design study. *JMIR Aging*, 4(1), e21461. DOI: 10.2196/21461 PMID: 33404509

Landström, H., & Winborg, J. (1996). *Financial bootstrapping in small businesses-a resource-based view on small business finance*. Scandinavian Institute for Research in Entrepreneurship. Universidad Halmstad

Langford, A. (2020). *Agri-food transformations in Northern Australia* (Doctoral dissertation, The University of Queensland).

Langhof, J. G., & Güldenberg, S. (2020). Servant Leadership: A systematic literature review—toward a model of antecedents and outcomes. *German Journal of Human Resource Management: Zeitschrift Für Personalforschung*, 34(1), 32–68. DOI: 10.1177/2397002219869903

Lawler, E. E., Porter, L. W., & Tennenbaum, A. (1968). 'Managers' attitudes toward interaction episodes. *Journal of Applied Psychology*, 52(6p1), 432. https://doi.org/ DOI: 10.1037/h0026504

Leat, P. M., Lamprinopoulou-Kranis, C., Revoredo-Giha, C., & Kupiec-Teahan, B. (2011). *Agri-food supply chains and sustainability-related issues: evidence from across the Scottish agri-food economy.*

Lee, A., & Ride, K. (2018). Review of nutrition among Aboriginal and Torres Strait Islander people. *Australian Indigenous Health Reviews*, 20, 1–48.

Lee, J., & Park, S. (2022). Government incentives and their effects on organizational pro-environmental practices: A policy analysis. *Business Strategy and the Environment*, 31(2), 184–198.

Lee, P.-C., Huang, C.-Y., Huang, M.-H., & Hsu, M.-J. (2023). The behavioral intention of hospitals to promote sustainable development of green healthcare from the perspective of organizational stakeholders during the COVID-19 epidemic: A case study of hospitals in Taiwan. *Sustainability (Basel)*, 15(5), 4521. DOI: 10.3390/su15054521

Lee, R. M. (2019). Unobtrusive Methods. In Liamputtong, P. (Ed.), *Handbook of Research Methods in Health Social Sciences* (pp. 491–507). Springer. DOI: 10.1007/978-981-10-5251-4_85

Lee, Y. J., & De Young, R. (1994). Intrinsic satisfaction derived from office recycling behavior: A case study in Taiwan. *Social Indicators Research*, 31(1), 63–76. DOI: 10.1007/BF01086514

Lee, Y. J., de Young, R., & Marans, R. W. (1995). Factors Influencing Individual Recycling Behavior in Office Settings: A Study of Office Workers in Taiwan. *Environment and Behavior*, 27(3), 380–403. DOI: 10.1177/0013916595273006

Leka, S., & Houdmont, J. (Eds.). (2010). *Occupational health psychology*. Wiley Blackwell.

Le, N. T. T., Nguyen, Q. N., Phien, N. N., Duong-Trung, N., Huynh, T. T., Nguyen, T. P., & Son, H. X. (2019). Assuring non-fraudulent transactions in cash on delivery by introducing double smart contracts. *International Journal of Advanced Computer Science and Applications*, 10(5). Advance online publication. DOI: 10.14569/IJACSA.2019.0100584

Lewicki, R. J., Saunders, D. M., & Barry, B. (2015). *Negotiation: Readings, Exercises, and Cases*. McGraw-Hill Education.

Lian, H., Wang, D., & Li, H. (2020). Waste sorting and its effects on carbon emission reduction: Evidence from China. *Zhongguo Renkou Ziyuan Yu Huanjing*, 18(1), 26–34. DOI: 10.1016/j.cjpre.2021.04.027

Li, S., Huang, H., Liu, X., & Chen, Z. (2024). The power of visuals in destination advertising. *Annals of Tourism Research*, 107, 103790. DOI: 10.1016/j.annals.2024.103790

Liu, B., Moyle, B., Kralj, A., & Li, Y. (2023). Celebrity endorsement in tourism: Attention, emotional arousal and familiarity. *Tourism Management*, 98, 104750. DOI: 10.1016/j.tourman.2023.104750

Liu, B., Moyle, B., Kralj, A., & Li, Y. (2024). *Eye-Tracking in Tourism, Cognitive Psychology and Tourism* (Vol. 27). Tourism Social Science Series. Emerald Publishing Limited., DOI: 10.1108/S1571-504320240000027020

Liu, L., Han, M., Zhou, Y., Parizi, R. M., & Korayem, M. (2020). *Blockchain-Based Certification for Education*. Employment, and Skill with Incentive Mechanism., DOI: 10.1007/978-3-030-38181-3_14

Liu-Lastres, B., Mariska, D., Tan, X., & Ying, T. (2020). Can post-disaster tourism development improve destination livelihoods? A case study of Aceh, Indonesia. *Journal of Destination Marketing & Management*, 18, 100510. DOI: 10.1016/j.jdmm.2020.100510

Liute, A., & De Giacomo, M. R. (2022). The environmental performance of UK-based B Corp companies: An analysis based on the triple bottom line approach. *Business Strategy and the Environment*, 31(3), 810–827. DOI: 10.1002/bse.2919

Liu, W.-J., Chiu, W.-Y., & Hua, W. (2024). Blockchain-enabled renewable energy certificate trading: A secure and privacy-preserving approach. *Energy*, 290, 130110. DOI: 10.1016/j.energy.2023.130110

Liu, Y., & Whatson, S. (2020). Whose leadership role is more substantial for teacher professional collaboration, job satisfaction and organizational commitment: A lens of distributed leadership. *International Journal of Leadership in Education*. Advance online publication. DOI: 10.1080/13603124.2020.1820580

Li, W., Sun, K., Liu, X., Wang, Z., & Li, G. (2023). What attributes of mandatory waste management policy can enhance the separation intention of residents in China? A behaviour choice experiment. *Journal of Material Cycles and Waste Management*, 25(4), 2365–2380. DOI: 10.1007/s10163-023-01695-8

Li, W., Su, Z., Li, R., Zhang, K., & Wang, Y. (2020). Blockchain-Based Data Security for Artificial Intelligence Applications in 6G Networks. *IEEE Network*, 34(6), 31–37. DOI: 10.1109/MNET.021.1900629

Li, X., Cifuentes-Faura, J., & Tan, Y. (2023). Analyzing the low carbon and pro-environment behavior of agricultural enterprises based on organizational commitment and role models' guidance. *Environmental Science and Pollution Research International*, •••, 1–13. DOI: 10.1007/s11356-023-31302-0 PMID: 38079039

Li, Y. W., & Wan, L. C. (2025). Inspiring tourists' imagination: How and when human presence in photographs enhances travel mental simulation and destination attractiveness. *Tourism Management*, 106, 104969. DOI: 10.1016/j.tourman.2024.104969

Lockie, S., Fairley-Grenot, K., Ankeny, R., Botterill, L., Howlett, B., Mcbratney, A., ... & Woodhead, I. (2020). *The future of agricultural technologies*. Australian Council of Learned Academies (ACOLA).

Lohmer, J., & Lasch, R. (2020). Blockchain in operations management and manufacturing: Potential and barriers. *Computers & Industrial Engineering*, 149, 106789. Advance online publication. DOI: 10.1016/j.cie.2020.106789

Loloi, J., Berstein, A., & Dubin, J. (2023). „Likes" in Social Media: Does it carry any implications? *Société Internationale d'Urologie Journal : SIUJ*, 4(2), 105–111. DOI: 10.48083/KTOL8925

Lopez-Cabrales, A., Bornay-Barrachina, M., & Diaz-Fernandez, M. (2017). Leadership and dynamic capabilities: The role of HR systems. *Personnel Review*, 46(2), 255–276. DOI: 10.1108/PR-05-2015-0146

Lo, S. H., Peters, G. J. Y., & Kok, G. (2012). A Review of Determinants of and Interventions for Proenvironmental Behaviors in Organizations. *Journal of Applied Social Psychology*, 42(12), 2933–2967. DOI: 10.1111/j.1559-1816.2012.00969.x

Losada Crespo, B., & Briz Clariget, M.J. (2024), “La gestión de conflictos laborales. Habilidades necesarias para el mediador laboral”. *Revista de Derecho (Universidad Católica Dámaso A. Larrañaga, Facultad de Derecho)*, (29), e3694. Epub 01 de junio de 2024.https://doi.org/DOI: 10.22235/rd29.3694

Lourenção, M., de Moura Engracia Giraldi, J., & de Oliveira, J. H. C. (2020). Destination advertisement semiotic signs: Analysing tourists’ visual attention and perceived ad effectiveness. *Annals of Tourism Research*, 84, 103001. DOI: 10.1016/j.annals.2020.103001

Lugo, S. D. R., Kimita, K., & Nishino, N. (2023). Characteristics of decision process towards circular food economy: A review. *Cleaner Logistics and Supply Chain*, 7, 100104. DOI: 10.1016/j.clscn.2023.100104

Maden, A., & Alptekin, E. (2020). Evaluation of factors affecting the decision to adopt blockchain technology: A logistics company case study using Fuzzy DEMATEL. *Journal of Intelligent & Fuzzy Systems*, 39(5), 6279–6291. Advance online publication. DOI: 10.3233/JIFS-189096

Makhal, A., Robertson, K., Thyne, M., & Mirosa, M. (2021). Normalising the “ugly” to reduce food waste: Exploring the socialisations that form appearance preferences for fresh fruits and vegetables. *Journal of Consumer Behaviour*, 20(5), 1025–1039. DOI: 10.1002/cb.1908

Manika, D., Wells, V. K., Gregory-Smith, D., & Gentry, M. (2015). The Impact of Individual Attitudinal and Organisational Variables on Workplace Environmentally Friendly Behaviours. *Journal of Business Ethics*, 126(4), 663–684. DOI: 10.1007/s10551-013-1978-6

Manzoor, S., Fayaz, U., Dar, A. H., Dash, K. K., Shams, R., Bashir, I., Pandey, V. K., & Abdi, G. (2024). Sustainable Development Goals Through Reducing Food Loss and Food Waste: A Comprehensive Review. *Future Foods : a Dedicated Journal for Sustainability in Food Science*, 9, 100362. DOI: 10.1016/j.fufo.2024.100362

Maqueira Marín, J. M., De Oliveira-Dias, D., Jafari Navimipour, N., Gardas, B., & Unal, M. (2022). Cloud computing and human resource management: Systematic literature review and future research agenda. *Kybernetes*, 51(6), 2172–2191. DOI: 10.1108/K-05-2021-0420

Marans, R. W., & Lee, Y. J. (1993). Linking recycling behavior to waste management planning: A case study of office workers in Taiwan. *Landscape and Urban Planning*, 26(1–4), 203–214. DOI: 10.1016/0169-2046(93)90017-8

Maraslis, K., Cooper, P., Tryfonas, T., & Oikonomou, G. (2016). An Intelligent Hot-Desking Model Based on Occupancy Sensor Data and Its Potential for Social Impact. *Lecture Notes in Computer Science*, 9860, 142–158. DOI: 10.1007/978-3-662-53416-8_9

Marcos, M.-C., & González-Caro, C. (2010). Comportamiento de los usuarios en la página de resultados de los buscadores. Un estudio basado en eye tracking. *El Profesional de la Información*, 19(4), 348–358. DOI: 10.3145/epi.2010.jul.03

Marder, B., Erz, A., Angell, R., & Plangger, K. (2021). The Role of Photograph Aesthetics on Online Review Sites: Effects of Management- versus Traveler-Generated Photos on Tourists' Decision Making. *Journal of Travel Research*, 60(1), 31–46. DOI: 10.1177/0047287519895125

Mariappanadar, S., & Kramar, R. (2014). Sustainable HRM. *Asia-Pacific Journal of Business Administration*, 6(3), 206–224. DOI: 10.1108/APJBA-03-2014-0039

Marrucci, L., Daddi, T., & Iraldo, F. (2021). The contribution of green human resource management to the circular economy and performance of environmental certified organisations. *Journal of Cleaner Production*, 319, 128859. DOI: 10.1016/j.jclepro.2021.128859

Marrucci, L., Daddi, T., & Iraldo, F. (2023). Institutional and stakeholder pressures on organisational performance and green human resources management. *Corporate Social Responsibility and Environmental Management*, 30(1), 324–341. DOI: 10.1002/csr.2357

Martinez, A., & Gomez, M. (2023). Measuring the effectiveness of behavioral interventions in promoting pro-environmental behaviors: A meta-analysis. *Environmental Psychology Review*, 45(4), 302–318.

Matiku, S. M., Zuwarimwe, J., & Tshipala, N. (2020). Sustainable tourism planning and management for sustainable livelihoods. *Development Southern Africa*, 38(4), 524–538. DOI: 10.1080/0376835X.2020.1801386

Matzke, U. (2018). Personalgewinnung und -bindung im Wandel. In Simon, A. (Ed.), *Akademisch ausgebildetes Pflegefachpersonal* (pp. 115–136). Springer. DOI: 10.1007/978-3-662-54887-5_9

McCarthy, B., Kapetanaki, A. B., & Wang, P. (2020). Completing the food waste management loop: Is there market potential for value-added surplus products (VASP)? *Journal of Cleaner Production*, 256, 120435. DOI: 10.1016/j.jclepro.2020.120435

McEachan, R. R. C., Lawton, R. J., Jackson, C., Conner, M., Meads, D. M., & West, R. M. (2011). Testing a workplace physical activity intervention: A cluster randomized controlled trial. *The International Journal of Behavioral Nutrition and Physical Activity*, 8(1), 1–12. http://www.ijbnpa.org/content/8/1/29. DOI: 10.1186/1479-5868-8-29 PMID: 21481265

McGrath, D. (2021). *Watch my waste: how self-auditing affected Australian food-service food waste* (Doctoral dissertation, RMIT University).

McKenzie, F. C., & Williams, J. (2015). Sustainable food production: Constraints, challenges and choices by 2050. *Food Security*, 7(2), 221–233. DOI: 10.1007/s12571-015-0441-1

McKenzie, N. N., Jacquier, D. D., Isbell, R. R., & Brown, K. K. (2004). *Australian soils and landscapes: an illustrated compendium*. CSIRO publishing. DOI: 10.1071/9780643100732

McKinsey & Company. (2020). *The future of work in Europe: Automation, workforce transitions, and the shifting geography of employment*. https://www.mckinsey.com/featured-insights/future-of-work/the-future-of-work-in-europe

McKinsey Global Institute. (2023). *Generative AI and the future of work in America* (Informe). Recuperado el 10 de junio de 2024, de https://www.mckinsey.com/~/media/mckinsey/mckinsey%20global%20institute/our%20research/generative%20ai%20and%20the%20future%20of%20work%20in%20america/generative-ai-and-the-future-of-work-in-america-vf1.pdf

McMahon, L. (2000). Bullying and harassment in the workplace. *International Journal of Contemporary Hospitality Management*, 12(6), 384–387. DOI: 10.1108/09596110010343666

Measuring digital development - Facts and Figures 2023. (2023, noviembre 27). ITU; ITU/UN tech agency. https://www.itu.int/hub/publication/d-ind-ict_mdd-2023-1/

Mena, C., Terry, L. A., Williams, A., & Ellram, L. (2014). Causes of waste across multi-tier supply networks: Cases in the UK food sector. *International Journal of Production Economics*, 152, 144–158. DOI: 10.1016/j.ijpe.2014.03.012

Méndez Zamora, E. (13/06/2019), "La inteligencia artificial en el arbitraje internacional", available at LexLatin | La inteligencia artificial en el arbitraje internacional

Mendez, J. (2006), *Approaches and models for the development of competence*. https://www.icam.com.mx/canales6/rrhh/gestion-y-desarrollo-de-competencias.htm (2006).

Messner, R., Johnson, H., & Richards, C. (2021). From surplus-to-waste: A study of systemic overproduction, surplus and food waste in horticultural supply chains. *Journal of Cleaner Production*, 278, 123952. DOI: 10.1016/j.jclepro.2020.123952

Mesterházy, Á., Oláh, J., & Popp, J. (2020). Losses in the grain supply chain: Causes and solutions. *Sustainability (Basel)*, 12(6), 2342. DOI: 10.3390/su12062342

Metallo, C., Agrifoglio, R., & Maria, F. (2021). Effective Management of a Remote Workforce for Covid-19: A Proposed Research Model Toward Smart Working Adoption Within Organizations. *HR Analytics and Digital HR Practices*, 101–126. https://doi.org/DOI: 10.1007/978-981-16-7099-2_5

Mexico, how are we doing? (2024, April 30). *National and state growth of the Mexican economy*. https://mexicocomovamos.mx/publicaciones/2021/08/crecimiento-nacional-y-estatal-de-la-economia-mexicana/#:~:text=La%20econom%C3%ADa%20mexicana%20tuvo%20un,4.5%25%20anual%20de%20forma%20sostenida

Meza-Rodríguez, E. (2023, 22 de marzo). Emprender es más difícil: México baja en el índice de creación de negocios [Entrepreneurship is more difficult: Mexico descends in the business creation index]. *El Economista*. https://www.eleconomista.com.mx/el-empresario/Emprender-es-mas-dificil-Mexicobaja-en-el-indice-de-creacion-de-negocios-20230321-0098.html

Mičík, M., & Mičudová, K. (2018). Employer brand building: Using social media and career websites to attract generation Y. *Economia e Sociologia*, 11(3), 171–189.

Midgley, J. L. (2014). The logics of surplus food redistribution. *Journal of Environmental Planning and Management*, 57(12), 1872–1892. DOI: 10.1080/09640568.2013.848192

Miellet, S., Zhou, X., He, L., Rodger, H., & Caldara, R. (2010). Investigating cultural diversity for extrafoveal information use in visual scenes. *Journal of Vision (Charlottesville, Va.)*, 10(6), 21–21. DOI: 10.1167/10.6.21 PMID: 20884570

Mihalič, T. (2014). 3. Tourism and Economic Development Issues. In R. Sharpley & D. Telfer (Ed.), *Tourism and Development: Concepts and Issues* (pp. 77-117). Bristol, Blue Ridge Summit: Channel View Publications. https://doi.org/DOI: 10.21832/9781845414740-005

Millward, L. J., Haslam, S. A., & Postmes, T. (2007). Putting Employees in Their Place: The Impact of Hot Desking on Organizational and Team Identification. *Organization Science*, 18(4), 547–559. DOI: 10.1287/orsc.1070.0265

Minz, R., Grüttner, D., & von Heusinger-Lender, M. (2023). Krankenhaus 2030 – Was sich ändern muss. *Gefässchirurgie*, 2(28), 98–107. DOI: 10.1007/s00772-023-00986-6 PMID: 36945660

Mion, G., & Loza Adaui, C. R. (2020). Understanding the purpose of benefit corporations: An empirical study on the Italian case. *International Journal of Corporate Social Responsibility*, 5(1), 4. DOI: 10.1186/s40991-020-00050-6

Mirosa, M., Pearson, D., & Pearson, R. (2016). Ethics of food waste. In *The Routledge Handbook of Food Ethics* (pp. 400–408). Routledge.

Mohamad, A. M. (2024). *Using ATLAS.ti Desktop for literature reviews.*

Mohammad Azahari, A., Ahmad, A., & Rahayu, S. B. (2021). *Contactless Attendance Method with Face Recognition.* Body Temperature Measurement and GPS System Using Blockchain Technology., DOI: 10.1007/978-981-33-6490-5_8

Mohiuddin, M., Al Mamun, A., Syed, F. A., Mehedi Masud, M., & Su, Z. (2018). Environmental knowledge, awareness, and business school students' intentions to purchase green vehicles in emerging countries. *Sustainability (Basel)*, 10(5), 1534. DOI: 10.3390/su10051534

Mololoth, V. K., Saguna, S., & Åhlund, C. (2023). Blockchain and Machine Learning for Future Smart Grids: A Review. *Energies*, 16(1), 528. DOI: 10.3390/en16010528

Mondal, S. R., Di Virgilio, F., & Das, S. (Eds.), *HR Analytics and Digital HR Practices*. Palgrave Macmillan., DOI: 10.1007/978-981-16-7099-2

Moore, C. W. (2014). *The Mediation Process: Practical Strategies for Resolving Conflict*. Jossey-Bass.

Moral-Muñoz, J. A., Herrera-Viedma, E., Santisteban-Espejo, A., & Cobo, M. J. (2020). Software tools for conducting bibliometric analysis in science: An up-to-date review. *El Profesional de la Información*, 29(1). Advance online publication. DOI: 10.3145/epi.2020.ene.03

Moreau, V., Sahakian, M., van Griethuysen, P., & Vuille, F. (2017). Coming Full Circle: Why Social and Institutional Dimensions Matter for the Circular Economy. *Journal of Industrial Ecology*, 21(3), 497–506. DOI: 10.1111/jiec.12598

Moreddu, C. (2016). *Public-Private Partnerships for Agricultural Innovation: Lessons From Recent Experiences", OECD Food, Agriculture and Fisheries Papers, No. 92*. OECD Publishing., DOI: 10.1787/5jm55j9p9rmx-

Morgan, D., Moore, K., & Mansell, R. (2005). Adventure tourists on water: Linking expectations, affect, achievement and enjoyment to the sports tourism adventure. *Journal of Sport & Tourism*, 10(1), 73–88. DOI: 10.1080/14775080500101593

Morrar, R., Arman, H., & Mousa, S. (2017). The fourth industrial revolution (Industry 4.0): A social innovation perspective. *Technology Innovation Management Review*, 7(11), 12–20. DOI: 10.22215/timreview/1117

Morrison, R. L., & Macky, K. A. (2017). The demands and resources arising from shared office spaces. *Applied Ergonomics*, 60, 103–115. DOI: 10.1016/j.apergo.2016.11.007 PMID: 28166868

Mouloudj, K., Bouarar, A. C., & Mouloudj, S. (2023b). Extension of the theory of planned behaviour (TPB) to predict farmers' intention to save energy. In *AIP Conference Proceedings* (Vol. 2683, No. 1). AIP Publishing. https://doi.org/DOI: 10.1063/5.0125022

Mouloudj, K., & Bouarar, A. C. (2023). Investigating predictors of medical students' intentions to engagement in volunteering during the health crisis. *African Journal of Economic and Management Studies*, 14(2), 205–222. DOI: 10.1108/AJEMS-08-2022-0315

Mouloudj, K., Bouarar, A. C., Bovsh, L. A., Zikii, N., & Kebab, M. (2023a). Investigating the Antecedents of Eco-Friendly Vehicle Purchase Intentions: An Extension of the Theory of Planned Behavior. In Masengu, R., Bigirimana, S., Chiwaridzo, O., Bensson, R., & Blossom, C. (Eds.), *Sustainable Marketing, Branding, and Reputation Management: Strategies for a Greener Future* (pp. 1–16). IGI Global., DOI: 10.4018/979-8-3693-0019-0.ch001

Mouloudj, K., Njoku, A., Asanza, D. M., Bouarar, A. C., Evans, M. A., Mouloudj, S., & Bouarar, A. (2023c). Modeling predictors of medication waste reduction intention in Algeria: Extending the theory of planned behavior. *International Journal of Environmental Research and Public Health*, 20(16), 6584. DOI: 10.3390/ijerph20166584 PMID: 37623170

Mourad, M. (2016). Recycling, recovering and preventing "food waste": Competing solutions for food systems sustainability in the United States and France. *Journal of Cleaner Production*, 126, 461–477. DOI: 10.1016/j.jclepro.2016.03.084

Muduli, A., Trivedi, J., & Pingle, S. (2021). Social media recruitment and culture: An empirical study. *International Journal Indian Culture and Business Management*, 22(3), 364–382. DOI: 10.1504/IJICBM.2021.114085

Munesue, Y., Masui, T., & Fushima, T. (2015). The effects of reducing food losses and food waste on global food insecurity, natural resources, and greenhouse gas emissions. *Environmental Economics and Policy Studies*, 17(1), 43–77. DOI: 10.1007/s10018-014-0083-0

Murillo, G., & Barroso, F. (2012). *Design of a test for critical thinking* [Software]. Unpublished work. Universidad Anáhuac Mayab, Mérida, Yucatán, Mexico.

Murillo-Ramos, L., Huertas-Valdivia, I., & García-Muiña, F. E. (2022). Exploring the cornerstones of green, sustainable and socially responsible human resource management. *International Journal of Manpower*, 44(3), 524–542. DOI: 10.1108/IJM-12-2021-0696

Murphy, S. J., & Wright, A. T. (2019). Employee behavior and food waste reduction in Australian corporate cafeterias. *Waste Management (New York, N.Y.)*, 92, 55–62.

Napier, E., Liu, S. Y., & Liu, J. (2024). Adaptive strength: Unveiling a multilevel dynamic process model for organizational resilience. *Journal of Business Research*, 171, 114334. DOI: 10.1016/j.jbusres.2023.114334

Nappi, I., & de Campos Ribeiro, G. (2020). Internet of Things technology applications in the workplace environment: A critical review. *Journal of Corporate Real Estate*, 22(1), 71–90. DOI: 10.1108/JCRE-06-2019-0028

Näswall, K., Hellgren, M., & Sverke, M. (2008). *The individual in the changing working life*. Cambridge University Press. DOI: 10.1017/CBO9780511490064

National Academies of Sciences, Engineering, and Medicine. (2014). *Revisiting the STEM workforce: A companion to science and engineering indicators 2014*. National Academies Press. https://www.nap.edu/catalog/18953/revisiting-the-stem-workforce-a-companion-to-science-and-engineering

National Food Waste Strategy. (2017). Halving Australia's Food Waste By 2030. Accessed from https://www.agriculture.gov.au/sites/default/files/documents/national-food-waste-strategy.pdf

National Science Board. (2020). *Science and engineering indicators 2020: The state of U.S. science and engineering*. Recuperado el 10 de junio de 2024, de https://ncses.nsf.gov/pubs/nsb20201

Navarro-Navarro, J., Juárez-Tárraga, F., Ramón-Rodríguez, A. B., & Perles-Ribes, J. F. (2023). The life cycle and competitive position of tourism destinations: A global empirical approach. *Current Issues in Tourism*, •••, 1–17. DOI: 10.1080/13683500.2023.2280161

Ndraha, N., Hsiao, H. I., Vlajic, J., Yang, M. F., & Lin, H. T. V. (2018). Time-temperature abuse in the food cold chain: Review of issues, challenges, and recommendations. *Food Control*, 89, 12–21. DOI: 10.1016/j.foodcont.2018.01.027

Negi, S., & Anand, N. (2016). Factors leading to losses and wastage in the supply chain of fruits and vegetables sector in India. *Energy, Infrastructure.Transport Challenges: Way Forward*, 1, 80–105.

Nencková, L., Pecáková, I., & Šauer, P. (2020). Disposal behaviour of Czech consumers towards textile products. *Waste Management (New York, N.Y.)*, 106, 71–76. DOI: 10.1016/j.wasman.2020.03.001 PMID: 32222682

Neu, C. V., Gibson, J., Lunardi, R. C., Leesakul, N., & Morisset, C. (2023). *A Blockchain-Based Architecture to Manage User Privacy Preferences on Smart Shared Spaces Privately*. DOI: 10.1007/978-3-031-25734-6_9

Neuber, L., Englitz, C., Schulte, N., Forthmann, B., & Holling, H. (2022, March 04). Colinda Englitz, Niklas Schulte, Boris Forthmann & Heinz Holling (2021) How work engagement relates to performance and absenteeism: A meta-analysis. *European Journal of Work and Organizational Psychology*, 31(2), 292–315. Advance online publication. DOI: 10.1080/1359432X.2021.1953989

Ng, H. S., Kee, P. E., Yim, H. S., Chen, P. T., Wei, Y. H., & Lan, J. C. W. (2020). Recent advances on the sustainable approaches for conversion and reutilization of food wastes to valuable bioproducts. *Bioresource Technology*, 302, 122889. DOI: 10.1016/j.biortech.2020.122889 PMID: 32033841

Ng, S. L. (2023). Knowledge–intention–behavior associations and spillovers of domestic and workplace recycling. *The Social Science Journal*, 60(2), 254–273. DOI: 10.1080/03623319.2020.1735857

Nguyen, O. S., & Smith, P. D. (2022). Green initiatives and their impact on food waste in office settings. *Sustainability*, 14(5), 2900.

Nicastro, R., & Carillo, P. (2021). Food loss and waste prevention strategies from farm to fork. *Sustainability (Basel)*, 13(10), 5443. DOI: 10.3390/su13105443

Niu, Q., Nagata, T., Fukutani, N., Tezuka, M., Shimoura, K., Nagai-Tanima, M., & Aoyama, T. (2021). Health effects of immediate telework introduction during the COVID-19 era in Japan: A cross-sectional study. *PLoS One*, 16(10), e0256530. DOI: 10.1371/journal.pone.0256530 PMID: 34624027

Njoku, A., Mouloudj, K., Bouarar, A. C., Evans, M. A., Asanza, D. M., Mouloudj, S., & Bouarar, A. (2024). Intentions to Create Green Start-Ups for Collection of Unwanted Drugs: An Empirical Study. *Sustainability (Basel)*, 16(7), 2797. DOI: 10.3390/su16072797

Nolan, J. M., Schultz, P. W., Cialdini, R. B., Goldstein, N. J., & Griskevicius, V. (2008). Normative social influence is under-detected. *Personality and Social Psychology Bulletin*, 34(7), 913–924. DOI: 10.1177/0146167208316691 PMID: 18550863

Nong, S. Z., & Fong, L. H. N. (2021). Eye tracking in tourism. *Information Technology & Tourism*, 23(4), 633–635. DOI: 10.1007/s40558-021-00210-9

North, M. S., & Fiske, S. T. (2012). An obstacle race: Ageism and its impact on older adults. *Perspectives on Psychological Science*, 7(3), 264–269. PMID: 26168463

Norton, T. A., Parker, S. L., Zacher, H., & Ashkanasy, N. M. (2015). Employee Green Behavior: A Theoretical Framework, Multilevel Review, and Future Research Agenda. *Organization & Environment*, 28(1), 103–125. DOI: 10.1177/1086026615575773

Obeidat, S. M., Abdalla, S., & Al Bakri, A. A. K. (2023). Integrating green human resource management and circular economy to enhance sustainable performance: An empirical study from the Qatari service sector. *Employee Relations*, 45(2), 535–563. DOI: 10.1108/ER-01-2022-0041

Obu, U., Ambekar, Y., Lingam, R., Borikar, Y., Yadav, R., & Dongre, S. (2023). Blockchain System Against Gender Bias and Other Discriminatory Practices in Workplaces. *2023 IEEE 3rd International Conference on Technology, Engineering, Management for Societal Impact Using Marketing, Entrepreneurship and Talent (TEMSMET)*, 1–6. IEEE. DOI: 10.1109/TEMSMET56707.2023.10150193

Odhiambo, G. M., Waiganjo, E., & Simiyu, A. N. (2023). Incentivizing Employee Pro-Environmental Behaviour: Harnessing the Potential of Green Rewards. *African Journal of Empirical Research*, 4(2), 601–611. DOI: 10.51867/ajernet.4.2.60

OECD. (2019). *Skills outlook 2019: Thriving in a digital world.*https://www.oecd.org/education/skills-outlook-2019/

OECD. (2021). *Skills outlook 2021: Learning for life.*https://www.oecd.org/education/skills-outlook-2021-learning-for-life.htm

OECD. (2022). *PISA 2022 Results*. OECD Publishing. https://www.oecd.org/pisa/publications/pisa-2022-results.htm

Ofstad, S. P., Tobolova, M., Nayum, A., & Klöckner, C. A. (2017). Understanding the Mechanisms behind Changing People's Recycling Behavior at Work by Applying a Comprehensive Action Determination Model. *Sustainability 2017, Vol. 9, Page 204, 9*(2), 204. DOI: 10.3390/su9020204

Oggier, W. (2015). *Gesundheitswesen Schweiz*. Hogrefe.

Okano, M. T., & Santos, H. de C. L. dos, Honorato, W. J., Viana, A. M., &; Ursini, E. L. (. (2020). Impacts of the Covid-19 pandemic on large companies: Evaluation of changes in technology infrastructure for telework under the optics of theories of dynamic capacity and adaptive structure. *Research. Social Development*, 9(9), e756997852. DOI: 10.33448/rsd-v9i9.7852

Oke, A. (2015). Workplace Waste Recycling Behaviour: A Meta-Analytical Review. *Sustainability 2015, Vol. 7, Pages 7175-7194, 7*(6), 7175–7194. DOI: 10.3390/su7067175

Oke, A., McDonald, S., Korobilis-Magas, E., Osobajo, O. A., & Awuzie, B. O. (2021). Reframing Recycling Behaviour through Consumers' Perceptions: An Exploratory Investigation. *Sustainability 2021, Vol. 13, Page 13849, 13*(24), 13849. DOI: 10.3390/su132413849

Oke, A. E., & Stephen, S. S. (2024). Smart Contract for Sustainable Infrastructure Management. In *A Digital Path to Sustainable Infrastructure Management* (pp. 75–83). Emerald Publishing Limited., DOI: 10.1108/978-1-83797-703-120241008

Oke, A., McDonald, S., & Korobilis-Magas, E. (2021). Demystifying the complexity and heterogeneity of recycling behavior in organizational settings: A mixed-methods approach. *Waste Management (New York, N.Y.)*, 136, 337–347. DOI: 10.1016/j.wasman.2021.10.020 PMID: 34752973

Okumus, F., Köseoglu, M. A., Chan, E., Hon, A., & Avci, U. (2019). How do hotel employees' environmental attitudes and intentions to implement green practices relate to their ecological behavior? *Journal of Hospitality and Tourism Management*, 39, 193–200. DOI: 10.1016/j.jhtm.2019.04.008

Oliver, M. A., Bishop, T. F., & Marchant, B. P. (Eds.). (2013). *Precision agriculture for sustainability and environmental protection* (pp. 1–283). Routledge. DOI: 10.4324/9780203128329

Olsen, A., & Huang, F. (2019). Teacher job satisfaction by principal support and teacher cooperation: Results from the Schools and Staffing Survey. *Education Policy Analysis Archives*, 27, 11. DOI: 10.14507/epaa.27.4174

Omarova, L., & Jo, S. J. (2022). Employee pro-environmental behavior: The impact of environmental transformational leadership and GHRM. *Sustainability (Basel)*, 14(4), 2046. DOI: 10.3390/su14042046

ONTSI. (2022) El teletrabajo en España antes, durante y después de la pandemia. https://www.ontsi.es/sites/ontsi/files/2022-06/teletrabajoenespana.pdf

Oosterkamp, E., van der Sluis, A., van Geffen, L., Aramyan, L., & Bos-Brouwers, H. (2019). *Cosmetic aspects in specific marketing standards for fruit and vegetables: removing cosmetic aspects from the EU marketing standards: implications for the market and impact on food waste* (No. 2019-014). Wageningen Economic Research.

Ordelin Font, J. L. (diciembre de 2021) "El uso de la inteligencia artificial en la mediación: ¿Quimera o realidad?", *Revista IUS,* Vol. 15, pp. 357-382.

Oreg, S. (2006). Personality, context, and resistance to organizational change. *European Journal of Work and Organizational Psychology*, 15(1), 73–101. DOI: 10.1080/13594320500451247

Orgaz Agüera, F., & Moral Cuadra, S. (2016). El turismo como motor potencial para el desarrollo económico de zonas fronterizas en vías de desarrollo. Un estudio de caso. *El Periplo Sustentable*, (31). https://www.redalyc.org/articulo.oa?id=193449985009

OzHarvest. (2023). Inquiry into food security in Australia. *Accessed from*https://www.ozharvest.org/app/uploads/2023/03/221209-Inquiry-into-Food-Security-in-Australia-OzHarvest-submission-v2.pdf

Ozkan, S., Tari Selcuk, K., & Kan, Z. E. (2024). Is green behaviors of health professionals related to green practices in the workplace? Multicenter study in Turkey. *International Journal of Environmental Health Research*, 34(2), 898–910. DOI: 10.1080/09603123.2023.2185209 PMID: 36854645

Page, M. J., McKenzie, J. E., Bossuyt, P. M., Boutron, I., Hoffmann, T. C., Mulrow, C. D., Shamseer, L., Tetzlaff, J. M., Akl, E. A., Brennan, S. E., Chou, R., Glanville, J., Grimshaw, J. M., Hróbjartsson, A., Lalu, M. M., Li, T., Loder, E. W., Mayo-Wilson, E., McDonald, S., & Moher, D. (2021). The PRISMA 2020 statement: An updated guideline for reporting systematic reviews. *BMJ (Clinical Research Ed.)*, (71), n71. Advance online publication. DOI: 10.1136/bmj.n71 PMID: 33782057

Paillé, P., Raineri, N., & Boiral, O. (2019). Environmental Behavior On and Off the Job: A Configurational Approach. *Journal of Business Ethics*, 158(1), 253–268. DOI: 10.1007/s10551-017-3758-1

Paiola, M., & Gebauer, H. (2020). Internet of things technologies, digital servitization and business model innovation in BtoB manufacturing firms. *Industrial Marketing Management*, 89, 245–264. DOI: 10.1016/j.indmarman.2020.03.009

Palacios, L. (1999). *Popular wisdom in Venezuelan business*. Universidad Católica Andrés Bello.

Pan, J., Cho, T. Y., Sun, M., Debnath, R., Lonsdale, N., Wilcox, C., & Bardhan, R. (2023). Future workspace needs flexibility and diversity: A machine learning-driven behavioural analysis of coworking space. PLoS ONE, 18(10 October). https://doi.org/DOI: 10.1371/journal.pone.0292370

Panday, R., Almira, S., & Navanti, D. (2022). Employer branding and social media as an attractive job seeker to e-commerce companies for Z generation. *American Journal of Humanities and Social Sciences Research*, 6(7), 141–150.

Pannell, D., & Rogers, A. (2022). Agriculture and the environment: Policy approaches in Australia and New Zealand. *Review of Environmental Economics and Policy*, 16(1), 126–145. DOI: 10.1086/718053

Pan, S., Lee, J., & Tsai, H. (2014). Travel photos: Motivations, image dimensions, and affective qualities of places. *Tourism Management*, 40, 59–69. DOI: 10.1016/j.tourman.2013.05.007

Pan, X., Zhong, B., Sheng, D., Yuan, X., & Wang, Y. (2022). Blockchain and deep learning technologies for construction equipment security information management. *Automation in Construction*, 136, 104186. DOI: 10.1016/j.autcon.2022.104186

Papargyropoulou, E., Steinberger, J. K., Wright, N., Lozano, R., Padfield, R., & Ujang, Z. (2019). Patterns and causes of food waste in the hospitality and food service sector: Food waste prevention insights from Malaysia. *Sustainability (Basel)*, 11(21), 6016. DOI: 10.3390/su11216016

Parfitt, J., Barthel, M., & Macnaughton, S. (2010). Food waste within food supply chains: Quantification and potential for change to 2050. *Philosophical Transactions of the Royal Society of London. Series B, Biological Sciences*, 365(1554), 3065–3081. DOI: 10.1098/rstb.2010.0126 PMID: 20713403

Paul, J., & Criado, A. R. (2020). The art of writing literature review: What do we know and what do we need to know? *International Business Review*, 29(4), 101717. DOI: 10.1016/j.ibusrev.2020.101717

Paul, J., Lim, W. M., O'Cass, A., Hao, A. W., & Bresciani, S. (2021). Scientific procedures and rationales for systematic literature reviews (SPAR-4-SLR). *International Journal of Consumer Studies*, 45(4). Advance online publication. DOI: 10.1111/ijcs.12695

Pearson, D., Mirosa, M., Andrews, L., & Kerr, G. (2017). Reframing communications that encourage individuals to reduce food waste. *Communication Research and Practice*, 3(2), 137–154. DOI: 10.1080/22041451.2016.1209274

Pearson, T. (2002). Falling Behind: A Technology Crisis Facing Minority Students. *TechTrends*, 46(2), 15–20. https://www.learntechlib.org/p/95168/. DOI: 10.1007/BF02772070

Pérez Alonso, Y., & Gadea Peiró, I. (2021). *Bretxa digital de gènere en la Comunitat Valenciana – Informe 2021*. Universitat de València., DOI: 10.7203/10550.82251

Pérez Tortosa, F. (2022), "Personas con discapacidad intelectual y mediación: especial referencia a la mediación electrónica", available at https://riuma.uma.es/xmlui/handle/10630/24516?show=full

Pérez, M. A., & Kwortnik, K. J. (2021). Tourism development and employment: Evidence from emerging markets. *Journal ofDestination Marketing & Management*, 19, 100–112. DOI: 10.1016/j.jdmm.2021.100112

Pérez, M. P., Sánchez, A. M., De Luis Carnicer, P., & Vela Jiménez, M. J. (2005). The differences of firm resources and the adoption of teleworking. *Technovation*, 25(12), 1476–1483. DOI: 10.1016/j.technovation.2005.04.002

Perlmutter, H. V. (1969). The tortuous evolution of the multinational corporation. *The Columbia Journal of World Business*, 4(1), 9–18.

Petry, T. (2019). *Digital Leadership: Erfolgreiches Führen in Zeiten der Digital Economy*. Haufe.

Pham, N. T., Hoang, H. T., & Phan, Q. P. T. (2019). Green human resource management: A comprehensive review and future research agenda. *International Journal of Manpower*, 41(7), 845–878. DOI: 10.1108/IJM-07-2019-0350

Philip Chen, C. L., & Zhang, C.-Y. (2014). Data-intensive applications, challenges, techniques and technologies: A survey on Big Data. *Information Sciences*, 275, 314–347. DOI: 10.1016/j.ins.2014.01.015

Picatoste, X., Mesquita, A., & González-Laxe, F. (2023). Gender wage gap, quality of earnings and gender digital divide in the European context. *Empirica*, 50(2), 301–321. DOI: 10.1007/s10663-022-09555-8 PMID: 36471732

Pieroni, M. P. P., McAloone, T. C., & Pigosso, D. C. A. (2019). Business model innovation for circular economy and sustainability: A review of approaches. *Journal of Cleaner Production*, 215, 198–216. DOI: 10.1016/j.jclepro.2019.01.036

Pittock, J., Hussey, K., & Stone, A. (2016). Groundwater management under global change: Sustaining biodiversity, energy and food supplies. *Integrated groundwater management: Concepts, approaches and challenges,* 75-96.

Ployhart, R. E. (2006). Staffing in the 21st century: New challenges and strategic opportunities. *Journal of Management*, 32(6), 868–897. DOI: 10.1177/0149206306293625

Pollard, C. M., & Booth, S. (2019). Food insecurity and hunger in rich countries—It is time for action against inequality. *International Journal of Environmental Research and Public Health*, 16(10), 1804. DOI: 10.3390/ijerph16101804 PMID: 31117216

Pollard, G., Roetman, P., Ward, J., Chiera, B., & Mantzioris, E. (2018). Beyond productivity: Considering the health, social value and happiness of home and community food gardens. *Urban Science (Basel, Switzerland)*, 2(4), 97. DOI: 10.3390/urbansci2040097

Polo García-Ochoa, C., De Pablos Heredero, C., & Blanco Jiménez, F. J. (2020). How business accelerators impact startup's performance: Empirical insights from the dynamic capabilities approach. *Intangible Capital*, 16(3), 107–125. DOI: 10.3926/ic.1669

Pomfret, G. (2006). Mountaineering adventure tourists: A conceptual framework for research. *Tourism Management*, 27(1), 113–123. DOI: 10.1016/j.tourman.2004.08.003

Popp, M., & D'Angelo, R. (2021). The evolving landscape of tourism employment: Opportunities and challenges. *Journal of Hospitality and Tourism Management*, 49, 251–263. DOI: 10.1016/j.jhtm.2021.07.012

Porat, M., & Efrat, A. (2018). Consumer behavior and food waste: A review of recent research. *Food Policy*, 82, 32–40.

Porat, R., Lichter, A., Terry, L. A., Harker, R., & Buzby, J. (2018). Postharvest losses of fruit and vegetables during retail and in consumers' homes: Quantifications, causes, and means of prevention. *Postharvest Biology and Technology*, 139, 135–149. DOI: 10.1016/j.postharvbio.2017.11.019

Porter, S. D., Reay, D. S., Bomberg, E., & Higgins, P. (2018). Avoidable food losses and associated production-phase greenhouse gas emissions arising from application of cosmetic standards to fresh fruit and vegetables in Europe and the UK. *Journal of Cleaner Production*, 201, 869–878. DOI: 10.1016/j.jclepro.2018.08.079

Pretty, J. (2018). Intensification for redesigned and sustainable agricultural systems. *Science*, 362(6417), eaav0294. DOI: 10.1126/science.aav0294 PMID: 30467142

PwC. (2024). *27th Annual Global CEO Survey: Thriving in an age of continuous reinvention*. Recuperado el 10 de junio de 2024, de https://www.pwc.com/gx/en/ceo-survey/2024/download/27th-ceo-survey.pdf

Queensland Government. (2024). Food waste facts. *Accessed from*https://www.qld.gov.au/environment/circular-economy-waste-reduction/reduction/reduce-food-waste/facts

Quested, T. E., Ingle, R., & Parry, A. D. (2013). *Household food and drink waste in the UK: Quantification and analysis*. WRAP Report.

Raak, N., Symmank, C., Zahn, S., Aschemann-Witzel, J., & Rohm, H. (2017). Processing-and product-related causes for food waste and implications for the food supply chain. *Waste Management (New York, N.Y.)*, 61, 461–472. DOI: 10.1016/j.wasman.2016.12.027 PMID: 28038904

Rahman, M. M., Azam, M. M., & Sanjida Chowdhury, F. (2022). Secure Complaint Management System against Women Harassment at Workplace Using Blockchain Technology. *International Journal of Electrical and Computer Engineering Systems*, 13(3), 209–217. DOI: 10.32985/ijeces.13.3.6

Rai, A. K., Bana, S. R., Sachan, D. S., & Singh, B. (2023). Advancing sustainable agriculture: A comprehensive review for optimizing food production and environmental conservation. *International Journal of Plant and Soil Science*, 35(16), 417–425. DOI: 10.9734/ijpss/2023/v35i163169

Rakić, T., & Chambers, D. (2010). Innovative techniques in tourism research: An exploration of visual methods and academic filmmaking. *International Journal of Tourism Research*, 12(4), 379–389. DOI: 10.1002/jtr.761

Ramachandran, R., Babu, V., & Murugesan, V. P. (2023). The role of blockchain technology in the process of decision-making in human resource management: A review and future research agenda. *Business Process Management Journal*, 29(1), 116–139. DOI: 10.1108/BPMJ-07-2022-0351

Rasmussen, K. B., & Thimm, H. (2015). Circumventing nonresponse - upgrading traditional company survey data with unobtrusive data from company websites. *Bulletin of Sociological Methodology. Bulletin de Methodologie Sociologique*, 127(1), 85–96. DOI: 10.1177/0759106315582198

Raut, R. D., Gardas, B. B., Narwane, V. S., & Narkhede, B. E. (2019). Improvement in the food losses in fruits and vegetable supply chain-a perspective of cold third-party logistics approach. *Operations research perspectives, 6,* 100117.

Raut, R., & Gardas, B. B. (2018). Sustainable logistics barriers of fruits and vegetables: An interpretive structural modeling approach. *Benchmarking*, 25(8), 2589–2610. DOI: 10.1108/BIJ-07-2017-0166

Refrigerated Warehouse & Transport Association of Australia Ltd-RWTA. (2023). The Australian Cold Chain: Confidence in Food Quality, Every Day. *Accessed from*https://www.rwta.com.au/australian-cold-chain-summary

Reingold, E. M., Sheridan, H., Meadmore, K. L., Drieghe, D., & Liversedge, S. P. (2016). Attention and eye-movement control in reading: The selective reading paradigm. *Journal of Experimental Psychology. Human Perception and Performance*, 42(12), 2003–2020. DOI: 10.1037/xhp0000291 PMID: 27643527

Renwick, D. W. S., Redman, T., & Maguire, S. (2013). Green Human Resource Management: A Review and Research Agenda*. *International Journal of Management Reviews*, 15(1), 1–14. DOI: 10.1111/j.1468-2370.2011.00328.x

Reynolds, C. J., Piantadosi, J., & Boland, J. (2015). Rescuing food from the organics waste stream to feed the food insecure: An economic and environmental assessment of Australian food rescue operations using environmentally extended waste input-output analysis. *Sustainability (Basel)*, 7(4), 4707–4726. DOI: 10.3390/su7044707

Reynolds, C., Goucher, L., Quested, T., Bromley, S., Gillick, S., Wells, V. K., Evans, D., Koh, L., Carlsson Kanyama, A., Katzeff, C., Svenfelt, Å., & Jackson, P. (2019). Consumption-stage food waste reduction interventions–What works and how to design better interventions. *Food Policy*, 83, 7–27. DOI: 10.1016/j.foodpol.2019.01.009

Reynolds, S. (2024). Adapting to technological change: A qualitative investigation of digital transformation in supply chain operations. En *Preprints*. https://doi.org/ DOI: 10.20944/preprints202406.1115.v1

Ridoutt, B. G., Juliano, P., Sanguansri, P., & Sellahewa, J. (2010). The water footprint of food waste: Case study of fresh mango in Australia. *Journal of Cleaner Production*, 18(16-17), 1714–1721. DOI: 10.1016/j.jclepro.2010.07.011

Ringle. C. M. Wende. S. and Will A. SmartPLS 3.0 M3, 2005.

Robbins, S., & Judge, T. (2009). *Comportamiento Organizacional* [Organizational Behavior]. 13th ed.). (Brito, J. L., Trans.). Pearson-Prentice Hall.

Rochecouste, J., & Crabtree, B. (2014). *Conservation agriculture in Australian dryland cropping*. Conservation agriculture: global prospects and challenges.

Rodríguez Bolívar, M. P., Scholl, H. J., & Pomeshchikov, R. (2021). *Stakeholders' Perspectives on Benefits and Challenges in Blockchain Regulatory Frameworks*. DOI: 10.1007/978-3-030-55746-1_1

Rodríguez, E. (2024). Critical thinking and creativity, indispensable skills in the era of Artificial Intelligence. *ISDI Digitalent Group*. https://www.isdi.education/mx/blog/pensamiento-critico-y-creatividad-las-skills-indispensables-en-la-era-de-inteligencia-artificial

Rodríguez, S. (2024, May 30). Unemployment decreases. It reaches a rate of 2.6% of the EAP in April 2024. *Forbes*. https://www.forbes.com.mx/disminuye-desempleo-alcanza-tasa-de-2-6-de-la-pea-en-abril-de-2024/#:~:text=En%20abril%20de%202024%2C%201.6,Poblaci%C3%B3n%20Econ%C3%B3micamente%20Activa%20(PEA)

Rodríguez-Espíndola, O., Chowdhury, S., Dey, P. K., Albores, P., & Emrouznejad, A. (2022). Analysis of the adoption of emergent technologies for risk management in the era of digital manufacturing. *Technological Forecasting and Social Change*, 178, 121562. DOI: 10.1016/j.techfore.2022.121562

Rodríguez-Modroño, P., & López-Igual, P. (2021). Job Quality and Work-Life Balance of Teleworkers. *International Journal of Environmental Research and Public Health*, 18(6), 3239. DOI: 10.3390/ijerph18063239 PMID: 33800995

Rogers, C. A. (2019), "*Arbitrator Intelligence: From Intuition to Data in Arbitrator Appointments", New York Dispute Resolution Lawyer,* vol. 11 No.2, available at https://papers.ssrn.com/sol3/papers.cfm?abstract_id=3113800

Rogers, W. A., & Fisk, A. D. (2010). Human factors for engineers and designers: The role of age and ability. En *Handbook of Human Factors and Ergonomics*.

Rohm, H., Oostindjer, M., Aschemann-Witzel, J., Symmank, C., & Almli, L., V., De Hooge, I. E., ... & Karantininis, K. (. (2017). Consumers in a sustainable food supply chain (COSUS): Understanding consumer behavior to encourage food waste reduction. *Foods*, 6(12), 104. DOI: 10.3390/foods6120104 PMID: 29186883

Rojas-Perez, H. L., Díaz-Vásquez, M. A., Díaz-Manchay, R. J., Zeña-Ñañez, S., Failoc-Rojas, V. E., & Smith, D. (2024). Nurses' Environmental Practices in Northern Peruvian Hospitals. *Workplace Health & Safety*, 72(2), 68–74. DOI: 10.1177/21650799231163130 PMID: 37016802

Rojo-Ramos, J., Gómez-Paniagua, S., Guevara-Pérez, J. C., & García-Unanue, J. (2023). Gender Differences in Adventure Tourists Who Practice Kayaking in Extremadura. *International Journal of Environmental Research and Public Health*, 20(5), 3889. DOI: 10.3390/ijerph20053889 PMID: 36900899

Roland Berger Krankenhausstudie. (2022). *Zeit für Lösungen. Warum der Umgang mit COVID, Fachkräftemangel und Ambulantisierung für deutsche Kliniken zur Existenzfrage wird.* Roland Berger.

Roopa, C., Suganthe, R. C., & Shanthi, N. (2020). Blockchain based certificate verification using ethereum and smart contract. *Journal of Critical Reviews*, 7(09). Advance online publication. DOI: 10.31838/jcr.07.09.71

Rosbergen, E., Pieters, R., & Wedel, M. (1997). Visual attention to advertising: A segment-level analysis. *The Journal of Consumer Research*, 24(3), 305–314. DOI: 10.1086/209512

Roxas, F. M. Y., Rivera, J. P. R., & Gutierrez, E. L. M. (2020). Mapping stakeholders' roles in governing sustainable tourism destinations. *Journal of Hospitality and Tourism Management*, 45, 387–398. DOI: 10.1016/j.jhtm.2020.09.005

Roy, M., & Medhekar, A. (2024). Green Supply Chain, Circular Economy, and Technological Innovation: Challenges and Opportunities for Developing Countries. Green Supply Chain Management Practice and Principles, 102-124.

Roy, P., Mohanty, A. K., Dick, P., & Misra, M. (2023). A review on the challenges and choices for food waste valorization: Environmental and economic impacts. *ACS Environmental Au*, 3(2), 58–75. DOI: 10.1021/acsenvironau.2c00050 PMID: 36941850

Roy, S., Dryl, W., & de Araujo Gil, L. (2021). Celebrity endorsements in destination marketing: A three country investigation. *Tourism Management*, 83, 104213. DOI: 10.1016/j.tourman.2020.104213

Ruiz, G., García, C., & Covarrubias, R. (2017) Environmental Assessment for Health Tourism in Baños de Agua Santa, Ecuador. *Journal of Environmental Protection*, 8, 799-809. https://doiDOI: 10.4236/jep.2017.87050

Saleem, M., Qadeer, F., Mahmood, F., Ariza-Montes, A., & Han, H. (2020). Ethical Leadership and Employee Green Behavior: A Multilevel Moderated Mediation Analysis. *Sustainability 2020, Vol. 12, Page 3314, 12*(8), 3314. DOI: 10.3390/su12083314

Saleem, M., Qadeer, F., Mahmood, F., Han, H., Giorgi, G., & Ariza-Montes, A. (2021). Inculcation of Green Behavior in Employees: A Multilevel Moderated Mediation Approach. *International Journal of Environmental Research and Public Health 2021, Vol. 18, Page 331, 18*(1), 331. DOI: 10.3390/ijerph18010331

Saleh, R. M., Anuar, M. M., Al-Swidi, A. K., & Omar, K. (2020). The effect of awareness, knowledge and cost on intention to adopt green building practices. *International Journal of Environment and Sustainable Development*, 19(1), 33–58. DOI: 10.1504/IJESD.2020.105468

Sales, F. C. V., De Souza, M., Trento, L. R., Pereira, G. M., Borchardt, M., & Milan, G. S. (2023). Food Waste in Distribution: Causes and Gaps to Be Filled. *Sustainability (Basel)*, 15(4), 3598. DOI: 10.3390/su15043598

Salvador-Oliván, J. A., & Agustín-Lacruz, C. (2015). Correlación entre indicadores bibliométricos en revistas de Web of Science y Scopus. *Revista General de Información y Documentación*, 25(2). Advance online publication. DOI: 10.5209/rev_RGID.2015.v25.n2.51241

Salvador, R. O., & Burciaga, A. (2020). Organizational environmental orientation and employee environmental in-role behaviors: A cross-level study. *Business Ethics (Oxford, England)*, 29(1), 98–113. DOI: 10.1111/beer.12241

Samadhiya, A., Agrawal, R., Kumar, A., & Garza-Reyes, J. A. (2023). Blockchain technology and circular economy in the environment of total productive maintenance: A natural resource-based view perspective. *Journal of Manufacturing Technology Management*, 34(2), 293–314. DOI: 10.1108/JMTM-08-2022-0299

Sanad Alsbu, R. A., Yarlagadda, P., & Karim, A. (2023). Investigation of the factors that contribute to fresh fruit and vegetable losses in the Australian fresh food supply Chain. *Processes (Basel, Switzerland)*, 11(4), 1154. DOI: 10.3390/pr11041154

Sanciolo, P., Rivera, E., Navaratna, D., & Duke, M. C. (2022). Food Waste Diversion from Landfills: A Cost–Benefit Analysis of Existing Technological Solutions Based on Greenhouse Gas Emissions. *Sustainability (Basel)*, 14(11), 6753. DOI: 10.3390/su14116753

Santos, R. (2011). *Entrepreneurial skills of young people and opportunities for job development in their region. The case of the Mayan area called Camino Real de Campeche*. Unpublished doctoral thesis. Universidad Anáhuac Mayab, Mérida, Yucatán, México.

Saphores, J. D. M., Nixon, H., Ogunseitan, O. A., & Shapiro, A. A. (2006). Household willingness to recycle electronic waste: An application to California. *Environment and Behavior*, 38(2), 183–208. DOI: 10.1177/0013916505279045

Saphores, J. D. M., Ogunseitan, O. A., & Shapiro, A. A. (2012). Willingness to engage in a pro-environmental behavior: An analysis of e-waste recycling based on a national survey of U.S. households. *Resources, Conservation and Recycling*, 60, 49–63. DOI: 10.1016/j.resconrec.2011.12.003

Saqib, N. (2019). A positioning strategy for a tourist destination, based on analysis of customers' perceptions and satisfactions: A case of Kashmir, India. *Journal of Tourism Analysis*, 26(2), 131–151. DOI: 10.1108/JTA-05-2019-0019

Sarkar, A. (2022). Minimalonomics: A novel economic model to address environmental sustainability and earth's carrying capacity. *Journal of Cleaner Production*, 371, 133663. DOI: 10.1016/j.jclepro.2022.133663

Sarker, A. H., Bornman, J. F., & Marinova, D. (2019). A framework for integrating agriculture in urban sustainability in Australia. *Urban Science (Basel, Switzerland)*, 3(2), 50. DOI: 10.3390/urbansci3020050

Savelyeva, T., & Park, J. (2022). Blockchain technology for sustainable education. *British Journal of Educational Technology*, 53(6), 1591–1604. DOI: 10.1111/bjet.13273

Schneiders, K., & Schönauer, A.-L. (2022). Fachkräftemangel in der Sozialwirtschaft: Empirische Befunde zu Ursachen und Handlungsbedarfen. In Gehrlach, C., von Bergen, M., & Eiler, K. (Eds.), *Zwischen gesellschaftlichem Auftrag und Wettbewerb* (pp. 355–370). Springer. DOI: 10.1007/978-3-658-35381-0_21

Schoner-Schatz, L., Hofmann, V., & Stokburger-Sauer, N. E. (2021). Destination's social media communication and emotions: An investigation of visit intentions, word-of-mouth and travelers' facially expressed emotions. *Journal of Destination Marketing & Management*, 22, 100661. DOI: 10.1016/j.jdmm.2021.100661

Schultz, P. W., Oskamp, S., & Mainieri, T. (1995). Who recycles and when? A review of personal and situational factors. *Journal of Environmental Psychology*, 15(2), 105–121. DOI: 10.1016/0272-4944(95)90019-5

Schwartz, S. H. (1973). Normative explanations of helping behavior: A critique, proposal, and empirical test. *Journal of Experimental Social Psychology*, 9(4), 349–364. DOI: 10.1016/0022-1031(73)90071-1

Schwartz, S. H. (1977). Normative influences on altruism. *Advances in Experimental Social Psychology*, 10, 221–279. DOI: 10.1016/S0065-2601(08)60358-5

Selvi A, J. A., Rajan Y, P., & Geetha, M. (2023). The mask of hidden knowledge behind advanced technologies: A case of distress, unlearning and knowledge transfer. Journal of Information Technology Teaching Cases, 20438869231210577.

Selwyn-Rowland, T. (2021). Impact of Hotdesking on team cohesion. *Journal of Asia Entrepreneurship and Sustainability*, 17(5), 123–152.

Semenzin, S. (2023). 'Blockchain for good': Exploring the notion of social good inside the blockchain scene. *Big Data & Society*, 10(2), 20539517231205479. Advance online publication. DOI: 10.1177/20539517231205479

Shakhbulatov, D., Arora, A., Dong, Z., & Rojas-Cessa, R. (2019). Blockchain Implementation for Analysis of Carbon Footprint across Food Supply Chain. *2019 IEEE International Conference on Blockchain (Blockchain)*, 546–551. IEEE. DOI: 10.1109/Blockchain.2019.00079

Sheffey, S., & Tindale, R. S. (1992). Perceptions of Sexual Harassment in the Workplace. *Journal of Applied Social Psychology*, 22(19), 1502–1520. DOI: 10.1111/j.1559-1816.1992.tb00963.x

Shen, Y., Lever, M., & Joppe, M. (2020). Investigating the appeal of a *visitor guide: A triangulated approach. International Journal of Contemporary Hospitality Management*, 32(4), 1539–1562. DOI: 10.1108/IJCHM-03-2019-0281

Sheremata, S. L., & Silver, M. A. (2015). Hemisphere-Dependent Attentional Modulation of Human Parietal Visual Field Representations. *The Journal of Neuroscience : The Official Journal of the Society for Neuroscience*, 35(2), 508–517. DOI: 10.1523/JNEUROSCI.2378-14.2015 PMID: 25589746

Shetye, I., Morwadkar, S., Chavan, B., Rajole, S., & Kulkarni, S. (2024). *Literature Survey: Complaint Management System Using Blockchain Technology*. DOI: 10.1007/978-981-97-1313-4_29

Shinde, P. P., & Shah, S. (2018). A Review of Machine Learning and Deep Learning Applications. *2018 Fourth International Conference on Computing Communication Control and Automation (ICCUBEA)*, 1–6. IEEE. DOI: 10.1109/ICCUBEA.2018.8697857

Shipman, K., Burrell, D. N., & Huff Mac Pherson, A. (2021). An organizational analysis of how managers must understand the mental health impact of teleworking during COVID-19 on employees. *The International Journal of Organizational Analysis*. Advance online publication. DOI: 10.1108/IJOA-03-2021-2685

Short, J. C., McKenny, A. F., & Reid, S. W. (2018). More than words? Computer-aided text analysis in organizational behavior and psychology research. *Annual Review of Organizational Psychology and Organizational Behavior*, 5(1), 415–435. DOI: 10.1146/annurev-orgpsych-032117-104622

Si, H., Shi, J. G., Tang, D., Wen, S., Miao, W., & Duan, K. (2019). Application of the Theory of Planned Behavior in Environmental Science: A Comprehensive Bibliometric Analysis. *International Journal of Environmental Research and Public Health 2019, Vol. 16, Page 2788, 16*(15), 2788. DOI: 10.3390/ijerph16152788

Sidique, S. F., Joshi, S. V., & Lupi, F. (2010). Factors influencing the rate of recycling: An analysis of Minnesota counties. *Resources, Conservation and Recycling*, 54(4), 242–249. DOI: 10.1016/j.resconrec.2009.08.006

Si, K., Jalees, T., Zaman, S. I., Alam, S. H., & Khan, S. (2023). The role of communication, informativeness, and social presence play in the social media recruitment context of an emerging economy. *Cogent Business & Management*, 10(3), 2251204. DOI: 10.1080/23311975.2023.2251204

Simon, M. (2021). *Das Gesundheitssystem in Deutschland.* Hogrefe. DOI: 10.1024/86147-000

Sims, S. (2017). TALIS 2013: Working conditions, teacher job satisfaction and retention. *Department for Education Statistical Working Paper*. Londres: Department for Education. Recuperado el 10 de junio de 2024, de https://eric.ed.gov/?id=ED604491

Smith, F. P., Prober, S. M., House, A. P., & McIntyre, S. (2013). Maximizing retention of native biodiversity in Australian agricultural landscapes—The 10: 20: 40: 30 guidelines. *Agriculture, Ecosystems & Environment*, 166, 35–45. DOI: 10.1016/j.agee.2012.01.014

Smith, J., Brown, R., & White, A. (2021). *Food Recovery and Redistribution: Addressing Hunger and Waste in Australia*. Environmental Sustainability Publications.

Smith, K., & White, A. (2023). The effects of waste management policies on recycling behavior: A quantitative assessment. *Waste Management (New York, N.Y.)*, 114, 62–74.

Smith, L., & Jones, R. (2022). The impact of food safety regulations on surplus food redistribution: Balancing safety and sustainability. *Journal of Food Policy*, 92, 104–116.

Smith, R., Johnson, L., & Brown, A. (2022). The influence of pro-environmental behavior on environmental policy outcomes: An empirical analysis. *Policy Studies Journal: the Journal of the Policy Studies Organization*, 50(2), 225–244.

Smyth, S. J., Webb, S. R., & Phillips, P. W. (2021). The role of public-private partnerships in improving global food security. *Global Food Security*, 31, 100588. DOI: 10.1016/j.gfs.2021.100588

Sodhi, M. S. (2015). Conceptualizing Social Responsibility in Operations Via Stakeholder Resource-Based View. *Production and Operations Management*, 24(9), 1375–1389. DOI: 10.1111/poms.12393

Sofronov, B. (2017). The economic impact on global tourism. Annals of Spiru Haret University. Economic Series, 17(2), 127-139. https://www.ceeol.com/search/article-detail?id=561416

Son-Turan, S. (2022). Fostering Equality in Education: The Blockchain Business Model for Higher Education (BBM-HE). *Sustainability (Basel)*, 14(5), 2955. DOI: 10.3390/su14052955

Soosay, C. (2013). Improving Sustainable Development in Australia's Agrifood Supply Chains. *Sustainability and Collaboration in Supply Chain Management: A Comprehensive Insight into Current Management Approaches, 43.*

Sparks, B. A., & Wang, Y. (2014). Natural and Built Photographic Images: Preference, Complexity, and Recall. *Journal of Travel & Tourism Marketing*, 31(7), 868–883. DOI: 10.1080/10548408.2014.890155

Spence, M. (1973). Job Market Signaling. *The Quarterly Journal of Economics*, 87(3), 355–374. DOI: 10.2307/1882010

SRHM. (2022). *SHRM Body of Applied Skills and Knowledge*. https://www.shrm.org/content/dam/en/shrm/credentials/shrm-certification/shrm-bask.pdf

Sroufe, R. (2017). Integration and organizational change towards sustainability. *Journal of Cleaner Production*, 162, 315–329. DOI: 10.1016/j.jclepro.2017.05.180

Stancu, V., Haugaard, P., & Lähteenmäki, L. (2016). Determinants of consumer food waste behavior: A review. *Sustainability*, 8(6), 1377.

Stanford University. (2021). Bloom, N. Hybrid in the future work. Available at: https://drive.google.com/file/d/1U8NeVFONOHO0rHQq6A4hytlm3I1wio0T/view (URL date accessed on 31 July 2023). Publication based on the Working Paper https://www.nber.org/papers/w28731

State of NSW and Environment Protection Authority (2018). Love Food Hate Waste Tracking Survey Report 2017.

Statistische Ämter des Bundes und der Länder. (2023). *Verzeichnis der Krankenhäuser und Vorsorge- oder Rehabilitationseinrichtungen.* https://www.statistikportal.de/de/veroeffentlichungen/krankenhausverzeichnis

Štefko, R., Šambronská, K., Matušíková, D., Šenková, A., & Tumpach, M. (2021). Analytical study on adventure tourism destination management concerning expenditure on adventure activities. *Polish Journal of Management Studies*, 24(1), 373–391. Advance online publication. DOI: 10.17512/pjms.2021.24.1.22

Steg, L., & Vlek, C. (2009). Encouraging pro-environmental behaviour: An integrative review and research agenda. *Journal of Environmental Psychology*, 29(3), 309–317. DOI: 10.1016/j.jenvp.2008.10.004

Stipanović, C., Rudan, E., & Zubović, V. (2019). Development concept of adventure tourism for the purposes of destination competitiveness. In *Proceedings of the International Scientific Conference* (p. 163). https://fet.unipu.hr/images/50033564/Conference_Proceedings_2020.pdf

Stoian, C.-A., Caraiani, C., Anica-Popa, I. F., Dascălu, C., & Lungu, C. I. S. (2022). Telework Systematic Model Design for the Future of Work. *Sustainability (Basel)*, 14(12), 7146. DOI: 10.3390/su14127146

Subramanian, N., & Suresh, M. (2022). The contribution of organizational learning and green human resource management practices to the circular economy: A relational analysis – Part I. *The Learning Organization*, 29(5), 428–442. DOI: 10.1108/TLO-12-2021-0143

Sustainability Victoria. (2023). SV's State of Sustainability Report 2023: Are Victorians living sustainably? *Accessed from*https://assets.sustainability.vic.gov.au/susvic/Document-SV-State-of-Sustainability-Report.pdf

Tang, G., Chen, Y., Jiang, Y., Paillé, P., & Jia, J. (2018). Green human resource management practices: Scale development and validity. *Asia Pacific Journal of Human Resources*, 56(1), 31–55. DOI: 10.1111/1744-7941.12147

Tang, X., Qiu, J., Zhang, W., Toure, I., Zhang, M., Messina, E., & Yu, S. (2019). The Internet of Responsibilities - Connecting Human Responsibilities using Big Data and Blockchain. *2019 IEEE International Conference on Big Data (Big Data)*, 6226–6228. IEEE. DOI: 10.1109/BigData47090.2019.9006521

Tanwar, S., Bhatia, Q., Patel, P., Kumari, A., Singh, P. K., & Hong, W.-C. (2020). Machine Learning Adoption in Blockchain-Based Smart Applications: The Challenges, and a Way Forward. *IEEE Access : Practical Innovations, Open Solutions*, 8, 474–488. DOI: 10.1109/ACCESS.2019.2961372

Taşkıner, T., & Bilgen, B. (2021). Optimization models for harvest and production planning in agri-food supply chain: A systematic review. *Logistics (Basel)*, 5(3), 52. DOI: 10.3390/logistics5030052

Tatar, U., Gokce, Y., & Nussbaum, B. (2020). Law versus technology: Blockchain, GDPR, and tough tradeoffs. *Computer Law & Security Report*, 38, 105454. DOI: 10.1016/j.clsr.2020.105454

Teece D, Pisano G, Shuen A. Capacidades, recursos y concepto de estrategia de la empresa: cuatro paradigmas de la gestión estratégica. Documento de trabajo de la CCC. Universidad de California en Berkeley, Centro de Investigación en Gestión, Consorcio sobre Competitividad y Cooperación; 1990.

Teece, D. J. (2007). Explicating dynamic capabilities: The nature and microfoundations of (sustainable) enterprise performance. *Strategic Management Journal*, 28(13), 1319–1350. DOI: 10.1002/smj.640

Teece, D. J. (2014). A dynamic capabilities-based entrepreneurial theory of the multinational enterprise. *Journal of International Business Studies*, 45(1), 8–37. DOI: 10.1057/jibs.2013.54

Teece, D. J., Pisano, G., & Shuen, A. (1997). Dynamic capabilities and strategic management. *Strategic Management Journal*, 18(7), 509–533. DOI: 10.1002/(SICI)1097-0266(199708)18:7<509::AID-SMJ882>3.0.CO;2-Z

Teleoacă Vartolomei, B. O. (2020). Considerations Regarding Work from Home and Telework. *Proceedings of the International Conference on Business Excellence*, 14(1), 1217–1221. https://doi.org/DOI: 10.2478/picbe-2020-0115

Teller, C., Holweg, C., Reiner, G., & Kotzab, H. (2018). Retail store operations and food waste. *Journal of Cleaner Production*, 185, 981–997. DOI: 10.1016/j.jclepro.2018.02.280

Tengjian, Z., Gokhan, E., & Gerard, G. (2018). The capacity to innovate: A meta-analysis of absorptive capacity. *Innovation (North Sydney, N.S.W.)*, 20(2), 87–121. DOI: 10.1080/14479338.2018.1428105

Teng, Z., Guo, C., Zhao, Q., & Mubarik, M. S. (2023). Antecedents of green process innovation adoption: An AHP analysis of China's gas sector. *Resources Policy*, 85, 103959. DOI: 10.1016/j.resourpol.2023.103959

Testa, F., Todaro, N., Gusmerotti, N. M., & Frey, M. (2020). Embedding corporate sustainability: An empirical analysis of the antecedents of organization citizenship behavior. *Corporate Social Responsibility and Environmental Management*, 27(3), 1198–1212. DOI: 10.1002/csr.1875

The Conference Board (2023). *TED: Summary tables and charts*https://www.conference-board.org/retrievefile.cfm?filename=TED_SummaryTables_Charts_april20231.pdf&type=subsite

Thøgersen, J. (2006). Norms for environmentally responsible behaviour: An extended taxonomy. *Journal of Environmental Psychology*, 26(4), 247–261. DOI: 10.1016/j.jenvp.2006.09.004

Thomé, A. M. T., Scavarda, L. F., & Scavarda, A. J. (2016). Conducting systematic literature review in operations management. *Production Planning and Control*, 27(5), 408–420. DOI: 10.1080/09537287.2015.1129464

Thompson, A. (2024). *Digital 2024: 5 billion social media users*. We Are Social UK; We Are Social. https://wearesocial.com/uk/blog/2024/01/digital-2024-5-billion-social-media-users/

Thyberg, K. L., & Tonjes, D. J. (2016). Drivers of food waste and their implications for sustainable policy development. *Resources, Conservation and Recycling*, 106, 110–123. DOI: 10.1016/j.resconrec.2015.11.016

Tiitta, I., Cubelo, F., McDermott-Levy, R., Jaakkola, J. J., & Kuosmanen, L. (2024). Climate change integration in nursing education: A scoping review. *Nurse Education Today*, 139, 106210. DOI: 10.1016/j.nedt.2024.106210 PMID: 38643656

Tiron-Tudor, A., Deliu, D., Farcane, N., & Dontu, A. (2021). Managing change with and through blockchain in accountancy organizations: A systematic literature review. *Journal of Organizational Change Management*, 34(2), 477–506. DOI: 10.1108/JOCM-10-2020-0302

Tirrel, H., & Winnen, L. (2024). Digital Corporate Identity. In *Reference Modul in Social Sciences*. DOI: 10.1016/B978-0-443-13701-3.00068-2

Tirrel, H. (2023). *Working flexibly: A study on German SMEs in relation to information and communication technology and leadership*. University of Nicosia.

Tirrel, H., Kaufmann, H. R., & Winnen, L. (2021). Why not to work in flexible workplaces? A systematic literature review and development of a conceptual framework for SMEs. *International Review of Entrepreneurship*, 19(4), 555–584.

Tirrel, H., & Winnen, L. (2019). Die digitale Identität der DAX-30-Unternehmen aus Sicht des Personalmarketings 2.0. In Winnen, L., Rühle, A., & Wrobel, A. (Eds.), *Innovativer Einsatz digitaler Medien im Marketing: Analysen, Strategien, Erfolgsfaktoren, Fallbeispiele* (pp. 29–46). Springer Gabler., DOI: 10.1007/978-3-658-16774-5_3

Tirrel, H., Winnen, L., & Baumann, R. (2022). Durch Social Media Personal gewinnen. *Personalführung*, 55(5), 10–11.

Todorova, G., & Durisin, B. (2007). Absorptive capacity: Valuing a reconceptualization. *Academy of Management Review*, 32(3), 774–786. DOI: 10.5465/amr.2007.25275513

Tokarchuk, O., Gabriele, R., & Neglia, G. (2021). Teleworking during the Covid-19 Crisis in Italy: Evidence and Tentative Interpretations. *Sustainability (Basel)*, 13(4), 2147. DOI: 10.3390/su13042147

Toma, L., Costa Font, M., & Thompson, B. (2020). Impact of consumers' understanding of date labelling on food waste behaviour. *Operations Research*, 20(2), 543–560. DOI: 10.1007/s12351-017-0352-3

Torralba, A., Oliva, A., Castelhano, M. S., & Henderson, J. M. (2006). Contextual guidance of eye movements and attention in real-world scenes: The role of global features in object search. *Psychological Review*, 113(4), 766–786. DOI: 10.1037/0033-295X.113.4.766 PMID: 17014302

Ture, R. S., & Ganesh, M. P. (2018). Pro-environmental behaviours at workplace: An empirical study in Indian manufacturing organizations. *Benchmarking*, 25(9), 3743–3766. DOI: 10.1108/BIJ-07-2017-0193

Uggerslev, K. L., Fassina, N. E., & Kraichy, D. (2012). Recruiting through the stages: A meta-analytic test of predictors of applicant attraction at different stages of the recruiting process. *Personnel Psychology*, 65(3), 597–660. DOI: 10.1111/j.1744-6570.2012.01254.x

Ullah, M., & Ullah, R. (2015). *Erfolgsfaktor Candidate Experience: Der Perspektivwechsel im Recruiting*. Schäffer-Poeschel Verlag.

UN. (2015). *Transforming Our World: The 2030 Agenda for Sustainable Development. Resolution Adopted by the General Assembly on 25 September 2015.*

UNCTAD. (2020). Report about digital economy. https://unctad.org/webflyer/digital-economy-report-2020

Underwood, G., & Foulsham, T. (2006). Visual saliency and semantic incongruency influence eye movements when inspecting pictures. *Quarterly Journal of Experimental Psychology*, 59(11), 1931–1949. DOI: 10.1080/17470210500416342 PMID: 16987782

UNESCO. (2019). *Teaching and Learning in the Digital Age*. UNESCO Publishing.

UNESCO. (2022). *Transforming Technical and Vocational Education and Training for successful and just transitions: UNESCO strategy 2022-2029*. UNESCO Publishing.

United Nations. (2021). The 17 Goals. Retrieved from https://sdgs.un.org/goalsUsman, M., Rofcanin, Y., Ali, M., Ogbonnaya, C., & Babalola, M. T. (2023). Toward a more sustainable environment: Understanding why and when green training promotes employees' eco-friendly behaviors outside of work. *Human Resource Management, 62*(3), 355-371.

United Nations. (2023). Department of Economics and Social Affairs.

Urien, B. (2023). Teleworkability, Preferences for Telework, and Well-Being: A Systematic Review. *Sustainability (Basel)*, 15(13), 10631. DOI: 10.3390/su151310631

Van Boxstael, S., Devlieghere, F., Berkvens, D., Vermeulen, A., & Uyttendaele, M. (2014). Understanding and attitude regarding the shelf life labels and dates on pre-packed food products by Belgian consumers. *Food Control*, 37, 85–92. DOI: 10.1016/j.foodcont.2013.08.043

van Eck, N. J., & Waltman, L. (2010). Software survey: VOSviewer, a computer program for bibliometric mapping. *Scientometrics*, 84(2), 523–538. DOI: 10.1007/s11192-009-0146-3 PMID: 20585380

Vargas, F. (2006). Competencies in training and human talent management. *Annals of common education.Third Century*, 2(5), 147–163.

Vartiainen, M. Telework and Remote Work. Oxford Research Encyclopedia of Psychology. Retrieved 7 Jan. 2022, from https://oxfordre.com/psychology/view/10.1093/acrefore/9780190236557.001.0001/acrefore-9780190236557-e-850

Vassanadumrongdee, S., & Kittipongvises, S. (2018). Factors influencing source separation intention and willingness to pay for improving waste management in Bangkok, Thailand. *Sustainable Environment Research*, 28(2), 90–99. DOI: 10.1016/j.serj.2017.11.003

Veleva, V., Bodkin, G., & Todorova, S. (2017). The need for better measurement and employee engagement to advance a circular economy: Lessons from Biogen's "zero waste" journey. *Journal of Cleaner Production*, 154, 517–529. DOI: 10.1016/j.jclepro.2017.03.177

Venkatesh, V., & Bala, H. (2008). Technology acceptance model 3 and a research agenda on interventions. *Decision Sciences*, 39(2), 273–315. DOI: 10.1111/j.1540-5915.2008.00192.x

Verghese, K., & Lewis, H. (2015). Promoting sustainable food practices through consumer behavior change. *Sustainability*, 7(6), 7910–7927.

Verghese, K., Lewis, H., Lockrey, S., & Williams, H. (2015). Packaging's role in minimizing food loss and waste across the supply chain. *Packaging Technology & Science*, 28(7), 603–620. DOI: 10.1002/pts.2127

Vida Fernández, J. (2022, March). La gobernanza de los riesgos digitales: Desafíos y avances en la regulación de la inteligencia artificial. *Cuadernos de Derecho Transnacional*, 14(1), 489–503. DOI: 10.20318/cdt.2022.6695

Vidmar, M., Rosiello, A., & Golra, O. (2020). Resilience of New Space Firms in the United Kingdom During the Early Stages of COVID-19 Crisis: The Case for Strategic Agility. *New Space*, 8(4), 172–178. DOI: 10.1089/space.2020.0057

Vidyasagar, T. R. (1999). A neuronal model of attentional spotlight: Parietal guiding the temporal. *Brain Research. Brain Research Reviews*, 30(1), 66–76. DOI: 10.1016/S0165-0173(99)00005-3 PMID: 10407126

Vinezuela-Cabezas, A., Osejo-Taco, G., Unda-López, A., Paz, C., & Hidalgo-Andrade, P. (2022). A Comparison of Working Conditions and Workers' Perceptions among On-Site, Telework, and Hybrid Workers in Ecuador during the COVID-19 Pandemic. *International Journal of Environmental Research and Public Health*, 19(21), 14337. DOI: 10.3390/ijerph192114337 PMID: 36361220

Voigt, D. (2022). *Digitalisierung im Sozial- und Gesundheitswesen*. Springer. DOI: 10.1007/978-3-658-38360-2

Vozzi, A., Ronca, V., Aricò, P., Borghini, G., Sciaraffa, N., Cherubino, P., Trettel, A., Babiloni, F., & Di Flumeri, G. (2021). The sample size matters: To what extent the participant reduction affects the outcomes of a neuroscientific research. A case-study in neuromarketing field. *Sensors (Basel)*, 21(18), 6088. DOI: 10.3390/s21186088 PMID: 34577294

Wang, B., Wang, X., Guo, D., Zhang, B., & Wang, Z. (2018). Analysis of factors influencing residents' habitual energy-saving behaviour based on NAM and TPB models: Egoism or altruism? *Energy Policy*, 116, 68–77. DOI: 10.1016/j.enpol.2018.01.055

Wang, X., Feng, L., Zhang, H., Lyu, C., Wang, L., & You, Y. (2017). Human Resource Information Management Model based on Blockchain Technology. *2017 IEEE Symposium on Service-Oriented System Engineering (SOSE)*, 168–173. IEEE. DOI: 10.1109/SOSE.2017.34

Wang, Y., & Hsu, C. H. C. (2022). The effect of tourism on rural employment: A comparative study of Asia and Africa. *Journal of Rural Studies*, 89, 88–98. DOI: 10.1016/j.jrurstud.2022.02.012

Wang, Y., & Sparks, B. A. (2016). An Eye-Tracking Study of Tourism Photo Stimuli: Image Characteristics and Ethnicity. *Journal of Travel Research*, 55(5), 588–602. DOI: 10.1177/0047287514564598

Wang, Y., Zhang, L., & Chen, J. (2020). The effect of pro-environmental consumer behavior on waste reduction: A quantitative approach. *Waste Management (New York, N.Y.)*, 102, 45–56.

Wan, X., Teng, Z., Zhang, Z., Liu, X., & Du, Z. (2023). Equity financing risk assessment based on PLTS-ER approach in marine ranching from the ecological and circular economy perspectives. *Annals of Operations Research*. Advance online publication. DOI: 10.1007/s10479-023-05222-8

Waqas, M., Honggang, X., Ahmad, N., Khan, S. A. R., & Iqbal, M. (2021). Big data analytics as a roadmap towards green innovation, competitive advantage and environmental performance. *Journal of Cleaner Production*, 323, 128998. DOI: 10.1016/j.jclepro.2021.128998

WCED. (1987). Our common future. World commission on environment and development. *Sustainable Development*, 154, 1–374.

Webb, E., Campbell, D. T., Schwartz, R. D., & Sechrest, L. (1966). *Unobtrusive measures: Nonreactive research in the social sciences*. Rand McNally.

Wedel, M., & Pieters, R. (2008). Eye Tracking for Visual Marketing. *Foundations and Trends® in Marketing, 1*(4), 231-320. https://doi.org/DOI: 10.1561/1700000011

Wedel, M., & Pieters, R. (Eds.). (2007). *Visual marketing: From attention to action* (1st ed.). Psychology Press., DOI: 10.4324/9780203809617

Wei, F., & Pokrovskaia, N. N. (2017). Digitizing of regulative mechanisms on the masterchain platform for the individualized competence portfolio. *2017 IEEE VI Forum Strategic Partnership of Universities and Enterprises of Hi-Tech Branches (Science. Education. Innovations) (SPUE)*, 73–76. IEEE. DOI: 10.1109/IVForum.2017.8246055

Wei, G. (2019). A Map of Bibliometrics and Scientometrics in Journals of Various Disciplines Excluding Library and Information Science From 2009 to 2018. SSRN Electronic Journal. https://doi.org/DOI: 10.2139/ssrn.3557950

Weidinger, L., Löschnigg-Tausz, M., & Hausmann, D. (2022). Fachkräftemangel in der Pflege – ein Blick über Österreichs Grenzen hinaus. *Procare : das Forbildungsmagazin fur Pflegeberufe*, 27(3), 48–51. DOI: 10.1007/s00735-022-1540-9

Weitzel, T., Maier, C., Weinert, C., Pflügner, K., Oehlhorn, C., & Wirth, J. (2020). *Mobile Recruiting: Ausgewählte Ergebnisse der Recruiting Trends 2020, einer empirischen Unternehmens-Studie mit den Top-1.000-Unternehmen aus Deutschland sowie den Top-300-Unternehmen aus der Branche IT und der Bewerbungspraxis 2020, einer empirischen Kandidaten-Studie mit Antworten von über 3.500 Kandidaten.*https://www.uni-bamberg.de/fileadmin/uni/fakultaeten/wiai_lehrstuehle/isdl/Recruiting_Trends_2020/Studien_2020_02_Mobile_Recruiting_Web.pdf

Wesselink, R., Blok, V., & Ringersma, J. (2017). Pro-environmental behaviour in the workplace and the role of managers and organisation. *Journal of Cleaner Production*, 168, 1679–1687. DOI: 10.1016/j.jclepro.2017.08.214

West, E. G., Lindberg, R., Ball, K., & McNaughton, S. A. (2020). The role of a food literacy intervention in promoting food security and food literacy—OzHarvest's NEST Program. *Nutrients*, 12(8), 2197. DOI: 10.3390/nu12082197 PMID: 32718054

Whitmarsh, L. E., Haggar, P., & Thomas, M. (2018). Waste reduction behaviors at home, at work, and on holiday: What influences behavioral consistency across contexts? *Frontiers in Psychology*, 9(DEC), 417854. DOI: 10.3389/fpsyg.2018.02447 PMID: 30574111

WHO. (2017, February 7). Environmentally sustainable health systems: a strategic document. https://www.who.int/publications/i/item/WHO-EURO-2017-2241-41996-57723

WHO. (2023, October 12). Climate change. https://www.who.int/news-room/fact-sheets/detail/climate-change-and-health

Wieser, L., & Abraham, M. (2024). Employee acceptance of digital monitoring systems while working from home. *New Technology, Work and Employment*, 39(1), 109–142. DOI: 10.1111/ntwe.12280

Wilkinson (2024). Ugly fruit and vegetables sold at discount prices in Odd Bunch campaign by Woolworths. *Accessed from*https://www.news.com.au/lifestyle/food/ugly-fruit-and-vegetables-sold-at-discount-prices-in-odd-bunch-campaign-by-woolworths/news-story/e9a9d2527fbba38dd92ad7db1a8e4f1b

Williams, J., Alter, T., & Shrivastava, P. (2018). Systemic governance of sustainable agriculture: Implementing sustainable development goals and climate-friendly farming. *Outlook on Agriculture*, 47(3), 192–195. DOI: 10.1177/0030727018795907

Williams, S. R., Zhu-Barker, X., Lew, S., Croze, B. J., Fallan, K. R., & Horwath, W. R. (2019). Impact of composting food waste with green waste on greenhouse gas emissions from compost windrows. *Compost Science & Utilization*, 27(1), 35–45. DOI: 10.1080/1065657X.2018.1550023

Winans, K., Kendall, A., & Deng, H. (2017). The history and current applications of the circular economy concept. *Renewable & Sustainable Energy Reviews*, 68, 825–833. DOI: 10.1016/j.rser.2016.09.123

Winnen, L., Schrader, S., & Tirrel, H. (2021). Der Einfluss von Social Media (im Employer Branding) auf den Stellenbesetzungserfolg: Eine quantitative Analyse. In Tirrel, H., Winnen, L., & Lanwehr, R. (Eds.), *Digitales Human Resource Management. Aktuelle Forschungserkenntnisse, Trends und Anwendungsbeispiele* (pp. 173–194). Springer., DOI: 10.1007/978-3-658-35590-6_11

Winnen, L., Tirrel, H., & Mertens, A. (2024). Digitale Identität ausgewählter Organisationen der Sozialwirtschaft: Eine quantitative Analyse des digitalen Personalmarketings. *PERSONALquarterly*, 76(2), 36–41.

Wisnujati, N. S., Sangadji, S. S., & Handriana, T. (2024). Assessing the Role of Marketing Communication in Shaping Tourist Intentions to Morotai Island. *International Journal of Sustainable Development and Planning*, 19(5), 1845–1854. DOI: 10.18280/ijsdp.190522

Woiceshyn, J. (2005). Integrative capability and technology adoption: Evidence from oil firms. *Industrial and Corporate Change*, 14(2), 307–342. DOI: 10.1093/icc/dth053

Wood, R., Lenzen, M., Dey, C., & Lundie, S. (2006). A comparative study of some environmental impacts of conventional and organic farming in Australia. *Agricultural Systems*, 89(2-3), 324–348. DOI: 10.1016/j.agsy.2005.09.007

Woolworths Group. (2021). Reducing hunger and food waste. *Accessedfrom*https://www.woolworthsgroup.com.au/au/en/sustainability/Planet/food-waste.html

World Bank. (2019). *World development report 2019: The changing nature of work.* https://www.worldbank.org/en/publication/wdr2019

World Economic Forum. (2022). *3 ways the circular economy is vital for the energy transition.*

World Economic Forum. (2023). *The future of jobs report 2023.* https://www3.weforum.org/docs/WEF_Future_of_Jobs_2023.pdf

World Health Organization. (2019). *Global action plan on physical activity 2018-2030: More active people for a healthier world*. World Health Organization. https://iris.who.int/handle/10665/272722

World Health Organization. (2021). Global strategy on digital health 2020–2025. World Health Organization. https://iris.who.int/handle/10665/344251

World Tourism Organization. (2016). *Panorama OMT del turismo internacional, Edición 2016*. UNWTO., DOI: 10.18111/9789284418152

World Tourism Organization. (2020). *UN Tourism | Bringing the world closer*. UNWTO. https://www.unwto.org

World Tourism Organization. (2021). *Impact assessment of COVID-19 on tourism employment*. United Nations World Tourism Organization. https://www.unwto.org/resources/impact-assessment-covid-19-tourism-employment

World Tourism Organization. (2023). *International Tourism to End 2023 Close to 90% of Pre-Pandemic Levels*. https://www.unwto.org/

World Travel & Tourism Council. (2023). *Travel & Tourism set to Break All Records in 2024*. https://wttc.org/news-article/travel-and-tourism-set-to-break-all-records-in-2024-reveals-wttc

World Travel and Tourism Council (WTTC). (2017) Travel and Tourism Economic Impact Caribbean. World Travel and Tourism Council, London. https://www.slovenia.info/uploads/dokumenti/raziskave/world2017.pdf

Wübbelt, A., & Tirrel, H. (2022). Attracting members of generation Z to companies via social media recruiting in Germany. *Human Technology*, 18(3), 213–233. DOI: 10.14254/1795-6889.2022.18-3.2

Xie, J., Tang, H., Huang, T., Yu, F. R., Xie, R., Liu, J., & Liu, Y. (2019). A Survey of Blockchain Technology Applied to Smart Cities: Research Issues and Challenges. *IEEE Communications Surveys and Tutorials*, 21(3), 2794–2830. DOI: 10.1109/COMST.2019.2899617

Xie, Y., Chen, Z., Tang, H., Boadu, F., & Yang, Y. (2023). Effects of executives' pro-environmental education and knowledge sharing activities on eco-friendly agricultural production: Evidence from China. *Journal of Cleaner Production*, 395, 136469. DOI: 10.1016/j.jclepro.2023.136469

Xu, B., Gao, X., Cai, W., & Jiang, L. (2022). How environmental leadership boosts employees' green innovation behavior? A moderated mediation model. *Frontiers in Psychology*, 12, 689671. DOI: 10.3389/fpsyg.2021.689671 PMID: 35153882

Yahia, E. M., & Mourad, M. (2020). Food waste at the consumer level. In *Preventing food losses and waste to achieve food security and sustainability* (pp. 341–366). Burleigh Dodds Science Publishing. DOI: 10.19103/AS.2019.0053.14

Yalabik, Z. Y., Rayton, B. A., & Rapti, A. (2017). Facets of job satisfaction and work engagement. *Evidence-based HRM*, 5(3), 248–265. DOI: 10.1108/EBHRM-08-2015-0036

Yang, W., Chen, Q., Huang, X., Xie, J., Xie, M., & Shi, J. (2022). Image and text presentation forms in destination marketing: An eye-tracking analysis and a laboratory experiment. *Frontiers in Psychology*, 13, 1024991. DOI: 10.3389/fpsyg.2022.1024991 PMID: 36536866

Yavuzkurt, T., & Kiral, E. (2020). The Relationship Between Workplace Friendship and Job Satisfaction in Educational Organizations. *International Journal of Progressive Education*, 16(5), 404–425. DOI: 10.29329/ijpe.2020.277.25

Ye, H., & Tussyadiah, I. P. (2011). Destination visual image and expectation of experiences. *Journal of Travel & Tourism Marketing*, 28(2), 129–144. DOI: 10.1080/10548408.2011.545743

Yi, G. (2021). From green entrepreneurial intentions to green entrepreneurial behaviors: The role of university entrepreneurial support and external institutional support. *The International Entrepreneurship and Management Journal*, 17(2), 963–979. DOI: 10.1007/s11365-020-00649-y

Yong, J. Y., Yusliza, M.-Y., & Fawehinmi, O. O. (2019). Green human resource management. *Benchmarking*, 27(7), 2005–2027. DOI: 10.1108/BIJ-12-2018-0438

Yuan, J. J., Yi, S., Williams, H. A., & Park, O. H. (2019). US consumers' perceptions of imperfect "ugly" produce. *British Food Journal*, 121(11), 2666–2682. DOI: 10.1108/BFJ-03-2019-0206

Yu, H., Salman Shabbir, M., Ahmad, N., Ariza-Montes, A., Vega-Muñoz, A., Han, H., Scholz, M., & Safdar Sial, M. (2021). A Contemporary Issue of Micro-Foundation of CSR, Employee Pro-Environmental Behavior, and Environmental Performance toward Energy Saving, Carbon Emission Reduction, and Recycling. *International Journal of Environmental Research and Public Health*, 18(10), 5380. DOI: 10.3390/ijerph18105380 PMID: 34070088

Yüksel, D. (2023). Investigation of web-based eye-tracking system performance under different lighting conditions for neuromarketing. *Journal of Theoretical and Applied Electronic Commerce Research*, 18(4), 2092–2106. DOI: 10.3390/jtaer18040105

Yuriev, A., Boiral, O., Francoeur, V., & Paillé, P. (2018). Overcoming the barriers to pro-environmental behaviors in the workplace: A systematic review. *Journal of Cleaner Production*, 182, 379–394. DOI: 10.1016/j.jclepro.2018.02.041

Zahra, S. A., & George, G. (2002). Absorptive capacity: A review, reconceptualization, and extension. *Academy of Management Review*, 27(2), 185–203. DOI: 10.2307/4134351

Zahra, S. A., & Hayton, J. C. (2008). The effect of international venturing on firm performance: The moderating influence of absorptive capacity. *Journal of Business Venturing*, 23(2), 195–220. DOI: 10.1016/j.jbusvent.2007.01.001

Zatyko, N., Caldera, S., & Desha, C. (2023, July). Closing the Loop on Food Waste: Stakeholder Views and Experiences from Southeast Queensland, Australia. In *Waste* (Vol. 1, No. 3, pp. 640-653). MDPI.

Zavala, J. (2012). *Think like Silicon Valley being anywhere.*

Zeweld, W., Van Huylenbroeck, G., Tesfay, G., & Speelman, S. (2017). Smallholder farmers' behavioural intentions towards sustainable agricultural practices. *Journal of Environmental Management*, 187, 71–81. DOI: 10.1016/j.jenvman.2016.11.014 PMID: 27883941

Zhang, J., & Chen, Z. (2024). Exploring human resource management digital transformation in the digital age. *Journal of the Knowledge Economy*, 15(1), 1482–1498. DOI: 10.1007/s13132-023-01214-y

Zhang, K., Zhang, J., & Yang, J. (2023). The influence of human elements in photographs on tourists' destination perceptions and intentions. *Tourism Management*, 95, 104684. DOI: 10.1016/j.tourman.2022.104684

Zhao, X., Zhang, X., & Zhang, Y. (2021). Employment trends in the tourism industry post-pandemic: An analysis of recovery patterns. *Tourism Management*, 83, 104219. DOI: 10.1016/j.tourman.2020.104219

Zhou, A. J., Fey, C., & Yildiz, H. E. (2020). Fostering integration through HRM practices: An empirical examination of absorptive capacity and knowledge transfer in cross-border M&As. *Journal of World Business*, 55(2), 100947. DOI: 10.1016/j.jwb.2018.05.005

Zupic, I., & Čater, T. (2014). Bibliometric Methods in Management and Organization. *Organizational Research Methods*, 18(3), 429–472. DOI: 10.1177/1094428114562629

About the Contributors

Cristina Carrasco Garrido is a Professor and Researcher at the King Juan Carlos University in Madrid, Spain where her research focuses on telework, the welfare and health of workers in the workplace, and the organization and management of companies. She is also a member of the high-performance research group of the URJC Open Innova. Dr. Carrasco also obtained degrees in economics and in the law, and practiced as an auditor at Deloitte Consulting before obtaining her PhD in Business Organization. She earned honors and international mention for her PhD work. After Deloitte, she founded a fintech where she worked as a lawyer to help over-indebted people restructure their debts through the "second chance" law in Spain. Dr. Carrasco also has worked with colleagues in other distinguished universities on special projects including telework at the University of Birmingham (UK) and on workplace mental health at the University of California, Berkeley (USA).

Antonio Martínez Raya holds a Ph.D. degree (EQF level 8) with honors in European studies on Transportation Economics from UNED. Furthermore, he graduated with a degree in Aeronautical Engineering (EQF level 7) together with a minor in aircraft and space vehicles from UPM. He has also earned a Bachelor of Arts Degree in Economics (EQF level 6) and majored in European Union (EQF level 7) with a focus on economic and political levels from UNED in both degrees. Currently, he works as an Associate Professor at Universidad Politécnica de Madrid (UPM).

Carmen De-Pablos-Heredero is Full Professor of Business Administration at the Rey Juan Carlos University, Spain. Coordinator of the High Performance Research Group OPENINNOVA. Director of the Master Degrees in Business Organization & Logistic Processes Management SAP. She has published articles in impact-indexed journals. WIDS Ambassador. Editor of ESIC Market Journal.

***

Delwar Akbar is a full professor at the School of Business and Law, Central Queensland University, a regional economist, and a leader in supply and value chain research. His research during the last decade has focused predominantly on rural and regional economics, value chain analysis, property and health economics, economic impact assessment and regional development. Since his joining CQU in 2008, he has been successful in gaining 73 research and consultancy projects and have obtained over $11 million research income either as a Chief Investigator and/or Project Leader, which includes four Category-1 research grants. He has integrated economic models with supply chain, services and planning models. Recently, he has been developing and testing collaborative business models that could boaster rural economic dynamics and international trade. Over his academic career, he has published over 140 refereed papers, book chapters and project reports.

Jesus Barrena Martinez I am an Associate Professor in the Department of Business Management at the University of Cadiz, Spain. My teaching and research interests include Human Resource Management, Corporate Social Responsibility, Sustainability and Intellectual Capital. I work in the University of Cadiz since 2009, participating in international and national research projects, transference agreements with companies as well as publishing several articles and chapters. Some of these publications can be check in my google academic profile.

Ahmed Chemseddine Bouarar is a Professor of English, accounting, and marketing at University of Medea, Algeria. He received his Ph.D. in sciences commerciales from the University of Algiers 3 at Algiers in 2016. Bouarar has made over 40 scholarly contributions, including nearly 25 peer-reviewed research papers.

María-José Foncubierta-Rodríguez Associate Professor. Full-time profe Nowssor. Department of Management, University of Cádiz (UCA). Her research lines goes in direction with innovative fields: the competencies of the PI as a leader of research groups, and the competencies of leaders to manage employee Happiness and Well-being at work. In both cases, the aim is to help comply with SDG-8 and SDG-3. She transfered the research findings through articles, books, book chapters (WoS, Scopus, Scielo, Latindex, etc), conferences, research meetings, and media. She collaborated with transfer actions to the social environment: Collaboration with the City Council of Algeciras (projects "Algeciras Digital Challenge", of the EU, and "Agenda 2020"); Evaluator in R+D+i Awards of the Technological Campus Foundation of Algeciras. -Training of young researchers, being co-director of two doctoral theses already defended and three theses in progress. -From the 1996 to

2020 holding positions as manager at the University of Cádiz: a) Sub-coordinator of Studies at the University School EUEJE (UCA); b) Coordinator of the Business Economics Area at University School EUEJE (UCA) until 2010; c) Director of the Headquarters of the Faculty of Economic and Business Administration Sciences at the Bahía de Algeciras Campus since April 2012 to December 2020. - Principal Investigator (PI) of the Research Group SEJ 058 "Cátedra de Estudios Jurídicos y Económicos delCampo de Gibraltar "Francisco Tomás y Valiente",PAIDI, Junta de Andalucía (Spain).

Cristina Gallego-Gomez Master Degree in Business Organization and another one in Business Communication at the Rey Juan Carlos University. She is a doctoral candidate in the Business Administration PHD Program at the Rey Juan Carlos. She is an IT organizational Consultant in the digital areas of firms from 2008. She works at Capgemini, Spain, where she is specialized in channels in the Financial Services for big size firms leading their industries. She has done research in the management of CRM and ERP systems where she has published articles in indexed journals and presented communications in International venues.

José Luis Gilabert Villard is a Ph.D. candidate, focusing on the study of emerging psychosocial risks in the digital age and how education plays a dual role, both as an affected sector and a control tool. He holds a degree in Business Administration and Management and an MBA from the University of Cádiz. He has over 15 years of teaching experience in various management areas, including Strategic Management, Fundamentals of Management, Human Resources Management, Managerial Skills, Entrepreneurship, and Production Management. He also has more than 15 years of experience teaching Secondary Education, High School, and Vocational Training programs in both the public and private sectors. Additionally, he has held positions in administration and finance departments of national and multinational companies and served as a local employment promotion agent in the city of Cádiz. He is an expert in advising and guiding entrepreneurial initiatives and regional business development. Committed to education and business development, he is an author passionate about sustainable economic development, eager to share his extensive experience and knowledge.

Marta Gonzalo Quiroga is Professor of International Private Law. Rey Juan Carlos University of Madrid. ORCID ID: 0000-0002-6553-3268. PhD in Law from the Complutense University of Madrid (UCM). Professor of Private International Law at the Universidad Rey Juan Carlos (URJC), specific profile in ADR: Negotiation, Mediation and Arbitration: Director of the URJC Mediation Expert Degree and Coordinator of the Arbitration and Mediation Module of the

URJC Master's Degree in Access to the Legal Profession. Medal of Professional Merit 2020 for his promotion of Negotiation, Mediation, Dialogue and the Culture of Peace. International Mediator and Arbitrator. E-mail: marta.gonzalo@urjc .es. This publication is part of two research projects: 1. Project "ODS, ADR and ODR: Justice, Human Rights and Culture of Peace", directed by the author within the R+D+I Research Project of the Universidad Rey Juan Carlos (URJC 2021-24) and 2. FEMGEN Project: High Performance Research Group on Gender and Feminism of the URJC (2022-2025), directed by Dr. Laura Nuño Gómez, to which this contribution is attached from a gender perspective.

Stefanie Hohenhorst holds a Master of Science in Human Resources Management from the FOM University of Applied Sciences in Münster (Germany) as well as a Bachelor of Science in Psychology and Management from the International School of Management (ISM) in Dortmund (Germany). Her research focuses on Personnel Marketing, Recruiting and (Digital) Employer Branding. Moreover, she works as a Human Resources Specialist in Personnel Marketing at the University Hospital Münster.

Doruntina Kabashi was born in Peja on April 24, 1993. She completed her primary education in Peja and graduated from the Medical High School, specialising in Pharmacy, in 2012. In the academic year 2012-2013, she enrolled in the Faculty of Medicine, Department of Physiotherapy at the University of Prishtina "Hasan Prishtina." In April 2016, she graduated with a Bachelor's degree in Physiotherapy.In the academic year 2022-2023, she enrolled in the Master's programme at the Faculty of Medicine "Fehmi Agani" in Gjakova, specialising in Health Management. She is scheduled to defend her Master's thesis before the relevant committee in September. Currently, Doruntina works as a physiotherapist at "Fizioterapia Kabashi" clinic in Klinë and also serves as the project coordinator and physiotherapist for the "Health and Well-being of Students in the Municipality of Peja" project. This project is a result of her collaboration with the Municipal institutions of Peja following research she conducted in several schools in the Municipality.

Dachel Martínez Asanza is an esteemed academic and public health expert, currently affiliated with the National School of Public Health (ENSAP) in Cuba and the University of Medical Sciences of Havana. She has contributed significantly to the field of dentistry, publishing over 40 peer-reviewed articles and participating in numerous national and international conferences.

Medina Ayta Mohammed holds a PhD in Business and Economics from Universidad Rey Juan Carlos. She also have a Bachelor's degree in Business Administration and a Master's degree in Business Organization.

José-Luis Montes-Botella is a Professor of Advanced Statistics and Econometrics at the Rey Juan Carlos University in Madrid (Spain). He holds university degrees in Engineering (Industrial Organization), Business administration, and Economics (Ph.D.). He is a researcher and consultant to international corporations and public administrations. His areas of interest include structural equation modeling, data science econometric modeling, and statistics. He has published articles in scholarly journals. His current research focuses on forecasting and structural equations modeling.

Belen Maria Moreno-Cabezali obtained a double degree in Business Administration and Management and Law from Rey Juan Carlos University in Spain in 2016. In 2018, she earned a Master's degree in Auditing and Higher Accounting from Rey Juan Carlos University. In 2023, she was awarded a Doctorate in Management Engineering from the Polytechnic University of Madrid. Since the academic year 2020-2021, she has been teaching at the Department of Business Economics (ADO), Applied Economics II, and Fundamentals of Economic Analysis. Her research and publications focus on applying fuzzy logic approaches to risk analysis in engineering projects, as well as human resources management in the engineering sector. The results of her research have been published in high-impact international journals: Computers & Industrial Engineering (Q1, JCR) and Journal of Cleaner Production (Q1, JCR). She also has a strong interest in the military field, focusing on risk analysis in military operations and additive manufacturing projects. The results of this research have culminated in the publication of an article in the Aeronautics and Astronautics Journal of the Spanish Air and Space Force.

Kamel Mouloudj is a Professor in the College of Economics at the University of Medea in Algeria. His research primarily focuses on predicting individual behavior across various contexts, including customer interactions, employee dynamics, and student engagement. He earned his Bachelor of Science in Commercial Sciences and his Master's in Marketing from the University of Blida, followed by a Doctorate in Marketing from the University of Algiers 3. With over 19 years of teaching experience, he has published more than 45 research papers. Prof. Mouloudj has also participated in three significant research projects at the University of Medea, concentrating on industrial marketing, energy, and green start-ups. Since 2019, he has served as the Chair of the Doctoral Training Committee in the Department of Commercial Sciences and continues in this role through 2026.

Lydia Murillo-Ramos, Ph.D., is a researcher in Business Organization at the University Rey Juan Carlos. Her work delves into innovative aspects of green human resource management, responsible leadership, and environmental citizenship behaviours within the hotel sector.

Cristina Pérez-Pérez, Ph.D., is a lecturer at the Department of Management at Rey Juan Carlos University (Madrid, Spain). The main focus of her research is the Sharing Economy and its different associated processes, especially the internationalization processes, as well as entrepreneurship and sustainability.

Mallika Roy is an associate professor (study leave) at the Department of Economics, University of Chittagong, Bangladesh. Mallika graduated with Honours (Economics) and Masters' (Economics) from the University of Chittagong, followed by earning her M. Phil (Economics) from the City University of Hong Kong. She achieved the Prestigious Prime Minister Gold Medal Award Bangladesh for her scholastic academic results. She was also awarded a Hong Kong government-funded scholarship for her M. Phil study and Industry and a CQUniversity-funded Elevate scholarship and International Excellence Award for her PhD Program. Her research interests include Agricultural Economics, Supply Chain, Environmental Economics, Economic Development, and Macroeconomics. She has teaching experience of above 13 years. After working as a faculty member at Islamia University College for 2 years and 4 months and subsequently at BGC Trust University Bangladesh for about 1 year, she has been serving as a faculty member at the University of Chittagong for over 11 years. While working as a faculty member at the University of Chittagong, she additionally served as an adjunct faculty in multiple universities in Bangladesh. She worked as a research fellow and teaching assistant at the Department of Economics and Finance of the City University of Hong Kong for 2 years. She completed three research projects by UGC Bangladesh in the role of a project director. She published 23 research papers in national, and international journals and books.

Henning Tirrel is affiliated with the FOM University of Applied Sciences in Münster (Germany) as a lecturer. He holds a PhD from the University of Nicosia (Cyprus, EU). Henning does research in Strategic Human Resource Management as well as Business Administration, considering issues of Leadership, Trust, (Digital) Employer Branding and Workplace Flexibility Practices. He is also an associate fellow of the EuroMed Academy of Business.

Lothar Winnen is a lecturer in the Department of Mechanical Engineering at the University of Applied Sciences Südwestfalen in Iserlohn. He teaches in the field of business administration, particularly in the areas of marketing, entrepreneurship and accounting. Lothar Winnen conducts research in the fields of strategic human resource management and marketing. Lothar Winnen studied business administration at RWTH Aachen University and later at the Business and Information Technology School, Iserlohn. At the end of 2015 he successfully completed his doctoral programme at the Universidad Europea Madrid in the subject area of human capital management.

Index

A

B

C

D

E

F

G

H

I

J

L

M

N

O

P

R

S

T

V

W

www.ingramcontent.com/pod-product-compliance
Lightning Source LLC
LaVergne TN
LVHW080346011026
849161LV00009B/2208